Conflict Diagnosis and Alternative Dispute Resolution

Conflict Diagnosis and Alternative Dispute Resolution

Laurie S. Coltri

Department of Legal Studies

University of Maryland, University College

PEARSON

Prentice Hall

Upper Saddle River, New Jersey

Library of Congress Cataloging-in-Publication Data

Coltri, Laurie S.
   Conflict diagnosis and alternative dispute resolution and mediation / by Laurie S. Coltri.
     p. cm.
   Includes bibliographical references.
   ISBN 0-13-098109-5
   1. Dispute resolution (Law) 2. Mediation. 3. Negotiation. 4. Conflict management. I. Title.
   K2390 .C655 2004
   303.6'9—dc21

2003010821

Acquisitions Editor: Elizabeth Sugg
Editor-in-Chief: Stephen Helba
Editorial Assistant: Cyrenne Bolt Freitss
Managing Editor (Production): Mary Carnis
Production Editor: Brian Hyland
Director of Production and Manufacturing:
  Bruce Johnson

Manufacturing Buyer: Ilene Sanford
Design Director: Cheryl Asherman
Design Coordinator: Christopher Weigand
Cover Design: Joe DiPinho
Composition/Full-Service Project Management:
  Carlisle Communications, Ltd.
Printer/Binder: Courier Westford

Credits and acknowledgments borrowed from other sources and reproduced, with permission, in this textbook appear on appropriate page within text.

Pearson Education LTD.
Pearson Education Singapore, Pte. Ltd
Pearson Education, Canada, Ltd
Pearson Education—Japan

Pearson Education Australia PTY, Limited
Pearson Education North Asia Ltd
Pearson Educación de Mexico, S.A. de C.V.
Pearson Education Malaysia, Pte. Ltd

10 9 8 7 6 5 4 3 2
ISBN 0-13-098109-5

To my father, who taught me to love learning.

Brief Contents

Contents

4   Conflict Diagnosis   49

5   Recurrent Themes in Conflict Diagnosis   62

PART II

THE STEPS OF CONFLICT DIAGNOSIS 91

6

Step 1. Describe the Conflict 92

7

Step 2. Identify the Sources of the Conflict 103

11   Step 6. Assess the Impediments to Resolving the Conflict   192

12   Step 7. Assess the Negotiation Styles and Practices of the Participants   215

13 Step 8. Assess Power and Alternatives to a Negotiated Agreement 234

14 Step 9. Consider Diversity Issues at Play in the Conflict 263

PART III

ALTERNATIVE DISPUTE RESOLUTION PROCESSES 303

15

Mediation: An Introduction 305

20   Nonbinding Evaluation   462

21   Mixed (Hybrid) and Multimodal Dispute Resolution Processes   476

PART IV

PUTTING IT ALL TOGETHER   515

22

Power Tools and Magic Keys: Using Conflict Diagnosis to Manage Legal Disputes and Select ADR Processes   516

APPENDIX A
Alternative Dispute Resolution Act of 1998   562

APPENDIX B
Alternative Dispute Resolution Act of 1996 (Selected Provisions)   566

APPENDIX C
Uniform Mediation Act (Selected Provisions)   573

APPENDIX D
Federal Arbitration Act (Selected Provisions)   577

Preface

In 1975, when I began the study of law at the University of Southern California, there were virtually no law school courses that taught the law and practice of Alternative Dispute Resolution (ADR). But soon thereafter, a revolution took place in the legal systems of the United States and other westernized nations: potential litigants and their attorneys began to let go of the view that a lawsuit is the inevitable conclusion to an unsettled dispute.

In the 1970s, the ADR revolution began, almost timidly, as a counterculture oddity, with a few community mediation centers springing up in big cities, and a few divorce professionals experimenting with alternatives to the adversary process for families seeking "friendly divorces." I myself joined this experiment in 1983, obtaining graduate training and becoming a divorce mediator in those early years when divorce mediators were about as common as a six-toed cat. Proving that it was not a passing fancy, ADR gathered steam throughout the 1980s, and exploded into mainstream legal practice in the 1990s. By the turn of the twenty-first century, every federal trial court and nearly every state court had some sort of ADR program. Virtually all law schools had courses in ADR, and many offered elective concentrations and clinical programs in the field. Thanks to the work of visionaries, geniuses, and pioneers of ADR—Robert Baruch-Bush, Former Chief Justice Warren Burger, Roger Fisher, Stephen Goldberg, Kimberly Kovach, Kenneth Kressel, Lela Love, Carrie Menkel-Meadow, Len Riskin, Frank E. A. Sander, William Ury, and James Westbrook, plus my own mentors, Elizabeth Koopman and Joan Hunt and others too numerous to mention—it seems clear that ADR is here to stay.

And, yet, it is still unsettled just what sort of legacy these trail-blazers will leave behind. ADR gives us a dazzling array of choices when a dispute arises or a transaction runs into trouble. Our decades of reliance on adversarial methods of settling interpersonal conflicts has left fallout: our view of conflict is blinded by our narrow past experience. The application of ADR processes to legal disputes that would otherwise have been litigated (or settled "on the courthouse steps") may turn out to have profound implications, both on the personal-client level and on a broader societal level; beyond the savings of cost and time, the choice, selection, and presentation of ADR processes to disputants has the potential to transform culture, for good or ill.

But despite the potentially monumental nature of the transformation on which our legal system is embarking in the ADR revolution, there is a tendency to use ADR processes without a careful understanding of their uses, applicabilities, and impacts on individual disputants and on the legal system and society as a whole. The lack of appreciation for the subtle distinctions among ADR processes is part of a bigger problem: we do not have firmly in place methods of understanding interpersonal conflict so that we can select, or design, optimal methods of handling them, nor would most of us recognize a good strategy if we saw it. Add to this deficit the Western cultural reliance on "rugged individualism" and the American belief that competition is integral to social organization, and a serious blind spot is created, one that often prevents us from selecting dispute-resolution processes well and wisely. Indeed, these lapses are often invisible players in the decisions our government makes when it designs and funds dispute resolution programs, as well as in decisions about how our law schools teach new lawyers to use ADR. Thus, early in the ADR revolution, many experts in the field wonder whether the true potential of ADR as a tool that can be tailored to individual conflicts will ever be realized.

This textbook is an effort to fill this void, by presenting a method of understanding interpersonal conflict and ADR that transcends the existing blinders. The method, referred to in the text as *conflict diagnosis,* enables the user to clarify the reasons for the conflict, the deep-seated goals and interests of the disputing parties, and the impediments to effective resolution, with a level of complexity that real-life conflict presents and demands. Knowing the conflict at this level of detail and objectivity enables practitioners of conflict diagnosis—whether disputing parties, attorneys, paralegals, ADR screeners, or ADR neutrals—to tailor the very best process to meet the needs of those with whom they are concerned. It also allows the user–particularly if he or she is embroiled in a dispute—to develop better strategies for addressing the conflict. These intentional and rational strategies move beyond the knee-jerk reaction or the "fight or flight" response. Most of the ideas that make up conflict diagnosis are not new; what is new is the logical organization and level of detail in which they are presented, as well as the transformation of these ideas from cerebral theory into hard, practical skill.

This book started out simply as an ADR textbook for students of law and legal studies. It features a particularly thorough and comprehensive survey of ADR processes: mediation, arbitration, nonbinding evaluation, and hybrid processes, and stands alone in that role. But the book is unique in its use of the principles of conflict diagnosis to better achieve the goal of surveying and understanding the ADR field. I began the task of writing this book because, as an educator teaching ADR to legal studies students and legal professionals, I found that none of the available texts adequately explained how to match a specific conflict to an optimum ADR process and provider. Conflict diagnosis is the missing link, giving the reader an understanding of why particular dispute-resolution processes work very well in some cases, but not so well in others, and revealing side effects, both positive and negative, that accompany the application of particular dispute resolution processes to conflicts. Conflict diagnosis provides a theoretical and practical basis for understanding the major ADR forms, their advantages and disadvantages, and their indications and contraindications. Many works attempt to describe ADR processes without the theoretical basis provided by conflict diagnosis, or with only sparse and shallow use of some of its concepts. But in my opinion, trying to select a dispute resolution process without understanding its conflict diagnosis implications is like trying to select a treatment for a sick patient without knowing the illness—it's risky at best.

So ADR and conflict diagnosis are intricately intertwined. The field of ADR offers people who are involved in conflicts, either as disputants or as agents, advocates, neutrals, and others, many alternatives to the litigation process. Conflict diagnosis, on the other hand, offers people the tools for charting a path from impasse to solution and suggests dispute resolution strategies and options, including the use of ADR, that are most appropriate in addressing the conflict.

This book, mirroring the reality of the relationship between conflict diagnosis and ADR, deals with both topics together. It begins with an in-depth explanation of conflict diagnosis. Using the theories from which conflict diagnosis has been developed as an explanatory base, the book gives a thorough treatment of the relationship between ADR processes, variants, and specific features, and the pros, cons, and specific applicability of each process. The conflict diagnosis paradigm sets out the needed information in a straightforward and systematic way for practitioners and disputing persons to apply. The student of interpersonal conflict and ADR will be able to understand the intricacies of ADR processes only by understanding the nature of the problems and challenges that each process responds to.

But conflict diagnosis is much more than a pedagogical device for teaching ADR. Indeed, although I developed conflict diagnosis from available conflict-resolution theory and research as a way to convey information about ADR to my legal studies students, I simultaneously discovered an invaluable tool for my own work as a professional mediator. As I began applying the techniques of conflict diagnosis to my own cases and clients, I discovered a powerful tool for understanding and dealing with difficult conflicts. As an attorney and mediator, and as an individual with conflicts in my personal, family, and professional life, I have personally found that applying conflict diagnosis is a critical step in the process of responding to conflict efficaciously. Conflict diagnosis is a kind of recipe for gaining understanding of a conflict, achieving useful emotional distance and objectivity, and selecting appropriate approaches to its resolution. It's a deliberate, structured, sometimes plodding process. But when it's used, seemingly magical things can happen. A rigorous application of conflict diagnosis techniques can lead to sudden enlightenment about the conflict—a sort of "aha" effect. When this happens, it is almost like stumbling on a set of magic keys—the keys to transforming a conflict from impasse to opportunity. Conflict diagnosis can often light the way from a seemingly impossible situation to a solution. It is my hope that, in making a commitment to using the techniques of conflict diagnosis, you, the reader, will have many "aha" experiences of your own, and that you and the people around you will be the glad and enriched beneficiaries.

In short, although this book is intended for students, conflict diagnosis can benefit anyone, because everyone interacts with others and therefore encounters conflicts. Whether you are a lawyer, a teacher, a parent, an employee, a middle manager, a legal assistant, a chief financial officer, a neighbor, a judge, or a college student, conflicts are inevitable, and into each life conflict will inevitably enter. This book presents and provides information about the range of ADR processes available to address legal disputes, but beyond this, the book presents a coherent and comprehensive method of understanding and responding to conflicts of all sorts. Whether the majority of conflicts in your life more closely resemble fender-benders, contract disputes, health insurance claims denials, office politics problems, multinational corporate merger transactions, or dueling preschoolers (or, if you are very, very busy, all of the above), this book aims to provide you with the means to find the "magic keys" for resolving differences.

I confess to being an idealist. Armed with the ideas and skills that comprise conflict diagnosis, and with a truly comprehensive grasp of the promise of alternative dispute resolution, each of us can find the magic keys to unlocking tough conflicts. An army of legal professionals, carrying this knowledge, can take law practice to the next level, serving clients with an effectiveness and an efficiency we could not have dreamed of a half-century ago. But the usefulness of conflict diagnosis does not end with legal disputing. As individuals, friends, family members, parents, and consumers we can use the ideas of conflict diagnosis to handle everyday conflict more effectively. And as members of the collective enterprises in which we inevitably are a part, we can better make the tough decisions that we must make to create a better and more peaceful world.

A brief note about ADR terminology. Alternative Dispute Resolution is a relatively new, rapidly evolving, and interdisciplinary field, and, perhaps because of its rapid growth, it is marked by confusion over terminology. An effort has been made to identify and rigorously define ADR-related terms, both in the glossary that follows the chapters, and in boxes embedded in the text. To make for easier understanding, definitions provided in the chapters are accompanied by graphical icons that identify the field from which each term is taken:

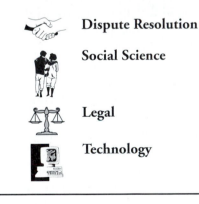

Dispute Resolution

Social Science

Legal

Technology

SUPPLEMENTS

Guidance and support for classroom and CLE courses include:

- ◆ An Instructor's Manual with lecture notes, tests, and additional cases
- ◆ Online materials for distance learning programs

- Lexiverse CD-ROM with LexBrief Case Briefing Software and the Lexiverse digital law dictionary
- Pearson Legal series super web site with course support for students and instructors including a newsletter, state-specific information, research access, and more. Visit *www.prenhall.com/legal_studies.*

ACKNOWLEDGMENTS

I feel honored and proud to have been a part of an interconnected web of dedicated, talented, and caring individuals, without whom this book would never have come into being.

Adelaide Lagnese, Director of Legal Studies at the University of Maryland, University College, has stood by me throughout my teaching career. She believed in my vision to publish a textbook from the idea's inception, and put me in touch with the editors of several publishers who could make the vision a reality. Without her, this book would remain a wish unrealized.

Diane Bridge, my colleague at the University of Maryland, is, in a metaphoric sense, a co-parent of the Alternative Dispute Resolution course that formed the basis for this textbook. She is a woman of incredible energy, talent, intellect, assertiveness, and warmth and has given me such unwavering support that she made it possible for me to juggle the demands of work, writing, and family life. Her voice wafts through this volume.

I am profoundly indebted to three groups of people, many of whom modestly prefer that I not include them by name here. The first are those who have been my mediation clients. Some of their stories are the basis for ideas and anecdotes that appear in this textbook. In the face of seemingly intractable situations, these courageous people have shown a creative genius and a tenacity that should be honored as heroic. The other group consists of my students, current and former. As with my former clients, some of my former students' stories are adapted for use here, and like my clients, a great many of my students have struggled against, and overcome, challenges that I as a person of relative privilege cannot imagine. In a very real sense, both my clients and my students have been my most important teachers. They constantly remind me of the messy diversity of real life, of the need to get and be real, of the extraordinary courage of ordinary people, and of the constant need to transcend egocentrism. Those who see the outlines of their own experiences in these pages are witness to the profound influence they have on me: their experiences have been my guides and have become a part of me.

One group provided pointed feedback on every topic in this book. This group brought focus specifically to the content of this work. These people include, but are not limited to, Linda Cabral Marrero, Mercy College; Otis Grant, Indiana University-South Bend; and David J. White, Southern Missouri State University-West Plains.

I wish to especially pay tribute to my two mentors in the Alternative Dispute Resolution field, Elizabeth Koopman and Joan Hunt. Elizabeth Koopman is a true visionary of incredible strength, creativity, and intellectual prowess. Her unwavering sense of right and wrong is a model for everyone whose lives she touches.

I aspire to be even a shadow of the positive force she exerts on earth; and even now, after time and distance have separated us, her good works touch me every day in the work I do and the thoughts I think. Elizabeth deserves a place in the pantheon of leading lights of the dispute resolution field. Fiercely principled, Elizabeth is willing to sacrifice everything to do what is right. She has paid many prices for her integrity, and I profoundly wish that this book will pay tribute to her.

Joan Hunt, who passed away in the spring of 2003, was my academic advisor and my guide throughout graduate school. She was a person of such astounding fidelity, integrity, intellectual prowess, warmth, and iron resolve that everyone around her inevitably became a better person. She is my model as a professor and my role model as a human being, and in this and uncountable other ways, her legacy lives on today.

Dr. Robert Hardy, who became my graduate advisor after Dr. Hunt left the University of Maryland, had the political smarts to shepherd my dissertation through the process of review and defense, making it possible for me to get my Ph.D. and get on with teaching. He stood by me and supported my efforts to juggle childbirth and new parenting with dissertation work. I also wish to acknowledge colleagues Fran Favretto, Meta Lagerwerff, Angela Miotto, and Robin Majeski. Their friendship and collegiality have been invaluable. Pat Martin, another colleague, has also become like family to me, and I would like to honor her; her husband, John Caughey; and their daughter, Ananda. They have made life bearable during the long authorship process, and have rescued me more than once from logistical challenges that threatened to derail me. Carol Wilner has given me emotional support and needed objectivity. In addition, I would like to honor Guy Williams and Edith Thompson for their important contributions to the book.

The members of my family have made many sacrifices to allow me the time and space to complete a project the size of this textbook. My mother and father, Ruth and Mike Schalit, and my brother, Mark, are a well of daily love and support that I feel even when we don't speak. Julia and Robin, my two wonderful children, have had to put up with a lot—a mom absent from school activities, inconsistent guidance and supervision, mom's bad moods and writer's blocks, and incomprehensible dinner conversation, just to name some of the discomforts of living with an author. Julia has been a source of constant and quiet love, wisdom, and sophisticated insight greatly beyond her years. Robin has always been there with a smile, a hug, and a compliment when I most needed it. Julia and Robin have taught me many things, and continue to teach me how to love and be loved.

My loving husband Alan has perhaps been the most indispensable of all. He has been mother and father to our children, cook and housekeeper, technical advisor, sounding board, and emotional support person. All this was done in his spare time after his demanding workday. And all this he did, not for financial gain, but simply because he knew that writing this book was what I aspired to do. A greater demonstration of love, strength, and determination cannot be imagined. When I was twenty and single, waiting to take the elavator to work, I used to imagine that my dream-husband-to-be was waiting for me on the other side of the door. But in my wildest and most romantic dreams, I could not have cooked up Alan, nor the magical path we have taken together.

About the Author

Laurie S. Coltri was born and raised in Los Angeles, California. She received her bachelor's degree in English from the California Institute of Technology, in Pasadena, California, in 1974. Thereafter, she attended law school at the University of Southern California, graduating with a J.D. in 1979.

After several years of general law practice specializing in complex case preparation and legal research and writing, Coltri and her legal advocacy career came to a parting of the ways. In the early 1980s, after moving to Maryland, she began taking courses in the mediation of divorces. After a year of graduate work, she received a graduate concentration in divorce mediation from the University of Maryland at College Park, and began one of the earliest private mediation practices in the state. She mediated virtually the first court-referred child custody case in the Maryland trial courts in the mid-1980s, and directed a telephone-based visitation mediation service for the Prince George's County Department of Child Support Enforcement.

Returning to graduate school, Coltri received her doctorate in Human Development from the University of Maryland, College Park, in 1995. Her graduate work focused on the resolution of conflict and the impact of dispute resolution processes on individual development. Since 1996, Dr. Coltri, an Associate Professor, has taught for the University of Maryland, University College, in its highly regarded Legal Studies program. She has received the university's Teaching Recognition Award for her work and has published several articles and book chapters in the field of Alternative Dispute Resolution.

Dr. Coltri shares a home in Columbia, Maryland, with her husband, Alan; their daughters, Julia and Robin, born in 1990 and 1994; and an assortment of slightly offbeat animal companions.

PART I

INTRODUCTION

In this textbook, you will have an opportunity to learn about the process of understanding interpersonal conflicts and of selecting tactics and processes to address them. The conflicts to which this book is addressed include disputes, particularly disputes in the legal arena, as well as transactions, which are the development or adjustment of working relationships between people with both divergent and complementary interests and goals. The process of understanding interpersonal conflicts, prefatory to selecting methods for dealing with them, is called conflict diagnosis.[1] The processes available for dealing with these conflicts in a controlled and civil manner are collectively known as dispute resolution, and those dispute resolution processes other than taking a dispute to court are known as alternative dispute resolution, typically abbreviated as ADR. Chapter 1 will provide rigorous and explicit definitions for the varieties of interpersonal conflict and the persons involved in conflict, and Chapter 2 will conceptually describe the major forms of dispute resolution. You will need these definitions to understand and work with the concepts and skills considered in the remainder of the textbook.

This book may differ in an important respect from textbooks you may have become used to. In most textbooks, the principle idea is to acquire knowledge. Students often like to think of learning as a form of consumption: the mind is opened and the facts and ideas are poured in. In the study of conflict diagnosis and alternative dispute resolution, the opening of the mind is as important as the pouring in of new matter. Before fresh ideas can enter, you must *unlearn* some old beliefs and preconceptions. Specifically, you must become aware of the nearly universal propensity to view all conflicts as win-lose situations resolvable only through competition. This propensity underlies much of law and judicial process in the Western world, particularly in the United States. Chapter 3 will introduce the idea that this set of beliefs is unduly limiting: it acts as an invisible veil, blinding us to better opportunities for managing conflict effectively.

---

[1] In recent years, more and more alternative dispute resolution scholars have begun to adopt the term *conflict diagnosis* to describe some or all of the analytical processes presented in Part II of this text. Unfortunately, like much of the ADR field, the term *conflict diagnosis* means slightly different things to different people. For purposes of this textbook, the term will refer to the ten-step process presented in Chapter 4.

Chapter 4 will introduce the concept of conflict diagnosis. Conflict diagnosis is both a valuable skill and a set of ideas underpinning the ADR field. It can help lift the invisible veil and guide the diagnostician in developing effective ways to approach and resolve conflict. You will get an initial sense of what conflict diagnosis is and why it can be beneficial. You may find that, unlike the material in some other textbooks, the benefits of learning conflict diagnosis can be highly personal: some learners experience the conflict diagnosis materials as a kind of self-help guide. Chapter 4 contains an outline of the process of conflict diagnosis. You will find that Part II of the textbook is organized so that each chapter deals with one step in the outline.

Chapter 5 will introduce some recurrent themes of conflict diagnosis, themes that have their origins in the social sciences. These themes address the reasons that interpersonal conflict is so problematic and why people observing conflict in themselves and others so often misread it. This information is critical for understanding why conflict diagnosis is useful and why our assumptions about the efficacies of various dispute resolution processes may be off-base. The recurrent themes allow us to open our minds to new possibilities and to become receptive to some of the more radical forms of alternative dispute resolution.

1

Basic Definitions

"All men are caught in an inescapable network of mutuality."

—Martin Luther King, Jr.

In this chapter, you will learn ...

- ◆ A number of terms related to the study of conflict and conflict resolution.
- ◆ The basic attributes of interpersonal conflict.
- ◆ About interdependence and about the mixed nature of interdependence in virtually all interpersonal conflict.

Jeff is a junior at State University. Jeff's all-consuming hobby is designing computer games. In fact, over the past four years, he has poured all his free time and a lot of money into his passion.

Recently, Jeff developed an innovative game he calls Digi-Date. Modeled after TV shows popular to the seventeen-to-twenty-three crowd, Digi-Date allows the user to input his or her own physical, intellectual, and personality attributes. The computer allows the user to design a "dream date," or the computer can design one for the user. The user can select a number of first-date scenarios. Similar to the popular "Sim" software products, the computer presents a variety of challenges and problems for the virtual couple to deal with (such as "you forget your credit card" or "date reveals she has herpes"). The software is notable in its slick and sophisticated uses of artificial intelligence and eye-popping 3-D graphics.

Jeff showed the software to a friend, Marsha, who got very excited about its potential marketing possibilities. She, in turn, spoke to her dad, who agreed orally to provide financial backing. Marsha and Jeff agreed to work together on producing and marketing the work for commercial sale. Unfortunately, Marsha and Jeff were so excited about the possibilities for getting rich that they failed to consider the details of their arrangement: their ownership agreement, largely oral, is vague and sketchy. Now, after Jeff has worked over nine months to perfect the product and Marsha has put a similar amount of time into market research, they are disputing over how much of the revenues from product sales will go to each of them. Because they have been unable to agree, Marsha's dad says he will withdraw financial support. Meanwhile, the software market continues to evolve. If the product is not launched soon, it is likely that someone else's product will take over the market.

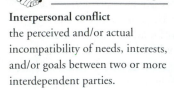

Interpersonal conflict
the perceived and/or actual incompatibility of needs, interests, and/or goals between two or more interdependent parties.

Jeff and Marsha's disagreement is an example of an **interpersonal conflict.** Conflict is so ubiquitous that we usually don't think about what it is: instead, we "know it when we see it." But, before we can begin the study of either conflict diagnosis or alternative dispute resolution, we must first define some terms. We will start with a rigorous definition of the term *interpersonal conflict.* From this definition will follow some basic attributes of conflict. Our discussion of definitions will give us a common language, which we will use to share thoughts and information about this exciting, challenging, and critically important field.

INTERPERSONAL CONFLICT

Adversarial
a quality of some interpersonal conflicts, in which participants treat one another as enemies or adversaries.

When we think of interpersonal conflict, what comes to mind is often a violent argument, a fistfight, or a war. Although dictionary definitions of *conflict* typically refer to its **adversarial,** competitive, or violent manifestations, the issues addressed in this book require a more rigorous yet generalized definition. That's because we want to be able to consider conflict in all its guises.

BASIC ATTRIBUTES OF CONFLICT

The primary requisite to the existence of interpersonal conflict is an *incompatibility of needs, interests, and/or goals* among participants in the conflict. Thus, conflict is not necessarily characterized by the presence of violence, coercion, or even open disagreement.

Before Marsha and Jeff ever clashed over the sharing of revenues, or even knew they disgreed on this issue, they already had an interpersonal conflict, because each had a different, and incompatible, goal concerning the sharing of sales revenues from Digi-Date. Following is another example to illustrate this aspect of conflict:

> Doreen and Don Prather are buying their first house. Today, they saw a beautiful home that, except for some minor water damage, seemed to be just what they want. The home is owned by Arnold and Lonnie Jones. The Jones' agent has reassured the Prathers that it's a terrific deal, but they don't know whether to trust her. Doreen and Don don't know how to go about protecting themselves in the purchasing process.

The homebuying effort of Doreen and Don qualifies as an interpersonal conflict despite the lack of an outright dispute, because some of the interests of Doreen and Don (to purchase a top-quality home at a great price) are divergent from some of the interests of the Joneses and their agent (who would all like to sell the house for the maximum possible price, despite any defects). In fact, conflict, by this definition, need not be even conscious. Parties with an actual incompatibility of needs, interests, or goals can be in conflict even if they have never thought of themselves as being in conflict. Take the following scenario:

> Harriet works as a human relations specialist at Ahalt & Blackletter, P.C., a civil litigation firm in Metropol. Recently, one of the associates, Karen, complained

that she was being sexually harassed by a fellow associate, Mark. When questioned, Karen stated that the two work in close physical proximity and that Mark frequently tells offensive jokes, which she is sure she is meant to overhear. Karen seemed very stressed over her workload and high expectations of new associates, and Harriet wondered whether she was blowing the harassment issue out of proportion. Harriet went to Mark, who said he had no idea that Karen was offended by his behavior. He explained that joking is one of the ways he lets off steam in his extremely stressful work environment. Three weeks prior to the conversation with Karen, Harriet had recommended reassigning the two associates to separate departments, so that Karen would no longer work in proximity to Mark, but the partners have not followed through on her recommendation. Harriet has also noticed a rise in complaints by other associates and junior partners against one another.

Latent conflict
an interpersonal conflict of which no participant in the conflict is aware.

Interdependent
parties related to one another such that what happens to one is likely to affect the state, attributes, resources, or well-being of the other.

Contriently interdependent
a state of interdependence such that one party's efforts to satisfy needs, interests, or goals adversely affects those of the other.

Zero-sum
a conflict state in which the more one person gets, the less the other has.

True or (veridical) conflict
a conflict situation in which there are real incompatibilities of goals, needs, and interests between the parties to a conflict.

In this example, there are obvious conflicts between Karen and Mark. However, until confronted by Harriet, Mark may not have known that a conflict existed. Additionally, it is likely that the associates, as well as Harriet herself, have incompatible goals (and hence a conflict) with the law partners over the management of associates at the law firm. It's possible, even likely, that none of the individuals involved has even thought of there being a conflict between the partners and the associates. A conflict in which none of the involved parties is aware of the divergence of goals, needs, or interests is known as a **latent conflict** (Deutsch 1973, 14)—a conflict "lying in wait" for outward expression.

A second important point to be taken from the definition of interpersonal conflict is that, for needs, interests, or goals to be incompatible, the parties to the conflict are necessarily **interdependent**. *Interdependence* simply means that what happens to one party to a conflict will affect the other parties. Persons who have no actual or perceived effect on one another cannot be in conflict. In the words of conflict theorist Morton Deutsch, parties to a conflict are (actually or apparently) **contriently interdependent** (Deutsch 1973, 20). *Contrient interdependence* means that goals are incompatible: the efforts by Party A to satisfy his or her needs, interests, or goals actually—or apparently—impede the ability of Party B to satisfy his or hers (Deutsch 1973, 21). In other words, to the extent that parties are contriently interdependent, the conflict can be resolved either by having a winner and a loser or by "splitting the difference." Contrient-interdependence situations are also known as **zero-sum** situations. The term comes from the idea that the well-being of the disputing parties sums to zero: the more Party A gets out of the deal, the less Party B gets.

Third, look at the language "perceived and/or actual incompatibilities." The incompatibilities can be real, but they need not be. A situation involving actual incompatibility of needs, interests, or goals is defined as a **true**, or **veridical**, **conflict.** On the other hand, parties may think a conflict exists, whereas, in fact, none does—for example:

Lisa and her husband, Mark, go out to dinner twice a month. Tonight, Mark would really like to have Italian food, but Lisa nearly always prefers

False conflict

a conflict situation in which the incompatibilities of goals, needs, and interests are perceived, but not real.

Disputants

participants in a conflict who have actual or perceived incompatibilities of goals, needs, and/or interests with one another.

Transactions

interpersonal conflicts in which disputants work to create arrangements that transfer resources, delineate responsibilities, or otherwise create or adjust an interdependent relationship. Transactions are characterized by disputants' emphasis on mutually complementary needs, goals, and interests and a deemphasis on incompatible goals, needs, and interests.

seafood. Mark is anticipating the usual spat over where to go for dinner; however, unbeknownst to Mark, tonight Lisa actually wants pasta.

Thus, from Mark's perspective, a conflict exists. However, the incompatibility of goals is not "actual"; it's merely "perceived." This sort of conflict, which disappears when all the facts come out, is known as **false conflict** (Deutsch 1973, 14).

Let's also look at the word *parties* in the definition. In this book, we will call the parties with divergent goals, interests, or needs the **disputants**. Disputants may be individuals, as in most of the scenarios. However, disputants may also be organizations. Consider the following situation:

> The S Corporation is the manufacturer of a device called an S-Chip, used in the manufacture of cellular telephones. S Corporation's marketing department has located a potential buyer, B Corporation, a manufacturer of cellular telephones. A meeting has been scheduled to negotiate the sale of the S-Chip. S Corporation has sent its research vice president, Samantha (nicknamed Sam) to perform the negotiation, along with its corporate counsel, Sean, to act as legal advisor. B Corporation has sent its purchasing vice president, Bob, to negotiate, along with B's corporate house counsel, Bea. Back at the corporate headquarters of S Corporation, Sue, Sam's staff assistant, is responsible for supporting the negotiation efforts, whereas, at B Corporation, Ben, the executive secretary in charge of the purchasing department, provides support for Bob during the negotiation. The directors of each corporation believe that the proposed sale is potentially advantageous, provided that a good deal can be struck.

In the sale of the S-Chip, the disputants (the prospective seller and buyer of the merchandise) are corporations, not individuals, although the corporations are composed of individuals and do their business through the activities of individuals. Situations such as treaty development between countries, international disputes, and wars are important examples of conflict in which the disputants are generally not individuals, although typically there will also be ancillary conflicts that exist among individuals that are participating in the larger conflict.[1]

There is also a qualitative difference between the S-Chip and home sale scenarios, on the one hand, and the law office and computer game scenarios, on the other. The S-Chip and home sale scenarios are not "conflicts" by our commonsense dictionary definition: they involve no obvious disagreements. They are **transactions**: forward-looking arrangements made by parties who recognize that making such arrangements will satisfy mutually complementary goals, needs, or interests. However, because transactions virtually always involve divergent as well as complementary goals, needs, and interests, they are interpersonal conflicts, according to our definition. For example, in both scenarios, the seller typically wants to get the highest possible price for his or her

---

[1] In international conflict, the disputants are often countries. Obviously, however, individuals and subgroups within the countries are also likely to have divergent or conflicting goals, needs, and interests. A typical multiparty conflict presents a complex situation in which there are many conflicts, each with a set of disputants. We'll look further at this phenomenon in a later chapter.

item, whereas the buyer wants to get the product or item as cheaply as possible. Transactions are not usually recognized as conflicts unless the divergent goals, needs, or interests become more important or noticeable to the participants than the mutually complementary goals. Thus, the home sale transaction would probably be recognized as a conflict if the buyers made an offer that the sellers rejected as ridiculously low.

If a conflict is not defined primarily by forward-looking complementary goals, needs, or interests but, instead, by the presence of incompatible goals, needs, or interests, that conflict is identified as a **dispute.** The term *dispute* implies that the incompatibilities are conscious on the part of at least one of the parties to the conflict and that the incompatibilities—rather than the complementary goals, interests, or needs—are uppermost in the minds of those involved in the conflict. Disputes often relate to grievances arising from behavior or events that occurred in the past. For example, once Jeff and Marsha realized they disagreed over revenue sharing, their conflict became a dispute.

A critical point, one crucial to the effective management of conflict, is that virtually all conflicts, including virtually all disputes, contain *both* divergent and incompatible goals, needs, or interests (otherwise, they would not be conflicts) *and* compatible, complementary goals, needs, or interests. At the least, virtually all disputes involve parties who would benefit from the dispute being efficiently resolved; thus, this element of the parties' interests, at least, is compatible and complementary. Parties whose individual efforts to advance their own needs, goals, or interests promote the other's goals, needs, or interests are said to be **promotively interdependent** (Deutsch 1973, 21). Since both transactions and disputes generally contain a combination of compatible and incompatible goals, needs, or interests, they carry within them the seeds of both destructive conflict escalation and mutually beneficial resolution.

A conflict with a combination of both compatible and incompatible goals, needs, or interests—that is, a conflict in which the disputants are *simultaneously* contriently and promotively interdependent—is called a **mixed-motive situation.** In the situation that opened this chapter (the Digi-Date revenue dispute), Jeff and Marsha have an element of contrient interdependence in that, the greater the proportion of revenues received by one, the less the other will get, yet there are also promotive dimensions to the situation. If Jeff and Marsha can maximize the total sales of Digi-Date, both will receive more profit, regardless of the revenue-sharing arrangements. Also, if, as a result of their impasse, Marsha's dad backs out of the deal, they'll both lose out. A conflict in which promotive interdependence is recognized, and in which the disputants anticipate being able to settle on a solution that improves everyone's situation, is known as a **positive-sum situation.** For example, if Jeff and Marsha can quickly and amicably resolve their dispute over how to divide their income from the software, they can probably regain Marsha's dad's financial backing and enter the software market at an opportune time, making a huge profit for both of them. The alternatives, giving up on the project altogether or resolving the dispute through a lengthy lawsuit, are likely to serve neither of them as well. A central goal of dispute resolution professionals is to "mine" every

---

Dispute
a nonlatent interpersonal conflict characterized by the disputants' emphasis and concentration on incompatible needs, goals, and interests.

Promotively interdependent
a state of interdependence in which improvements to one party's needs, goals, or interests tend to improve or enhance the needs, goals, or interests of the other party.

Mixed-motive situation
a conflict situation characterized by a combination of contrient and promotive interdependence.

Positive-sum situation
a promotively interdependent situation. Efforts by both parties to help themselves, and each other, effectively improve joint resources.

Promotive Interdependence Doesn't Mean You're Buddies!

Imagine being marooned on a small desert island with nothing but the shirt on your back—and your worst enemy. Most likely you and this person (let's call him Fred) will have a great deal of difficulty surviving without the other's cooperation. It's a lot easier building lean-tos, killing wild boar with makeshift spears, avoiding being eaten by leopards, and signaling for help from passing ocean liners when there are two of you. Despite the fact that you can't stand Fred, you and he are promotively interdependent—what's good for Fred is also good for you.

Real-world conflict often presents similar situations. For example, a quarter-century ago, the United States vigorously supported Osama Bin Laden in his efforts to oust the Soviet Union from Afghanistan. At that time, it was the opinion of those making U.S. foreign policy that our nation was in a promotively interdependent relationship with the person who is now our deeply vilified enemy. According to Yael Shahar of the International Policy Institute for CounterTerrorism, the U.S. Central Intelligence Agency spent some $500 million annually, starting in 1979, to help Bin Laden in his successful quest to rid Afghanistan of the Soviets. (*Source:* Osama Bin Laden. Marketing terrorism, *28 August 1998, http://www.ict.org.il/articles/bin-ladin7.htm cited 27 August 2002.*)

Promotive interdependence can sometimes exist between hostile disputants, as the experience with Osama Bin Laden demonstrates. Corbis/Bettmann

---

Cause of action

a group of operative facts giving rise to one or more bases for suing; a factual situation that entitles one person to obtain a remedy in court from another person (*Black's Law Dictionary*, 7th ed, s.v. "cause of action").

Legal dispute

an interpersonal conflict that can be expressed as one or more causes of action.

interpersonal conflict for its positive-sum attributes, so that solutions can be "win-win" for all concerned.

The Digi-Date, law firm, and dinner scenarios are all examples of disputes, although the software scenario started out as a transaction.[2] Two of these scenarios, the software scenario and (probably) the law office scenario, involve disputes that could be taken to court and litigated. In other words, some aspect of the parties' incompatible goals, needs, or interests could be expressed as one or more **causes of action.** A conflict that can be, or is being, expressed as a cause of action will be referred to in this book as a **legal dispute.**

Figure 1-1 shows the relationship between interpersonal conflict and its subsets, false and veridical conflicts, transactions, disputes, and legal disputes.

---

[2] In the case of the dinner dispute, the conflict is false but perceived as a dispute on the part of Mark, who wants Italian food but thinks his wife won't go along with his preferences.

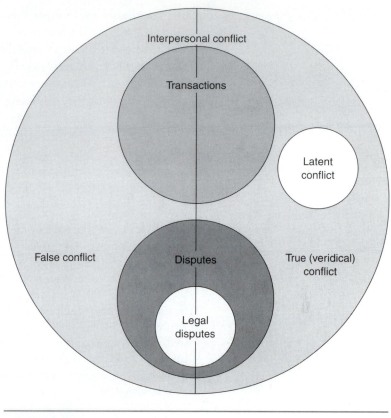

◆ **FIGURE 1-1**

Forms of Interpersonal Conflict

PARTIES TO CONFLICT

Agent
someone who "stands in the shoes" of a disputant during an interpersonal conflict, acting in the disputant's behalf.

Advocate
someone who acts as an agent for a disputant during an interpersonal conflict, and who is ethically obligated to represent the interests of the disputant zealously and competently.

If you review the examples in the preceding section, one thing you may notice is the presence of people other than the disputants. At least two disputants are necessary for a conflict to be created, but frequently other interested parties are involved.

The home sale scenario (involving Doreen and Don Prather) illustrates one sort of conflict participant: the **agent**. Agents are people (or, occasionally, groups of people) that stand in the shoes of a disputant. In the Prather scenario, the seller's realtor occupies such a role. In the S-Chip scenario, both Sam and Bob, the respective corporate vice presidents, are acting as agents, despite the lack of an explicit "agent" designation—their status as corporate vice presidents entitles them to act as such. In the Digi-Date scenario, if Jeff were too embarrassed to confront Marsha about their disagreement but, instead, sent his less-sensitive brother-in-law to lean on her, the brother-in-law would be acting as his agent.

Advocates are one variety of agent. An advocate is an agent who has an ethical and/or legal duty to represent the interests of his or her principal, the

Constituent

a party whose interests, goals, or needs will be affected by the process or outcome of a conflict.

Stakeholder

a constituent who is powerful enough to significantly alter the course of a conflict.

disputant, zealously and competently. In the S-Chip scenario, the two attorneys, Sean and Bea, occupy the role of advocate for their disputant clients.[3]

The term **constituent** is applied to parties who are not directly involved in a conflict but whose interests may be affected by the process or outcome of the conflict, or who may themselves affect the course of the conflict. In the S-Chip scenario, Sue and Ben, the administrative support people for the agents, Sam and Bob, can be considered constituents.

Another term often used to designate interested parties is **stakeholder.** A stakeholder is generally a constituent whose interests will be dramatically affected by the outcome of a conflict and who is sufficiently powerful or authoritative that he or she may affect how a conflict plays out. In Digi-Date, Marsha's father can be identified as a powerful stakeholder. Consider the following example:

> The Rodericks own a townhome in Middlesex, a large, middle-class, sub-urban community on the West Coast. Approximately 1/4 mile from their home is an undeveloped parcel of property covered with orange groves. The parcel was recently purchased by Amalgamated, Inc., which plans to build a heavy industrial plant on the site. The Sierra Club has threatened to sue Amalgamated, claiming that the plans violate federal and state environmental regulations. The state environmental agency, which is charged with enforcing its antipollution regulations, is planning a public hearing to air all concerns. If the plans of Amalgamated are found to violate the regulations, the agency has the authority and responsibility to stop the project altogether.

Focusing our attention on the conflict between the state agency and Amalgamated, we find that the Rodericks are likely to be affected by the outcome of the conflict; accordingly, they are constituents.[4] The Sierra Club, as well as the Middlesex homeowners association, are constituents with considerable power to impact the course of the conflict. As such, these entities are considered stakeholders.

WHAT TO MAKE OF THIS CHAPTER

What should you make of this chapter? There are a lot of definitions and new terminology to sort through. However, as the conflict diagnosis process unfolds over the next several chapters, the definitions will prove invaluable.

In a revealing way, this book represents an interpersonal transaction between reader and author. The relationship of reader and author is an interdependent

---

[3] This definition of the term *advocate* is slightly different than, albeit related to, the everyday usage of the term. Advocates for the homeless, the poor, children, the disabled, and other disempowered groups also act on behalf of those they represent and advance their interests. However, they do not act under a legal or an ethical obligation to do so, nor do they necessarily always act in an interpersonal conflict setting (although they often do).

[4] As with many conflict situations, there are potentially a number of interpersonal conflicts in this scenario. Depending on which conflict is the focus, the individuals involved will take on different roles.

one: the author's purpose is to convey thoughts, ideas, and information to the reader, and the reader's purpose is typically to obtain information, training, knowledge, and motivation from the author's written materials. These purposes are primarily promotive (reader generally wants to learn, and author wants to convey knowledge to the reader), although there are also some contrient aspects of the relationship (for example, the reader typically will want to pay as little as possible for the book, whereas the author will want to receive as much as possible when it is sold). A hallmark of effective conflict prevention and management is clear communication. The purpose of this chapter has been to set the stage for clear communication between author and reader, so that the thoughts, ideas, and information contained in succeeding chapters can be conveyed efficiently and accurately. You are encouraged to return to this chapter later if clarification is needed, just as disputants often have to go back to an agreement to review the details of a settlement. As you go forward in the book, you may notice ways that the book tries to minimize misunderstanding, foster trust, acknowledge your frame of reference, create receptivity to the author's frame of reference, and draw you in to the validity of the content of the book. All of these are goals of effective conflict resolvers.

EXERCISES, PROJECTS, AND "THOUGHT EXPERIMENTS"

1. Select a news item that seems to involve an interpersonal conflict. Identify the conflicting goals that make this situation an interpersonal conflict, and, to the best of your ability, identify the disputants and, if any, the agents, advocates, constituents, and other stakeholders. Note that it is often difficult to distinguish among disputants, agents, and constituents. Compare notes with fellow class members and share with one another your justifications for the identifications you made.

2. In the news item you identified in question 1, identify any complementary or shared goals that make the situation mixed-motive rather than zero-sum. Think hard about this; it is often hard to see complementary or shared goals without a lot of deliberation. Are you surprised that the disputants in this conflict have some shared goals? Do you think they're aware of them?

3. A conflict journal is an invaluable tool for learning about interpersonal conflict, sensitizing yourself to the nuances of conflict, and learning how to diagnose and deal with conflict. To begin your conflict journal, select an actual ongoing interpersonal conflict—a dispute, transaction, or conflict-ridden relationship—in which you're involved. It's best if you're a disputant, but you may also be an agent, an advocate, a constituent, or another stakeholder. A conflict journal works best if the conflict you've chosen is likely to persist for a long time—weeks, months, or years. If your conflict resolves more quickly, choose another conflict and continue the exercise. Some examples of suitable conflicts include disputes with merchants, ongoing disputes with family members, difficult relationships with coworkers, disputes

with homeowners associations, and ongoing conflicts with neighbors. You may, but need not, select a legal dispute. The first entry in your journal should be a description of the conflict and its participants. Be sure to describe the conflicting goals that produce the interpersonal conflict. **Continue your conflict journal** by making frequent entries—every time there is a new development. Each entry should include the following parts:

a. *Substantive.* Describe what new development has occurred.

b. *Relationship.* How has the new development affected relationships between conflict participants?

c. *Self.* How is the conflict affecting you?

Every chapter in Part II contains exercises for use in your conflict journal. These exercises will encourage you to apply conflict diagnosis techniques to your conflict and to assess how well they are working.

4. Describe the differences among an interpersonal conflict, a dispute, and a transaction.

5. Debate or discuss the merits of the following statement: "Part of the role of a legal advocate is to determine whether the disputant is involved in a true (veridical) or a false conflict." Consider whether taking on such a role is consistent or inconsistent with the ethical obligation of a lawyer to act as a legal advisor to the client.

6. In our description of the Digi-Date scenario, there were two disputants, Jeff and Marsha, as well as a constituent/stakeholder, Marsha's dad. Specify the conflicting goals that created the interpersonal conflict between Jeff and Marsha.

7. Do the facts suggest any other interpersonal conflicts between Jeff and Marsha? If so, describe them, and identify the disputants and the conflicting goals.

8. In question 6, you were asked to specify the conflicting goals that made the Digi-Date situation an interpersonal conflict between Jeff and Marsha. What elements of the conflict made the situation mixed-motive, rather than zero-sum?

RECOMMENDED READINGS

Deutsch, M. 1973. Introduction. In *The resolution of conflict: Constructive and destructive processes.* New Haven, CT: Yale University Press.

Rubin, J.Z., D.G. Pruitt, and S.H. Kim. 1994. Overview. In *Social conflict: Escalation, stalemate, and settlement.* New York: McGraw-Hill.

2

Dispute Resolution Processes: An Introduction

"A brook would lose its song if God removed the rocks."

—Proverb

In this chapter, you will learn ...

The basic forms of dispute resolution:

- Adjudication and negotiation.
- Assisted and unassisted (simple) negotiation.
- Agent- or advocate-assisted negotiation.
- Mediation.
- Nonbinding evaluation.
- Litigation, agency adjudication, and arbitration.
- Mixed, or hybrid, dispute resolution forms.

The Digi-Date saga continues. Jeff, our would-be software developer, is too busy with his hobby and, unconsciously, too uncomfortable with personal confrontation to discuss the revenue conflict directly with Marsha, so he calls his brother-in-law, Max, asking him to talk to Marsha for him. Max calls Marsha, only to be roundly shouted at—"If he wants to work this thing out, he should call me himself!" is her reply. Nonetheless, Max manages to get a meeting worked out between Jeff and Marsha. Max offers to act as a sort of mediator, or go-between, to help them settle their differences.

Max, a born entrepreneur, sees dollar signs: he hopes to get into the deal himself as a marketing agent.

Jeff spends all night and the next day tinkering with a software project, loses track of time, and is forty minutes late to the meeting, which is being held at a local hangout for university students, called Treasures. By the time Jeff arrives, frazzled and sleepless, Max has had a few snootfuls and is acting belligerently. Marsha is in the process of being picked up by a local. Accompanied by her new date, Eric, she charges over to Jeff. "You're a great one. An hour late? What kind of crap are you trying to pull?" Jeff responds dully that he's sorry—in fact, he hadn't realized that he was late at all. The three of them start to talk about the Digi-Date project, but Jeff immediately clams up—he doesn't want Eric, a stranger, in on the deal. It soon becomes apparent that none of them is in any condition to talk about money. Jeff leaves the bar and goes home. Marsha is too drunk and too involved to be much good, anyway. Max is too busy directing his entrepreneurial zeal toward conquering the opposite sex.

The next day, Jeff is staggered to find a message from Marsha on his answering machine after class. Eric, it turns out, is a law student. He has suggested that Marsha take Jeff to court to enforce her interpretation of their royalty agreement. "Stop playing around; think big, Marsha," he said to her after a night of tender moments and conversation. "Don't bother to call me," she says in the message. "You'll hear from me soon enough."

Chapter 1 introduced the features of interpersonal conflict and the terms used to describe the roles of participants in conflict. With this basic understanding, we now have enough common language to sketch out and identify the various means by which conflict is resolved.

In this chapter, we will consider the overall landscape of conflict resolution processes and define them conceptually. These definitions will help us make sense when we are discussing the steps of conflict diagnosis. We will return in detail to the dispute resolution processes when we address alternative dispute resolution (ADR) in Part III. As we explore dispute resolution processes, see if you can pick out examples of some of these processes in the Digi-Date story.

FORMS OF DISPUTE RESOLUTION

Dispute resolution
the methods that people use in an effort to resolve interpersonal conflicts.

Alternative dispute resolution (ADR)
generally, the dispute resolution processes used in the resolution of legal, business/commercial, and other interpersonal conflicts, other than litigation, other than doing nothing, and other than illegal or violent approaches such as extortion or assault.

The ways that people deal with conflict are known broadly as **dispute resolution**. There is a virtual rainbow of possible ways to address conflicts and disputes. In this book, we will limit ourselves to the forms of dispute resolution that are commonly used to address disputes and transactions in legal, business, and interpersonal settings. We will generally exclude from consideration "extra-legal" and "illegal" forms of dispute resolution, such as war, physical violence, extortion, and other similar processes.

It's important to be able to distinguish among the basic forms of dispute resolution, because each form has particular advantages and disadvantages for particular situations. The field of **alternative dispute resolution (ADR)** is characterized by looseness and misuse of identifying terminology, as well as controversy over how to define the processes. In part, these controversies and uncertainties reflect the perspectives of the diverse professionals involved in the field, and, in part, the controversies probably reflect "turf battles" and entrepreneurial decisions to name processes in the most marketable fashion. The result is that the same term is often used to denote quite different processes.

Knowing the basic varieties of dispute resolution processes conceptually will help the diagnostician select the best process to address the conflict, regardless of

> ### *Factors that Distinguish Dispute Resolution Processes*
> ◆ Who decides the outcome of the interpersonal conflict
> ◆ Who participates in the process
> ◆ Under what auspices the process is provided

the name given to it. In selecting a particular ADR provider, it is always important to clarify the conceptual variety of the process that the provider is offering, regardless of how he or she has named it.

The universe of dispute resolution processes can be distinguished according to the factors shown at the top of the page. The major dispute resolution forms each represent a combination of these factors. Dispute resolution processes can be further subdivided based on the auspices under which the process is provided (governmental or private sector) and on a number of procedural details.

NEGOTIATION AND ADJUDICATION

Dispute resolution processes can be divided into two main categories, according to the identities of the persons who decide the outcome. These two categories are *negotiation* (Figure 2-1) and *adjudication* (Figure 2-2). In negotiation, disputants (or their representatives) engage in a dialogue aimed at resolving the conflict. The dialogue may be verbal and face-to-face, may be written, may occur by telephone, or may use one of the many technologies available for communication purposes, such as e-mail, instant messaging, or videoconferencing. The disputants are in control of the outcome of the conflict: it is their decision whether to settle. In adjudication, on the other hand, a neutral third party, an adjudicator, decides the outcome. (Litigation—trying a case in court—is the most well-known form of adjudication.) Thus, *the*

◆ **FIGURE 2-1**

Negotiation

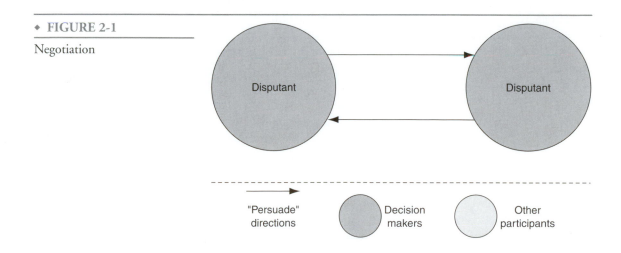

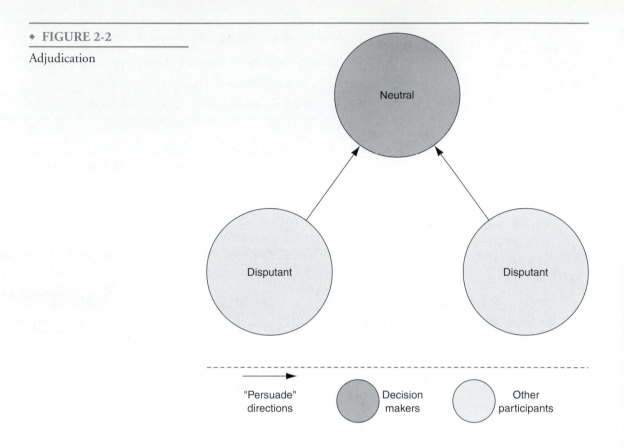

principal distinction between negotiation and adjudication is the person in charge of deciding the outcome: in negotiation, it is the disputants; in adjudication, it is the neutral.

Forms of Negotiation. There are numerous forms of **negotiation.** In fact, many of the most innovative forms of ADR are variants of the negotiation process. In this introductory section, the major conceptual variations of the negotiation process will be defined.

Negotiation may be unassisted or assisted. Unassisted negotiation is referred to in this text as **simple negotiation** (Figure 2-1). In this form of negotiation, the disputants are the only participants. For example, the scenario in Chapter 1, of the husband and wife discussing where to go for dinner, demonstrated a simple negotiation.

Negotiation may also be assisted, or facilitated. There are three principal variations. The most common form of assisted negotiation, at least in the United

Negotiation

the process in which disputants seek to resolve an interpersonal conflict through dialogue or another form of communication. In negotiation, the disputants themselves decide mutually whether, and on what terms, the conflict should be resolved.

Simple negotiation

negotiation in which the only participants are the disputants.

◆ **Negotiation:** The disputants decide.
◆ **Adjudication:** A neutral third party decides.

◆ **FIGURE 2-3**

Negotiation with Agents or
Advocates

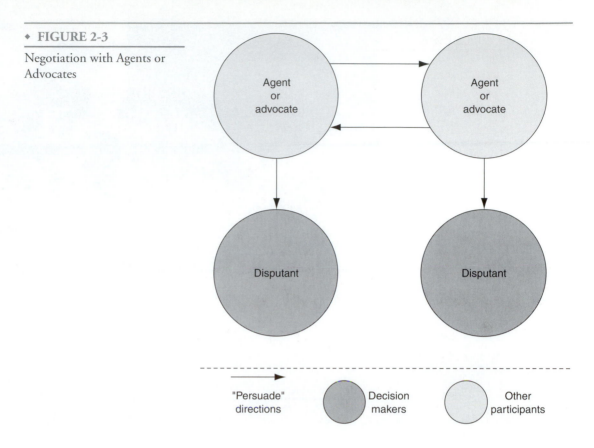

Agent
or
advocate

Agent
or
advocate

Disputant

Disputant

"Persuade"
directions

Decision
makers

Other
participants

**Agent- or advocate-assisted
negotiation**

negotiation in which one or both
disputants are represented in the
negotiation by an individual who
acts on the disputants' behalf. The
disputants retain the ultimate
authority to accept or reject a
settlement.

Mediation

assisted negotiation in which the
disputants, either alone or assisted
by agents or advocates, negotiate
in the presence of a neutral
professional (or panel of
professionals), called a mediator
(or mediation panel). The
mediator's role is to assist the
disputants in their negotiation.

States, is **agent-** or **advocate-assisted negotiation** (Figure 2-3). In this form of negotiation, one or more of the disputants are represented by assistants who "stand in the shoes" of the disputants and negotiate on their behalf. In the S-Chip scenario (Chapter 1), the two corporate disputants are represented by *both* agents and advocates. In agent- and advocate-assisted negotiation, the disputant retains the authority to accept or reject a given settlement, although the disputant may instruct his or her representative on a range of acceptable settlements before or during negotiation.

Mediation (Figure 2-4), the second variety of assisted negotiation, has become increasingly important in the resolution of legal disputes. In mediation, the disputants' negotiation is facilitated by a neutral third party, whose role is to help the disputants in their negotiation. The disputants retain all control over whether to settle their conflict and the details of their settlement. The disputants may attend mediation on their own, they may attend with their agents or advocates, or their representatives may mediate in their place. Mediation itself is a highly diverse process, with each variation having important uses, strengths, and weaknesses. These variations will be considered in detail in Chapter 15. In our Digi-Date scenario, the brother-in-law, Max, evidently has it in mind to mediate the dispute between the disputants Jeff and Marsha—although he could hardly be considered neutral.

Negotiation is often assisted by advocates. Michael Newman, PhotoEdit

---

Mediation

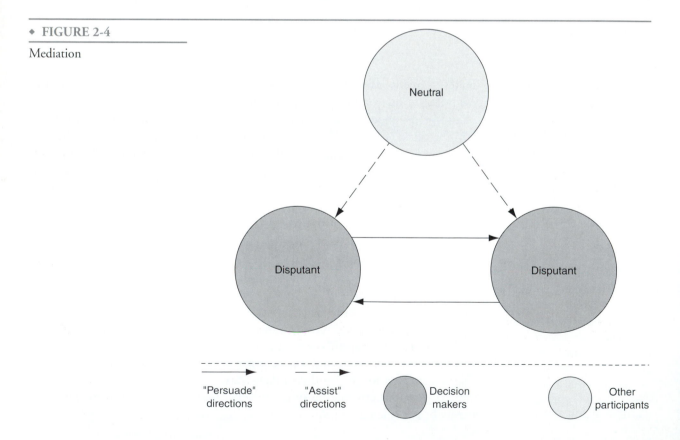

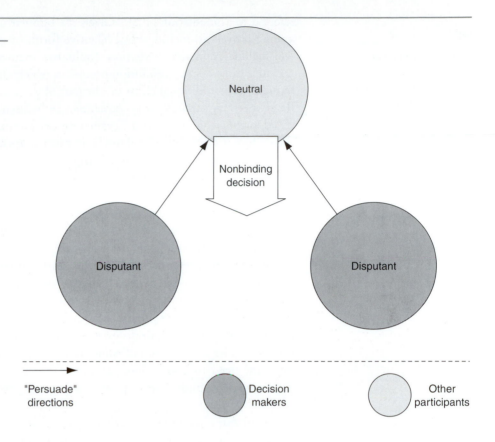

Nonbinding evaluation

assisted negotiation in which the disputants present their conflict to a third party or a panel of third parties. The third party's role is to render a nonbinding decision or opinion about the conflict.

The third variety of assisted, or facilitated, negotiation is **nonbinding evaluation** (Figure 2-5). In this form of negotiation, the disputants (either on their own or, more commonly, represented by advocates or other agents) present their side of the dispute to a third party or a panel of third parties. The third party is usually neutral, but, in some variants of the process, the panel is comprised of groups of persons who are directly interested in the outcome (such as directors or executive officers for corporate disputants). In a proceeding that often resembles adjudication, the third party renders a decision or an opinion about the appropriate or expected outcome of the conflict, but this decision or opinion is not binding on the disputants, as it is in adjudication. The disputants use the nonbinding evaluation as information to assist them in their continuing negotiations. There are numerous forms of nonbinding evaluation, the most popular of which will be described in detail in Chapter 20.

Some variants of mediation are difficult to distinguish from nonbinding evaluation. These involve the mediator issuing an opinion about the likely outcome of the dispute, should it be submitted to a court. Some legal scholars—most notably, law professors Kimberlee Kovach and Lela Love (1996), have recommended that this "evaluative" variety of mediation, which is increasingly popular in business, commercial, and governmental agency settings, not be

Evaluative mediation
mediation in which the mediator issues one or more opinions or evaluations about the likely outcome of the conflict, should it be taken to court, or about the strengths and weaknesses of each disputant's case. It is distinguished from nonbinding evaluation in that the evaluation is not the centerpiece, or endpoint, of the process.

Litigation
an adjudication process that proceeds under the auspices of state or federal law in a court.

Adversary process
an approach to handling interpersonal conflict in which each person presses for an advantage at the expense of the other's interests—in other words, competition is used to resolve the conflict.

referred to as mediation at all.[1] Given the popular usage of the term *mediation* among lawyers to include this evaluative form, the term *mediation* in this text will include evaluative mediation. **Evaluative mediation** will be defined in this text to mean a dispute resolution process in which an evaluation is accompanied by significant additional effort on the part of the neutral party to facilitate a settlement, whereas *nonbinding evaluation* will be used to describe a process of assisted negotiation in which the evaluation predominates, and generally serves as the endpoint of, the process. However, it bears repeating that, if choosing a dispute resolution process, it is always important to get the details of any proposed process or provider's services to determine what sort of dispute resolution is being considered.

So far, we have defined the forms of negotiation primarily based on who participates in the process and how, if at all, negotiation is facilitated. What about who sponsors, promotes, or provides the processes? In general, negotiation is considered a private process. Any disputants can consent to a negotiation and can hire an agent, an advocate, a mediator, or a nonbinding evaluator to assist in the process. However, some court systems, in recognition of some of the benefits of using negotiation processes to settle conflicts (Chapter 21), have ordered disputants to participate in negotiation, mediation, and nonbinding evaluation processes. The same is true of some local, state, and federal agencies that confront the need to resolve interpersonal conflict. Hence, negotiation may, but need not, occur under the auspices of a court or governmental agency.

Forms of Adjudication. As previously stated, in adjudication (Figure 2-2), unlike negotiation, the decision maker is a neutral third party, rather than the disputants. There are three major forms of adjudication.

Adjudication performed under the auspices of the government is the dispute resolution that we think of as "normal" and "usual." (The overwhelming prevalence of this sort of adjudication in the public consciousness is why other dispute resolution processes are thought of as "alternative.") The most familiar form of adjudication for most people is **litigation,** which is, of course, what Marsha has now threatened Jeff with in the Digi-Date dispute. Litigation is simply a lawsuit, culminating in a trial by judge or jury—the adjudication of an interpersonal conflict under the auspices of a court system. Litigation is characterized, in the United States, by a formalized and ritualized adversary procedure, including carefully prescribed rules of evidence and procedure. These rules are designed to promote a controlled **adversary process** and to ensure that each litigant's rights and interests are protected by the application of due process of law under the Fifth and Fourteenth Amendments to the United States Constitution and analogous state law. The types of disputes that may be submitted to litigation, as well as the sorts of outcomes that a court may prescribe, are also defined strictly by law. A dispute that a court is empowered to pass upon in litigation is called a cause of action, and an outcome that a court can provide to an applicant to a

---

[1] The term *evaluative mediation* was coined by law professor Leonard Riskin and presented in his classic article "Understanding Mediator Orientations, Strategies, and Techniques: A Grid for the Perplexed" (1996).

Legal remedy

an outcome that, by law, a court can provide to a party in litigation, such as a legal pronouncement or money damages.

Agency adjudication

an adjudication process that proceeds under the auspices of agency law or regulation and features an adjudicator and adjudicatory procedures specific to that agency.

Arbitration

an adjudicatory process that proceeds under the auspices of a private contract. The neutral decision maker is referred to as an arbitrator.

Mixed, or hybrid, dispute resolution processes

any one of a number of ADR processes that feature a combination of two or more basic dispute resolution processes.

court is called a **legal remedy.** There are many interpersonal conflicts that either cannot be expressed as causes of action, do not have effective solutions that courts are empowered to provide as remedies, or both, and this limitation of the litigation process is one reason for the growing popularity of ADR processes. For example, if former spouses have a dispute about whom their children will live with, they may have a legal basis for going to court to determine child custody. However, if they have a disagreement over the types of foods one or the other parent feeds the children when they are with that parent, or over bedtimes or how often the children get bathed, there is probably no legal recourse to resolve it, even though these "minor" disputes may cause just as much grief, aggravation, and damage as the disputes that can be considered by a court.

Governmental agencies may also have legally prescribed adjudicatory processes. This **agency adjudication** is generally somewhat less formal than litigation, although it may be very similar in complexity and formality. Like litigation, agency adjudication occurs under governmental auspices, is restricted in the types of disputes that the adjudicator (often called a *hearing officer*) is empowered to resolve, and is restricted in the sorts of remedies the adjudicator is empowered to provide. For example, many states provide that drivers who accumulate too many traffic tickets have their licenses suspended or revoked, and this process of suspension or revocation is usually done through an *administrative hearing process* performed by the state agency charged with regulating motor vehicles.

Agency adjudication and litigation are not considered ADR processes. However, the third type of adjudication is. This very popular form of dispute resolution is called **arbitration.**

Arbitration is characterized by two attributes. First, it is a form of adjudication, in which the disputants present their cases to a neutral third party, called an arbitrator, who issues a binding decision in the matter. Second, arbitration occurs not under governmental auspices (as it does for litigation and agency adjudication) but, instead, under private auspices. Arbitration occurs because disputants have *contracted* (agreed, in a legally enforceable manner) to have it occur, either pre-dispute, in an effort to manage future conflicts, or after the dispute has arisen.[2]

MIXED, OR HYBRID, DISPUTE RESOLUTION PROCESSES

So-called **mixed, or hybrid, dispute resolution processes** are processes that combine the attributes of two or more of the major forms of dispute resolution. For example, "med-arb," in which mediation is followed by arbitration if the mediation does not result in settlement, and "ombuds," in which an individual is

---

[2] Despite the conceptual distinction between arbitration, in which the neutral party decides the outcome of the conflict, and nonbinding evaluation, in which the decision is in the hands of the disputants, there is a form of ADR referred to (unfortunately) as "nonbinding arbitration." This process is a type of nonbinding evaluation and frequently occurs under the auspices of a court system.

vested with the power to counsel disputants and suggest or refer to other ADR processes, are considered mixed, or hybrid, processes.[3]

A SUMMARY OF DISPUTE RESOLUTION PROCESSES

Considering only the sorts of dispute resolution that individuals and organizations tend to use in civil, business, commercial, and legal settings, dispute resolution processes can be divided conceptually into negotiation, in which disputants have the authority to decide on the outcome of their conflict, and adjudication, in which the authority to decide on an outcome is granted to a third party. Negotiation, in turn, can be divided into simple negotiation, in which the disputants are the only participants, and assisted, or facilitated, negotiation, in which other participants help one or both disputants. Assisted, or facilitated, negotiation is divisible into subcategories that reflect the identity and role of the facilitators, including agent- or advocate-assisted negotiation (in which people negotiate "in the shoes" of the disputants), mediation (in which a neutral third party facilitates negotiation), and nonbinding evaluation (in which a neutral third party issues a nonbinding opinion or decision to the negotiators). Adjudication, in turn, can be distinguished in terms of the auspices under which it occurs, including litigation and agency adjudication, in which particular disputes are submitted to a governmental entity for determination, and arbitration, in which the disputants contract to submit a case to a private adjudicator. Figure 2-6 diagrams this summary, and

◆ **FIGURE 2-6**

Basic Dispute Resolution
Forms

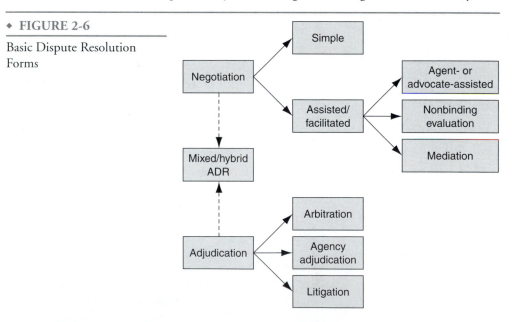

---

[3] In the ADR field, nonbinding evaluation is usually included in the list of hybrid processes because it is a type of negotiation, yet it often resembles adjudication in form. This categorization, unfortunately, adds to the confusion and misunderstandings surrounding ADR processes. In this text, *nonbinding evaluation* is defined separately, in recognition of its conceptual characteristics as an assisted negotiation process and in recognition of the fact that the uses, strengths, and drawbacks of nonbinding evaluation processes differ from those of true mixed, or hybrid, processes.

Table 2-1 describes the relationship between the basic forms of dispute resolution and the three factors (who participates, who decides, and under what auspices) that determine the distinctions between the forms.

◆ **TABLE 2-1**   Forms of Dispute Resolution: Characteristics

DISPUTE RESOLUTION FORM	WHO DECIDES?	WHO ELSE PARTICIPATES?	AUSPICES	COMMENTS
Simple negotiation	Disputants	No one	Private	
Agent-advocate-assisted negotiation	Disputants	Agents or advocates (or both)	Private	Agent/advocate may participate alongside or in place of one or both disputants.
Mediation	Disputants	A neutral, called the mediator, whose role is to facilitate negotiation	May be private or governmentally encouraged, sponsored, or mandated	Agents/advocates may also be present.
Nonbinding evaluation	Disputants	A neutral, whose role is to issue a nonbinding evaluation or decision	May be private or governmentally encouraged, sponsored, or mandated	Agents/advocates may also be present. Process may resemble advice-giving, court trial or jury trial.
Litigation	Judge	Disputants and, often, their agents and/or advocates	State or federal judicial system	There are very rigid rules of procedure and evidence and very rigorous rules concerning right to litigate and remedy if cause of action is established.
Agency adjudication	Hearing examiner or similar agency official	Disputants and, often, their agents and/or advocates	Agency law or regulatory structure	Process is usually less rigid procedurally than litigation.
Arbitration	Arbitrator	Disputants and, often, their agents and/or advocates	Private: disputants contract to submit to arbitration	It may be highly formalized, extremely informal, or in between.
Mixed, or hybrid, ADR	Depends on the process and the stage; usually, disputants at some stage in the process and adjudicator at another stage	Disputants and, often, their agents and/or advocates; neutral, such as an evaluator or a mediator, may also participate	May be private or governmentally encouraged, sponsored, or mandated	The specifics vary greatly with the form of hybrid ADR.

The Cartoon Bank

EXERCISES, PROJECTS, AND "THOUGHT EXPERIMENTS"

1. Ed found the following ads on the Internet for dispute resolution providers. Given their descriptions of what they offer, identify each proprietor's process as *arbitration, mediation, nonbinding evaluation*, or *mixed/hybrid process*.

   a. *Cyber Court.* Here's how it works! You and your opponent agree to submit your case to the Cyber Court and set the stakes. The appropriate party sends us a check for the stakes. We keep it in escrow at (name of bank). You and your opponent provide written statements of your cases. You can fax documentary evidence to us, and, for an extra fee, we will schedule a real-time hearing using Internet conferencing with "whiteboard" and document-sharing facilities. Our panel of trained dispute resolvers reviews your case and votes on the best outcome. We send the winner the award and return any additional escrowed funds to the payor. You have real peace of mind, knowing that your issues will be resolved and your problems will be put behind you.

   b. *Internet Jury.* A jury of your peers is available to solve your problems. Our jury pool is made up of people, just like you. When you have a conflict, you are assigned a jury, who will hear your arguments. The Internet Jury makes a decision and posts it in your own personal "cyber-courtroom." Then you can use the decision to help you settle your case. Our case analysis shows that 90 percent of cases submitted to the Internet Jury settle for the amount determined by the Internet Jury!

   c. *World Wide Web Dispute Resolution Services.* Our panels of trained professionals will help you work out your own settlements wherever you are by assisting with the negotiation process. Recognizing the global economy, we are proud to present this service for the global community. You get the help you need but stay in charge of the solution.

   d. *Byte-Peace.* We use the sophistication of the modern cyber-world to resolve your dispute. Here's how it works: Each disputant is assigned a private "cyber-workspace." Working step by step with our exclusive computerized analysis system, each disputant answers a series of questions designed to uncover his or her exact interests. We keep this information strictly private at Byte-Peace. When both disputants have completed their submission, our advanced mathematical model determines whether there is "overlap" in your positions. If there is, the model reports the midpoint to both disputants.

2. Research the World Wide Web for organizations devoted to the practice of dispute resolution. Write a summary of a website you find. What services are provided by this organization that would be useful to legal assistants or paralegals, and why would these services be useful?

3. Legal research. Research the process known as Michigan mediation. What ADR process is this? Is it mediation under the definition this book uses? Is Michigan mediation privately or governmentally sponsored? If the latter, what governmental entity oversees it?

4. Go to your local trial court of general jurisdiction and ask the clerk to pull the file of a civil case that has been litigated to completion. Study the file thoroughly. From a public policy perspective, are there any reasons that this dispute should have been encouraged to settle? What are they? Are there other public policy reasons that this case is better off being litigated? What are they? Overall, in comparing these public policy considerations, is society better off for having had this case go to trial, or would it have been better for society if the case had settled? Compare your reasons with those of other class members who have done this exercise to develop a list of public policy reasons for encouraging cases to either litigate or be settled.

5. Consider the following disputes. Should each be encouraged to go to litigation or to settle? In answering this question, take the following perspectives: (1) each of the disputants; (2) a settlement conference judge trying to determine how to handle the logistics of trying the case; (3) a legislator considering legal reform legislation:

   a. *Case 1, Smith v. Jones.* Smith was proceeding southward on Interstate 95 just above the Route 50 interchange. Smith states that he was properly in the lane adjacent to the fast lane when he was struck by Jones along the left side of his vehicle. Smith was slightly injured and states that he spent $2,000 on medical care. His vehicle was damaged and was repaired for $1,500. Jones was uninjured and suffered $750 in damages to his right front bumper. Smith contends that Jones, originally in the fast lane, entered Smith's lane at a high rate of speed and hit Smith. Jones contends that he remained in his own lane, driving within the speed limit, and that Smith changed lanes to hit his vehicle without first checking his "blind spot."

b. *Case 2.* This is the same as Case 1, except that Smith, a twenty-four-year-old healthy male at the time of the accident, was seriously injured, incurring $500,000 in medical expenses and severe permanent disability. Smith's total damages claim of $2 million is *not* in dispute.

c. *Case 3, Brown v. Board of Education (a famous case, decided by the United States Supreme Court, 347 U.S. 483, 1954).* It is the 1950s. A group of African-American parents contend that the widespread practice of segregating their children in colored-only schools is wrong. The government contends that the practice is perfectly acceptable and that, legally, it's a "slam-dunk" due to *Plessey v. Ferguson* (also a real case, 163 U.S. 537, 1896).

d. *Case 4, Burnwell v. Hayden.* In 1965, Ernest Burnwell, then a student in London, met Gloria Hayden. They soon became romantically involved and moved in together, but never married. In their many years together, Burnwell worked himself up to a middle-management position at a multinational food service corporation, being paid by a number of its subsidiaries around the world. Hayden freelanced as a writer, making a very modest income while she raised their two children. The couple acquired a flat in Madrid, a tiny house in Brazil, a modest home in Mexico, and another flat in Bombay. They were unable to take the time to sell these residences, as Burnwell's frequent job moves were sudden and unanticipated. In 1998, while the couple was living in Portugal for a six-week assignment, the relationship fell apart and the couple separated. Now they have to decide how to allocate their joint property, with a net worth of about $200,000 U.S.

Note: you are not expected to know how the law resolves issues of which jurisdiction's law should be applied in international disputes.

e. *Case 5, Doe v. Drugco.* Drugco released its new diet drug, Thinisin, for prescription sale in 1996. The drug was in extreme demand, owing to an intensive and sophisticated media campaign directed at consumers and physicians alike. More than 5 million obese patients were prescribed the drug, and Drugco made over $500 million in profits over a five-year period. In late 1999, an obscure journalist broke the story of several Thinisin users who had died of a rare and extremely virulent form of pancreatic cancer. This journalist implied that the drug had caused the deaths, but Drugco denied the claim, citing numerous drug trials that had found the medicine to be perfectly safe. Then, in September 2000, a disgruntled former employee at Drugco alleged that Drugco had had experimental evidence of Thinisin's carcinogenic properties as early as 1995 but had destroyed all traces of the drug trials that pointed to the drug's problems. If the claims of the journalist and employee are correct, there are several million citizens who are now at high risk for deadly pancreatic cancer as a result of their exposure to Thinisin.

6. What dispute resolution process would you recommend, and why, if you occupied each of the following roles in the Digi-Date conflict?

    a. You are an advocate for Marsha.

    b. You are an advocate for Jeff.

    c. You are a close friend of *both* Marsha and Jeff.

    d. You are Max, the brother-in-law of Jeff who offered to intercede.

7. Put yourself in the role of a managing paralegal at a large urban law firm. Your state bar governing body has just adopted an ethical rule obligating all attorneys to inform their clients of dispute resolution options, including ADR. Develop the text of a brochure that your firm will distribute to clients to help satisfy this disclosure obligation. What else will advocates have to do to satisfy such an obligation, and why?

RECOMMENDED READINGS

Kubey, C. 1991. *You don't always need a lawyer: How to resolve your legal disputes without costly litigation.* Yonkers, NY: Consumer Reports Books.

Nolan-Haley, J. M. 2001. Dispute resolution in the court system. Hybrid dispute resolution procedures. In *Alternative dispute resolution in a nutshell.* St. Paul, MN: West.

3

Of Artisans, Invisible Veils, and Philosophical Maps: Our Preconceptions About Conflict and How They Shortchange Us

"Everyone's objectivity is seen through their own prism."

—Anonymous sports fan, radio sports talk show, Baltimore, Maryland, 28 April 2001

"Very early in my life I saw that what people in different cultures consider given—just the way things are— is not the same everywhere."

—Anthropologist Riane Eisler (1988, xiii)

"When the only tool you have is a hammer, every problem begins to resemble a nail."

—Abraham Maslow

In this chapter, you will learn . . .

- How approaching interpersonal conflict is like being a craftsman, using blueprints and tools learned from parents, school, friends, the media, and societal institutions.
- How we acquire our conflict blueprints and toolboxes.
- How Bronfenbrenner's ecological theory of development helps explain the persistence of the prevailing conflict blueprint—that conflict is a contest with only one winner and one loser—and the prevailing conflict toolbox— competitive strategies and tactics.

- ◆ How the legal system helps perpetuate our conflict blueprints and toolboxes.
- ◆ How our conflict blueprints and toolboxes are unduly limiting, preventing us from resolving conflict more effectively.
- ◆ Some perspectives people may take in assessing whether conflict is being handled effectively.

Interpersonal conflict is all around us.[1] We confront interpersonal conflict when we decide who will do the housework, attend staff meetings, negotiate for a raise, or discipline a child. Anytime we deal with another person, the possibility of incompatible goals raises the possibility of conflict. Since human beings are social creatures, much of what we do on a moment-to-moment basis involves conflict—heading it off, recognizing it, avoiding it, managing it, resolving it.

Before embarking on a study of conflict and the processes of resolving it, it is necessary to appreciate that people—particularly people from westernized cultures, such as the United States—have a narrow perspective on what conflict is and how it is best managed and resolved. This narrowness, fostered by our cultural beliefs and practices, seriously impairs our ability to understand and choose methods of resolving conflict, as well as our ability to choose dispute resolution processes and providers. To make things worse, the narrowness of our perspective is practically always invisible to us. It is almost as if we have tunnel vision and have gotten so used to it that we no longer notice. Our narrow perspective acts as an invisible veil, blinding us to many of the possibilities we have to manage conflict effectively and creatively. One of the objectives of this chapter is to lift the veil and widen the scope of your understanding of conflict and how it can be resolved.

ARTISANSHIP AND THE CRAFT METAPHOR

It is useful to think of a craft metaphor when we try to understand our perspective on conflict. To be a master artisan, creating products at the highest possible level, we need three things. First, we need an effective plan, or idea, for how to build or create our craft. We'll call this plan or idea the *blueprint*. Next, we need a *toolbox*—a set of tools well suited for this sort of craft. Finally, we need *proficiency*—a high level of expertise in using the tools to translate the plans in the blueprint to the finished craft. The high level of expertise enjoyed by a master artisan can come only from lots of practice. We'll return to this recipe for mastery repeatedly throughout our discussion of conflict diagnosis.

Practice makes perfect, and, over a lifetime of dealing with a particular set of blueprints and tools, we can get very good at producing the product described. But what happens when the tools or the blueprint is changed? Let's imagine we are carpenters who have mastered the art of cabinetry. If we have

---

[1] Interpersonal conflict is to be distinguished from "inner conflict," the sort of internal strife we feel when we are uncertain about what to do.

Recipe for Mastery
◆ A plan or blueprint
◆ A toolbox
◆ Proficiency at interpreting the blueprint and using the tools

learned to make a particular sort of cabinet using old-style tools and, over a long time, have mastered our craft, we will falter if we are suddenly given a new set of tools—for example, power tools with computerized controls—to make a cabinet. We lack the *proficiency* to use the new tools well. If we do not observe well-respected masters successfully making cabinets using these new tools, we are not likely to be motivated to develop the proficiency needed to use the new tools effectively. Instead, we are very likely to abandon the new tools and go back to the old ones, complaining that the new tools aren't any good. Similarly, if we are given a new and potentially better blueprint for making a different sort of cabinet, we may not be able to see the advantages of the new blueprint, because our inappropriate toolbox and lack of proficiency keep us from producing as good a product as when we make old-style cabinets in the design we're used to making. Unless we have specific information to indicate that either the new blueprint or the new set of tools is better in some way than our comfortable old versions, it's likely we'll conclude that the old blueprint and the old tools are just plain *better.*

It is equally likely, however, that we have failed to develop the *proficiency* to use the new plans and the new tools effectively. From our perspective as masters of the old equipment, we are likely to blame the new blueprint or the new tools, rather than to realize that it is our lack of proficiency that holds us back.

What does cabinetry have to do with alternative dispute resolution? Each of us receives a set of blueprints for managing interpersonal conflict. We get these blueprints largely from our parents and other caregivers, with help from siblings, teachers, peers, the mass media, governmental institutions, and other sources, who, in turn, got their blueprints from their parents, caregivers, siblings, teachers, and so on. The people who teach us how to manage conflict have acquired a high degree of proficiency in applying particular tools to deal with conflict. The contents of their toolboxes have evolved to fit their blueprints, and they have developed a high level of proficiency in using those tools to resolve conflict according to the blueprints they have acquired. We learn the same tools by observation; by imitation, a process called *role modeling;* and by practice in situations that require using the tools. As human, social creatures, we encounter interpersonal conflict with such frequency that we gain massive amounts of experience applying our acquired blueprints and toolbox for handling conflict. To the extent that our blueprint is limited, we acquire and become proficient at only a small toolbox of conflict-handling tools. Once we master our preferred blueprint and our toolbox, we are likely to experience any alternative blueprints and toolboxes as inherently inferior to the ones we are used to.

CULTURAL INFLUENCES ON THE BLUEPRINT AND TOOLBOX

There are bigger forces at work, as well, influencing which blueprints and which tools we acquire in the handling of interpersonal conflict. The blueprints our parents and others around us apply to conflicts usually reflect the practices predominating in the society at large.

Uri Bronfenbrenner, an eminent developmental psychologist, named the overall social structure that acts as a source of blueprints for individuals the **macrosystem** (Bronfenbrenner 1979). The macrosystem includes the important institutions in which we operate—the court system, the governmental structure, and so on. In his influential theory of Social Ecology, Bronfenbrenner postulated that there is a synergistic relationship between the macrosystem and the individual. Think of it as a chicken-egg relationship. The macrosystem is structured to reflect the cultural belief systems of its inhabitants—that's because a society is composed of its individual members, and their collective efforts maintain the macrosystem. Since most of the individuals in a society possess these culturally predominant beliefs, those individuals tend to interact with, and therefore maintain, the macrosystem in a manner reflective of these beliefs. Because of this consistent input from society's members, the macrosystem evolves a particular structure. The macrosystem's structure generates situations in which individuals, to survive and do well, must adopt blueprints and use tools consistent with the

Macrosystem

the part of a person's environment consisting of overall societal social structures, including the government, the mass media, cultural attitudes, and overarching social and governmental institutions, such as the predominant school organization, the justice system, the manner in which people acquire goods and services, and the Internet.

Parenting and Interpersonal Conflict

Unless we are orphaned, we usually have our first interpersonal conflicts with our parents, and, since we interact a lot with our families, as children we probably have more conflicts with parents (and siblings) than with anyone else. Styles of parenting probably act as blueprints for conflict resolution, and observations of our parents teach us the tools we need to act according to the blueprints. *Authoritarian* parents, who are strict and demanding but not very sensitive or responsive, teach children that only one person wins a conflict, the strong one. Children of authoritarian parents learn dominating behavior by watching their parents discipline them, and these children learn submissive, obliging behavior as it is demanded of them. *Permissive* parents, who are warm and responsive but demand little from their children, teach their children that they can exercise power through manipulation. Children of permissive parents also become proficient in a toolbox of dominating and submissive behavior, except that they learn submission by observation and are encouraged to practice dominating themselves. Children of both authoritarian and permissive parents have very similar patterns of social adjustment. Neither tends to be effective in leadership roles, both often have difficulty getting along with others, and neither tends to be academically competent. *Authoritative* parents, on the other hand, are strict and demanding yet also warm and responsive. These parents teach their children that all disputants' needs matter when there is a conflict, and they learn techniques of social problem solving from seeing their parents do it and from being forced to do it themselves. Coming into an essentially individualistic social system, children of authoritative parents get plenty of training in dominance and submission, anyway, but, having been given a different blueprint from their parents, they suffer less from the tunnel vision about conflict resolution that afflicts most of us. These children tend to grow up more socially and academically successful than their counterparts, at least in mainstream American culture.

overall cultural belief systems. Thus, they will become more proficient in using blueprints and tools that reflect prevailing cultural beliefs than in others. When these individuals grow up and attain positions of power and influence, they tend to make decisions that reinforce the existing macrosystem blueprints. Thus, the macrosystem influences individuals, and individuals reinforce the macrosystem.

A society's approach to dealing with conflict is one important aspect of the macrosystem. American society, along with most other Western nations, has been reported to be highly individualistic[2] (see, e.g., Leung and Lind 1986) and reflects an ethic of adversary process and competition as the best—indeed, the only—way to resolve a conflict that has reached an impasse. Because of the prevalence of this blueprint for handling interpersonal conflict, the macrosystem process developed to handle interpersonal conflict, the court system, is competitive and adversarial. As the theory of social ecology would predict, this macrosystem structure is reflected in the proficiencies, attitudes, and behaviors of individuals. People—including those whom we interact directly with—get lots of practice handling competition, adversary processes, dominance, and submission. If you have a legal dispute and wish to resolve it, you must bargain "in the shadow" of a competitive, adversarial legal system.[3] This belief system also

[2] In empirical studies assessing the cultural attitudes of the members of numerous nationalities, in the dimension of individualism, the United States has consistently been rated first of all the countries studied (Leung 1988).

[3] The phrase "in the shadow of the law" comes from the classic 1979 article by Robert Mnookin and Lewis Kornhauser, "Bargaining in the Shadow of the Law: The Case of Divorce." The premise of the work is that individuals who are attempting to negotiate a resolution of their conflict bargain "in the shadow" of our adversarial legal system.

American culture is known for its reference of ragged individualism and vigilante approaches to conflict, as epitomized by Sylvester Stallone's classic character Rambo.
Photofest

trickles down to our other social institutions, including school systems (in which assignments and grades are primarily individually based), many religious structures (based on hierarchical forms of organization), beloved national competitive sports (such as football), and the media (in which extreme individualism and violent domination using deadly weapons are frequently displayed as the pinnacle of heroism). Americans have plenty of opportunity to observe others using

Recognizing the Influence of Individualism in the American Legal System

If you were born and raised in the United States, you may have difficulty with the proposition that its legal system is unusual, apart from the lesson, learned in school, that it is "best." Whether or not "best," the American legal system is, in fact, extreme, compared with other nations, with respect to its emphasis on individualism, individual rights, and the role of competition.

One measure of the individualistic bent of American culture is how it does, or does not, export itself to other nations and cultures. In a classic comparative study of legal systems, sociologist Robert W. Benjamin illustrated the changes that a less individualistic culture might bring upon Westernized legal precepts. Following World War II, the U.S. occupation of Japan brought about the imposition of an American model of adversary criminal justice on Japan, an Eastern, more collectivist nation. Some twenty-five years later, Benjamin compared the Japanese system, with this model in place, with a state court in the American Midwest. He found profound differences in the manner in which these systems, virtually identical in their inception, were actually practiced. The Japanese population of legal professionals Benjamin studied (judges, defense counsel, prosecuting attorneys, and public defenders) were more likely than their American counterparts to agree with statements that defense counsel ought to act more as a "coach" than an advocate, preparing the client to meet behavioral standards and attitudes acceptable to criminal law officials. The American legal professionals were much more likely than their Japanese counterparts to agree with a statement that the role of defense counsel is to protect the interests of the client, regardless of the interests of others or the state. And the Americans were much less likely to agree with statements that the defendant's role is to seek a settlement that will bring substantial justice to both the client and the society and that defense counsel's role is to assure that the best law, rather than the law most favorable to the client, is applied (Benjamin 1975).

competition to address conflict and to hone competitive skills in the face of tasks that require individual accomplishment and recognition. There is relatively little opportunity to acquire alternative blueprints for living; even if such blueprints are made available, it is usually so difficult to develop enough proficiency at using the necessary tools to make them work that they are largely abandoned. Relationships built on mutual cooperation and support are considered "weak" and "feminine" and receive little reward in the society at large. Consider, for example, the differences in salary levels between nursery school teachers, who provide nurturance and support, and professional sports figures, whose job is to compete. Even in collectivist ventures, such as corporate organizations, individual success is typically won in competition. Hence, the tendency for individuals to learn and practice competitive conflict resolution is constantly reinforced in the society at large. When people raised in this fashion enter the productive phase of adulthood, in which they are in the position of maintaining, perpetuating, and reforming social institutions, their decisions are reflective of their experience. They tend to maintain the macrosystem structures according to the blueprint they are used to. Thus, the ethics of adversary process and competition tend to be perpetuated. Figure 3-1 illustrates this cycle of perpetuation of the adversary, competitive ethic.

◆ **FIGURE 3-1**

How the Conflict Blueprint
Perpetuates Itself

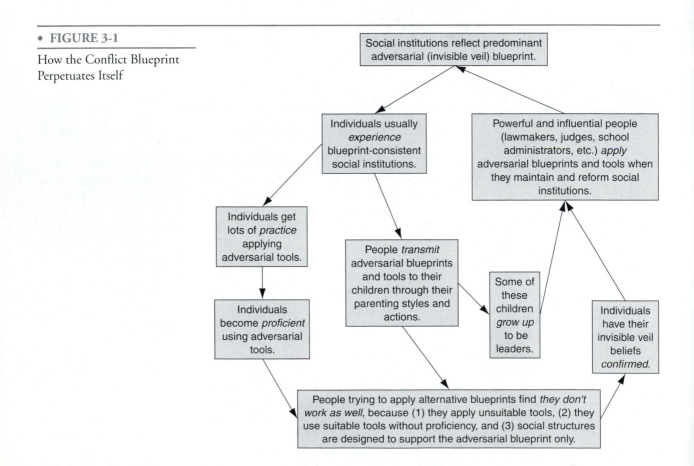

THE INVISIBILITY OF THE DOMINANT BLUEPRINT

Perhaps the most important aspect of the process of blueprint confirmation is the blueprint's invisibility. People raised in a particular culture do not grow up conscious of the values and beliefs promoted by the culture; they take them as "given" and "the only way to do things." The lack of experience and proficiency in alternative blueprints creates independent verification of the "truth" of the dominant blueprint. In this sense, then, a culture is self-conserving, and its members operate beneath an invisible veil of culturally induced beliefs.

Efforts to apply alternative blueprints largely fail. There are *four principal reasons* for this failure. First, people who recognize the possibility of an alternative means of resolving conflict receive little support from others, because others are viewing the world through the invisible veil created by the traditional blueprint. Thus, an individual who comes to believe that cooperation is a better approach to resolving conflicts is likely to encounter sustained resistance from others. Second, the effort to try an alternative blueprint is doomed, because people apply the wrong tools—they try to address an alternative blueprint using the old, familiar tools applicable to the prevailing macrosystem blueprint for conflict. Third, people may try to use the right tools but lack proficiency in using them. And fourth, people often fail to apply an alternative blueprint effectively because the existing social structures are constructed to support the predominant blueprint, not the alternative blueprint. However, instead of understanding that the failure is due to lack of proficiency, poor tool choice, and lack of support, they are likely to conclude that the alternative blueprints themselves are

---

How the Preexisting Social Structure Inhibits the Effort to Adopt New Blueprints: An Example from the Field of Mediation

The alternative dispute resolution (ADR) field is rife with examples of how the prevailing adversary blueprint prevents effective application of an alternative blueprint for resolving conflict. One example of this phenomenon is the impact of legal ethical rules on the practice of divorce mediation.

The ability of mediators to provide effective mediation services to disputants who want it is compromised by existing rules developed to regulate the legal profession in an adversary context. For example, lawyer-mediators who draft the settlement agreement reached by the clients are vulnerable to accusations of "legal representation" of clients with conflicting interests. Thus, in many instances, mediators (who are themselves lawyers) protect themselves by drafting a written document, often called a "memorandum of agreement," or "MOU," only to have the document redrafted as a binding agreement by independent legal counsel. The second drafting adds a significant expense to the process and opens it up to conflict escalation, as legal counsel attempt to interject a client-friendly interpretation on the settlement. The mediator's inability to provide such services is a significant barrier to the usefulness of mediation.

There is no reason that lawyer-mediators cannot be held to an ethical obligation to produce an agreement that faithfully represents the clients' intent as expressed in mediation sessions. However, the existing legal structures do not provide for such an orientation; instead of creating one, most jurisdictions have chosen to rely on existing rules that suit a society built on adversary conflict resolution. In short, old tools are being used to implement a new blueprint, and the result is less than satisfying.

> ### *Why Reform Is Hard: Lessons from Blueprint and Toolbox Analysis*
>
> - ◆ Lack of support from others, who are blinded by their invisible veils
> - ◆ Tools adapted to the old blueprint used for the new blueprint
> - ◆ Lack of proficiency in using tools adapted to the new blueprint
> - ◆ Existing social structures usually supporting and reinforcing the old blueprint, not the new one

inadequate.[4] Thus, the predominance of the adversarial, competitive blueprint for handling conflict is a self-fulfilling prophecy.[5]

CONFLICT AS BATTLE

Our acceptance of conflict as synonymous with competition between individuals is so deep-seated that it is even reflected in the dictionary. *Merriam-Webster's Collegiate Dictionary* (online edition 2002, s.v. *conflict*) defines conflict as

   1: fight, battle, war
  2a: competitive or opposing action of incompatibles: antagonistic state or action (as of divergent ideas, interests, or persons) **b:** mental struggle resulting from incompatible or opposing needs, wishes, or external or internal demands
   3: the opposition of persons or forces that gives rise to the dramatic action in a drama or fiction

Members of our social system have plenty of experience with competitive conflict and plenty of opportunity to practice skills related to this sort of social system. Because of this familiarity, individuals faced with conflict typically react by conceptualizing the situation as competitive. In other words, when confronted with a conflict, people ordinarily view the situation as having limited resources

---

[4] The tendency to attribute outcomes caused by situational factors to innate characteristics is a well-known phenomenon in the social psychology of stereotyping and is known as the fundamental attribution error (Darley and Fazio 1980). This phenomenon is described further in Chapter 14. The tendency to attribute to a blueprint intrinsic merit rather than to recognize errors of selection of, or proficiency in using, the tools used to execute alternative blueprints can be understood as a more generalized version of this attribution error.

[5] The picture painted by Bronfenbrenner's paradigm is grim, indeed, for people who wish for a less adversarial society in the future. However, the theory of developmental ecology is bidirectional. Despite the pressures at work that tend to reinforce the status quo, it is also true that reforms attempted at any level of the social system create their own pressures on the macrosystem to change. The forces of reform encounter the resistance of an entrenched macrosystem, yet sustained reform efforts do create social change. One has only to look at such reform movements as the women's liberation, civil rights, and labor movements to see these changes at work. It is safe to say that the advent of the ADR movement has meant both the "adversarializing" of ADR and the "de-adversarializing" of social systems in general. Only time will tell how the society at large will absorb these pressures and changes.

and only one possible winner. As you will recall from the previous chapter, in conflict resolution parlance, this sort of situation is called zero-sum. Interpersonal conflict is also emotionally challenging. The strong frustration, fear, and anger that come from being in a conflict reinforces this negative, threatening view of the conflict as having only one possible winner and motivates the people involved to protect themselves from harm by using competitive, dominating tactics designed to "win" a contest instead of "resolving" a conflict. Thus, each time they encounter conflict, the experience reinforces their view of conflict as a competition and gives them practice using the tools of competitive conflict resolution.

THE INFLUENCE OF AMBIGUITY

Social interaction is very complex: we cannot hope to take in and understand fully everything that happens. This is even more true for conflict, an arena in which people are often suspicious, secretive, and ambivalent. We are often unaware of, or unsure of, even our own motives, and this lack of certainty goes double for other people we interact with. Empirical research demonstrates a systematic tendency to misunderstand others in a conflict. When dealing with others in the complex environment surrounding a conflict, we tend to oversimplify and misunderstand the motives of others. This oversimplification tends to be in keeping with the overall blueprint of conflict as implying competition for fixed resources. When we encounter conflict, we are likely to interpret the other person's behavior as threatening to us. While we would ordinarily interpret compliance as meaning there is no conflict at all, our response to threat is usually either fight or flight. Hence, our response to the conflict behavior of others usually reflects the basic blueprint of conflict as competition for fixed resources. Thus, our own responses to interpersonal conflict often perpetuate the blueprint.

LAWYERS AND THE AMERICAN LEGAL SYSTEM

In the American system of government, the formalized structure built to handle disputes that people have been unable to resolve on their own is the judicial system. Of all the social systems that reflect the competitive/adversarial blueprint for conflict resolution, the American judicial system is the most stark. American legal process is an adversary process built on the notion that justice is achievable only through competition. The judicial system even has a name reflective of this blueprint: the adversary system.

Law professor Roberta K. Flowers notes that the adversary system has historical roots in actual battle:

> The trial process in America has been referred to as "a battle of adversaries" or "legal combat." The adversarial system assumes that truth emerges from the confrontation of opposing views. In its earliest form, brought to England by William the Conqueror, the accused would physically battle with

his accuser. The underlying belief was that "heaven would give the victory to him who was in the right." (Flowers 1996, 923)

The idea that might makes right evolved into a belief that the verbal clash of legal adversaries in zealous advocacy is the best way to ensure that the truth is revealed during litigation. Put simply:

> [the] fundamental assumption of the adversary system is that a clash of equally matched adversaries will produce truth. (Taslitz 1998, 237)

This premise is deeply woven into the fabric of American jurisprudence. The United States Supreme Court, in *Gardner v. Florida,* 430 U.S. 349, 360 (1977), stated that "[d]ebate between adversaries is often essential to the truth-seeking function of trials." In *Mackey v. Montrym,* 443 U.S. 1, 13 (1979), the court went further, stating that "[o]ur legal tradition regards the adversary process as the best means of ascertaining truth and minimizing the risk of error." Subsequently, in *Polk County v. Dodson,* 454 U.S. 312, 318 (1981), the Court pronounced, "The system assumes that adversarial testing will ultimately advance the public interest in truth and fairness."

Lon Fuller and John Randall (1958) further expand on this assumption, explaining that, if adjudication is used to resolve conflict, an adversarial process is necessary to reveal unbiased truth. Fuller and Randall argue that the adjudicator, the person whose job it is to decide the conflict—must listen to both sides in turn and sequentially turn a most sympathetic ear to each side. To avoid being swayed unduly by the arguments of one side or the other, it is argued, each disputing party must put his or her side of the case in the best possible light. "The arguments of counsel hold the case, as it were, in suspension between two opposing interpretations of it" (1160).

Thus, these writers imply that the adversarial legal system was developed as a method of dealing with disputes that individuals are unable to resolve on their

A common presumption holds that, in legal disputing, the truth is best determined through the vigorous clash of legal adversaries. Michael Herron, Pearson Education/PH College

own and assumes that the only alternative to self-regulation is to submit the dispute to a neutral third party to decide instead. It is further assumed that the only effective method of resolving the dispute is to first discover the truth about the dispute and that the adjudicator has the best chance of discovering this truth if informed about the case by zealous advocates on all sides (Leung and Lind 1986; Vidmar and Laird 1983).

The premise that the adversary system is the best guarantee of truth in an interpersonal conflict has its detractors, however. David Luban, writing about legal philosopher Lon Fuller in the *Georgetown Journal of Legal Ethics* in 1998, notes that:

> [w]hen Fuller writes, "Each of these [representative] roles must be played to the full without being muted by qualifications derived from the others," he is presupposing that the inquiry proceeds best by unmuted adversary presentation, in which case, of course, an inquisitorial investigation becomes by definition a mere copy of the real thing. In *The Adversary System,* Fuller likewise insists that decision-makers must be able to hear each side's position stated in its strongest form, which only partisan advocacy provides. But is it not equally possible that a decision-maker can form a more reliable picture if the opposed positions are muted by qualifications derived from each other? After all, the strongest form of each side's case may be strongest because it is exaggerated and misleading—"to use a harsher expression, biased." The opponent may be able to smoke out the exaggeration, but there will inevitably be cases in which the decision-maker simply cannot sort through the exaggerations, strategic omissions, and false implications, and as a result decides wrongly. (Luban 1998, 822)

Luban further asserts (1998, 824) that whether the adversary system is effective in discerning truth is not a matter for speculative debate but, rather, for empirical research. There is little empirical support for the assumption that *truth* is best determined through the competition between vigorous and zealous adversaries. Anecdotal accounts of biased conclusions reached as a result of adversary processes have been confirmed in social science research (Vidmar and Laird 1983). It is an appropriate generalization that the adjudicator often does not have the full factual truth before him or her. Moreover, he or she usually can discover the truth about the law only (if at all) by conducting independent legal research. Law professor Stephen Goldberg comments that:

> I am prepared to concede that trials are not perfect (maybe not even very good) truth-finding devices, but so what? Truth finding is not the primary purpose of the common-law trial. (Goldberg 1997, 677)

Empirical assessment bears out this account of the judicial system. In a study of 178 business lawyers, members of inhouse legal departments and outside counsel, as well as business executives,

> most respondents said that the legal system is not a good mechanism for finding the truth. Forty percent of outside counsel believed that the legal

system correctly determines the truth more than half the time, compared with 38% of inside counsel and 28% of executives, suggesting little confidence in this aspect of the justice system. Indeed, many respondents laughed cynically when the proposition was posed to them. (Lande 1998, 29)

It might be more accurately said that the protective function of zealous advocacy is not so much to reveal truth but, rather, to prevent exploitation by one side of the dispute. There is also evidence that, when disputants do not have control over outcomes, they prefer adversary processes because of a perception that this allows them process control (Leung and Lind 1986).

Lawyers are steeped in this adversarial, competitive, adjudication-dependent blueprint from the moment they enter law school. Throughout their law school and subsequent legal careers, lawyers exist in a world of pending litigation, adversarial communication, strategic use of the English language to gain the upper hand, and competition-based hearings and trials. Both the cause and the effect of this experience is the acquisition of a blueprint of adversarial approaches to disputes, a toolbox of competitive skills, and extreme proficiency in using these competitive tools.[6]

The blueprint used by lawyers to understand conflict is so important and so pervasive that it has even been given a name. Leonard Riskin coined the phrase "lawyer's standard philosophical map" to describe the two basic assumptions that he believes lawyers make when dealing with disputes:

> (1) that disputants are adversaries—*i.e.,* if one wins, the other must lose— and (2) that disputes may be resolved through applications, by a third party, of some general rule of law. (Riskin 1982, 44–45)

Having acquired the adversarial blueprint for understanding conflict, lawyers, like nonlawyers, then tend to overapply it, presuming that it is the only fair and effective way to resolve a conflict that has not been settled amicably by the disputants. In Riskin's words,

> [t]he problem is that many lawyers, because of their philosophical maps, tend to suppose that these assumptions are germane in nearly every situation that they confront as lawyers. The map, and the litigation paradigm on which it is based, has a power all out of proportion to its utility. (Riskin 1982, 45)

In other words, the problem is not in the existence of adjudication, or in the adversary procedures applied to adjudication; it is the notion that the adversarial system is always the highest and best means of conflict resolution that is flawed. The argument that adjudication requires the participation of zealous advocates to avoid exploitation of the litigants certainly has merit. And the argu-

---

[6] Law schools that have attempted to counteract this prevailing blueprint by making minor curriculum modifications have met with significant failure (see Coben 1998). Such failure is predictable, given the invisibility and ubiquity of the prevailing blueprint in society.

How the Adversarial Blueprint Is Taught to Law Students

Law students are taught by multiple means that their highest and best talents should be applied to the zealous advancement of their client's case by any legitimate means necessary. This education occurs, in part, directly and didactically, through ethics courses discussing the adversarial system and the duty of zealous advocacy. The adversarial blueprint is also transmitted indirectly using the tactics of law school education.

In the casebook method school of acquiring legal knowledge, the substantive content of the law is given to students primarily through the study of appellate court opinions. In this way, students experience, over and over again, litigant contentions and countercontentions, as well as the adjudicator's resolution of the competition, and come to see the legal field as a process of presenting and resolving competing legal positions.

Law students also learn the adversarial blueprint by practicing contentious wordplay in the classroom. Law professors typically lecture using the *Socratic method.* In the Socratic method, the professor challenges his or her students with a question, calling on students to provide answers and dressing down the responder for any flaws in the response. A successful response is generally rewarded with an additional, and harder, challenge question. The Socratic method is an efficient way of teaching students an important tool of the adversary process, argument and counterargument, while continuing to reinforce the world of the legal system as one built on competition between adversaries.

Finally, the adversarial blueprint is reinforced by the traditional law school grading system. Traditional courses are graded strictly on the curve. In other words, it does not matter how well a student learns the material in absolute terms; rather, it is only important whether the student expresses his or her learning better or worse than others in the class. This grading system prepares the law student to view conflict not in terms of what is best in absolute terms but, rather, in terms of whether one side is deemed to have done better than the other. The strict curve system also reinforces the world view that professional life will consist of zero-sum situations, in which advantages to one participant will inevitably create equivalent disadvantages to others.

ment that processes of adjudication should be available for disputants to use seems beyond refute: all organized societies have adjudication; indeed, it is hard to imagine a civilized society without it. The problem is that these highly competitive, adversary processes provide the basic model or blueprint for conflict resolution in general, for both legal professionals and the lay public alike, and this is despite the fact that the vast majority of interpersonal conflicts are not adjudicated (Coben 1998). Riskin's point in developing his concept of the philosophical map is that it acts as an invisible veil, blinding lawyers to the alternative visions of their client's problems that would enable them to respond to client interests more effectively.

In short, our cultural blueprint of an adversarial approach to conflict is insufficient to handle appropriately the range of interpersonal conflicts we confront. Where we as a society have been derailed is *not* in including the adjudication/adversarial blueprint among our panoply of conflict resolution techniques but, rather, in concluding that the adjudication/adversarial blueprint represents the *highest and best* form of dispute resolution in *most or all* cases. It is not surprising that this conclusion has become integrated into our belief systems, given the competitive and individualistic blueprint we have of conflict resolution in general. If conflict is perceived as a zero-sum situation and if competition is the only way to deal with conflict, then adjudication is the best way to resolve conflict in a fair manner. If adjudication is used to resolve conflict, it follows that the litigants need zealous legal advocacy to avoid being beaten.

As we will see in this text, processes such as adjudication, which rely on competition to resolve conflict, have many contraindications. Given what is known, empirically and scientifically, about conflict and the best ways of resolving it, competitive and adversary processes are most often the worst choices for addressing conflict, not the best. Thus, basing our panoply of conflict resolution processes on the false ideal of adjudication perpetuates many unnecessarily poor outcomes. This text will present theoretical and empirical material that will reveal a wider set of blueprints. We will consider some of these alternative blueprints, as well as the tool needed to use them. The text will also provide the information needed to select the best blueprint, and best tools, for each job.[7]

GOOD AND BAD CONFLICT

The preceding discussion presumes that we make certain judgments about conflict and how it is managed. To concern ourselves with the invisible veil means that we care about the ways conflict is handled, which presumes, in turn, that some courses and outcomes of conflict are better than others. The evaluation of conflict represents another instance in which we often suffer from preconceptions that blind us to opportunities and possibilities. Let's look at this issue.

To illustrate the nature of the usual preconception, try completing the following sentence: "Conflict is . . . ." Frequently, the first things that come to mind in completing the sentence are negative. Some examples are included in the left-hand side of Table 3-1. In keeping with our cultural blueprint of conflict as a competitive situation requiring an adversarial approach, and producing a winner and a loser, we tend to see conflict as destructive, damaging, and scary. And this vision of conflict certainly has a basis in reality. We have only to glance at a newspaper to see the unfortunate results of interpersonal conflict in terms of social unrest and violence, war, and other examples of human brutality.

Some of us, however, recognize the possibility of conflict as a force for good. Take a look at the examples of how others have completed the sentence "*Conflict is . . . ,*" shown in the right-hand column of Table 3-1. These responses reflect the nature of conflict as a source of social change and reform. Much of human innovation is the result of interpersonal conflict. In fact, it is safe to say that, without the struggles between human beings as a motivating force for change, human cultural and technological evolution would not have occurred. The civil

---

[7] In that one of the primary goals of this book is to describe a process of selecting appropriate dispute resolution processes and providers, this book has many commonalities with the classic law review article published in 1994 by Frank E. A. Sander and Stephen B. Goldberg, "Fitting the Forum to the Fuss: A User-Friendly Guide to Selecting an ADR Process." The premise of the article is vital, and its contents make a wonderful beginning to the issue. However, an effective choice of a dispute resolution process and provider requires a closer examination of the characteristics of the conflict, the disputants, and the features of the many dispute resolution processes available. This book will take you step by step through what you need to know. Nonetheless, "Fitting the Forum to the Fuss" is recommended reading.

◆ **TABLE 3-1**   Some Ways People Complete the Sentence "Conflict Is . . . ."

NEGATIVE	POSITIVE
Violent, a war	A way to clear the air
Expensive and time-consuming	Personal "voice"
	Needed to get personal needs out on the table
Dangerous, potentially fatal	A way to spur reforms
Emotionally painful relationships	The path to creative improvements in
Damaging	A way to improve society
A Waste of resources	An opportunity for individual development and betterment
Personally devastating	
Destructive to relationships	
Harmful to trust.	

rights movement and development of the modern legal system are but two of the most obvious examples of cultural innovations that have resulted from persistent interpersonal conflict.

What determines whether a conflict can be described as a positive or a negative force? There are two ways to answer this question. The first is to consider the perspective from which the question is asked, and the second is to consider the actions that can be taken to influence whether conflict is resolved in a primarily good or a primarily bad way.

PERSPECTIVES ON "GOOD" AND "BAD" CONFLICT

It should go without saying that whether a conflict is judged as good or bad depends on the point of view of the person making the judgment. Conflict-resolution scholars (Hunt et al. 1989) have recognized a number of dimensions that make up this point of view.

First, someone evaluating how well a conflict is being dealt with may be considering the conflict from a *short-term,* an *intermediate-term,* or *long-term* perspective. A conflict's course may seem quite constructive in the short term, only to prove quite the reverse in the long term, or vice versa. For example, consider the Israeli-Arab conflict. In the immediate aftermath of the 1967 war, there was overwhelming consensus among sympathizers of Israel that the hard-line, dominating, militaristic approach taken by Israel against Arab opponents was extremely effective in deterring continued aggression by the latter, and the approach was almost universally hailed by Israel's allies. It can be argued, however, that the same hard-line approach set the stage for the wave of Intifada activities that occurred early in the twenty-first century, as well as for the erosion of world support for Israel. Frequently, coercive approaches to addressing conflict stop unwanted behavior in the short run, but exacerbate competitive or even violent conflict in the long run. The converse is frequently true as well:

expensive or time consuming efforts (such as negotiating a provision to pre-scribe what disputants will do if a new conflict should erupt) that seem to have little effect on the course of a conflict other than to drive up costs may save the day down the line.

Judgments about good and bad conflict may also depend on which person's goals, needs, and interests are being considered. Often this point of view reflects the professional role of the evaluating person.

Individual disputants are likely to evaluate the conflict from their own per-spectives: "Was the result good for me?" Similarly, in a legal dispute, lawyers are likely to base their assessment of the conflict on whether the outcome was in the best interests of their own client. However, other professionals take other, and broader, person perspectives. Professionals working with conflicted couples, for example, are more likely to take a *joint-client* focus: rather than focusing on whether one client is now better or worse off, these professionals are more likely to focus on whether the two clients, *as a unit,* are better off. Still other profes-sionals have more of a *systemic* focus. For example, a family counselor may con-sider not only the impact of the conflict on the couple with whom he or she is working, but also the impact on the couple's children, who are constituents in the conflict. Some professionals may even take a *society-wide* focus in conflict. For example, the transformative mediation movement, as exemplified by Robert Baruch-Bush and Joseph Folger's classic work, *The Promise of Mediation* (Baruch-Bush and Folger 1994), advocates that conflict resolution processes should be evaluated, in part, based on the overall improvement to society brought about by the transformation of individual disputants.

Persons considering how well conflict is being dealt with may also focus on either *process* or *outcome.* Obviously, participants in an interpersonal conflict tend to look at the result of the dispute resolution process and ask themselves whether the result is acceptable or unacceptable. Participants in a conflict always prefer an outcome that suits them well.

However, in many cases, disputants must submit to a dispute resolution process, such as litigation, that vests the power to determine outcome in a third party, such as a judge. In such cases, the disputants want the process to be fair, even if they cannot guarantee what the outcome will be. There is, for example, some evidence that, in the United States, individuals are likely to perceive the process control that comes from adversary participation in adju-dication to be a necessary precondition to "good conflict resolution" if a con-flict is submitted to adjudication (Leung and Lind 1986). Even in processes in which the disputants retain the authority to consent to settlement, dis-putants do not generally get everything they want, and, in the absence of a perfect result, disputants generally are more satisfied with a process they per-ceive as procedurally just.

Moreover, a dispute resolution process may have its own intrinsic merits and disadvantages apart from its relationship to fair or unfair outcomes. The **process** of resolving a dispute is a significant event in its own right. Dispute resolution requires a monetary outlay, an investment of time, and frequently emotional anguish.[8] Furthermore, the process itself may carry significant implications for the relationships among participants, being a force for either the healing or destruction of intimate or working relationships and having an impact on the personal, professional, and economic lives of participants. Thus, apart from its connection to outcome, a dispute resolution "process" may be worth evaluating as it stands on its own.[9] Scholars of justice theory, which examines the cognitive and attitudinal underpinnings of the sense of justice and injustice, as well as scholars of therapeutic jurisprudence, a discipline that examines the reform of the law and the judiciary to make it a more healing process, are both concerned with the process end of evaluating conflict.

Dispute resolution processes can also be evaluated on the basis of what substantive issues are resolved. Is the evaluation *narrow* (based on an assessment of whether a specific issue was resolved effectively) or *broad* (based on an entire relationship among participants)? Should the evaluation consider the effectiveness of the settlement of *economic, monetary* issues alone, or should the evaluation also consider the *nonmonetary* aspects of the conflict? And should the evaluation be *retrospective,* considering how well the past behaviors of the participants were dealt with, or should it be more *prospective,* asking whether conflict prevention and prospective dealings have been enhanced for the future? Each of these considerations influence the judgment of a particular interpersonal conflict and the way it is dealt with.

AN EVALUATION OF INTERPERSONAL CONFLICT DEPENDS ON HOW IT IS HANDLED

Regardless of the points of view taken, one's ultimate judgment about an interpersonal conflict depends on just one thing: **how the conflict is handled.** Conflict does not have intrinsic good or evil: its propensity to heal and improve things and, alternatively, its propensity to harm and destroy depend on its course, management, and resolution. In a sense, this entire book deals with the specific issue of how to improve the likelihood that conflict will be good conflict through the selection of strategies, tactics, and processes that are well suited to addressing the specific attributes of the conflict in question. Working toward good conflict

---

[8] The most famous illustration of the stand-alone impact of a dispute resolution process is probably the fictional lawsuit at the center of Charles Dickens' scathing novel *Bleak House.*

[9] For an example of a dispute resolution scholar's evaluation of the intrinsic merits of a dispute resolution process, see Gerald Williams' article in the 1996 issue of the *Journal of Dispute Resolution,* "Negotiation as a Healing Process." Williams' thesis is that a negotiation process can have important positive effects on individuals who have been involved in an interpersonal conflict. Conversely, the process of resolving conflict itself can create damage. In the field of medicine, practitioners call a medical intervention that produces harm *iatrogenic,* and no study of dispute resolution processes should omit the potential iatrogenic effects of the processes themselves. For example, business disputants who suffer bankruptcy from taking a dispute to expensive and time-consuming litigation are suffering iatrogenic effects of dispute resolution. Similarly, a nation that uses atomic weapons to wage a war suffers iatrogenic effects if its bombs cause radiation poisoning of its own people.

is the essence of the field of conflict resolution. The specific process that can be used to develop a sense of the attributes of a given conflict so that it can be matched to a set of strategies, tactics, and processes is **conflict diagnosis,** discussed further in the next chapter.

EXERCISES, PROJECTS, AND "THOUGHT EXPERIMENTS"

1. Keep a log of the television programs you watch for one week. For each program, keep track of the interpersonal conflicts shown and how they are resolved. In your log, describe each conflict, identifying what makes the situation an interpersonal conflict. Is the conflict resolved? If so, how?

2. Using the log you developed in question 1, examine each situation to determine what conflict blueprint and conflict resolution toolbox are depicted. Is the depiction realistic? What would this depiction teach someone about conflict resolution?

3. In real-world international conflicts, policymakers conclude, often erroneously, that punitive sanctions will be effective in getting other nations to change their behaviors and policies. Researchers Myron Rothbart and William Hallmark (1988) tested this effect in a research study. They asked undergraduates to imagine that they were citizens of one of two imaginary countries. The undergraduate subjects were given a description of a conflict over military buildups between the countries. The subjects were asked to consider five possible disarmament strategies. Some were asked which strategy would be most effective for their own country to use to limit military expansion by the other, whereas others were asked which strategies the other country could use most effectively to limit its own country's buildup. The strategies ranged from coercive, as in "increase military buildup and threaten to use weapons unless country disarms," to conciliatory, as in "unilaterally stop production of weapons with the expectation that the other country would act in kind." The subjects who were asked what techniques would be most effective for their own country to use to disarm the other rated coercive strategies as more effective. But the subjects who were asked what techniques would be most effective for the other country to use in disarming its own country rated conciliatory strategies as more effective. This effect held true regardless of which imaginary country the subjects were assigned to. What mechanism do you think is responsible for this difference in beliefs about the effect of coercion on one's own "in-group," as contrasted with beliefs about its effects on the "out-group"?

4. *Internet activity.* Search for the term *parenting style* using an online search engine. Select one of the "parenting style quizzes" or questionnaires. A good one can be found at Parent's Club, *http://www.activeparenting.com/parents.htm.* If you are a parent, take the test. If you are not a parent, take the test to assess one or both of your parents' style, or (even better) ask your mother and/or father to take the test and share their results with you. Study the results

closely. What blueprint for human relationships does the test suggest is being transmitted in your family to your children (or was transmitted by your parents to you)? Make a list of the parenting tactics and techniques associated with your or your parents' parenting style. Do you think these tactics and techniques are effective in perpetuating the parenting blueprint?

5. Attend a civil trial. Keep a log of the trial. See if you can determine what interpersonal conflicts are at play in the litigation. Do you think a better alternative than litigation might do a better job of resolving this conflict? Why or why not? Is there anything about the litigation process that limits your ability to consider what alternatives might be preferable?

6. Debate and discuss the following proposition: "Undergraduate college courses should be graded on the curve." There should be two groups in this discussion: one group should defend the proposition and one should defend the opposite proposition. One individual should moderate the discussion, and one or two people should keep a list of the interests, principles, and values that underly each position statement. Post these interests, principles, and values on large sheets of paper around the room or on the chalkboard. After the debate, brainstorm some possible grading methods that meet all the expressed interests, principles, and values.

7. One reader of this chapter commented, "It's all well and good to talk about friendship and cooperation, but not everyone is sweetness and light. These radical types are just dreamers. They talk a good talk, but if everybody acted that way we'd all get taken advantage of. There's a good reason that the adversarial system of justice has been around as long as it has—it works, and it works better than any alternative." What would you say to this reader? Do you agree? Or is this reader suffering from the blindness that comes from growing up in a culture that prefers adversarial blueprints for handling conflict? Does your own cultural background prevent you from knowing for sure?

8. If you apply nonadversarial blueprints to an interpersonal conflict, does it increase the risk of your getting taken advantage of? Would a strategy of applying an adversarial blueprint to all conflicts reduce your risk of exploitation? Would such a strategy raise any other important risks? If we as a society were much less likely to apply adversarial blueprints to legal disputes, would it increase the likelihood of disputants' exploiting one another? Why or why not?

RECOMMENDED READINGS

Bronfenbrenner, U. 1979. *The ecology of human development.* Cambridge, MA: Harvard University Press.

deWaal, F. 1989. *Peacemaking among primates.* Cambridge, MA: Harvard University Press.

Eisler, R. 1988. *The chalice and the blade: Our history, our future.* San Francisco: Harper & Row.

Chapter 3

Fiss, O. 1984. Against settlement. *Yale Law Journal* 93:1073–90.

Fuller, L. L., and J. D. Randall. 1958. Professional responsibility: Report of the Joint Conference. *ABA Journal* 44:1159–61.

Gilligan, C. 1982. *In a different voice: Psychological theory and women's development.* Cambridge, MA: Harvard University Press.

Mnookin, R., and L. Kornhauser. 1979. Bargaining in the shadow of the law: The case of divorce. *Yale Law Journal* 88:950–97.

Riskin, L. 1982. Mediation and lawyers. *Ohio State Law Journal* 43:29–60.

Strick, A. 1978. *Injustice for all: How our adversary system of law victimizes us and subverts justice.* New York: Penguin Books.

Williams, G. R. 1996. Negotiation as a healing process. *Journal of Dispute Resolution,* 1996:1–66.

4

Conflict Diagnosis

"99% of the game is half mental."

—Yogi Berra

In this chapter, you will learn . . .

- The ten steps of conflict diagnosis.
- How everyone can benefit from learning how to diagnose a conflict.
- That beliefs about the usefulness of alternative dispute resolution (ADR) fall into two camps—an "efficiency" camp, seeing ADR as a way to reduce time and costs, and a "radical" camp, seeing ADR as a way to better resolve conflict.
- How conflict diagnosis can help legal professionals and others select the right ADR process and provider for each client and situation.

We closed Chapter 3 with a discussion of good conflict—the perspectives people take in assessing it and what it takes to recognize it. Whether good conflict is achieved, we concluded, depends on how it is handled; however, to handle conflict effectively, we have to plan and execute effective blueprints for conflict handling. And being a complex, human problem, conflict is not one size fits all. Each conflict must be understood and treated uniquely.

Conflict diagnosis is a structured process for understanding and responding to interpersonal conflicts, disputes, and transactions. Conflict diagnosis provides a rigorous and clear framework for understanding and appreciating the multiple facets of any conflict. It also serves as a clear guide for the development of strategies for addressing conflict, including the selection of dispute resolution processes and providers. In a sense, conflict diagnosis provides the basis for designing methods of producing maximally good conflict in any conflict situation. The steps of Conflict Diagnosis, are listed below, and discussed in detail in Part II of this book.

The Steps of Conflict Diagnosis

1. Map out the conflict, identifying the roles of the participants.

2. Identify the sources and causes of the conflict.

3. Identify each participant's aspirations, positions, interests, principles and values, and basic needs, and consider how they interrelate logically. Identify any linked conflicts and consider how the conflicts affect one another. Identify the divergent, conflicting interests held by the participants in the conflict. Identify the common, convergent interests held by the participants in the conflict.

4. Characterize the conflict as cooperative, competitive, or in between. If a cooperative conflict, identify attributes of the situation that could cause it to become competitive. If competitive, identify points of influence in the situation that could create greater cooperativeness.

5. Analyze the kinds and levels of trust present in the relationship between the disputants and other participants in the conflict. Develop plans to increase trust appropriately.

6. Identify any impediments to cooperative settlement.

7. Assess the negotiation styles of the participants in the conflict, consider how these styles have an impact on the conflict, and, if possible, develop plans for encouraging cooperation and collaboration among the participants.

8. Analyze each participant's power. Analyze the sources of power, the ways in which each participant could exercise each source of power, the likely impact of its exercise, and ways that this source of power could be increased.

9. Develop a list of alternatives to a negotiated agreement, including the best alternative to a negotiated agreement, or BATNA. If you are a disputant, an agent, or an advocate, develop plans for clarifying these alternatives and improving them. Also, identify the alternatives to a negotiated agreement for the "other side" in the conflict.

10. Choose a dispute resolution process, or a series of processes, appropriate to the conflict diagnosis. Select practitioners best able to meet your goals in the process. If necessary, negotiate the dispute resolution selection process with other conflict participants.

Conflict can be like the elephant in the old parable about the blind men and the elephant. Get a group of people in a room to examine a conflict, and they will each perceive something completely different. The disputing parties will tend to see only the righteousness of their own perspective and the wrongfulness of their opposition. The lawyer, relying on his or her standard philosophical map, will see only the legal issues presented in the conflict, as well as the facts pertinent to the legal issues alone, from the perspective of his or her client's interests. The psychiatrist may see only the individual psychopathologies of the disputing parties. The therapist may see primarily the psychodynamics of the interpersonal relationship. The CPA may see the tax consequences of various proposals. The friend of one disputing party may see only the potential threat to the friend. Seeing the conflict from only one narrow perspective limits the viewer's ability to develop effective strategies for dealing with the conflict. It is as if the elephant is suffering from the flu and the expert assigned to treat the elephant has contact with only the elephant's tail. The advantage of conflict diagnosis is that, instead of a restrictive, focused perspective, the process enables a diagnostician to view the conflict from many appropriate and useful perspectives. This diversity of perspective enables the development of creative, effective approaches to resolving the conflict. Moreover, the perspectives are tailored specifically to the nature of conflict itself. The need for a conscious analysis of the conflict in order to choose an appropriate intervention is noted by a number of experts in the field. (See Dezalay and Garth 1996; Guthrie 2001; Moore, 1996; Nolan-Haley 2001; Riskin 1982; Sander and Goldberg 1994; Schneider 2000; Wade 2001; Wolfe 2001.)

WHO NEEDS TO KNOW ABOUT CONFLICT DIAGNOSIS?

Everyone can benefit from understanding conflict diagnosis. Obviously, legal and dispute professionals, such as lawyers, paralegals, professional negotiators, and others involved in dispute resolution, need to know the principles of conflict diagnosis, so that they can do their job intelligently. But conflict diagnosis is useful in other situations as well, including many situations in which professional dispute resolution processes would never be used.

CONFLICT DIAGNOSIS FOR CONFLICT GAMERS AND CONFLICT PHOBICS

When conflict arises, how do you react? Before framing your answer, consider the following analogy from television:

> Consider the Crocodile Hunter, the host of a popular show on the Animal Channel, a cable television station owned by Discovery Channel. His idea of a good time is to wrestle crocodiles. Large, scary looking ones. Accompanied by his intrepid female companion, he displays obvious enjoyment when grappling with the wild, thrashing crocs before displaying them to the viewing audience. Then he releases them and suavely steps back, barely avoiding their angry strikes. Similar encounters involve deadly snakes, scorpions and vicious mammalian carnivores (like Tasmanian Devils). He never flinches and is always smiling. To reach the locations of his encounters with

Steve Irwin, The Crocodile Hunter
Justin Sullivan/Getty Images

the fauna, the Crocodile Hunter likes to hike through uncharted jungle choked with venomous frogs and poisonous plants, and to scale vertical rock faces, particularly the slick and crumbly ones.

One of the reasons the Crocodile Hunter is so entertaining is that very few of us would willingly trade places with him. There may be striking resemblances between the Crocodile Hunter and certain conflict professionals, who will be referred to here as conflict gamers.[1] Conflict gamers love interpersonal conflict and feel the most alive when up to their necks in it. They don't seem to need to prepare for a negotiation—their innate personality and temperament alone seem to be preparation enough. They jump at the chance for a rumble. In a negotiation, they seem utterly fearless. They are always ready to inflict punishment on their adversaries. They make extreme demands. They don't take notes but can remember everything said and can instantly fathom all the strategic implications of every development. They seem to know how to exploit their opponent, yet they give no clues about how the opponent can exploit them back. They always seem to know what moves to make, no matter how intense the situation—they think on their feet with the agility of a mountain lion. They are the people who look

---

[1] Legal studies scholar Gerald Williams, in his classic study of lawyers (Williams 1983), found that a minority of lawyers could be described in this sort of manner and named this category of lawyers the Gladiators.

steadily at their opponent and threaten to walk out of a negotiation. If they can't get what they want, they don't hesitate to raise the stakes by suing.

After litigation is over, win or lose, over drinks or lunch, conflict gamers express what a profound pleasure it all was, what a rush, and how it resembled the happy days they once spent in high school, lettering on the squad—baseball, football, or lacrosse. They assume their opponents feel the same way. Conflict is their element, and their highest thrills come from life on the edge. They are perfectly comfortable trying to wring their opponent's neck one minute, and slapping him or her on the back over beers the next. High-stakes, adversarial conflict is intrinsically rewarding for conflict gamers.

An experienced divorce mediator recalls how, as a young attorney, she assisted a veteran trial attorney in litigating a nasty insurance fraud case. After two years of contentious pretrial maneuvering followed by a bitter two-week trial (in which their client lost big), the litigator and his young attorney assistant found themselves eating dinner together. The litigator told her that he had been discussing the trial with a local judge who had mentored her some years before. The litigator and the judge, both conflict gamers, had come to the certain conclusion that the trial must have sealed for all time the young lawyer's wish to become a litigator and repeat this happy experience many times. He was incredulous when she told him that she had endured the entire trial in agony, mortified and almost physically ill. Obviously, the young lawyer was not a conflict gamer. Conflict gamers are probably in the minority, except perhaps in professions such as litigation, which often attracts such people. Whether layperson or legal professional, conflict is scary for most of us, and, for some of us, conflict is terrifying and abhorrent.

For the typical person caught in a conflict, coming out of it with a sense of success is frequently elusive, and some of us will do almost anything to avoid conflicts altogether. Do you fit this description? Do you subconsciously search for ways to postpone an important negotiation? Are you secretly relieved when the opponent gets held up in traffic and can't make it? Is buying a car (and having to bid down the dealer) a trauma you *try* never to have to endure? For you, does a tense negotiation feel more like torture than like a competitive sport? Is it worth the loss of money not to contest the extra charges on your bill?

If this description fits you, then you are probably like most of us, more on the conflict-phobic side of things. If you are conflict-phobic, then conflict diagnosis has many important advantages to offer you. It will give you clear guidance when conflict arises. It will help you understand what to do when you feel you are unprepared but don't know how to prepare. Nongamer legal studies students frequently comment that the ideas presented in this book help them stay calm and focused when they have to confront a conflict. This, alone, helps them make better decisions. You will also receive information to guide you in coping with the twists and turns of conflict processes, so you'll be less likely to feel alone and desperate.

Conflict diagnosis can be invaluable even if you're a conflict gamer. Have you begun to sense that your "iron-fisted" approach is not always the best one to take?[2] Perhaps you see yourself developing a reputation as someone who can't be dealt with. Perhaps your negotiations are limited by the lack of trust you engender in others. Or perhaps you sense that the range of possible solutions to the conflicts in which you are involved are not explored because every conflict turns into a battle. Conflict diagnosis can suggest alternative ways to assert your interests without giving in. It can indicate the best times to turn on your game and the best times to ease off.

Conflict Diagnosis for Conflict Professionals

Conflict diagnosis is also for conflict professionals and professionals-in-training seeking to enrich their understanding of their field. Whether you're planning a career as a lawyer, a paralegal, a judge, an arbitrator, a hearing examiner, a mediator, or a professional negotiator, this book will provide you with a rigorous framework in which to analyze disputes and transactions and to evaluate and choose the best dispute resolution processes and providers for each client's problem. Applying this system to conflicts enables conflict professionals to find the magic keys to unlocking their clients' potential power to settle their differences. The conflict diagnosis process also helps users avoid being swept up in the emotional turmoil of the conflict, and to choose the best way to handle conflicts with colleagues, neighbors, and even family members.

CONFLICT DIAGNOSIS AND ALTERNATIVE DISPUTE RESOLUTION

Conflict diagnosis and ADR are intertwined. There is no way to understand the implications of the many dispute resolution processes and variants available today without first understanding the principles of conflict diagnosis. This conclusion is by no means without controverts, however. To understand why, it is useful to delve a bit into the history of the ADR movement.

Although ADR processes such as mediation and arbitration are ancient methods of coping with human conflict, ADR in the United States has enjoyed an unprecedented explosion in popularity in the last quarter-century. This is particularly true for so-called legal disputes. Mediation, arbitration, and other forms of ADR have existed worldwide for centuries, but recently these processes have become more and more widely used, particularly in commercial disputes; in labor, sports, and entertainment disputes; in family law disputes; and in international legal disputes of all kinds. Moreover, courts throughout North America are

---

[2] If so, you're probably right: evidence from social psychology and related research suggests that, over time, a highly contentious approach to resolving conflict does not provide the best outcomes. If you are perfectly satisfied with your approach, read on: you'll learn that it's probably limiting your success.

incorporating ADR into their systems to an ever greater degree, and many jurisdictions, including most U.S. federal courts, mandate the availability of, and frequently the referral of, entire classes of cases to ADR. Employers and commercial
entities are also incorporating agreements to engage in ADR—particularly, arbitration and often along with waivers of jury trials—into employment and commercial contracts.

Underlying the popularity explosion are two disparate activist movements, which, ironically, are frequently in conflict with one another. (See
Menkel-Meadow 1991 for an alternative account of these movements.) The
first, which can be referred to descriptively as the "efficiency" wing of the ADR
movement, is typified by former Supreme Court Chief Justice Warren Burger's
many pronouncements on the subject (Burger 1982). In this root of the ADR
tree, ADR is seen primarily through the prism of efficiency. Bemoaning the
high cost and extreme delays inherent in today's overcrowded court system,
the "efficiency" wing touts ADR processes as a cheaper, quicker, and less formal route to disposing of the overwhelming backlog of cases clogging our nation's dockets. From this perspective, the type of ADR used is less important
than the availability and use of ADR in any form. The important factor to
keep in mind is that a case disposed of using an ADR process, preferably a private process paid for directly by the disputing parties, is not present in the
courts to slow things down.

The second, more "radical" wing of the ADR movement takes a very different perspective. This wing, typified perhaps most starkly by ideas advanced by
the "transformational" ADR scholars Robert Baruch-Bush and Joseph Folger
(1994), focuses on the effects and implications of various dispute resolution
processes on individuals, communities, and societies and considers some types of
ADR—most often, mediation—to be intrinsically superior to litigation and
other traditional adversary processes. Under this wing of the ADR movement,
the specific type of ADR relied on, and its unique features, are not only relevant
but utterly critical to understanding the effect of using the process on individuals, groups, and society at large.

There has been a tendency for the efficiency ADR advocates to be more
powerful than the radicals in influencing the course of adoption and use of ADR
in the United States. There are two main reasons for this trend. The first is simple: money talks. It is relatively easy to demonstrate the desirability of a program
that, for example, eliminates the need for the hiring of additional judges or that
seems to have produced a reduction in time from filing a court action to a trial
on the merits. On the other hand, the radicals have a difficult time proving just
what, apart from time and cost savings, makes certain types of ADR better than
others. Client satisfaction can be assessed, but it is merely a rough proxy for the
sort of benefit touted by the radical wing. The problem is compounded by a difficulty with language. Because the efficiency wing has been more influential, and
because this wing cares less about the form of ADR used, a certain looseness with
ADR terminology is rampant. Indeed, many professional people, who should
know better, still confuse mediation with arbitration, two processes that are as

different as night and day.[3] Thus, research into the effect and efficacy of ADR processes sometimes fails to consider the subtle but important differences between processes and programs tagged with the same name.

The second reason for the predominance of the efficiency wing is more subtle: it is the invisible veil, introduced in Chapter 3. Our society in general has difficulty accepting the premise that conflict can be resolved through any means other than competition. The legal profession, in whose control the management of legal disputes rests, is built on the idea that the clash of adversaries is the only way to resolve conflict. Although this ideal is the basis for our largely very effective system of justice, it tends to blind legal professionals to alternatives (Baruch-Bush and Folger 1994). Thus, when nonadversarial alternatives to litigation are considered, they are viewed through a prism of adversary process; seen this way, there are very few advantages to ADR processes except efficiency. (Indeed, when professionals with an adversarial perspective engage in ADR, they tend to "adversarialize" the process in question, masking the distinctions.) Both the narrowness of the research and the perceptual limitations of the legal profession have created the false impressions that all ADR processes are similar and that the differences are obvious and easy to apply.

The radical wing, on the other hand, views seemingly small variations in ADR processes as producing profound differences. These views are the result of fine theoretical exploration, by and large, but difficult to verify through empirical research. For example, Baruch-Bush and Folger not only prefer mediation to arbitration but also consider mediation in which the goal is to produce collaboration between the disputing parties to be suboptimal, compared with mediation that leads to "empowerment" of each disputant and "recognition" of each disputant by the other (Baruch-Bush and Folger 1994). It would be extremely difficult even to accurately characterize such distinctions among mediation programs, processes, and practitioners so that the potential differences between them could be explored.[4] Moreover, the radicals point not only to the personal benefits of ADR processes but also to cultural and societal reforms that can result from altering societal emphasis from litigation to nonadversarial ADR processes. Radicals believe that deemphasizing adversary processes and emphasizing nonadversary processes may help increase communitarian values, which, it is believed by some, are unduly suppressed by the American emphasis on rugged individualism and laissez-faire capitalism. Of course, not everyone sees such an ideological shift as even desirable. And yet trying to prove that a particular ADR program or process might have such a far-ranging effect on society is virtually impossible, even if the goal of a more collectivist social structure were a matter of universal consensus.

---

[3] For the classic exposition of this perceptual limitation suffered by the legal profession, the classic law review article by Leonard Riskin, "Mediation and Lawyers" (1982), is must-reading.

[4] This work is now being attempted. The "transformative mediation" process envisioned by Professor Baruch-Bush has been institutionalized as the REDRESS™ program of the United States Postal Service, which offers conflict resolution to postal employees. This program is undergoing an extensive evaluation by scholars at the University of Indiana (Indiana Conflict Resolution Institute 2001).

A student of ADR will find that both the efficiency and radical wings of the ADR movement provide useful perspectives. However, one undeniable contribution of the radical wing is the assertion that the desirability and efficacy of particular ADR programs and processes in individual cases depend critically on the specific structure and features of the process being used. Although it is true that a dispute effectively resolved outside of court will not clog the docket, it is also true that some forms of dispute resolution are more effective than others for particular situations. A process that provides a well-thought-out and well-tailored resolution to a difficult conflict is less likely to lead to litigation down the line, and disputing parties who feel they have had an important hand in choosing the outcome of a dispute are less likely to feel disgruntled about it in the future and find something else to fight about. On the other hand, a process that most disputing parties consider a waste of time and money, a resolution coercively imposed upon the participants, or a process that perpetuates existing power inequities is unlikely to have the same sorts of salutary effects. Thus, although a quick and cheap dispute resolution process is not necessarily effective, neither is it necessarily efficient. Good conflict resolution, on the other hand, is efficient in an important way, in that it may prevent future conflicts and case filings and may, moreover, lead to better allocation of societal rights, obligations, and resources. Hence, whatever you think about the radical vision of a more communitarian society, the radicals are on target when they assert that choosing a high-quality form of conflict resolution, tailored to the situation at hand, is important.

There is evidence that the sort of intelligent and reasoned choice of dispute resolution processes advocated by the radical wing of ADR proponents is *not* now taking place on a widespread basis. For example, Judge Wayne Brazil of the federal bench, a leading proponent of ADR, reported evidence that federal court referrals to ADR do not vary based on the characteristics of the dispute and disputants but, instead, depend on what processes are available in the particular court system and on the preferences of the judge making the referral (Brazil 2000). Additionally, it appears that choices of both court-connected and private ADR are made not so much based on the needs of specific clients but, rather, on the cultural predilections and emotional reactions of the practitioners who make referrals. For example, attorneys working with commercial clients sometimes assert that some forms of ADR are too "touchy-feely" for their clients, despite a clear basis for concluding that these forms are well suited to their issues, which often involve the need to preserve a working relationship with suppliers, subcontractors, and customers. Thus, there is little evidence at this time that the true promise of ADR is being realized, beyond diverting legal disputes out of the litigation system.

Another unfortunate result of the lack of emphasis on careful conflict diagnosis is the slow but inexorable adversarialization of ADR. Because most people who are in a position to provide funding for ADR programs operate in the efficiency wing of the movement, ADR programs are often reduced to nothing more than *litigation lite* (a term coined by law professor Jack

M. Sabatino 1998), a less formal and less careful version of the same old adversary process. This point is reiterated by Professors Lela P. Love and Kimberlee K. Kovach (2000), who caution that without taking more care to consider and preserve the unique characteristics of the many varieties of ADR, the benefits that each unique process offer will be lost. The 1983 lament of history professor Jerold Auerbach is, perhaps, overstating the point, but correct in its overall concern:

> "[W]hile the forms of alternative dispute settlement still flourish, its substance recedes to the vanishing point. The relentless force of law in American society can be measured by its domination, and virtual annihilation, of alternative forms of dispute resolution. (Auerbach 1983, 15)

The radicals assert that the careful application of ADR processes to disputes both transforms the handling of specific disputes and, more broadly, transforms legal and non-legal culture. This general assertion is no doubt true, although exactly what form this transformation may take is certainly controversial and will probably remain unclear for many years to come. Individuals with conflicts, disputes, and pending transactions, as well as conflict and dispute professionals, need to have as much information as possible about the impact of various dispute resolution processes to make enlightened decisions about how to select and participate in them. Thus, the superficial efficiency treatment of ADR by some—the characterization of ADR as nothing more than "litigation on the cheap"—is insufficient and dangerous. There are many, more enlightened texts dealing with ADR.[5] Some are cited in this book. You are encouraged to delve more deeply into the subject by reading them.

The noted law professor Frank E. A. Sander (1976) has taken the notion of tailoring a dispute resolution process to a specific situation a step further in suggesting that courts should have a "multidoor" aspect to them: that disputing parties should have available to them a whole variety of dispute resolution processes, both traditional and alternative. Sander's extensive work suggests that the optimal dispute resolution process is different for different types of cases (Sander and Goldberg 1994, note v). Social and developmental psychology theory and research strongly bear this assertion out. The notion of tailoring the dispute resolution process to the specific characteristics of the conflict and its participants is also behind the idea of conflict diagnosis.

The concept of a multidoor courthouse is now present in the free market. Although most court systems at this time have available at most only a few "alternatives" to litigation, a plethora of private, entrepreneurially based alternatives, each with their own stated goals, processes, and practitioners, exists,

---

5 For other excellent works that present a deeper view of ADR processes, try Leonard L. Riskin and James E. Westbrook's (1997) law school textbook, *Dispute Resolution and Lawyers,* and Baruch-Bush and Folger's *The Promise of Mediation* (1994). Many excellent law review and social science articles, too numerous to list, also attempt to deal with the issue of the deeper ramifications of ADR, including Sander and Goldberg (1994, *supra*).

"*Judge Wycoff is a strong advocate of swift justice.*"

The Cartoon Bank

particularly in large metropolitan areas. With little consensus about what these processes are, or the implications of using each one, entrepreneurs and others offering services are typically loose with terminology (thus, for example, a practitioner offering "mediation" will frequently be found to be offering nonbinding evaluation). Legal professionals are called on increasingly to select, recommend, or evaluate ADR choices for their clients.[6] Trying to make such a choice among multitudinous options, each having been given a nonrigorous, commercially motivated title, can be a quagmire. By using conflict diagnosis, with its underpinning of theory and research, these professionals can better predict how idiosyncratic characteristics of specific ADR processes will impact the course, process, and outcome of conflict. Thus, using conflict diagnosis can enable legal professionals to make better choices about selecting and using ADR.

SUMMARY

Conflict diagnosis provides a step-by-step process for analyzing and understanding interpersonal conflict. Grounded in tested theory and research, and backed by experience, the process of conflict diagnosis enables the user to better understand the forces that drive the conflict and impede its resolution. Conflict-phobics often find that having a straight-forward system of analyzing conflict can help them confront difficult or frightening situations and become more calm, deliberate, and pro-active. Conflict-gamers, on the other hand, can benefit from

---

[6] In some jurisdictions, discussing and recommending ADR to clients is evolving to become an ethical obligation for lawyers. This issue is discussed in more detail in Chapter 22.

the broader perspective that comes from pausing to evaluate the situation from the conflict-diagnosis perspective. In either case, conflict diagnosis can enable participants in conflict to achieve more flexibility and adaptability. What works very well in one situation may be disastrous in another situation, but conflict diagnosis helps the user identify a panoply of possible strategies, and to determine when a strategy will work, and when it won't.

Conflict diagnosis also informs the study of ADR. As many scholars in the field have pointed out, ADR, like conflict itself, is not "one size fits all." Familiarizing yourself with conflict diagnosis before embarking on the study of ADR will help you appreciate the sometimes subtle differences between forms of ADR and why these differences are important.

Finally, conflict diagnosis enables more effective selection and use of ADR. Conflict diagnosis can help shed light on whether ADR is appropriate, on what ADR processes and providers would lead to "good conflict," and on what strategies and tactics will best meet the goals, interests, and needs of the parties involved. In this modern age of expansion of the ADR movement, conflict diagnosis is a critical tool in the legal and conflict professional's arsenal of skills.

EXERCISES, PROJECTS, AND "THOUGHT EXPERIMENTS"

1. Think back on the last interpersonal conflict in which you were involved. (You may use your conflict journal topic for this exercise.) How did it feel when you first realized a conflict was occurring? What steps did you take to handle the conflict? What does this information tell you about your overall attitude toward conflict? Are you a conflict gamer, a conflict-phobic, or something in between? Think hard about what the advantages are of your overall approach to conflict. What are the disadvantages? What can you do to minimize these disadvantages while retaining the advantages?

2. Having identified your predominant attitude toward conflict in question 1, interview someone who you believe holds a very different attitude. (For example, if you consider yourself to be a conflict gamer, interview someone you think is probably conflict-phobic.) Try to find out whether your belief about this person is accurate. How does he or she feel when dealing with interpersonal conflict? What do you see as the advantages and disadvantages of the person's approach?

3. Whom does the traditional legal system benefit more—disputants who are conflict gamers or people who are conflict-phobic? Explain your answer. Compare your answer and rationale with that of your classmates.

4. Which of the following statements are you in more agreement with? Discuss your decision with your classmates.

    a. "As a society, we need to realize that litigation is not a very good way of dealing with most disputes. We need to develop other ways of handling legal disputes, so that these disputes can be resolved more effectively."

b. "Our judicial system is seriously underfunded and understaffed. It remains the best way to resolve legal disputes, and we should do a better job of providing it with resources."

5. Review the steps of conflict diagnosis. See box on p. 51. Which of these activities or skills appear to be consistent with the traditional roles of an attorney? Which of these activities or skills appear to be activities that attorneys don't normally do? Which of these activities or skills are contrary to the traditional roles of an attorney?

6. Put yourself in the role of an attorney who handles civil litigation, mostly business contract actions. You have learned all about conflict diagnosis and think you would like to put these skills to use with your clients.

a. Is it ethical for you, or for experts you retain for the purpose, to diagnose your clients' conflicts without first informing them of your intentions? Why or why not?

b. How do you think your clients will feel if you bill them for the time and effort you spend diagnosing their conflicts?

c. Is there a way to market conflict diagnosis to this customer base? Design a brochure that convinces potential clients of the advantages of conflict diagnosis.

d. Would your answers to these questions change if you specialized in child custody cases? Why or why not?

RECOMMENDED READINGS

Auerbach, J. S. 1983. *Justice without law: Resolving disputes without lawyers.* New York: Oxford University Press.

Brazil, W. D. 2000. Symposium: Continuing the conversation about the current status and the future of ADR: A view from the courts. *Journal of Dispute Resolution* 2000:11–39.

Burger, W. W. 1982. *Isn't there a better way?* Annual Report on the State of the Judiciary, presented at the 1982 midyear meeting of the American Bar Association, Chicago, 24 January. Reprinted as Burger, W. W. 1982. Isn't there a better way? *A.B.A. Journal* 68 (March):274.

Riskin, L.L., and Westbrook, J.E. 1997. *Dispute resolution and lawyers.* 2d ed. St. Paul, MN: West.

Sander, F. E. A. 1976. *Varieties of dispute processing.* 70 *Federal Rules Decision* 111.

Schneider, A. K. 2000. Building a pedagogy of problem-solving: Learning to choose among ADR processes. *Harvard Negotiation Law Review* 5 (spring):113–135.

Wade, J. 2001. Don't waste my time on negotiation and mediation: This dispute needs a judge. *Mediation Quarterly* 18 (spring):259–280.

Williams, G. R. 1983. *Legal negotiation and settlement.* St. Paul, MN: West.

5

Recurrent Themes
in Conflict Diagnosis

*Common sense is the collection of prejudices
acquired by age eighteen.*

—Albert Einstein

In this chapter, you will learn …

- ◆ How our mental and perceptual limitations produce bias and inaccuracy when we are involved in an interpersonal conflict.
- ◆ The seven steps taken by conflict participants in responding to the actions of others involved in the conflict.
- ◆ The ten recurrent themes of conflict diagnosis.

In the chapters that constitute Part II of this book, you will be introduced, step by step, to the process of conflict diagnosis. A number of recurrent themes and assumptions run through this material. These are based on common and basic tenets of general, social, and developmental psychology. The elements of conflict diagnosis will make more sense if these themes and assumptions are kept in mind. Thus, this chapter provides crucial grounding material for the study of conflict diagnosis.

The themes you'll be learning about in this chapter specify the circumstances in which human beings misperceive, misinterpret, and misreact during interpersonal conflict. If you are a student of human nature, the humanities, or the natural or social sciences—or if you enjoy situation comedy—you'll probably discover that the themes of conflict diagnosis are endlessly fascinating.

THE SEVEN STEPS OF SOCIAL BEHAVIOR

It helps in the analysis of behavior during a conflict to break it down into its component parts. Confusion, subjectivity, and ultimately bias and error enter an individual's responses at multiple stages in his or her reactions. Thus, examining these responses at each step is extremely revealing: we can discover how, why, and when an individual can be led astray.

Developmental and basic psychological theories can provide just such a step-by-step model of conflict response. Figure 5-1 summarizes the model we will use in the discussion that follows.[1]

To understand these steps better, let's use an example. Do you remember the Digi-Date dispute introduced in Chapter 1? Let's focus on an incident that could have taken place in the bar where our conflict participants, Jeff, Marsha, and Max, had planned their settlement meeting. You'll recall that Marsha became acquainted with Eric while waiting for Jeff to arrive.

Marsha and Eric were at a table, sharing beers, when Jeff finally arrived. The clock on the wall read 6:20. Marsha looked up, an eyebrow raised—her Palm Pilot had indicated that the meeting was to be held at 5:30, and she'd checked the device at least four times in the past forty minutes while

◆ **FIGURE 5-1**

Interpersonal Conflict: Steps in Social Behavior

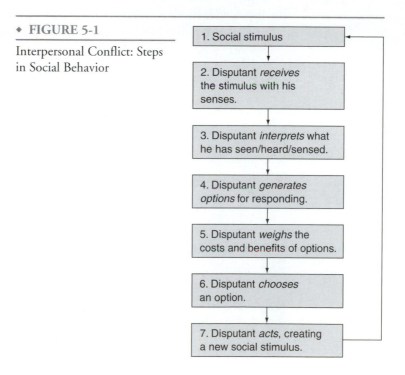

1. Social stimulus

2. Disputant *receives* the stimulus with his senses.

3. Disputant *interprets* what he has seen/heard/sensed.

4. Disputant *generates options* for responding.

5. Disputant *weighs* the costs and benefits of options.

6. Disputant *chooses* an option.

7. Disputant *acts*, creating a new social stimulus.

---

[1] If you are a psychology buff, you may be interested to learn that this model of human response to interpersonal conflict integrates Albert Bandura's social learning theory (Bandura 1971) with several information-processing developmental theories.

talking with Eric and downing beers. She rose from the table and walked briskly (if unsteadily) over to Jeff, pumping her arms energetically as if to quicken her stride and increase its power. Stopping about a foot away from Jeff, she thrust a finger within 4 inches of his nose. "You're a great one. An hour late? What kind of crap are you trying to pull?" Jeff shrank back with a look that might have meant fear, defensiveness, or arrogance. "I'm sorry," he said in an inflectionless voice. "Do you still want to have this meeting?" Marsha wavered slightly and rolled her eyes back. "Anything you say."

Let's put ourselves in Marsha's shoes for a moment. What were her internal reactions to Jeff's arrival at the bar? What led her to respond the way she did?

STEP 1: SOCIAL STIMULUS

Stimulus
in the field of psychology, any event or circumstance that elicits a response in someone who experiences it.

Jeff's entry into the room is the starting point for our analysis. It's the occurrence of an actual event in a conflict. Psychologists call such an event, which stimulates a reaction in someone, a **stimulus**. A stimulus that constitutes part of a social interaction is known as a **social stimulus**. Not only is Jeff's physical entry into the room part of a stimulus, but anything that accompanies this action can be considered a part of the stimulus: his body language, his clothing, the state of his hair, the bags under his eyes, others' reactions to his entrance, the temperature of the room—anything that Marsha might experience along with the event.

STEP 2: STIMULUS RECEPTION

Social stimulus
a stimulus that consists of a social event—that is, of one or more people behaving in a way that intentionally affects others.

The second step in social interaction during conflict is for the perceiver (in this case, Marsha) to see, hear, or otherwise use her senses to *receive* the social stimulus. Steps 2 and 3, combined, are what we generally think of as *perception*. However, although we generally think of both of these steps as a single action, it is extremely important to distinguish the *reception* of a social stimulus (step 2) from its *interpretation* (step 3), because each step introduces unique risks for error, ambiguity, and confusion.

Perception
◆ Reception
plus
◆ Interpretation

To clarify the differences between reception and interpretation, consider the face shown in (Figure 5-2). If one is in a dimly lit room, one might not receive the stimulus well. The failure to receive the stimulus effectively would be a problem with reception—step 2. However, even in bright light, putting a label on this person's facial expression is not straightforward. Is he smiling or grimacing? Your decision is the *interpretational* part of social perception—step 3.

◆ **FIGURE 5-2**

Is this man smiling or grimacing? The answer is a matter of stimulus interpretation.

Social Stimulus Interpretation in Psychological Research

Social psychologist Yaacov Trope (1986) explored stimulus interpretation by showing people photos of other people, accompanied by verbal descriptions of their situations. The viewers were consistent in their assessments of the emotional states of the models in the photos whose facial expressions were unambiguous. However, when shown photos of ambiguous faces, viewers interpreted the facial expressions in terms of context. For example, a photo of a model shown with a description such as "this man just received a birthday gift" tended to elicit a description of "happy," "surprised," or "pleased," whereas the same photo accompanied by a description such as "just learned he had to work late" elicited a description of "angry," "frustrated," or "sad."

Let's return to the conflict between Marsha and Jeff to explore further the process of stimulus reception (step 2). Step 2 involves Marsha's senses' receiving information. For example, if Jeff has used particular words, facial expressions, and gestures, some aspects of his behavior will be picked up by Marsha's eyes and ears. Additionally, other parts of the environment, such as the music, smells, actions of other people, taste of Marsha's drink, and anything else that happens to drift into Marsha's sensory view, will be picked up. (It remains to be seen whether Marsha will attend to, or ignore, each sense impression she receives—that determination is made in step 3.)

At step 2, features of both the environment (here, Jeff, the bar, and anything else relevant to the situation) and the perceiver (Marsha) combine to produce error and subjectivity. The stimulus itself, and the context in which it occurs, may be ambiguous for the person who perceives it. In Marsha's case, since the bar is likely to be dark and noisy, Jeff's nonverbal cues may be difficult to read, and, if he says anything, she may not be able to hear it accurately. This sort of mistake can be generated by the "signal-to-noise" ratio (soft voice, loud background), by problems in the communicator's speech patterns, and by problems in the listener's ability to accurately pick up the intended message (for a fascinating account of these sorts of communication problems, see Krauss and Morella 2000, 131–43).

Consider another example of subjectivity in the reception of social stimulus. Remember the law firm dispute first introduced in Chapter 1, in which Karen

Context influences the way our minds interpret the information taken in by our senses, as optical illusions demonstrate. Here, two adult women sit in opposite corners of an 'Arnes Room' at the Science Museum of Virginia. Cyane Lowden

believes she has overheard her colleague, Mark, making sexually offensive comments? If Karen, overhearing Mark in a noisy office, thinks he has said a word demeaning to women sexually (step 2), when, in fact, he has said something different altogether, she may misinterpret his intent as fraught with offensive content, when, in fact, something else was intended.[2] The misperception may then feed her sensitivity to other elements of Mark's behavior.

The perceiver's ability to absorb fully and accurately a social stimulus is also affected by factors that impede the perceiver's ability to pay attention and to devote mental resources to perception. We'll refer to these factors as "attention-robbers." In the Digi-Date scenario, for example, Marsha will be less able to listen and watch Jeff attentively if she is pleasantly distracted by Eric. And she will be further impaired mentally if she's had quite a few beers. In the law firm example, Karen is more likely to make mistakes about Mark's behavior if she's otherwise stressed out by her work or if she's already emotionally upset about what she thinks Mark is doing.

STEP 3: STIMULUS INTERPRETATION

Following the perception of a social stimulus, people interpret what they've experienced. This means that people assign meaning to what they've sensed. Much of the difficulty and error in social perception involves this step.

---

[2] Technically, the issue of what word is heard by a listener is often both a step 2 and a step 3 problem. Suppose Mark had said the word *limbo*, but Karen had heard the word *bimbo* (a word demeaning to women). Part of the problem may be signal-to-noise ratio: in a noisy office, perhaps Mark's speech was difficult to hear clearly. However, Karen's mental interpretation of the ambiguous stimulus (step 3—stimulus interpretation) does the rest.

Interpersonal conflict is an inherently stressful and difficult situation, as everyone who has ever experienced conflict (in other words, everybody) is sure to recognize. For this reason, those involved in a conflict use every clue at their disposal to try to make sense of the conflict, so that they can minimize their stress and make effective decisions. Marsha is likely to be trying to "read" the situation so that she can comprehend "where Jeff is coming from" in order to protect herself and manage the conflict most effectively.

Social stimuli that take place during a conflict can be interpreted in different ways by different people in different circumstances, and here's why. First, the actor him- or herself may not have intended his or her actions. Consider Jeff's arrival at the bar. Marsha may interpret his lateness as purposeful—his attempt to manipulate her—when, in fact, it was actually the result of his forgetting the time. But let's take it a step further. Suppose Jeff had not intended to attend at all—he had forgotten all about the meeting, had intended instead to go to a restaurant after a long day of software programming, and had wandered into the bar by mistake. If Marsha interprets his arrival as signaling his intent to meet with her, she will be mistaken. Errors, ambiguities, and confusions originating in the perpetuator of the social stimulus are the first source of mistakes and misunderstanding during interpersonal conflict.

In virtually all social interactions, people are forced to make frequent guesses about the internal states of others. It's an essential part of effective social functioning, and it occurs because we need to know what motivates the other disputant, but we can't read one another's minds. People construct what they believe to be objective reality by applying mental shortcuts, or rules of thumb, that enable them to make guesses about what they don't know. In the human behavioral sciences field, these shortcuts are called **heuristics.** (For a thorough treatment, see Fiske and Neuberg 1990, 1–74.)

To understand the ubiquity of these heuristics in human behavior, consider the following example. You are alone and walking down an empty street in a bad part of town. It is very late at night. Peering into the darkness, you see the form of someone walking toward you. What are you thinking at this point? Most likely, your mind is preoccupied with whether this person presents a danger to you. How would you assess the threat? Would you stop the person and engage in conversation? Would you ask for a family history? Would you take two weeks to research his or her criminal record? Obviously not. In such a circumstance, as in practically any situation in which people must interact on a relatively brief or immediate basis, there are insufficient resources and time to conduct a thorough investigation. Additionally, considerations of politeness and social convention usually prevent us from asking most of the questions we have about others directly. Instead, people use heuristics to estimate what an individual's motivations and next moves are likely to be. In the case of the dark and empty street, you may base your next move on a set of stereotypes. Stereotypes—which are guesses about people's traits, states, motivations, and attributes based on membership in an

Heuristics
generally rules of thumb; in social psychology, mental shortcuts that people use to make quick assessments of other people during social interactions.

identifiable social group—are a very commonly used heuristic.[3] For example, you may change to the other side of the street if the person walking toward you appears to be a young adult male. Consider how your reaction might change if the person walking toward you appeared, instead, to be a toddler. And consider how your reaction might change if the setting were different—if, for example, you were walking along a busy street at midday in the middle of the business district. The same tendency to apply heuristics operates in interpersonal conflict. In our law firm example, Karen may identify Mark as the sort of guy likely to commit sexual harassment, because she has learned that he was a "football jock" in college, and she harbors negative stereotypes about such people. Having so labeled Mark, Karen may be more likely to interpret as offensive a word she was not able to hear clearly. Moreover, Karen may perceive jokes made by Mark as directed at her, when, in fact, he is not intending for her to overhear them.[4]

A different set of heuristics is likely to operate when people with substantial relationship histories interact. These heuristics are based on how things have gone between them in the past. For example, in the Digi-Date case, Marsha may have developed a belief about Jeff—that "he just wants to take advantage of her"—and, so, interprets his lateness as an intentional manipulation rather than an inadvertent mistake. As we will see in Chapter 9, the presence of interpersonal conflict and the course of the conflict profoundly alter the perceptual frames of the disputants and change the nature of the heuristics brought to bear in the interaction. In a conflict that is escalating out of control, these heuristics can become terribly destructive.

Heuristics, particularly stereotypes, can have a self-fulfilling aspect. There is overwhelming evidence that perceivers engage in a number of practices, including selective attention, "explaining away," and misattribution, that cause their interpretation of others' behavior to be consistent with their heuristic assumptions. These processes, which will be discussed in more detail in Chapter 14, interfere with a conflict participant's objective assessment of a conflict situation. One ubiquitous heuristic during interpersonal conflict is *demonization*. It's natural for people involved in an interpersonal conflict to tag the other disputant as "evil" if the conflict has escalated and to tag themselves and members of their "team" as "good." Thus, Marsha (of Digi-Date) and Karen (of the law firm) are likely to see the actions of Jeff and Mark, respectively, as evil if they are experiencing the conflicts as intractable. You'll learn more about this phenomenon in Chapter 14.

Heuristics are most likely to be used instead of a more systematic way of trying to understand a situation when a disputant doesn't have a lot of time, energy, or attention to pay to the situation. Thus, interpretation is affected by

---

[3] See Chapter 14 for a detailed discussion of the impact of stereotypes and other heuristics on interpersonal conflict.

[4] Karen may be correct in her assessment that the jokes are, in full or part, directed at her. A heuristic does not always yield an incorrect conclusion.

factors that affect a disputant's attention and mental energy. Heuristics are generally relied on more in situations in which the perceiver is tired, ill, hungry, emotionally upset, distracted, stressed out, or confronted with a very complex situation. Unfortunately, interpersonal conflict is nearly always stressful and complex.

What determines the sorts of heuristics and other subjective interpretations that a conflict participant applies? Contextual influences—a person's *background, experiences, current sensitivity,* and *current social context*—are powerful determinants of these effects. Context is an important influence on the manner in which disputants frame (that is, describe and identify) a conflict, as well as an important influence on the meaning individuals ascribe to the conduct of others. Many experts in the conflict field assert that the lack of consensus in framing conflicts is one of the most important and pervasive impediments to resolving them.

A classic example of contextual influences on perception occurred during the O. J. Simpson murder investigation in the mid 1990s. A huge number of Americans watched the television coverage of Simpson's "Bronco chase" down the Los Angeles freeways in 1994. When asked about Simpson's likely guilt or innocence, European Americans, who as a group do not have many experiences with police brutality, overwhelmingly gave the opinion that Simpson was guilty; among the chief reasons for their opinion was his flight from police as evidence of "consciousness of guilt." On the other hand, the majority of the African Americans who were asked the significance of Simpson's flight from the police did not see the event as suggesting guilt at all. Members of this group, used to a lifetime of experiences with or stories of police harassment, assumed that Simpson's behavior merely reflected the emotional response of any citizen to being pursued by police.

Individual experiences as members of cultural or ethnic groups may influence beliefs about the implications of behavior, as illustrated by racial differences in reactions to the O. J. Simpson "Bronco Chase." The Outlook/Rich and Hartog, Corbis/Sygma

There are both short-term and long-term contextual influences. Contextual influences can "leap to the head of the line," so to speak, by being important in recent experience or having garnered the perceiver's attention repeatedly. This phenomenon is called *salience.* For example, in the law firm scenario, Karen may be more sensitized to the possibility of sexual harassment as a reason for Mark's behavior if she has recently attended a seminar on the subject, has been the victim of sexual assault, or has seen a particularly dramatic movie or television show depicting sexual harassment. She might then be more likely to interpret Mark's behavior as consistent with sexual harassment. Salience is also influenced by immediate social context, such as the order and organization of the environment. For example, the issue of sexual harassment would probably be more on everyone's mind if Karen were the only female in the office.

Finally, motivational factors, both stable and transient, affect how the perceiver interprets the situation. Available social psychology research suggests that, the more important a situation is to the perceiver, the greater is the motive to be accurate in the person's perceptions. However, this motivation can be counterbalanced by other motives, such as the motive to appear strong to others and the motive to be internally consistent.

It is not correct to view the interpretational process as a merely intellectual exercise. Accompanying the disputant's interpretation of social stimulus is a package of emotional reactions. For example, in the Digi-Date conflict, Marsha, seeing Jeff enter the bar and interpreting his behavior as manipulative, probably feels a flash of rage. This, added to her interpretation, colors what she decides to do next.

STEP 4: DISPUTANT GENERATES OPTIONS FOR RESPONDING

Steps 2 and 3 constitute the disputant's efforts to understand and conceptualize the situation in which he or she finds him- or herself. The disputant is involved in constructing reality—that is, he or she is using the evidence before him or her and trying to solve the mystery of what it means.

In step 4, the disputant begins the process of responding to the social stimulus. Steps 4, 5, 6, and 7 are discrete elements in the disputant's response. Sometimes, they are taken slowly and with great deliberation. Other times, they are highly abbreviated and fleeting. (In particular, step 5—in which the disputant evaluates the costs and benefits of available options—may be very minimal.) But they are present in every case. And each step introduces a unique collection of errors and biases.

The first element of responding is to generate some possible response options. Perceivers will not act unless they first contemplate the possibilities. For example, Marsha, feeling angry and dealing with what she has concluded is a manipulative, recalcitrant adversary, will begin to generate some options for how to alleviate her rage and deal with Jeff.

To say that a disputant has to contemplate options before acting in no way implies that response to conflict is always thoughtful, measured, or deliberate.

Option generation ranges from careful study, debate, and discussion all the way to an immediate and subconscious selection of a single option for action. In Marsha's case, it's clearly more like the latter: she sees Jeff and reacts in a flash. Compare this sort of behavior with the lengthy and public process that the United States engaged in after the September 11 attacks to develop a response to threats posed by so-called rogue nations. In the case of U.S. foreign policy, a series of communications among members of the government, its citizens, and advocacy groups—the United States "team"—took place, apparently directed at generating and evaluating the numerous options available to achieve the crucial goal of preserving the nation's viability and strength on a long-term basis.

Option generation is a mental process. Just as with the reception and perception of the social stimulus, option generation is vulnerable to subjectivity and error. Transient factors—such as lack of time, attention-robbers, distractedness, illness, emotional arousal, and fatigue—can affect the thoroughness of the process. Moreover, the perceiver's emotional state can bring some aspects of the conflict to the forefront at the expense of other aspects, and this can lead to the perceiver's entirely missing viable options. This is a common phenomenon during escalated conflict between divorcing parents. In the typical scenario, Mom and Dad are disputing over everything, including how to parent the children. One of the parents (let's assume it's Mom, for purposes of discussion) has had her working hours changed and needs more child support because she has to hire child care. Dad wants more time with the children. Mom's hostility toward Dad prevents her from seeing an alternative option: allowing Dad to provide the child care himself. In the Digi-Date case, a similar phenomenon may take place: a sort of a short-circuit of most of the option generation. Marsha's reaction to Jeff, taking place in a split second, may be something like the following:

1. "Boy, he makes me mad!"
2. "I want to get back at him!"
3. "How can I do that?"
4. "I could yell!"

STEP 5: DISPUTANT WEIGHS THE OPTIONS

In step 5 of the response process, the disputant weighs the costs and benefits of using the options he or she has generated. If the disputant has thought of only one option, this process may be very abbreviated, as in "I have no choice but to do X." However, many times, a disputant has more than one possibility in mind—such as "Well, I could just take my lumps, I could write him a threatening letter, or I could sue." What ultimately determines the disputant's choice takes place in step 5.

Weighing and assessing options involves the disputant's considering the pros and cons of each possible action. Where do the pros and cons come from? Some of them are more or less objective, as in "I'm sure that suing him would cost me at least $10,000 in legal fees." But many of the pros and cons, and all of the weight assigned to them, are personal to the disputant. They come from the disputant's underlying interests, needs, and values. Thus, although it would be nice if the weighing of options were an objective, scientific process, it's really quite subjective, like the other steps of response to a social stimulus.

The Effect of Attention-Robbers and Lack of Mental Resources. What gets disputants into trouble during the weighing of options? First, the problem of selecting a response often requires a slow, thoughtful, intensive process of research, information gathering, and deliberation, and many disputants don't have that kind of time or energy. This problem is particularly acute during ongoing, day-to-day relationships. For example, imagine you are a parent, and are grocery shopping with your six-year-old. She wants the candy bar she's just seen at the check-out counter. You have to decide whether giving her this candy now will hurt her teeth or her appetite for dinner; whether you'll be setting a bad precedent for later on; whether the good job she did cleaning her room is a sufficient "special case" to remove the general rule against buying candy at the check-out counter; whether this is a good "teachable moment" for teaching self-restraint; whether, if you relent and buy the candy, big sister will claim unfair prejudice; and so forth. All these issues are present in a split-second moment of decision. Usually, a parent can't do a particularly good job of balancing the pros and cons under these circumstances. Attention-robbers—such as items spilling out of your shopping cart or your preoccupation with a simmering argument you're having with the child's other parent—as well as factors that impair thinking processes—such as being up the previous night with a child who had a nightmare—also have an impact on this process.

Factors in the Weighing of Options for Action. Other considerations affect which factors are applied and how much weight they are given. Transient, contextual factors—what's been going on and how it's affected the disputant—make a difference. Recall our parent/candy dispute. If your child has been irritable and cranky all day, and has worn your patience thin, you may place less importance on being kind to her and more importance on making sure your general rule against buying candy at the counter isn't violated. Similarly, in our workplace sexual harassment example, Karen, the potential victim, may place more salience and weight on options that feature adversary processes if she has recently attended a seminar that emphasizes going after harassers. She may be more likely to consider cooperation and conciliation if she is coming up for a promotional evaluation and doesn't want to rock the boat. And she may place more importance on cooperation if she's taking alternative dispute resolution courses. These factors are transient in the sense that their influence may fully or partially fade with time. The familiar experience of going grocery shopping while hungry—and finding that one has spent twice as much as usual—illustrates this point. Sharp negotiators use this fact about people when they plan strategy. For example, a business-person in California who has to negotiate with another businessperson visiting from Florida may push for the negotiation session to occur just before the latter's plane flight back is scheduled to depart. By doing so, the negotiator manipulates the situation to increase the value of quick resolution to her Florida counterpart.

Stable factors may also influence the weighing process. Some of the most important have to do with the individual's entrenched beliefs about conflict—his or her conflict blueprints. An individual who believes that conflict is principally a contest is unlikely to give a great deal of weight to cooperation as a goal. Disputants who believe that maintaining interpersonal harmony is extremely important (this belief system is common in individuals from Eastern cultures—see Chapter 14) are more likely to emphasize options that avoid outward strife and hostility. Along with the conflict blueprint, beliefs about the conflict toolbox—beliefs about what techniques are likely to be effective in what situations—affect the weighing process. For example, a consumer with a $60 dispute over dry cleaning, and who has spent many hours watching courtroom reality TV—"If you can't get him to give you what you deserve, take him to court!" (slogan from the television program "People's Court")—is likely to take the perspective that litigation is the best tool for obtaining relief.

Each individual's beliefs and personal values about the costs and benefits of various options are guided by complex internal factors. For example, consider the decision to buy a car. When Jane goes shopping, she is looking for a subcompact vehicle with a small price tag, a minimum of special features, and a large trunk to store her golf clubs. Andy's priorities are to get a vehicle that will function in an off-road environment and seem sexy to the young women he dates. Joe is looking for an upscale car with leather upholstery and an aesthetically pleasing paint job—white or silver. Rhonda also wants an aesthetically pleasing paint job but can't stand either white or silver—she prefers blue. Rhonda won't buy anything that won't hold all of her five children in the back in car seats. Attitudes about the costs of achieving a goal are also very individual. Joe's idea of "too expensive" is about four times as high as Jane's. For Rhonda, the tradeoff of a beautiful interior against the lack of safety features is intolerable.

This cost-benefit analysis results from a complex mixture of environmental, cognitive, and emotional/attitudinal factors. For example, Rhonda's desire for a vehicle that seats five children and has all sorts of safety features is partially dependent on her status as the mother of five, a role that young bachelor Andy can't even fathom. And the distinction between Joe's and Jane's concept of "too expensive" may depend, in part, on the differences in their incomes. Rhonda may also have specific statistical information about crash injuries, which her friend, Ethel, also a parent, has not seen and therefore does not appreciate.

Attitudinal factors are also important, however. Two people may have identical disposable income, for example, but one may be much more willing than the other to spend most of this wealth on an upscale car. Why? Gabriel may have the same resources with which to buy a car as Mel, but Gabriel may be a more anxious and risk-averse person and therefore may place more importance on safety features and a price that allows him to live within his financial means.

Every individual is unique, but social and developmental psychological theories have much to say about the development of personal attitudes and can help us make some educated guesses. We will turn to some of these theories for guidance in Chapter 7.

Expectancy of reinforcement
a person's belief about the likely personal rewards and drawbacks of an action he or she is contemplating.

Expectancy of Reinforcement and Perceived Self-efficacy. A disputant cannot perform the necessary cost-benefit analysis of possible actions unless he or she makes assumptions about what *results* his or her actions will have. To determine what is likely to happen, the individual *calls on other preexisting blueprints and associated toolboxes* related to the situation the person believes he or she is confronting. This assessment of what is likely to happen—and how it will affect the disputant—is known in psychological terms as the **expectancy of reinforcement.**

Since each conflict participant must engage in a mental process to assess the expectancy of reinforcement, the conflict participant relies on his or her subjective perceptions of the conflict situation to understand the options. Thus, the same factors that influence the accuracy of a person's interpretation of reality also influences the accuracy of his or her expectancy of reinforcement. For example, in our sexual harassment example, Karen may believe that, if she asks Mark to stop making off-color jokes, he will ridicule her—part of her beliefs about Mark's attitudes toward her. This expectancy of the reinforcement Karen will receive if she talks to Mark comes from Karen's beliefs about Mark. She may believe that her only viable option is to file an employee grievance against Mark—but her belief may be in error. In our Digi-Date scenario, Marsha may have come to the conclusion that Jeff is out to cheat her—and, accordingly, that a confrontational, hostile approach would protect her interests better than a conciliatory, cooperative one. This interpretation may, or may not, be accurate.

There are many additional components of the expectancy of reinforcement that are subjective. The conflict participant's background and experience influence what options he or she considers viable in the situation. In other words, the individual's background influences the blueprints he or she believes are appropriate to apply in the conflict and his or her beliefs about what they will do. Thus, for example, if our possible sexual harassment victim, Karen, was raised to believe that adversary processes are the best way to address social grievances, this background may influence her to think that filing a grievance is the best way to handle her concerns about Mark. However, there may be other, more appropriate blueprints that Karen has failed to consider.

A final note about the expectancy of reinforcement has to do with the degree of its conscious deliberateness. The expectation of reinforcement may be conscious, but it need not be. Sometimes—in fact, most times—a person's expectancy of reinforcement develops more or less automatically and unconsciously. Moreover, multiple expectancies may be operating at once, some on a conscious level and some unconscious. In any interpersonal conflict, a conflict diagnostician should expect to find a complex interplay of personal goals and reinforcement expectations—some overt and expressed, some hidden from public view, and some unacknowledged even to the self.

Individuals also have beliefs about their abilities to execute particular strategies and tactics; in other words, they have beliefs about their mastery of particu-

Perceived self-efficacy
a person's beliefs about his or her ability to carry off a contemplated action—his or her belief about how well he or she can use a given tool from his or her toolbox of strategies and tactics.

lar blueprints and toolboxes. This belief system is called **perceived self-efficacy.** An individual bases the expectancy of reinforcement on his or her perceived self-efficacy in executing particular blueprints and using particular tools. Perceived self-efficacy may be accurate or inaccurate. An individual may inappropriately reject using a particular technique because she mistakenly believes that, although it's the best tool for the job, she won't be able to make it work. Another individual may inappropriately use a technique he doesn't really know how to use effectively. In both cases, the individuals have made poor choices about how to handle the conflict. Because perceived self-efficacy is a mental process, it is affected by all the same things that affect the perception of the conflict situation itself: the individual's background and experience, the stress of the moment, the presence of attention-robbers, and the salience of goals, needs, and interests for that person, at that moment.

STEP 6: DISPUTANT CHOOSES AN OPTION

Step 6, choosing an option, is the result and culmination of all the steps that preceded it. At each step along the way, the disputant has had to interpret ambiguous or hidden information, has probably had to cut corners due to lack of time or resources, has been influenced by contextual features of the environment and the disputant's recent history, and has made decisions based on beliefs and attitudes personal to him or her. The time between step 1 and step 6 may be ten years or a split second, but, in some form, all the elements of steps 1 through 5 are present by the time disputant makes the choice to act.

How did these complex elements play out for Marsha in Digi-Date? As observers, we can only speculate. Perhaps she did very little option generation, being impaired by alcohol, distracted by Eric, and enraged by Jeff's lateness. It's possible to speculate that her action—which was to march over to Jeff, shake her finger at him, and scold him for his manipulative behavior—was motivated by a simple process. Given time constraint attention-robbers, and the influence of beer, it's likely she could generate only a single option: to scold him. It may have felt better emotionally to her to think about releasing her anger that way than having him approach her to make the first move, and therefore that was her choice. On the other hand, we cannot read Marsha's mind. Thus, if we were to *assume* that this was the process she used to decide on her actions, we would be vulnerable to the same sorts of mental errors and biases that might have gotten Marsha into trouble.

Before action occurs, the disputant more or less plans the steps that he or she will use in taking action. This planning process may start during option generation (step 4) and may inform the weighing process of step 5. Sometimes, poor or absent planning leads to errors in step 5, as the costs and benefits of taking the steps needed to exercise a particular option are not adequately taken into account.

STEP 7: DISPUTANT ACTS, CREATING A NEW SOCIAL STIMULUS

In step 7, the disputant puts the decision reached in step 6 into practice. Even here, there is opportunity for error, subjectivity, and bias to creep in.

Actual self-efficacy
a person's actual ability to carry out a contemplated action.

Actual Self-efficacy (Proficiency). Actions are not always the ones that have been intended, nor do they always have the expected effect. One reason is deficiencies of **actual self-efficacy.** Actual self-efficacy is an individual's ability to successfully carry out the behavior he or she has set for him- or herself. Actual self-efficacy in a given situation is determined by both stable factors (such as strength, intelligence, verbal ability, and knowledge) and transitory factors (such as fatigue, illness, hunger, stress, and emotional arousal).

Actual self-efficacy is also known in the behavioral sciences as *proficiency.* Social scientist Patrice Miller, studying the development of complex skills in children, has identified a multistage process in the development of proficiency (Berk 1997, 267–68):

Step 1: In a situation requiring an individual to dig into his or her toolbox, he or she is unable to find any tools to use.

Step 2: The person has learned to use a tool but often applies it in the wrong situation.

Step 3: The person has learned when to apply a given tool appropriately, and applies it, but is not yet good enough at it to have it help him or her.

Step 4: The person is able to use the tool appropriately and skillfully (attainment of proficiency).

What does this stage theory have to do with conflict diagnosis and ADR? The resolution of conflict is an extremely difficult process, even for the most expert diplomats and mediators. Proficiency is acquired gradually and in stages, and the mere learning of the tools of dispute resolution does not necessarily translate into an ability to use them appropriately and skillfully. Moreover, proficiency is not a stable trait. An individual who develops a particular proficiency level in applying a particular tool to interpersonal conflict will find it decreases when he or she enters a highly challenging situation. It is very common for people to become barely proficient at using a tool, only to have their new-found skill seemingly abandon them during a conflict. This phenomenon is well-known to parents who vow never to do to their children what their own parents did to them. These new, young parents learn some new disciplinary tools—from books, classes in parenting, and so forth—only to find that, when faced with their child's misbehavior at a stressful time, they are doing just what they vowed never to do: use the old, bad tools their parents used on them. Similarly, people who become professional dispute resolvers after working for a period of time in a related field, such as law or counseling, often find that they have misapplied techniques from their old profession in an ADR case.

Failures of Proficiently Executed Tactics. Despite high levels of proficiency, actions may nonetheless fail to have the intended effect. This failure may be due to errors in interpretation or judgment made by the disputant about the situation, mistaken beliefs about the effectiveness of various blueprints and their tools, and even changes in the situation that render a previously good idea bad. Actions may also fail because the disputant knew at the outset there was a chance of failure. In football, for example, the decision to try for a 45-yard field goal may be a valid one, even though the chance of succeeding is less than fifty-fifty; similarly, during interpersonal conflict, there are tactics that are worth trying even if they fail.

Actions Become Social Stimuli. It's critical to recognize that, each time a disputant acts, the action becomes the social stimulus for the other disputant or someone else on his or her "team." One of the most important failures of objectivity during interpersonal conflict is created by the belief, by one disputant, that the actions and effects of the other disputant's actions are wholly intentional and purposeful. As we have seen in our review of the seven steps of social behavior, they seldom are. In the Digi-Date conflict, it is likely that Jeff, our slightly confused software developer, will use Marsha's scolding as evidence for his interpretation of what she must be thinking and feeling. If Jeff was merely forgetfully late to the meeting, only to have Marsha tear into him, finger wagging and name-calling, he is likely to misinterpret Marsha's behavior as unjustifiable aggression rather than as the frustrated and self-protective response to misunderstood behavior that it evidently was. And so it goes in interpersonal conflict.

SUMMARY: THE SEVEN STEPS OF SOCIAL BEHAVIOR

Table 5-1 summarizes the seven steps of social behavior, and lists the factors that contribute to bias and error during conflict. Because social behavior in conflict is so vulnerable to these distorting forces, it can be risky to base judgments about participants in conflict on their actions. On the other hand, knowing about the factors that promote bias and error can serve as a red flag, enabling the careful conflict participant to avoid snap judgments, and to perform further investigation where needed. Overall, knowing where perceptual error and bias is likely to occur can help the conflict participant to reach his/her own goals, or those of his/her client or principal, more effectively.

◆ **TABLE 5-1**   Sources of Bias and Error During Social Behavior

Social Behavior Step	Stable and Transient Sources of Bias and Error* These refer to perceptions and actions of Disputant #2 unless otherwise specified.	
Step 1. Stimulus: action of Disputant #1	Biases and errors in Disputant #1's perceptions and decisions will influence his/her action.	
Step 2. Reception: Disputant #2 receives stimulus	Stable	• Sensory deficits (e.g., hearing impairment)
	Transient	• Attention-robbers (e.g., fatigue, illness, hunger, intoxication) • Cognitive overload factors (e.g., situational complexity, distractions, emotional arousal) • Contextual factors affecting stimulus reception (e.g., positions of disputants in room)

Step 3. Interpretation: Disputant #2 interprets behavior of Disputant #1	Stable	• General experiences and development
		• Past experiences with Disputant #1
		• Cognitive capacity
		• Heuristics governing social perception (e.g., "If he is silent in this situation, he must be angry")
		• Cultural context (e.g., "a passionate delivery of argument denotes dishonesty")
		• Simplification heuristics in conflict situations:
		  • Behavior is always what was intended
		  • Motives for behavior are simple
		  • Behavior is directed at the other disputant
		• Overall conflict blueprint (e.g., "all conflict is competitive")
		• Language and dialect differences

	Transient	• Current state of conflict (contained or escalated) • Other current social context (e.g., in a singles bar, shouting expected) • Time limitations • Cognitive overload and attention-robbing factors • Factors affecting salience of social cues (e.g., just watched romantic movie; flirtatious behavior very salient)
Step 4. Option Generation. Disputant #2 generates options for responding	Stable	• Past history & experience: conflict toolbox • Past history with Disputant #1 • Cognitive capacity • Cultural context
	Transient	• Time limitations, cognitive overload, and attention-robbing factors • Current state of conflict • Other current social context
Step 5: Weighing Options. Disputant #2 weighs options	Stable	• Pleasure principle: universal drive to maximize gain and minimize gain • Long-standing values • Drives, needs, and life challenges
	Transient	• Time limitations, cognitive overload, and attention-robbing factors • Factors affecting immediate salience of weighting factors (eg., wallet is empty, so making large profit more salient) • Current state of conflict (e.g., in escalated and intractable conflict, hurting other disputant takes on more importance)

SOCIAL BEHAVIOR STEP	STABLE AND TRANSIENT SOURCES OF BIAS AND ERROR* These refer to perceptions and actions of Disputant #2 unless otherwise specified.	
Step 6: Choice: Disputant #2 chooses an option	Stable	• Perceived self-efficacy
	Transient	• Time limitations, cognitive overload, and attention-robbing factors
Step 7: Action: Disputant #2 acts, becoming the stimulus for Disputant #1	Stable	• Proficiency (actual self efficacy)
	Transient	• Biases and errors in Steps 1-6 • Changes in situation • Challenging situation impairing proficiency • Chance (anticipated uncertainty)

* For steps 1 and 7, refers to factors that influence whether behavior matches what actor intended. For steps 2–6, refers to factors that cause bias and error in perception and response.

THE TEN THEMES OF CONFLICT DIAGNOSIS

Now that we've reviewed the steps of social behavior, we can apply them to an understanding of conflict diagnosis. Ten themes that recur throughout the study of conflict diagnosis. These themes are summarized below.

Recurrent Themes in Conflict Diagnosis

1. An individual will behave in ways that make sense to him or her.

2. Each individual's interpretation of reality is subjective.

3. Conflict participants use the conflict itself to make judgments about the motives of the other conflict participants.

4. The influence of mental processes on the perception of reality in interpersonal conflict is largely unconscious and automatic.

5. Expect interpersonal conflict to be characterized by widespread subjective perception and misperception on the part of the conflict participants, which, in turn, contributes to the persistence of conflict.

6. Each individual is motivated to improve basic well-being, happiness, comfort, and pleasure and to minimize discomfort, pain, and damage to the self.

7. Individuals' expectations about the results that their behavior will produce are subjective.

8. Individual choices in a conflict will be the result of reconciling numerous, diverse, frequently unconscious, and often contradictory motivations.

9. Individuals in a conflict frequently don't attain their intended goals.

10. Interpersonal conflict tends to be a self-fulfilling prophecy.

THEME 1: BEHAVIOR MAKES SENSE

People do things to achieve results. This fundamental assumption, underlying all behavioral sciences, may seem obvious. Another, and perhaps more useful, way of stating this basic assumption about human behavior is contained in the following epigram:

> If you know a person's situation and his background and experience, his actions will always make sense to you. (Koopman personal communication, 1983)

This assumption sounds an implicit cautionary note to conflict diagnosticians to resist the temptation to ascribe the seemingly irrational behavior of others to stupidity, ignorance, or evil. An astute conflict diagnostician always seeks to find rationality and sense in the behavior of all conflict participants, even if agreement with their actions does not follow. The discovery of an explanation for behavior, however irrational the behavior first seems, is a necessary precursor to dealing effectively with the behavior.

THEME 2: EACH INDIVIDUAL'S INTERPRETATION OF REALITY IS SUBJECTIVE

This theme reflects a long and venerated line of social psychological research and is supported by examining the seven steps of social behavior. In all human behavior, and particularly in interpersonal conflict, the reality understood by each participant is highly subjective. Legal professionals, such as lawyers and judges, and conflict professionals, such as mediators and arbitrators, encounter this phenomenon on a regular basis. A judge hearing a particularly intractable dispute may say that, if the plaintiff and defendant had not sat in the same courtroom at the same time and said they were talking about the same situation, the judge would not have been able to tell it from their accounts. Sometimes, it seems as if "plaintiffs are from Mars, and defendants are from Jupiter."

THEME 3: USE OF CONFLICT TO FORM PERCEPTION

One of the most important elements of social context is the conflict itself. Since conflict is a difficult, stressful, and often risky or even dangerous event, disputants are quite anxious to know what is happening in the mind and heart of the other disputant and his or her "team." The problems that people have misinterpreting and misunderstanding each other come from a very simple fact: they can't read each other's minds. Because they can't, they act like detectives, looking for clues to the inner workings of the other disputant and his "team" in the conflict itself—the participants' words, expressions, body language, behavior, and so forth.

As we will see when we turn to the issue of cooperation and competition, one's interpretation of a conflict directly influences his or her interpretation of the motives of others in the conflict. Engaging in conflict is like putting on funny glasses—it distorts perception—and this distortion is predictable, causing conflict participants to oversimplify their opponent, pass moral judgment, emphasize the struggle over scarce resources, magnify differences with the other disputant, and fail to see areas of agreement. And this tendency to use the conflict to reveal the motives of the participants tends to create a self-fulfilling prophecy: people generally tend to behave in the way we believe they are behaving, because our responses to what we think they are doing compels such a response. We will examine this issue in detail in Chapter 9. For the moment, suffice it to say that the importance of what is happening in the conflict for creating beliefs about the motives of conflict participants should not be underestimated.

THEME 4: PERCEPTUAL BIASES ARE UNCONSCIOUS

By now, you will have begun to see the complexity of everyday social perception. Social interaction, and particularly interpersonal conflict, is a highly complicated and difficult situation to assess accurately. As social beings, we are all built to interpret social interaction on a continuing basis and to bring our considerable intellectual skills to bear on this highly complex task. We also make a lot of mistakes when we perform this interpretive act. Unfortunately, we are seldom aware of these mistakes. The interpretation of interpersonal conflict is done almost entirely at the unconscious and automatic level. Conflict participants don't think of their conclusions about a conflict as interpretations or perceptions; they think of them as objective facts. Because the participants are unaware of the subjectivity inherent in their social perceptions, there is little incentive for people to work at improving things.

Thus, during an interpersonal conflict, when a participant confronts another individual whose frame of reference is very different, each is unlikely to attribute the other's attitudes and behaviors to diversity of perception: instead, not realizing that their conclusions are based on their own unique frames of reference, they are likely to attribute the other's conflict behavior to stupidity, ignorance, or illegitimate or evil motives or intentions. Recall our law firm sexual harassment example. Assuming that Mark does, in fact, like to engage in "locker-room humor" at the office, Mark may view his off-color jokes as completely harmless—"after all, they aren't directed at Karen." Given this frame of reference, which Mark perceives as "obvious," he may make some inappropriate assumptions about why Karen is raising a fuss about it. For example, he might conclude that Karen is competing with him for a partnership position and wants him out of the way. Karen, on the other hand, viewing her conclusion that off-color joking is "obviously" offensive and makes her life difficult, may attribute Mark's intransigence on the topic as indicating misogyny—"the fewer females who are in professional positions, the more he likes it." These misattributions of evil motive, fed by the differences between Karen's and Mark's frames of reference, allow each to feel justified in competitive, defensive, or damaging behavior against the other. Hence, the misattributions feed the conflict and help it escalate out of control.

THEME 5: PERCEPTUAL BIASES FEED CONFLICT

What we have learned in theme 4 leads inextricably to theme 5. Each time a disputant misinterprets the actions of another disputant, his or her reactions are very likely to be misunderstood by the original actor. Thus, as conflict unfolds, misunderstanding and misattribution accrete to the conflict in layers. These layers of mental mistake intermingle with resultant rage, mistrust, and a sense of betrayal to create a situation that becomes harder and harder to disentangle. In a very escalated conflict (such as the longstanding dispute between Israel and Arab nations), truth on both sides is long lost. As each disputant or group of disputants verbalizes its polarized beliefs about "the enemy," the distortions in these beliefs (which are always demonizing) feed the negative stereotypes held about them by the other side. For example, in the aftermath of the 9/11/01 terrorist attacks on the World Trade Center and Pentagon, a rumor circulated in the Arab world that 4,000 Jewish occupants of the World Trade Center evacuated the building before the impacts. This rumor, layered on top of the Arab demonization of Israelis that has come from decades of escalated conflict in the Middle East, fed Arab beliefs that are held to this day—that Islamic extremists were not responsible for the attacks. Americans who learn of these seemingly intransigent Arab beliefs, in the face of what they considered to be incontrovertible proof to the contrary, have their negative stereotypes about Arabs reinforced. Meanwhile, most Americans unquestioningly assumed that the terrorist group al Qaeda was responsible for the attacks even before hard evidence appeared. Citizens of Arab nations who disagree with the American perspective react to American intransigence, in the face of what they consider to be overwhelming proof to the contrary, by having their beliefs that all Americans are anti-Islamic bigots reinforced.

THEME 6: THE PLEASURE PRINCIPLE

Theme 6 expresses a basic tenet of social learning theory (Bandura 1977), an important wing of the field of developmental psychology. The assumption is that, at some level, people try to act in their own best interests: they minimize pain and maximize gain. Social learning theorists believe that an individual mentally assesses what the likely outcomes of potential behavior options might be to produce an assessment of the expectancy of reinforcement. An individual's expectancy of reinforcement is generally the result of a largely automatic and unconscious cost-benefit analysis of the likely outcomes of the various options the participant is considering.

In the rush and chaos of an ongoing conflict, disputants are often without the time and resources to perform a full-blown cost-benefit analysis of their options. In ordinary conflict, the assessment of costs and benefits may be instantaneous, unconscious, and very incomplete. We have already seen an example of this phenomenon, in the context of the Digi-Date conflict. Full-blown legal disputes and transactions, on the other hand, evolve over time and offer the disputants opportunities to engage in more thoughtful and complete analysis of the expectancy of reinforcement.

THEME 7: SUBJECTIVITY OF EXPECTATIONS ABOUT RESULTS

This theme is explained in more detail in our discussion of step 5 of social behavior. To determine what he or she should do, a conflict participant assesses various options, guessing at what will happen if he or she reacts in certain ways, ultimately selecting an option. This assessment is based on the mental construction the individual placed on reality in steps 2 through 5, and is therefore subjective.

THEME 8: COMPLEXITY AND INCONSISTENCY OF MOTIVATION

It is typical for an observer of behavior to attribute that behavior to a very simple set of motives. In practice, this assessment is usually wrong. Individuals involved in conflict are usually beset with multiple, often inconsistent, motives. For example, in our law firm sexual harassment scenario, Mark may have simultaneous motives of lightening the office environment with his joking, engaging in a bit of male bonding, and getting Karen's attention. He may like Karen and not want to offend her, yet this motive may seem to conflict with his desire to use a familiar tactic, off-color joking, to reinforce friendships with male associates. Moreover, many motives are unconscious, and, because the person making behavioral choices is unaware that they are operating, such unconscious motives may be influential. For example, Mark may additionally have an unconscious motive to establish himself as a powerful male in the office, and intimidating female associates into a subordinate position may be a way he learned to achieve this position. The subtle disempowerment of females as a method of consolidating male power may be a blueprint he has experience with as an observer of male relatives, friends, and role models in the media. Because this motive is both unconscious and linked to Mark's sense of self-confidence, it will likely be a powerful force in Mark's behavior. It will also likely be a motive Mark will deny. Because the motive operates below consciousness, Mark's denial will be honest, albeit mistaken. Moreover, given this disparate, and sometimes inconsistent, set of motives, the behavior Mark actually engages in may reflect his ambiguity about his motives. For example, Mark may tell dirty jokes at a volume that he is unsure whether Karen is able to hear. Unless Karen is able to read Mark's conscious and unconscious mind, and realize the muddle from which his behavior springs, she is likely to misconstrue his motives.

Environmental factors that affect the expectancy of reinforcement are critical to understanding the ultimate behavior of disputants in a conflict. The course of the conflict itself causes profound changes to occur in the motivations of the disputants, as we will see in Chapter 9. Destructive and escalating conflict causes the disputants to shift from an individualistic, "maximize personal gain" orientation to an adversarial, "I've got to do better than he or she does" orientation. In its most extreme form, escalated conflict causes those trapped in it to value damage to or the destruction of the other disputant over everything else. People, groups, and nations that seem to be locked into an irrational pattern of attack and counterattack are often suffering from the shift in cost-benefit valuation that comes from spending time in an intractable conflict.

THEME 9: ACTUAL AND INTENDED RESULTS OF ACTION MAY DIFFER

This theme was introduced in our discussion of step 7 of social behavior. When disputants react in a conflict situation, their goals are often not met in the actions they have taken. Broadly, there are five reasons for this sort of failure.

First, conflict participants may have misinterpreted the situation initially. In our law firm sexual harassment example, if the human relations specialist flatly dismisses Karen's concerns despite a real pattern of sexual innuendos on Mark's part, her approach to resolving the situation is very likely to backfire.

Second, a conflict participant may have applied an inappropriate blueprint for resolution. For example, consider a dispute between neighbors over loud noises. One neighbor resents the other's choice of playing the stereo very loudly every night while the first is trying to sleep. If the resentful neighbor has only a "take it to court" blueprint for resolving conflicts with people he doesn't know very well, he may decide that the only effective way to deal with this neighbor is to sue him. Unfortunately, this sort of lawsuit cannot be pursued in small claims court, and most trial courts of general jurisdiction would discourage neighbors from using the court system to resolve this sort of problem. The resentful neighbor is very likely to come out of court with a defendant's verdict, a big legal bill, and a neighbor who is now motivated to make him as miserable as possible.

Third, the conflict participant may have applied an appropriate blueprint but an inappropriate tool. This choice of tools may come from inaccurate perceived self-efficacy, from errors in choices of tools, or from errors in perception about the situation. A conflict-resolution specialist recounts a favorite example of a mistaken choice of tools, which was told to her by a friend. This friend was, at the time, the mother of a four-year-old and a two-year-old. One day, the four-year-old smacked the two-year-old, as preschoolers sometimes will. The four-year-old's decision to hit his baby brother was at odds with Mom's blueprint, which was to raise nonviolent children, hence the interpersonal conflict. Mom rushed over to the oldest child, gave him a whack on the hand, and shouted: "In this family, we do not hit!" Almost immediately, she said, she realized that the tool she had used to discipline her child was probably the worst one she could have chosen, since she herself had used the forbidden behavior even while speaking the message that the family should not use it.

Fourth, individuals are not always able to engage successfully in the conduct in which they intend to engage. For example, in the Karen-Mark scenario, a human relations specialist who has been asked to intervene in the conflict might misjudge her ability to be persuasive with Karen, based on her lack of experience managing in diversity settings. Or she may be extremely busy just now and not able to devote the time required to handling the situation effectively. Or the individual's expectation of reinforcement may be wrong. For example, Karen may misinterpret the situation as involving bigoted, rather than merely insensitive, colleagues. Based on her misinterpretation, she may believe that taking the issue to a formal grievance procedure is likely to win her back pay and an apology, an assessment she may be very wrong about.

Fifth, the conflict participant may have done all the mental calculations right and merely tried to achieve a goal that he or she knew from the beginning was uncertain. All assessments of the expectation of reinforcement are, in fact, assessments of *probabilities* of various potential outcomes. Thus, the fact that one is trying to attain a particular goal in a conflict does not mean that one's actions will necessarily achieve them or even will help one move in that direction. Thus, *chance* is an important element determining whether the results a conflict participant expects will actually come to pass.

Consider the implications of theme 9 for theme 3 (the fact that participants in a conflict use the conflict itself as evidence for the motivations of other participants). Each participant in a conflict is engaged in various behaviors aimed at meeting particular goals. Other participants observing these behaviors are likely to presume that the individual is intending the results of his or her behavior. If this presumption is not accurate, as we have seen is a strong possibility, then the other participants will be mistaken about the motivations of the individual they are observing. Since this phenomenon is widespread in interpersonal conflict, participants are frequently mistaken about the motives of others. These erroneous judgments usually go unchecked and uncorrected. Since the behavior of one disputant becomes the trigger for behavior by the other disputant, errors tend to be perpetuated and magnified.

THEME 10: THE SELF-FULFILLING NATURE OF CONFLICT

Because there are many subjective elements that affect interpersonal conflict, and because conflict participants try to draw inferences about the situation from the behaviors of the other conflict participants, these subjective elements tend to create their own reality. Hence, a conflict becomes what its participants think it is.

This self-fulfilling aspect of conflict can have a positive or a negative impact on the participants in the conflict. But an effective conflict diagnostician can use this information to his or her advantage. By knowing this recurring theme of interpersonal conflict, the diagnostician can call on his or her knowledge of conflict to develop strategies that divert the situation from a destructive path to a more constructive one. Moreover, as we will see in Part III of this book, the self-fulfilling aspect of conflict is an important tool used by savvy ADR practitioners to alter the course of conflict, making the process and outcome more constructive.

PUTTING THE THEMES TOGETHER

The recurrent themes of conflict diagnosis demonstrate the inherent subjectivity of the process of interpersonal conflict. Table 5-2 summarizes these themes and provides examples of how the themes operate in real-life conflicts.

We have seen that conflict can be a minefield of confusion and inadvertent mutual deception for the individuals involved. When one disputant performs actions in a conflict, those actions are subjected to a series of interpretations and analyses. Distortion and error almost invariably creep into the process of receiving, digesting, and responding to the action. Yet, when the disputant ultimately acts on what he or she has understood, the other disputant will most likely interpret the conduct using his or her own, very different frame of reference. The disputant observing the conduct will usually assume that the motives of the actor are perfectly expressed in the action, are very simple, and are directed at the observer, whereas the actions are often unintended, are typically the result of multiple and often contradictory motives, and are usually directed at protection of the actor. It bears remembering, as well, that the action of a disputant in a conflict serves as the information that the other disputant uses to interpret the situation and to respond: thus, the distortions and errors that occur during the course of a conflict are often amplified and inflict damage on a widening scale.

CONCLUSIONS: THEMES OF CONFLICT DIAGNOSIS

Stepping into an interpersonal conflict is a little like being one of the blind men examining an elephant. As we have discovered, there are numerous ways that our perceptions and mental processes trick us into thinking we know what is going on in a conflict, when, in fact, nothing could be further from the truth. Conflict diagnosis helps us recognize subjectivity and put it in its place. Conflict diagnosis allows us to shed light on a specific conflict—or, at the very least, it helps us to recognize when we're flying blind. With the help of conflict diagnosis, we can better assess what is going on in the conflict, avoid the otherwise inevitable perceptual distortion that conflict creates, and develop effective strategies for turning adversity into opportunity. In Part II, we will explore the steps of conflict diagnosis in more detail. This exploration will allow you to better understand conflict and to strategize approaches to dealing with it. The information on conflict diagnosis will also make it possible for you to evaluate and understand the approaches to dispute resolution that are discussed in Part III, in a manner that illuminates their uniqueness, differences, and specific indications and contraindications.

RECURRENT THEME	EXAMPLE
An individual will behave in ways that make sense to him or her.	A divorcing mother, whose alcoholic father beat and traumatized her, mistakenly believes that her children's father, a "social drinker," has become an alcoholic and, accordingly, files suit to deny him all contact with the children. From the father's perspective, the mother's conduct is completely irrational.
Each individual's interpretation of reality is subjective.	In the early twenty-first century, many Israelis believed they were innocent victims of Palestinian terrorism, whereas many Palestinians believed they were innocent victims of Israeli oppression.
Conflict participants use the conflict itself to make judgments about the motives of the other conflict participants.	Jim, a client in a tort action, is questioned by Grant, counsel for opposing client George in a deposition. Being vigorously cross-examined, Jim concludes that George hates him and is intentionally and maliciously trying to paint him as a liar and perjurer. In fact, Grant had developed the questions on his own, without knowing Jim personally, and Grant had not consulted George about them at all.
The influence of mental processes on the perception of reality in interpersonal conflict is largely unconscious and automatic.	There is some evidence that many whites who formed an opinion that the police had used justifiable force in the subduing of suspect Rodney King unconsciously believed that King was more "in control" during the altercation than he really was.
Expect interpersonal conflict to be characterized by widespread subjective perception and misperception on the part of the conflict participants, which, in turn, contributes to the persistence of conflict.	There is evidence that Israelis and Palestinians each attribute violence of unknown origin to members of the other group, thus confirming the opinion of the members of each group that the other is at fault in the conflict.
Each individual is motivated to improve basic well-being, happiness, comfort, and pleasure and to minimize discomfort, pain, and damage to the self.	A client in a child custody case fails to attend a negotiation session, as directed by his attorney. Although initially he states that he was busy and forgot the appointment, he later realizes that his failure was due to his aversion to facing his child's mother across the negotiation table.
Expectations held by individuals, about the results that their behavior will produce, are subjective.	Many Americans believe that, if military force is used against governments known to be sympathetic to the aims of Islamic militants, the overall safety to Americans will improve. There is no firm evidence that this is the case.
Individual choices in a conflict will be the result of reconciling numerous, diverse, frequently unconscious, and often contradictory motivations.	Dora pursues a small claims action against an automobile dealership she blames for unnecessarily high repair bills. She thrusts herself enthusiastically into the task of preparing her case, only to become distracted by a family emergency. When the date of trial arrives, Dora is unprepared. Her motivation, so intense at the commencement of litigation, has been sapped by other life experiences.
Individuals in a conflict frequently don't attain their intended goals.	Blair files a civil action against the manufacturer of his television. He has prepared carefully and is ready for trial, except that he has lost the paperwork demonstrating sale of the television and cannot obtain them from the dealer from whom he bought the item. Although he has an otherwise airtight case against the manufacturer, his case is thrown out when he is unable to demonstrate a chain of purchase.
Interpersonal conflict tends to be a self-fulfilling prophecy.	A father who wants additional help in getting special accommodations for his special-needs third-grader, expects the school to be uncooperative. As a result, the father is abrasive, hostile, and pushy with the principal and third-grade teaching team. This conduct alienates the school personnel, who react by concluding that the father's demands are extreme and finding reasons to deny the father what he seeks.

EXERCISES, PROJECTS, AND "THOUGHT EXPERIMENTS"

1. *Conflict journal.* Think back to the last time you took any action in your chosen conflict. In a written essay, identify and describe the following:

   a. The social stimulus, including any context that was relevant to your reaction.

   b. What you saw, heard, and otherwise sensed. Try as best as you can to avoid interpretation at this stage. For example, "he smiled" is usually a description, providing that the facial expression was unambiguous, whereas "he was happy" is interpretation.

   c. How you interpreted the social stimulus (now you can interpret).

   d. The option or options you considered for responding to the social stimulus (ignoring it or doing nothing is one such option).

   e. The process you used for deciding which option to exercise.

   f. What you did in response. Were you able to respond in the way that you had planned, and did the response have the effects you intended?

   g. How the other conflict participants interpreted your actions. You may have to speculate. Do you think their interpretation was accurate? If not, would it help the course of the conflict for you to clarify your intentions?

2. *Conflict journal.* Write an essay applying the ten recurrent themes in conflict diagnosis to your chosen conflict. Look closely for ways in which they apply—they are powerful largely because they are automatic and unconscious. Does the writing of this essay empower you to make better decisions in the conflict?

3. Using the Internet, research an international peace movement or organization devoted to resolving a hot conflict, such as the Israeli-Palestinian conflict. An example of such an organization is Americans for Peace Now (*http://www.peacenow.org/index.html*). Examine the programs undertaken by the organization you choose. Do you see instances in which the activities of this organization could be viewed as attempts to counteract the biases and errors discussed in this chapter? For example, an organization that sponsors ongoing dialogue between groups in conflict might be seen as making an effort to counteract errors of interpretation of a social stimulus. Find as many such instances as you can, and describe how they address these biases and errors.

4. *Part A.* Imagine yourself in the following situation:

   > You are driving north on the highway. You enter an intersection at a green light to turn left. You wait, since there are oncoming cars. The light turns yellow, then red, and you start your left turn to clear the intersection. But the oncoming car fails to stop at the red light. It comes right for you, and only quick reflexes on your part keep you from colliding.

Before going on to read Part B of this question, put the book aside and write down your attitudes and feelings about this other person. Are you making any assumptions about what this person is like?

Part B. Now read the following paragraph. It describes what is going on in the mind of the driver of the other car.

> I am driving home from the hospital. Three days ago, my fiancé of five years and I were coming back from our wedding rehearsal dinner with our families. We are devout Christians who do not drink. On the way home, our car was struck by a drunk driver. The car hit us on the driver's side. I was shaken but not seriously hurt. My fiancé was hit on the side and was thrown against the windshield. In the hospital, the doctors have been trying everything. They operated to set his broken tibia. They have performed a number of scans to try to figure out why he hasn't regained consciousness. They put in a tube so he could breathe. They fed him through an IV. I have stayed by his side every moment. I've heard that, if you talk to the person and tell him you love him, there is a better chance of his waking up. But this morning they said the latest MRI looked very bad. They say he really doesn't have any chance of ever waking up. I am just in shock. They won't let me stay with him anymore; they say I should go home and get some rest. My whole life is over. He was my whole life.

Does this new information cause you to consider revising your assumptions about what caused this driver to nearly hit you? Does the new information change the way you think about this person? If so, how? What does this exercise have to do with the themes of this chapter?

5. Suppose you are an attorney. A new client comes to see you. She wants to sue a former friend for harassment. The story goes that she and the former friend had children in school together. They worked together on school committees and had their kids over for play dates at one another's home. Then your client started getting suspicious that the friend was cheating with your client's husband. Her husband started hanging up the phone when she entered the room, and, about the same time, her friend seemed to become more distant. Finally, she says, she confronted the friend and accused her of adultery. The friend categorically denied it and acted very offended. The angry confrontation ended the friendship. Then, the client reports, she started getting phone calls at all times of the day and night. When she picks up the phone, there's no one there. She *just knows* that this is the work of her former friend, trying to get back at her. The situation is totally intolerable, complains the client, and she wants to sue to get the friend to stop. What do the recurrent themes of conflict diagnosis tell you about the client's account of harassment? What, as an attorney, would you do to assist her? (Although the details have been changed, this story is an adaptation of a real-life conflict situation. Assume, for purposes of this exercise, that there

is a cause of action for harassment if one person misuses the telephone to harass or intimidate another.)

6. Discuss the roles of inaccurate perceived self-efficacy and deficient proficiency in creating bias and error during interpersonal conflict.

7. Put yourself in the position of a managing paralegal at a large law firm. The firm has invested time, money, and effort in integrating conflict diagnosis elements into the practice, in an effort to serve their clients better. They have given you the responsibility for developing a handbook to explain to other paralegals how to prepare cases and clients to minimize the perceptual and interpretational biases and errors that are created during interpersonal conflict. List the specific guidelines you would include, and justify each one.

8. Debate or discuss the following statement: "The information contained in this chapter has no relevance for commercial legal disputes and transactions." If you do this exercise on your own, share your comments with those of your classmates. Are you all in agreement? Do their answers surprise you?

RECOMMENDED READINGS

Bandura, A. 1977. *Social learning theory.* Englewood Cliffs, NJ: Prentice-Hall.

Fiske, S. T., and S. L. Neuberg. 1990. A continuum model of impression formation from category based to individuating processes: Influences of information and motivation on attention and interpretation. In *Advances in experimental social psychology,* Vol. 23, edited by M.P. Zanna (pp. 1–74). San Diego: Academic Press.

Krauss, R. M., and E. Morella. 2000. Communication and conflict. In *The handbook of conflict resolution,* edited by M. Deutsch and P. T. Coleman (pp. 131–43). San Francisco: Jossey-Bass.

Part II

The Steps of Conflict Diagnosis

Part I framed our discussion of the major topic of this book, interpersonal conflict. After an introduction to basic concepts and definitions in Chapters 1 and 2, you confronted in Chapter 3 the challenging notion that most of us have an unduly narrow conception of what conflict and its resolution can be. In Chapter 4, you learned that gaining proficiency in a technique called conflict diagnosis can set the stage for a deeper and more comprehensive understanding of interpersonal conflict.

Part II will take you, step by step, through the process of conflict diagnosis. Each chapter is devoted to a separate step in the process. Conflict diagnosis is a skill, yet it is heavily based on theory and empirical data hailing from a number of social science disciplines. You will find that the skill of conflict diagnosis lies primarily in learning to apply theoretical material to conflict facts. A conflict diagnostician, proceeding step by step through conflict diagnosis, creates a rigorous description of an interpersonal conflict. This detailed description is then matched with the dispute resolution strategies, tactics, and processes best designed to produce good conflict from the diagnostician's point of view and role in the conflict. The dispute resolution processes, and how they match with the characteristics of conflicts, are addressed primarily in Part III of this book. Conflict diagnosis, in addition to serving as a skill you can apply directly to personal and professional conflicts, will also be helpful in explaining the attributes and functions of the ADR processes we will examine in Part III.

6

Step 1. Describe the Conflict

"Well begun is half done."

—Aristotle

In this chapter, you will learn . . .

- How to describe an interpersonal conflict using a diagramming system.
- How to learn more about the interested parties in a conflict to make your diagram more complete.
- That the diagram you develop is affected by which interpersonal conflict you choose as a focus.
- Some of the benefits of diagramming a conflict.

The first step in conflict diagnosis is to describe the conflict. Putting the situation into words will help you clarify in your own mind what the conflict is about. Describing the conflict will also help you begin to formulate an analysis of who is involved in the conflict and what their interests are. It will also help you identify where you need additional information about the conflict to help you understand it better.

It is important to write down your description and put it aside for a time—at least twelve hours is a good recommendation. Then reread the description. Is it clear what divergent goals, interests, or needs exist that make this situation a conflict? If it isn't clear, either you need more information, or the situation may not be an interpersonal conflict after all. The following example illustrates this point.

A college student was bothered by what she felt was a conflict with her mother over her career plans. When she began diagnosing the conflict, her first step was to write the following:

> My mother and I disagree over what I should be doing with my life. My mother seems to think very highly of me and thinks I'll go far, but I have so many self-doubts that I am not so sure. I live at home, and my mother

has been very supportive of my efforts to get a university education. I haven't decided on a major yet, and I can't decide whether I want to go into psychology or elementary education. Mom doesn't seem to be pressuring me in any way, but I feel as if I have to choose something to appear grown-up and mature in her eyes. Often, I can't sleep at night, because I keep turning this decision over and over and mentally I keep seeing my mother's judging stare. It causes me a lot of stress and turmoil.

When this student reread her description the next morning, she realized that she did not have a conflict with her mother. The pressure she was feeling about choosing an academic major was self-generated: she was having an internal, *intra*personal conflict, not an *inter*personal conflict. Whenever her self-critical attitude started to bother her, she thought of how her mother must be judging her. Having written the description and having had this insight, the student realized that, far from having a disagreement with her mother over college and career, her mother was someone she could count on to support her during her efforts to make this difficult career choice.

Once the conflict description has been completed and you have verified that you are dealing with an actual interpersonal conflict, the next step is to map out the conflict. The conflict map (or **sociogram**, as it is termed in the field of psychology) supports the process of defining the roles and interests of the conflict participants. In a very simple interpersonal conflict, this step may seem superfluous and unnecessary, but in more complicated situations it is critical. The conflict map helps reveal the influence of stakeholders and other constituents, linked conflicts, and conflicts of interest among disputants and their own agents and advocates. As such, the map helps highlight some of the complexities that might otherwise cloud the situation and prevent constructive intervention. The map also points the way to areas in which more information is needed.

The best way to describe the mapping process is to use some examples. We will begin by examining the S-B corporate transaction scenario introduced in Chapter 1. The description is repeated here. Imagine that you are on the staff of S Corporation, and you have been assigned the task of assisting with the development of a strategy for successfully negotiating a deal with B Corporation:

> The S Corporation is the manufacturer of a device called the S-Chip, used in the manufacture of cellular telephones. The individuals at S Corporation responsible for marketing have located a potential buyer, B Corporation, a manufacturer of cellular telephones. A meeting has been scheduled to negotiate the sale of the S-Chip. S Corporation has sent its research vice president, Samantha (Sam), along with its corporate counsel, Sean, to act as legal advisor. B Corporation has sent its purchasing vice president, Bob, to negotiate, along with B's corporate house counsel, Bea. Back at the corporate headquarters of S Corporation, Sue, Samantha's staff assistant, is responsible for supporting the negotiation efforts, while at B Corporation, Ben, the executive secretary in charge of the purchasing department, provides support for Bob during the negotiation. The directors of each corporation believe that the proposed sale is potentially advantageous, provided that a good deal can be struck.

Sociogram

a diagram or chart that shows individuals and their relationships to one another.

Let's map this transaction. Right now what you know is that individuals within both corporations are attempting to make a deal for the purchase and sale of the S-Chip from one corporation to the other. Thus, the transaction itself is corporate; any eventual deal will be between the corporate entities, and, accordingly, the disputants are the two corporations. Each disputant wants to obtain the best deal for itself in the transaction, and, since price is one element of the deal, there is at least one set of incompatible goals between the disputants, rendering this a true interpersonal conflict. Each corporate disputant in our scenario has an agent, an attorney/advocate, and a constituent.

To map conflicts in this book, we will use *circles* to identify the participants. We will use a *double-ended block arrow* to represent interpersonal conflict and *straight lines* to represent relationships between the disputants and their own agents, advocates, and constituents. Since an actual negotiation is planned, we will add one element of complexity to the map: we will indicate *communication lines* between representatives of different disputants by one-tailed arrows. A map of the S-B corporate transaction is shown in Figure 6-1.

So far, the mapping of this conflict has been fairly straightforward. However, it is likely that more people are affected by, and can have an impact on, this transaction than the map shows. How can a conflict diagnostician learn more about who is involved in the conflict and how each participant relates to the main conflict? The answer is that any diagnostician trying to map a conflict needs to do careful research.

As a conflict diagnostician, you would most likely interview as many people as you could find to grant you the time and give you information. The following is an example of what you might find out researching a conflict like this one:

Interviewing Sam, the corporate research vice president, you learn that she considers herself the principal investigator who invented and developed the S-Chip. The chip has been a three-year project for her, and she is extremely proud of it. You sense that Sam's ego is riding on this project and that she will be devastated if the chip is rejected or sold at a bargain price. Interviewing Steve, the CEO, you learn that, after consultation with the board, Steve brought Sean, the lawyer, up to date on his concerns about Sam and asked Sean to find a way to rein in Sam's push to get a ridiculously high price for the chip. The board of directors unanimously concurs that they'd like the chip ultimately sold to B Corporation, but they realize that the price Sam expects is totally unreasonable. Additionally, the board heard a presentation from quality control (QC), casting some doubt on the current readiness of the chip for market. Sam has reassured the board that it is ready, but the QC people think it needs another three to six months in reliability testing. There is no hard evidence of reliability problems, just a lack of appropriate data. Nonetheless, a premature release and failure of the chip could seriously damage S Corporation's reputation in the business community. Other board members, fearing a poor earnings report will scare away shareholders, are pushing for some sort of immediate sale to fatten the corporate asset/liability statement. The compromise the board reached was to sell now, to hide their desire to foot-drag, and then to offer a delayed pro-

◆ **FIGURE 6-1**

Map of S-B Corporate
Transaction

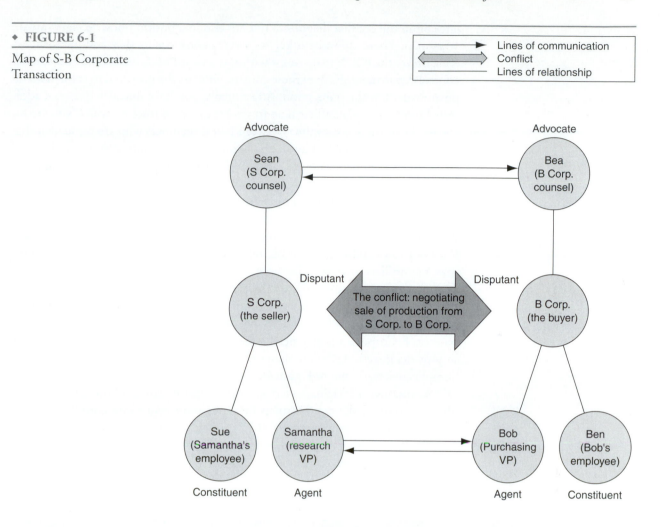

duction schedule in exchange for some better terms. (In other words, the board hopes that B Corporation would also hope for a slight delay and wants to determine if they can "have their cake and eat it, too.") If they can't get mileage out of the "do it now" position, they will agree to some discounting if production is delayed a bit.

You also interviewed Sean, and learned that he has a reputation as a peacemaker, which he wishes to preserve. However, Sean sees opposing counsel, Bea, as having a vested interest in preserving her "tough as nails" reputation, which she uses in marketing her services. You sense real animosity in Sean against Bea, and, in checking with some friends of yours in the legal community, you learn that Sean once commented that Bea reminded him of his exwife, with whom he had had a protracted, expensive, and agonizing divorce.

Now you have some more information that illuminates the likely behavior, attitudes, and motivations of some of the participants. You would certainly want to keep careful notes of this additional information: it will come in very handy later on in the conflict diagnosis. You are also in a position now to elaborate on your map. There are some other important constituents that you have uncovered: Steve, the CEO; two groups within the board of directors; plus the quality control department. Each of these constituents has the potential to influence and possibly disrupt the transaction. Additionally, you have uncovered several additional interpersonal conflicts that are *linked* to the conflict on which you are focusing. First, there is a conflict between board members who are persuaded that sale of the S-Chip should await the completion of quality control testing and those board members who are more concerned that any delay in making a sale will scare off possible shareholders. Second, there appears to be a personality conflict between Sean and Bea. Third, there is a conflict between Sam, who wants an extremely high price for the S-Chip for ego reasons, and S Corporation, whose desire for a high price is tempered by a need for the sale to go through and the need to establish an amicable relationship with B Corporation. And there may be conflicts of interest between the attorneys, who have an interest in taking a certain approach to the transaction in order to protect their professional reputation and their clients: for example, S Corporation may need Sean to be tougher than he would prefer to be to preserve his peacemaker reputation, whereas B Corporation may need a more conciliatory stance than Bea is willing to provide. If we add all these elements to the map, it becomes substantially more complicated, as shown in Figure 6-2.

As you might imagine, as a diagnostician gains more and more information about a conflict, the conflict map becomes more and more complex. As you gathered information about the S-B Corporate transaction, you would probably transfer your conflict map to a large sheet of paper or presentation board to give you room for all the complexities.

Primatologist Franz de Waal (seen here in scientific observation) describes many conflicts and their resolution, but, unlike most conflict diagnosticians, his study population is chimpanzees and other primates. Digital Vision Ltd.

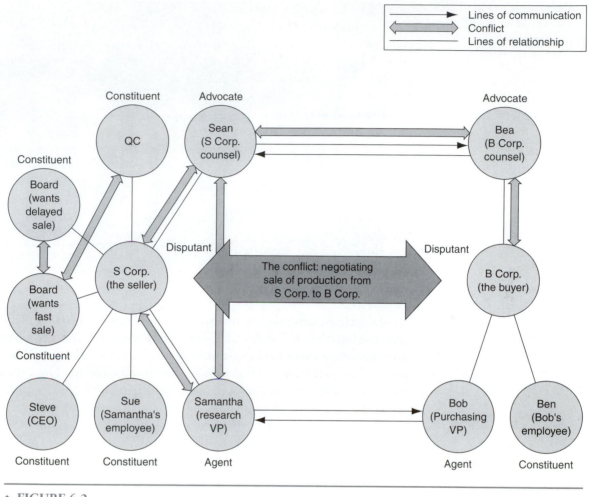

	Lines of communication
	Conflict
	Lines of relationship

◆ **FIGURE 6-2**

Revised Map of S-B Corporate Transaction

Let's see how the conflict map applies to another interpersonal conflict. Consider the following description written by Ed, a father of three:

My wife left me six weeks ago, saying she wanted a divorce. We have three adorable children: Joe, age twelve; Marjorie, age six; and Jennie, age five. I still can't figure out why Ellen left. I thought the marriage was OK, although I admit it wasn't perfect. I do not want the marriage to end, and I want to fight her all the way. The kids are with Ellen. Ellen seems very angry and accuses me of never supporting her or being emotionally available during the marriage. I couldn't disagree more—I spent seventy hours a week working two jobs just to support the family and keep them safe and secure. Every nonworking moment awake I spent with them. Maybe she is having an affair, or maybe her sister has convinced her to leave—Gloria has always hated me and tried to turn Ellen against me. I am really worried that, with my work schedule and Ellen's rigid attitude, I'll never see the kids.

Constituents, such as children in a divorce dispute, can affect, and be affected by conflict. Michael Newman, PhotoEdit

Ed is clearly describing an interpersonal conflict—in fact, there may be more than one interpersonal conflict. Ed is in shock about the recent separation. Right now, he is clear about the fact that his wife wants the separation and he doesn't, and he fears a possible conflict over time with the children. Thus, there are at least two sets of divergent goals that define the conflict between Ed and Ellen. However, Ed is likely to gain additional insights into the nature of the conflict as time goes by, clarifying some divergent goals, needs, and interests; adding some; and finding that others don't apply. The written description of the conflict should be a working document: as you gain information about the conflict, you should expect the description to evolve and change. Keep earlier versions of your description: it will shed light on the course and evolution of the conflict and on the effect the conflict is having on your perceptions and attitudes.

At this point, Ed knows that he and Ellen are the principal disputants in what is primarily a marital conflict, so, on his map, he draws Ed and Ellen as the disputants and his sister-in-law (Gloria) and children as constituents. He is not sure, however, whether Gloria is also acting as an informal advocate for Ellen, so he labels her as both a constituent and a possible advocate. He links the children as constituents to both Ellen and himself, to reflect their close relationship with both their mother and father. He also adds a conflict arrow between Gloria and himself to reflect their disagreement and her possible involvement in the breakup. His diagram is shown in Figure 6-3.

You may have noticed that each of the conflict maps has more than one conflict arrow. Conflict maps frequently show more than one conflict, because multiple conflicts are often linked. This feature of conflict relates, in part, to the fact that divergent goals, needs, and interests are so common that nearly everyone involved in a conflict has some sort of conflict with nearly every other participant. But also, linked conflicts tend to propagate when a conflict is unresolved and escalating, as we will see in Chapter 9. The conflict that is chosen as the

◆ **FIGURE 6-3**

Maps of Ed-Ellen Conflict

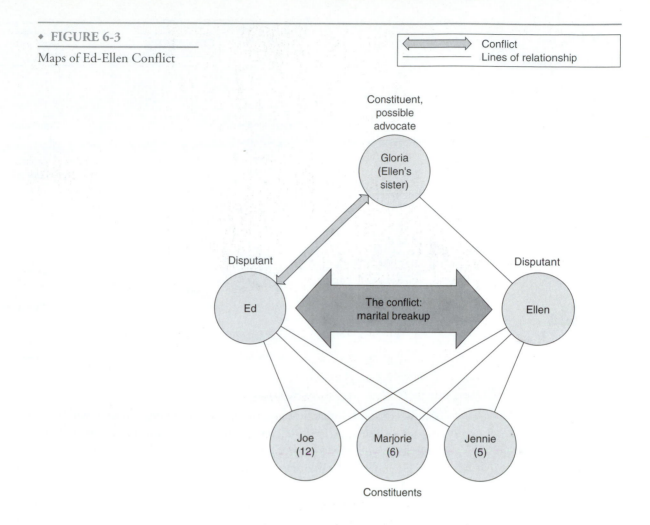

main focus of a conflict map depends on the goals of the conflict diagnostician. For example, in the Ed-Ellen-Gloria situation, we have been looking at the conflict from Ed's perspective. However, if Gloria had a husband who was being affected by Gloria's conflict with Ed, Gloria's husband might draw a map showing Ed and Gloria as the disputants and he and Ellen as constituents. Such an alternative map would show the Ed-Ellen conflict as a linked conflict, affecting and perhaps exacerbating the conflict between Ed and Gloria. Compare Figure 6-4 with Figure 6-3.

Note that, in the new map, in Figure 6-4 Gloria has been reidentified as a disputant and Ellen has been reidentified as a constituent. Since Ed and Ellen's children are affected by the conflict (albeit indirectly, through the Ed-Ellen conflict), they are still shown as constituents, but it is the conflict diagnostician's judgment call whether to include constituents with very attenuated relationships to the main conflict. The diagnostician will want to include constituents and stakeholders who have the potential to affect the course of the conflict on which the diagnostician is focusing or on the participants that the diagnostician is concerned

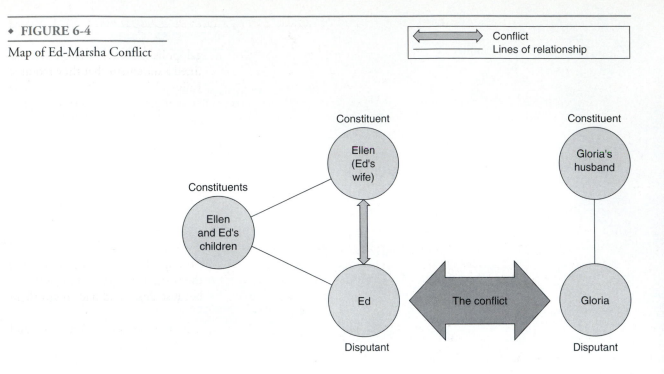

about. Thus, if Gloria's husband thinks Ed and Ellen's children will not have any impact on the course of the conflict between Ed and Gloria, he may choose to leave them out. However, if Gloria's husband cares about the way the conflict affects Ed and Ellen's children, or if he feels the children will get swept up into the conflict between Ed and Gloria, he will probably want to include them.

To recap what we have learned so far, the first step in the process of conflict diagnosis is to describe the conflict. The diagnostician should put the conflict into words and create a conflict map, or sociogram. Completing these tasks will help the conflict diagnostician achieve the following goals:

- The diagnostician will be able to determine more clearly whether an interpersonal conflict, in fact, exists.
- The diagnostician will be able to more clearly determine relationships between participants and therefore to identify the relevant sources of conflict (see Chapter 7).

If, in fact, there is an interpersonal conflict, the tasks of describing and mapping the conflict will help the diagnostician identify and describe the most obvious divergent interests, goals, and/or needs that create the interpersonal conflict.

The tasks of describing and mapping the conflict will help the diagnostician begin understand and articulate the multiple interests, goals, and needs of each participant in the conflict, a critical topic to which we will turn in Chapter 8.

Conflicts Involving Corporations: Percy's Stereo Dispute

A month ago, Percy purchased a new set of stereo speakers from Music Megalopolis (M&M), a large national chain selling stereo and video components. The box the speakers came in contained a statement that they required a special kind of speaker wire (sold by the speaker manufacturer) for compatibility with his existing system. The salesperson at M&M, after trying unsuccessfully to convince Percy to upgrade to a more modern receiver, said he "supposed" the special wire requirement was just a come-on by the speaker vendor to get buyers to spring for extra money for speaker wire. The special wires were extremely pricy, $75 to hook up to Percy's system. Percy, partially trusting the salesperson and partially having a case of wishful thinking, took the speakers but not the wire. He felt reassured that the worst that would happen would be that he would need to return to the store to get the new wires if they turned out to be necessary.

At home, Percy connected the speakers using his existing speaker wires, but they sounded highly distorted. He returned to M&M and purchased the $75 speaker wires, but the situation was not improved by the new wires. Percy then tried to return the speakers and wires to the store. The service department at M&M verified that the speakers were not functioning properly and agreed to submit them for warranty service. A week later, Percy called M&M, only to be told that the manufacturer had refused to take the speakers back. It claimed that Percy's decision to try to use the speakers with the inferior wires had voided the warranty. Percy is out $600 for the two speakers and $75 for the wires, which the store refused to take back because Percy had had to cut them to install them.

Percy feels he has either been misled by the salesperson at M&M or lied to by the speaker manufacturer and that, either way, he is due a replacement set of speakers. He has no way to refute the manufacturer's claim that it was the improper installation, rather than a preexisting defect, that created the problems. He has visited the store on several occasions to speak to the salesperson who sold him the speakers but has not been able to locate him and does not have his name. He has called the speaker manufacturer, but no one has returned his calls. Percy is at a loss for what to do now. He does not understand why no one wants to do the right thing by him.

Percy's dilemma is partially due to the fact that his conflict is with a corporate entity—actually, at least two corporate entities, the stereo store and the speaker manufacturer. Each human being he will have to deal with has motives and employee responsibilities Percy is not privileged to know. One way to address this lack of knowledge is simply to sue both entities in small claims court and to let the court system sort it all out via the adversary process. Given his very busy schedule and the disputes of fact, Percy is very reluctant to take that step. Percy could gain some further understanding of why he is being treated the way he is by developing a sociogram of the conflict. He should include all the individuals who have been involved in his dispute, including the salesperson, the manager at the store where he bought the product, and anyone he can conclude is involved from the manufacturer. He needs to understand the goals, needs, and interests of the individuals involved in the conflict if he is to motivate them to negotiate with him. For example, the manager at M&M probably gains nothing in terms of personal success by putting a lot of time or money into helping Percy—in fact, the manager probably loses profitability by doing so, and the fact that the store is part of a large national chain may mean that individual customer satisfaction is not an important consideration. Moreover, the salesperson may have been paid a commission for selling the speakers—but not the wires. The salesperson therefore may have been motivated to find some way, short of legally actionable fraud, to induce Percy to buy the speakers. If he could persuade Percy to take a chance on buying the speakers without the wires, without actually lying or concealing any known information, it may have been worth some income to him. To have any chance of success, Percy will have to overcome such impediments to cooperation. Mapping the conflict will help Percy begin to understand which individuals are involved in the process of deciding whether, and how, to respond to John's complaints, and in what way they are motivated to respond.

EXERCISES, PROJECTS, AND "THOUGHT EXPERIMENTS"

1. *Conflict journal exercises.*

    a. In your journal, describe the incompatible goals that make this situation an interpersonal conflict.

    b. Map your conflict. Make a sociogram, as shown in Figures 6-1 through Figure 6-4. Identify the individuals in your diagram as disputants, agents, advocates, and constituents.

    c. Are there any additional conflicts? Pay careful attention to possible incompatible goals among members of a single disputant's team, or between a nondisputant of one team and someone on another team. How does the presence of these additional conflicts complicate the picture and prevent easy resolution?

    d. Think carefully about all the participants you have put in the diagram. Are there ways in which their goals are either similar (as in "both want to avoid going to court") or compatible (as in "the china is more important to her, and the linens are more important to him")? How might a dispute resolver use this information to address the conflict?

2. Choose an interpersonal conflict described in the newspaper or on the Internet. (For this exercise to be useful, there should be a detailed account of the conflict and of the expressed opinions, attitudes, and positions of the participants.) Cut out or print the article(s) that describe the conflict. Then, follow the same steps shown in Exercise 1 for the conflict journal. Does your analysis suggest an approach to the conflict that hasn't been tried yet?

3. Attend a civil court or jury trial. Do your best to apply steps a through d from exercise 1 to the dispute being litigated. Do you think any action other than litigation could have been effective in resolving this dispute? Why or why not?

4. Interview a mediator, counselor, or complaint handler at an organization that handles and processes consumer complaints. Examples of such organizations include the Better Business Bureau and the department of consumer affairs in your state. (Often, consumer affairs are handled as part of the attorney general's office.) How does this person perform his or her duties? Ask this individual to articulate what he or she does to motivate large commercial enterprises to settle consumer complaints. What is his or her success rate? What, according to this individual, prevents him or her from being more effective?

5. Review the description of the Digi-Date conflict. (See pages 3, 14–15, and 63–64.) Using this information, construct a diagram of the Digi-Date conflict.

7

Step 2. Identify the Sources of the Conflict

"It is essential to the sanity of mankind that each should think the other crazy . . ."

—Emily Dickinson, notebook, c. 1880.

In this chapter, you will learn . . .

- How the obvious cause of an interpersonal conflict is seldom the only cause, or even the most important one.
- Which sources of conflict lawyers are usually most comfortable dealing with.
- About the need to determine and understand the many sources of conflict.
- About twelve important sources of many conflicts.

The "source" of an interpersonal conflict is the underlying reason that there is conflict. Although it is simple to explain away all conflicts as simply "incompatible goals," this explanation does nothing to move us along to the point of being able to develop strategies for the conflict's resolution. Understanding, and conceptually organizing, the sources of a conflict can greatly improve the chances that effective means for managing and resolving the conflict can be found and implemented.

Understanding human behavior can help reveal the motivations of the individuals involved in a conflict and can further efforts to develop appropriate approaches to resolution. In Chapter 8, discussing the analysis of participant interests, this individual-by-individual approach to understanding conflict will be presented. While interests analysis illuminates the motivations of *individual* conflict participants, the process of identifying the sources of conflict illuminates the *features of the relationship* between conflict participants that foster conflict. A conflict diagnostician will find that identifying the sources of a conflict, and performing interests analyses for the conflict participants, go hand in hand. In practice, a conflict diagnostician does both simultaneously.

103

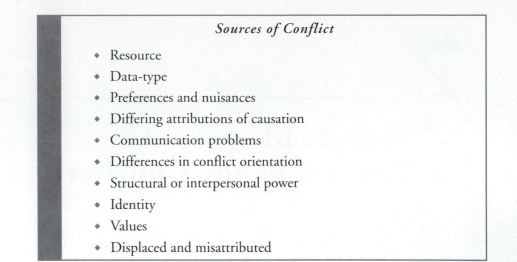

Sources of Conflict

- Resource
- Data-type
- Preferences and nuisances
- Differing attributions of causation
- Communication problems
- Differences in conflict orientation
- Structural or interpersonal power
- Identity
- Values
- Displaced and misattributed

A critical point is that **there are usually multiple sources of any given conflict.** Certain sources of conflict are obvious and easy to spot, whereas other types of conflict sources often remain hidden from view. In legal disputes, there are two major obvious sources of conflict. First, many legal disputes are perceived and framed as differences over resource ownership or control (known as "resource conflicts"). For example, if a divorcing couple is disputing over entitlement to pension rights, it is easy to brand this conflict as a resource conflict, which is a conflict involving the right to control a resource, such as money, property, or intangible valuables. "Data-type conflicts" (disputes over facts or law) are also easy to spot in the legal domain. In our divorce example, the legal basis for determining the disputed entitlement will always boil down to either a determination of disputed facts ("What proportion of the time period during which this pension was earned took place during the disputants' marriage?") or law ("In a divorce, how is the entitlement of each spouse to a pension determined?").

However, the obvious or presenting source of a conflict is seldom the only, or even the most important, source. Finding and understanding all the sources of conflict, even those that are hidden from view, leads to a richer understanding of the conflict and to a better idea of how to cope with it. Thus, in our divorce example, the more important reasons that the spouses are disputing over the pension might remain hidden from those who don't go looking more deeply. Perhaps the reason that the pension is such a hotly contested issue for these spouses, for example, relates to the identities of the two spouses. It is common for husbands' self-concepts to be tied up primarily with their careers, whereas wives commonly have more diffuse identities involving nonpaying home and parenting responsibilities, as well as career involvement. Thus, the husband may see the wife's claim for half his pension as a direct threat to his life's work and therefore to his sense of self, whereas the wife may see the husband's belief that he should keep the entire pension as evidence that he devalues her important nonmonetary contributions to the marriage. Both spouses experience the issue of the pension as a threat to the sense of self, and, as long as the conflict is treated as a simple resource or data-type conflict, it will tend to be resistant to resolution. Recognizing this conflict for what it really is may hold important keys to creative, effective, and efficient settlement possibilities. For example, the husband may have an easier time giving up an asset not as closely tied to his personal identity, such as a bank account or real property, in a monetary exchange for the value of the wife's interest in his pension rights.

The lawyer's standard philosophical map (Riskin 1982; see Chapter 3) has been identified by Leonard Riskin as a force blinding legal professionals to the influence of important conflict sources. Lawyers are taught, in law school and by means of on-the-job training, to identify and focus on only those sources of conflict directly relevant to the establishment of, or defense against, causes of action: resource and data-type conflicts. Each of these sources of conflict relates directly to the art and skill of the litigator: resource conflicts illuminate the types of remedies the lawyer should be seeking, whereas conflicts over facts or law (data-type conflicts) define the causes of action the client or opponent might have, as well as the best defense to the opponent's positions. Thus, if a lawyer focuses on only these specific conflict sources, it makes his or her work in representing a client in litigation more efficient. It is important to note, however, that although these categories of conflict sources are usually obvious and are the stuff of most legal activity, they may not be the most important sources on which to focus for the overall welfare of the client. Law students in recent years are being taught to identify other sources of conflict, so that their representation of clients may be more holistically supportive of their interests.

In this chapter, a typology of conflict sources will be presented, with helpful examples you might find interesting, enlightening, and even entertaining.[1] The conflict sources will be addressed roughly in order of their obviousness, with the most obvious sources considered first. A brief summary of this typology, along with examples, is presented in Table 7-1.

RESOURCE CONFLICTS

As previously stated, resource conflicts are conflicts over the ownership or control of something of value—such as a tangible object or money—or of an intangible item of value—such as the right to spend time with a loved one. Resource conflicts are probably the most obvious sources of conflicts, and most interpersonal conflict involves a conflict over resources. However, although it is important to understand what resources disputants are fussing over, this knowledge, *in*

---

[1] A number of scholars have developed other typologies, including preeminent conflict theorist Morton Deutsch (1973), from which some of these elements have been taken.

◆ **TABLE 7-1**   Sources of Conflict (Summary)

CONFLICT TYPE	EXPLANATION	EXAMPLES	USEFUL APPROACHES
Control over resources	Disputants disagree over control of valued items or struggle over ownership of scarce commodities.	The dispute is between neighbors over property boundaries.	Many conflicts that appear at first glance to be resource conflicts can be resolved by understanding and dealing with deeper sources of conflict that may be operating. Integrative tactics (tactics aimed at "expanding the pie") can also be useful.
Data-type conflicts: conflicts over facts	The conflict is over reality, either past or present.	Two drivers disagree over who drifted into whose traffic lane.	Sometimes, a focus on satisfying the underlying interests of the disputants avoids the need to resolve the factual issue. If not, these types of conflicts can be resolved through factfinding, nonbinding evaluation, or adjudication. Many disputes over facts mask other, deeper conflicts.
Data-type conflicts: conflicts over law	The disagreement is over how the law impacts the relationship between the disputants.	The disagreement is between divorcing spouses over the appropriate appraisal and allocation of pension rights or between separating gay partners over property division and support payments.	Ironically, litigation is probably the least desirable way to handle most of these kinds of conflicts, because they typically arise when the law is vague. Often, the best tactic is for the disputants to educate themselves about the law (to verify the degree of uncertainty), then to engage in principled negotiation aimed at developing solutions that accommodate mutual interests. Litigation should be used primarily when the legal conflict masks a dispute over social structure and interpersonal power imbalance.
Preferences and nuisances	One disputant's behavior disturbs the other.	Factory runoff pollutes the stream of a landowner who loves to fish.	These types of disputes are particularly amenable to creative problem solving that acknowledges and seeks to preserve the underlying interests of the disputant but rearranges the environment, modifies people's schedules, and so on.
Communication difficulties	The meanings of language and behavior may be misunderstood.	Frequently, self-interested tactics on the part of one disputant are misunderstood by an opponent as motivated by malice.	Approaches include becoming familiar with the other disputant and his or her cultural practices; using active listening; hiring a mediator, an agent, a consultant who shares the cultural background of the other disputant, or a translator.
Differences in conflict orientation	There are differences in the basic approach to relationships.	One disputant sees the relationship of the parties as mutually cooperative. The other disputant is basically competitive.	It helps resolve the conflict if the disputants recognize the style differences to miminize communication difficulties that result from differences in conflict orientation. The cooperative disputant can refuse to negotiate unless the parties agree to use a set of objective principles to guide the negotiation. The cooperator may need to signal a willingness to fight hard if the other disputant fails to act cooperatively.

CONFLICT TYPE	EXPLANATION	EXAMPLES	USEFUL APPROACHES
Values	Conflicts are over personal beliefs and deeply held values.	Ongoing Middle-East conflicts have religious origins, which include values conflicts.	Sometimes, values conflicts can be resolved if the disputants can agree to disagree about the underlying values, as when a disputant agrees to go along with a settlement without admitting liability. Values conflicts are difficult to resolve peacefully if the values involved are central to the self-concepts or world views of the disputants or if coupled with many other sources of conflict, such as disputes over limited resources.
Threats to self-concept and world view	One disputant's viewpoint threatens the other disputant's central ideas about him- or herself or about how the world works.	In a medical malpractice case, the patient's allegations of negligence threaten the physician's self-concept as a competent professional. An employee's allegation of racism on the part of a supervisor threatens the supervisor's self-concept as racially tolerant and his concept of American society as color-blind and fair.	As with values conflicts, occasionally these conflicts can be managed by having the disputants agree to disagree while implementing a solution that threatens neither disputant's self-concept or world view. It helps to use negotiation tactics that confirm and protect the dignity of each participant. Sometimes, these conflicts can be handled through the use of negotiating agents. Conflicts based on the negative stereotypes held by one social group about another social group are very difficult to resolve.
Structural and interpersonal power issues	A disputant perceives an unjust balance of power and struggles to rectify it.	School integration and affirmative action disputes are examples.	The more powerful disputant is generally unwilling to give up power and may honestly fail to see that a power imbalance exists. If this disputant is made aware of the imbalance, sometimes he or she can be convinced to give up power to preserve long-term social structure, avoid violent struggle, or make his or her own actions consistent with deeply held values (as when discriminatory laws are pointed out as being inconsistent with national values of equality and equal rights). Frequently, however, appeal to a more powerful authority (e.g., litigation) is the only method that produces lasting change.
Differing attributions of causation	Each disputant believes that the existing state of affairs is due to a different cause and hence warrants a different remedy.	In a products liability case, the manufacturer contends that the product was treated improperly, whereas the consumer contends that the product is defective.	Some attributional disputes boil down to a data-type conflict (did the consumer kick the washing machine or didn't she?), whereas other attributional disputes are really values conflicts (yes, she kicked it, but the washing machine should be built to handle occasional violent outbursts). The most effective treatments depend on which kind of attributional conflict is involved.

(Continued)

◆ **TABLE 7-1**   Sources of Conflict (Summary)   *(continued)*

CONFLICT TYPE	EXPLANATION	EXAMPLES	USEFUL APPROACHES
Displaced conflict	There is an unacknowledged conflict; the disputants are disputing over something else.	Business partners who have an unacknowledged conflict over the allocation of rights and responsibilities dispute about a minor aspect of the business.	The underlying conflict should be uncovered and diagnosed. A mediator is often useful in such situations. Unfortunately, the underlying conflict is often deep-rooted and difficult to resolve (otherwise, it would not have stayed hidden).
Misattributed conflict	There is an unacknowledged conflict; one disputant picks a fight with someone else.	A teen living in the inner city under circumstances of grinding poverty, oppression, and racism loses his temper and fights with a neighbor.	It is important to uncover the "real" conflict to avoid repetitions of misattributed conflict. Often, the underlying conflict is a structural/power issue that the disputant feels powerless to change. Sometimes, the former disputants, once aware of the misattribution, can band together to address the real problems with the formerly unacknowledged disputant.

and of itself, does relatively little to help a conflict diagnostician come up with an effective strategy for dealing with the conflict. It tells one only that each disputant wants all or part of the same thing. Thus, focusing only on the resource aspects of a conflict tends to mislead the observer into thinking that the conflict is intractable. A conflict resolver might use this knowledge to help the disputants fashion a compromise or to do some "logrolling" (trading off some of this resource against entitlement to another resource of greater value to the disputant who is giving up his or her entitlement). However, in general, knowing the other sources of conflict can lead to greater understanding and more effective solutions.

The divorce field frequently exemplifies the sort of harm that focusing only on a resource conflict can have. In a typical contested divorce, each spouse feels angry and betrayed by the other, creating a desire for vengeance. Since each spouse finds making the other spouse feel good unpalatable, there is a tendency for resource conflicts to proliferate as spouses try to deny one another what they say they want. When the issue is child custody and visitation, for example, the spouses frequently tiff over the amount of time each gets to have with the child, as if the child were a sort of trophy whose possession is awarded to the victor. Lawyers are often prone to take the same, zero-sum perspective on child custody. For example, Penelope Bryan, a law professor, criticizing the use of mediation to handle custody disputes, explains that child custody is often used as a bargaining chip in negotiation because

> if the wife has the children 300 days of the year, the husband can only have them for 65 days. If she bargains for more than 300 days, he necessarily loses. (Bryan 1992, p. 478, note 56)

This perspective posits child custody disputes as a pure matter of resource allocation—"either you can see him, or I can see him, and the more I win the more you lose."

In a child custody situation, however, the resource conflict is almost never the whole story, and focusing only on the resource conflict can lead to poor outcomes for all concerned. Assuming for a moment that neither parent is abusive, neglectful, or severely mentally ill, a parent who has effective parenting as an important life goal generally satisfies this goal more effectively by giving the child liberal access to the other parent. This is because children of divorce are generally known to do better if they have substantial and meaningful relationships with both parents (Wallerstein & Kelly 1980). Minimizing the time the child spends with one parent undercuts this vital parenting goal. Moreover, a child typically senses the reason for the dispute, and, if vindictiveness is at the heart of the custody dispute, the child will come to feel exploited and used by both parents. Because this sense of exploitation is deeply harmful to a child's healthy development, the vindictive effort to curtail parental access is actually bad parenting, and again the goal of being an effective parent is undercut. But there are more selfish reasons for the parent not to try to curtail the child's access to the other parent. First, experts in child development have found that, by adolescence and young adulthood, children who have been denied time with a visiting parent in childhood often idealize the absent parent, rather than joining in vilifying the parent (Wallerstein & Kelly, 1980, 256), and generally refuse to remain in alliances with one parent against the other (Ibid, 88). Thus, a primary caregiver whose underlying reason for curtailing access is to "win" the child as a trophy can end up losing the war in the end. Since parenting is a heavy burden, the parent with the lion's share of day-to-day caregiving responsibilities can often gain immediate personal benefit if the other parent shares the parenting. Thus,

Many conflicts are about much more than claiming entitlement to resources, as child custody disputes often demonstrate. Leland Bobbe, Getty Images Inc.—Stone Allstock

cooperation between parents to provide the child with liberal access to both parents is usually better for all concerned, including the parent who is trying to curtail access.

This is not to say that lopsided parenting arrangements that give one parent almost all of the caregiving responsibilities are always wrong; it is merely to say that focusing on only the resource goal can lead the client badly astray, undercutting his or her overall best interests. Legal and other conflict professionals should take care to look behind resource conflicts to ensure that other, more fundamental disputant interests are being served.

DATA-TYPE CONFLICTS

Pleading
a document, filed in court, that starts litigation or a document that answers a pleading that starts litigation.

Motions
requests for judicial action. Motions are brought in the context of a pending lawsuit. The sorts of requests that may be brought up via a motion include a request to have a case determined without trial, to have the litigation dismissed, to compel one of the litigants to produce information, and to penalize a litigant for misconduct in relation to the pending litigation. Motions may be brought before, during, and after trial.

Data-type conflicts are disagreements over facts or law. Like resource conflicts, they are also relatively obvious. For example, suppose two disputants have been involved in a fender-bender. If one disputant thinks he was going below the speed limit and that the other entered his lane, but the other disputant disagrees and thinks she was cut off illegally, the situation involves a dispute over facts. On the other hand, if how the accident came about is not in dispute, but there is a disagreement over who has the right of way in the sort of intersection in which the accident occurred, this disagreement is over the applicable law. Much, if not most, personal injury litigation involves a combination of disputes over facts and law.

Lawyers generally feel quite comfortable handling data-type conflicts: they are the essence of what lawyers deal with in their practices. Lawyers frame disputes in data-type terms, so that the viability of any causes of action can be evaluated; if a cause of action or defense is warranted, this knowledge is used to determine the contents of **pleadings, motions** for judgment based on legal arguments, and evidentiary considerations.

Simple data-type conflicts are amenable to resolution using nonbinding evaluation processes, as well as binding adjudicatory procedures, such as litigation and arbitration. The nonbinding processes inform the parties of the most likely outcome, should they decide to take the action to court. Not wishing to invest the time and resources in litigation, many disputants will settle the dispute at or near the decision of the evaluator. Arbitration, like its cousin, litigation, will impose an authoritatively binding decision about the data-type conflict, should that conflict be amenable to submission to the adjudicatory process.

However, as with focusing attention on resource conflicts, concentrating on the data-type sources of a conflict can often shortchange a disputant. Since data-type issues are usually obvious, there is a natural tendency to stop there and not go deeper to determine whether other sources of conflict are also present. Because there are always other, often deeper reasons for the conflict, deciding it on this sort of basis often misses opportunities for more holistic, creative, effective, mutually beneficial, and permanent resolution. In fact, it can be argued that data-type conflicts are the least important sources of conflict from the perspective of disputant interests. To illuminate this point, consider this: data-type conflicts are practically never pursued unless another source of conflict is present. If, for example, two drivers disagree about who swerved into whose lane of traffic, neither is likely to pursue any action against the other unless one of them is harmed in some way. And "what the law is" on some point is unlikely to matter to them (unless they happen to be law buffs and are just curious) unless a matter of real substance turns on the interpretation of the law.

PREFERENCES AND NUISANCES

In conflicts over preferences and nuisances, one disputant is doing something that harms, bothers, or irritates the other. A typical example is a neighborhood dispute in which barking dogs or loud, squealing tires disturb the sleep of a neighbor.

This category of conflict source is usually obvious: the client goes to a lawyer directly, complaining about the nuisance. Frequently, these kinds of conflicts are amenable to settlements that "restructure the environment"—for example, if the problem is a barking dog, the answer may be a sound-reducing barrier, paid for by both neighbors.

However, creative, effective, and progressive solutions are often missed by focusing only on the preferences-and-nuisances aspect of a conflict. For example, at an alternative dispute resolution conference many years ago, Ray Shonholtz (1986), who directed a preeminent community mediation (dispute resolution) program, told the story of two residents of an apartment building, each of whose noisy activities disturbed the other. In mediation, it came out that each resident's schedule and typical activities were dictated by his fear of the neighborhood—one of the disputants was a person of color and the other was a white gay man, and both had been suffering from repeated intimidation, harassment, and threats to personal safety on the street. By identifying this underlying source of conflict (in this case, a threat to basic safety needs, which created a misattributed conflict[2]), the two disputants were able not only to develop a schedule that minimized the nuisance that each imposed on the other but also to cofound a grass-roots activist program to fight hate in the community. This outcome went far beyond merely fixing the presenting problem: it also improved the quality of life for both disputants, provided a basis for an ongoing and caring relationship between them and others in the activist group, and had the potential for reforming the community as a whole.

DIFFERING ATTRIBUTIONS OF CAUSATION

In conflict over differing attributions of causation, the disputants disagree about the cause of some outcome. For example, suppose a baby is born with the umbilical cord wrapped around her neck, with the resulting loss of brain oxygenation responsible for cerebral palsy and developmental delays. Even though there may

---

[2] Misattributed conflict, a conflict in which the disputants and underlying problem are misidentified, is defined and discussed later in this chapter.

be no data-type conflict (in other words, everyone agrees about what happened), there may be a difference of opinion concerning how to attribute causation: the physician and hospital may attribute the outcome to an act of God (the presentation of the fetus at delivery), whereas the family may attribute the outcome to the doctor's failure to perform a Cesarean section. This sort of difference in attribution is really a conflict over values and, in this example, a data-type conflict over law. In some societies (indeed, in some U.S. communities), this sort of event would be considered an unfortunate outcome of a natural phenomenon, whereas, in most U.S. jurisdictions, if it were reasonable to expect the physician to be able to diagnose the problem and intervene, given modern technology, the physician would be held to a legal duty to do so.

Frequently, law (statutory law and common law) exists to resolve attribution conflicts. (Of course, it is possible for the parties to differ over whether relevant statutes exist or apply to the situation at hand—in which case, there is a data-type conflict as well.) If there is no relevant law, a **matter of first impression** is created. In such a situation, disputants will confront a dilemma: whether to endure litigation, possibly including appellate litigation, to resolve the legal issue or instead to create a settlement that meets the interests of all concerned to the extent possible.

Matter (issue) of first impression a legal issue not covered by statute and not previously decided by an appellate court of the jurisdiction in which the matter has come up. Thus, existing law offers no guidance to the court that must apply the law in the situation.

COMMUNICATION PROBLEMS

In some interpersonal conflicts, the meaning of language or behavior may be misunderstood, creating conflict. These differences may be due to environmental forces, language problems, cultural differences, or differences in communication style.

An example of a communication problem occurred in a small claims dispute mediated many years ago. A landlord and tenant were in an angry dispute: the tenant had wanted something in the apartment fixed, and, having had no response from his complaints, he withheld rent. In fact, when the tenant had discovered the problem in the apartment, he had left a message on the landlord's answering machine describing the problem and asking for help, but the machine had malfunctioned and the message had been lost. Then, the tenant had sent a letter to the landlord, and, by unfortunate coincidence, that letter had been misdirected and lost as well. By the time the tenant actually made direct contact with the landlord, he was so angry that his tone with the landlord was nasty and arrogant. The landlord became hostile in return and was in no hurry to respond to the request. Litigation followed. Only when each party to the dispute learned of the interrupted communication, and was able to acknowledge to the other that it was reasonable for the other in the circumstances to feel angry and frustrated, was the dispute able to move forward to an eventual settlement.

An example of a culturally based communication problem is presented by Thomas Hochman in his book *Black and White: Styles in Conflict* (1981). Hochman is a white college professor who taught college in multiracial New

York City in the 1970s. As a sociologist, it was his professional habit to make observations about the behaviors of subcultures within his student body, and the book arose from his observations. Hochman observed that, for his white middle-class students, when an argument became loud and verbally abusive, this characteristic usually signaled that violence was about to erupt. For inner-city African Americans, this pattern did not hold. In general, he observed that African-American arguing could become extremely loud and verbally abusive without erupting into violence. However, for his African-American students, imminent violence was signaled by physical movement, however slight.

Hochman generalized his observations from his classroom to American society in general. He interprets an incident occurring during a 1977–1978 NBA game as follows:

> [A]ctual violence [could not be averted] between Kermit Washington, a black player, and Rudy Tomjanovich, a white one. According to Tomjanovich, he tried to break up a fight that he thought was about to erupt between Washington and someone else [because he saw loud and abusive argument and interpreted the situation as imminently violent]. Washington, however, interpreted Tomjanovich's movement toward him as provocative, signaling an [imminent] intent to hit him. Washington swung first and broke Tomjanovich's jaw. (Hochman 1981, 47)

In situations ripe for communication problems, it can help to include a "translator" in any dialogues between disputants. Intermediaries such as mediators and facilitators, hailing from all the represented cultures if the difference is culturally based, can be quite helpful in interpreting past or present communication and sidestepping this sort of problem, or at least helping the disputants come to some sort of peace with one another based on their mutual understanding and acknowledgment of what went wrong in the communication process.

Professor Thomas Kochman believes the violent conclusion to this altercation between NBA players Rudy Tomjanovich (shown going down, at right) and Kermit Washington (throwing the punch) resulted from cultural differences in interpreting nonverbal communication. NBC, Corbis Bettmann

DIFFERENCES IN CONFLICT ORIENTATION

Differences in conflict orientation are differences in the way people preferentially or automatically respond to conflict. These differences can cause communication problems and leave disputants feeling aggrieved and betrayed.

Conflict orientation frequently causes disturbance in a relationship when one disputant prefers the rough and tumble of a competition, whereas the other disputant prefers a cooperative, mutually collaborative approach. The competitive disputant's orientation blinds him or her to solutions that would benefit everyone. If the cooperator proposes a settlement, the competitor is likely to see the offer as a come-on or ruse[3] since, in general, the competitor expects others to compete with him or her, or, if the competitor believes its sincerity, as an opportunity to exploit an easy mark. Either response on the part of the competitor will typically leave the cooperator feeling betrayed and disempowered, leading to a withdrawal of cooperation and the creation of impasse.[4]

Many times, a difference in conflict orientation can lead to communication problems. As with other similar conflicts, the use of an intermediary, such as a mediator, can help disputants effectively interpret one another's tactics and avoid misunderstanding and needless conflict escalation. Unfortunately, if one disputant loves competition, it may not be easy to convince him or her to modify that orientation. This unfortunate generality is due to the fact that adversarial interaction is an inherently positive goal for this disputant. To persuade him or her to depart from the orientation, the person has to first be made aware of the nature of his or her preferences (sometimes disputants have no idea that they have such an orientation) and then convinced that, overall, he or she would be better served by cooperating. If the competitive orientation is habitual, even this effort may not succeed.

STRUCTURAL AND INTERPERSONAL POWER CONFLICTS

Structural and interpersonal power conflicts involve inequalities of power, choice, and freedom. In these conflicts, a more powerful disputant and a less powerful disputant are in a relationship harmful to the less powerful disputant. Disputes break out when the less powerful disputant becomes self-aware about the discrepancy and moves to find a remedy for the situation. Conflicts over affirmative action, equal-pay, and civil rights abuses are perfect examples. In these conflicts, one disputant (or disputant group) has more power than the other, leading to inequities, oppression, harm to the less powerful disputant(s), and, in time, harm to the social structure as a whole.

---

[3] This tendency for people in a competitive orientation to distrust the cooperative moves of the other disputant is referred to as "reactive devaluation." This concept will be discussed in detail in Chapter 9.

[4] These sorts of differences in negotiation orientation can be culturally or ethnically based. For examples of this sort of mismatch between Hispanic and white disputants, see Rack 1999.

These conflicts are often invisible to the more powerful disputants, due either to subconscious denial or to an authentic failure, arising out of the limitations brought on by a privileged background and experience, to see the inappropriateness of the existing social structure. Powerful disputants are also, naturally, reluctant to give up the power associated with privileged status. Indeed, if the power imbalance is longstanding and has been very harmful to the disempowered disputants, the more powerful disputants may fear retaliation if they allow the other group to gain enough strength to retaliate. Moreover, there may be a data-type conflict, with the less powerful disputant seeing a structural or interpersonal power conflict and the more powerful disputant seeing the existing structure as equitable and problems, if any, attributable to other features, such as genetic inferiority or counterproductive social behaviors.

Take the following example:

> An employment dispute has developed between a Ron, a white/European-American male supervisor, and Stella, his African-American, female staff member. Stella, challenged to fit into an office consisting largely of white coworkers, has been denied advancement. She entered the office on fairly good terms, but seemed to keep to herself. The other employees complained that she is aloof, and she failed to acquire the knowledge she needed to fit effectively into the office environment and become proficient in her responsibilities. Thus, the quality of her work was mediocre, at best. Stella, with her lifetime of experience of racism and gender discrimination, perceives the problem as one of her exclusion from the social circle of the office, her denial of essential on-the-job training, and the acquiescence of the supervisor in her difficulties. In contrast, Ron, with his privileged background, does not have past experience being the victim of discrimination, and accordingly concludes that her difficulties must result from personality issues with Stella ("Everyone else gets along, so it must be her. She is always complaining!").[5]

Stella, the African-American employee, perceives her inability to advance in her career, as well as her isolation from others in the office, as clear evidence of invidious racism. Ron, her (white) supervisor, as a member of a privileged class who has never first-hand been victimized by bigotry, assumes that the cool demeanor of others in the office toward the employee, as well as her slowness to climb the corporate ladder, is due to the employee's withdrawn and suspicious personality.[6]

Structural/interpersonal power conflicts are among the hardest to resolve via settlement. Most often, they require the intervention of a powerful and authoritative figure, such as a court, legislative enactment, or a constitutional amendment.

---

[5] This scenario is adapted from Howard Gadlin's excellent example in his article, "Conflict, Cultural Differences, and the Culture of Racism" (Gadlin 1994).

[6] Both may be right in the sense that the uncomfortable, avoidant, and ostracizing conduct of those in the office may create a mistrustful and withdrawn attitude on the part of the employee. So-called self-fulfilling prophecies, of which this situation is an example, are well documented in the arena of race relations.

IDENTITY CONFLICTS

Identity can be understood as the features one attributes to oneself. Identity can also include a judgment about self: *self-worth* and *self esteem,* as well as important roles that the individual plays, such as *student, mother, husband, sales manager,* and so forth.

Identity conflicts are conflicts in which a disputant's personal identity is threatened by the other disputant. Identity conflicts are usually very difficult to resolve. Maslow's needs theory (see Chapter 8) can help explain this intransigent feature of identity conflict. Developmental psychologist Abraham Maslow conceptualized a hierarchy of needs and postulated that human beings are driven to satisfy the needs that are most basic on the hierarchy before they move on to higher-order needs. The need for a positive and consistent self-concept is considered a primary and deeply seated human need, superseded in importance only by the most basic physiological (food, shelter, sleep, etc.) and safety needs (Goble 1970). Identity functions as a "theory of self," making deliberate action possible (Epstein 1973). Without a consistent identity, individuals cannot plan their daily activities, since they cannot predict how their own actions will affect them. Conflicts that threaten the sense of identity and self-worth are therefore experienced as profoundly threatening.

LOSS OF FACE

One extremely important and common identity conflict prevalent in legal disputing is the problem of loss of face. This identity conflict is the almost inevitable product of the most common ways we have of expressing disputes. *Face* in this context refers to the dignity and respectability of the social presence displayed by an individual to others. The loss of face, with its accompanying sense of shame and embarrassment, is intolerable to most individuals (in the literature of collectivist societies, such as Asian countries, the suicide of a character who has experienced a loss of face is common). During **positional bargaining**, once a disputant sticks his or her neck out by taking a position, moving off that position is often experienced as a loss of face and as an intolerable threat to the self-concept. For example, a defendant in a tort case tells the other side that she'll pay no more than $5,000 to settle the case. Later, legal research by her attorney reveals that, in fact, she is likely to lose much more if she takes the case to court. Unless her lawyer can find a way to help her present her new position as one of strength rather than of losing face, she is unlikely to budge. Loss of face is a particular problem in the United States, where adversarial negotiation is the predominant method of resolving conflicts; therefore, disputants tend to negotiate by "drawing lines in the sand."

Positional bargaining
a common type of negotiation style characterized by the negotiator taking firm stands using a series of demands or positions.

RELATIONSHIP BREAK-UPS AND IDENTITY CONFLICTS

Conflicts that involve the end of an ongoing and important relationship present another variety of identity conflict and offer some of the most difficult identity conflicts to manage. Multiple threats to identity are often involved:

- ◆ The loss of a predominant life's work
- ◆ Profound disruption of roles critical to identity
- ◆ Direct attacks and counterattacks on the self-concepts of each disputant by the other

For example, consider the case of longstanding business partners who have a falling-out that threatens the viability of the venture. The enterprise itself may comprise a large element of the identity of one or both disputants, and the threat of its loss can therefore cause a disputant to feel as if his or her life's work is being obliterated, and, accordingly, that he or she is being erased from existence. Moreover, if the dispute disrupts ongoing business activities, then familiar, everyday roles played by each partner will be impeded. Not only is an identity threat created by this loss of crucial roles, but the loss of familiar, everyday life structure also undermines each disputant's ability to engage in rational and effective behavior. These losses and disruptions leave the affected disputant disoriented, confused, and disempowered at the precise time that he or she most needs to have his or her wits intact. Moreover, if the dispute is accompanied by accusations of incompetence or bad character, then the recipient of the accusations will experience a direct verbal assault on self-esteem and self-concept.

Divorce cases provide a wellspring of similar sorts of threats to identity and self-esteem. If one spouse announces to the other that he or she no longer wants to be married, it is often a devastating blow to the self-esteem of the "left" spouse. There is the obvious pain of a profound rejection: the leaving spouse has been as close as anyone ever has been, and the rejection implies that his or her most deep, private, and important attributes have been judged as wanting. At the same time, the everyday roles of the spouses in a marriage—who takes out the garbage, feeds the children, mows the lawn, and so forth–are swept away, leaving both spouses disoriented, bereft, and confused. (Indeed, according to Isolina Ricci (1980), vulnerability to accidents surges in the period right after a marital separation.) If the spouse derived a great deal of self-worth from the role of husband or wife, the blow can be even more devastating. Then there can be specific disputes related to the divorce that are experienced as a threat to identity, such as when one spouse wants to limit the other's time with the children, threatening his or her identity as a parent.

"MEN ARE FROM MARS . . . ": SEPARATION AND INDIVIDUATION ISSUES IN IDENTITY CONFLICT

Another variety of identity-based conflict, separation and individuation problems, applies primarily to intimate relationships between males and females and might be appropriately described as the "men are from Mars/women are from Venus" (Gray 1992) phenomenon.[7]

These problems arise when deep-seated tendencies to connect and disconnect with others are in conflict at a time of great crisis. Psychologists (such as Gilligan 1982) have theorized that, because small children are cared for primarily by their mothers, little girls (who are "like Mommy" in terms of gender) tend to develop an identity of "merging with the beloved," whereas little boys (who are "unlike Mommy" in terms of gender) tend to develop an identity of "separating from the beloved." When little girls and little boys grow up and take mates or partners, these hidden features of their identities can cause problems, as women tend to want close intimacy and communication with their partners, whereas men tend to want clear boundaries with their partners.

These disputes are sometimes managed in an ongoing relationship through compromise, recourse to friends and relatives, or simply an uneasy adjustment to personality differences. But sometimes the differences are so large as to be unresolvable. Moreover, when an intimate relationship ends, the mental and emotional functioning of members of the couple tends to be compromised by the relationship crisis, bringing out these differences at a moment of great psychological vulnerability for both. This phenomenon can create conflict, causing either or both disputants to have difficulty disconnecting from the relationship and moving on. In a divorce in which separation/individuation problems are significant, the wife tends to want continuing, sometimes unnecessary communication with the husband, whereas the husband tends to avoid communication, even to the point of leaving essential issues unresolved. Thus, the wife often tries to initiate or perpetuate contact with the husband even for matters of dubious relevance to the substantive issues they need to resolve. The husband, who typically fears being "swallowed up" by the wife's incessant intrusions, tends to avoid communication altogether. Moreover, even when the husband can bring himself to negotiate with the wife, he tends to find agreement on anything intolerable (because it means he is "like her" on the issue in question). Since the content of the wife's communication includes matters of dubious relevance, the husband is able to rationalize his own avoidance of contact and agreement as "more reasonable," so he can paint his own behavior as rational and healthy and the wife's behavior as irrational or even as indicative of mental illness. On the other hand, the husband's avoidance, even of relevant issues, "proves" to the wife that the hus-

---

[7] These identity conflicts are most common in the divorce context, given the extreme intimacy of the relationships involved, but they can occur whenever a longstanding and important relationship ends and the disputants are of different genders or are at different extremes of this psychological dimension.

band is the unreasonable or "sick" one and that her own attempts to make contact should be continued, or even escalated. A vicious circle results. The wife seeks to fulfill her deep-seated need for fusing with the person to whom she is attached by seeking communication with the husband, while the husband seeks to fulfill his deep-seated need to separate himself from the person to whom he is attached by seeking curtailed communication with the wife.

A key point is that, in this sort of dispute, both disputants intensely resist finalizing any settlement. The wife has a desperate need to avoid finalizing settlement because "then the relationship will truly be over and I'll be cut off forever," while the husband is desperate to avoid being "smothered" or "swallowed up" ("any time I agree with her, it feels like 'being like her,' which is utterly intolerable"). It cannot be overemphasized that, although it would appear irrational to observers of such couples, from the vantage of the disputants themselves the stakes are survival itself. Both the wife and the husband truly feel that they will be annihilated if (from the wife's perspective) the issues are settled and the relationship ends, or (from the husband's perspective) communication occurs and a connection is made. These couples are immensely frustrating to conflict professionals because they actively seek out professional intervention to help them with their disputes, yet simultaneously at a deep level they want NOT to resolve their disputes and move on.

These can also be the couples we read about in the homicide section of the newspaper. It takes a skilled professional to manage these sorts of deep-seated issues of separation and individuation.

WORLD VIEW AND IDENTITY

World view is closely tied to identity because, first, one's world view defines how one sees oneself in relation to the world and, second, because one's world view directly influences one's sense of self-worth and self-esteem. A stable world view also enhances self-confidence by giving a person reassurance that he or she will be reasonably able to anticipate what will happen and, so, will be prepared to deal with life challenges. Conflicts over world view, therefore, often present difficulties similar to conflicts over identity.

An example may be helpful. In the employment dispute between Ron and Stella (page 115), both self-esteem and world view are on the line for both disputants.[8] The manager, Ron, has developed a world view clustered around the basic concept that people succeed by merit and hard work. This gentleman, moderately successful on his job, hails from a privileged background in which discrimination based on substantively irrelevant factors such as gender, skin

---

[8] We will be imposing assumptions about the world views of these individuals. These assumptions are consistent with the background of each person, but they are not intended to imply that others in their position would necessarily hold the same world views. In general, it is not known with statistical accuracy what sorts of world views are held by various gender and ethnic groups.

color, or religious background is not directly experienced. It enhances Ron's self-esteem to have this merit-based world view, since it implies that his success on the job is due to who he is as an individual.

Similarly, employee Stella's world view and self-esteem are closely linked. In a position subordinate to the manager, and moving through life with the dual identities "woman" and "black," she has lived in a very different world than the manager: repeatedly, she has seen hatred and bigotry applied to herself and others with physical appearances similar to hers. For this woman, even if she is fairly successful, disappointment is an expected phenomenon, and it serves her self-esteem well to hold the world view that people are frequently victimized by bigotry, a process beyond their control, and that their progress is impeded, despite their hard work and merit.[9]

Both Stella and Ron have been operating using world views that, if not wholly accurate and healthy, have supported their senses of self-worth and self-confidence. Accepting the argument of the other disputant is a direct threat. In arguing that her troubles are caused by racism, Stella raises to Ron the possibility that his neat and tidy, merit-based world view is flawed. This, in turn, raises the disturbing possibilities that he has not gotten to his present level of success strictly by merit but, instead, has been the recipient of privilege. This conclusion leads to the further conclusion that he is not as "meritorious" as he had previously believed. Moreover, if merit does not routinely lead to advancement, the manager is less able to predict whether, if he has been working hard, his director will promote him next time around. Similarly, the employee, by having her victimization world view challenged by the manager, is faced with the possibility that she is personally deficient in some way that she did not previously see and that this deficiency is what has held her back from greater advancement on the job. Thus, each disputant in this example has a vested interest in maintaining his or her existing world view and, thus, in rejecting the idea that the other disputant's world view explains the situation. Each disputant's world view maintains high self-esteem and provides a sense of predictability. It is hard to reach a settlement when beliefs so critical to self-worth and the basic predictability of the future are at stake.

A favorable resolution to a conflict over world view must take into account the identity issues hidden in the outward dispute. For example, in the employment example, both of these disputants must be given support in their senses of self-worth (for example, by encouraging each disputant to give honest and substantive compliments to the other during the settlement process), so that they can rationally consider the possibility that this situation is, at least, an exception to their overall world view. As a possible increased benefit to settling the employment dispute, each disputant has the opportunity to enrich and improve the accuracy of his or her world view, coming to recognize that there are important

---

[9] No opinion as to the merit of either world view is implied by this discussion. It is virtually impossible to accurately determine the extent to which either world view is valid.

exceptions to the rule he or she has lived by, realizing that some situations can have multiple causes, and discovering that rigidly holding to his or her world view can occasionally blind him or her to the truth. Each might thereby become more able to cope with new situations as they arise in the future.

VALUES CONFLICTS

In a values conflict, disputants are in conflict over deeply held personal, community, or societal beliefs and values. For example, in a divorce, one spouse's strong traditional beliefs about the inappropriateness of extramarital sex may set the stage for a custody conflict, particularly when the other spouse begins dating.

Some values conflicts can be resolved by an agreement to disagree. For example, in the custody example, the parents could settle the case by agreeing that, regardless of the personal beliefs of each, neither parent will bring home a date for the night while the children are in the home. The parent with less traditional beliefs suspends his or her lifestyle choice during the period that his or her children are in the home for the sake of lessened parent-to-parent conflict.

Values conflicts can also be settled using creative approaches that respect and put into practice the conflicting values. For example, a divorcing couple in a real-life mediation disagreed concerning whether one of the spouses contributed on an equal basis to the marriage, home, and parenting. The accusing spouse, Janet, argued that the other spouse, Brad, failed to work as hard as she did in the marriage. Consequently, Janet argued, Brad should not receive half the marital property. Brad, naturally, disagreed vehemently with this assessment. Rather than have a court decide the issue—with the time, expense, and emotional damage litigation would likely impose—this couple came up with the idea that Janet would keep half the marital property, Brad would receive one-third, and the remaining one-sixth would be put into trust for the children. Janet was comfortable with this outcome, because it put her beliefs about fault in the marriage into concrete terms. On the other hand, Brad could live with this arrangement, since he intended the children to eventually receive a substantial share of the parents' property, anyway, and he had the strength of character to realize that the financial settlement did not have to have the meaning for him that it held for Janet.

Despite the preceding examples, many values conflicts are extremely difficult to resolve because of the close connection between values and personal identity. Some of the most difficult situations are those in which the values involved are social group values held by groups to which the disputants belong and with which they have strong identification. Again, Maslow's needs theory can help us understand this phenomenon (Goble 1970). Maslow assigned the need for self-esteem, esteem from others, and belongingness to the category of intermediate needs, just above the most basic physiological and security needs. Thus, threats to these needs are experienced deeply. And people obtain a strong sense of self-worth and belongingness from being a member of a social group with which they identify intensely. For example, devoutly religious people often derive great self-worth and belongingness from their religious affiliation. The sense of belonging and identification is further strengthened and deepened when the group members band together against a common enemy (often called an "outgroup"). Thus, having a dispute with a member of an outgroup, engaging in intergroup struggle, and triumphing over the outgroup, whether by means of substantive or psychological put-downs, makes group members feel more accepted, loved, and righteous.[10]

For example, consider the Palestinian-Israeli conflict. The Israeli notions of a homeland in the geographic location known previously as Palestine, and of historical Jewish oppression and victimization, are essential components of Israeli identity. The alleged evil of the Jews having wrested away Palestine from the Arab population is an essential component of Palestinian identity. Each group thus gains esteem, love, and belongingness, as well as strengthens important aspects of group identity, by making war against the other. The conflict is deepened —inflamed—by the identity implications of having, and being denied, a geographic homeland and made more difficult to cope with because basic safety and security needs are perceived as being threatened. This conflict has proven to be intractable: a legion of conflict resolution experts has tried for decades to help the parties involved to come to a settlement, without much success. However, any conflict resolution process will be more successful if it takes into account, and works with, the group identities of the involved disputants. A conflict resolver working with the Israelis might, for example, emphasize the Jewish identity components of intellectualism, tolerance, progressivism, and activism, rather than those elements of identity tied up with a sense of historical victimization and anti-Semitism.

The Palestinian-Israeli conflict exemplifies the profound influence of values, self-concept, and world view on the persistence of violent and destructive conflict. Here, young Palestinian children take an active part in honoring suicide bombers and other anti-Israeli activists. AP/Wide World Photos

---

[10] For a discussion of ingroup and outgroup conflict behavior, see Deutsch 1973, 25–31.

DISPLACED AND MISATTRIBUTED CONFLICT

Displaced and misattributed conflicts are "the wrong conflicts." In a displaced conflict, the disputants, for some reason, aren't fighting about what's really bothering them. For example, a tenant who is unhappy with a rent increase but, instead, raises a fuss about chipped paint is involved in a displaced conflict.

Misattributed conflicts are similar to displaced conflicts, except that, instead of the right people fussing over the wrong conflict, the fight is being picked with the wrong people. Typically, there is a reason that disputants are avoiding the underlying conflict. For example, in a real estate office, the broker gave his top agent the task of training a newly hired agent but paid the employees a percentage of commissions and did not give the top agent any additional wages for her training efforts. The experienced agent had a Hobson's choice: train the trainee poorly, keeping the business for herself, or train the trainee well and impair her own earnings. Reluctant to complain about her overall job responsibilities for fear of being fired, the top agent ended up bickering with the trainee over a host of minor issues. The real conflict, in this case, was between the top agent and her boss, who had put her into this dilemma with his decisions about job responsibilities and compensation.

Displaced conflicts and misattributed conflicts share many similarities. In the first place, generally there is some very important reason the real conflict is either not recognized by the disputants or, if recognized, not overtly acknowledged. There may be fear of repercussions (as with the real estate office example). There may be threats to basic needs involved or underlying motivations of which the disputants are unaware. In any case, displaced and misattributed conflicts are generally easy to resolve, once the underlying conflict can be recognized and acknowledged. (The underlying conflict, however, is often a much different story.) Nonetheless, to achieve lasting and effective conflict resolution, the falsity of displaced and misattributed conflicts must be discovered and the nature of the underlying conflict must be identified.

USING SOURCES OF CONFLICT TO UNDERSTAND AND DIAGNOSE CONFLICT

It should be clear from the foregoing discussion that most interpersonal conflicts go far beyond disputes over money, what the witnesses would say, or the appropriate law to apply to a situation. Although conflict diagnosticians need to consider data-type and resource aspects of a conflict, particularly in the case of legal conflicts that might eventually be litigated, a holistic approach to serving a disputant's legal needs should never stop there. An in-depth consideration of the sources of a disputant's conflict is an essential step in understanding how the motivations of each disputants and his or her important underlying interests and needs are juxtaposed with those of others in the conflict, as well as in developing the most efficient and effective strategies for achieving a just, effective, humane solution.

EXERCISES, PROJECTS, AND "THOUGHT EXPERIMENTS"

1. *Conflict journal.* Identify the sources of conflict at play in your main conflict (the conflict you have decided to focus on, if there are several conflicts among participants). Typically, a conflict has an obvious, or "presenting," cause, such as a dispute over resources, preferences and nuisances, facts, or law. Justify your identification of this source of conflict. Then go further. Applying the categories discussed in this chapter, identify *all* the sources of conflict you can. Can you uncover any hidden sources of conflict? How do you think these hidden factors complicate the conflict or make it harder to resolve? Do you think that knowing about these hidden sources of conflict will help you find a better way to resolve it? Be sure to keep sources of conflict in mind as you proceed with the journal project. As you continue to have experiences and acquire additional information, you may uncover yet more hidden sources of conflict.

2. Do you agree or disagree with the following statement? "To serve a client adequately, a lawyer should consider all sources of the client's dispute, not just those legal issues that may be relevant to a cause of action." Note reasons in support of the statement, as well as reasons in opposition to it.

3. Imagine that you are a benevolent despot, capable of reforming the legal system with just a royal declaration. How could you improve the legal system so that underlying sources of conflict in legal disputes were dealt with? Consider formal methods of dispute resolution, as well as lawyer-client relationships and legal ethics.

4. Peruse a newspaper or an Internet news site. If you can, find and write down an example of each of the twelve sources of conflict described in Table 7-1.

5. In an effort to maintain control over potentially damaging admissions by clients, lawyers often ask their clients to stop communicating directly with the other disputants or their legal representatives: during the pendency of legal representation, communication generally is performed only by the lawyers. Do the ideas presented in this chapter suggest that this practice will reduce, or exacerbate, interpersonal conflict? Explain your answer.

6. Consider one of the following two conflicts: (1) the so-called war against terrorism or (2) the Israeli-Palestinian conflict. Write an essay discussing all of the sources of your chosen conflict. In your conclusion, speculate on how understanding these sources of the conflict could help resolve it. Be specific.

7. Harry, a paralegal, has come to your law office complaining about a dispute between himself and attorney Rona Rhododendron. Harry was employed by Rona's law office. Harry recently went to Rona, complaining that his

level of responsibility in the office was inconsistent with his high degree of training, and he demanded additional responsibilities and a 30 percent raise. Rona acknowledged his qualifications but refused to give him the promotion. According to Harry, her comments were demeaning to him. Harry erupted in anger and Rona fired him for his insubordination. In explaining his angry outburst, Harry comments, "It's not the money; it's that Rona refused to give me the recognition I deserved. I have been a paralegal for over ten years, and I'm more highly qualified than 99 percent of the other paralegals in the community. She utterly failed to acknowledge my superiority by giving me the promotion I deserve." Discuss the sources of conflict at play in this dispute.

8. Each of the following statements describes a disputant's point of view about the source of a conflict. For each one, *take the disputant's statement at face value.* What is the source of conflict implied by each statement?

   a. "Georgiana and I are fighting because I want the piano and so does she."

   b. "I'm fighting with him over ownership of the piano because he is responsible for our breaking up, and he shouldn't be rewarded for his bad behavior. He admits he caused the breakup but says it shouldn't matter who was responsible and that we should just divide our property 50/50. Neither of us cares about what the law is on this issue."

   c. "I really lost my temper when he refused to pay a reasonable price for the business. This is my life's work, and the price he offered was a personal insult to me."

   d. "We don't disagree about what happened. We are in conflict over the negligence standard to be applied to my behavior."

   e. "This situation escalated into a conflict because he never returns my phone calls."

RECOMMENDED READINGS

Deutsch, M. 1973. *The resolution of conflict: Constructive and destructive processes.* New Haven, CT: Yale University Press.

Epstein, S. 1973. The self-concept revisited or a theory of a theory. *American Psychologist* 28:405–16.

Gilligan, C. 1982. *In a different voice.* Cambridge, MA: Harvard University Press.

Hochman, T. 1981. *Black and white: Styles in conflict.* Chicago: University of Chicago Press.

Pruitt, D. G., and P. V. Olczak. 1995. Behond hope: Approaches to resolving seemingly intractable conflict. In *Conflict, cooperation and justice: Essays inspired by the work of Morton Deutsch* (pp. 59–92), edited by B. B. Bunker, J. Z. Rubin, and Assoc. San Francisco: Jossey-Bass.

Rothman, J. 1997. *Resolving identity-based conflict.* San Francisco: Jossey-Bass.

Rubin, J. Z., D. G. Pruitt, and S. H. Kim. 1994. Nature and sources of conflict. *Social Conflict: Escalation, stalemate, and settlement* (pp. 11–26). New York: McGraw-Hill.

8

Step 3. Perform an Interests Analysis

"The shortest and best way to make your fortune is to let people see clearly that it is in their best interests to promote yours."

—LaBruyere, "Of the Gifts of Fortune," *Characters,* 1688 (Gross 1987, 90)

"It is easier for a camel to pass through the eye of a needle if it is lightly greased."

—Kehlog Albran

In this chapter, you will learn …

- ◆ The layers of interests held by conflict participants, from positions and aspirations down to the most deeply seated human needs.
- ◆ The advantages of understanding a disputant's underlying interests in an interpersonal conflict.
- ◆ The advantages of understanding the interests of agents, advocates, constituents, and members of "the other team."
- ◆ Building an interest tree to clarify a disputant's interests and how they are interconnected.
- ◆ Developmental theories that can give a conflict diagnostician valuable clues to the underlying interests of conflict participants.

One day, a young man visited a lawyer to have a will prepared. The lawyer, who specialized in estate planning, usually interrogated new clients with a long series of questions about family status and spent several weeks researching a client's financial and tax situation. The client just wanted the will, and he wanted it tomorrow. The lawyer started preparing the will as directed by the client, but with misgivings about his lack of the usual preparation. Finally, fearing malpractice, the lawyer refused to proceed further. But the client insisted. Finally, the lawyer asked, "Why on earth are you so anxious to have a will so fast? Do you have a terminal illness?"

"No!" the man replied. "I'm very healthy—right now, that is."

"Well, why, then?"

"Because my wife has hired a hit man to take me out!" replied the man.

This story illustrates the importance of the topic to which we turn next: interests analysis. Interests analysis is perhaps the most critical step in the conflict diagnosis process, and the most highly skilled negotiators are those who can perform accurate and complete analyses of the interests of each conflict participant. An effective interests analysis can mean the difference between grudging settlement and real satisfaction. The client in the preceding example would have gotten better and faster help with his legal problem if the lawyer had begun by calling the police and state prosecutor.

In the words of Roger Fisher, William Ury, and Bruce Patton of the Harvard Negotiation Project,

> [i]nterests motivate people; they are the silent movers behind the hubbub of positions. Your position is something you have decided upon. Your interests are what caused you to so decide. (Fisher, Ury and Patton 1991, 41)

Thus, *what* people normally say they want out of a conflict are **positions**, whereas the *why* of what people say they want are **interests**. Briefly stated, interests analysis is the development of an accurate and complete understanding of each conflict participant's positions, aspirations, interests, needs, and values in relation to the interpersonal conflict. Interests analysis includes an explication of all the underlying interests, needs, and values of each conflict participant, as well as an exploration of how all link together and are organized. In other words, interests analysis is an exploration of a conflict participant's motivations in the conflict.

Position

the stances or demands taken by disputants (or their agents or advocates) in an interpersonal conflict.

Interests

the considerations that motivate people in a conflict: the reasons underlying the positions that people take in a conflict. For purposes of this book, the term *interests* also includes principles, values, and needs.

WHAT IS THE PURPOSE OF INTERESTS ANALYSIS?

The idea that someone involved in a conflict should be concerned about underlying interests is foreign to many people. Why is it useful to perform an interests analysis? There are a number of good reasons.

ANALYZING YOUR TEAM'S INTERESTS

If you are a disputant, it is crucial to understand thoroughly the interests of your own team.[1] When you are involved in an interpersonal conflict, your thought processes are often clouded or diverted by strong emotions and stress. (This phenomenon is like the lawyer who represents him- or herself—and has a fool for a client!) As we will see in later chapters, people caught up in a conflict often focus on the lines they have drawn in the sand—their positions—and on beating the other disputant—rather than on getting what is best for them. Performing an interests analysis helps you understand more clearly and accurately what you really want and need, enabling you to meet your most critical needs and interests more effectively.

Moreover, interests analysis allows you to distinguish interests you wish to pursue in this conflict from interests it would be better to meet another way. For example, imagine a child custody dispute in which a father and mother are each seeking sole custody. Often, underlying the desire for sole custody is a basic esteem need: the parent's deep-seated desire to have his or her stature as a wonderful parent confirmed by the court's award of sole custody.[2] When a parent realizes that this basic need underlies his or her demand for custody, he or she can determine whether the desire for esteem could, or should, be better met by other means (for example, by joining a single-parent support group) rather than through expensive and traumatic litigation that could result in curtailment of involvement by the other parent.

Analyzing your interests also allows you to develop flexibility in your bargaining position, so that you can find better ways of attaining an agreement. Consider, for example, the S-B corporate transaction described and diagrammed in Chapter 6. Your discovery that the S Corporation has interests beyond getting a maximally high price for the S-Chip—including assuring the reliability of the chip, showing additional assets on the corporate balance sheet as soon as possible, and establishing a good working relationship with B Corporation—allows you to be more creative in a negotiation with B Corporation. There are many dimensions on which a good agreement can be developed besides the dimension of sales price. In fact, it may turn out that price is not the most important consideration.

Finally, using interests analysis allows you to avoid the negative consequences of drawing lines in the sand, known in the conflict resolution field as *positional bargaining*. There are three principal negative consequences of positional bargaining: (1) becoming locked into position psychologically, (2) becoming blinded to issues unrelated to your position, and (3) seeing the other disputant as the enemy.

---

[1] In this text, the term *team* will refer to a particular disputant and the agents, advocates, and constituents with whom that disputant is associated. The terms *other disputant* and *other team* will be used in preference to more popular, but emotionally loaded terms, such as *adversary, enemy,* and *opposition.* Using such terms, which connote the idea of conflict as a competitive battle or war, contributes to the invisible veil and would work at contrary purposes to this textbook.

[2] So-called esteem needs and other basic human needs will be covered later in this chapter. For the moment, it suffices to say that esteem needs relate to the need to feel good about oneself.

> ### *Advantages of Knowing Your Team's Interests*
>
> ◆ Gain a clearer understanding of your goals
> ◆ Clarify what interests would be best met in resolving this conflict and what interests would be better met elsewhere
> ◆ Develop flexibility in bargaining, so that a good settlement is more attainable
> ◆ Avoid the problems of positional bargaining

In a negotiation, people who take a position, particularly when they do so publicly, paint themselves into a corner. Once a position has been taken, departing from that position feels like loss of face, and people are strongly motivated to avoid it. In Fisher, Ury, and Patton's words,

> [w]hen negotiators bargain over positions, they tend to lock themselves into those positions. The more you clarify your position and defend it against attack, the more committed you become to it. The more you try to convince the other side of the impossibility of changing your opening position, the more difficult it becomes to do so. Your ego becomes identified with your position. You now have a new interest in "saving face"—in reconciling future action with past positions. (Fisher, Ury, & Patton 1991, 4–5)

Moreover, taking a position causes people to engage in dangerous, one-dimensional thinking. Disputants who are engaged in positional bargaining tend to focus their attention only on the issue represented by the position. For example, if negotiators for S Corporation enter the negotiation taking the position "$25 per chip, and not one penny less," they will tend to ignore other, equally important considerations, such as payment method and due date, delivery arrangements, delays to permit quality control assessment, and so forth. In most negotiated agreements, "the devil is in the details": failing to make effective arrangements for delivery, payment, and so forth can make the difference between a good sale and a very bad one. Thus, taking positions can lead to very costly errors. Performing an interests analysis first helps a disputant keep these other important dimensions in mind.

Finally, positional bargaining makes enemies. Since your ego tends to become entangled with your position, any effort by the other side to move you off your position necessarily becomes personal—it's a direct attack on your ego. As enmity between the disputants builds, it becomes more and more difficult to get any resolution of the conflict at all. In the terms introduced in Chapter 7, positional bargaining can turn any interpersonal conflict into an identity conflict.

These considerations relate to a disputant's own interests analysis. They apply as well to an agent or advocate's analysis of his or her principal's interests. If you are representing someone else, it's critical to understand that person's interests. In fact, since you cannot read your principal's mind, you cannot determine his or her interests without a thorough investigation. The only way to know what

What's Wrong with Positional Bargaining?

♦ Danger of becoming locked into position psychologically—regardless of whether a better option is available

♦ Danger of becoming blinded to important issues unrelated to your position

♦ Tendency to see the other disputant as the enemy, leading to an unnecessary impasse and additional "spinoff" conflicts

---

the disputant's underlying interests are is to discuss these issues with him or her and to perform a careful interests analysis. And if the principal is a corporation or other multi-party entity, ascertaining interests will be a complex process of understanding the interests of the important individuals, as well as their power and influence on the decisions of the principal.

ANALYZING THE OTHER DISPUTANT'S INTERESTS

Beyond analyzing one's own interests and those of one's principal, it is also important to analyze the interests of the other disputant. Really understanding what motivates the other side gives a disputant, an agent, or an advocate the power to understand the significance of the other side's maneuvers and to respond effectively. There are five major reasons.

First, in a negotiation, you are most effective if you can craft proposals that appeal to the other team while still serving your side's interests. The old adage about honey catching more flies than vinegar is applicable: negotiation is more successful if you can craft creative ways of responding to the other disputant's underlying interests while serving your own interests as well. For example, if you

Is It Ever Good to Take a Position?

It's seldom advantageous to use positional bargaining as your primary negotiation strategy, or even as an isolated tactic, for the reasons we've discussed. However, there are at least three situations in which taking a position—"drawing a line in the sand"—can be useful.

The *first* is the situation in which you can't get the other disputant's attention. Every attorney who has ever dealt with civil litigation can recite several instances in which the other party came to the bargaining table only after a "litigation line" was drawn in the sand—a lawsuit was either threatened or actually filed.

The *second* is the situation in which the other disputant has a strong interest in delay. Examples are individuals whose liability to pay a sum of money is clear but who will not actually be "on the hook" until a settlement negotiation is concluded. These disputants may need a kick-start to get negotiations going.

The *final* situation is the one in which you or someone depending on you is actually being harmed by the other disputant and the latter won't stop committing harmful acts voluntarily. In this situation, it's not so much a matter of drawing a line in the sand as it is a matter of taking unilateral, assertive action to protect yourself or your charge. Taking a clear, concrete position—often, a threat—may get the other person to stop.

There are two major challenges in making this sort of line-drawing effective. The first is that, as we saw in Chapter 5, and will explore further in Chapter 9, being involved in an interpersonal conflict can mislead us about what's really happening. We may conclude in error that the other disputant is out to harm us, won't cooperate, or won't pay attention to us and think that line-drawing is necessary when it really isn't. The other problem is that taking a position will typically elicit similar behavior in the other disputant, leading to all the problems with positional bargaining we've already discussed. It sometimes helps to make an outright explanation of your motives as you take your position and to offer to use a more interest-based method of negotiation thereafter.

Some feel that having a firm position is useful to avoid appearing weak, or knuckling under too fast. Fisher, Ury, and Patton (1991), the authors of *Getting to Yes,* argue that using the line in the sand approach makes the disputant vulnerable to either too much or too little flexibility in bargaining, because a position is, essentially, arbitrary. A better approach, argue the authors, is to discover and use one's Best Alternative To a Negotiating Agreement (BATNA). This important skill is addressed in Chapter 13.

> ### *Advantages of Understanding the Other Disputant's Interests*
>
> - Ability to craft proposals the other disputant will want to accept
> - Ability to take advantage of opportunities created by concordant interests
> - Avoidance of later sabotage of the settlement by a disputant forced into an undesirable settlement
> - Avoidance of positional bargaining by appealing to the other disputant's interests
> - If coercion needed, ability to design more coercive strategies

are on the S Corporation negotiation team and discover that members of the B Corporation team are anxious to demonstrate their negotiation prowess to their superiors, you may be able to get a better deal by offering, through informal channels, to put on a display of tough bargaining with the B team—a sham, in essence, designed to make the other team look good in exchange for your own side's receiving additional benefits in the bargain.

Second, knowing the other disputant's underlying interests also allows you to avoid making costly errors of judgment. Such errors can lead to less effective resolution of the conflict. For example, suppose B Corporation has no upfront cash to bring to the table, so that B Corporation has an interest in delaying aspects of performing the contract. S Corporation may thus have a golden opportunity to trade a delayed transaction date (which is good for S Corporation, anyway) against a higher sales price. This opportunity may well be lost if this aspect of B Corporation's interests are not discovered.

Third, if you are the stronger of the disputants and are able to impose a solution without that disputant's most important interests having been met, invariably those deep-seated interests will express themselves, anyway, and it is likely that they will be expressed through sabotage of the solution you imposed. For example, it is common in divorce cases for a spouse who is unhappy with custody or visitation arrangements to sabotage the parenting arrangements or support obligations or to decide to contest other issues more vigorously. It is quite typical for parents who feel disempowered in a custody conflict to react by creating inconvenience in transporting children from one home to the other, by being "fashionably late" in paying child support or other obligations, and even by taking legal action about issues they otherwise might have chosen to leave alone.

Fourth, as with the analysis of your own interests, developing an accurate and complete analysis of the other disputant's interests allows the disputants to avoid positional bargaining, with the negative consequences already described.

Finally, if you have determined that you must put pressure on the other team to force them to do something that they have refused to do, having an accurate interests analysis allows you to select your weapons with greater surgical precision. Thus, interests analysis is valuable even for the most competitive of negotiators.

ANALYZING THE INTERESTS OF CONSTITUENTS AND STAKEHOLDERS

Constituents and stakeholders are affected by the course and outcome of a conflict; in turn, their connection to the disputants can lead to their significantly affecting the settlements, or potential settlements, made by the disputants, for good or for ill. For example, in the S-B Corporate transaction, it is likely that the staff members operating under the negotiating vice presidents, Sue and Ben, have interests that must be addressed to ensure that they cooperate in making the sale work. Imagine, for example, that Sue, Sam's underling, is overworked and overwhelmed by Sam's enthusiasm for her invention and her insistence on Sue's dropping everything to make sure the sale is successful. If Sue's need for balance in her worklife isn't addressed, she is likely to sabotage the transaction by failing to meet expectations for her work, such as the failure to meet due dates for written correspondence.

Similarly, in Ed and Ellen's divorce case (diagrammed in Chapter 6), the children's interests should be analyzed carefully. Apart from the moral responsibility of the adults in the situation to act in the best interests of these children, it is highly likely that, without an understanding of the children's interests, the children will themselves contribute to the destruction of the agreements made by the grownups. For example, it is well established that children frequently suffer separation anxiety during a marital separation and often react to their distress by attempting to reunite the parents. Many children attempt to create contact between Mom and Dad by engineering arguments between them. Children also attempt to create a secure relationship between themselves and each parent by telling each parent what the children think the parent wants to hear. In many cases, this translates into the child's "telling tales" about each parent to the other (Ricci 1980, 182–84). Without understanding the role of the children's underlying interests in the conflict, the parents may not be aware of the children's active role in stirring up controversy, and the result may be an exacerbation of the grownups' interpersonal conflict.

ANALYZING THE INTERESTS OF AGENTS AND ADVOCATES

Finally, an interests analysis should explore the interests, values, and needs of the agents and advocates on all sides of the conflict. The principal reason that interests analysis should include the agents and advocates of one's team is to clarify whether they have problematic conflicts of interest with their principal. For example, in the S-B Corporate transaction, Sam, the agent acting on behalf of S Corporation, has interests in satisfying her own ego needs with an astronomical chip price, which potentially conflict with the corporation's goal of establishing a long-term, amicable relationship with B Corporation. Moreover, the attorneys for both corporations have potential conflicts of interest with their clients: they have professional reputations that depend on a specific negotiation stance. If their clients' needs require a different strategy, they may be reluctant to adopt it. A disputant needs to determine whether a conflict of interest can be worked around, or whether it's so intractable that replacing the representative must be considered.

Conflicts of Interest Between Attorneys and Their Clients

Attorney-client relationships present special conflict-of-interest problems, which must be recognized and dealt with in the diagnosis process. Ronald J. Gilson and Robert H. Mnookin (1994) have written an excellent and thought-provoking analysis of how the differences between the interests of attorneys and those of clients might have an impact on the resolution of a client's dispute ("Disputing Through Agents: Cooperation and Conflict Between Lawyers in Litigation"). Gilson and Mnookin, noting the popular notion that the lawyer's interest in legal fees might create incentive to exacerbate conflict, also comment on the influence of the need to protect professional reputations: a lawyer with a reputation as a gladiator may be reticent to take a conciliatory approach, even if the client needs one, and vice versa. Client self-selection may remedy this situation somewhat, but the client may not always be the best judge, going in, of the best approach to take, and the authors also point out that a conciliatory approach to legal advocacy may be more difficult to handle economically (they note that the gladiator approach may allow a law firm to bill more services to inexpensive associates and paralegals than does a conciliatory approach).

◆ **TABLE 8-1**　Advantages of Interests Analysis

The Disputant	Clarifies what the disputant really wants and needs
	Enables the disputant to consider whether interests, values, and needs would be better met outside the conflict
	Enables greater flexibility and creativity in crafting solutions
	Avoids the pitfalls of positional bargaining
The Other Disputant	Enables the negotiator to craft appealing proposals
	Avoids errors of judgment about how to resolve the conflict
	Avoids sabotage by a disputant whose deep-seated interests are not addressed by the resolution of the conflict
	Avoids the pitfalls of positional bargaining
	Enables the negotiator to (if necessary) tailor coercive measures to the disputant's interests
Constituents and Stakeholders	Allows action to be taken up front to avoid later sabotage of or damage to the settlement
Disputant's Own Agents and Advocates	Reveals possible conflicts of interest requiring replacement of representative
Agents and Advocates for the Other Disputant	Reveals possible conflicts of interest and how they may make resolution more difficult or complex

An interests analysis should also include the agents and advocates for the other disputant. This is because the interests of other participants in the conflict can add to the complexity of motivations driving behavior in the conflict. For example, it helps S Corporation negotiators to know that there is a personal conflict between the two lawyers representing the corporate entities. The conflict may add unnecessary animosity to the negotiation and prevent the S-Chip transaction from being successfully consummated.

Table 8-1 summarizes the many reasons for performing an interests analysis.

PERFORMING AN INTERESTS ANALYSIS: THE CONFLICT ONION AND INTEREST TREE

Interests exist at multiple levels and are logically connected. To perform an interests analysis, a conflict diagnostician usually starts at the most obvious level and works deeper and deeper to uncover the more fundamental and basic interests, such as principles, values, and basic human needs. The more deep-seated interests drive the shallower interests: they are the *reasons* for the interests and positions that lie nearer the surface. In a sense, performing an interests analysis is a little like peeling an onion: you peel back each layer to reveal a deeper set of interests. That's why it's useful to refer to the hierarchy of interests associated with any conflict participant as the *conflict onion* (Figure 8-1 and Table 8-2).

Conflict Onion

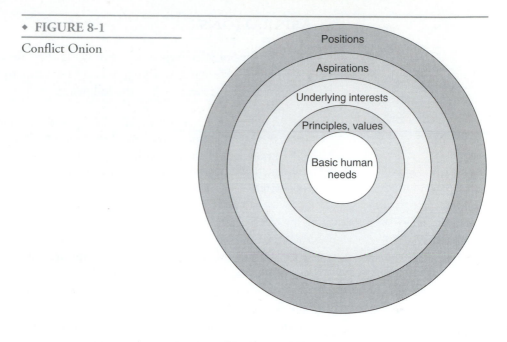

◆ **TABLE 8-2** Interests and the Conflict Onion

KIND OF INTEREST	DEFINITION
Position	The demand the disputant makes to others
Aspiration	The bottom line the disputant is looking for
Underlying interests	The reasons for the aspirations
Principles and values	Beliefs and moral codes that influence the interests
Basic human needs	Underlying needs that drive the motivations of the disputant

POSITIONS

The most obvious element of the conflict onion is what is visible to the perceiver: the individual's *position*. Positions are what people enter a conflict saying that they want.[3]

For example, sixty-two-year-old Sol Silverman is trying to sell his successful restaurant business to a prospective buyer. Sol has asked his own lawyer to demand $1.5 million, payable immediately in cash, for the business. These three elements—the price ($1.5 million), the type of payment (cash), and the time of payment (immediately)—constitute Sol's position.

---

[3] Nondisputants in a conflict may not have positions, *per se*. They are more likely to have specific aspirations for the process and outcome of the conflict. The same techniques would be used, however, to perform their interests analysis.

ASPIRATIONS

To represent Sol effectively as a client, his lawyer[4] decides to perform an interests analysis.[5] He starts by asking Sol *why* he wants to take this position. Sol is likely to give an answer such as the following:

> Well, I want to get at least $1 million for the business and I want to get the money as soon as possible. I made the $1.5 million demand because I know I need to start with a higher demand than I think I'm going to get. If the buyer is a sucker and will go with $1.5 million, so much the better.

This response (assuming it is complete and honest[6]) has gotten Sol's lawyer to the next layer of the onion: *aspirations*. Aspirations are the practical hopes that drive the individual's position. Aspirations are what the disputant hopes to get out of the conflict, on a very concrete level.

It is important for a conflict diagnostician to organize the interests analysis information. One effective way to do this is to create an interest tree. An interest tree is a diagram that shows the relationships among the various aspects of the participant's interests. It connects interests that are logically related to one another and it organizes the interests by level. So far, Sol's interests analysis can be diagrammed as shown in Figure 8-2.

◆ **FIGURE 8-2**

Sol's Interest Tree, in Progress

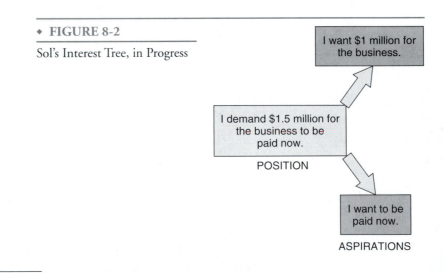

---

[4] It has not been traditional for lawyers to perform interests analyses. However, the June 2001 issue of the *ABA Journal*, the magazine of the American Bar Association, reports (Keeva 2001) on a highly successful lawyer, Arnie Hertz, whose success is attributed to his ability to look behind initial client positions to uncover deep-seated motivations and goals (discussed in more detail in Chapter 22).

[5] Sol himself could, of course, act as his own conflict diagnostician. In that case, the following steps might occur introspectively.

[6] Concerns about the accuracy of the interests analysis are, of course, more pronounced when the diagnostician is a member of one disputant's team and is attempting to analyze the interests of members of the other disputant's team.

Disputants, such as hypothetical restaurant owner Sol Silverman, have a variety of interests that affect the sorts of settlements that will best suit them. David Leach, Getty Images Inc., Stone Allstock

UNDERLYING INTERESTS

A conflict diagnostician could stop analyzing at the level of positions and aspirations, but it would leave a very incomplete picture of Sol's interests. Based on this information, there would be little a disputant, an agent, or an advocate could do other than barter over positions. As we have seen already, limiting the discussion to jockeying over positions would have many disadvantages.

Thus, an effective conflict diagnostician would go further. It makes sense to probe Sol gently for further information. Conflict diagnosticians usually use open-ended "why" questions to probe for underlying interests. Questions such as "What prompted you to choose $1 million as the price?" and "Why is getting paid now important to you?" may yield critical information about the *underlying interests* that drive Sol's aspirations:

> I want to be paid $1 million because I think that's what the business is worth. Besides wanting to get what the business is worth, I'm pretty proud of what I built over all these years and it would make me proud to get the money.

Probed further by his lawyer over coffee at the restaurant, Sol reveals some additional important information:

> I had some bad news from my doctor last week. I have Parkinson's disease, an illness that affects the ability of people to use their muscles to walk, hold things, and even speak and swallow. I waited until my symptoms were pretty bad to see the doctor. He says I can take medication that will help, but it's not going to be enough to let me keep up the pace at the restaurant. Parkinson's is progressive and incurable, and eventually I will become completely disabled. I need immediate help if the business is going to survive

and maintain its value. Also, this diagnosis has gotten me worried about the future. I've been ignoring retirement and now I have to face it. A great investment opportunity has come up for me, but it will be available only for a little while. I really need to cash out while the restaurant is still going well and get someone else to take over the day-to-day stuff in the business.

With this additional information, the conflict diagnostician can add considerably to the interest tree. Sol has a number of underlying interests, which have now been identified: to keep the asset from being impaired by his impending disability, to get paid fair value for the business, to gain recognition for his accomplishment in developing the restaurant, to fund his retirement, to take immediate advantage of an available investment opportunity, and to get someone to take over for tasks that, because of his illness, Sol can no longer handle. Sol's lawyer uses this information to add to Sol's interest tree, as shown in Figure 8-3.

It is possible, and valuable, to delve still deeper into Sol's motivations. Understanding more deeply seated (and therefore more basic and important) aspects of Sol's motivations will help the diagnostician understand where and when Sol will resist compromise, why some seemingly reasonable options will not be acceptable to him, and what other options will be equally satisfying.

PRINCIPLES AND VALUES

Conflict participants have underlying principles and values at play in their motivations. For instance, Sol's diagnostician can infer some of these from what Sol has already said. Sol obviously believes that people should be paid fairly for what

---

◆ **FIGURE 8-3**

Sol's Interest Tree (Next Step)

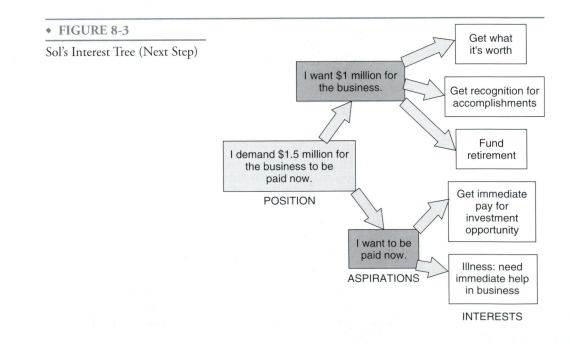

they are selling. He also obviously believes that people should be recognized for important accomplishments and life's work. These are *principles and values*. Important, fundamental, and basic principles, values, and deep-seated beliefs are not subject to compromise, because they make up a fundamental element of the self-concept, a fact of conflict that can be recognized by the persistence of protracted disputing when "it's the principle of the thing" that matters most.

Disputants may express principles and values disingenuously, as rationalizations for a position, rather than as honest expressions of deeply held beliefs. A conflict diagnostician must be able to distinguish between legitimately held principles and values and those that are trotted out as argument. Often, principles and values used as rationalizations can be identified as such because of the breezy ease with which a disputant who has shown a desire to focus on positions verbalizes them, as in "I demand at least $1,000 for the piano; it's fair compensation for the money I put into it." Occasionally, such rationalizations are actually based on true principles and values. The conflict diagnostician will need to engage in some further probing to distinguish truth from rationalization.

Principles and values are closely tied to basic human needs. We will see later in the chapter that the need for the esteem of others and a stable, positive sense of self are among the most important and deeply seated basic human needs. Thus, when a conflict participant evidences a legitimate preoccupation with principles and values, one can be certain that underlying human needs for esteem, stable identity, and "face" are responsible.

Considerations of "Justice" and Basic Principles and Values. A sense of justice, of having and doing justice, is an intrinsic part of almost all interpersonal conflict. Each participant in a conflict seeks justice for him- or herself, and an outcome that violates a participant's sense of justice is almost sure to fall apart later on.

Justice scholars generally identify two major types of justice, *distributive justice* and *procedural justice*. Distributive justice is concerned with whether the outcome of a conflict is fair. According to the scholarly research on justice, there are three basic principles generally called upon to determine distributive justice, each of which tends to be more important in particular sorts of situations. *Equity* considerations, which allocate resources based on the contributions of the participants, are often most relied upon when groups of people must be motivated as a group, such as when a corporation awards a bonus to an employee whose idea produces the greatest improvement in manufacturing efficiency. *Equality* considerations, which indicate that resources should be allocated equally, are generally most prominent when there is a high need for group cohesion, such as when professional sports team members are rewarded with identical bonuses for winning a championship together. Finally, *need* considerations suggest that resources should be allocated to those who need them most, as when a judge orders child support to a child based on the need of the family the child is living with. Many decisions about distributive justice are a combination of two, or even all three, considerations. For example, states now have child support guidelines that determine the level of child support based on the needs of the child *and* the ability of the payor parent to pay, but they make the support levels *the same for all families* in similar financial positions. And professional sports teams generally pay their players an equal bonus for winning a championship but pay individual players very different salaries, depending on their expected contributions to team success.

Procedural justice refers to the fairness of the *process* used to reach a given outcome. Procedural justice is extremely important in lending a sense of legitimacy to a conflict resolution process that imposes an outcome, or exerts some other sort of pressure or influence, on the disputants. It allows each disputant to enter the conflict resolution process with a fair degree of security and to achieve psychological closure in the conflict despite doubts about the merits of the outcome.

A sense of justice, whether having distributive or procedural considerations as its source, is essential to the effective resolution of conflict in the same manner as other principles, values, and beliefs. A process or an outcome that violates a disputant's sense of justice also violates his or her sense of self—it is experienced as humiliating and a loss of face. Such a resolution is almost certain to lead to trouble later.

BASIC HUMAN NEEDS

Lying even more deeply at the heart of the conflict onion than principles and values are *basic human needs*. Generally, people are not able to verbalize easily the basic human needs that lie at the heart of a conflict onion: they must be inferred from what people say and do and the circumstances they are in.

A good interests analysis should include basic human needs. Basic human needs are *basic*, and a failure to deal with and address them creates pressure for them to be expressed in other ways. Numerous examples of this phenomenon pepper the literature in conflict resolution. Ongoing international conflicts in the Middle East, Northern Ireland, Africa, and the Balkans, for example, often feature seemingly intractable conflicts over basic human needs for food, shelter, and basic security from physical attack. The race riots of the latter half of the twentieth century in U.S. cities can be attributed to efforts to apply law-and-order solutions to repress conflict without addressing the underlying needs of the groups who later rioted. These are the conflicts that persist and worry negotiators. The failure to consider and address basic human needs contributes to the persistence, evolution, transformation, and escalation of conflict everywhere.

Each conflict diagnostician brings his or her own skills and perspectives to the task of drawing inferences about underlying basic human needs. However, two major theories from the field of developmental psychology prove extremely useful in helping with this process. They are *Maslow's needs theory* and *Erikson's psychosocial theory*. Each deals directly with, and aids in the assessment of, basic human needs.

Maslow's Needs Theory. Abraham Maslow, a psychologist working in the first half of the twentieth century, presented a theory to explain the behavior and de-

Intractible Conflict over Basic Human Needs

Occasionally during conflict, horrific events—such as the 9/11/01 destruction of the New York World Trade Center and the attack on the Pentagon—shock the world. Although it is natural to react to such events by dehumanizing and demonizing those responsible, reactions like these detract from our ability to understand, cope with, and prevent such events from occurring in the future.

What threats to basic human needs led one group of people to give up their lives in an act of mass murder and another group of people to provide support and succor to the perpetrators? No lasting solution to the problem of international terrorism is possible without exploring this fundamental question. Although the perpetrators of such an act must be brought to justice, it is equally true that those for whom the act represented a cry for help must be listened to and understood. In this age of highly advanced weaponry, ease of international travel, and the information highway, only the principles and practice of conflict resolution can provide a lasting solution.

Greg Martin, Corbis/Sygma

velopment of mentally healthy adults. Maslow theorized that people have a drive to satisfy human needs and that these needs are organized hierarchically. He believed that the most basic needs are the physiological needs (such as needs for air, food, shelter, and sleep) and that, until these needs are satisfied, people are not motivated to address other needs or desires. The next most basic need on Maslow's hierarchy is for safety and security. Maslow termed the physiological and safety/security needs "deficiency needs," meaning that they are so basic that human existence is in jeopardy until they are satisfied. Once they are, Maslow believed, individuals next turn to the need for love and belongingness (love needs), followed next by the need for self-esteem and esteem by others (esteem needs). Finally, should these other needs be attained, Maslow believed that individuals seek to satisfy the need for something he called "self-actualization"—essentially, the ability to be all you can be as a unique individual. It should be noted that the need for "justice" is listed as one of these self-actualization needs. Maslow's needs hierarchy is presented in Table 8-3.

Maslow believed that one is not motivated to satisfy the higher needs until and unless more basic needs are satisfied. On the other hand, one might expect that, when a need is "just barely" satisfied, one might be motivated to consolidate that need even while addressing higher-level needs. For example, a man who is insecure about his love needs may marry and have them satisfied but might persist in worrying about losing the love he has attained. He may move on to address his esteem needs yet, at the same time, may be working to further address his love needs.

◆ **TABLE 8-3**   Maslow's Needs Hierarchy, with Examples from Sol Silverman's Restaurant Sale

LEVEL	NEED	INTERPERSONAL CONFLICT EXAMPLE
Growth, Achievement, or Self-Actualization Needs	Truth, Goodness, Beauty, Aliveness, Individuality, Perfection, Necessity, Completion, Justice, Order, Simplicity, Richness, Playfulness, Effortlessness, Self-sufficiency, Meaningfulness	Sol asks as a condition of sale that the new owner continue his tradition of featuring displays of local artists as décor on the walls of the restaurant.
Intermediate needs	Self-esteem, Esteem by others	Sol asks that the restaurant be sold "for what it's worth" because "people should be recognized for their work." Sol also worries that he will not be able to keep his role as head of his household if he loses the restaurant.
	Love and belongingness	Sol unconsciously resists closing the deal because he will no longer be a member of the community restaurant association and will no longer attend meetings with his peers.
Basic needs	Safety and security needs	Sol's concern for getting a good deal on the restaurant rests, in some measure, on his concern that he will no longer be able to afford the security measures he and his wife h'ave gotten used to.
	Physiological needs: Air, Water, Food, Shelter, Sleep, Sexuality	Sol's concern for getting a good deal on the restaurant also rests on his concern that he will not be able to afford to take care of himself. This concern is made more extreme by his illness, which will eventually become totally disabling.

Adapted from: Goble, 1970.

What happens when a need is being satisfied, but then it is threatened? This situation is very common in conflicts. One would expect that the response to a threat to a basic need would depend on the nature of the need and the severity of the threat. For example, one might expect that Sol is concerned with basic deficiency needs because of the severity, incurability, and progressive nature of his illness: he expects not to be able to work and support himself in the future. His threat to basic deficiency needs would be greatly lessened if his illness were, for example, the flu. One would expect also that someone whose confidence in her ability to meet her needs is shaky would react more intensely to the threat of loss than someone whose confidence is greater. For example, a woman who is insecure about her attainment of her love needs in the first place would be likely to react more intensely to a threat to this basic need than someone who felt her love needs were well met prior to the threat. In a custody case, for example, a father who feels comfortable with his relationship with his child is likely to react less defensively to his wife's filing for visitation rights than a father who is insecure about his child's love for him in the first place.

Maslow's needs theory is important to effective conflict diagnosis because it can provide insight into the deeply held motives of the persons involved in the conflict. Although nearly any legal conflict can be characterized as a dispute over the allocation of monetary resources, underlying this surface characterization there is always a problem with the attainment of, or threat to, basic needs. And Maslow would predict that the precise nature of the motivational set of the persons involved in the conflict depends on their developmental status at the time the conflict arises (in other words, the extent to which each level of need has already been attained), as well as the nature of the threat.

Legal disputes often present a combination of threats to basic human needs, with money standing in for a variety of needs. In many such disputes, money represents deficiency needs, as when an accident victim asks for compensation because she can no longer earn a living. Money may also represent love needs—the ability to be generous to others, the belongingness of the individual to an aristocratic family, and so on. Money may also represent esteem needs, representing the individual's success or social status. It may represent the esteem needs of disputants who see the attainment of net worth as the evidence of their "worth as a person." Finally, getting a really good deal may represent evidence that the individual is not a "sucker"—thus meeting his or her esteem need for self-respect, as well as so-called "face needs", or respect by others.

For example, a plaintiff in a fender-bender with a back injury may feel that his ability to earn a living is potentially impaired (threatening a physiological need for food and shelter). He will also feel his esteem needs threatened—in our adversarial society, it is common to feel profound shame and humiliation if one does not get the last dime from a defendant in a tort case. The defendant, similarly, has her deficiency needs threatened by the accident because she may be required to pay the other party and/or a lawyer lots of money. In addition, the defendant may feel her esteem needs threatened by the allegations of the plaintiff that she is guilty of a wrongful act, as well as being threatened by the loss-of-face esteem needs that accompany having to pay out.

Erikson's Psychosocial Theory. Another theory that can illuminate the deep-seated motivations of persons involved in conflict is the psychosocial theory of Erik Erikson (Erikson 1950, ch. 7). Erikson's theory, which is based fundamentally on the work of Sigmund Freud, posits that healthy development over the human life span follows a set course of development, in which particular life stages are associated with particular sets of overriding concerns. Thus, knowing Erikson's theory and the approximate ages of the individuals involved can provide some clues into deep-seated motivations. It provides a means of interpreting the statements and behaviors of individuals in conflict to tap into deeply held, and often unconscious, motivations. Many conflict professionals find that using Erikson's theory to suggest the possible motivations of disputants enables them to unlock many doors to resolving conflicts.

Erikson posits eight developmental stages extending over the human life span—four in childhood, one in adolescence, and three in adulthood. In each stage, the individual confronts a fundamental life challenge, with which he or she is preoccupied. A balanced, positive resolution of this life challenge enables the

Erik Erikson's Stages of Psychosocial Development

Stage 1 *(birth to 1 year)*—"trust versus mistrust." The individual's life challenge is to develop a healthy and realistic ability to trust others in his or her world, particularly an ability to trust the primary caregiver.

Stage 2 *(1 to 3 years)*—"autonomy versus doubt and shame." The individual's life challenge is to learn to act in an autonomous manner, to exercise control over him- or herself.

Stage 3 *(3 to 6 years)*—"initiative versus guilt." The individual's life challenge is to develop a sense of potency over his or her environment, to be able to act on the environment in creating situations and plans, without impinging on the rights and needs of others in the social system. It is here that the developing individual first confronts the limits of social organization and interpersonal conflict first appears.

Stage 4 *(6 years to adolescence)*—"industry versus inferiority." The individual's life challenge is to develop a mastery of the academic, social, and vocational skills that will be needed in adulthood.

Stage 5 *(adolescence and very young adulthood)*—"identity versus role confusion." The individual's life challenge is to develop a strong and stable sense of self with clear values, a sense of vocational identity, a social identity, and so forth.

Stage 6 *(young adulthood)*—"intimacy versus isolation." The individual's life challenge is to develop enduring intimate relationships, such as marriages.

Stage 7 *(middle adulthood)*—"generativity versus stagnation." The individual's life challenge is to find a way to make a lasting contribution to others and to society in general. This stage often includes an emphasis on procreation and the raising of children.

Stage 8 *(late adulthood)*—"ego integrity versus despair." The individual's life challenge is to find a way to reconcile and find peace and satisfaction with the manner in which he or she has lived life and to find meaning for the experience.

---

individual to move on to the next stage in a psychologically healthy manner. And clues to difficulties in the present day can be found in unsuccessful resolutions of prior developmental stages.

How can Erikson's psychosocial theory aid us in understanding conflict? Let's turn again to Sol Silverman's transaction. Sol is sixty-two years old and a successful restauranteur. One could expect his principal concerns at this stage of life to be related to stages 7 and 8 issues. One would expect Sol to be very concerned, first, with ensuring that the restaurant continue to be successful and viable or, if it does not, that he receive appropriate compensation to reflect his life's work (the fruits of his generativity). One might also expect him to be very concerned that he receive the recognition he deserves for his life's work, so that he can find peace with his overall life course.

There may be other ways of meeting these needs if they are not available in connection with cash payments for the restaurant: for example, Sol's children might be able to carry on in the business, with his retaining ownership, or it might be possible to organize some sort of lifetime achievement award for Sol. Brainstorming such creative approaches to meeting Sol's basic human needs can improve the situation for Sol without sacrifice on the part of the potential buyer, making success in the transaction more feasible. But notice that such a creative approach depends on our knowing where Sol is in a developmental sense. Were Sol twenty-five years old, one might expect a different motivational set: one

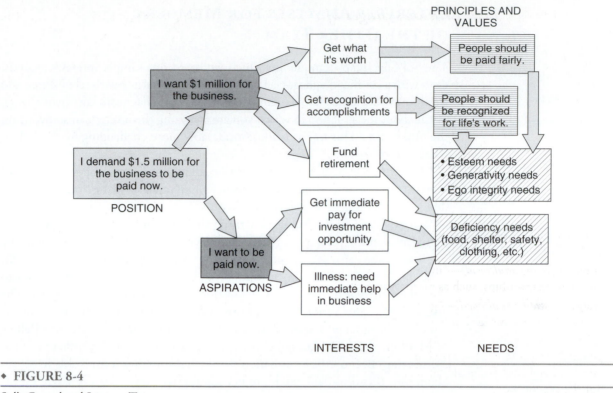

PRINCIPLES AND VALUES

Get what it's worth

People should be paid fairly.

I want $1 million for the business.

Get recognition for accomplishments

People should be recognized for life's work.

I demand $1.5 million for the business to be paid now.

Fund retirement

• Esteem needs
• Generativity needs
• Ego integrity needs

POSITION

Get immediate pay for investment opportunity

Deficiency needs (food, shelter, safety, clothing, etc.)

I want to be paid now.

ASPIRATIONS

Illness: need immediate help in business

INTERESTS   NEEDS

◆ **FIGURE 8-4**

Sol's Completed Interest Tree

might expect to see Sol more concerned with identity issues (such as getting a great price for the restaurant to prove his effectiveness as an entrepreneur) or intimacy issues (such as proving to a mate or potential mate that he has what it takes to be a successful businessman). Sol at twenty-five might be satisfied with a different set of alternatives than Sol at sixty-two.

It should be noted that other psychologists working since Erikson have proposed both alternative and complementary stage theories in an attempt to explain adult development. You are encouraged to get more information about these developmental stage theories—any of them can be useful in augmenting the process of determining a disputant's motivational stance.

We are now ready to draw some inferences about Sol's underlying basic human needs that are driving his interests in the restaurant transaction. His drive to satisfy his principles and values (that people should be paid fairly and that they should receive recognition for their life's work) can be inferred to spring from basic esteem needs for recognition by his peers and by society in general. His drive to establish his retirement, protect the value of the restaurant until it can be sold, and take advantage of the currently available investment opportunity may spring from threats to his basic deficiency needs prompted by his illness. With these new and tentative conclusions about Sol's most basic needs, Sol's attorney is ready to develop a draft of the completed interest tree. It is shown in Figure 8-4.

Interests Analyses for Members of the Other Team

The Sol Silverman example, on which we based our sample interests analysis, dealt with a conflict diagnostician who could communicate with relative ease and freedom with the disputant (who, after all, was the diagnostician's own client). What about the situation in which you are analyzing the interests of someone on the other team? This task is made considerably more challenging by the lack of reliable information.

In a typical legal dispute or transaction, the teams view the open exchange of honest information about one another's interests as dangerous and self-destructive. This is because legal conflict is seen as essentially adversarial. Scholars Gary Bellow and Bea Moulton, writing about the process of legal negotiation, point out that the primary sources of information that each team has about the interests of the other are the positions taken in the negotiation (1981, 27–35). Each disputant wants the other disputant to think he or she is more resistant to movement than he or she really is, so positions are structured to be deceptive. The goal of legal maneuvering for each team is, first, to learn the truth about the interests of the other and, second, to hide the truth about its own interests (Bellow & Moulton 1978). Additionally, as we will learn in Chapter 9, conflict itself has a distorting effect on the information that each disputant's team is able to obtain about the other disputant and his or her team. If you are trying to analyze the interests of members of the other team, there are four tactics you can try to use to get around these obstructions.

First, you may be able to convince the other team that sharing information will be in their best interests. One way to further this goal is to explain the merits of sharing interests and offering up information of your own. It helps to reassure the other team that you are not asking for an honest bottom line and to refuse to divulge a bottom line of your own. Reassuring the other team that, although you wish to have your own interests satisfied, you would prefer to satisfy their interests as well can sometimes improve the flow of information.

Second, the distorting effect of conflict can be partially countered by the conflict diagnosis process itself. In performing an interests analysis for the other disputant and his or her team, it is vital to keep in mind that systematic biases in perception created by the conflict itself affect the inferences that one draws. Specifically, persons from one team observing members of another team are likely to draw overly simplified conclusions about the meaning of behavior, and these conclusions tend to be biased toward the conclusion that the other team members are acting out of malice or devious intent. This perceptual bias, and the reasons for it, will be discussed in more detail in Chapter 9. Conflict diagnosis helps a diagnostician counter conflict's inherent tendency to create subjectivity in one's understanding of the situation.

Third, as part of diagnosing the conflict, you can perform a factual and legal investigation. For example, if you are a member of the S Corporation team and attempting to learn about the interests of B Corporation, you could take a look at previous profit/loss and asset statements, plus annual reports to stockholders, to learn more about the corporate financial position. You might do media research to determine whether there are any news articles relevant to B Corporation's status. If you are looking at B Corporation's attorney's interests, you may be able to get "through the grapevine" information from other legal colleagues. In general, information you are able to get from outside the context of the conflict is probably more reliable than anything you are able to learn by inference from the team members' behaviors in the conflict.

Finally, there are alternative dispute resolution processes—most notably, mediation (Chapters 15 through 18)—that focus participants on the sharing of underlying interests. Mediation should be considered as an option whenever interests analysis is important but the disputants are reluctant to reveal information about themselves.

SUMMARY

An interests analysis is always a work in progress. Human motivation is a dynamic variable affected by changes in the situation, as well as by the individual's perceptions of the situation, evolving beliefs, development, levels of stress, and emotional status. Moreover, an interest tree should be reexamined frequently to determine whether it is complete and accurate. Much of the information on any interest tree is inferential and subject to error. This is particularly true of the analysis of the other team members' interests. As a conflict diagnostician continues to observe and gather information, he or she should be ready to revise and improve the interest tree. The more accurately the conflict diagnostician can analyze interests, the more helpful the analysis will be.

IDENTIFYING DIVERGENT AND COMPLEMENTARY INTERESTS

A complete and accurate interests analysis is the first step in clarifying the nature of the conflicts at work in the situation you are diagnosing. It's very useful to uncover both divergent interests and complementary interests. Divergent interests between disputants define the conflict itself. They also define any associated and linked conflicts that might complicate resolution or provide opportunities for creative trade-offs. Divergent interests among members of the same team are red flags: they signal conflicts of interest that could impede effective resolution. Divergent interests involving nondisputant members of different teams may constitute linked conflicts that could complicate matters and prevent resolution. The interests analysis also gives you the raw information you will need to uncover complementary interests. These complementary interests, whether

◆ **FIGURE 8-5**

Brief Summary of S-B
Interests Analysis

BRIEF SUMMARY OF S-B INTERESTS ANALYSIS

S Corporation (Disputant)
- Get most $$ for product
- Establish amicable relationship with B
- Get immediate sale for balance sheet
- Delay production if possible
- Bind B Corporation to purchase its requirements of S-Chip
- Retain ability to sell S-Chip to others
- Retain freedom to provide less than B Corporation requirements

Sam (Agent)
- Esteem needs: get huge offer for chip
- Conduct successful deal: increase stature in employer's eyes
- Preserve health of S Corporation to improve job security

Sean (Advocate)
- Zealously represent client
- Take down Sam's inflated ideas
- Make lots of attorneys fees
- Preserve peacemaker reputation

Sue (Constituent)
- Get deal done/lower workload
- Preserve health of S Corporation to improve job security

QC Board Faction and QC Department (Constituents)
- Preserve health of S corporation to improve job security
- Delay deal so that QC testing can be completed/reduce risk of product reliability problems

Finance Board Faction (Constituent)
- Preserve health of S Corporation to improve job security
- Expedite deal so that balance sheet can reflect additional receivables

B Corporation (Disputant)
- Get product for least $$
- Establish amicable relationship with S
- Delay payment if possible
- Bind S Corporation to provide all S-Chip supplies needed
- Retain ability to buy comparable chips from others

Bob (Agent)
- Display negotiating prowess by getting great deal for B Corporation: impress boss; preserve job security and increase chances for raise; consolidate esteem needs; provide for family; show potency and power
- Hurt Sam (reminds him of ex-wife)
- Preserve health of S Corporation to improve job security

Bea (Adovcate)
- Zealously represent client
- Make lots of attorneys fees
- Preserve "Rambo lawyer" reputation
- Hates Sean—feels he deceived her in another case

Ben (Constituent)
- Preserve health of S Corporation to improve job security

between disputants or between nondisputant members of different teams, contain the seeds of truly creative and constructive conflict resolution.

The first step in identifying divergent and complementary interests is to list the interests you developed in the interests analysis. To give you a flavor for what the completed list might look like, and to give an example for how to conduct the next step, a list of interests for the S-B Corporate transaction, performed by a conflict diagnostician for S Corporation, appears in Figure 8-5. Let's look at the interests of each conflict participant to learn about their divergent and complementary interests.

The interpersonal conflict on which the diagnostician is focusing is based on the sale of the S-Chip. The divergent interests that create the interpersonal conflict can be determined by comparing the interests in the respective disputants' boxes and identifying those that are inconsistent:

◆ S Corporation wants a high price for the S-Chip, whereas B Corporation wants a low price.[7]

◆ S wants to force B to purchase its entire requirements for the chip from S (creating a sort of "captive customer"), whereas B would prefer to be able to shop the market for chips on a continuing basis.

◆ B would prefer to bind S to provide all the chips B asks for (creating a sort of "captive supplier"), whereas S would prefer to be able to produce only so many chips as it prefers.

Note that, although there are a number of divergent interests, there are also a number of convergent, complementary interests:

◆ S and B both want the sale to take place.

◆ S and B both want to establish a constructive business relationship with one another. Each can provide something the other wants, and, the more amicable the relationship, the more efficient and pleasant transacting business with one another will be.

◆ Both corporations want a delay in causing this transaction to play out— S because the chip has not been through quality control testing and B because it needs time to amass some upfront cash.

Now, let's turn to the relationships among the members of the S Corporation team. All the team members want to accomplish the sale of the S-Chip to B Corporation. Also, each team member has a vested interest in the health and viability of S Corporation, since each derives income from it. Thus, each team member is helped by a deal that is good for S Corporation. However, beyond these commonalities, there are a number of conflicts of interest among members of the S Corporation team. Sam, the principal negotiator, has a personal esteem need for recognition for her development of the S-Chip. Unless this esteem need is somehow accommodated or otherwise handled, it has the potential to wreck the deal, as Sam is likely to take offense at contract prices unless they are (perhaps unrealistically) high. Sean, the lawyer, has been instructed to "handle" Sam; thus, one would expect the possibility of overt disputing between Sam and Sean. Sue, Sam's secretary, may create problems if she fails to do the background work of

---

[7] Of course, corporations don't "want," "need," or "prefer" things, since they are not individual human beings. We will use the terms *want, need,* and so forth to designate goals that have been attributed to the corporate entities by the human beings that constitute their leadership and decision-making arms.

"It's a fabulous deal. You'll make peanuts."

The Cartoon Bank

making the deal (such as typing any necessary paperwork) promptly and effectively. And, if potential deals don't simultaneously accommodate the interests of the divergent board of director factions, there is likely to be controversy as each faction advocates for or against proposals. Finally, there is a potential conflict of interest between the attorney for S Corporation, Sean, and the corporation itself: should the corporation need an adversary approach to deal making in this instance, Sean would have to behave in a manner contrary to his own reputation as a cooperator. This change of style would compromise Sean's ability to market himself as a peacemaker to future clients. A similar conflict of interest exists between Bea and B Corporation.

There are also linked conflicts between members of the S and B teams that threaten the deal-making process. Bob has unconscious personal animosity toward Sam—Sam reminds Bob of his ex-wife. For Bob to close a deal on the S-Chip means either amicable cooperation with Sam (which he may find difficult) or going around Sam and working with another member of the team (which is likely to antagonize Sam). It is likely that Bob is unaware of the reason he finds Sam so unpleasant. Like most people, Bob is unlikely to feel good about himself if he sabotages the deal with S Corporation out of spite. Therefore, wanting to preserve his positive self-concept as a rational and reasonable guy, Bob is likely to find reasons for his hatred in the current negotiation behavior of Sam (for example, Bob is likely to be hypercritical of Sam's proposals). Given that Sam hopes for unreasonably high offers, Bob is not likely to be disappointed in finding things to criticize.

Bea and Sean also have divergent interests unrelated to the conflict at hand: Bea hates Sean for a supposed deception in another matter they handled together. Because people generally don't like to admit to themselves that they are acting out of spite, Bea, rather than acknowledging her hostile feelings as borne of a past incident, is likely to look to Sean's conduct in the current negotiation for reasons to be critical of how he is conducting herself.

What initially looked like a simple conflict over price has turned out to have numerous hidden complexities. Moreover, as the negotiation proceeds, additional complexities will probably appear. As discussed in Chapter 4, people inevitably use their experiences in a conflict to make judgments about the people they are dealing with, further adding information to their assessment of other participants' interests. Chapter 4 also proposed that conflict itself introduces a whole variety of perceptual and judgmental biases into the conflict participants; thus, the judgments that people make about others during a conflict are often questionable. In Chapter 9, we will delve into this topic, learning some fascinating facts about conflict and the biases it creates in the people who participate in it.

EXERCISES, PROJECTS, AND "THOUGHT EXPERIMENTS"

1. *Conflict journal.* This chapter's conflict journal exercises are extensive.

   a. Build an interest tree that represents your interests (if you are the disputant) or the interests of your disputant (if you are an agent, an advocate, or a constituent). Suggestion: use a computer presentation program that enables you to create text boxes that you can reorganize. You may have to use a very small typeface to fit your tree on a single page. Or hand-create your interest tree, using a very large sheet of paper and making rectangular boxes of interests, which you can organize and reorganize before you glue them down.

   b. Build interest trees that represent the interests of the other disputants.

   c. If you are comfortable sharing your results with a trusted friend, fellow student, or colleague, do so. Explain what the interest tree is intended to do. Get some feedback concerning the logic of the items (for example, whether the items labeled as values are really values) and whether the connections you display have a logical rationale. Revise your trees as needed.

   d. Study the results closely. Does the information help you brainstorm some creative ideas for resolving the conflict? Do the trees empower you in any way?

   e. Keep revising and perfecting your interest trees as you deal with the conflict.

2. Twenty-five-year-old Arnold takes his clothing to the Spotstown Dry Cleaners and pays $15 to have them cleaned. When his clothes are returned, there

is a spot still on his pants, and his two work shirts (which cost $25 apiece but were three years old and rather well used) are missing. Arnold is mad, but also very busy, and loses his dry cleaning slip. He returns to the cleaners, angrily demanding $200 to cover the cost of buying two new shirts, plus one pair of new wool pants to replace the ones that have spots. The owner refuses, stating that there is no guarantee against spot removal and that, according to her records, no shirts were ever brought in. Arnold now wants to take the Spotstown Dry Cleaners to the cleaners, as it were. He's willing to pay the $300 in filing fees that it will take to file a complaint in small claims court, despite the fact that he's unlikely to get it back and, because he has no record of the transaction, he has little chance of winning. Arnold's case is diverted to a court-connected ADR service, and you are the coordinator.

    a. Based on the information given, build an interest tree for Arnold. You may draw any reasonable inferences and make any educated guesses necessary to the task.

    b. Would your tree be different if Arnold were a sixty-five-year-old man? Why or why not?

3. If you're reading this textbook as part of a course, imagine that you, the rest of the class, and the professor are about to negotiate a policy to cover timeliness and late penalties for homework assignments and projects.

    a. Build an interest tree that represents your aspirations, interests, principles and values, and basic needs in this transaction. Be careful—remember that the policy will apply to all students, not just yourself. You may want to consider how you will feel if you turn in papers on time and others turn them in late, as well as the fairness implications of having the professor grading papers all at once, versus a few at a time.

    b. Compare your tree with those of your classmates. Having seen other responses to the task of building this interest tree, would your interest tree better represent your interests if modified? Perform the modifications needed.

4. Consider, write about, discuss, or debate the following questions: "What does it mean to say that a corporate entity or other group has 'interests'? How does one determine what the interests of such an entity are? In resolving conflict that involves such an entity, doesn't it make more sense to consider the interests of the individuals you will be dealing with, and those of the persons to whom the former individuals will be accountable?"

5. Consider the following ethical dilemma. Pearl is a paralegal working in a small law firm. She attended the initial client interview conducted by her supervisor, attorney Arlene, with potential divorce plaintiff Pam. Pam, a fairly wealthy woman, made it clear that she wanted the case to settle with a minimum of expense paid to legal fees. Pearl has since had the impression that Arlene is fanning the flames of the conflict. Arlene has filed numerous motions in the case, some of which seem unnecessary, and she seems to be

inflaming passions in her letters and phone calls. Arlene charges by the hour, which is typical in divorces. Might Arlene be violating any ethical obligations? What should Pearl do, and why?

6. Would your answers to the questions in exercise 5 change if Pam, the client, were the person pushing for litigation and Arlene, the attorney, were the conciliatory one? If so, why is this a different situation?

7. Choose one of the current longstanding international conflicts. Build interest trees for each of the participants. Conduct factual research to assist you in this task. Include the disputants and any stakeholders, agents, advocates, and constituents you can identify. In an accompanying essay, explain and justify your interest trees in detail. The key to doing an effective job on this project is to be as objective as possible. It helps to exchange your trees with another student whose position on the conflict is different from your own.

RECOMMENDED READINGS

Erikson, E. 1950. *Childhood and society.* New York: W.W. Norton.

Fisher, R., W. Ury, and B. Patton. 1991. *Getting to yes: Negotiating agreement without giving in.* 2d ed. New York: Penguin Books.

Goble, F. G. 1970. *The third force: The psychology of Abraham Maslow.* New York: Pocket Books.

Keeva, S. 2001. What clients want. *ABA Journal* 87 (June):48–52.

Mnookin, R. E. 1993. Why negotiations fail: An exploration of the barriers to the resolution of conflict. *Ohio State Journal on Dispute Resolution* 8(2):235–49.

Riskin, L. L., and J. E. Westbrook. 1997. In *Dispute resolution and lawyers* (pp. 80–147). St. Paul, MN: West.

Rubin, J. Z., D. G. Pruitt, and S. H. Kim. 1994. *Social conflict: Escalation, stalemate, and settlement.* New York: McGraw-Hill.

Sandy, S. V., S. K. Boardman, and M. Deutsch. 2000. Personality and conflict. In *The handbook of conflict resolution: Theory and practice* (pp. 289–315), edited by M. Deutsch and P.T. Coleman. San Francisco: Jossey-Bass.

9

Step 4. Assess the Character of the Conflict as Constructive or Destructive

"I am become mine enemy."

—Source unknown

*"Grief and disappointment give rise to anger,
anger to envy, envy to malice, and malice to grief again,
till the whole circle be completed."*

—Hume, *A Treatise of Human Nature* (1739)

In this chapter, you will learn …

- The four components of Morton Deutsch's theory of constructive and destructive conflict.
- Why Morton Deutsch theorized that cooperation is more likely than competition to produce constructive conflict.
- Why conflict has the amazing capacity to become what the disputants think it is.
- Why it's easier for a cooperative conflict to become competitive than vice versa.
- Some criteria for assessing a conflict as cooperative or competitive.
- Strategies and tactics for turning a competitive conflict into a cooperative one.

"I thought I knew him, but I was wrong." If you've ever been unfortunate enough to be caught up in a destructive conflict with a former friend, coworker, lover, or spouse, you are probably familiar with this sentiment. Disputants involved in longstanding relationships that are going bad frequently express a sense of shock, grief, and betrayal as the person they thought was so good, trustworthy, and predictable seems to reveal him- or herself as a wolf in sheep's clothing.

Do people routinely cover up their evil side, only to reveal it in times of conflict? It sometimes seems that way. All of us are familiar with destructive conflict—we see it in our personal lives, in literary fiction and film, in the news media. It is a hallmark of destructive conflict that each side conceives of the other as evil and sees its own violent or coercive behavior as self-defense or righteous retribution.

Social scientists have puzzled over what characteristics make conflict destructive and why some forms of conflict seem to be associated with such extreme polarizations of perspective and attitude. The leading light in this field, for a period approaching half a century, is clinician and scholar Morton Deutsch (Bunker, Rubin & Associates 1995). In this chapter, we will explore his seminal theory of cooperation and competition and uncover some of the insights his theory holds for conflict diagnosticians.

MORTON DEUTSCH'S THEORY OF CONSTRUCTIVE AND DESTRUCTIVE CONFLICT

Deutsch's ideas about what makes conflict constructive and destructive are well summarized in his 1973 work, *The Resolution of Conflict: Constructive and Destructive Processes.*[1] Although Deutsch's work is complex and scholarly, it can be condensed into four basic premises:

1. Conflict is either cooperative or competitive.
2. Cooperation tends to be constructive, and competition tends to be destructive.
3. Cooperation and competition tend to be self-fulfilling prophecies: perception becomes reality.
4. Cooperation easily turns into competition, but not vice versa.

Each of these premises has important and useful implications for conflict diagnosticians.

---

[1] For an enlightening review of the life of Morton Deutsch, see Bunker, Rubin & Associates 1995, xix–xxv.

PREMISES OF DEUTSCH'S THEORY

Premise 1: Conflict Is Either Cooperative or Competitive. Deutsch started with the premise that any conflicted relationship is either primarily cooperative or primarily competitive. As you will recall from Chapter 1, interpersonal conflict is characterized by *interdependence*; that is, what one disputant does affects the other disputant, either actually in fact or according to the perceptions of the parties. *Deutsch believes that all interpersonal conflict can be categorized as cooperative or competitive,* depending on the nature of their apparent interdependence.

Cooperative conflict is characterized by the disputants' beliefs that interdependence is primarily *promotive*: in other words, the belief that what each disputant does affects the other disputant in a positive manner. If I am a disputant in a cooperative conflict, I will tend to believe that, if you, the other disputant, try to help yourself, it will tend to promote my interests, and *vice versa*.

Competitive conflict, on the other hand, is characterized by the disputants' beliefs that interdependence is mainly *contrient*: what each disputant does affects the other in a *negative* manner. If I am in a competitive conflict, I will tend to believe that, if you, the other disputant, try to help yourself, it will tend to harm me and, if I try to help myself, it will tend to harm you.

Deutsch describes ten essential characteristics of cooperation and competition. These characteristics flow from the differences in apparent interdependence.

How the Conflict Is Characterized in the Minds of the Disputants. Since a cooperative conflict is perceived as promotively interdependent, the disputant perceiving a conflict as cooperative will tend to see the conflict as a joint problem to be solved: that is, if the problem is solved for one disputant, it will also tend to be solved for the other. Metaphorically, if the situation is thought of as a tug-of-war, the disputant will think of the other disputant as being on his or her side, pulling in the same direction. In a competitive conflict, the opposite is true. Since the disputant in a competitive conflict sees him- or herself as vulnerable to harm if the other disputant's interests are addressed, a competitive conflict is usually perceived as a contest, with one winner and one loser.

Communication in Cooperation and Competition. Since the disputant in a cooperative conflict sees the goals of the other disputant as promoting his or her own interests, it appears to be in his or her best interests to share as much information as possible. Thus, *cooperation is characterized by open, honest communication of relevant information.* In contrast, since the interests of disputants in a competitive conflict are seen to be in opposition, *competition is characterized by efforts on the part of the perceiving disputant to avoid open and honest communication.* In competitive conflict, disputants tend to be suspicious of one another, fearing that information they share will be used against them. A disputant who sees him- or herself in a competition will communicate as little as possible. In addition, since their interdependence is contrient, there is a tendency for disputants in a com-

---

Cooperative conflict
a conflict in which the disputants believe that, when one disputant helps him- or herself, the other disputant is also helped.

Competitive conflict
a conflict in which the disputants believe that, when one disputant helps him- or herself, the other disputant is harmed.

petition to believe that they can protect their own interests by misleading the other disputant. Accordingly, disputants in competition are likely to lie or mislead one another about information relevant to the conflict.

Lack of communication in a competitive conflict breeds a phenomenon known as **autistic hostility.** In autistic hostility, the taciturn reactions of the disputants to the escalating conflict keep them from clearing the air. The result is that disputants, suspicious of one another's motives in every action, don't have an opportunity to have their suspicions allayed by explanation. Hence, suspicions tend to fester and multiply. The following is an example, from a divorce mediation, which shows how anger can prevent disputants from clearing the air:

Autistic hostility

a phenomenon in which hostile feelings promote a lack of communication, leading to negative attributions about the acts, attitudes, and motivations of the other person. Because of the lack of effective communication, neither disputant is able to correct the resulting misperceptions.

The husband and wife, both employed full-time, trying to manage their own businesses on the side, and the parents of two lively, elementary-aged kids, entered the mediation session in a state of mute rage and fear. When prodded by the mediator, each had their own version of a vicious confrontation that had recently occurred at the family home. After a period of angry accusations, the mediator asked the couple to begin to think more in terms of what each needed from the other, so that they could function more effectively.

"Stop treating me like a thief," said the husband immediately.

"Could you be more specific?" asked the mediator.

The husband bitterly related his humiliation when, as he went from room to room to retrieve belongings, so that he could move them to his new residence, the wife hovered over him, watching every move.

"Could you perhaps arrange to be out of the house while Gene gets his things, so that the two of you aren't there to argue with each other?" the mediator asked the wife.

"Absolutely not," she replied. "I want to see everything he takes out." This reply drew a stony glare from Gene.

"Why?" asked the now discouraged mediator. Evidently, thought the mediator, Laura really thinks he's out to steal her blind. This was one of those moments of mediator bafflement. What should she do next?

It took several unsuccessful attempts by the wife to discuss the situation. The husband's feelings were so deeply hurt by apparently being accused of theft that he was unable to allow Laura to get more than a few words out before reacting in anger.

Finally, after about the fifth try, the wife was able to get an entire paragraph out unimpeded. "I need to see everything he takes," she said with a degree of exasperation at the interruptions and the mediator's slow-wittedness, "because I can't find anything as it is. The only way I can figure out whether something is gone from the house or just lost, is to watch to see whether he takes it. We have two kids and four jobs, and I can't find anything from one minute to the next. I don't care what he takes and I'm not at all worried about his 'stealing' stuff. He needs something to live on, too. If I can't find the kid's socks, I just need to know whether they're here somewhere or whether he took them to his house, so I know whether I have to replace them."

This revelation brought down the house. After a period of helpless laughter, the couple was, with the mediator's help, able to develop an agreement that allowed Laura an opportunity to review what Gene was taking. More-over, the episode served as a way for the couple to remind themselves that they were able to work together constructively when, later in the mediation, other impasses arose.

In the preceding example, the husband misinterpreted the wife's actions as hostile and insulting, whereas she was apparently only trying to manage the mess. The fact that the husband was feeling humiliated colored the few words he chose to direct to his spouse, and she was no more successful at being civil and amicable with him. Since the lines of communication between them had been severely disrupted, neither spouse had been able to clear up the misunderstanding until mediation provided a controlled forum for this to occur.

Coordination of Effort in Cooperation and Competition. Since a disputant who sees the conflict as cooperative believes that the other disputant's efforts will help him or her, the disputant will tend to try to coordinate his or her efforts with those of the other disputant. *Thus, cooperation is characterized by efforts by the disputants to pool their efforts to gather information and solve the problem.* For example, if a conflict involves the sale of property, cooperating disputants are likely to join to-gether to choose an appraiser to value the property. In contrast, disputants in competition are more likely to mistrust the efforts of one another to resolve the conflict and to believe that efforts to help the other disputant will be personally harmful. Hence, *competition is characterized by duplication of effort and ineffi-ciencies in time and money* spent in gathering relevant information and getting the problem resolved. If the sale of property involves disputants who believe they are competing rather than cooperating, each is likely to want to hire his or her own appraiser; when the appraisals are completed, the disputants are likely to spend time battling over whose appraisal is accurate.

Efforts of the Disputants on One Another's Behalf. Obviously, a disputant who be-lieves that meeting the other disputant's interests will meet his or her own inter-ests has good reason to help the other disputant: it will help him or her as well. Thus, *cooperation is characterized by efforts by the disputants to help one another.* In contrast, *competition is characterized by efforts by each disputant to obstruct the other,* since the disputant sees meeting the other disputant's interests as person-ally harmful. Since cooperating disputants try to help one another, they tend to accumulate real-world evidence that the relationship is, in fact, cooperative, whereas competing disputants tend to have their beliefs confirmed that the other disputant is trying to undermine them.

Responses to the Suggestions of the Other Disputant. The reactions of one disputant to suggestions by the other disputant are controlled by the attitudes engendered by their perceptions. In cooperative conflict, a disputant will tend to see the sug-gestions of the other disputant as motivated by a sincere desire to help, since everyone's goals are perceived to be complementary. Accordingly, *in a cooperative conflict, suggestions tend to be welcomed, approved of, or at least taken at face value.*

Reactive devaluation

a phenomenon present in escalating conflict, in which a suggestion made by one disputant, or members of his or her team, is met with suspicion or incredulity by the other disputant, or members of his or her team.

The contrary tends to be true during competition. Since the disputant believes that the other disputant is motivated to do him or her harm, he or she will tend to mistrust, and be suspicious of, suggestions that the other disputant makes. *The discounting of suggestions made by the other disputant in a competitive conflict is referred to as* **reactive devaluation**.

Reactive devaluation can lead to some seemingly absurd results. Imagine that Browne and Greene had an auto accident, which resulted in personal injury to Browne and damage to his car. They have been involved in an acrimonious and hostile negotiation for the past six months. Browne has had his vehicle examined and has sought medical care. His attorney concludes that he should get about $50,000 from Greene for damages. Now, suddenly, after months of contentious thrust and counter-parry, Greene offers Browne the $50,000 he has hoped for. Reactive devaluation is likely to prompt Browne to question the original assessment from the attorney. Suspicious of anything Greene does, Browne will probably wonder: Is there something his attorney missed? Does Greene have an ulterior motive? Does Greene have some sort of sabotage in mind? In fact, Greene may simply have evaluated the merits of his position and decided to settle at a reasonable sum. But, instead of accepting the offer graciously and ending the conflict, Browne is likely to delay while his attorney conducts a reevaluation, or even to reject the offer altogether. Greene is likely to resent this reaction to his offer, and the delay in responding may even prompt him to withdraw it.

Feelings of the Disputants for One Another. There is a great deal of evidence from social psychological research indicating that disputants in a cooperative relationship tend to develop feelings of friendliness and positive regard for one another. If the disputant feels that helping the other disputant has personal advantages, he or she will tend to do many things, in his or her own apparent self-interest, that help the other disputant. The other disputant is likely to notice these friendly and helpful efforts, and they tend to breed positive regard. This positive regard, in turn, promotes friendly behavior in the second disputant and increased feelings of friendliness in the first disputant. *Thus, cooperation tends to breed feelings of friendliness.* Similarly, a disputant who sees a conflict as competitive will tend to behave in a way that obstructs and misleads the other disputant, promoting the belief on the part of the other disputant that he or she is "the enemy." *In short, competition tends to breed feelings of enmity and hatred between disputants.* In an extreme case of escalated conflict, disputants are apt to *demonize* one another—that is, to see one another as inherently evil.

Effect of Cooperative Behavior on the Disputants' Egos. In a cooperative conflict, cooperating with the other disputant is a comfortable outgrowth of the self-interest of each disputant. The feelings of friendliness that tend to grow out of a cooperative relationship further motivate the disputants to be helpful to one another. *Thus, in a cooperative conflict, cooperating with the other disputant gives a boost to the ego.* In contrast, the feelings of enmity engendered by competition, as well as the conceptualization of competitive conflict as a contest, produce a much different effect on the disputants' egos. In a competitive conflict, cooperating with the other

Cooperation can promote feelings of friendliness among disputants. Lockyer Romilly, Getty Images Inc.—Image Bank

disputant is emotionally tantamount to "sleeping with the enemy." And, since the conflict is seen as a contest with a winner and a loser, the act of cooperating with the other disputant creates a profound sense of loss of face. *Hence, in a competitive conflict, cooperating with the other disputant can often be psychologically intolerable.* For this reason, it is extremely difficult to convince disputants to adopt cooperative stances once a conflict has become competitive.[2]

Perception of Similarity and Difference. The positive and negative regard that cooperating and competing disputants hold for each other have implications for their perceptions about one another. People who like one another tend to focus on, and even inflate, mutual similarities, while they tend to ignore differences. The old adage "love is blind" refers to the tendency for people who have a high regard for one another to ignore shortcomings and obsess on wonderful and heroic qualities seemingly possessed by one another, as well as the ways in which the loved one seems just like the self. *Thus, cooperation is characterized by the perception of similarities among disputants.* In contrast, when a relationship sours, as in competitive conflict, these biases fade and are replaced by an opposing set of biases that emphasize apparent differences between people. These biases, both in favor of those we like and against those we dislike—are probably the result

---

[2] Some mediators recognize that, to counter this tendency, tactics can be used that convince the disputant that somehow his or her cooperative conduct makes the disputant "better than" the enemy.

A Brief Cognitive Dissonance Exercise

Think of a politician, a talk-show host, an activist, or another public figure whom you particularly dislike. On an empty sheet of paper, draw a line down the center. On one side of the paper, write down all the qualities of that person that are similar to yours. On the other side, write down qualities that are unlike yours. Compare the list. Is the list of unlike qualities longer than the list of like qualities? That's to be expected. Now look at the list of like qualities. Do they make you uncomfortable? Do you want to explain them away? That's the cognitive dissonance effect.

Now try the same exercise using someone you like very much. How do the results differ? Can you see a cognitive dissonance effect at work here, too? In what way?

of efforts to minimize "cognitive dissonance"—the uncomfortable state in which one's thoughts seem internally inconsistent. *Thus, in competitive conflict, disputants tend to ignore similarities and focus only on differences.*

Note how these biases operate when disputants consider deep-seated values and principles. A disputant who perceives a conflict as cooperative is likely to notice, emphasize, and focus on those values that he or she and the other disputant hold in common. Since the disputant notices that the other disputant shares many deep-seated values, he or she is likely to approve of the overall approach and world view of the other. In a competition, the opposite tends to be the case. Because Disputant X sees Disputant Y's deep-seated values as antithetical, Disputant X tends to *demonize* Disputant Y. This judgment allows Disputant X to dehumanize Disputant Y, making inhumane, violent, mean-spirited, or retributive treatment of Disputant Y seem more appropriate. Disputant Y, seeing Disputant X behave in this manner, has some basis for concluding that Disputant X is, in fact, morally inferior to him- or herself, setting the stage for a similar judgment and similarly reprehensible action. In short, both disputants now have ample evidence to prove to each the inhumanity and inherent evil of the other. These reciprocal actions tend to escalate the negative judgments and, hence, the conflict.

Task Focus in Cooperation and Competition. Because the disputant who perceives a conflict as cooperative believes that he or she helps him- or herself by helping the other disputant, he or she tends to stay focused on the task at hand. *Thus, cooperation tends to be characterized by task focus and efficiency.* On the other hand, because of the perception of a competitive conflict as a contest, as well as because of the hostile feelings created by competition, *competition tends to be characterized by a focus on beating the other disputant.*

How does this focus on winning operate in practice? In a conflict characterized by competition, doing better than the other disputant becomes an independent disputant interest. Thus, the disputant becomes willing to trade off other interests in order to see that the enemy suffers a defeat. Consider, for example, our divorce case between Ellen and Ed (introduced in Chapter 6). If Ed is caught up in a competitive conflict with Ellen, he may assert a claim for sole custody of the children, not because he particularly wants the children to live primarily with him but, rather, because it would defeat Ellen's expressed desire for sole custody. In taking this adverse position, Ed compromises important interests in effective parenting and in shared responsibility for custody. (Ed will probably rationalize some substantive reasons to support his sole custody claim in order to preserve his "good parent" self-concept.)

Productivity, Containment, and Escalation of Cooperative and Competitive Conflict. A cooperative conflict tends to be characterized by contained size and maximal productivity. There are several reasons for this feature of cooperative conflict.

First, because the conflict is conceptualized as a joint problem to be solved, the disputants tend to work with focused efficiency to resolve it. The disputants stay with the issue at hand and tend not to get off track. Since they tend to work together and share information openly, communication tends to create a minimum of misunderstanding and little duplication of effort. Since feelings of friendliness are generated, there is little likelihood of associated conflicts' being generated and little likelihood of personality conflicts' being created. Moreover, because of the tendency for cooperating disputants to focus on similarities and minimize differences, they will tend to make light of, or minimize, collateral or linked conflicts that exist between them or the members of their teams. Thus, overall, the forces at work in a cooperative conflict all tend to contain the conflict and lead to its rapid resolution.

In contrast, a competitive conflict tends to be characterized by impaired productivity, conflict escalation, and spreading. The reasons for this feature mirror those just described for cooperative conflict.

Because the conflict is conceptualized as having only one winner and one loser, disputants are necessarily in the business of impeding each other's efforts to reach their goals. They attempt to impede one another through false and misleading communication, lack of communication, and direct efforts to thwart one another's goals. Each of these processes directly impairs productivity. Moreover, because each disputant tries to thwart the other's goals in the conflict, conflicts over the handling of the main conflict are generated. A conflict (including a dispute) over the handling of another conflict (dispute) is called a **meta-conflict (meta-dispute)**, and competitive conflicts feature an abundance of these. Each meta-conflict complicates the picture, further impeding the resolution of the main conflict and adding to the evidence that each disputant has about what a bad person the other disputant is. Meta-conflicts also add to the disputants' already escalating tendency to focus on differences and deemphasize similarities between them; thus, collateral and linked conflicts take on increasing importance in the minds of the disputants. The motivation that each disputant has to keep the other from attaining his or her goals is exacerbated by the bad feelings each has about the other. The more competition, the greater the degree of enmity; the more enmity, the more competitive the conflict gets.

Moreover, as the hostile feelings of each disputant increase, people outside of the immediate dispute feel pressure to take sides. To avoid being perceived as unkind, friends and friendly acquaintances of each disputant usually feel compelled to express emotional support. Members of the other team see this support

Meta-conflict (meta-dispute) an interpersonal conflict (dispute) over the way another interpersonal conflict is being handled.

◆ TABLE 9-1   Features of Cooperation and Competition

FEATURES OF COOPERATION	FEATURES OF COMPETITION
The conflict is seen as a joint problem to be solved.	*The conflict is seen as a contest, with a winner and a loser.*
It is characterized by open, honest communication of relevant information.	It is characterized by avoidance of communication, miscommunication, and misleading communication.
Disputants pool efforts to gather information (efficient in time, money).	Disputants duplicate efforts to gather information because they mistrust one another's efforts (inefficient in time, money).
Disputants try to help one another.	Disputants try to obstruct one another.
It generates feelings of friendliness; disputants tend to see one another's similarities and not see differences.	It generates feelings of enmity, hostility; disputants tend to ignore one another's similarities and focus on differences.
The dispute tends to be contained in size and tends not to spread.	Meta-conflicts and beliefs about the hostile intentions of the other disputant cause original conflict to spread and escalate.
One disputant's suggestions for resolving dispute are welcomed and respected by other disputant.	One disputant's suggestions for resolving dispute are mistrusted by the other and are seen as a devious effort to gain the upper hand (reactive devaluation).
Cooperating with the other gives an ego boost.	Cooperating with the other feels like losing face and is psychologically intolerable.
Disputants tend to be task-oriented.	"Defeating the enemy" becomes more important than staying on task.
Total productivity is maximized.	Total productivity is impaired.

as an all-out alliance—"if you're not with me, you're against me." Thus, competitive conflict tends to draw others into the escalating conflict. This phenomenon is called "polarization" (Rubin, Pruitt, & Kim 1994, 107–8). Thus, competitive conflict tends to escalate and spread, not only beyond the original boundaries of the conflict itself but also beyond the original disputants. One has only to examine the course of the twentieth century's major military conflicts to see ample evidence of this phenomenon.

Table 9-1 summarizes the major features of cooperation and competition.

Premise 2: Cooperation Tends to Be Constructive, and Competition Tends to Be Destructive. Deutsch's second major premise is that cooperation tends to be constructive, whereas competition tends to be destructive.[3] The many benefits of using cooperation, rather than competition, to resolve conflict follow directly from the ten major features of cooperation and competition.

First, cooperation is *more efficient* than competition. Because disputants are motivated to help one another, there is more effort directed at resolving the conflict. In a competition, in contrast, disputants are motivated to keep one another from reaching their goals, so they spend additional time and resources trying to

---

[3] Deutsch qualifies his assertion by noting that it is not invariably the case that all competition is destructive and further notes that, in some cases, some amount of competition is needed to induce disputants to adopt co-operative behaviors (Deutsch 1973).

impede and undermine one another. The motivation to do harm is exacerbated by the enmity each disputant comes to feel toward the other. Thus, in a competition, time and resources otherwise available to resolve the conflict are diverted to the purpose of undermining the other disputant.

In competition, there is also greater duplication of effort. Since disputants distrust one another, each gathers information independently, instead of coordinating efforts, and more time and money is spent attacking the findings of the other disputant and his or her experts. These tendencies create additional inefficiencies in the conflict resolution process.

Cooperation is also more efficient because of the nature of the information flow between disputants. Cooperating disputants are motivated to share relevant information openly and honestly, because they believe that their counterparts can better assist them in reaching their goals with more information. Thus, cooperating disputants tend to communicate efficiently and effectively. In contrast, competing disputants try to hide relevant information from one another, so the flow of information needed to resolve the conflict is impeded. It becomes expensive and time-consuming to gather the data needed to resolve the conflict.

A renowned mediator many years ago provided the following example of this relative inefficiency of competition:

> A couple came to the mediator's office to settle a divorce. As with many divorcing couples, this one entered mediation in a deeply competitive mindset, and bickered over almost everything. At some point, the dialog turned to the kitchen appliances and cookware. They had recently bought a blender, and each wanted it. The couple engaged in heated argument over the item and couldn't seem to make any progress. Finally, the mediator was able to get a word in edgewise. "You're paying me $75 an hour for mediation services. I have seen the same blender in the store

Escalating conflict causes predictable and destructive changes in the disputants' attitudes, perceptions, and interactions. Bruce Ayres, Getty Images, Inc.—Stone Allstock

for $30, but I'm happy to take your money. After all, I have mouths to feed and a child who will be going to college in a few years." After some moments of embarrassment, the couple agreed to flip a coin and buy a new blender for the loser. E. J. Koopman, (personal communication 1985.)

In addition to being more efficient, cooperation tends to *produce more effective outcomes* than competition. Because cooperating disputants see the conflict as a joint problem, rather than as a contest, their efforts tend to be devoted to solving the problem in the best way possible. Because cooperating disputants tend to be open and friendly with one another, they are more likely to share information about underlying goals, interests, values, and needs. With this information in mind, they can target their efforts to fashioning arrangements that meet those considerations effectively. Moreover, because cooperation is more efficient, more resources can be devoted to meeting the needs of both disputants effectively. Thus, cooperating disputants have the luxury of devoting more time and energy to the details that can make or break an effective outcome. In competition, on the other hand, disputants are thrown off track by the lack of reliable information and by the focus on beating the other disputant. Disputants trapped in a competition become more and more focused on simply coming out ahead of the opponent, rather than doing well in an objective sense.

Competition promotes a sort of "binary thinking" (Menkel-Meadow 1996) by promoting a focus on the conflict as a contest: "Either I win and you lose, or you win and I lose." Thus, disputants tend to characterize the conflict as "either my position wins" or "the other position wins," without any thoughts of alternative options other than perhaps the possibility of splitting the difference. Because of this binary thinking, competition has a tendency to produce less creative, less optimal, and less appropriately detailed outcomes. As an example of the limits that binary thinking imposes on competing disputants, consider the following tale popular with mediators:

> Two customers at a local library are disputing over whether to leave the window open. Dick is too hot, so he opens the window. Rene's book flaps open whenever the breeze from the open window hits it, so she closes it. After Rene closes the window, Dick becomes angry and opens it again. Rene emphatically closes it again. They try various compromises involving partially opening the window, but these satisfy neither patron. Sensing an impending riot, the librarian enters the room. Asking each customer what the problem is, she promptly walks into an adjacent room and opens the window there—problem solved. (Adapted from Fisher, Ury & Patton 1991, 40)

Cooperation is also less likely than competition to lead to *escalation and spreading of the conflict*. Cooperation is less likely than competition to lead to additional conflict. Cooperative conflict stays well contained, whereas competitive conflict escalates and spreads, creating additional problems that must be resolved.

One of the most striking examples of the tendency for competition to escalate and spread was seen in a Maryland trial court in the latter half of the twentieth century. A disgruntled spouse filed for divorce, and the proceeding became highly contentious and acrimonious. Each litigant was so competitive that the divorce was marked by many times the usual number of ancillary proceedings, such as petitions for support, modification, enforcement, contempt proceedings, and appeals. Unlike the typical contested divorce case that usually fits into a file less than 1 inch thick, this divorce filled about a foot of file space at the courthouse. The most amazing thing about the case was that, even after the death of the former spouses, the heirs of the litigants carried on the battles, recasting issues that had been pending in the domestic relations system as estates and trusts issues suitable for litigation in the Orphan's Court.[4] The dispute was known by many who worked in the courthouse as an infamous example of litigation that would never die.

Cooperation is also more *protective of relationships* than competition. The forces that lead to feelings of animosity and hostility in competitions do not operate in a cooperative conflict; on the contrary, cooperative conflict is marked by feelings of friendliness and closeness on the part of the disputants. If the disputants have an ongoing relationship to protect, this aspect of cooperation can be extremely important. Examples of disputants who need to protect ongoing relationships include divorcing parents of minor children, business partners, those attempting to establish or maintain a business relationship (such as repeat buyers and sellers), employers and employees, schools, parents, teachers and students, and landlords and tenants. The positive regard promoted by cooperation can improve relationships on multiple fronts; thus, the advantages go beyond the immediate conflict itself to improving the relationship altogether.

Even disputants whose relationships will be temporary have an interest in sustaining positive mutual regard for the duration of their conflict, in order to take advantage of the other positive and constructive aspects of cooperation. It is easier to sustain a cooperative interaction when the disputants or their teams are not distracted by negative feelings toward those on the other team. Moreover, it is easier to get your interests satisfied by a disputant on the other team whose regard for you is positive.

Finally, outcomes achieved in a cooperative conflict tend to be *more durable* than outcomes reached in a competitive conflict. There are several reasons for this phenomenon. First, as previously noted, outcomes achieved via cooperation tend to be better suited to each disputant than outcomes achieved via competition. Hence, each disputant has less reason to stop abiding by arrangements reached in a cooperative process.

Second, disputants who reach an agreement using a cooperative process tend to feel that they were responsible for the development of the particulars of the arrangement: they feel that the agreement was the result of the exercise of their own personal power. Conflict resolution specialists call this phenomenon **psychological ownership.** People who feel psychological ownership of an outcome are more likely

---

Psychological ownership
a phenomenon in which a disputant feels that the outcome of a conflict is psychologically "his or her own."

---

[4] In Maryland courts, the Orphan's Court is responsible for handling matters involving decedents' estates.

to want to preserve and protect it. In a cooperative conflict, both disputants tend to feel psychological ownership of the outcome. In a competitive conflict, an outcome tends to be psychologically owned by, at most, one of the disputants. The other disputant tends to feel that the outcome was imposed by "the enemy" and will take every available opportunity to sabotage, impede, or challenge its terms. Psychological ownership is closely related to another concept called **quality of consent,** which is the extent to which the process used to resolve conflict, and the conflict, ultimate outcome, were freely consented to by the disputants.

Quality of consent

the extent to which the conflict resolution process and outcome are freely consented to by the disputants. Processes that possess a high quality of consent tend to yield outcomes that are psychologically owned by the disputants. (See a more detailed discussion in Chapter 16.)

Finally, because disputants in a cooperative conflict have more positive, friendly feelings toward one another, they are more likely to protect the terms of the arrangement they have reached in order to preserve the relationship. If a particular part of the agreement is less advantageous to one disputant, he or she tends to be more willing to overlook it in the interests of satisfying the other disputant. Even if an aspect of the arrangements they have made turns out not to function as well as expected, cooperating disputants are more likely to be able to negotiate a modification, thus allowing the overall arrangements to survive. Competitive disputants are more likely to gloat over a provision that causes disadvantage to "the enemy" and to be suspicious of any efforts by the other disputant to modify provisions. Overall, disputants in a cooperative conflict tend to be

- More satisfied with outcomes they have attained
- More likely to abide by and preserve the outcome they have attained

Premise 3: Deutsch's Crude Axiom: Cooperation Begets Cooperation and Competition Begets Competition. A disputant's perceptions regarding whether the conflict is cooperative or competitive will produce conduct that tends to reinforce this perception. In other words, cooperation and competition tend to be self-fulfilling prophecies. This premise is referred to as "Deutsch's Crude Axiom."

You'll recall that one recurring theme in conflict diagnosis is that conflict participants, who are unable to read the minds of other participants, tend to use the conflict itself as a source of information about their motivations. Imagine a disputant, Disputant X, who thinks of the conflict he is in as cooperative. This disputant will try to help the other disputant, Disputant Y, since he believes it will also help him. As Disputant X tries to help Disputant Y meet her interests and needs, Disputant Y will typically (unless other factors intervene) notice the helpful behavior.[5] Disputant Y will have evidence, and therefore probably infer, that Disputant X is motivated to help her. Thus, Disputant X's actions generate a belief in Disputant Y that their interdependence is promotive. Disputant Y will typically respond to this inference in the most self-interested fashion: by helping Disputant X.

A converse phenomenon occurs in competitive conflict. If Disputant X thinks of the conflict as competitive, he will tend to engage in obstructive,

---

[5] If the other disputant perceives the conflict as competitive, it may impede her ability to perceive the efforts of the first disputant to help her. This phenomenon is discussed later in the chapter.

misleading behavior, behavior that tends to impede rapid resolution of the conflict and to harm Disputant Y. Disputant Y, seeing this behavior, will probably conclude that, if she helps Disputant X, she will be harmed. Thus, to protect herself, Disputant Y is motivated to try to obstruct Disputant X from his goals. Disputant X has his suspicions confirmed by this behavior by Disputant Y, and so on.

Another way to express this premise is to describe both cooperation and competition as *cyclical processes* driven by the perceptions of the disputants. Figure 9-1 shows the cooperation cycle, and Figure 9-2 shows the competition cycle. It is worth studying these diagrams closely. Consider how each applies to situations and relationships you have experienced.

It is worth noting that, the more objective information about the conflict is possessed by each disputant, the less the disputant is likely to be swayed by the other's behavior in the conflict. The phenomenon of disputants using the conflict to make assessments about the conflict itself is exacerbated when participants are poorly informed about the conflict. A very well-prepared participant—one who has studied the situation, knows his or her own interests, and the interests of other participants, has learned as much as he or she can about the other participants, and knows where he or she stands in the conflict—has less need to draw inferences from the course of the conflict. Thus, being very well prepared is a factor insulating a conflict participant from being misled by the forces that influence perception in a conflict. In legal disputing, the gathering of information about the dispute is often called "case preparation." If you are a legal professional or have studied the legal process, you will be familiar with the steps of preparing a case:

◆ **FIGURE 9-1**

Cooperation Cycle

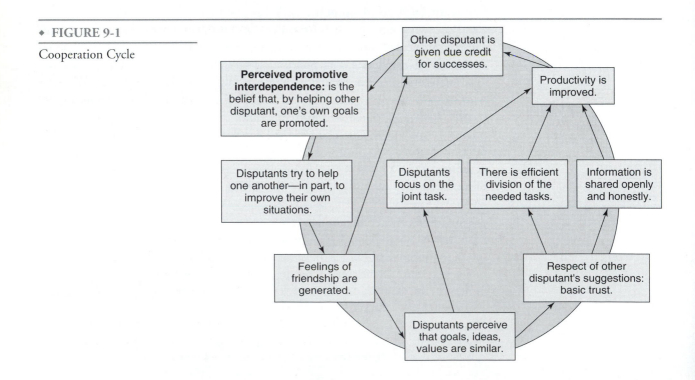

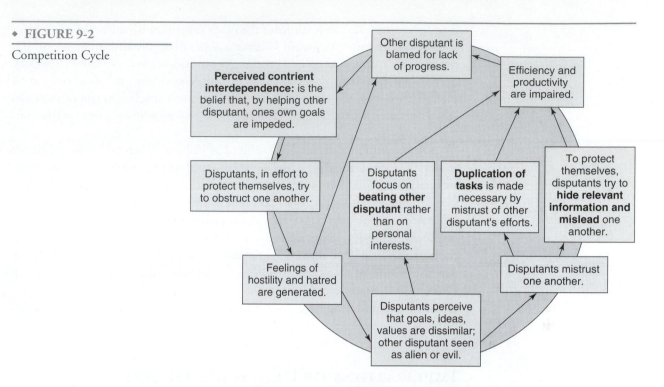

1. Researching the applicable law
2. Investigating the applicable facts
3. Interviewing and assessing the possible witnesses
4. Gathering and organizing the relevant documentary and other evidentiary materials

These steps, so essential to preparing a lawsuit for litigation, paradoxically have the power to minimize the destructive effect of competitive conflict. Since the person in possession of this information has less need to draw inferences about the conflict from the behavior of the other disputant, he or she is less likely to be drawn in by the perceptual distortions caused by competitive conflict. On the other hand, the more resources that are used to gather information about a legal dispute, the sillier it often seems not to pursue a lawsuit—"I've already done all the work to get it ready for trial; why not just go the last little bit and try the darn thing?" Rubin, Pruitt, and Kim (1994, 111–16), refer to this phenomenon as "overcommitment," an impediment to cooperation that will be discussed in Chapter 11.

Premise 4: It Is Easier to Move from Cooperation to Competition Than Vice Versa. Deutsch's final premise about cooperation and competition is that cooperation is relatively fragile. His studies indicated to him that it is easier to move from cooperation to competition than vice versa. People never have perfect knowledge about one another, and, in their fear and suspicion, they tend to set in motion protective actions that promote competition. For example, a disputant may hide the truth from the other disputant because, although he or she thinks the other disputant is being cooperative, the disputant is not 100 percent sure. Moreover, in any conflict, communication is typically imperfect. Betrayal of trust can occur through misunderstanding, the intervention of third parties, missed communication, and so on. A single betrayal of trust can set in motion the perceptual cycle leading to the beginnings of destructive conflict escalation.

On the other hand, once a conflict has become competitive, it is difficult to derail. Because the disputants are mistrustful of one another, they are likely to interpret one another's actions as maliciously motivated. Reactive devaluation and other similar processes prevent the disputants from recognizing or acknowledging one another's truly cooperative efforts; hence, efforts by one disputant to break a competition cycle may be ignored, denigrated, or exploited by a suspicious other disputant. Competition cycles tend to be marked by abortive efforts to break the cycle. Disputants who stick their necks out in an effort to cooperate, only to be rebuffed, are likely to become even more entrenched in competition, because they are likely to conclude that the other disputant is incorrigible.

IMPLICATIONS OF DEUTSCH'S THEORY FOR CONFLICT DIAGNOSIS

Deutsch's theory of constructive and destructive conflict has a number of implications for conflict diagnosticians.

The Desirability of Seeking a Cooperative Relationship. Competition is saddled with a number of significant disadvantages, compared with cooperation.

Deutsch himself notes that not all competitive conflicts are destructive. He states, first, that a benevolent and powerful disputant may be able to impose a useful solution and, second, that sometimes competition and the pain it causes are essential to motivate future cooperation (Deutsch 1973, 31–32). It might also be noted that not all cooperative conflicts are constructive: cooperative conflict resolution that involves a more powerful party's simply imposing its will, however unwelcome, on a disempowered and compliant other is clearly not what Deutsch had in mind for the paradigm of a cooperative conflict. Nonetheless, Deutsch recognized the inherent destructiveness of the competitive process, concluding that

> [t]here are pathogenic processes inherent in competitive conflict—such as perceptual distortion, self-deception, unwitting involvement—that tend to magnify and perpetuate conflict. (Deutsch 1973, 47)

In general, a principal task of a conflict diagnostician is to determine whether a conflict is caught in a competitive cycle, and to what extent. If it is caught, the conflict diagnostician often looks at whether there are steps that can be taken to break the cycle without causing harm to the participants. And, if the conflict is still cooperative, the conflict diagnostician will want to consider whether there are steps that can be taken to keep it that way.

Steps That Influence the Conflict Cycle. To determine what interventions should be applied to preserve or improve the constructiveness of a conflict, conflict diagnosticians rely on the idea that one can change the actual course of a conflict by changing the disputants' perceptions about the conflict. In other words, referring to the process shown in Figure 9-2, one can step in and break the cycle at any point. In particular, competing disputants can, with understanding, skill, and effort, be nudged into a more cooperative frame of mind if they can be made to change their perceptions about the conflict. Table 9-2 lists some useful approaches.

A very common method of refocusing disputants away from competitive perception is simply for the conflict professional to avoid using language that suggests that the conflict is a competition or battle. For example, an expert ADR professional will often avoid words such as *opponent, adversary, plaintiff,* and *defendant* or similar emotionally loaded terms to identify disputants, using instead words such as *partner, other disputant,* or *codisputant,* or simply the individual's name. An ADR professional may also engineer activities specifically designed to alter perceptions. For example, a skilled mediator often assigns an easy task to the disputants, one that the disputants are required to complete together to move forward in the mediation. If the disputants are successful, the mediator will immediately call the disputants' attention to the fact that the actions of one disputant had the effect of improving the status of the other disputant. This tactic is designed to focus the disputants on promotively interdependent aspects of their relationship. Another common mediator tactic is to find a way to ally the two disputants against a common enemy—for example, if the disputants are in conflict about dividing an asset, the mediator may recast the issue into a problem of minimizing the tax liability of the allocation (refocusing the disputants against the IRS). In a different tactic with the same aim, the mediator may make an outrageous suggestion for resolving the conflict, creating an alliance of the two disputants against the mediator. In either case, the tactic is designed to interrupt that part of the competition cycle at which the disputant are focused on difference and dissimilarity and to replace that perception with one of similarity. Moreover, there is a vast body of social psychological evidence that placing people in a single group allied against another group creates amicable feelings, cooperativeness, and a sense of similarity. Thus, this tactic also improves the feelings of the disputants toward one another and imparts a sense that their goals and values are similar.

Resolve Conflicts Early (but Not Too Early). Another important point to take from Deutsch's work is that it is important to try to resolve conflicts fairly early, while they are still cooperative. Since cooperative relationships become competitive easily, but not vice versa, early intervention helps prevent conflict from entering a competitive cycle. This point has relevance when deciding at what point to begin an ADR process or another intervention, and it is of particular significance in legal disputes.

◆ **TABLE 9-2** Techniques That Can Interrupt the Competitive Conflict Cycle

TECHNIQUE	STEP IN COMPETITION CYCLE AFFECTED	EXAMPLE
Choose language with care	Perception of contrient interdependence	Instead of calling the disputants "opponents," call them "Mary" and "Jane." Instead of referring to the conflict as a "dispute," refer to it as "the problem we need to solve." Instead of asking disputants to "state their positions," ask them to "talk about their goals for the process."
Assign joint tasks	Perception of contrient interdependence *and* perception of inefficiency in conflict resolution	Business partners disputing over the appropriate assignment of the venture's profits are assigned to interview jointly a CPA to learn some steps they can take to increase overall profitability.
"Expand the pie"	Perception of contrient interdependence	Spouses disputing over a property settlement are encouraged to characterize a payment as alimony—the wealthier spouse receives a tax deduction bigger than the tax the other spouse will have to pay on the amount received. The overall benefit is allocated between the spouses, so both are better off.
Establish ground rules for civility in communication	Perception of enmity between disputants	An ADR neutral requires each disputant to refrain from "bad-mouthing" the other and takes the time to guide each disputant in using complimentary, polite discourse.
Create or focus on a common enemy	Perception of enmity; hostility; perception of contrient interdependence	In a custody dispute, the parents' advocates reframe the issue into a problem of how the parents can convince a mother-in-law who has created friction in the past of the merits of a proposed parenting plan.
Point out areas of agreement	Perception of difference in values and principles	The disputant's advocate makes sure to comment, "So, you agree about that," each time the disputant mentions something that has already been resolved.
Focus blame away from the disputant and toward process	Perception that other disputant is at fault for failure to progress in a conflict	In response to a disputant's complaint about the other disputant's not complying with a prior agreement, counsel says, "So those arrangements didn't work for you. Let's work on making some new, more effective, and workable arrangements."
Prepare "the case"	Minimization of the impact of Deutsch's Crude Axiom	The disputant is encouraged to get all the information he or she can about the factual and legal aspects of the dispute and to perform an in-depth conflict diagnosis.
Use trust-building exercises	Lack of trust between disputants	Disputants are encouraged to confirm the accuracy of one another's statements. The ADR professional gently guides the suspicious disputant into realizing that the other disputant has, in fact, been behaving as the disputant would have, had he or she believed the same thing.
Set up structure to create sharing of information	Tendency to obfuscate or mislead	The mediator requires the sharing of tax forms to confirm the income information of the disputants. The mediator asks each disputant to back up claims about expenditures with receipts and other documentation.

Litigation is an adversary process—which means that it is competitive. It has a winner and a loser, and the process involves a contest between adversaries. As such, litigation is fraught with all the disadvantages attributable to competitive conflict in general.

Experts in conflict resolution often use a variety of tactics to influence the disputants into believing the situation is cooperative, thus taking advantage of Deutsch's Crude Axiom. Bob Dammrich, The Image Works

The Ubiquitous Language of Competition in Legal Negotiation

A couple with two children sought help from a mediator to ensure that their impending separation and divorce did not become locked into an escalating and destructive cycle. In the initial mediation session, the clients and mediator discussed the use of the separation agreement that would be developed in mediation. The mediator explained to them that the finished document would render the divorce uncontested and that the usual practice was to attach a copy of the agreement to the initiating pleading, the complaint for divorce.

The eyes of one of the spouses, a professional writer, widened. "If there are no contested issues left, why do they still call it a complaint?" he asked incredulously.

The mediator could give no answer other than to reaffirm the adversarial focus of the legal system, and the client could only shake his head in disbelief. "Isn't that ridiculous? That's why we are in mediation!"

In any legal dispute, litigation is on the horizon, so, even if disputants aren't already in court, their negotiations take place in the knowledge that a competitive process looms on the horizon. One seminal piece of scholarship called this phenomenon "bargaining in the shadow of the law" (Mnookin & Kornhauser 1979). Thus, legal disputants are pushed toward competition even when they are trying to avoid court. ADR reformers have tried to make litigation less inevitable, and ADR processes more mandatory, for just this reason.

On the other hand, litigation provides important fairness protections for litigants: evidentiary and discovery rules, the right to a neutral forum, and the right to place one's case in the best possible light. Legal policymakers are still struggling to balance the need to make legal disputing less competitive with the due process protections the adversarial legal system provides.

If parties to a legal dispute get too far into a litigation process, they tend to get frozen into their competitive orientation. Moreover, the substantial

"This is where your mother and I had our first argument."

The Cartoon Bank

investment of time and money into preparing for battle may create overcommitment, a feeling that the disputants have come too far to turn back. But, if disputants start a dispute settlement process too early, the disputants may not be emotionally ready to settle (Pruitt & Olczak 1995, 59–92, refer to this readiness as "ripeness"; see Chapter 11), and they may not yet have the information they need to make a good decision.

EXERCISES, PROJECTS, AND "THOUGHT EXPERIMENTS"

1. *Conflict journal.*
   a. Assess whether the main conflict is primarily competitive or cooperative. Using the definitions of *cooperation* and *competition* advanced in this chapter, justify your answer.
   b. Explain how each of the ten essential characteristics of cooperation and competition are playing out in the main conflict. You should *apply* the characteristics to your conflict and be specific about how these characteristics manifest themselves in your conflict.
   c. Considering the ideas in this chapter, do you think you could improve the situation by changing the overall orientation of the conflict (for in-

stance, if the conflict is primarily competitive, would it help to make it more cooperative)? Why?

   d. Consider Deutsch's Crude Axiom. Looking at each "node" in the cooperation and competition cycles (each box in Figure 9-1 and Figure 9-2), identify a specific act you, or your team, could do that would influence the conflict to become more cooperative by altering that node.

   e. How could you influence the conflict to become more "ripe" for cooperation?

2. Is it practical to try to make a legal dispute more cooperative once the dispute has entered litigation? Why or why not?

3. Patty Plaintiff and Donnie Defendant are in settlement negotiations over a fender-bender. Patty has demanded $15,000 for medical expenses and damage to her car. Donnie has been unwilling to offer more than $1,000. After two weeks without any communication, Donnie's attorney, Debbie, has just called and abruptly offered Patty $14,950 to settle the case.

   a. If the disputants and their lawyers are in a cooperative relationship, how is Patty most likely to react?

   b. Would your answer change if the disputants and their lawyers were in a highly competitive relationship? Why or why not?

4. What are the risks to the client for attorneys to attempt cooperative approaches to resolving conflict? What are the risks to the client for attorneys *not* to make a diligent effort to cooperate in settling the client's dispute? Where should attorneys draw the line between protecting the client from exploitation and protecting the client from escalating and destructive conflict?

5. Consider the issues presented in exercise 4. Are there ways that the client can get the best of both worlds by having a cooperative but protective attorney engaged in a process that both can be assured will have cooperative features? One solution, suggested by others, is the concept of "collaborative law" (discussed further in Chapter 22). The organizations HALT (*http://www.halt.org/FLIP/CLP.cfm*) and the Collaborative Law Institute (*http://www.collaborativelaw.org*) post information and links where you can get more information about this innovation. Prepare a report discussing the advantages and disadvantages of collaborative law for improving the constructiveness of legal disputes.

6. Consider the Israeli-Palestinian dispute. What signs do you see that the conflict is in a destructive cycle? (You should look at the ten essential characteristics of cooperation and competition and apply each of them to the situation.) Can you think of ways that the United States, or other countries, might be able to influence the course of the conflict by effecting a change to a "node" (one of the boxes in Figure 9-1 and Figure 9-2) of the cooperation or competition cycle?

7. During the months leading up to Operation Desert Storm in 1990–1991, President George H.W. Bush made a number of diplomatic moves, which

he said were designed to avoid going to war with Iraq. However, he also announced publicly that he would not allow Saddam Hussein to save face. Were President Bush's comments about saving face consistent with his stated goal of avoiding military confrontation? Why or why not? Use the ideas you have learned in this chapter to justify your assertions.

8. How important is cooperation in a workplace environment? (Look at the ten essential characteristics of cooperation and competition and assess their relevance to the workplace.) Do you think those at the top of a business organization would want to improve cooperation among employees in the workplace? Why? Is there any danger to individual employees in a move to increase workplace cooperation? What steps might be taken to protect the interests of workers while facilitating an environment of cooperation?

RECOMMENDED READINGS

Bunker, B. B., J. Z. Rubin, and Associates (eds.). 1995. Cooperation. In *Conflict, cooperation and justice: Essays inspired by the work of Morton Deutsch* (pp. 133–257). San Francisco: Jossey-Bass.

Deutsch, M. 1973. *The resolution of conflict: Constructive and destructive processes.* New Haven, CT: Yale University Press.

Deutsch, M. 2000. Cooperation and competition. In *The handbook of conflict resolution: Theory and practice* (pp. 21–40), edited by M. Deutsch and P. T. Coleman. San Francisco: Jossey-Bass.

Rubin, J. Z., D. G. Pruitt, and S. H. Kim. 1994. *Social conflict: Escalation, stalemate, and settlement.* New York: McGraw-Hill.

10

Step 5. Assess the Levels of Trust and Develop Strategies to Increase or Preserve It

"It takes years to build up trust, and only seconds to destroy it."

—Author unknown

"A verbal contract isn't worth the paper it's written on."

—Samuel Goldwyn

In this chapter, you will learn …

- That, according to one prominent theory, there are three levels of trust: calculus-based trust, knowledge-based trust, and identification-based trust.
- That some forms of trust are harder to establish than others.
- That some forms of trust are more useful than others.
- That lack of trust is not the same thing as active distrust.
- That high levels of trust carry distinct advantages for disputants.
- That high levels of trust are not always attainable.
- That a "business relationship" can protect disputants when trust is low or distrust is high.

Aretha and Rae have been best buddies since middle school. Now they are sophomores together at a large state college. They used to do everything together—they studied together, ate together, and relied on one another to keep each other's most intimate thoughts and secrets.

Last semester, Aretha confided in Rae that she has become interested in Josh, a junior in their geology class. Aretha hasn't had the guts to reveal her feelings to Josh yet. At the Christmas dance, Aretha noticed Rae, who had had rather a lot to drink, spending a considerable amount of time with Josh. Since then,

Josh, who had been friendly, seems more distant from Aretha. She has begun to suspect that Rae is hitting on Josh. Aretha confronted Rae, who angrily denied it. But doubt has begun to poison Aretha's feelings about Rae. Anytime she and Rae are apart, she imagines her friend and Josh together. Rae has started to pull away. Is it because she, Aretha, has changed her behavior or because Rae is seeing Josh? Aretha can't tell. She only knows that she feels that she no longer knows or trusts her good friend. The sense of betrayal in her heart follows her wherever she goes, and she can say without reservation that her life has changed for the worst.

Trust
a state of mind in which a person believes that another person intends to be helpful and, accordingly, that it is appropriate to take risks in the relationship.

The behaviors essential to maintaining a constructive and cooperative relationship involve an element of risk. To risk the open communication and altruistic behavior that makes cooperative sharing of tasks possible, each disputant must believe that the other will not exploit the situation. The attitude that allows this risk taking behavior is known as *trust*.

Trust, for purposes of this discussion, is defined as

> a state of mind in which a person believes that another person intends to be helpful and that, accordingly, it is appropriate to take risks in the relationship.

Even a single threat to mutual trust can turn a cooperative relationship into an escalating competition. One unreturned phone call, careless remark, failure to share information, or erroneous factual representation can have the effect of betrayal. Once trust has been damaged, a suspicious disputant begins to question the motives of the other, leading to inefficiencies in information gathering, obstacles to free information sharing, and erosion of friendly feelings. The competition cycle, with its "pathogenic perceptual distortions," is set in motion.

When trust is threatened, the mistrustful person suspects that the other may harm or exploit him or her, and risky behaviors, such as information and effort sharing, are abandoned as dangerous. Moreover, a mistrustful person in a conflict is likely to see his or her own well-being as dependent on self-defense. Mistrust is therefore associated with aggressive behavior and the escalation of destructive conflict.

LEVELS OF TRUST

Organizational and management psychologists Debra Shapiro, Blair Sheppard, and Lisa Cheraskin (1992) propose that there is great utility in identifying several kinds, or levels, of trust. Some are easier to attain than others, and some serve broader interests than others. The levels of trust are:

- Calculus-based trust
- Knowledge-based trust
- Identification-based trust

CALCULUS-BASED TRUST

The first, and most basic level of trust is called *calculus-based trust* (Lewicki & Bunker 1995).[1] Calculus-based trust is trust based on knowledge of the consequences of compliance or noncompliance. Shapiro, Sheppard, and Cheraskin (1992, 366–67) give the following vivid example of calculus-based trust. During the Cold War, leaders of both the United States and the Soviet Union negotiated the so-called Mutually Assured Destruction policy to institute calculus-based trust between the two hostile nations. Upon the policy's implementation, members of each country could be assured that any nuclear-missile-based aggression by one country could mean their complete destruction—the missile treaties that had been negotiated by the two nations disallowed any effective missile defense. Since no one wants to be destroyed, members of each nation could count on the other nation to refrain from any intentional efforts to launch nuclear missiles at the other. Thus, the Mutually Assured Destruction policy depended on calculus-based trust to operate effectively.

In legal disputes, provisions founded on calculus-based trust are common in settlement agreements and court judgments. For example, agreements calling for payments often include clauses requiring the payment of interest and penalties if payments are late. Disputants are made aware of the fact that refusal to comply with settlement provisions can mean being hauled into court, made to produce information about assets, and even forced to sell property. These threats of inconvenience and penalty are usually enough to promote compliance and to create minimal levels of peace of mind in those insisting on their inclusion.

The incentives that can produce calculus-based trust are as varied as the individuals involved, and they do not always involve money. An attorney explains that she had this point brought home to her when she was a neophyte attorney and volunteer for Legal Aid. In her very first trial, she was asked to represent a penniless client who had spent her last bit of money to purchase a mobile home so defective that it was uninhabitable. The lawyer worked hard on the case and

---

> ### *Calculus-Based Trust*
>
> * Trust based on knowledge that the other person won't want to incur the consequences of betrayal
> * Narrow applicability to the action for which consequences are in place
> * Easiest type of trust to establish

---

[1] Shapiro, Sheppard, and Cheraskin (1992), who developed the stage theory of trust, called this stage "deterrence-based trust" and defined it as trust based on consequences of noncompliance. Lewicki and Bunker (1995, 133–74), in their extension of Shapiro's model, generalized deterrence-based trust to the broader calculus-based trust, which added the positive consequences of compliance to the negative consequences of noncompliance.

won easily in small claims court against the mobile home seller, but the defendant had no particular motivation to pay: he seemed to have no scruples whatsoever—that is, not until, in desperation, the lawyer filed for supplementary proceedings (which are court proceedings in which the defendant is required to answer questions under oath, in court, about his or her assets). The night before the supplementary proceedings were scheduled, the owner of the dealership delivered a cashier's check for the amount of the judgment to the lawyer, personally, at her home. The defendant had meetings scheduled throughout the following day and could not afford to take the morning off to spend it in court. This gentleman was unconcerned about his reputation for delivering defective goods and probably would not have minded lying under oath about his assets (since he had evidently twisted the facts freely at trial), but he had a busy life and considered its interruption to be a significant deterrent.

Calculus-based trust is the easiest type of trust to create. All you need is an enforceable contract and some basic knowledge of the kinds of deterrents and incentives that are likely to be effective. Generally, establishing calculus-based trust requires only a minimal acquaintance with the other disputant: enough acquaintance to verify the impact of any incentives and penalties built into the arrangements. Shapiro and colleagues (1992) also comment that more broad-based trustworthy behavior can be the result of calculus-based trust. The termination of a profitable relationship can act as the deterrent that creates calculus-based trust. Thus, if disputants develop a longer-term or multifaceted relationship, the overall disadvantages of doing something to destroy the relationship can create incentives to behave in a broader, more trustworthy manner. Further, individuals operating in a public arena, such as businesses that transact with many other entities, risk loss of reputation if they breach trust. Thus, the loss of reputation can also act as the source of calculus-based trust.

On the other hand, calculus-based trust does relatively little to build a relationship beyond preventing the open outbreak of conflict. Indeed, packing a contract with a lot of penalty clauses may have the opposite effect: it is likely to encourage hostility between the disputants and therefore may promote the competition cycle. Moreover, calculus-based trust often has only narrow applicability. It will promote rewarded conduct and prevent the other disputant from engaging in the behavior to be penalized, but it will not prevent the other disputant from exploiting or harming in other areas (unless the parties are engaged in a continuing course of dealing with intrinsic advantages for both). For this reason, calculus-based trust is not the best choice if other levels of trust are attainable and appropriate.

KNOWLEDGE-BASED TRUST

The second level of trust is known as *knowledge-based trust.* Knowledge-based trust is based on one disputant's knowledge and understanding of the other disputant. For example, if a woman needs to leave her children with their regular baby-sitter while she attends a business meeting, she can trust that the baby-sitter will keep them safe because of her longstanding history of having done so in the

> ### *Knowledge-Based Trust*
>
> ◆ Trust based on knowledge of the other person's habits, traits, attitudes, principles, and values
>
> ◆ Applicability to all actions about which relevant characteristics of the person are known
>
> ◆ Establishment dependent on knowing the other person well enough to acquire the relevant knowledge

past. The mother may also have knowledge of the baby-sitter's background, skills, education, and apparent values, as displayed in numerous social contexts in which the mother has observed her in the past.

Obviously, you cannot establish a relationship that relies on knowledge-based trust if you do not know the other disputant, or if the other disputant has been acting in ways that cause you to question your knowledge. Thus, the establishment of knowledge-based trust is usually unwarranted in new relationships, in very short-term relationships, and in relationships caught up in a competition cycle.[2] For these situations, it is usually more appropriate to rely on calculus-based trust. After a period of effective functioning, relationships expected to be needed for the long term can begin to convert to a greater reliance on knowledge-based trust. The advantages of knowledge-based trust include the ability to function in a less formalized manner (for example, being able to rely on oral or implicit agreements rather than formalized, written agreements that take time to structure and follow) and the broader applicability of the trust to all areas in which the disputants have knowledge of one another's attitudes, motives, education and training, skills, and abilities.

IDENTIFICATION-BASED TRUST

The highest level of trust is *identification-based trust*. Identification-based trust is founded on the disputants' sense of identification with one another. Because the disputants identify with one another, they tend, as do all groups with a sense of solidarity, to see themselves as being "as one" in their goals, values, and needs (Hamilton & Trolier 1986, 127–63; Wilder 1981, 213–57). Thus, it is intrinsically satisfying to a disputant in a relationship characterized by identification-based trust to meet the perceived needs of the other disputant.

Business organizations that indoctrinate their new employees into the company, and devote resources to building company spirit, are exploiting the advantages of identification-based trust. By helping employees build a strong sense of identification with the organization, employers hope that these employees will

---

[2] Disputants caught up in a competition cycle are prone to believe that the other disputant's actions constitute betrayal, as discussed in Chapter 9.

> ### *Identification-Based Trust*
>
> - Trust based on a sense of identification, or "oneness," with the other person
> - Broad applicability to entire relationship
> - Establishment is very difficult: requires a period of intimacy, partnership during a crisis, or another intense interconnection

Identification-based trust makes productive interaction much easier to accomplish. John Labbe, Getty Images Inc.—Image Bank

come to see corporate goals as synonymous with their own, so that they will be motivated to act in a trustworthy manner. Because identification-based trust affects a disputant's entire identity, it applies broadly to an entire relationship. Thus, once established, it is the most effective and useful kind of trust to have. Identification-based trust obviates much of the need for formality and even overt communication: people who identify with one another just simply want to help one another in any way they can.

In intimate relationships, such as those between family members, preserving identification-based trust is more important than the specific substantive agreements reached. For example, two spouses who are arguing over the best color to paint a bedroom generally have a much greater need to preserve their mutual sense of identification with one another than to resolve the issue of the paint color. Thus, a spouse who unilaterally paints the room while the other is out of town for the weekend ends the dispute but clouds the larger relationship with a sense of betrayal and mistrust. On the other hand, in nonintimate relationships, the establishment of identification-based trust is highly utilitarian, and wonderful if it can be achieved, but not central to the purpose of the relationship. Sometimes, the desire to regain identification-based trust can even be damaging. For example, formerly intimate disputants whose intimate relationship has gone bad, such as divorcing spouses, often unconsciously expect to be able to rely on identification-based trust and experience the failure of identification-based trust as a painful betrayal. Thus, a conflict diagnostician should consider what sort of relationship the disputants have or are trying to establish. A conflict diagnostician who is diagnosing conflict in an intimate relationship, one that the disputants expect to continue, would see a greater need to establish or preserve identification-based trust than if he or she were diagnosing a conflict between nonintimate disputants. Disputants who are ending an intimate relationship may have to be guided explicitly into a lower level of trust, one more suited to their new connections.

Identification-based trust is the most difficult of all types of trust to establish, particularly for people who have a history of mistrust and mutual suspicion. For extremely short-term relationships, it can be very difficult to use at all—although, in some lucky happenstances, disputants have a commonality that a dispute resolution professional can exploit to create identification-based trust.

Table 10-1 summarizes the levels of trust and gives examples of how they function in potentially conflicted relationships.

◆ **TABLE 10-1**   Kinds and Levels of Trust According to Shapiro, Sheppard, and Cheraskin (1992)

LEVEL OF TRUST	DEFINITION	EXAMPLE
Calculus-based	Trust based on the knowledge of the effect of compliance or noncompliance	A consumer signs an auto loan that states that, should the buyer default on the loan, the car can be repossessed and the buyer held liable for all costs of repossession and sale, including attorney's fees; the seller trusts the buyer's intention to repay the purchase price because of the consequences of failing to do so.
Knowledge-based	Trust based on the knowledge that the disputant has of the other disputant	One partner in a restaurant gives a large amount of cash to the other partner to deposit at the bank, knowing that, in the twenty years they have worked together, the other partner has never misappropriated funds.
Identification-based	Trust based on the feelings of oneness of identity, goals, and/or purpose that the disputant feels for the other disputant	New employees of a fast-food establishment are given a four-week indoctrination into the values of the company. They are taken to a forest retreat and participate in a lengthy and emotional program whose purposes are to promote mutual trust among employees and to foster a strong sense of identity with the company.

MISTRUST

Is mistrust merely the absence of each of the three levels of trust? Lewicki and Wiethoff (2000, 86–107) regard mistrust as a separate phenomenon. Although a relationship with low levels of all kinds of trust may mean uncertainty for disputants, actual mistrust is considered a state in which one individual actively believes that the other is likely to do him or her harm. Thus, disputants in a state of mistrust are actively motivated to protect themselves from the other disputant. On the other hand, although trust and mistrust are separate phenomena, clearly they are related in the sense that trust is more difficult to establish when mistrust is present. In that sense, they are mutually exclusive.

ORIGINS OF TRUST

Trust comes from a variety of sources. Calculus-based trust can come directly from provisions in contracts that give people incentive not to harm one another, as when an agreement specifies penalties for breach. Since a contract is all that is needed to create this form of trust, it is relatively easy to establish. It can be created even between hostile adversaries using a penalty system. Calculus-based trust can also come from the course of dealing itself: in a continuing relationship, often each disputant can count on the other disputant to preserve the course of dealing because of its intrinsic advantages for those involved.

Knowledge-based trust comes from any situation in which people become well acquainted with one another—a longstanding business relationship, a friendship, and so on. Knowledge-based trust need not be based on intimate knowledge of the other disputant: it may be relatively narrow and based on a course of dealing. Knowledge-based trust can also come from any situation in which it's clear that interests are not in conflict. Shapiro and colleagues (1992) note that the cooperation cycle itself tends to promote knowledge-based trust, since it tends to promote the belief in each disputant that the other is acting and will act in a trustworthy way.

Since knowledge-based trust can come from the experience of dealing with a person whose motives and behaviors are otherwise unknown, a course of dealing based originally on calculus-based trust can ultimately produce knowledge-based trust. Thus, disputants who expect to enter a long-term relationship sometimes establish a contractual relationship based on calculus-based trust. A period of successful relations based on abiding by the contract often produces knowledge-based trust. Shapiro and colleagues (1992) note that promoting a structure of regular communication also promotes knowledge-based trust, as does engaging in "courtship" processes (such as pre-contract meetings), conducting research about the other disputant, performing interests analyses, and performing other activities designed to increase one's knowledge of the other disputant.

Knowledge of the sort required to establish knowledge-based trust can also be obtained in some cases through investigation and research. For example, a job applicant may be able to obtain enough information about his or her prospective employer to determine the employer's likely course of dealing, likely salary and benefits offer, and likely job environment; thus, in working out the details of an employment contract, research about the potential employer can enhance the candidate's knowledge-based trust of the employer.

Identification-based trust is hardest to establish. It is most commonly found in intimate and well-functioning family relationships, as between lovers, spouses, and parents and children. It is also created in situations involving a joint venture that both disputants care about deeply (for example, participants in the space program), as well as in situations in which disputants share clear values (such as when they are both members of the same advocacy group). Identification-based trust may be founded on mutual involvement in a serious crisis or test of survival, as when neighbors endure a natural disaster together or college freshmen are thrown together in their first year of independent living. Identification-based trust is also created by a long-functioning cooperation cycle. You will recall that the cooperation cycle promotes both good feelings between disputants and the tendency to focus on shared goals and values to the exclusion of divergent and conflicting goals and values. These two elements, positive regard and unity of purpose, support the creation of identification-based trust.

EFFECTS OF TRUST

For a number of reasons, it is very useful to operate with high levels of trust, particularly with identification-based trust. First, the higher the level of trust, the greater the likelihood of perpetuating a cooperation cycle. Considerable trust can help buffer disputants against inadvertently betraying one another. For example, imagine how the U.S. government is likely to react to a "friendly fire" incident caused by its Canadian or British allies, with whom a high level of trust has been established, compared with its likely reaction to the same incident committed by the Russians or the Chinese. High levels of trust also obviate the need for much of the formality required in a relationship marked by low levels of trust. Since the disputants know that the other disputant is likely to be helpful, there is reduced need to document the parties' decisions. Thus, highly trusting disputants tend to work very efficiently together. High levels of trust eliminate a lot of the risks and guesswork of working with strangers. And high levels of trust are just downright pleasant.

What about the impact of low levels of trust? Typical situations in which there is little or no trust include brand-new relationships, such as transactions between strangers, situations in which an intimate relationship goes bad, and situations in which a betrayal of trust occurs in a cooperative relationship. The effect is to move the disputants into a competition cycle and toward a state of active mistrust. And the advent of competitive behavior further erodes trust. Because of the hostile feelings that are generated, any identification-based trust is destroyed. The undermining behavior created by the competitive cycle destroys knowledge-based trust as well. Thus, a single apparent betrayal of trust can lead to the entire relationship's unraveling and the creation of active mistrust.

Low levels of trust and active mistrust are associated with the competition cycle. A mistrustful disputant believes that he or she cannot count on the other disputant to be helpful and may fear that the other disputant actively wants or intends to harm him or her. Thus, mistrustfulness creates a perception of contrient interdependence: the belief that the other disputant is motivated to harm one. The competition cycle is set in motion by this perception. Moreover, distrust creates the perception that the actions of the other disputant cannot be taken at face value—that one must be suspicious of everything the other disputant does. Thus, mistrust creates the impetus to hide information and duplicate effort, both of which escalate the competition cycle.

IMPLICATIONS FOR CONFLICT DIAGNOSIS

All other things being equal, it is clearly better for disputants to have appropriately high levels of trust in one another. The greater the level of trust, the better the mutual feelings of amicability, the less formality the arrangement needs, and the more cooperative the disputants are likely to be. On the other hand, if high levels of trust are not warranted in the situation, it is dangerous to act as if they are. Thus, the tasks of a conflict diagnostician are to evaluate the levels of trust that exist between the disputants and the degree of mistrust and to determine whether there are any ways to enhance trust appropriately.

In some situations, such as in continuing relationships between family members, the relationship is more important to the people involved than is resolving particular conflicts. In other words, the trust, rather than the agreement, is the goal. In this sort of situation, the failure to establish, or to reestablish, identification-based trust is an indication that the relationship has failed. In this sort of case, typically an intervention focused directly on the interpersonal relationship—such as counseling—is the best option.

In many cases, however, either there never was an intimate relationship or the intimate relationship that there was previously has been irretrievably destroyed (as in a divorce or a business partnership that has ended). If a relationship has gone sour, achieving identification-based trust is often impossible. If there has been no intimate relationship, there is no particular reason for each person to trust each other's goodwill.

Thus, what should be the goal in *this* sort of situation? A resourceful conflict diagnostician will carefully evaluate the situation to consider possible sources of each level of trust. These can be exploited to create a climate ripe for the creation of trust. For example, a conflict diagnostician might note the political persuasions of the disputants. Even though the disputants are not in conflict over politics, if they are both active in the same political movements, this mutual identification might be exploited to increase trust.

What about situations involving active mistrust? These relationships tend to be resistant to efforts to create identification-based trust and even knowledge-based trust. The existence of the competition cycle focuses these disputants on their differences and dislikes, and the perceptual distortions of the competition cycle makes it likely that each will misinterpret the other's actions, making knowledge-based trust harder to establish. In these kinds of cases, it is useful to consider the concept of a "business relationship."

THE BUSINESS RELATIONSHIP

A business relationship is designed for people who must be involved in a relationship but who have very low levels of trust in each other. A business relationship has the following components:

- ◆ Explicit and detailed agreements
- ◆ Formality
- ◆ Restraint of emotional expression
- ◆ Balanced, neutral factfinding and evaluation

Table 10-2 summarizes the elements of a business relationship.

◆ **TABLE 10-2** 　Components of a Business Relationship, with Examples of Nonbusiness and Business Approaches

COMPONENT	EXAMPLE OF NONBUSINESS RELATIONSHIP APPROACH	EXAMPLE OF BUSINESS RELATIONSHIP APPROACH
Explicit and detailed agreements	Joe agrees to sell a piano to Jane for $800.	Ann agrees to sell a piano to Linda for $800, one-half payable by cashier's check on or before July 1, 2004, and one-half payable by cashier's check on delivery of the piano. The deal is void if the first check is not received by the date specified. The piano is to be delivered by Ann or her agent on or before July 8, 2004, to Linda's living room. Linda has the option to terminate the contract and receive a full refund within five business days if delivery is not on the date specified. The piano is sold as-is, and Linda waives any right to compensation or return of the piano for defects or problems.
Formality	Joe agrees to sell a piano to Jane for $800. The deal is oral.	The Ann-Linda deal is in writing and signed by both Ann and Linda.
Restraint of emotional expression.	In a child custody case, the father of the children uses the telephone calls he makes to schedule time with the children to express his sorrow and anger to the children's mother that the marriage ended.	In a child custody case, the father of the children is careful not to discuss his feelings about the ending of the marriage with the children's mother.
Balanced, neutral factfinding and evaluation	In a deal for the sale of homebuilding struts, the buyer and seller make a five-year contract in which the price per unit for the first year is $5 and the price for subsequent years "will be determined by an appraiser chosen by the seller."	In a deal for the sale of homebuilding struts, the buyer and seller make a five-year contract in which the price per unit for the first year is $5 and the price for subsequent years "will be at the prevailing market price as set forth in the [name of trade journal publishing such information] for the prior year as a national market price for that component."

Chapter 10

Achieving a Business Relationship Through Effective Agreement Drafting

Nothing destroys trust quite as fast as the belief that the other disputant has flagrantly violated a hard-won settlement agreement. Unfortunately, poor agreement drafting can lead to misunderstandings over the terms of a settlement. In a climate of low trust or mistrust, a difference of interpretation can be perceived as a betrayal. For this reason, effective agreement drafting is a required skill for all legal and dispute resolution professionals.

Effective agreement drafting is an acquired skill. Traditional legal drafting has the goal of developing a legally enforceable document favoring the client as much as ethically possible. But effective agreement drafting as understood in the conflict resolution context is different: it is intended to meet the following goals:

- *Accuracy and completeness.* The resulting agreement should correctly and completely set down the agreement of the parties. It is critical to represent the settlement with complete faithfulness and accuracy and not to expand upon or alter the results of negotiation. If an item has been omitted from the settlement, it's vital to get the consent of all disputants before adding it. A good practice that improves the odds of an accurate, complete agreement is to draft clauses that settle issues during, or immediately after, the negotiation at which the settlement occurs. It's also important to circulate the draft among the parties to cross-check its accuracy.
- *Clarity and certainty.* The agreement should make all rights, responsibilities, and procedures clear, including minutiae such as the manner of payment, payment due date, delivery date, responsibility for shipping goods, and risk of damage during shipment. The devil is in the details. Ensuring clarity and certainty begins during negotiation.
- *Flexibility.* The agreement should be workable despite unforeseen developments that might occur in the future. Flexibility and certainty are often traded against one another in a case-by-case balancing process. But, to the extent possible, the agreement should anticipate events that might render the arrangements inappropriate and should provide contingencies or an opportunity to reopen negotiations.
- *Legal enforceability.* The agreement should preserve or attain the legal status of a contract, and the limits of legal enforceability should be specified where necessary. The appropriate signature lines, seals, and acknowledgment forms should be used as required. Dates of inception and expiration should be specified where the terms are limited in time.
- *Relationship preservation.* The resulting agreement should avoid damaging relationships by preserving fairness, by avoiding inflammatory, insulting, or demeaning language, and by minimizing the likelihood of misinterpretation. If possible, the language of the agreement should protect and emphasize the positive elements of the relationships of the persons involved. It helps to recite the underlying, shared principles and values that led the disputants to settle in the specified manner: in addition to adding to the dignity of the process, such a recitation also reinforces the disputants' psychological ownership of the outcome and guides them, should there be a dispute over interpretation of the agreement in the future.

EXPLICIT AND DETAILED AGREEMENTS

A business relationship takes nothing for granted. All details are made explicit. The disputants must be prepared to clarify and reclarify to avoid misunderstandings.

FORMALITY

A business relationship makes use of *formal, preferably written methods of communication* (with confirming letters when communication is oral). The use of formal communication minimizes the possibility of misunderstanding, thus lowering the likelihood of unnecessary betrayals of trust.

In a business relationship, mutual rights and responsibilities are made explicit, detailed, and formal to prevent misunderstandings and support calculus-based trust. Stephen Marks Inc., Getty Images Inc.— The Image Bank

RESTRAINT OF EMOTIONAL EXPRESSION

A mistrustful relationship is marked by intimacy: the disputants frequently communicate their emotions to one another. Unfortunately, these emotions are usually reflective of the unhappy nature of the relationship, and they prompt counterattack and conflict escalation. In a formerly intimate relationship, this sharing of emotion is a special problem: the disputants are in the habit of sharing feelings, but, unfortunately, now the contents of the communication have become incendiary. In a business relationship, all sharing of emotion is kept to a bare minimum.

BALANCED, NEUTRAL FACTFINDING AND EVALUATION

The use of *balanced, neutral methods of factfinding and evaluation* (for example, using an independent consultant to value assets) is very useful in low-trust situations. The reliance on neutral, objective factfinding methods avoids the need to dispute over whose opinion is to be believed.

If the disputants were formerly intimate or informal partners, embarking on a business relationship can seem strange. In fact, formerly intimate partners often read emotional content into the act of engaging in a business relationship ("He sent me a formal letter about the children. It sounds as if he doesn't trust me at all. How insulting!"). But a business relationship has worthwhile payoffs. Calculus-based trust is built in: it is understood that both disputants want the arrangements to work and would be penalized by its falling apart, and there may be explicit rewards and penalties built into the agreement to ensure compliance. The successful operation of a business relationship also provides an opportunity to build knowledge-based trust, over time, if dealings are smooth. The more explicit and formal the disputants' agreements, the more likely it is that the dealings of the parties won't contain any unpleasant surprises. Since the arrangements are very precise and clear, the possibility of misunderstanding is minimized, and accordingly, the likelihood of breaches of trust is minimized.

After a long period of successful businesslike relations, *sometimes* the relationship builds a sufficient level of trust that formalities can be gradually dropped. This increasing casualness can reduce the cost and inefficiency of interacting. Often, however, either the brevity or the nature of the relationship precludes dropping formalities. In short, high levels of trust are nice to have, and essential in continuing love relationships, but not the most appropriate goal in everyday business and legal conflict resolution. In most legal disputes, only calculus-based trust plays an important role, and business relationship techniques should be used. In ongoing relationships, knowledge-based trust and even identification-based trust may be appropriate, or even essential, and should be nurtured.

EXERCISES, PROJECTS, AND "THOUGHT EXPERIMENTS"

1. Jill is in an interpersonal conflict with her next-door neighbor, Ned, over her wish to construct a fence between their properties. The situation is conflictual because Ned enjoys the open space of the neighborhood, but Jill desires to put up a fence so she can get a dog for her five-year-old son. Identify the types of trust displayed by Jill in the following subparts, as calculus-, knowledge-, or identification-based. Justify your responses.

   a. Jill trusts Ned because Ned and the members of Jill's family have known one another since Jill was little. Ned cares deeply for Jill, her husband, and little son and wants the family to have whatever it takes to make them happy.

   b. Ned and Jill are not close family friends. Ned and Jill have entered into a written agreement providing that Jill will have the right to put up the fence. In return for specific restrictions on the type of fence Jill will erect, the contract waives any right on Ned's part to contest the fence. Should he impede her erection of the fence in any way, Jill is granted the right to seek an injunction and damages.

   c. Ned and the members of Jill's family are not close or intimate, but they have known one another for years. Jill's experience with Ned is that he never raises a fuss, even if he's unhappy about what's happening. Accordingly, she believes that, even if she erects a fence Ned doesn't like, Ned won't create any problems about it.

2. *Conflict journal.*

   a. What level of trust exists for the disputants in your main conflict? Give explicit and detailed support for your assertion.

   b. Is the level of trust you see in the conflict appropriate or inappropriate? Support your assertion.

   c. What amount of distrust exists in the main dispute? Give explicit examples.

   d. List specific recommendations for dealing with the trust situation in your conflict. These recommendations should be realistic and implementable by you. (In other words, responses such as "the other disputant should start believing what I say" are inappropriate.)

3. Why is it so hard to implement a business relationship when one is in the middle of an escalating and destructive conflict? Try to analyze and respond to this question by considering the relationship between trust and the competition cycle.

4. Does competition itself create changes in trust? Explore this question in a written essay. Use your knowledge of trust and your knowledge of Deutsch's theory. Hint: consider Deutsch's Crude Axiom.

5. Is it ever possible to protect oneself in a low-trust situation while maintaining high levels of cooperation? Explain your answer using the ideas in this chapter and in Chapter 9. If you feel that it is possible to be self-protective and cooperative in a low-trust situation, try to list some situations in which it might happen.

6. *Internet exercise.* Using any Internet search engine, search for the term *trust exercises* or *trust-building exercises.* One good set of exercises can be found at the PTC Consulting Partners website (*http://ptcpartners.com/Team/hpt_tbe.htm*) Locate a site that describes trust-building exercises. How do these sorts of exercises relate to the information discussed in this chapter? Can you adapt any of the exercises for use by disputants in a pre-existing conflict? Be creative.

RECOMMENDED READINGS

Lewicki, R. J., and B. B. Bunker. 1995. Trust in relationships: A model of development and decline. In *Conflict, cooperation and justice: Essays inspired by the works of Morton Deutsch* (pp. 133–73), edited by B. B. Bunker, J. Z. Rubin and Associates. San Francisco: Jossey-Bass.

Lewicki, R. J., and C. Wiethoff. 2000. Trust, trust development, and trust repair. In *The handbook of conflict resolution: Theory and practice* (pp. 86–107), edited by M. Deutsch and P. T. Coleman. San Francisco: Jossey-Bass.

Shapiro, D. L., B. H. Sheppard, and L. Cheraskin. 1992. In Theory: Business on a handshake. *Negotiation Journal* 8(4):365–77.

11

Step 6. Assess the Impediments to Resolving the Conflict

"The ultimate measure of a man is not where he stands in moments of comfort and convenience, but where he stands at times of challenge and controversy."

—Martin Luther King, Jr.

"If a man empties his purse into his head, no man can take it away from him. An investment in knowledge always pays the best interest."

—Benjamin Franklin

In this chapter, you will learn …

- ◆ Fourteen important factors that impede the resolution of conflicts.
- ◆ What you can do about each impediment.

When participants in a conflict realize that they need help resolving it, that usually means that they have already tried, and failed, to handle it themselves. Thus, a central step in any conflict diagnosis is to determine what factors are impeding resolution of the conflict.

As we saw in Chapter 9, one important reason that conflicts fail to be resolved is that the competition cycle is easy to trigger, and, once this happens, the conflict tends to escalate out of control. Thus, a diagnostician should always look for evidence of pressure in the conflict toward the competition cycle.

However, legal and social science scholars and conflict practitioners have recognized a number of other, more specific factors that contribute to difficulties in

---

Impediments to Resolving Interpersonal Conflict

- ◆ Motivation to seek vengeance
- ◆ Meta-disputes
- ◆ Mistrust
- ◆ Vastly different perceptions of reality
- ◆ Overcommitment and entrapment
- ◆ Lack of ripeness
- ◆ Jackpot Syndrome
- ◆ Loss aversion
- ◆ Linkages
- ◆ Conflicts of interest among team members
- ◆ Excluded stakeholders
- ◆ Disempowered disputant
- ◆ Unpleasant disputant
- ◆ Competitive culture or subculture

---

resolving conflict.[1] The most important of these are listed in this chapter, along with some strategies that a conflict diagnostician or dispute resolution practitioner can use to ameliorate the situation.

MOTIVATION TO SEEK VENGEANCE

A disputant who is motivated to seek vengeance is likely to sacrifice the advantages of cooperation to punish the other side. This phenomenon often occurs after a conflict has been in a competitive cycle and has escalated and spread.

Disputants have many reasons to seek vengeance (Kim and Smith 1993). Some may believe that revenge is necessary to rectify an injustice that has been perpetrated on them. Disputants often seek revenge to resurrect a sense of self-worth that has been damaged in the conflict. And disputants may believe that punitive action must be taken to prevent the other disputant from wreaking further havoc. As a conflict becomes increasingly competitive, disputants tend to experience the other disputant's conduct as motivated by hostility or hatred; thus, they are more likely to see the behavior as unjust and humiliating and are more and more likely to respond by wanting revenge.

It can be difficult to admit to vengeful feelings, because they are considered socially unacceptable in many circumstances. For that reason, disputants often rationalize vengeful feelings and actions as being defensive. For example, in eth-

---

[1]Legal and ADR scholars Frank E. A. Sander and Stephen B. Goldberg compiled much of the information presented in this chapter in their immensely popular article "Fitting the Forum to the Fuss: A User Friendly Guide to Selecting an ADR Process" (1994).

nic conflict, an "ethnic cleansing" often is rationalized, not as an act of revenge but, rather, as a response to perceived threats to property rights or personal safety.

The motivation to seek vengeance is a difficult impediment to deal with. Often, legal disputants with this motive categorically reject seemingly rational and cooperative approaches to resolving the conflict in favor of potentially damaging and expensive litigation. These disputants feel that, if only their story were told, the authoritative judge would agree with them that the other disputant deserves to be punished. Frequently, that isn't the case, and the vengeful disputant is deeply disappointed with the adversarial approach to conflict resolution. Other vengeful disputants may feel justified in resorting to extra-legal measures, such as threats, intimidation, and violence. Still others recognize that their behavior is counterproductive but can't resist taking measures that are unpleasant to the other side.

> In negotiations between separated spouses, a husband insisted on receiving the lion's share of the marital property "because you wanted the divorce, not me." When it was suggested that he would probably not receive as much in court as he was demanding, and would have to pay thousands in attorney's fees to litigate, he said that he was aware of that but didn't care. Later, in mediation, he confided to the mediator that, when he sat face to face with his wife, he was unable to resist making demands he knew were unlikely to be met: his anger toward his wife was so overwhelming that he just couldn't help himself. After a long period of cooling off, this husband was able to reach agreement with his wife in mediation, but only by using a format in which she was not physically in the same room but, instead, participated via conference call. The mediation almost fell apart when, after all the major financial issues had fallen into place, the husband refused to give his wife back her guitar. "I promised myself I would learn to play it after the divorce," the husband rationalized. He was able to relent and agree to return the guitar only after his wife had hung up the telephone and he could speak with the mediator alone.

Assuming that the disputants can be convinced, or coerced, into participating, mediation has proven to have particular power in helping reorient disputants away from vengeful behavior and toward more constructive approaches to conflict resolution (McEwen & Milburn 1993). Kim and Smith (1993) recommend, in any conflict resolution process, that steps be taken to support the self-worth of each disputant, that vengeful feelings be carefully diagnosed (since they are often hidden), and that apology be encouraged whenever possible. A skilled mediator will often structure the negotiation to create these opportunities for coping with vengefulness.

META-DISPUTES

Meta-disputes (see Chapter 9) are disputes about the way a conflict is being handled. Unresolved and escalating conflict breeds meta-disputes, and, the more such disputes there are, the more difficult and conflicted the disputants' relationship.

Following is a classic and common example of how a meta-dispute can develop:

> The disputants are spouses who are separating and headed for a divorce. Right now, they aren't angry, just sad and confused. After the husband

moves out, the wife, in an effort to protect herself and behave rationally, goes to a lawyer. After a brief initial client interview, the lawyer, having minimal information about the wife's situation, and seeking to protect the wife's legal rights while he conducts an investigation, advises (1) that the wife change the locks on the house (just in case the husband decides to hide assets); (2) that the wife stop talking to her husband (a very common recommendation to protect the client from accidentally jeopardizing her case); and (3) that the lawyer file a petition for divorce (so that the requisite paperwork is in place). The next day, without any warning, the husband receives an intimidating visit from the sheriff, who serves him with divorce pleadings. The pleadings are accompanied by twenty-five **interrogatories** that ask, among other things, about his past five years' sexual partners and whether he has been hiding assets. The wife has no knowledge of these inquiries, having only briefly glanced at the documents after they were sent, and the lawyer sees these questions not as personal accusations but merely as "boilerplate" materials he sends to all the spouses of his divorce clients to ensure that he exercises due diligence in representing the client. The husband calls the wife in shock and anger, only to have the wife refuse to speak to him. He rushes over to the house and finds the locks have been changed. The husband is outraged—there are now at least four new "hot" conflicts—over the locks, over the sudden appearance of "the law" at his door, over the insulting interrogatory questions, and over the wife's refusal to talk.

The best way to deal with meta-disputes is to prevent them in the first place. A cooperative conflict cycle minimizes meta-disputes by encouraging free and open communication and by protecting the disputants from negative attributions of one another's behaviors. Once meta-disputes begin to accumulate, it is hard to avoid conflict escalation unless they're dealt with directly.

Often, meta-disputes reveal themselves to be misunderstandings, but they can be hard to untangle without the help of a neutral third party, such as a mediator. In the preceding divorce example, a mediator could help the husband understand that the wife's actions were the result of "standardized" tactics on the part of the lawyer, not motivated by ill will on the wife's part. A mediator could also help the wife appreciate the impact that the actions had on the husband. Often, a sincere apology from someone in the position of the wife can open many doors to removing the impediment.

Interrogatories
written questions sent to a litigant, asking him or her to answer questions relevant to a pending lawsuit. Lawyers use them to gather information about the facts of a case.

MISTRUST

Trust and mistrust were considered in detail in Chapter 10. Mistrust and low levels of trust are the engines driving conflict escalation: low levels of trust create the suspicion, circumspection, and defensive tactics that promote inefficiency, bad feelings, and disputants' efforts to undermine one other. Mistrust is created by competitive conflict, and it is fed by vengeful behavior and meta-disputes. Obviously, tactics that build trust (discussed in Chapter 10) are vital in counteracting mistrust and facilitating the resolution of conflict.

VASTLY DIFFERING PERCEPTIONS OF REALITY

When disputants have dramatically differing perceptions of the facts or law that underlie the conflict, they usually have trouble achieving resolution without help. If each person has a strong, honest belief that his or her point of view is the correct one, then it is difficult to convince the person to decide otherwise. Rational individuals are not likely to settle a dispute for a lot less than they think they would get if the dispute were resolved in a court.

When differing perceptions are the result of factual or legal error or insufficient information, they are very easy to resolve through processes that clarify facts or law, such as nonbinding evaluation. For example, if the parties disagree about how to place a value on the pain and suffering of an accident victim, they can each present a summary of their evidence before a group of individuals selected from a jury pool to render a nonbinding opinion.[2] The trouble is that many differing perceptions of reality arise not out of error or ignorance but, rather, out of the perceptual distortions inherent in the competition cycle, and nonbinding evaluation processes do little to counteract them. A disputant in an escalating competition who has staked his or her ego on a position usually interprets reality to be consistent with his or her judgmental attitude toward the other disputant. The key to removing such an impediment to conflict resolution is to find a way for the disputant to back away from his or her extreme position without losing face. An example from child custody mediation is helpful:

> Two parents were referred to child custody mediation in a midwestern urban court system. The father was suing for full custody and wanted to terminate all unsupervised visitation between the six-year-old child and the child's mother. In the initial interview with the mediator, the parents' acrimonious relationship was immediately obvious from body language and the hostile words they exchanged.
>
> The mediator asked the father why he believed that the mother should lose all rights to time alone with the child, and the father replied that there had been physical child abuse. The mother adamantly denied that any child abuse had taken place. The mediator recognized that somewhere in the conflict was probably a vast difference in perception. Pressed further for details by the mediator, the father said that the mother had not actually committed the abuse but had stood by and allowed someone else caring for the child to abuse him. The father finally admitted that the only incident of which he was actually aware involved the child, left with a baby-sitter while the mother ran an errand, being hit with some snowballs by a much older boy. The father then softened his position somewhat and argued that this incident proved the mother's poor judgment in her selection of a baby-sitter. Ultimately, with the mediator's gentle assistance, the father came to acknowledge that completely cutting the child off from his mother would be counterproductive under the circumstances. The child's mother offered

---

[2] Such a proceeding, known as a summary jury trial, will be discussed further in Chapter 20.

an agreement to involve the father in the choice of the child's caregivers; in fact, however, having had the opportunity to express his angry and mistrustful feelings, the father abandoned his demands for control in this area, and the parents were ultimately able to reach a shared parenting agreement.

OVERCOMMITMENT AND ENTRAPMENT

A disputant "overcommits" when he or she pours so much time, money, and energy into preparing for a battle that it is seemingly wasteful to back out of the project. The result is that the disputants feel trapped.

To model this phenomenon, social scientist Martin Shubik developed the Dollar Auction Game (Rubin, Pruitt, & Kim 1994, 111–12). A dollar bill is auctioned off to a group of bidders. The rules award the dollar bill to the highest bidder, but *both* the highest and second-highest bidders must pay the amounts of their bids to the auctioneer: if the highest bid is $1, the winner just breaks even and the second-highest bidder loses the amount of his or her bid. Thus, the game simulates the reality that negotiations often involve significant and mounting costs to the disputants. The bidding generally starts out low and brisk, but, as the bidding approaches $1, bidders begin to fear that they will end up with the second-highest bid. Some bidders drop out, but a few stick with it, in the hope that they will be the highest bidder. As the bidding exceeds $1, the issue is no longer winning but cutting losses. Thus, the bidding tends to continue past the $1 break-even point as each bidder tries to avoid being the second-highest bidder. As the bidding continues, however, it is believed that the entrapped bidders shift their focus from minimizing losses to ensuring that they lose less than the other side (Rubin, Pruitt, & Kim 1994, 111–13)—in other words, a motive to harm the other party appears. According to Shubik, the winning bid for the $1 bill is often $5 or $6.

How does overcommitment and entrapment appear in real-life interpersonal conflicts? Consider the following example, adapted from a real trial, with the details modified to preserve client confidentiality:

> Acme, a large national real estate brokerage business, contracts with Dolores Merriwether to act as an agent. She begins with plenty of enthusiasm but not a whole lot of skill, and, after a year or so, her production drops off to a barely adequate level. Eventually, Acme's regional manager, Grant Beasley, encourages her to look elsewhere for a career. Thereafter, Dolores continues to act as an Acme agent, but she finds that support from the agency, formerly spotty at best, becomes inadequate.
>
> In anger, Dolores finally ends her contractual relationship with Acme and consults a lawyer. Some weeks later, Acme's regional manager receives a letter from the lawyer, stating Dolores' contentions that Acme systematically withheld commissions from buyers who worked with Dolores but consummated a deal with another agent. The lawyer demands $50,000 in immediate settlement damages. Acme's house counsel hires outside counsel to defend the accusations. Initial interviews with Grant and his staff produce rolling eyes and guffaws: Dolores was a poor agent and they were lucky to finally have her gone. Grant convinces the attorneys that Dolores

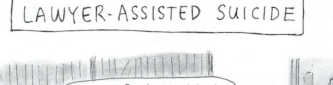

The Cartoon Bank

does not have a leg to stand on—the client files will prove it. Thus, Acme's lawyer contacts Dolores' lawyer and informs him that Acme refuses to consider negotiation.

Dolores then sues Acme, seeking compensatory damages of $100,000 and unspecified punitive damages. Acme's counsel then conducts more extensive interviews with Acme's personnel and discovers that the case is not as black and white as it first appeared. Dolores was a poor agent, to be sure, but she is able to make an argument that her lack of immediate revenues was due to her building up goodwill for Acme. Grant is absolutely convinced that the argument is silly, but it might play with a jury. Also, substantial legal research must be conducted in light of ambiguities in the contractual relationship between Acme and Dolores.

As Acme's legal bill approaches $10,000, Acme's lawyers receive word from the regional office that Dolores' client files have been archived; it will take at least eight weeks to retrieve the materials. Another several thousand dollars are spent contesting numerous preliminary motions brought by Dolores' attorney. Ten weeks later, the regional office managers begin to express some doubts about whether they know the actual location of about 60 percent of the client files in question. Without the client files, the likelihood of Acme's prevailing in litigation is called into a bit more doubt. In fact, the "outrageously high" demand Dolores' lawyer made eight months ago (for

$50,000) is starting to look almost attractive; however, now that the legal bill is around $20,000, Acme sees as the only rational choice to press on—there's still a pretty good chance that it will win.

As trial approaches and Acme's legal team perfect their legal research and factual analysis, the probability of winning at trial becomes more and more uncertain. Pre-trial requests for legal rulings in Acme's favor have either failed altogether or have been rebuffed by the motions judge as being premature. As the trial date approaches, it becomes evident that the client files are unrecoverable. Grant's job is on the line: if he admits that the client files are lost, he believes he is likely to lose his job. At least if the case is tried, and Acme wins, he will have total vindication; if it is tried and Acme loses, he is not very much worse off than if the case settles. Besides, Dolores' initial demand of $50,000 in damages, initially seen as ridiculous, has now been withdrawn. Dolores' legal team has spent hundreds of hours preparing the case and sees no reason not to take a chance with litigation.

The trial takes two weeks. Each legal team sends two lawyers and a paralegal to the courthouse for twelve- to fourteen-hour days. At the end of trial, the jury awards Dolores $40,000 in compensatory damages and $200,000 in punitive damages. Acme also has $40,000 in legal fees and spent hundreds of employee hours preparing the case. Moreover, the case has substantial precedential value: it means that Acme will have to recompute the commissions of every entry-level agent in its pool. The computation itself will cost thousands of manpower hours and potentially cost the company billions. Dolores has spent over $55,000 in lawyer's fees as well.

Overcommitment is a toxic combination of inattention and fear of losing face. It is insidious: it happens inch by inch, creating entrapment by degrees. The best ways to combat entrapment are to make disputants attentive to the process of commitment and to avoid the loss of face issue that comes with it. Rubin, Pruitt, and Kim (1994, 114–16) recommend four tactics designed to avoid overcommitment and entrapment.

First, before entering into a negotiation, it helps to set some boundaries on how much the disputant will lay on the line. By setting limits, the conflict participant establishes a sort of "trip wire," which alerts him or her to the potential danger of entrapment. For example, in the Acme example, the attorneys for Acme might have been instructed to invest no more than $5,000 in legal research and then to meet with Acme personnel to decide what to do next.[3]

Second during the negotiation, one can schedule "points of decision," at which the decision to stay involved is periodically reevaluated. This tactic counteracts the tendency to ignore issues of cost-effectiveness until overcommitment has already occurred. For example, the Acme legal team could have scheduled bimonthly teleconferences with the board to discuss progress to date, costs, and possible decisions to settle.

---

[3] One kind of limit, called the Best Alternative To a Negotiated Agreement (BATNA) is discussed in Chapter 13.

Third, attention should be paid, during analysis of whether to continue committing resources to a conflict, on the costs, nonmonetary and monetary, of continuing the conflict. Any evaluation of the merits of continuing a dispute should always include cost estimates. In the Acme case, it would have been helpful if the legal team had been required to estimate the costs of each step of the process and to report to the Acme board whenever the estimates seemed to be in question.

Fourth, it's very useful to build in ways to save face wherever possible. As entrapment builds, the participants continue to persist in the dispute to avoid loss of face. In the Acme case, it would have been useful to have members of the corporate structure not associated directly with the regional office involved in the decision making, so that Grant's psychological and personal needs did not interfere with decisions made for Acme as a whole. Also, if possible within the participants' professional roles, Grant's esteem could have been supported directly, perhaps by reassuring him that his position was not in jeopardy despite the snafu. If Grant were a generally competent individual, he could even be made responsible for overhauling the client-file storage and retrieval system: this move could preserve his image and benefit the company as a whole.

LACK OF RIPENESS

Often, resolving a conflict is perceived as costly, difficult, scary, or intolerably unpleasant—and sometimes it is. Many times, disputants won't confront the work needed to resolve a conflict until they feel there is no other alternative. This characteristic of conflict is called "ripeness."

Dean Pruitt and Paul Olczak, who write about seemingly intractable conflict, list the following sources of ripeness (Pruitt and Olczak 1995, 68–69):

- The disputants are at an impasse and failing to resolve the conflict is doing significant continuing damage. Pruitt and Olczak refer to this phenomenon as "hurting stalemate."

- "Recent catastrophe or near catastrophe"—a consequence or near-consequence, of the conflict—stuns the participants into the need for immediate resolution.

- "Impending catastrophe or deteriorating position"—the parties in the conflict become aware that failing to resolve the conflict is creating the likelihood of imminent disaster.

- The presence of an "enticing opportunity"—an opportunity arises to resolve the conflict that could yield terrific benefits but is available "for a limited time only."

In legal disputing, ripeness is often created by the proximity of trial. A trial usually has many unexpected twists and turns; it is expensive, time-consuming, and emotionally harrowing. As a trial date approaches, disputants formerly noted for their intransigence often find heretofore hidden flexibility in their negotiating positions. The common practice of "settling on the courthouse steps" illustrates the truth of the proposition that, for many litigants, trial is the impending catastrophe needed to spur them into settling their legal dispute. However, it is less expensive, less harmful to relationships, more efficient, and more constructive to find a way to ripen a legal dispute before the participants have invested the considerable time and money required to prepare for a trial.

Sometimes, disputants perceive the possible development of a competition cycle as the impending catastrophe needed to create ripeness. Many divorce mediation clients enter the mediation process expressing fear that, if they cannot resolve the issues around their divorce themselves, the case will be run away with by the lawyers. Although these disputants' perceptions about lawyers may not be wholly accurate, their conceptualization of the competition cycle as impending catastrophe is laudable. It allows resolution of the conflict while it is still in a cooperative cycle.

If disputants appear to be intransigent, a conflict diagnostician can look for sources of ripeness that the parties have overlooked, develop strategies to create awareness of existing sources of ripeness, or even, as appropriate, develop strategies to create sources of ripeness. If possible, this effort is better done before a competition cycle begins, by educating the disputants to the likely damage that would be done if the conflict were to escalate, thus encouraging the perception of a competition cycle as an impending catastrophe. In our example of the real estate commissions dispute, a conflict diagnostician could have alerted the parties to a hurting stalemate by calling their attention to the escalating legal costs, for example, and the uncertainty of outcome. In recent years, U.S. presidents have attempted to create enticing opportunities for the resolution of difficult international conflicts by engineering special time-limited summit negotiations.

JACKPOT SYNDROME

The Jackpot Syndrome, identified by prominent law professors Frank Sander and Stephen Goldberg (Sander & Goldberg 1994), involves apparently irrational behavior by a disputant who is risk-tolerant. Disputants afflicted with this syndrome believe that they have a chance of "winning big" if they hold out and refuse to settle. The irrationality comes because their chances of actually getting the big payoff are miniscule. For example, consider a disputant who believes he has a shot at winning tens of millions of dollars if he takes his grievance to court. The other side believes that his chances of being struck by lightning are better than his chance of winning the litigation, yet, dazzled by the thought of riches beyond the dreams of avarice, he persists in the lawsuit.

An apparent case of Jackpot Syndrome should be carefully diagnosed. If the disputant is not clear about the apparent worthlessness of the case, he or she needs to be educated: rather than Jackpot Syndrome, this is a case of differing views of reality. Of course, if the conflict is marked by mistrust among disputants, a neutral or an advocate of the misinformed disputant will have to be the bearer of the bad news. Some cases of apparent Jackpot Syndrome arise from a litigant's failure to appreciate the truly hopeless position he or she is in if he or she tries to go to court. Nonbinding evaluation processes can be of great help in making the disputants aware of their true interests in settling the dispute amicably. In other cases, apparent Jackpot Syndrome is, in reality, a disputant bent on vengeance: his or her focus on the high payoff is a rationalization for behavior really meant to punish the other disputant. In the case of true Jackpot Syndrome, a visionary mediator, or another conflict resolver, can sometimes intuit the psychological needs underlying the disputant's compulsion to gamble and can find creative ways to meet those needs. This tactic allows the disputant to have his or her needs met but act rationally in the conflict. However, sometimes a case of Jackpot Syndrome can be resolved only through litigation: the disputant will agree to participate in no other process, and, in fact, such a disputant gains independent satisfaction from rolling the dice in court. To persuade such an individual to settle out of court, one must make a case for the proposition that the benefits of settlement outweigh the intrinsic satisfaction the disputant gets from gambling.

LOSS AVERSION

Loss aversion is the propensity of many people to prefer to gamble on an uncertain outcome rather than to take on a certain but manageable loss. For example, imagine a dispute over a fender-bender. Mary, whose car suffered the most damage, sues Ernie for $10,000. Mary then demands $2,000 to settle the case. Ernie may prefer to chance court, rather than to take on a definite loss of $2,000, even if he is likely to lose more than $2,000.

Loss aversion is the complement of Jackpot Syndrome; it involves people who would rather gamble, knowing they have a good chance of losing, than give up a sure thing of lesser value. As with Jackpot Syndrome, if the loss aversion amounts to ignorance, a good approach is to educate the disputant about the real chances and costs of litigation.

Loss aversion may also be a coverup for an identity issue. It may be difficult to settle a case because of the loss of face that attends agreeing to pay a settlement. The disputant may prefer to take his or her chances and gamble on a big loss, rather than admitting he or she did wrong upfront. If this issue is lurking behind a disputant's intransigence, establishing face-saving measures (such as payment without an admission of liability or an agreement not to make the settlement public) may be helpful.

LINKAGES

A linkages problem (Sander & Goldberg 1994) occurs when the conflict under consideration is interlinked with other conflicts and other parties. The implications of settlement may be hard to clarify or may overwhelm the stakes in the current conflict. It may seem safer just to avoid settlement altogether. For example, in the real estate commissions dispute example described earlier in this chapter, the outcome of the dispute had the potential to affect commission arrangements across the nation. The pending dispute had received media coverage in trade newspapers and was being followed by the specialized legal community that dealt with real estate commission contracting. At one point in the dispute, Acme's leadership met to consider settlement but concluded that settling would make them appear "soft" and would leave them vulnerable to attacks by other agents. As things turned out, however, the litigation produced an outcome that made Acme even more vulnerable.

Class action lawsuits and similar massive conflicts involving multiple parties and incidents present prime examples of linkages. Consider, for example, the tobacco litigation that occurred in the last half-decade of the twentieth century. Individual tobacco firms were in danger of incurring dangerous precedents whether they settled or litigated. In an effort to create more certainty and limit losses, the companies offered a broad-based settlement with limited future liability in exchange for huge initial financial outlays. Among individual litigants, politicians, and advocacy groups, there were so many conflicting interests that the broad-based settlements could not be accepted. The tobacco litigation is still being resolved, on the whole, one case or class of cases at a time.

Linkages are a reality of many interpersonal conflicts. An effective conflict diagnostician deals with linkages by performing detailed interests analyses to determine the nature of each interdependent relationship affecting the conflict. Sometimes, linkages can be turned to advantage—for example, by providing other dimensions on which a constructive outcome can be fashioned. For example, rather than hashing out the real estate commissions dispute in court, perhaps Dolores, who was struggling as an agent, anyway, could have been receptive to a consulting deal that gave her a lucrative position working with Grant and Acme's house counsel to redesign their agency agreements and client file storage system. Dolores could receive a good salary and valuable experience in the industry, and Acme could prevent such disputes from arising in the future by improving its contracts and record-keeping functions.

CONFLICTS OF INTEREST AMONG TEAM MEMBERS

Nondisputants can put a variety of barriers in the way of conflict resolution. Constituents, agents, and other influential parties can all impede the otherwise effective work of disputants.

Constituents often have interests that conflict with those of others on their disputant's team. Some examples of this phenomenon were presented in Chapters 6 and 8, when we discussed the S-B Corporate transaction. Sue, the officeworker for S Corporation and a constituent, is likely to give less than her full attention to the work needed to make the transaction work—she's overworked and just wants the whole transaction to "go away." Similarly, agents and advocates may have interests that conflict with their principals. In the real estate commissions dispute, Grant, the regional manager and agent for the disputant, has a personal interest in

Conflicts of interest among members of a negotiation team can ruin settlement efforts. Eye Wire Collection, Getty Images—Eye Wire, Inc.

concealing the loss of the client files. This personal interest—in not losing his job—creates an irresistible urge to conceal the truth and to convince the rest of his team to pursue litigation: after all, he reasons, he can't lose much more by litigating and being fired if they lose than he can by settling and probably being fired, anyway.

Individuals who are not participating in the negotiation may also have conflicts of interest with members of either or both teams. Following is an example that involves identity conflict (see Chapter 7):

> A skilled and experienced facilitator for a state public health agency related a saga involving efforts to create standards for improving consumer protection against fraudulent claims by weight-loss businesses. These standards were promulgated through a process of negotiation between interested stakeholders. The facilitator's responsibilities were to ensure that the proper parties were involved in the decision-making process, to structure a series of meetings to create a likelihood of settlement, and to protect the state's interests in properly meeting the objectives required by its public health and consumer protection laws.
>
> The facilitator identified a number of state agencies, industry representatives, and consumer health advocacy groups who were likely to feel the need to be heard on the issue. A problem ensued that involved a certain advocacy group. With its "cultural history" of advocacy, its approach was to characterize its work as a struggle against victimization by "forces of evil" at work in government and private industry. The group could not be seen as cooperating with "the enemies," else its identity as a champion

of the oppressed would be threatened. The facilitator was at a loss for what to do: the advocacy group seemingly refused both to participate and to be left out of the negotiation. The group preferred a milieu of struggle and revolution; peaceful negotiation itself was antithetical to their core identity. The facilitator dealt with this seemingly intractable situation by publicly honoring the group's commitment to consumer health protection, graciously inviting the group to participate in the negotiation process, and then quietly proceeding without them when they refused to participate.

Conflicts of interest can sometimes be treated as separate interpersonal conflicts, subject to creative resolution. When advocates and agents have clear conflicts of interest with their disputants, sometimes they must withdraw from representing the disputants to prevent the conflict of interest from doing harm to those they ostensibly represent.

EXCLUDED STAKEHOLDERS

Another group of people who frequently impede the smooth resolution of a conflict are those who are not at the negotiation table but feel they should be. In a complex conflict, sometimes the disputants are difficult to identify. There may be a number of advocacy groups, each of which claims to be an interested party. Or, within a single group of disputants, there may be conflict over who should be physically performing the negotiation of the conflict.

Any individual who feels a need to contribute to the resolution of a conflict, but who isn't invited to do so, is likely to feel slighted about the lack of consideration. This psychological sting typically prompts the person who has been left out to dislike any settlement being considered (in a phenomenon closely related to reactive devaluation), and this person will often seek to sabotage the settlement process. Following is a common example from divorce mediation:

> A divorced mother and father go to mediation to resolve issues concerning the parenting of their two children. They work in mediation for a number of sessions and are in the process of developing what appears to the mediator to be a logical and workable parenting plan. Part of the plan involves the children going to the father's house after school two days a week. When the fourth session begins, the father announces that the plan they are negotiating is unacceptable. The father offers no real substantive reasons for his rejection of the parenting plan, until he finally admits that his current wife has refused to perform any of the transportation that the agreement requires. Everyone is completely surprised by the developments, because, until they entered mediation, the wife presented herself as devoted to the children and willing to do everything she can to be an exemplary stepmother.

When a conflict diagnostician uncovers an excluded individual, often the most effective way to deal with the situation is to include him or her in some meaningful way in the negotiation. Imagine, for example, if the stepmother case had instead gone this way:

> In the initial session, the mediator uncovers the presence of the stepmother and her apparent involvement in parenting. She also notes a degree of friction between the stepmother and the children's mother. She recommends involving the stepmother in the mediation process to prevent the possibility of sabotage and develops a plan with the parents for how to involve her. She carefully prepares the mom and dad for how she will involve the stepmom and why it is important to make sure she feels involved. She reassures the mom that the stepmom does not have any actual decision-making authority—they are the parents, not her—and wryly asks the mom to keep her tongue firmly bitten throughout the next mediation session.
>
> The stepmom is invited to the next mediation session. The mediator welcomes the stepmom to the session and comments that she has heard from the parents how important she is to the lives of the children. Without telling the stepmom that she will have any power to make decisions about the evolving parenting plan, the mediator validates the stepmom's importance in making the parenting arrangements work and compliments the stepmom on her commitment to the children's welfare. When invited to share her opinion regarding how she can help make the parenting arrangements work, the stepmom herself notes that she is home in the afternoons and could provide transportation. She also asks that the father give her increased authority to discipline the children when they are at Dad's house and Dad is not at home. The final parenting plan, negotiated by the parents without the stepmom present, incorporates both these suggestions and expressly notes that the stepmom suggested them. Feeling a strong sense of psychological ownership of the arrangements, the stepmom works hard to keep the parenting plan, as a whole, working smoothly.

DISEMPOWERED DISPUTANT

A disempowered disputant is a disputant who feels he or she has insufficient power in the relationship with the other disputant.[4] A disempowered disputant fears coming to agreement, because he or she is afraid to be taken advantage of and doesn't know how to protect him- or herself. Often, the disempowered disputant cannot assess the utility of a proposed settlement, because he or she lacks essential knowledge. A disempowered disputant is very likely to dig his or her heels into the sand and become paralyzed.

A seeming paradox is that a very powerful disputant in negotiation with a very disempowered disputant often benefits from conferring power on the latter. This is particularly the case if the more powerful disputant loses more in the failure to reach agreement than the less powerful disputant.

> Spouses enter mediation at the behest of the husband to resolve issues around their separation and eventual divorce. The husband has been active

---

[4] Power in interpersonal conflict is covered in Chapter 13.

in the business world and negotiates for a living. He has also handled the family finances. The wife has stayed home and raised the children. When they are asked to describe their goals, hopes, and dreams for the future, the husband responds with a specific proposal concerning who will get the house, where the children will live, and how the assets will be divided. He asserts that he has considered the wife's best interests in his analysis and that his proposal is fair. The wife, on the other hand, has no goals she is able to express and wants the mediator to tell her whether the husband's proposal is fair. The mediator refuses to do this, stating that this is not an appropriate function for a mediator and suggesting that the wife receive legal advice to help her gain the knowledge she needs to assess the fairness of the proposal and to clarify her own goals.

Three days later, the husband telephones the mediator in a frantic state: his wife has abandoned mediation and has retained her parents' lawyer, who does not even specialize in divorce law. The mediator comments to the husband that individuals who do not feel comfortable negotiating on their own are poor candidates for mediation but that she would suggest some options to facilitate an effective alternative. The mediator, then hearing from the wife, offers her the option of bringing the lawyer to mediation to help her negotiate, but she adamantly refuses all further efforts to participate in her own negotiation, even given assistance of counsel.

A conflict diagnostician who finds a disempowered disputant impeding settlement should look at ways that the disputant can be empowered. As will be seen in Chapter 13, often the most effective form of empowerment is the conferral of knowledge. The disempowered disputant gains an enormous amount of knowledge by having the conflict effectively diagnosed for him or her. With a complete conflict diagnosis, the disputant can decide effectively whether it is in his or her best interests to settle a conflict.

UNPLEASANT DISPUTANT

Some disputants are so irritating that no one wants to please them. Their unpleasant personalities generate intense hostility in those who have to deal with them. They push conflicts into a competitive cycle by directly generating enmity between the participants. Helping the irritating person may feel psychologically intolerable to the other participants (contrient interdependence results). Sometimes, the problem is "goodness of fit"—a disputant is only unpleasant to a single other disputant—but sometimes the unpleasant disputant is decried almost universally as impossible to work with.

Obviously, if a conflict diagnostician discovers this impediment operating, one possible solution is to put distance between the disputant who is inciting hostility and the other conflict participants. One way to make this happen, if the unpleasant disputant is able to acknowledge the impediment, is to hire an agent or advocate to act in the disputant's place. Another way is to create physical or technological distance. If face-to-face negotiation is too provocative, one might try the telephone; if the telephone is still too incendiary, letters or e-mail may work better. Mediation can help in such negotiations if it is structured so that the mediator acts as a "shuttle diplomat," meeting with the disputants separately and providing a communication conduit between them. (This mediation technique, called "caucusing," is discussed in Chapter 17.) Another way to manage a difficult disputant is simply to become aware of the ways in which the disputant annoys the other participants and to create awareness of and insight into the problem. Other participants in the process may be able to control their tempers long enough to obtain a resolution that is in their self-interest.

COMPETITIVE CULTURE OR SUBCULTURE

A competitive culture or subculture breeds competitive conflict escalation in numerous ways. The invisible veil discussed in Chapter 3 is at work in certain cultural or subcultural groups, whose members are expected to behave competitively, are very skilled in adversarial conflict behavior, and are usually in the habit of doing so. Alternative ways of behaving are misunderstood, decried, or ridiculed. Efforts to create a cooperation cycle are met with efforts to exploit the opening thus created. It is difficult to deal with conflict in such an environment without retreating to the self-protective illusion of competition.

The most common competitive subculture is the legal subculture. Lawyers are inculcated in the ways of competitive conflict resolution, as we saw in Chapter 3. Clients who access lawyers and the judiciary to have their disputes resolved typically see the dispute resolved through competitive processes, although recent reforms in the legal educational system are beginning to create inroads into this cultural belief system.

A competitive culture or subculture sometimes prevents cooperative settlement. This illustration depicts Aaron Burr duelling Alexander Hamilton with pistols. Corbis/Bettmann

Obviously, trying to establish a cooperative relationship within a competitive culture or subculture involves one of two approaches: either creating enough incentive for the other disputant to break cultural traditions or moving the site of the conflict out of the competitive setting. Both of these approaches are used for legal disputes. There is an increasing trend toward so-called collaborative lawyering, an effort to create a noncompetitive sub-subculture within the legal subculture (Tesler 1999). Additionally, the movement toward using mediation to resolve legal disputes is a clear effort to move these interpersonal conflicts outside of a competitive subculture and into a clearly noncompetitive subculture for resolution.

Table 11-1 briefly summarizes the impediments to settlement that have been discussed in this chapter.

◆ **TABLE 11-1**   Summary: Impediments to Cooperative Settlement of Interpersonal Conflict

IMPEDIMENT	EXPLANATION	EXAMPLE
Motivation to seek vengeance	A disputant wants retribution against another participant more than he or she wants a settlement.	Knowing she will lose in court, a plaintiff pursues a lawsuit because of the inconvenience she knows it will cause the defendant.
Meta-disputes	Conflicts and disputes that relate to how the main conflict is or has been handled.	During a labor dispute, one side accuses the other of unfair practices.
Mistrust	A disputant believes that the other disputant is likely to use a settlement process as an opportunity for exploitation.	During the Israeli-Palestinian conflict, the Israeli government is unwilling to take the word of Palestinian leadership that they will take care of anti-Semitic terrorists; as a result, Israel takes violent action against Palestinian militants.
Vastly differing perceptions of reality	Each side believes a completely different version of the situation.	An employee files a grievance, claiming discrimination on the basis of gender against her supervisor, who believes that no gender discrimination has taken place.
Overcommitment and entrapment	A disputant's team commits so much time, resource, or psychological energy to a competitive position that they feel that to settle would be a waste or would create intolerable loss of face.	After committing $50,000 to preparing for trial, a plaintiff refuses an eleventh-hour offer to settle for an amount the plaintiff originally felt would be in his best interests.
Lack of ripeness	One or both teams have not yet come to believe that there is an urgent need to settle.	An auto accident plaintiff has filed suit, the case is scheduled for trial in fifteen months, and the plaintiff's legal team sees no harm in letting the case sit. They use the requests for settlement discussions by the other side for strategic advantage, hoping that playing hard to get will sweeten the eventual outcome.
Jackpot Syndrome	One of the parties is willing to take a huge risk that he or she will lose for the opportunity to obtain a huge recovery.	A plaintiff sues for $10 million and refuses to settle, despite her attorney's warning that she's unlikely to beat the defendant's latest offer.

(Continued)

◆ **TABLE 11-1** Summary: Impediments to Cooperative Settlement of Interpersonal Conflict *(continued)*

IMPEDIMENT	EXPLANATION	EXAMPLE
Loss aversion	A disputant would rather gamble on a likely huge loss than pay out a smaller loss now.	A Defendant, faced with an offer of settlement if he pays $25,000, prefers to try the case although his lawyer warns that he's very likely to lose more than that.
Linkages	Settling this case will affect other situations in unpredictable or damaging ways.	A prosecutor refuses to accept a plea-bargain offer from a defendant accused of accounting fraud—even though the evidence in the case is weak—because of the slap-on-the-wrist message that might be sent to others with similar cases pending.
Conflicts of interest among team members	A settlement that addresses the interests of one team member well does a bad job of addressing the interests of another team member.	A mother refuses to settle a pending child custody case with her child's father because civility with this man enrages her present husband.
Excluded stakeholders	One of the important stakeholders in the conflict is left out of the negotiations and therefore sabotages efforts to complete a settlement.	During negotiations over custodial arrangements for a teenager, parental efforts to institute visitation arrangements fall apart when the teenager refuses to go to the mother's house as specified in the agreement.
Disempowered disputant	A disputant feels overmatched during a conflict and is fearful that agreeing to a settlement will harm him.	A major corporation can't convince a frightened consumer to settle a warranty claim despite the honest beliefs of corporate counsel that they have bent over backwards to accommodate the consumer.
Unpleasant disputant	A disputant, or a member of the disputant's team, is so unpleasant that settling with her leaves a bad taste.	A defendant can't bring herself to settle with the plaintiff: the latter has made the defendant's life so miserable that the defendant finds giving her any sort of satisfaction to be intolerable.
Competitive culture or subculture	A disputant or negotiator comes from a culture or subculture in which competition is the primary blueprint for conflict management.	In a dispute over baseball salaries, both owners and players believe that it is inappropriate to cooperate with the opposition.

EXERCISES, PROJECTS, AND "THOUGHT EXPERIMENTS"

1. *Conflict journal.*

   a. Consider each of the impediments to resolving conflict that are listed in this chapter. For each, determine whether it is applicable to your main conflict and, if so, how it applies. List and describe *all* the impediments to resolving the main conflict cooperatively.

   b. Now rate the importance of each impediment on a scale of 1 to 10, with 10 designating an impediment you consider to be critical in preventing the resolution of this conflict.

    c. In your journal, brainstorm some strategies and tactics you could use to overcome each of the impediments you found.

    d. Are any of the options you came up with in exercise c risky in any way? Consider the possible damaging effects of each option.

    e. If you decide that the benefits clearly outweigh the risks for one or more of the strategies and tactics you brainstormed in exercise c, try implementing the strategy and/or tactic to see if you can overcome the impediment to resolution. Write in your journal about how well the strategy or tactic worked and what applying it has taught you about conflict diagnosis and conflict resolution.

2. Identify as many impediment(s) to conflict as you can find in the following fact situation and suggest tactics that a conflict diagnostician could recommend for overcoming each impediment:

> *Tilly and Tom Tenant rent a rowhouse from Lonny and Lisa Landlord. The Tenants and the Landlords recently made a deal whereby the Tenants would paint the interior of the rowhouse and the Landlords would pay for the supplies. The Tenants did the painting, then presented a bill for supplies to the Landlords—for $800. In the opinion of the Landlords, the Tenants spent at least five times as much for these items as they should have. The Landlords had recently painted their own, much larger home for about $300. Unbenownst to them, the Tenants had never painted a house before and had been led into buying the expensive supplies by getting some bad advice from a salesperson at a high-end paint store. Lonny Landlord, in reply to the bill, left a nasty message on the Tenants' answering machine. "How dare you?" he said. "Your claim is absolutely ridiculous. It's a slap in the face." Several words and phrases inappropriate for polite company followed. Tilly Tenant listened to the message as she was giving her four-year-old and six-year-old snacks after school. "Outrageous," she thought, utterly shocked. "They know we have young children! What an unfeeling, inhuman thing to do—leaving such a message!" She expressed her rage and sadness to her husband, who vowed to get back at the Landlords for their abusive telephone message. Tilly saw a legal services lawyer the next day. He advised her to withhold rent and, if threatened by the Landlords, to claim that they were being forced out of the rowhouse by the Landlords' abusive behavior. Thus, the following month's rent check was for $26.50. This outraged the Landlords, who filed for an eviction. In landlord-tenant court, the parties were referred to mediation. However, the mediator was unable to make any headway with the dispute. The Landlords, without benefit of legal assistance, felt uncertain about whether to accept any proposed settlements, because they weren't sure whether they were being "taken," so the mediator suggested that the mediation go into recess to allow the Landlords to get some legal advice. Unfortunately, instead of talking to a lawyer, Lisa Landlord talked to*

her brother, who was firmly of the opinion that one should never coop-erate with one's adversaries. When the parties returned to mediation, proposals that seemed reasonable to Lonny Landlord were unacceptable to Lisa Landlord (who wanted to avoid ridicule from her family) and vice versa. Finally, after a short break, the Landlords were able to agree to propose paying the Tenants $650 to cover most of their paint expenses and to terminate eviction proceedings. Unfortunately, during the recess after the previous session, the Tenants had also been discussing the dis-pute with their family relations. One of them had suggested that the Tenants hold out for many thousands of dollars on the basis that the epithet-ridden telephone message had damaged the Tenants' young chil-dren. Thus, the mediation ended in impasse. Later, when the Tenants were evicted, Tilly Tenant commented to her husband that, although she knew her chances of such a huge recovery were small, she had felt that the opportunity was worth the risk of losing altogether.

3. Write an essay discussing the following questions, or use them as a basis for discussion or debate: "Which of the impediments to resolution do you be-lieve are currently operating to prevent resolution of the Israeli-Palestinian conflict? What can world leaders do to overcome these impediments?"

4. Refer back to the definitions of *mediation* and *nonbinding evaluation* set forth in Chapter 1. Consider each impediment to settlement individually. Which of these two ADR processes do you think would be best at over-coming each impediment to settlement? Why? Justify your responses. Com-pare your answers with those of other students. If your opinions differ, discuss the reasons for your differences.

5. Write about, discuss, or debate the following questions: "Should it be an at-torney's role to discover the impediments to cooperative settlement? Or should an attorney merely be a litigation specialist? Should there be attorney-specialists who litigate and others who hold themselves out as non-adversarial specialists who would evaluate impediments? What would be the advantages and the disadvantages of such a two-tiered system of lawyering?"

6. Is there a conflict of interest for lawyers between overcoming impediments to conflict—and serving the client's best interests effectively—and main-taining a busy litigation practice? Imagine yourself to be a lawyer. A client comes to you, contending that he was cut out of a deal for royalties on a compact disc produced by his band. The disc is hugely successful and he is out several million dollars. He wants to sue for breach of contract. Litigation would be long and expensive, and your client would most likely lose. As-sume for this exercise that the client has enough funds to pay any legal fees he incurs in litigation. Settling out of court is a possibility. Consider each of the following statements. If your advice to the client about the costs and benefits of litigating were limited to the statement, would you be behaving ethically? Why or why not?

    a. "I could represent you in court, and, if we win, you'll get at least $10 million and up to $7 million after fees and expenses are deducted. I advise you to do it."

    b. "I could represent you in court, and, if we win, you'll get at least $10 million and up to $7 million after fees and expenses are deducted. Whether you'll win is uncertain, given the contract you signed. It's up to you whether to go to court."

    c. "I could represent you in court, and, if we win, you'll get at least $10 million and up to $7 million after fees and expenses are deducted. But, given the contract you signed, there's very little chance you'll win, and, if you lose, you'll be out $2 to $3 million in fees and expenses. It's up to you whether to go to court, but, as your attorney, I'd advise you to seriously consider settlement."

    d. (Assume that you have made statement c but the client is still committed to going to court. You respond with the following statement.) "You know, many times, disputants want to go to court for a chance at a big recovery, despite the fact that the chance of that recovery is very small. I just want to warn you that I think you may be hurting your own financial interests very severely if you litigate this matter. You have about as much chance of winning as you do being struck by lightning. I'm still willing to try the case for you, but I'd urgently suggest you think twice about it."

7. Play the Prisoner's Dilemma game. Computerized versions are available at the following websites:

    a. Repeated Prisoner's Dilemma Applet, *http://www.gametheory.net/Web/PDilemma/default.htm*

    b. Serge Helfrich's Prisoner's Dilemma, *http://www.xs4all.nl/~helfrich/prisoner/index.html*

    c. LIFL—UPRESA Iterated Prisoner's Dilemma Game, *http://www.lifl.fr/IPD/applet-tournament.html*

    d. You Have Found the Prisoner's Dilemma (Grobstein & Dixon 1994), *http://serendip.brynmawr.edu/playground/pd.html*

    e. The Prisoner's Dilemma, *http://www.princeton.edu/~mdaniels/PD/PD.html* (Princeton University)

In what ways does the Prisoner's Dilemma accurately reflect real life? In what ways does it not reflect reality? What does the play of this game tell you about the conditions needed for cooperation to occur? How could you set up negotiation to create conditions that promote cooperation? If you use the Princeton University game, try each of "Albert's strategies." Which of Albert's strategies best reflect reality in the legal setting, and why? What strategies work best for you when dealing with each of Albert's strategies?

RECOMMENDED READINGS

Kim, S. H., and R. H. Smith. 1993. Revenge and conflict escalation. *Negotiation Journal* 9(1):37–43.

Mnookin, R. H. 1993. Why negotiations fail: An exploration of the barriers to resolution of conflict. *Ohio State Journal on Dispute Resolution* 8(2):235–49.

Pruitt, D. G., and P. V. Olczak. 1995. Beyond hope: Approaches to resolving seemingly intractable conflict. In *Conflict, cooperation and justice: Essays inspired by the work of Morton Deutsch* (pp. 59-92), edited by B. B. Bunker, J. Z. Rubin, and Associates. San Francisco: Jossey-Bass.

Sander, F. E. A., and S. Goldberg. 1994. Fitting the forum to the fuss: A user-friendly guide to selecting an ADR process. *Negotiation Journal* 10 (January):49–68.

12

Step 7. Assess the Negotiation Styles and Practices of the Participants

"To jaw-jaw is better than to war-war."

—Winston Churchill

In this chapter, you will learn …

- Why Deutsch's theory of cooperation and competition doesn't tell the whole story about behavior in a conflict.
- How it's possible to cooperate without being taken advantage of.
- The five negotiation styles.
- The best negotiation styles to use for preserving cooperation.
- The best negotiation styles to use for self-protection.
- The negotiation skills of the best negotiators.
- Some ways of assessing your own preferred negotiation style and those of your clients, associates, team, and other disputant team.
- Tactics that can be used to develop win-win solutions to conflict.

Most interpersonal conflicts are resolved through a process of discussion among the disputants. This includes more than nine out of every ten legal disputes that are filed in court in the United States. Even if a conflict must be resolved in court, or (as in international conflicts) through military intervention, the conflict almost always passes through a period of verbal or written discussion on the way. And virtually all cooperative conflicts are resolved through discussion. A discussion among disputants or their representatives, aimed at dealing with or resolving an interpersonal conflict, is known as **negotiation.**

Negotiation styles and practices determine how each conflict participant will respond to the others. Thus, knowing the nature of prior negotiation behaviors, and of the likely course of future negotiation behavior, lends insight into how the conflict itself is likely to proceed, whether it will escalate or be resolved, how it will be resolved, and whether the resolution is likely to be permanent or fall apart later.

Negotiation
a dialogue, discussion, or written exchange aimed at resolving a dispute or consummating a transaction.

NEGOTIATION THEORY AND DEUTSCH'S MODEL

One way to look at the negotiation behavior of disputants and their agents and advocates is to characterize the behavior as cooperative or competitive—according to Deutsch's model of conflict. Indeed, for many years, this was the predominant approach to characterizing negotiation.

This approach has some advantages. First, seeing negotiation behavior as either cooperative or competitive seems intuitively correct. Many studies have shown that people observing negotiating behavior tend to see the behavior as either cooperative or competitive (Coltri 1995; van de Vliert & Prein 1989). Additionally, understanding negotiation behavior as either cooperative or competitive can shed light on whether the overall course of conflict is likely to be constructive or destructive, as discussed in detail in Chapter 9.

On the other hand, there are a number of important limitations to applying Deutsch's theory. First, Deutsch intended the cooperation-competition model to refer to the overall course of conflict, rather than to the behaviors of individual disputants and their representatives. In fact, although the model is an accurate representation of the perception of *observers* of conflict behavior, it does not accurately describe the *self-perceptions* of people in conflict. For example, although observers of conflict will often interpret assertive behavior as showing intent to do harm to the other side, self-attribution of the same behavior is likely to be much more complex: disputants explaining their own assertive behavior will attribute motive to a mixture of self-protection, necessary response to an action of the other disputant, and appropriate levels of concern for the other disputant's welfare (van de Vliert & Prein 1989).

Second, the Deutsch model doesn't deal with the situation in which each team comes to the bargaining table using different strategies. *Cooperation* and *competition,* due to their cyclical nature, refer to the conflict, rather than to any individual disputant. Individual participants often enter a conflict with divergent strategies, and it is the interactions between these approaches that nudge the conflict into either a cooperative or a competitive course.

A third, and critical, limitation of the Deutsch model is the implication that there can be only one form of cooperation. In fact, there are very important differences among cooperative negotiation strategies. One form of cooperation might be deemed the "pushover" strategy: one can bow to the wishes of the other disputant, letting him or her have his or her way. But there is another option, albeit one that people are somewhat less familiar with: one can cooperate and still protect one's interests. This latter form of cooperation requires the disputant to treat the conflict as a joint problem to be solved: how to address one's own interests while meeting the needs and interests of the other disputant.

THE DUAL-CONCERN MODEL

To address the limitations of Deutsch's model, social and organizational psychologists working in the midtwentieth century (see Blake & Mouton 1964, 1970) developed a "dual-concern model of negotiation behavior.[1]

To understand this model of negotiation, it is useful to define two dimensions of concern for disputants.[2] The first dimension is concern for the satisfaction of one's own interests. Conflict theorists refer to this dimension as "assertiveness," "concern for self," or "agency." The other dimension is concern for the satisfaction of the interests of the other disputant. This dimension is referred to as "cooperativeness," "concern for other," "concern for relationships," or "communion."

A pervasive belief about the nature of conflict is that these two dimensions are polar opposites, as shown in Figure 12-1. Thus, if disputants are concerned about their own well-being, they will be willing to harm the other disputant; if disputants are concerned about the well-being of the other disputant, they will be willing to let the other walk all over them. Thus, in this model of the negotiation process, one can either act in one's self-interest, tough and nasty, or be cooperative, and risk losing all one has. An adaptation of an Old West expression fits this concept about negotiation: "There's not enough room in this conflict for the two of us. It's either you or me." This either-or proposition reflects the invisible veil, in which self-protective behavior in a conflict must always be competitive, or adversarial.

The leap made by scholars beginning with Blake and Mouton was the realization that these two dimensions do not represent opposites but, instead, independent dimensions of behavior. And disputants' behaviors can simultaneously reflect varying levels of both concerns. Thus, disputants can evidence high levels of concern for both self and other, or low levels of concern for both self and other, as well as a high level of one concern and low level of the other.

Developing practical meaning from this insight, the dual-concern theorists proposed five basic negotiation styles (also sometimes referred to as "conflict styles"):

1. The *avoiding style,* which represents a low level of concern for both self and other;

2. The *dominating* (or *competing*) *style,* which represents a high level of concern for self and a low level of concern for other

---

[1] The work of social psychologists in the field were presaged by political scientist Mary Parker Follett in the 1920s, who wrote about "constructive conflicts" and the need for integrative approaches (Menkel-Meadow 2000, 7–10).

[2] For this discussion, we will assume two disputants negotiating without agents or advocates. Note that the situation is made more complex if there are more than two disputants or if the negotiation involves representatives. A careful conflict diagnostician will consider the complexities.

◆ **FIGURE 12-1**

Deutsch's Cooperation-Competition Theory

COOPERATION
High concern for other

COMPETITION
High concern for self

3. The *obliging* (or *accommodating*) *style,* which represents a low level of concern for self and a high level of concern for other

4. The *integrating* (or *collaborating* or *problem-solving*) *style,* which represents a high level of concern for both self and other

5. The *compromising style,* which represents a moderate level of concern for self and other[3]

The Dual-Concern model is summarized in Table 12-1 and diagrammed in Figure 12-2.

The dual-concern model is easier to understand when discussed using a concrete example. See the box feature (p. 220) "The Parable of the Two Sisters and the Orange."[4] The parable contains several truths about interpersonal conflict. First, the avoiding style generally results in the *least efficient outcome* for all involved, in terms of whether the outcome meets the needs of the disputant. (This negative result may be partially offset, in the real world of legal disputing, by a reduction in the costs of disputing.) *Efficient* means, in this discussion, that the outcome takes best advantage of differing values placed on the resources of the disputants. If Enid highly values the juice and does not value the rind, whereas the opposite is true of Esther, the most efficient outcome is to allocate the juice to Enid and the rind to Esther. Economists refer to this form of efficiency as **Pareto-efficiency.**

Second, the *most Pareto-efficient* style, in terms of meeting everyone's underlying interests and needs, is integrating. The integrating negotiation style is associated with the most creative, effective, and efficient settlement outcomes.

Third, a *free flow of information* is required to use the integrating style successfully. Notice that, in order to create the conditions for an integrative resolution of the dispute, the two sisters had to share information about underlying interests. In the Two Sisters Parable, other creative and Pareto-efficient solutions may also exist and may be explored by means of interests analysis and the sharing of information about underlying interests. For example, if Enid needs the whole orange to accomplish some goal of hers—for example, making a cake requiring both juice

Pareto-efficiency

the quality of a settlement agreement or another social arrangement to maximize overall value to the participants by allocating specific resources to those who value them most.

---

[3] Some commentators maintain that compromising and integrating are not separate styles but, instead, represent the same style used to address conflicts that have different potentials for integrative resolution. However, given that compromising can be used to resolve conflicts that are amenable to more creative, integrative approaches, it is useful to conceptualize it as a separate style. Whether it is actually a style based on moderate levels of concern for self and other is yet unresolved.

[4] The parable is popularly attributed to Mary Parker Follett (Menkel-Meadow 2000, 8, note 39).

◆ **TABLE 12-1**   The Five Negotiation Styles

NEGOTIATION STYLE	CONCERN FOR SELF	CONCERN FOR OTHER	EXAMPLE
Avoiding	Low	Low	In response to concerns raised by Muriel to her workmate, Reginald, about who should take on phone duty in the office, Reginald says nothing and pretends she never spoke to him.
Obliging, accommodating	Low	High	In response to Muriel's request to Reginald that he take on phone duty in the office during lunch, Reginald does so.
Dominating, competing	High	Low	In response to Muriel's request to Reginald that he take on phone duty in the office during lunch, Reginald refuses and threatens to lodge a complaint against Muriel for dereliction of duty.
Compromising	Moderate	Moderate	Muriel and Reginald agree that Muriel will do phone duty on Mondays and Wednesdays, that Reginald will do phone duty on Tuesdays and Thursdays, and that they will alternate Fridays.
Integrating, collaborating, problem-solving	High	High	In recognition of the fact that, as administrative assistants, both Muriel and Reginald are overqualified to answer phones, they agree to approach their supervisor mutually to ask her to assign phone duty to an employee of lower rank.

◆ **FIGURE 12-2**

Dual-Concern Model
Adapted from Psenicka and Rahim 1989.

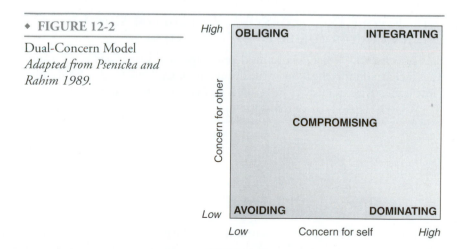

The Parable of the Two Sisters and the Orange

THE SITUATION

Two sisters who live together both go to the kitchen at the same time for an orange. Alas, there is only one orange in the refrigerator, so a dispute arises between them as to which sister should get the orange.

THE STYLES
(FOR SIMPLICITY, EXAMPLES SHOW BOTH SISTERS
USING THE SAME STYLE TO ADDRESS THE CONFLICT)

AVOIDING (LOW CONCERN FOR SELF AND OTHER)

The sisters do nothing, since they can't decide. Two weeks later, there are two dissatisfied sisters and one very moldy orange in the fridge.

We, the taxpayers, foot the bill for disposal of the wasted orange.

DOMINATING, OR COMPETING (HIGH CONCERN FOR SELF AND LOW CONCERN FOR OTHER)

The sisters agree to an arm-wrestling contest, with the winner taking the orange. Enid wins the orange, with Esther the loser. Enid juices the orange and drinks the juice. Esther is unhappy.

We, the taxpayers, foot the bill for disposal of the orange rind, which is better than wasting the whole orange.

OBLIGING, OR ACCOMMODATING (LOW CONCERN FOR SELF AND HIGH CONCERN FOR OTHER)

Enid says, "You take the orange, Esther." Esther replies, "No, no, deary, you take it. I want you to have it." Enid rejoins, "I couldn't possibly, Esther darling. You take it." Unless one or both sisters can recover from their case of terminal etiquette, the result will be the same as for avoiding.

Another possible outcome is that one sister relents and takes the orange, an outcome similar to that for dominating, except that animosity may be less.

COMPROMISING (MODERATE CONCERN FOR BOTH SELF AND OTHER)

The sisters agree to divide the orange in half. Enid juices her half and has a tiny glass of juice. Esther grates the rind from her half orange for a cake (except she doesn't have quite enough). The result is two half-satisfied sisters and a half-wasted orange.

We, the taxpayers, have about the same bill for waste disposal that we had for the dominating/competing outcome.

INTEGRATING, COLLABORATING, OR PROBLEM-SOLVING (HIGH CONCERN FOR BOTH SELF AND OTHER):

Enid asks Esther, "What do you need an orange for?" Esther replies, "I need the rind for my cake." (Integrating always includes an investigation of the disputants' underlying needs.) Enid smiles and says, "Then there is no problem. I just want a glass of juice." The result is two satisfied sisters and a fully utilized orange.

We, the taxpayers, have less waste to dispose of. (Now, if we could only find some use for the seeds!)

and rind—whereas Esther needs to bake a cake but knows how to make only orange cake—Enid might agree to help Esther with an equally delicious recipe not requiring an orange, with the result that Esther both meets her immediate needs and learns a new recipe. The possibilities for integrative solutions are limited only by the scope of the interests analysis and the creativity and time available to the negotiators.

CONSIDERATIONS INVOLVED IN USING THE FIVE NEGOTIATION STYLES

Conflict diagnosticians can gain more insight into the five styles by grouping them in three ways: according to (1) their *usefulness in inducing cooperation,* (2) their *self-protectiveness,* and (3) whether they can be *used without the consent of the other team.*

Usefulness in Inducing Cooperation. It follows from Deutsch's theory of cooperation and competition that those styles involving a high level of concern for other would be most likely to motivate cooperation in the other disputant. The two styles with the highest levels of concern for other are integrating and obliging, with compromising being moderately cooperative in orientation. These styles are all known as cooperative negotiating styles. Dominating, because its low degree of concern for other is coupled with a high degree of active engagement in the conflict, is least likely to produce a cooperative response in the other disputant.

Self-protectiveness. The styles that are the most obviously protective of a disputant's own interests are the dominating and integrating styles: each involves a high degree of motivation to promote self-interest. (Compromising is also self-protective, albeit to a lesser extent.) Avoiding and obliging are both styles that do little to protect the interests of the disputant using the style (though there may be times in which these styles protect interests better than any of the others). Although dominating is overtly protective of self-interest, it may produce a competitive response in the other disputant; accordingly, it may be seen as less self-protective than the integrating style.

We can conclude that, of the five styles, the one style that is most *protective of self-interest, while promoting a cooperative response in the other disputant,* is the integrating style. For this reason, most conflict resolution professionals advocate integrating as the negotiation style of choice when a choice is available. If all other things are equal, this is usually considered the best option.

Why is this so? First, integrating allows the disputants to seek out and take advantage of *integrative opportunities* in bargaining, those opportunities that address the unique interests of each disputant to maximize creatively the gains of each. This feature of integrating means that "the pie" can be expanded, so that each disputant can get more of the resources that are the most useful to him or her (in other words, the disputants can work at producing a Pareto-efficient settlement). Integrating also *builds relationships without self-sacrifice.* A disputant can be cooperative without knuckling under. A negotiator can be tough without appearing nasty. Integrating is also *generally less harmful than other styles in cases of power imbalance* to less powerful disputants because all interests are acknowledged and made important.

Integrating is, therefore, a very useful negotiation style. What is needed to set the stage for integrating? There are several essentials, including an interests analysis, the ability to cognitively multitask, and some cooperation.

No effort to use an integrating negotiation style can succeed unless each disputant conducts an effective interests analysis. This is because the negotiators need to be able to respond to the actual concerns of both disputants. Without an interests analysis, there is usually insufficient information about the disputants' real interests.

Integrating also requires the negotiators to be able to multitask. By definition, integrating involves the ability to concern oneself simultaneously with one's own interests and with the interests of the other disputant. Moreover, integrating requires the negotiators to abandon a preoccupation with bottom-line demands and to look for novel and creative solutions to the problem of meeting everyone's underlying interests. To meet these mental challenges, the negotiators must be able to retain and manipulate multiple, complex ideas in their minds. Integrating is difficult for people of limited cognitive capacities, such as small children, cognitively impaired persons, and individuals under extreme stress.

Finally, since integrating involves the honest sharing of information about individual interests, a certain degree of cooperativeness is needed. Enough trust between the disputants must exist so that they can share the necessary information. (Note that, for the integrating style to succeed, it is *not* necessary to reveal either bottom lines or aspirations. Thus, integrating can occur even with mistrustful disputants, assuming that they are able to find a way to safely share information about their interests.)

Mutual and Unilateral Styles. To engage successfully in both integrating and compromising, both disputants and their teams have to consent to using these styles at the same time. Thus, integrating and compromising require *mutuality*. An expert negotiator is adept at promoting the use of particular styles, such as integrating, to the other negotiator. A good negotiator will judiciously exercise his or her interpersonal power to convince the other negotiator that it is in his or her best interests to adopt a particular style. For example, a negotiator who wants to adopt integrating as a negotiation style, but is faced with a negotiator who wants to use dominating, might show the other that he or she is equally able to use dominating and that this course of conduct will result in personal loss to the other.

Frequently, however, a negotiator does not have a choice about which negotiation style to use. In such a situation, the negotiator is left with the styles that he or she can adopt, regardless of the style adopted by others—dominating and obliging. These styles require no concurrence of the other: they are *unilateral* styles. (Avoiding is only unilateral up to a point: if one disputant tries to engage another disputant in conflict resolution, the avoidant disputant can often be forced to choose between obliging and a coercive dispute resolution process, such as litigation.) Thus, although it is correct to say that integrating is a preferred style of negotiation overall, it is also correct to say that a negotiator should be fluent in using the unilateral, as well as the mutual, negotiation styles. And, in assessing a disputant's preferences about negotiation style, both the disputant's overall preferred style and the disputant's preferred unilateral style are important. The preferred unilateral style is the fallback style for the disputant if his or her initial efforts to use a preferred mutual style fail. Consider, for example, the following situation:

A disputant's preferred unilateral negotiation style will affect how she reacts when encountering resistance from the other disputant. David Young-Wolff, Photo Edit

A mother goes to a therapist, complaining that she is unable to get along with her adolescent daughter. The mother expresses a sincere desire to maintain a cooperative relationship with the girl and is baffled by the fact that they always seem to end up in screaming matches.

The therapist assesses the negotiation style of her client in relation to the daughter and discovers that, indeed, she has a cooperative orientation: integrating is her preferred style and compromising is her second choice. Far behind both integrating and compromising, dominating is her number-three negotiation style preference, with avoiding and obliging running behind that. Evidently, the daughter prefers avoiding, and the mother has been unaware of the need to convince the daughter to use either mutual style. Met with her adolescent brick wall, the mother finds herself slipping immediately into a dominating style. The therapist and mother work on teaching the mother how to persuade the daughter of the benefits of integrating, and they work on the patience the mother needs to see this through. The therapist also suggests the daughter participate in a high school peer mediation program to shore up her knowledge and skills in integrating.

What are some situations when integrating isn't possible? First, and probably most commonly, integrating can't be used when the *other disputant wants to compete and you aren't powerful enough to persuade the other* to use a cooperative method of resolving the conflict. Second, integrating may not be possible when the disputant is disempowered: when he or she *doesn't have enough information to act in his or her own self-interest* and has no practical way of getting the information. Of course, in this scenario, there is no way to ensure that one's interests

"Getting to Yes"

Probably the best and most widely known description of the integrating style of negotiation is presented in the classic book *Getting to Yes,* by Roger Fisher, William Ury, and Bruce Patton of the Harvard Negotiation Project (2nd Edition, 1991, New York: Penguin Books). The authors of this short, highly readable, and incredibly popular book (it's occasionally referred to as "the negotiation bible" by aficionados) present a clear, cookbook-style and deceptively simple approach to achieving an integrating style of negotiation. Called *"principled negotiation,"* the method recommended by the authors consists of just four steps (this list is from their extremely useful Table of Contents):

- *"Separate the people from the problem."*   The authors advocate being "soft on the person, tough on the problem", making it easy for the other side to save face and feel good about getting an agreement and fighting hard to prevent personal or personality issues from creeping into the decision.
- *"Focus on interests, not positions."*   The authors strongly advocate taking steps to reveal interests on all sides of the conflict.
- *"Invent options for mutual gain."*   The authors recommend brainstorming to create as long a list of potential settlements as possible to avoid disputants having their egos become tangled up with specific proposals.
- *"Insist on using objective criteria."*   When the going gets tough, as it does in most negotiations, the authors recommend tapping resources such as independent guidelines, independent appraisers, mathematical formulae, nonbinding evaluation, and other means by which proposals can be evaluated objectively. Use of objective criteria can help move disputants past impasse and avoid the situation in which a disputant hangs onto a poor proposal out of an aversion to losing face.

Getting to Yes is must-reading for anyone studying negotiation or ADR, and provides invaluable assistance to anyone wanting to become a better negotiator.

will be addressed whatever style is appropriated. Third, integrating may not be possible when the disputant is *forced into another mode,* as when a disputant is forced into litigation and can't persuade the other disputant to try settling using an integrating style. Fourth, integrating is often not an option when there are *severe constraints on time or mental energy.*

Overall, the very best negotiators are experts in using all five styles, in determining when it is most helpful to use each style, and in persuading other disputants to engage in a cooperative negotiation style, preferably integrating.

TACTICS USED IN INTEGRATING

Expert integrators are familiar with five common tactics that support the integrating style of negotiation (Rubin, Pruitt, & Kim 1994, 173–79):

- ◆ Expanding the pie
- ◆ Cutting costs
- ◆ Nonspecific compensation
- ◆ Logrolling
- ◆ Bridging

Expanding the Pie. Expanding the pie involves making the resource pool larger. For example, imagine business partners disputing over what percentage of revenues should go to each partner. Partner A accuses Partner B of falling down on his responsibility to market their product; thus, Partner A is claiming that Partner B should not receive the 50 percent they agreed would go to him. The partners agree to resolve the conflict by hiring a marketing expert. Partner B will receive 50 percent of product revenues, from which will be deducted the cost of retaining the marketing expert. If the marketing expert is effective, the revenues will increase overall, providing more resources to pay the marketing expert and both partners.

Cutting Costs. Cutting costs is the converse of expanding the pie: it relies on cost reduction to increase the net revenues available for distribution. A classic example of a cost-cutting opportunity occurs in divorce negotiations in which the spouses have highly disparate incomes. For example, imagine a young, childless married couple, Spouse A and Spouse B, who are splitting up. Spouse A will be paying Spouse B a sum to equalize the division of property; Spouse A is willing to pay only $80,000 but Spouse B wants $90,000. Further assume Spouse A makes $150,000 a year and Spouse B makes $20,000. If the spouses are able to structure a series of payments that can legally be characterized as alimony, Spouse A will be able to deduct the payments from her income tax. Spouse B will have to claim the payments as income, but, given his much smaller income, he will probably not pay nearly as much in taxes as Spouse A saves. The additional cost savings can be used to sweeten the deal for both disputants. Without characterizing the payments as alimony, there would be no tax consequence of the payments and, accordingly, no opportunity to realize these savings.

Nonspecific Compensation. Nonspecific compensation refers to giving the other disputant "unrelated" compensation for giving up something of value. For example, imagine that Jacob and Maggie are involved in a fender-bender. Maggie has cosmetic damage to her car and demands $2,000 in compensation.[5] For Jacob, money is extremely hard to come by: he is a young and up-and-coming carpenter and it's the off season. Jacob reveals his monetary difficulties to Maggie, and Maggie thereupon reveals that she has some remodeling that she needs to do but doesn't have the cash to pay a remodeler. They agree to settle the auto accident by having Jacob do thirty hours of free carpentry work for Maggie. Maggie is comfortable with foregoing the repairs to her car, since the damage is cosmetic only. Maggie gets her remodeling done, and Jacob, if he is a good carpenter, gets a reference as well as a cash break.

Logrolling. Logrolling is simply the exchange of items that have values personal to the disputants. For example, Ginger and Brittany are friends who collect

---

[5] For purposes of simplification, ignore the likely existence of insurance in this example.

Beanie Babies for fun—and profit. Ginger's collection is nearly complete and would be worth a lot more if she had a single variety that Brittany has in duplicate. Brittany, on the other hand, lacks a single Beanie Baby that Ginger has in duplicate. Obviously, by each giving up their duplicate Beanie Baby, both can greatly increase the value of their collections.

Bridging. Bridging is responding to underlying interests rather than to positions. In essence, every effective integrating negotiation is a bridging process. For example, a husband in divorce mediation entered the process asking that he be given title to the family home immediately, so that he could take advantage of low interest rates to refinance his wife off the mortgage. The wife demanded that her name remain on the home title. In mediation, the wife revealed that she did not wish to own the house, and she knew she would benefit from the husband's refinancing the mortgage, but she wanted to protect her right to have access to the house. The couple had teenage children, and the spouses' plan was to have the children stay in the family home, with each parent rotating time with them there. The wife was worried that the husband could use his sole ownership to deny her time with the children when they were at the family home. These mutual interests were addressed by developing a written contract granting to the wife the right to enter the family home for parenting purposes, regardless of how it was titled.

LIMITATIONS ON THE USEFULNESS OF THE DUAL-CONCERN MODEL

Three principal limitations constrain the usefulness of the dual-concern model. First, most of the assumptions about the appropriateness of the five styles in responding to particular situations are theoretical: the theory is relatively untested. Research in the field of negotiation is highly complex, and results vary with the specific situation being assessed. Accordingly, it is hard to generalize about the appropriateness of various negotiation styles, and most of the information about the relative merits of the styles is anecdotal. There is, of course, plenty of evidence of the destructiveness of competition as a course of conflict; since the dominating style is competitive, the desirability of avoiding dominating where possible should be regarded as empirically well supported.

Second, the dual-concern model is grounded on the supposition that orientation toward self and other during a negotiation is never negative—that is, a disputant either has a positive regard for the interests of the other disputant or has no concern for the other disputant at all. This supposition ignores the situation, common in escalated conflict, in which the disputant is actually motivated to harm the other disputant (sadism), as well as the less common situation in which the disputant actually wishes harm to self (masochism). If these negative attitudes are incorporated into the model, the result looks like that shown in Figure 12-3.

In effect, the dual-concern model assumes rational behavior: the disputant is either motivated to aid self, motivated to aid other, neither, or both. However,

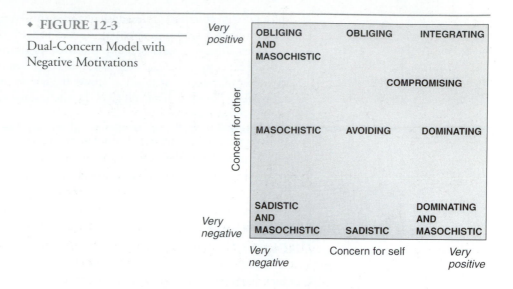

◆ **FIGURE 12-3**

Dual-Concern Model with Negative Motivations

in the real world, most of the time disputants in escalated conflict situations perceive the other team as having negative concern for the other—as operating somewhere in the bottom half of Figure 12-3. The dual-concern model would be more effective and useful if updated to include these negative, and apparently irrational, disputant motives.

The third limitation of the dual-concern model relates to the meaning of the term *negotiation style*. A negotiation style is an *overall strategy* for negotiating. A *strategy* is a general orientation. A strategy must be differentiated from a *tactic*—which is a specific behavior that someone uses to execute a strategy. A conflict diagnostician must take extreme care not to mistake one for the other. Consider the following example from a legal negotiation:

A young, inexperienced attorney was negotiating with her counterpart for a damages settlement of her client's medical malpractice claim. She wrote opposing counsel with her demand of $50,000 in compensatory damages, payable by the first of the following month by cashier's check, in exchange for her dismissal of the lawsuit and waiver of the right to ask for the defendant to pay court costs, and she briefly and cogently summarized the points in support of her assertion that her client had a very strong case.

A week later, the attorney was mortified to receive a scathingly hostile letter from opposing counsel. "How dare you" read the first words of the response, and the letter went on from there to accuse the attorney and client of everything from greed to stupidity. It suggested that opposing counsel had seriously considered taking the lawyer to the Attorney Grievance Commission to be professionally disciplined.

The attorney put the letter aside in shock and went home. The next day, in the quiet of early morning (after deciding not to change careers quite yet), she took out the letter again and reread it carefully. After all, she needed to determine whether she would be fired and reprimanded about whatever it was she had done wrong. She was relieved to see no actual substantive accusations of misconduct and surprised to discover that, in between volleys of acrimony, opposing counsel had accepted her offer! In talking to her supervisor later that day, the attorney learned that it is common practice for counsel in legal negotiation to couple an important concession to a show of apparent strength: it allows the lawyer to project a strong image to his or her own client and gives the client some satisfaction during the process of conceding.

In this example, the tactics used by opposing counsel seemed appropriate to a dominating style, yet the overall strategy of opposing counsel was to oblige. It's important never to mistake a tactic for a strategy.

MEASUREMENT OF NEGOTIATION STYLE PREFERENCES

Conflict diagnosticians need accurate ways to assess negotiation styles. What tools are available for assessing negotiation style preference in conflict participants?

A number of psychometric researchers have designed questionnaires, or "inventories," to assess the negotiation style preferences of individuals.[6] The best questionnaire, in terms of reliability and firm theoretical foundation, is the Rahim Organizational Conflict Inventory–II, or ROCI–II (Rahim 1983; Weider-Hatfield 1988). See Table 12-1. The questionnaire is designed to measure a disputant's preferences for using each of the five negotiation styles. For each of the five styles, the questionnaire yields a score, which represents the respondent's preference when playing a particular role in a negotiation with a particular other disputant. It does not purport to represent a person's negotiation profile generally.

There are several other negotiation style inventories that purport to measure similar negotiation style preferences (Putnam 1988). These include the Hall Conflict Management Survey, the Thomas-Kilmann Conflict MODE Survey, the Putnam-Wilson Organizational Communication Conflict Instrument (OCCI), and the Ross-deWine Conflict Management Message Style (CMMS).

However negotiation style is measured, it runs into problems when it is measured outside the business organizations context. In individual interper-

---

The Rahim Organizational Conflict Inventory–II

The Rahim Organizational Conflict Inventory–II can be purchased over the Internet from the Testing Materials Resource Book Online at *http://www.psychtest.com/curr01/CATLG003.HTM*, from Resources for the Study of Communication, at *http://www.uwec.edu/Sampsow/Resources/Measures.htm*, or in hard copy from the *Handbook of Tests and Measurement in Education and the Social Sciences,* Technomic Publishing Co. (Lester & Bishop 2001, 94–95).

---

[6] A psychometric researcher is a scientist who specializes in measuring psychological features, such as intelligence, attitude, and mental health.

Think of a person or an organization with whom you are currently having a dispute of concern to you. With this dispute in mind, read each of the following statements and decide how well or how poorly each describes your approach to this conflict. Use the following scale to give your answer:

6 = Describes your approach to the conflict extremely accurately

5 = Describes your approach to the conflict very accurately

4 = Describes your approach to the conflict somewhat accurately

3 = Describes your approach to the conflict somewhat inaccurately

2 = Describes your approach to the conflict very inaccurately

1 = Describes your approach to the conflict extremely inaccurately

6 5 4 3 2 1   1. I try to investigate an issue with _____ to find a solution acceptable to us.

6 5 4 3 2 1   2. I generally try to satisfy the needs of _____.

6 5 4 3 2 1   3. I attempt to avoid being "put on the spot" and try to keep my conflict with _____ to myself.

6 5 4 3 2 1   4. I try to integrate my ideas with those of _____ to come up with a decision jointly.

6 5 4 3 2 1   5. I try to work with _____ to find solutions to a problem which satisfy our expectations.

6 5 4 3 2 1   6. I usually avoid open discussions of my differences with _____.

6 5 4 3 2 1   7. I try to find a middle course to resolve an impasse.

6 5 4 3 2 1   8. I use my influence to get my ideas accepted.

6 5 4 3 2 1   9. I use my authority to make a decision in my favor.

6 5 4 3 2 1   10. I usually accommodate to the wishes of _____.

6 5 4 3 2 1   11. I give in to the wishes of _____.

6 5 4 3 2 1   12. I exchange accurate information with _____ to solve a problem together.

6 5 4 3 2 1   13. I usually allow concessions to _____.

6 5 4 3 2 1   14. I usually propose a middle ground for breaking deadlocks.

6 5 4 3 2 1   15. I negotiate with _____ so that a compromise can be reached.

6 5 4 3 2 1   16. I try to stay away from disagreement with _____.

6 5 4 3 2 1   17. I avoid an encounter with _____.

6 5 4 3 2 1   18. I use my expertise to make a decision in my favor.

6 5 4 3 2 1   19. I often go along with the suggestions of _____.

6 5 4 3 2 1   20. I use "give and take" so that a compromise can be made.

6 5 4 3 2 1   21. I am generally firm in pursuing my side of the issue.

6 5 4 3 2 1   22. I try to bring all our concerns out in the open so that the issues can be resolved in the best possible way.

6 5 4 3 2 1   23. I collaborate with _____ for a proper understanding of a problem.

6 5 4 3 2 1   24. I try to satisfy the expectations of _____.

6 5 4 3 2 1   25. I sometimes use my power to win a competitive situation.

6 5 4 3 2 1   26. I try to keep my disagreements with _____ to myself in order to avoid hard feelings.

6 5 4 3 2 1   27. I try to avoid unpleasant exchanges with _____.

6 5 4 3 2 1   28. I try to work with _____ for a proper understanding of a problem.

Source: Rahim, M. A. 1983. A measure of styles of handling interpersonal conflict. *Academy of Management Journal* 26(2):368–376.

sonal, nonbusiness contexts, these instruments tend not to be able to confirm the theoretical underpinnings of the dual-concern model, particularly with regard to the meaning of compromising (Hammock, Richardson, Pilkington, & Utley 1990; van de Vliert & Kabanoff 1990).[7]

Also, if a negotiation style questionnaire is used to assess an observed person, rather than to provide a self-report, it can result in missing the dual-concern aspects of the observed person's behavior. For example, in an unreported study by Coltri (1993), a small sample of ADR faculty members, who were asked to assess the negotiation styles of their mediation clients using the ROCI–II, tended to rate their clients as either displaying high concern for self and low concern for other or as displaying low concern for self and high concern for other, confirming Deutsch's one-dimensional model as applied to disputant negotiation styles. Other research (van de Vliert & Prein 1989, 51–66) confirms this general finding that, when observing others in conflict, people tend to see cooperation and self-assertion as mutually exclusive, and, since this phenomenon occurs with a variety of questionnaires and other methods used to assess negotiation style, it appears to be a problem with perception rather than with the questionnaires. The big question for conflict resolution researchers is whether this perceptual limitation can be reversed—through education and training, for example.

IMPLICATIONS FOR CONFLICT DIAGNOSTICIANS

A conflict diagnostician must always exercise caution not to confuse self-assertion with competitiveness and cooperativeness with weakness. The dual-concern model teaches us that high levels of concern for self (and, hence, high levels of assertiveness) can co-exist with altruism and a genuine desire to benefit the other disputant in the conflict. Research shows that we are better able to make this distinction when engaged in self-reflection than we are when we observe others. Thus, when a conflict diagnostician, particularly one who is a member of a disputant's team, is observing individuals from the other team, it is important to consider carefully whether the observations are being biased by oversimplification.

Since the integrating negotiation style has many benefits for disputants in conflict, a useful goal of a conflict diagnostician is to encourage negotiators to integrate. If the conflict diagnostician is a member of a disputant's team, there are two immediate goals: helping one's own side develop the skill and preparation needed to use the integrating style and convincing the other team to use integrating. However, since it is not always possible to accomplish either goal, the disputant's team should also develop the flexibility to use each of the five styles effectively.

---

[7] Factor analysis, a statistical process, is used to generate these conclusions.

EXERCISES, PROJECTS, AND "THOUGHT EXPERIMENTS"

1. *Conflict journal.*

    a. Take the ROCI–II, choosing the person with whom you have the most troublesome interactions in your conflict as the person "in the blanks." To score the ROCI–II,

        1. Add your scores for statements 3, 6, 16, 17, 26, and 27. Divide the total by 6. This is your score for *avoiding.*

        2. Add your scores for statements 2, 10, 11, 13, 19, and 24. Divide the total by 6. This is your score for *obliging/accommodating.*

        3. Add your scores for statements 7, 14, 15, and 20. Divide the total by 4. This is your score for *compromising.*

        4. Add your scores for statements 8, 9, 18, 21, and 25. Divide the total by 5. This is your score for *dominating/competing.*

        5. Add your scores for statements 1, 4, 5, 12, 22, 23, and 28. Divide the total by 7. This is your score for *integrating/collaborating/ problem-solving.*

    b. Interpret the scores.

    c. What was your highest score? What was your lowest score? What are the implications of these scores?

    d. What was your highest *unilateral* score? Given this score, what do you think you might do if the other disputant is unwilling to engage in the sort of negotiation you would prefer?

    e. Look at the five styles. Do you feel that you are proficient in using each of them?

    f. Given these results, do you see any need for you to work on increasing your proficiency or willingness to use any of the negotiation styles? Why or why not?

    g. Using the knowledge you have gained from this exercise, plan a strategy that you can use to improve your ability to fare well in this conflict.

2. The text states, *"[I] It follows from Deutsch's theory of cooperation and competition that those styles involving a high level of concern for other would be most likely to motivate cooperation in the other disputant."* Why is this so? Write a logical argument in support of this statement.

3. Spend an evening watching your favorite TV shows (fictional, not news or magazine shows). Keep a pad of paper and pencil on your lap. Divide the paper into five sections corresponding to the five negotiation styles. Each time you see an example of one of the five negotiation styles occurring in a show, under the appropriate section of the paper write down the name of the show, the characters involved, a brief description of the tactic the character used, the negotiation style you think the character was trying to use, and the

effectiveness of the tactic. (Incidents of physical violence should be placed under dominating/competing.) Reviewing the results of your investigation, what tactics and strategies predominated? Are you surprised? Which tactics and strategies appeared to be most effective? Did what you saw seem realistic? What macrosystem blueprints (Chapter 3) for resolving conflict were portrayed?

4. Repeat exercise 2 with a novel. Does this longer medium portray different conflict-handling blueprints?

5. Write about, discuss, or debate the merits of the following statement: "Negotiation style theory and skills should be taught to all students before they graduate from high school."

6. Identify each of the following statements of negotiators as more likely to represent efforts to use obliging/accommodating, avoiding, dominating/competing, integrating/collaborating/problem-solving, or compromising and justify your opinion. There may be more than one reasonable answer.

   a. A negotiator whose goal is to get $5,000 for medical expenses opens the negotiation saying, "I won't take a penny less than $100,000."

   b. A negotiator whose goal is to get $5,000 for medical expenses opens the negotiation saying, "I want $5,000 for my medical expenses."

   c. A negotiator whose goal is to get $5,000 for medical expenses opens the negotiation saying, "I won't take a penny less than $20,000." Then, after the other negotiator makes $100 her final offer, the first negotiator says, "I would consider settling at $12,000 just to get this case settled fast."

   d. A negotiator whose goal is to get $5,000 for medical expenses is told by the other party that he won't pay a penny. In response, the negotiator says, "If your position is based on reasons we can agree on, I'll say yes. Tell me the basis for that position."

   e. A negotiator who doesn't care when payment is made, within reason, says, "It's vitally important that I get paid immediately."

   f. A negotiator who doesn't care when payment is made says, "I care very much about the size of the payment, but I am not as concerned about when it is made."

   g. A negotiator threatens to walk out of the negotiation but, in fact, has no intention of doing so.

   h. In response to a request by the other disputant to engage in a negotiation session, a negotiator says, "My calendar is full. Let me get back to you on this next month." The negotiator has no firm plans to respond to the request and six weeks later has not yet called back.

   i. Same as situation h, except that the negotiator who is telephoned knows that the other disputant is desperate to get the case settled fast and wants to use the delay to get a better concession.

 j. A negotiator threatens to walk out of the negotiation unless the other party becomes more willing to explain her reasons for taking a position.

 k. A negotiator makes an important concession without any reason to expect a return.

 l. A negotiator asserts that the other side's case is weak and says, "If I walked out right now, I'd win twice as much in court."

 m. A negotiator makes an offer, which the other negotiator angrily rejects. The first negotiator expresses shock and comments that he could easily do better in court; however, then he immediately makes a more palatable offer. Assess the strategy of the *first* negotiator.

 n. There are two negotiators on each side of a dispute. When the defendant makes an offer, one of the plaintiff's negotiators turns beet-red, shouts embarrassing words at the defendant, and storms out of the room, slamming the door behind her. The other negotiator for the plaintiff shrugs her shoulders and gently says, "Well, what can I do? I'm stuck with her." Assess the likely strategy of the *plaintiff* team.

 o. In negotiation over the sale of an item in which price is an issue, a negotiator suggests submitting the issue of price to an independent appraiser selected by both parties' counsel.

 p. A negotiator insists on the other negotiator stating his "bottom-line offer," commenting that it would be impossible for the case to settle unless the offers were out on the table. Assess the likely strategy of the *first* negotiator.

RECOMMENDED READINGS

Blake, R. R., and J. S. Mouton J. S. 1964. *The managerial grid.* Houston, TX: Gulf.

Edwards, H., and J. White. *The lawyer as negotiator.* St. Paul, MN: West.

Fisher, R., W. Ury, and B. Patton. 1991. *Getting to yes: Negotiating agreement without giving in.* 2d ed. New York: Penguin Books.

Goodpastor, G. 1996. A primer on competitive bargaining. *Journal of Dispute Resolution* 1996:325–77.

Menkel-Meadow, C. 2000. Mothers and fathers of invention: The intellectual founders of ADR. *Ohio State Journal on Dispute Resolution* 16(1):1–37.

Riskin, L., and J. E. Westbrook, (eds.). 1997. Negotiation. In *Dispute resolution and lawyers* (pp. 148–311). St. Paul, MN: West.

Rubin, J. Z., D. G. Pruitt, and S. H. Kim. 1994. *Social conflict: Escalation, stalemate, and settlement.* 2d ed. New York: McGraw-Hill.

Van de Vliert, E., and H. C. M. Prein. 1989. The difference in the meaning of forcing in the conflict management of actors and observers. In *Managing conflict: An interdisciplinary approach* (pp. 51–63), edited by M. A. Rahim. New York: Praeger.

Weider-Hatfield, D. 1988. Assessing the Rahim Organizational Conflict Inventory–II (ROCI–II). *Management Communication Quarterly* 1(3):350–56.

13

Step 8. Assess Power and Alternatives to a Negotiated Agreement

"I don't know with what weapons World War III will be fought, but World War IV will be fought with sticks and stones."

—Albert Einstein

In this chapter, you will learn …

- That power is not merely about the ability to use physical force.
- That power exists in the personal, environmental, and relationship domains, with power during interpersonal conflict being exerted in the relationship domain.
- That coercive, reward, normative, referent, and expert power are all types of relationship power.
- That the varieties of relationship power are context-dependent for their effectiveness.
- That the use of each type of power is associated with predictable side effects, including the creation of alienation in the person on whom the power is exercised.
- That understanding your alternatives to a negotiated agreement, including the best alternative, can help you maximize your use of power in many ways.
- A step-by-step method of discovering the best alternative to a negotiated agreement and the benefits and drawbacks of conducting such an analysis.
- The problems created by power imbalance, along with appropriate approaches to redressing it.

For most people, the concepts of conflict and power are intertwined. The idea of conflict conjures up an image of two combatants, each seeking to use powerful means to gain an advantage over the other. The association of conflict with the use of force is inescapable in our culture: beginning with animated cartoons for preschoolers, we are taught that the highest form of heroism is to direct physical force against an evil foe. By these means, people learn that using force is the most efficient, the most effective, or, indeed, the only way to compel others to do what we wish.

Understanding power is essential to the study of interpersonal conflict, and diagnosing a conflict is impossible without also understanding power. However, like interpersonal conflict itself, our ideas about power have been distorted and made unduly narrow by the invisible veil. We cripple our ability to influence the course of conflict when we automatically equate power with the impulse to punish, harm, or destroy.

Consider the following examples:

1. A mother soothes her young infant with a gentle, enfolding embrace.
2. The members of a family whose home and town have been destroyed by a hurricane pull up stakes and move 20 miles to a new site to rebuild their lives.
3. A superstar athlete endorses a sports drink.
4. A revered teacher explains a difficult concept to a group of students.
5. Gary finally is able to quit smoking for good.
6. A Democratic Party website publishes information on political issues.
7. A lawyer, who has been negotiating fruitlessly with opposing counsel to settle an auto accident case, files suit for $5 million; a week later, opposing counsel calls with an offer to settle.

Power
deliberate or purposive influence.

You may be surprised to learn that all of these are examples of the use of power. Morton Deutsch (1973, 87) defined **power** as "deliberate or purposive influence." Thus, power need not have a destructive or coercive element. In fact, as we will see, although coercive forms of power are commonly used, they are typically not the best choice, in terms of the long-term impact on the course of conflict or the wielder of power.

DOMAINS OF POWER

When we talk about power, we may ask over what domain this deliberate or purposive influence is exercised. Deutsch (1973) and Coleman (2000, 108–30) identify three such domains:

1. *Environmental domain*—a person's surroundings
2. *Relationship domain*—a person's relationship to another person
3. *Personal*[1] *domain*—a person's own interests

You may want to examine the preceding seven examples to determine which domain each exemplifies. Personal and environmental power become more

---

[1] The term "personal power" is used in everyday communication to denote power of an individual in any of the three domains. This common usage is maintained throughout the text.

important when a disputant considers his or her alternatives to a negotiated agreement (discussed later in this chapter). However, of the three domains, relationship power is most obviously relevant to interpersonal conflict: since the disputants have conflicting goals, each disputant generally tries to exercise influence over the other.

KINDS OF POWER IN THE RELATIONSHIP DOMAIN

Many types of relationship power are available to disputants and their teams. An effective conflict diagnostician must think "outside the box" when it comes to considering the impact of power in a conflict. As we will see, equating powerfulness with the ability to inflict damage is unduly narrow, limiting the conflict participants to self-defeating, conflict-escalating choices. For this reason, a conflict diagnostician benefits from being aware of the many types of power and how each affects disputants and conflict. Like powerful pharmaceuticals, each type of power has unique uses, as well as its own set of harmful consequences if used inappropriately.

COERCIVE POWER

Coercive power is the type of power we are all most familiar with: the power to impose negative, damaging, or unpleasant consequences on someone else. Coercive power includes the power to kill or injure someone, to damage someone's property, to irritate someone, to create expensive outcomes, and so forth.

Coercive power often carries the greatest potential for immediate influence, particularly when the threat of harm is severe. However, coercive power also damages the ability of the disputant wielding the power to use other, more positive sources of influence later. Hence, an overreliance on coercive power actually disempowers the user, by denying him or her the ability to exercise any other types of power. Such a phenomenon has occurred in the Middle East. The process of engineering a lasting peace between Israel and the Palestinian people has been seriously compromised by the use of coercive power by both sides, with the Israeli government relying on institutional military and police power and selected Palestinian groups using terrorist attacks on Israeli civilians. The result has been an increase in pronouncements by leaders in both camps that the other side was never sincere about peace in the first place and that, in order to save themselves, it has been necessary to destroy the other side. Those groups of Israelis and Palestinians who wish to use nonviolent methods of protecting their own people through the development of a secure peace have lost any power they might have had to wield influence in the situation. As the Middle East conflict demonstrates, reliance on coercive power also has a tendency to lead to conflict escalation and the creation of a destructive competition cycle.

REWARD/EXCHANGE POWER

Reward/exchange power is the flip side of coercive power. Reward/exchange power is the ability to influence people by offering them something they value. Thus, a father offering his daughter money or a special treat in exchange for a good grade is exercising reward/exchange power. So is a disputant who offers to dismiss a lawsuit in exchange for a favorable settlement.

Coercive and reward/exchange power go hand in hand. Often, disputants in a conflict engineer situations that carry the threat of coercion, only to offer to withdraw the threat as a reward for a favorable outcome (as with the disputant who offers to dismiss his or her lawsuit). When reward/exchange power is wielded as threat withdrawal, it often creates the same problems that coercive power does. Additionally, as any parent can tell you, reward/exchange power becomes problematic when relied on repeatedly over time in a particular relationship. Offering a child a bribe for cleaning his room, for example, tends to work a few times, but typically more and more money has to be offered to produce the same behavior. On the other hand, reward/exchange power is very effective when there is a rational basis for concluding that the amount and type of reward is a just and fair exchange for items given up by the person being rewarded. In other words, reward/exchange power is most effective when the person being rewarded sees an intrinsic link between what is being offered and the overall just resolution of the conflict. For example, a child who is looking forward to a late afternoon play date can be rewarded with more time to play if she gets her room cleaned up quickly. Reward/exchange power is least effective, in the long run, when its use is perceived by the rewarded party as illegitimate, as in situations in which it is perceived as a bribe.

REFERENT POWER

Referent power is the power, held by attractive, charismatic people, to persuade and influence others. It is the power that drives the giant industry of celebrity product endorsement. The hundreds of millions of dollars paid to sports stars such as Tiger Woods and rock stars such as Britney Spears to appear with products as diverse as soft drinks, mutual funds, and underwear are a testament to the immense power of personal attraction.

Of course, not everyone possesses referent power, and, of those who do, their appeal is not to every audience. Thus, referent power must be used with some judiciousness. Also, referent power used in an illegitimate manner not only fails to persuade but also can undermine the power of the referent. For example, a mother who repeatedly uses her referent power over her small child to manipulate him covertly into meeting her personal needs—as in "If you really love me, you'll leave me alone so I can take a bath"—will eventually lose not only the ability to continue to do this but also a degree of referent power with the child she is manipulating.

NORMATIVE POWER

Normative power is the power of moral rectitude. Being on the "right" side of a moral issue gives the user the ability to convince others to serve the norm. For example, if I am your supervisor and you come to me, arguing that an employee of the opposite gender, of equal qualification and performance, is getting paid more than you, my commitment to gender equity is likely to convince me to increase your salary. You have successfully used your power of moral rectitude to influence me to meet your aspirations.

Normatively powerful people tend to acquire a certain degree of referent power by virtue of their noble or heroic positions with individuals or communities. Similarly, referently powerful people tend to gain normative power, as when an attractive or a charismatic public figure's stances on issues become more appealing because of the spokesperson. The power of rock groups and movie stars to collect funds for charitable causes demonstrates this relationship. Because of the close connection between normative and referent power, normatively powerful individuals can be influential regarding issues that lie outside the specific norms they are regarded as standing for. For example, in the 2000 presidential election, Ralph Nader's longstanding normative stature in the field of consumer protection gave him credibility with his followers to take stands on other issues, such as international affairs, for which he was not known to have expertise.

There are two sources of normative power, individual and group norms. If you try to convince someone to comply with your wishes based on that person's individual moral stance on an issue, you are using an individual-norm source of normative power. But, to wield normative power, it is not essential that the other disputant share the norm you are depending on, only that a large and influential group of people do so. For example, most people in the United States now express the opinion that people of color deserve the same civil rights as whites. If a disputant who claims that his or her civil rights as a person of color have been denied raises the issue with a racist governmental official, and can make a clear case that the norm has been violated, most likely the official will respond to the appeal, despite his or her personal attitude to the contrary. This is because public pressure to comply with prevailing norms will likely force the official into taking a step congruent with these prevailing norms.

There are two important limitations on the use of normative power. First, an appeal to prevailing norms taken to an individual disputant who does not hold to them will fail if the other disputant can rationalize that the norm is inapplicable. The ongoing debate over Affirmative Action demonstrates this point. Proponents of Affirmative Action argue that continuing remediation is needed to respond to ongoing threats to equal rights for all. If everyone agreed with this proposition, Affirmative Action would not be controversial. The problem is that Affirmative Action opponents make an appealing argument that Affirmative Action itself produces discrimination, precisely in opposition to the overall norm advanced by Affirmative Action's proponents. Each side in the debate is able to rationalize its stance by appealing to the same norm.

Second, obviously, the use of normative power will not be effective against an individual who holds to a contrary norm, if he or she has a significant support group. Indeed, in such circumstances, the use of normative power will only consolidate and harden the contrary group. For example, in the continuing controversy over abortion, an anti-abortion group that relies on lurid abortion-as-infanticide arguments in an attempt to persuade others is likely only to mobilize pro-abortion groups, which perceive this tactic as illegitimate. Similarly, efforts by abortion proponents to argue their position using arguments about back-alley abortions are likely to provoke only outrage and hardening from anti-abortion advocates. Thus, the use of normative power in such situations has the potential of creating an environment conducive to conflict escalation. To avoid this result, a careful interests analysis of the conflict participants can be helpful: even among disputants on opposite sides of the abortion debate, there are shared norms and values on all sides that can be articulated to serve effective conflict resolution.

EXPERT POWER

It is critical for legal professionals and other dispute resolvers to be familiar with expert power, the power of knowledge. Expert power is effective when the wielder has considerable knowledge and the person he or she is trying to influence comes to accept this degree of knowledge.

Expert power, used honestly to persuade others, is considered the least likely form of power (1) to disempower the person exercising the power and (2) to result in conflict escalation (Deutsch 1973, 87–93). It may also be the type of power most amenable to cultivation in many circumstances—it can be obtained simply by increasing one's knowledge.

The United States wielded considerable expert power throughout the twentieth century in such arenas as conflict resolution (as when it acted as a mediator in international conflicts), public health, and agricultural science and technology. It offered this expertise, often, in service of its own goals (for example, offering agricultural technology to prevent famine serves international security and economic stability). Turning to a more local venue, expert power is wielded by attorneys when they argue legal points with one another and before judges. Lawyers who can convince the other disputant that they have the correct interpretation of the law on their side can often obtain a favorable settlement for their clients. The following is an example of expert power used in a legal negotiation:

> A middle-aged man visited a legal clinic, complaining that he had been contacted by a bank about a past-due obligation. The debt was an auto loan for a car the client had owned jointly with his ex-wife over a decade ago. The man and his ex had entered into a separation agreement providing that the wife would receive title to the car and would accept responsibility for the auto loan. The husband turned over title and the wife began paying the loan. Sometime after the divorce, the ex-wife and car disappeared, and, reported the bank, the ex stopped paying the loan. The bank tried to find the ex-wife, but to no avail. The bank had a much easier time

The acquisition of information empowers disputants and improves their chances of a positive outcome. Here, a potential car buyer jots down price tag information, becoming a more informed consumer. Fay Torresyap, Stock Boston

finding the ex-husband, who, unfortunately, was still a co-obligor on the loan. Because of interest and penalties, the balance due had swelled to over $12,000.

The attorney's research paralegal verified that the ex-husband could be held liable for the unpaid loan because the separation agreement with the ex-wife did not bind the bank. The ex-husband had the option of paying the loan and subsequently suing his ex-wife for reimbursement under their contract, but, unfortunately, he had no better idea than the bank where she was. Moreover, the likelihood of her having the funds to pay him was slim.

Looking further at the law, however, the paralegal found evidence that the lending rate charged by the bank exceeded state legal standards. Hence, the loan could be considered "usurious" and held invalid. The attorney, with the paralegal's research memorandum in hand, contacted the bank. He presented the evidence to the lender that the loan might be considered illegal by a court. Two weeks later, the attorney received a letter from the bank, stating that, in return for the client's information about the last known whereabouts of the ex-wife, it would permanently waive any right to proceed against the ex-husband for the loan amount.

Expert power can be used illegitimately, and this misuse can create a sense of alienation in the person against whom it is used—for example, a daughter whose father requires her to engage in some action "for her own good," when, in fact, it obviously serves the father's interests, will cease to believe in the father's honest use of expert power. The illegitimate or dishonest use of expert power disempowers the wielder by creating the belief, on the part of the other disputant, that the claimed superior knowledge is a lie.

ECOLOGICAL POWER

Ecological power is the power to manipulate the environment. For example, imagine a dispute between two neighbors. Norman Neighbor is complaining that Perry Petowner's dog tramples Norman's vegetables. Norman exercises ecological power by erecting a fence to keep out the dog.

Although some social scientists (Deutsch 1973, 87) list ecological power as a separate type of power in the relationship domain, in fact, it functions in the environmental domain as a means of exercising other types of power. Disputants often use ecological means to exercise coercive power (as when the Israeli government bulldozed a Palestinian settlement it claimed was "illegal") or reward/exchange power (as when the settlement of a dispute involves one disputant's improving an aspect of another disputant's environment). Ecological power may also be exercised without influencing relationships, where a disputant changes the environment to better suit him or her. The Norman Neighbor-Perry Petowner fence is an example of such a use of ecological power.

Ecological power tends to be as harmful as the type of power it is used to impose. Ecological power used to coerce and ecological power perceived as illegitimately used by the other disputant tend to create conflict escalation and to eliminate the wielding disputant's ability to use broader power sources.

POWER AND ALIENATION

The term *alienation* refers to the extent to which a person becomes mistrustful of, hateful toward, and unwilling to assist another. It has been recognized that the six types of power have different intrinsic tendencies to create alienation in the person toward whom the power is exercised. Of the six types, coercive power is considered the most alienating; expert power, the least alienating. Any exercise of power that is perceived as illegitimate by the recipient also produces alienation.

Alienation is disempowering to the person exercising power. Imagine that Disputant A is attempting to influence Disputant B; in doing so, A alienates B. Alienation directly impairs Disputant A's referent power by causing Disputant B to dislike Disputant A. Moreover, by creating distrust, alienation also undermines Disputant A's normative and expert power. This leaves Disputant A with only coercive power, reward/exchange power, and ecological power used to promote coercive or reward/exchange goals. Indeed, alienation even damages reward power by creating the perception that the offer of reward is somehow tainted or illegitimate. This leaves Disputant A with coercive measures only, and, if Disputant A needs to continue to exercise power in the relationship with Disputant B, the latter is likely to become increasingly alienated as Disputant A is forced to limit his or her influence to the use of coercive tactics.

In a relationship already marked by high degrees of alienation, the use of coercive power may be appropriate if the relationship is likely to be very short-term, so that one coercive move is likely to be sufficient to produce desired results. Coercion may also be needed to convince a disputant to collaborate rather than to compete. However, it is a general rule that, in continuing relationships, and in conflicts that require significant negotiation, the exercise of coercive power should be considered a last resort.

SOURCES OF RELATIONSHIP POWER

We have considered six types of power that can be used in the relationship domain (see Table 13-1). Where do these forms of power come from?

Resources—including tangible assets, such as money—are one important source of power that operates in all domains. Money and other forms of wealth can be converted to other types of power. For example, cash can be used to purchase a

◆ **TABLE 13-1**   Types of Power in the Relationship Domain

TYPE OF POWER	DEFINITION	EXAMPLE	SOURCES OF POWER: EXAMPLES	LIKELIHOOD OF ALIENATION FROM USE
Coercive	The ability to influence others by coercing, threatening, harming, irritating	A disputant tries to get the other disputant to agree to his or her terms by threatening litigation.	Physical strength, weaponry, ability to file a lawsuit, ability to write threatening letters, having the law on one's side	Very high
Reward/ exchange	The ability to influence others by rewarding or withdrawing threats of coercion	A disputant offers to dismiss a lawsuit if the other disputant agrees to terms.	Coercive power, wealth, possession of something the other disputant wants	High
Referent	The ability to influence others based on charisma and attractiveness	The power of a father to influence his son is based on the son's looking up to the father.	Improvement of physical appearance, improvement of how one comes across ("charm school"), a charismatic spokesperson	Moderate
Normative	The ability to influence others based on high moral standing	A minister influences his penitent's important life choice.	Association with a "good cause," an influential spokesperson, "image handling"	Moderate
Expert	The ability to influence others based on availability of knowledge	A parent convinces a child to behave in a certain way, based on the parent's experience.	Research, investigation, formal learning, experts	Low
Ecological*	The ability to influence others by manipulating the environment	A disputant who wants to sell a used refrigerator cleans the kitchen to give the potential buyer the impression that the refrigerator has been well cared for.	Wealth, research into options, "elbow grease"	Dependent on what the power is exercised for

*Ecological power is listed as a form of personal relationship power by Morton Deutsch but functions in multiple capacities, depending on how it is used.

gun (coercive power), provide a bribe (reward/exchange power), erect a wall to keep out a nuisance (ecological power), hire a spokesperson (normative and/or referent power), or hire a lawyer or take a course in the subject matter of the conflict (expert power). Thus, wealth is a stand-in for the other sources of power. As part of conflict diagnosis, the diagnostician needs to consider the wealth of the participants, whether the participants are likely to be willing to expend wealth to gain power in the conflict, and in what kinds of power it would be most effective to invest.

Personal attributes also influence power. Characteristics such as physical appearance, mode of dress, articulateness, educational level, likeability, and emotional stability are important sources of normative, referent, and expert power. These sources of power are somewhat amenable to change: for example, a disputant involved in a trial may improve her referent power by rehearsing her testimony and wearing conservative business attire, and she may improve her expert power by studying documents supporting her claims.

Power also comes from the roles that people play in society and interpersonal relations. People are expected to behave in a particular manner when they occupy particular social roles, and they are typically penalized for stepping outside those boundaries. For example, secretaries are expected to serve coffee, behave deferentially toward their supervisors, sit at their desk during business hours, and so forth. Unless the employment situation is unusual, secretaries that depart from this pattern are often fired or kept from advancing in their positions. Similar and more egregious examples of power emanating from a social role include gender, racial, and ethnic role expectations. For example, a black person who commits a personal, violent crime against a white victim is likely to be punished more severely than if the victim had been black because of the common social role expectation that African Americans should not leave their social stratum.

Social role expectations often seem to create a scriptlike interaction between role participants (Coleman 2000, 108–30). For example, in a dispute over child custody, the mother of the children is likely to feel required to verbalize and commit to self-sacrifice in the name of the best interests of the children, whereas the father is generally not expected to make such a sacrifice. In a study comparing the reactions of undergraduates to child custody disputants portrayed in written mediation transcripts, Coltri (1995) found that the mothers were judged more arrogant, more selfish, and more vengeful and less cooperative, less child-focused, and less interested in achieving a harmonious result than the fathers exhibiting *identical* behavior. If these attitudes are mirrored in the attitudes of persons in the position of deciding custody disputes, such as judges, then it can be expected that fathers may be favored in judgments about attitudes relevant to child custody unless the mother-litigant behaves deferentially in court.

CONTEXT AND POWER

In the early 1960s, the U.S. government became increasingly concerned about what it saw as "creeping Communism" making inroads into several small, Southeast Asian countries. Most ominous to the United States was a

The experience of the United States military in Vietnam illustrates the strong influence of context on the ability to wield power. Here, American diplomat Henry Kissinger negotiates an end to the Vietnam conflict with his counterpart, Le Duc Tho.
AP/Wide World Photos

civil war being fought in the tiny country of Vietnam between the northerners, backed by Communist China, and their southern neighbors. The United States, as the world's richest, most militarily well-equipped country, made a decision to send military support to the south in an effort to quell the growing Communist uprising. The intervention was expected to be brief; after all, this was a true David-and-Goliath situation, with North Vietnam vastly overmatched by the huge Western world power.

True to the lessons of the biblical tale, over a decade later, the United States was forced to withdraw from Vietnam, its efforts an abject failure. Although it sported great wealth and military might, it was disempowered by an overall contrary world opinion, an inability to deal with guerilla tactics, and an unwillingness to commit to an all-out offensive, including the unpopularity of risking American lives in a venture that was controversial back home. The North Vietnamese, on the other hand, having less to lose, were willing to commit more fully to the war effort, and the South Vietnamese were, in the main, more concerned about survival than the specific governmental system under which they would live their lives. Vietnam remains Communist to this day.

As the lesson of Vietnam painfully demonstrates, power is context-dependent. Each of the six types of power exists to varying degrees depending on the specific other person toward whom the power is directed, as well as on the specific situation in which the power is sought to be exercised. For example, the gigantic standing U.S. army and air power proved largely irrelevant under the circumstances of the Vietnam conflict.

Powerful people and entities often have a lot to lose—because they have come to rely on their power and are comfortable with the choices and advantages it brings. A less powerful person, paradoxically, may be in a better position because he or she has little to lose. For example, a wealthy and powerful business executive who is caught engaging in white-collar crime would experience any jail time as a life-destroying punishment. An impoverished and homeless person who already has a criminal record, and who is caught stealing, might experience the same criminal sentence as a reward—no worse than an opportunity for a sheltered place to sleep and regular meals. Thus, it is often the case that a seemingly powerless disputant is able to bring a great power to its knees.

A conflict diagnostician must, therefore, go beyond merely assessing the types of power and levels of alienation. The conflict diagnostician must consider whether a given type of power is accessible for use in a particular situation with a particular other disputant and, if so, whether its potency is limited by the circumstances.

THE BATNA

So far, we have dealt primarily with the use of power to persuade and influence others. In an interpersonal conflict, does the exercise of power in the other two power domains, personal and environmental, have any relevance? The answer is yes.

Sometimes, a disputant finds that using negotiation to meet his or her interests and needs is not as useful as getting those goals attained some other way. For example, imagine that you have an old used car with a book value of about $1,000. You have advertised the car for a considerable period of time and finally have one serious potential buyer, Sandy. After considerable effort, you have negotiated Sandy up to $500, but this appears to be as far as she is willing to go. After some investigation, you discover that donating the car to charity will net you $300 in tax deductions. The charity is so worthwhile that it is worth a lot to you to help the charity. Moreover, if you donate the car, there is no concern about the car's being operable; on the other hand, if you sell it to Sandy, you will have to worry about her coming back to you with complaints if the car breaks down. Thus, you prefer this alternative to the deal Sandy has proposed. Unless she increases her offer, your best bet is to donate the car to the charity and forego the negotiation.

The option of donating the car to charity is referred to as an Alternative To a Negotiated Agreement, or ATNA (Fisher, Ury, & Patton 1991).[2] The best of all available ATNAs for any given disputant is referred to as the **Best Alternative to a Negotiated Agreement,** or **BATNA** (Fisher, Ury, & Patton 1991).

The used car example illustrates one obvious reason that it's useful for a disputant to know his or her BATNA: so that he or she can exercise it if the negotiation will not produce as good an outcome. But there are other very good reasons for knowing one's BATNA, even if the negotiation proceeds to settlement.

Best Alternative to a Negotiated Agreement (BATNA)

the best of all available alternatives to a negotiated agreement for any given disputant.

---

[2] The term *ATNA* was developed by the many scholars who wrote to comment on, critique, extend, and enlarge the concepts advanced by the Harvard Negotiation Project in its series of classic texts on negotiation, beginning with *Getting to Yes* (Fisher & Ury 1981).

First, knowing the BATNA protects a disputant, and the team, from irrational action. Trying to resolve a conflict without knowing the BATNA puts the team in the untenable position of not knowing whether to negotiate and, once negotiation has begun, when to stop. This uncertainty has two possible effects. First, the team may feel pressured to accommodate to the tactics of the other side. Without a clear goal in mind, the team may feel that offers and demands made by the others is the best they will be able to get. Alternately, the team may feel reticent to agree even to wonderful terms, because they are not sure it's the best they can do. Thus, without knowing the BATNA, a disputant and the team are likely either to settle prematurely or to resist settlement inappropriately. Moreover, without knowing the BATNA, the team is unlikely to have a clear picture of how to use the relationship power it has—it tends either to act too coercively or to refrain from using the power it does have. A team with a firm idea of its BATNA can use its power to influence the other team with surgical precision, exercising power where most useful while avoiding unnecessary harm that comes from the inappropriate use of power. Thus, knowing the BATNA is empowering—in the sense that the team can use its relationship power most efficiently and effectively.

Fisher, Ury, and Patton (1991) point out that many disputants deal with this pressure to act irrationally by developing a bottom line—that is, a sort of trip wire. If the negotiation leads to a deal that's as good as the bottom line, the negotiators will settle; otherwise, they won't. The difference between a bottom line and a BATNA is that a bottom line doesn't typically have a rational basis—it's arbitrary and may be either too optimistic or not optimistic enough. Fisher, Ury, and Patton also point out that a bottom line is unchangeable—it is not adaptable to information gained in the negotiation—and that a bottom line tends to inhibit the sort of creative brainstorming that's crucial to effective integrating negotiation. A BATNA, on the other hand, is a bottom line with a difference. It is based on a specific analysis of what you can get if you choose to use a means other than the negotiation to meet your goals. Thus, a well-developed BATNA is, by definition, "right."

Knowing the BATNA also helps a disputant and the team to act with efficiency. The team chooses to negotiate only if there appear to be potential benefits to negotiating, stays in negotiation only as long as it appears to be potentially beneficial, and gains a clear idea of what to do in the event that negotiation does not lead to settlement. There is less wasted time, money, effort, and emotional trauma.

ASSESSING THE BATNA

BATNA assessment follows a six-step process.

1. Conduct an Interests Analysis. If it has not been done before, BATNA assessment begins with an interests analysis. Why? Because there is no way to determine which alternative to negotiation is best without a clear picture of the disputant's interests, needs, and goals. Additionally, an interests analysis is needed to determine whether a proposed settlement in negotiation is better or worse than the BATNA.

2. Brainstorm the Alternatives to a Negotiated Agreement. In step 2, a diagnostician must consider what alternatives the disputant has to negotiating with this other disputant. Can the disputant meet his or her goals by exercising personal power? Can the disputant spend some money to get what he or she wants? Should the disputant consider holding out for another possible negotiating partner? Should the disputant consider litigation? The diagnostician should consider the alternatives creatively to assure that all possibilities have been explored.

3. Fine-tune the Alternatives. After a diagnostician has developed a list of the alternatives to a negotiated agreement, it is time to consider each one. Can it be improved? For example, if litigation is an option to consider, how can litigation be made more likely to succeed? If an alternative involves making a purchase (for example, perhaps an alternative to buying a hair salon business from this disputant is to buy one from another seller), the diagnostician might research the available alternatives. What is the very best the disputant is likely to be able to do with each alternative?

Personal power and environmental power are highly relevant to this stage of BATNA analysis. The diagnostician should take stock of the resources and support available to the disputant to improve each alternative to a negotiated agreement. For example, the hair salon seller might put together a glossy brochure showcasing the business, repaint the exterior to make it look more classy, or gather information to display the business's goodwill. A legal dispute can be organized and prepared for trial to improve the chances that, should this alternative be chosen, it is most likely to succeed. As a side benefit, in doing this trial preparation, the litigation team might also discover some sources of expert power that can be used to convince the other side to settle advantageously.

4. Assess Each Alternative Realistically. After a diagnostician has developed each alternative to the extent possible, it is time to be realistic about each one. How much would someone have to spend to buy the hair salon from someone else and how profitable is it likely to be? If litigation is an alternative, how likely is the disputant to prevail in the litigation, and how much is that person likely to be awarded if he or she wins? What are the costs of each alternative? In assessing both costs and benefits, it is important to avoid the temptation to limit the analysis to the monetary aspects of the alternative. Nonmonetary factors, such as the impact of the alternative on relationships, the potential for conflict escalation, and the grief and wasted time that some alternatives might produce, are equally important to consider.

5. Choose the Best Alternative. Step 5 is to compare the estimated costs and benefits of each alternative to the disputant's goals to determine which is the 'best'. This is the disputant's BATNA.

6. Regularly Reassess the BATNA. Situations change, new information becomes available, and disputant interests can evolve. Some alternatives that were formerly available may disappear, and others may develop. Circumstances may change

Using a BATNA

Imagine that you are a legal assistant working at a law firm consisting of two lawyers, another legal assistant, a secretary, and a receptionist.

Presently, you are making $24,000 a year, plus benefits. You have a performance evaluation coming up in four weeks. You wish to be promoted and to obtain a considerable raise.

The four weeks pass by, you get a very good performance evaluation, and you are now in the boss's office, requesting your raise. The boss has offered you $100 a month, or a 5 percent raise. Should you take the offer, continue negotiating, or reject the offer and do something else?

To answer this question, you can use BATNA analysis. Determining the BATNA answers the question "If I don't negotiate a deal with my boss, what's the best I can do otherwise?"

A really effective BATNA analysis takes time, so let's roll back several weeks. After completing an interests analysis, the first step in BATNA analysis is to identify the alternatives to a negotiated agreement. You might identify the following alternatives:

- Accept your current situation and do nothing
- Get another job with another firm
- Quit your job and stay home
- File a grievance with whatever entity (if any) can assist you in getting some sort of remedy for your lack of advancement

The next step is to maximize the alternatives. One step you can take is to make sure your performance evaluation is as positive as possible. You can be improving your performance, documenting anything you have done that distinguishes you in the workplace, and demonstrating your intent to improve yourself (for example, by taking the initiative to take paralegal courses). Another step you can take is to interview with other law firms. If you get job offers, these will provide you with clear alternatives to negotiating with your boss. You can also assess the pros and cons of staying home—perhaps you have underestimated the expenses of working, have a wealthy spouse, would do better as a mystery novelist, and so on. Finally, if filing an employee grievance is an option, you would want to investigate this option to determine whether the law and facts fall in your favor, what remedy would be available, and whether the remedy would be worth the relationship costs.

Once you've identified and maximized the alternatives, your next step is to choose the best one, using your interests analysis in this determination. You need to look at all the costs and benefits of each option—including those important, intangible factors, such as what you most love to do, the effect of your decisions on relationships that are important to you, the possibility of long-term advancement, and the time and trauma of adjudicating and finding a new job. When considering the grievance adjudication alternative, you must remember to factor in the uncertainty in obtaining the sought-after remedy. The best of these alternatives is your BATNA.

Finally, when you do enter negotiation, you should consider the boss's offer in light of the BATNA. Is it better? If so, you might not want to push your luck. You should keep negotiating, but be ready to settle if she seems to be digging in. If your BATNA is better than the boss's offer, you can be ready to terminate the negotiation, without settling, if she refuses to negotiate further or if it becomes clear that she will never be able to equal the BATNA. Knowing your BATNA will give you the clarity of purpose you need to be able to make such decisions calmly in the heat of a difficult negotiation.

that make certain alternatives to negotiation either more or less valuable. Moreover, as the conflict continues, the diagnostician may gain valuable information that changes the cost-benefit analysis performed in step 4. Therefore, BATNA assessment is a continuing process. The diagnostician should build in reassessment points, so that the BATNA is always assessed as accurately as possible.

KNOWING THE OTHER DISPUTANT'S BATNA

It is useful to know the other disputant's BATNA as well as your own. The better the other disputant's BATNA, the lower your team's chances of an excellent outcome in negotiation (unless the other disputant's team is unaware of their BATNA). If the other disputant's BATNA seems to be very poor—and the other disputant doesn't know it—you have expert power: you can improve your status in the negotiation if you can find a way to disclose what you know about the other disputant's BATNA (but, caution, the other team may mistrust your assessment).

Sometimes, you can use your own personal power to minimize the other disputant's BATNA. Doing this can be tempting: the lower the other disputant's known BATNA, the more flexible he or she is likely to be. However, reducing the other disputant's BATNA is an act of intentional harm and may produce highly negative consequences: alienation, conflict escalation, and a coercive response.

LITIGATION AND THE BATNA: PERFORMING CASE VALUATION

In most legal disputes, the choices will be either to settle with this disputant or to go to court. If a conflict diagnostician is assessing the BATNA of a potential claimant, the options often are to negotiate a settlement, to "lump it" (in other words, to walk away without compensation), or to file a lawsuit. The potential defendant often has no choice but to walk away, since filing a lawsuit is not within his or her personal control. If the defendant chooses not to settle, and the other party sues, the defendant has no choice but to defend or give up what the plaintiff claims in the litigation.

Thus, one ATNA in a legal dispute is always litigation, and litigation is frequently the BATNA as well. Thus, it is always important to assess the costs and benefits of litigating when a legal dispute is involved.

Assessing the costs and benefits of litigation is tricky because of the uncertainty involved. Consider the following example:

> Twenty-five-year-old Jane, a young doctor with a previously promising career as a neurosurgeon, has been diagnosed with a disabling and incurable autoimmune disorder that will permanently disable her from employment within the next decade and will probably render her unable to have children. She is faced with a lifetime of disability and suffering. Jane believes that her illness may have been caused by fumes emanating from her home. The house has always had odd smells, and, since moving into the residence three years ago, Jane has suffered increasingly from upper respiratory problems and rashes. She thinks the house may be afflicted with "sick house syndrome." Jane has done some Internet research to back up her belief.
>
> Jane has gone to an attorney to determine whether she can sue the homebuilder as well as the seller of the home. The attorney has advised Jane that her damages probably run to around $10 million, although she would have to hire an expert in autoimmune disorders, a vocational rehabilitation

expert, and an actuary to be sure. Net of costs and attorneys fees, Jane's recovery would be estimated to be between $5 million and $7 million. However, a suit based on sick house syndrome would be a matter of first impression, and there is no way to determine accurately Jane's chances of prevailing on the issue of liability—in other words, the attorney can't tell her with any degree of accuracy whether either the home seller or homebuilder would be held responsible for Jane's damages, even assuming she can prove that something in the house is the cause. The attorney's best guess is that Jane's chances of making new law in this case, and winning, aren't more than about 1 in 100 and might be much less. The lawyer could get a better sense of the chances by doing a lot of legal research, but the required research would be quite expensive, and the attorney would charge Jane upfront for the research time. Should Jane accept an offer of $10,000 from the homebuilder and $5,000 from the seller's liability insurer to settle the case and waive the right to file a lawsuit altogether?

What is the appropriate value to be assigned to the litigation alternative? Should Jane refuse to settle for any less than $5 million? Few clients or attorneys would take this position in light of the great uncertainty in whether she would recover at all. On the other hand, $15,000 sounds paltry, given Jane's suffering and disability. What is the appropriate value to place on the litigation alternative in this dispute?

Attorneys use a technique called *case valuation* to assign a monetary value to the litigation ATNA. Case valuation is a mathematical process based on the notion that a potential lawsuit should be assigned a value equal to the possible outcomes of the case multiplied by the probabilities of each outcome. The mathematical ideas behind case valuation also apply to any ATNA that involves uncertainty in what will happen if the alternative is exercised.

What does this mathematical process mean in concrete terms? A probability is a fraction that expresses the chance of a certain outcome. For example, the probability of flipping a coin and coming up with heads is 1 in 2, 1/2, or 50 percent. In practical terms, this means that, if you flip the same coin over and over again, you are likely to come up with heads about half the time.

Now suppose someone made the following offer to you: a machine will flip a coin (fairly; it's not rigged) 1,000 times. Before beginning, you call all the tosses. For example, you call heads. Each time the coin toss comes up heads, you win $1. If the coin comes up tails, you get nothing.[3]

How much is this opportunity worth to you? Since each coin toss gives you a 50 percent chance of winning, it is likely that the 1,000 coin tosses will net you in the neighborhood of $500—$1 times 1,000 times 50 percent. Thus, a bid of about $500 for this chance to bid against the machine would be about break-even, and paying substantially less than $500 for the opportunity is a savvy move.

What if, instead of 1,000 flips, the machine flipped a single coin only once? What would you pay for this opportunity? Now the question becomes harder.

---

[3] The coin-toss game presupposes only a single call for all 1,000 tosses. This supposition makes the explanation simpler. However, the same result obtains if you are allowed to call the toss separately each time.

Perhaps if you like gambling, you'd pay 50¢, or even more—anything short of $1. If you hate taking risks, or need to hold onto your change, you are likely to offer just a little or pass up the opportunity altogether. However, the principle that applied to 1,000 coin tosses still holds. You are more likely to come out ahead if you pay for the opportunity to toss the coin but bid less than 50¢. You are more likely to lose if you either forego the deal altogether or purchase the right to the coin flip for more than 50¢. In other words, the "value" of this coin toss game, in mathematical terms, is 50¢.

Metaphorically, real life consists of a series of single coin-toss opportunities. As individuals go through life, they are confronted with a series of choices, which they must make in situations in which the outcome is uncertain and beyond their control. Each such situation can be thought of as having particular possible outcomes with a probability for each outcome, like an individual coin toss. Although risk aversion, love of gambling, and cash flow considerations may affect motivation in individual choices, over a life span the individual will do best if he or she places value on the alternatives, assessing his or her BATNA and making negotiation choices, by multiplying the probability of the outcome by the amount of the outcome, as was done with the coin toss. Sometimes, this valuation leads to paying too much and sometimes to foregoing a profitable outcome, but, overall, if the individual accurately assesses both the size of each outcome and the probability of each outcome, he or she will do very well.

Attorneys often do very rough case valuation by guessing at the most likely monetary outcome of the case and multiplying it by the probability of the plaintiff's prevailing. For example, in the case of Jane and the sick house, Jane's attorney might estimate the value of her case as $6 million (his average estimate of what Jane would take home), multiplied by .5 percent (half of 1 percent, or 0.005—the attorney is guessing that the probability of her winning is less than 1 in 100). Using these figures, the attorney's case value estimate works out to $6 million multiplied by 0.005, or $30,000. Thus, by this estimate, the offer on the table ($15,000) looks low, but not ridiculously so. There may be room to negotiate.

Where do attorneys get their figures? Case valuation is a very inexact science. Attorneys use the following information to help them value a case:

- ◆ Their experiences with similar cases
- ◆ Their knowledge of, or research into, the applicable law
- ◆ Their knowledge of the presiding judge
- ◆ Their assessment of the believability and likeability of the witnesses
- ◆ Their assessment of the evidence
- ◆ Their assessment of opposing counsel
- ◆ Their intuition

Because there are so many variables and the need to apply intuition is so great, case valuation usually yields only a very rough estimate. (Techniques do exist for taking multiple potential outcomes, and other complexities, into account.) As an attorney prepares for and engages in trial, additional information is gathered, and the case valuation may become more exact.

DRAWBACKS OF BATNA ANALYSIS

Understanding and appreciating the BATNA has many advantages. Having a well-conceived BATNA in mind can lead to better decisions about whether to accept a settlement, "hang in" with a negotiation or end a negotiation, and can lead to a better and more efficient application of power in the relationship domain. Moreover, knowing the other disputant's BATNA can help you gain needed leverage and make more realistic assessments of the prospects of negotiation.

On the other hand, BATNA analysis has three drawbacks. The first is that it's often difficult to perform BATNA analysis accurately. And, when you misconstrue a BATNA, the effects can be unfortunate. For example, if you think your BATNA is better than it really is, you may pass up a golden opportunity to settle your conflict in favor of what turns out to be a very poor choice. For example, in late 1999, when Yasser Arafat rejected the terms of a peace proposal that, in essence, gave the Palestinians almost everything they had asked for, Arafat evidently thought his alternatives to settlement were better than the violence that they have suffered through since that time. Of course, it might be argued that any estimate of the BATNA, even if incorrect, is better than none at all.

A common mistake in BATNA analysis is to omit the nonmonetary implications of ATNAs, particularly the long-term nonmonetary implications. Potential litigants often fail to factor the extensive time, stress, and grief of a long lawsuit into their BATNA analysis, for example, and disputants often forget that there are long-term benefits to protecting a business relationship, which more than offset monetary sacrifices. It is also common to forget to factor in the cost of exercising the ATNA (such as attorney's fees, court costs, and so forth) and the possibility that a case will be appealed or that the other side will refuse to pay the judgment, go bankrupt, and so forth.

The second drawback to BATNA analysis is that it often takes a great deal of time, money, and resources to do well. This is particularly true when litigation is involved. Frequently, the only effective way to assess the litigation alternative is to prepare the case for trial. By the time the litigants realize that negotiation is preferable to litigation, it is too late: the costs of getting ready for trial are already spent, and there is a huge psychological investment in seeing it through. A conflict diagnostician must be sensitive to the costs of BATNA analysis and able to balance the uncertainty in assessing the BATNA against the cost of getting it right.

The third drawback to the BATNA is that, in some circumstances, it is not relevant. These circumstances usually relate to conflicts involving long-term, close, intimate, family relationships. Consider, for example, a dispute between a husband and a wife over whether to adopt a child. In this situation, any solution that does not involve achieving consensus is, by definition, a failure: either spouse exercising his or her BATNA is likely to create a serious rift in the marital relationship. In such a relationship, the ongoing ability to negotiate cooperatively and caringly is more important than the particular outcome of the decision about adoption. Some conflict resolution scholars and professionals argue that the BATNA is also irrelevant if the disputants, after being advised of the merits of BATNA analysis, deem it to be irrelevant. However, many attorneys, steeped in the practice of litigation, have a difficult time accepting the notion that a disputant can make an informed judgment about whether to settle a dispute without knowing the BATNA.

POWER IMBALANCE

In a technical sense, no two disputants have the same degree of power. Each interpersonal conflict brings together two or more persons or entities with complex patterns of power in each of the types and domains we have discussed. It is as impossible for two disputants to have exactly the same levels of power as it is for two people to have identical fingerprints.

Moreover, it's often tough to determine who has more power. Consider the following example, typical in divorce mediation:

> Paul and Denise enter divorce mediation with the desire to settle their parenting, child support, alimony, and property issues. Each admits that the other is an excellent parent. Both parents want sole custody of the children, and they are disputing about support and property division. During the marriage, Paul has been employed full-time and now makes $100,000 a year as a bank manager. Denise has an early childhood education degree but has worked only sporadically, as a nursery-school teacher. Paul has had relatively little to do with the children, who are girls, now ages ten and eight. Denise has extensively volunteered at the school and has gained considerable skill in fund-raising through her PTA work. Denise has paid the bills, although Paul has done the taxes every year. Denise has had extensive psychotherapy and is very comfortable in the mediation environment, particularly with Dr. Morris, their chosen mediator, who has a psychotherapy background. Paul is a man of few words and has refused, in fear, to participate in psychotherapy or counseling of any type. He has agreed only reluctantly to participate in mediation with Dr. Morris.

Paul and Denise each seem to display different amounts of power in different domains. Denise is comfortable in the mediation environment, and she shows clear advantages in terms of knowledge about, and a history of close contact with, the children. In a custody trial, her obvious closeness to the children would be strong evidence in her favor. On the other hand, Paul has a greater command of the monetary resources and is better able to earn additional funds in his job. The law is typically unsettled regarding whether a woman like Denise would be entitled to receive alimony and, if so, how long, and Paul might argue that Denise has gained job skills that she could use to make considerable income. Thus, Paul and Denise present a classic example of a couple with different, but not clearly unequal, levels of bargaining power.

Another example of different, but not necessarily unequal, bargaining power was on display in the international media during the O. J. Simpson murder trial in the mid-1990s. Simpson, the criminal defendant, was disadvantaged by the mere fact of his facing prosecution by the criminal department of the largest state in the nation, by his race, and by the publicity suggesting that considerable evidence pointed to his guilt. On the other hand, Simpson's massive wealth was able to buy him a legal defense to which few other litigants could ever aspire. The proof of this fact was in the ability of the defense to systematically dismantle a prosecution that probably would have seemed unassailable, had it been directed at a poor man. The degree to which it is hard to settle on who had more power in the Simpson criminal trial is reflected in the public controversy about the issue: many people thought Simpson had more power because of his wealth, whereas many others thought he had less power because of his race. The Simpson murder case illustrates why we must look deeply at conflict situations before pronouncing power to be unequal.

On the other hand, it is frequently true that disputants have obviously unequal amounts of power. For example, a divorcing woman in nineteenth-century America would have been clearly disempowered relative to her husband, who would have been entitled to all the property plus custody of the children. And individual consumers with complaints against huge multinational corporations are clearly up against a bigger adversary. What impact does power imbalance have on the course of conflict?

Power affects the choices that individual disputants are able to make and the degree of influence that one disputant can have on another. For example, if two neighbors are disputing over the boundary line between their properties, and Neighbor A makes ten times the annual income of Neighbor B, Neighbor A has all kinds of choices that Neighbor B does not have. Neighbor A can exercise more favorable BATNAs, hire a lawyer to argue on her behalf, or pay bribes to

The murder trial of O. J. Simpson demonstrates that it is sometimes impossible to determine the direction of a power imbalance. Myung J. Chun, AP/Wide World Photos

whomever will assist her in getting what she wants. The legal system has made an effort to compensate for individual power imbalance by supplying free legal representation in certain cases, but it is still true that a more powerful disputant is, on balance, able to get more of what he or she wants.

GROUP POWER IMBALANCE

A high-power group is highly likely to wield or threaten coercive, brutal, and sadistic power over a low-power group, as numerous classic experiments in social psychology demonstrate (Coleman 2000, 108–30). Group power imbalance sets in motion a series of processes that reinforce and increase the existing power imbalance. The high-power entity is able to control not only the overall interactions between the high- and low-power groups but also the perceptions about the groups and what they deserve. A high-power group will typically justify brutal or inhumane treatment of a lower-power group by engaging in a process of mental dehumanization, such as "They are less intelligent and therefore do not deserve equal opportunity" or "If we give them what they want, they will destroy society because they are innately brutal and violent." Because the lower-power group has fewer resources, it is difficult for them to counter these dehumanizing beliefs, which become incorporated into the overall culture through institutional and macrosystem processes such as the educational system and the mass media. Moreover, the treatment of the lower-power group tends to create a self-fulfilling prophecy. For example, in the eighteenth and nineteenth centuries, most free white Americans believed that Africans brought to the continent to act as slaves were inherently less intelligent and, accordingly, well suited to performing menial physical labor. Because of this prevailing belief, slaves were commonly forbidden to attend school or learn to read; in fact, in many states it was illegal to teach a slave to read or write. Accordingly, many slaves grew up lacking literacy, and nonslaves perceiving this widespread illiteracy concluded that, indeed, slaves were inherently less intellectually able.[4]

Once group power imbalance is in place, it can be very difficult to dislodge. Because the high-power group has typically engaged in behavior its members would consider immoral if committed against its own members, the high-power group has a strong psychological interest in distancing itself from such behavior—either by denying that it has taken place, by attributing it to a bygone era, or by justifying it by continuing to make negative attributions about the low-power group. This distancing is necessary to protect the positive self-concepts of the high-power members. It is often accompanied by a corresponding "victim" self-concept held by the low-power group, and this corresponding self-concept creates a sense of helplessness and paralysis in members of the

---

[4] This phenomenon will be discussed in the context of diversity conflict in Chapter 14.

Group Power Imbalance: The Divided Classroom

In a class conducted by third-grade teacher Jane Elliott in the 1960s and captured on documentary film by the Public Broadcasting System (*A Class Divided* 1987), third-graders (all white) were told that they would be engaging in a unit to study the teachings of Martin Luther King. The teacher then told the students that the brown-eyed students would henceforth be considered superior to the blue-eyed students. She required the "inferior," low-power students to wear an identifying collar, and, for one day, she imposed inequitable treatment, such as canceling their recess, denying equal resources, and constantly criticizing their performance. The next day, the roles were reversed, with the blue-eyed students' playing the high-power group. Within hours of each assignment, violent and hateful treatment by the high-power group of the low-power group broke out and became increasingly frequent and severe. A chilling side effect of the assignment was that students assigned to the low-power groups displayed substantially poorer scores on academic assessments, such as reading tests, than the high-power students. As the roles were reversed, these trends similarly reversed, demonstrating the power and pervasive damage caused by discriminatory treatment. The students were called back by the documentary filmmaker some two decades later for a viewing of the original film. The former students commented that the two-day experience had been one of the most formative of their lives.

The videotape *A Class Divided* is available through the Public Broadcasting Service.

---

low-power group. The high-power group also comes to rely on the advantages conferred upon it by its superior power and to fear retaliation by the lower-power group if it shares power.

These considerations can set the stage for explosive and violent clashes if the lower-power group ceases to accept its oppressed status and begins to insist on better treatment. The identity of the lower-power group members is transformed from "helpless victim" to "rights struggler," and the higher-power group correctly views this new attitude as a direct threat to its entrenched privileges. The identities of the struggling groups tend to perpetuate a protracted, competitive, and destructive conflict cycle.

BECOMING EMPOWERED

Power means choice. The more power you have, the better your range of choices, and the better the potential outcomes you have.

We usually think of people wielding power in the relationship domain to get the outcome they want, as in when they threaten one another or take a legal dispute to court to coerce a favorable outcome. But another important use of relationship power is to influence the other disputant to engage in the most desirable conflict resolution *process*. Thus, one important function of power is to encourage the adoption of cooperation and to persuade the other disputant to consent to the use of integrating or compromising negotiation strategies.

Power exercised in the personal and environmental domains can produce better alternatives to a negotiated agreement and, hence, better BATNAs. For example, if one alternative to a negotiated agreement to resolve a dispute with a neighbor is to move to another neighborhood, a disputant may enhance this alternative by painting and repairing the disputant's current house to get it ready to sell.

Changes wrought by the uses of power in the personal and environmental domains can also improve a disputant's ability to wield power in relationships. For example, a disputant who wishes to improve his or her referent power might visit an upscale clothing store to improve his or her physical appearance or consult an image expert to improve his or her demeanor.

Empowerment can be produced two ways: either the amount of power can be increased or the person's ability to use what power he or she has can be strengthened. For example, it is likely that the attorney for Jane, the "sick house" victim, would have his research paralegal conduct legal research to increase his team's expert power in the legal dispute over whether Jane should recover damages for her injuries. To improve the team's ability to use this expert power, the paralegal would organize her findings in an easy-to-read, clear memorandum and, in turn, would place the memorandum in a well-organized file that contains other material pertinent to Jane's claim.

Overall, it is often the case that expert power is more alterable than any other type of power—thus, overall relationship power can most frequently be increased by acquiring expert power. Since expert power is also the least likely form of power to create alienation, conflict participants who seek to empower themselves are smart to begin by increasing this form of power. Expert power can be increased by

- Better understanding the law (assuming the dispute is legal) and the facts underlying a dispute by conducting legal research and factual investigation; this understanding can be gained by personal research or through experts in the field, such as attorneys, investigators, expert consultants, and support staff, such as paralegals
- Gaining knowledge about the sort of factual evidence that supports each side of a dispute, including evidentiary considerations, such as the normative and referent power of supporting witnesses
- Organizing the factual and legal information for easy and efficient retrieval
- Conducting a complete conflict diagnosis; this diagnosis should include an assessment of the sources of conflict and the interests of all participants
- Getting an accurate sense of your team's BATNA, which necessarily involves investigating the resources at your disposal
- Getting a sense of the other disputant's BATNA

Other types of power can also be increased or made more useful. Some sources of these types of power were listed in Table 13-1.

DEALING WITH POWER IMBALANCE

Volumes have been written about the problem of power imbalance and how it should be dealt with. Legal scholars differ on whether power imbalance is best dealt with through zealous and adversarial advocacy or whether less competitive processes can be used effectively to handle power imbalance.

Some legal experts argue that the only effective means for dealing with power imbalance is to resort to the legal system—or to resort to extra-legal processes, such as violent or revolutionary struggle. This point of view is reinforced by experience tending to indicate that, overall, group power imbalance can be corrected only by structural changes mandated by courts or legislatures and evidence of social change produced by violent outbursts, such race rioting. Some examples of such structural changes include the famous litigation ending racial segregation in the public schools, *Brown v. Board of Education,* and the Thirteenth and Fourteenth Amendments to the Constitution, ending slavery and discrimination on the basis of race. There is a good argument that, whatever individuals choose to do to deal with conflict on an individual basis, their efforts are limited by overall societal power imbalances. However, these limitations exist in all forms of one-on-one dispute resolution, including the litigation and legislative processes. Unless a disputant is willing to take a dispute to court, is willing to pursue it through an appeals process, and is lucky enough to have the highest appellate court agree that a structural change is warranted, or unless the disputant has the political firepower to engineer legislative change, the disputant is likely to have the existing power imbalance reflected in the outcome of any adversarial dispute resolution process.

Assuming that institutional change through appellate litigation or legislative reform is not in the cards, disputants "on the short end" of a power imbalance are well advised to empower themselves as much as possible. This effort takes a thorough conflict diagnosis, as well as a creative approach to empowerment. The more effectively the disputant, or the conflict diagnostician, can analyze the disputant's power, and develop creative approaches to increasing and operationalizing that power, the less important is the power imbalance.

There is some argument that use of the integrating style of negotiation is most protective of a disempowered disputant. Integrating is a negotiation style that presupposes the importance of meeting everyone's interests; hence, if used, it has the potential to protect the interests of a lower-power disputant without threat to a higher-power disputant. Convincing a higher-power disputant to integrate, when it appears equally possible to dominate, is another matter. In a sense, a powerful disputant consenting to use integrating is sharing power with the disempowered conflict partner. The lower-power disputant must be well prepared with other types of power, so that he or she can demonstrate to the higher-power disputant that integrating is in the latter's best interests. Thus, frequently a lower-power disputant must be prepared to threaten the use of coercive power in order to demonstrate the utility of integrating. It also helps if the lower-power disputant can offer a long-term, holistic viewpoint to convince the other disputant to integrate. In other words, a lower-power disputant can sometimes convince a higher-power disputant to share power if the former can show the latter that, over the long term, the higher-power disputant will do better if power is shared. An example of this phenomenon occurred in the aftermath of the September 11, 2001, attacks on the World Trade Center and Pentagon. The United States, a leader in coercive power, was convinced to power-share on a number of fronts. For example, in addition to sending troops and munitions to Afghanistan in an effort to mount a military strike against suspected terrorists, the Bush administration in the fall of 2001 pushed to increase humanitarian aid to the Afghan people and paid the membership dues overdue from the United States to the United Nations. One might see these efforts as attempts to shore up long-term normative and referent power through the short-term sharing of personal resource power.

A higher-power disputant will often have difficulty seeing the need to power-share with a lower-power disputant. A conflict diagnostician should be prepared to help such a disputant review the conflict situation from all relevant vantages, including the long-term, holistic viewpoint. Ultimately, oppressive behavior by a higher-power disputant tends to be counterproductive in the long run. But it is frequently difficult to convince a high-power disputant to give up the immediate gains from entrenched power for the more ephemeral advantages of power-sharing.

IMPLICATIONS FOR CONFLICT DIAGNOSIS

The concept of power, applied to interpersonal conflict, goes far beyond the commonly held idea of physical force. A conflict diagnostician must be able to understand how power operates in each of the three major domains (relationship, environmental, and personal) and to identify the types of power available to the conflict participants in each domain.

Power is a context-specific attribute. A characteristic of an individual disputant, his or her resources and environment, or his or her team may spell out considerable power in one circumstance but helplessness in another. Moreover, considerable power of some types may turn out to be virtually useless because of the unintended side effects that the application of such power may carry. Thus, the mobilization of power must be done thoughtfully, with an eye to its applicability in specific situations and an eye to the consequences of its use. In general, the application of expert power is thought to be the least damaging to relationships and to the personal power of the wielder. Expert power can empower both the wielder and the recipient, resulting in an amicable resolution of the conflict and a better ongoing relationship. No other type of power has quite this set of advantages, although any type of power, perceived by its recipient as having been legitimately applied, can have positive effects.

There are no "magic bullets" that fix power imbalances. A conflict diagnostician needs to examine each situation and carefully consider the interests of the disputant. If a disputant has a high degree of interest in social reform—whether in keeping with deeply held values, individual identity, or a need to improve society—and if society in general seems ripe for the sought-after reforms, it may be in the disputant's interests (and in the interests of society at large) to pursue appellate or legislative approaches. If not, the disputant may wish to pursue a more individualized approach to dealing with power imbalance. In any case, it pays to maximize the sources of personal power, to make sure that existing types of power can be mobilized easily, and to be as clear as is feasible under the circumstances about the disputant's BATNA.

EXERCISES, PROJECTS, AND "THOUGHT EXPERIMENTS"

1. *Conflict journal.*

   a. Perform a relationship power analysis for your conflict. (If you are not a disputant, you have the option of performing the analysis for the disputant on your team.) Use five sheets of paper or five separate pages in your word-processing document file. Label each page with a different kind of relationship power: "Coercive," "Reward/Exchange," "Normative," "Referent," and "Expert." Each page should contain an analysis of that type of power, held by you in the conflict. Organize your analysis in the following sections:

      1. Describe your ability to wield this sort of power in this conflict. For example, if you are writing about a conflict with your boyfriend or girlfriend, and you feel that you can often get him or her to give in to your wishes by offering to take him or her to a nice restaurant, you would describe your ability under "Reward/Exchange Power." Include all instances of each kind of power that you can think of.

      2. Looking at your ability to wield each source of power, assess how much of each source of power you have. You can use words to describe it such as *a whole lot* or *almost none,* or you can use a numerical scale.

      3. Considering your personal power, and using creative brainstorming, include a section describing some ways that you could enhance each source of power. For example, under "Reward/Exchange Power," you might put "Contact his favorite restaurant to find out if they would be willing to cook him a special meal."

      4. Include a section discussing the potential negative side effects of using each source of power.

      Now review your analysis. What have you learned about what you can do to deal successfully with the conflict? Do you have any alternatives that allow you to exercise power while minimizing the risks of an escalated conflict?

   b. It is useful to perform the same power analysis for the other team's disputant.

   c. Consider whether clarifying the BATNA would be a useful effort for you or your disputant. (BATNA analysis is generally of limited use if preserving the positive intimacy of the relationship is of primary importance.) If so, estimate your BATNA, using the steps outlined in this chapter.

2. Assume you work as a paralegal in a busy law office. Madeline Dreyfus comes to your law office with a complaint about malpractice by a chiropractor. Madeline has recurring back problems and will probably need chiropractic care in the future, but she expresses a desire never to use this chiropractor again. The jist of her claim is that the chiropractor injured her shoulder in the course of treatment. Madeline's regular doctor is uncertain whether her

shoulder will heal completely with time, and it is causing her considerable discomfort but is not disabling her from her work activities. Your attorney-supervisor estimates the value of her case, if litigated, at $10,000. This figure does not account for Madeline's need to pay attorneys fees of 35 percent of the recovery, or an estimated $1,500 in fees and costs. Madeline can also pursue a complaint against the chiropractor through her state regulatory board. She can receive up to $5,000 by this means; by doing so, she waives the right to litigate. The attorney has agreed to offer her representation in this matter for 20 percent of recovery, and he thinks she has about a 60 percent chance of winning the $5,000 (so this option has a case value of $3,000, less attorney's fees). There is a flat $150 fee for this option. The chiropractor's lawyer has asked for a meeting to discuss possible settlement.

   a. What is Madeline's BATNA? Write an essay describing the analysis and your conclusion. (There is no right answer. Follow the process described in the chapter for finding the BATNA. You may invent necessary facts as long as they are realistic and you note in your essay when facts have been invented.)

   b. What steps could you take to clarify the BATNA further?

   c. What steps could you take to improve Madeline's BATNA?

3. Is an attorney ethically obligated to clarify the BATNA for the client?

   a. Research the American Bar Association's Model Rules of Professional Conduct (*http://www.abanet.org/cpr/mrpc/mrpc_toc.html*). How would you answer this question based on your interpretation of the Model Rules? Compare your interpretation with those of your classmates.

   b. If an attorney feels it would be in the client's best interests to evaluate the client's course of action in light of the BATNA (for example, if the attorney is concerned that the litigation option would serve the client poorly), may the attorney conduct a BATNA analysis even if the client does not want to know the alternatives to a negotiated agreement? May the attorney charge the client a fee for the analysis?

4. Consider the typical responsibilities of paralegals in preparing a case for trial. The National Federation of Paralegal Associations, NFPA, has a helpful discussion of paralegal responsibilities posted at *http://www.paralegals.org/Development/Handbook/litigate.htm#1*. Consider each of the responsibilities listed there. How does fulfilling each responsibility affect the personal power of the client? How does fulfilling these responsibilities affect clarification and maximization of the client's BATNA?

5. The violent conflict between Israel and Palestinians continues. During the violent Israeli-Palestinian Intifada that began in September, 2000, hundreds of Israelis have died in terrorist and suicide attacks. In 2002, Israel bombed a building that allegedly contained Palestinian civilians, including children. World opinion largely supported Israel's goal of stopping terrorism, but there was widespread condemnation of the bombing as an atrocity. Israel contended that the building was strongly suspected of harboring terrorist leaders who had been orchestrating the murder of numerous Israeli civilians. Several days after the bombing, Israel publicly apologized for the death of the Palestinian civilians. Do you think Israel's apology increased its power or decreased it? Justify your answer.

6. Turn to Chapter 1 and review the first interpersonal conflict that was described in the textbook (the conflict between Jeff and Marsha over the financing of their software venture). Pick one of the disputants and analyze his or her BATNA. As with any BATNA analysis, there is no correct answer: performing the process correctly is the vital part. Is there any really good ATNA? What can Jeff and Marsha do to preserve their negotiation alternative?

RECOMMENDED READINGS

A Class Divided. 1987. Part of the FRONTLINE video series, available through the Public Broadcasting Service.

Coleman, P. T. 2000. Power and conflict. In *The handbook of conflict resolution: Theory and practice* (pp. 108–30), edited by M. Deutsch and P. T. Coleman. San Francisco: Jossey-Bass.

Deutsch, M. 1973. Intergroup conflict. In *The resolution of conflict: Constructive and destructive processes* (pp. 67–123). New Haven, CT: Yale University Press.

Fisher, R., W. Ury, and B. Patton. 1991. What if they are more powerful? In *Getting to yes: Negotiating agreement without giving in.* 2d ed. (pp. 97–106). New York: Penguin Books.

Folger, R., B. H. Sheppard, and R. T. Buttram. 1995. Equity, equality, and need: The three faces of social justice. In *Conflict, cooperation and justice: Essays inspired by the work of Morton Deutsch* (pp. 261–90), edited by B. B. Bunker, J. Z. Rubin, and Associates. San Francisco: Jossey-Bass.

Kritek, P. B. 1994. *Negotiating at an uneven table: Developing moral courage in resolving our conflicts.* San Francisco: Jossey-Bass.

14

Step 9. Consider Diversity Issues at Play in the Conflict

*"I do not want my house to be walled in on all sides
and my windows to be stuffed. I want the cultures of all the
lands to be blown about my house as freely as possible.
But I refuse to be blown off my feet by any."*

—Mahatma Gandhi

*"In individuals, insanity is rare; but in groups,
parties, nations, and epochs it is the rule."*

—Friedrich Nietzsche, *Beyond Good and Evil*

In this chapter, you will learn …

- The influences of stereotyping, culture, and social-group power on interpersonal conflict.
- The reasons people stereotype others and why stereotypes are so resistant to change.
- "Red flags" that alert you to a situation in which you might be led astray by stereotypes.
- Tactics and strategies you can use to counteract the negative impact of stereotyping.
- How cultural and subcultural differences have an impact on the perception of and handling of interpersonal conflict.
- Some effective ways of minimizing damage due to the unrecognized and unacknowledged impact of cultural differences in conflicts.
- Some of the ways that racism and sexism affect the handling of conflict, and what to do about it.

On 1 April 2001, a United States Navy plane operating in the South China Sea collided with one of two Chinese fighter jets flying nearby. One of the Chinese planes was lost, with the pilot missing and presumed dead, and the American plane, which had been conducting surveillance and was loaded with sophisticated spying equipment, was severely damaged and almost crashed before making an emergency landing on Hainan Island, land under the sovereignty of mainland China.

In the immediate aftermath of the incident, it was apparent that neither the United States nor China was eager to provoke a serious confrontation. It was a very sensitive time in Sino-American relations, given the recent inauguration of a new U.S. president and a contemplated sale by the United States of weapons to Taiwan. Following the incident, the United States communicated its concern to the Chinese over the incident and asked that its crew be treated well ("U.S. Spy Plane, Chinese Fighter Collide" 2001).

From the beginning, responses to the incident reflected the differences in language and culture between the two nations. The United States issued a noncommittal but self-serving statement indicating that the plane was on a routine surveillance mission and that it was unclear whether the collision was an accident or the result of the Chinese jet's bumping the American plane purposefully ("Bush Statement on China, U.S. Spy Plane Incident" 2001). Western media indicated that the plane was in international airspace (although later reports indicated that the Chinese considered the territory their own), and U.S. military sources began to leak an opinion, widely held among those in the know, that the Chinese pilot who had hit the spy plane had a reputation as a "hot dog" whose prediliction for "buzzing" American planes had been the subject of a complaint to the Chinese some six months before ("U.S. Defense Secretary: Chinese Pilot Harassed U.S. crew" 2001).

On 2 April, the Chinese allowed U.S. diplomats to meet with the crew of the downed spy plane, who were being housed and questioned by the Chinese. The meeting went well, but thereafter China publicly referred to itself as the victim in the incident and called for the United States to take responsibility for the incident, reasoning that the missing jet and pilot were Chinese and the U.S. plane "entered Chinese air space in violation of relevant regulations and landed on Chinese territory without permission" ("Jiang Demands U.S. Apology for Plane Collision" 2001).

On 3 April, two days after the collision, President Bush publicly warned the Chinese that it was time for the return of the U.S. crew, as well as the plane itself. "We have allowed the Chinese government time to do the right thing," Bush said. "This accident has the potential of undermining our hopes for a fruitful and productive relationship between our two countries. To keep that from happening, our service men and women need to come home" ("Diplomats Visit, but China Still Holds U.S. Crew" 2001). U.S. officials, including those in the military, expressed puzzlement over what they viewed as an unacceptable delay in the Chinese response, and privately they regarded it as likely that the Chinese were using the delay to learn more about the plane's sophisticated technology. The Chinese did, in fact, assert a right to enter and inspect the aircraft.

In response to the Chinese demand for an apology, the United States, through its secretary of state, Colin Powell, expressed "regret" and called for an investigation and an exchange of explanations. However, Bush's spokesperson reiterated the president's stance that the United States had done nothing wrong and that the accident had taken place in international airspace. The Chinese, through their ambassador, Yang Jiechi, dismissed the expression of regret and commented, "The U.S. side should share all the responsibility and apologize to the Chinese side" ("Plane Deadlock Continues Despite 'Regret' " 2001).

Over time, it became clear that the apology was the principal sticking point in a deepening crisis. The United States refused to apologize without a prior finding of fault, and the Chinese insisted that an apology was necessary before anything further should be done. As the public rhetoric on both sides escalated, angry anti-American demonstrations broke out in China. Longstanding mistrust between countrypersons of both China and the United States fed the escalating standoff. Meanwhile, diplomats worked behind the scenes to defuse the situation. The Americans, in keeping with their principle that the facts must come out, recommended a joint Sino-American investigation of the incident. President Bush, for the first time, expressed regret over the apparent loss of life of the Chinese pilot. However, the Chinese continued to seek an apology. President Jiang Zemin commented, on a trip to Chile, "I have visited many countries and I see it as very normal that when people clash (bump in to each other), it is normal that these people apologize. Now, we see that these planes come in to our country and they don't want to ask forgiveness. Is that normal?" ("U.S. Considering Joint Investigation of Plane Collision" 2001).

Finally, on 11 April, an accord was reached. The crux of the deal was a brief letter issued by Joseph W. Pruehler, the U.S. ambassador to China, to Chinese Foreign Minister Tang Jiaxuan. The letter included the following passage: "We are very sorry the entering of China's airspace and the landing did not have verbal clearance, but very pleased the crew landed safely. We appreciate China's efforts to see to the well-being of the crew." The Chinese were able to use the text—translated in a manner the Chinese found acceptable—to imply that the United States had taken responsibility for flying into Chinese airspace, as it had contended, thus saving face for their country (Goldberg, K. 2001). The United States, on the other hand, also included the phrase "the full picture of what transpired is still unclear" (Prueher 2001), thus preserving its ability to maintain its position that the plane was flying appropriately when hit by the Chinese fighter jet and protecting the needs of its citizens for factual investigation before an assignment of responsibility. Based on the mutual preservation of face that the letter allowed, the crew was released by the Chinese and allowed to return home.

The Navy spy plane incident illustrates some of the complexities that cultural diversity imposes on interpersonal conflict. The predilections for people in both countries to fear the worst in the motives of the other undoubtedly arose in part from stereotypes held by all concerned—the Chinese saw the Americans as arrogant, aggressive, and insensitive, whereas the Americans saw the Chinese as inscrutable totalitarians bent on world domination. Beyond the issue of inappropriate attribution based on stereotypes, the spy plane controversy is an example of the trouble that confronts disputants when they have to deal with someone whose culture is different—whose language is not directly translatable, whose cultural values are different from one's own, and whose social context is very different. The U.S. interpretation of the Chinese response to the spy plane incident as "delayed" hardened the American side, with its rapid and goal-directed approach to conflict management. From the Chinese perspective, however, the time it took to resolve the incident was anything but delayed, given the comparatively relaxed attitude toward the passage of time in the typical Chinese approach to negotiation. Further, a language and etiquette problem was a crucial source of conflict: the Chinese demand for an apology from the United States, something apparently akin to saying "excuse me" when bumping into someone, was interpreted by U.S. leaders as something different, more similar to admitting legal liability for causing the incident. Thus, differences in style, language, and patterns of etiquette contributed to the standoff. Moreover, the need for the United States to get all the facts before allocating blame—and the need for the Chinese to interact in a manner that saves face—each of which went largely unacknowledged by the other—together probably constituted the largest single impediment to getting the plane's crew home. The Chinese loss of face was probably exacerbated by the power differences between the United States, generally regarded as the supreme superpower on Earth, and China, which, although huge, lacks the resources and might of the United States. Comments by the Chinese people about U.S. "arrogance" in the dispute were probably fed by the interaction between the refusal of the United States to apologize and Chinese shame in the face of an incident involving a more powerful rival.

This chapter will summarize some of the troublesome issues that confront conflict diagnosticians and conflict participants when dealing with a conflict involving people and groups from other cultures. The area of diversity issues in interpersonal conflict is among the most perplexing, yet fascinating, topics for the diagnostician.

DEFINITION AND SCOPE

For our purposes, a "diversity" issue is one involving the apparent or actual membership of conflict participants in diverse social groups. The term *social group* includes nationality, ethnicity, gender, race, cultural or subcultural affiliation, religious affiliation, and professional affiliation—any affiliation that involves the sharing of special values, communication styles, or patterns of behavior; tends to be the subject of stereotyping by others; or is associated with inequities of power, compared with other groups involved in the conflict.

Analyzing the impact of diversity is an important part of the conflict diagnosis process. Diversity considerations affect the choice of the most effective dispute resolution process, the most effective ADR process and provider (if any), and ways to prepare for the resolution of the conflict. Diversity considerations strongly affect the sources of conflict, differences of opinion over what the conflict is about, negotiation styles, power differences, and so forth. Thus, every legal professional, every person who negotiates frequently—in fact, increasingly in this day of globalization, *every* individual—needs to be aware of how diversity issues affect interpersonal conflict.

CATEGORIES OF DIVERSITY ISSUES

Diversity issues fall into three major categories. The first category is *stereotyping*. Stereotyping is the attribution of thoughts, qualities, behaviors, and attitudes to others based on their categorization into a social group. (For example, the attri-

---

Diversity Issues in Interpersonal Conflict

- ◆ Any issue involving the membership of one or more conflict participants in a social group
- ◆ Kinds of diversity issues
  - • Stereotyping
  - • Culture
  - • Power

bution of gentleness to a woman based on her gender is the application of a stereotype.) The second category includes considerations of *culture*. This category includes issues of language difference, cultural values and frames of reference, and cultural attitudes toward conflict, negotiation, and conflict resolution. The Navy spy plane crisis most profoundly reflects this category of diversity problem. The third category of diversity issue is the issue of *power*. Power problems in diversity conflicts include the disempowerment of particular social groups and the existence of bigotry and prejudice based on social group membership. A banker who insists on charging racial minorities a higher price for a home loan simply because he thinks he can get away with it is displaying this type of diversity issue. See Table 14-1 for a summary of these three categories of diversity issues.

Although they stand on their own as separate and independent sources of diversity problems in conflict resolution, the categories frequently influence one another. For example, the banker who discriminates against homebuyers on the basis of race may do so because of negative stereotypes he holds about the behaviors, values, and habits of the race he discriminates against. Because of these negative stereotypes, he may interpret culturally originating differences in language and style as reflective of the inferiority of the race, confirming his bigoted beliefs. Thus, a conflict diagnostician should look for all three categories of diversity issues and consider how they interact. Understanding this connection can help the diagnostician counter the negative effects of diversity in an interpersonal conflict and take advantage of the opportunities that diversity brings.

◆ **TABLE 14-1**   Three Categories of Diversity Issues in Interpersonal Conflict

DIVERSITY ISSUE	EXPLANATION	EXAMPLE
Stereotyping	Issues that arise because of the propensity to attribute behaviors, attitudes, and traits to people based on their membership in a social group	An attorney underestimates his opponent's ability to negotiate effectively for her client because he stereotypes women as soft and accommodating.
Culture	Issues that arise because of cultural differences in the framing of conflict, important values, negotiation style, communication, etiquette, and so on.	An Asian-American employee misinterprets her manager's questioning of her decisions as criticism, when, in fact, he is simply trying to learn from her expertise (*Rules of Engagement* 1997).
Power	Issues that arise because of inequalities in power that exist between members of social groups	A black job applicant is offered less than a comparable white applicant would be offered because the prospective employer knows that overall the job prospects for blacks are worse, and therefore the employer can get away with offering less.

STEREOTYPING

"First impressions are important," your mother may have said. Stereotypes are similar to first impressions; indeed, many first impressions come from stereotypes.

If you believe you're not one to stereotype, you're wrong. All human beings stereotype. The propensity to judge people based on stereotypes is believed to be hard-wired into the human cognitive system. Stereotypes serve a useful purpose for the human species: they allow us to make estimates or predictions about people we deal with in social interactions without having sufficient information to know for certain just what they are thinking or feeling. Since we can't mind-read, and since we don't know many of the people we have to deal with on an intimate basis, we need ways to guess at their motives, abilities, feelings, and likely behaviors. Stereotypes allow us to deal with social interaction in a rapid-fire, automatic fashion. Without stereotypes, social interaction would grind to a halt.

For example, if you enter an office to keep an appointment and see a woman sitting at a desk in the open, telephone on the desk, with a door behind her, you are likely to conclude subconsciously that she is the receptionist. This social category helps you make guesses and predictions about her behavior: that she will be relatively polite, docile, willing to help, and able to shepherd you to your appointment. Your ability to categorize this individual as a receptionist based on the limited number of visual clues (woman, desk in open, presence of phone, office door behind her) saves you valuable time and effort.

The Effect of Stereotypes. When we stereotype, we make estimates and predictions about people based on our expectations about members of their social group. In essence, stereotyping involves attributing to social group membership the characteristics, traits, and predicted behavior that, in fact, are due to individual background and experience. There are two major problems with this sort of attribution. *First, the attributions that one makes as the result of stereotyping may be totally wrong.* In general, relying on stereotypes to judge people involved in a conflict is a dangerous proposition, because it can lead to poor conflict diagnosis and, hence, poor strategic decision making. For example, suppose you are negotiating with a woman and you unconsciously assume, based on your stereotypes, that she will be compliant and gentle.[1] Such a woman, if she chooses to negotiate using adversarial tactics, is likely to catch you totally off guard.

Second, it is demeaning to be stereotyped. Being the subject of a stereotype—even a flattering one—is dehumanizing. And many stereotypes are viciously negative. Thus, besides being morally reprehensible, using a stereotype to judge or predict someone's behavior or characteristics in an interpersonal conflict is likely to generate considerable resentment. As you will recall from Chapter 9, the generation of personal animosity is likely to trigger the escalation of a conflict into a destructive competition cycle.

---

[1] In fact, there is no clear empirical evidence that women are more compliant or less competitive than men during negotiation.

> ### *Reasons to Be Concerned About Stereotyping During Interpersonal Conflict*
>
> - Stereotypes are often wrong, leading to bad strategy.
> - People are demeaned when they are stereotyped, making conflict escalation likely.

Red Flags: Recognizing When Stereotypes Are Most Likely to Be Applied. Stereotypes are used more in some situations than others. To clarify when stereotyping is most likely, it's helpful to refer to one of the currently dominant theories of social psychology, the dual-process theory (Fiske & Neuberg 1990, 1–74). The idea behind the dual-process theory is simple. When people are forming impressions about people and things in their world, they either gather the information they need "from scratch" or draw inferences about the person by fitting him or her into various categories, including his or her social category. The former type of impression formation is called *systematic processing,* whereas the latter is called *category-based processing.* Using stereotypes is a form of category-based processing.

When you first encountered the receptionist, you used category-based processing. First, you used readily handy clues to categorize the woman as "the receptionist," and then you used this social categorization to make predictions about how your social interaction would proceed. Suppose, instead, you decided to use systematic processing. You might begin by walking up to the desk and asking, "Are you the receptionist for Dennis Brown?" Her answer to this question would most likely provide the social category information you need to begin impression formation. But this social categorization does not necessarily mean that that she will be polite, competent, or helpful to you. Thus, as a systematic processor, you might ask others in the office about her professional competence and behavior, observe her behavior with others for a few hours, and obtain a complete job history with employment evaluations to determine whether she will be able to get Dennis Brown if asked, to pin down her personality characteristics, and to reassure you that she isn't dangerous.

Systematic processing seems silly in the case of the presumptive receptionist—after all, if she doesn't behave in accordance with your stereotypes, the consequences aren't very serious: she's unlikely to be a closet axe murderer and would have trouble pulling off a violent victimization in a public setting, anyway. In this case, the use of category-based methods of processing—of which stereotypes are a familiar example—is reasonable. But consider the following example instead:

> You receive a knock at the door and open it, to find a conservatively dressed, white-haired woman who looks to be about seventy-five. She identifies herself as a representative of the local Cancer Society. She has a wonderful offer. A generous donor has contributed a subdivided tract in Florida suitable for housing. She can sell you this real estate for a mere $15,000, one-fifth what it's worth, and she'll accept your credit card to make a modest downpayment. The proceeds will go to finding a cure for cancer.

Here, your use of category-based processing ("little old ladies are honest; she must be OK") could be seriously damaging to your wallet. You'd have a high motivation to verify that the person you're talking to is really the person she says she is, that she really is with the charity, and that the offer is legitimate. Here, systematic processing is called for.

The thinkers behind the dual-process theory view category-based and systematic processing as the poles of a continuum. Thus, in particular cases, a person who needs to form an impression of someone else in order to take action will engage in some category-based processing, plus a limited amount of systematic processing. For example, in the case of the presumptive receptionist, perhaps you sneak a peek at her desk and observe that she has Dennis Brown's schedule there. This information feeds your impression that she is probably his receptionist, and your next move may be to say to her, "I'm Jane Doe and I'm here for my appointment with Dennis Brown." Her response will provide further verification or refutation of your stereotype of this person as polite and able to help you. On the other hand, if, when you snuck a peek at her desk, you saw that she was engaged in complex mathematical calculations, your initial category-based impression would be challenged. Then you would have a motivation to seek more information. Perhaps a question addressed to the desk occupant, such as "Can you direct me to Mr. Brown's receptionist?" would give you enough information to give you the confidence you needed to take further action. Or if, when you ask for Dennis Brown, the woman responds loudly with language you wouldn't allow your twelve-year-old cousin to hear, your stereotype about her docile and helpful personality might be challenged, also prompting you to turn to a more systematic approach.

The dual-process theory relies on the so-called cognitive miser assumption. This assumption is, in essence, that, because category-based processing is a lot easier than systematic processing, category-based processing will be used unless the person forming the impression judges it to be insufficient under the circumstances. A person forming an impression will be motivated to use systematic processing if he or she is motivated to obtain a highly accurate result (as with our caller selling land in Florida)—this motivational set is called *accuracy motivation*.

Systematic processing may also be promoted by two other motivational sets: one designed to protect the impression former's deeply seated, deeply valued self-concepts if threatened, called *defense motivation*, and one designed to reach a conclusion that satisfies a social goal, such as agreeing with a more powerful person or going along with a group—called *impression motivation* (Chaiken, Gruenfeld, & Judd 2000, 144–65). The following is an example of defense motivation:

> Leonard has stereotyped Cynthia as a "typical female—a doormat." However, her behavior in negotiating a deal with him has been anything but accommodating: in fact, she has been a very hard bargainer. Leonard has reacted by being tough in return. However, he does not believe in "hitting a lady"—his tough response bothers him. He reacts by going beyond his stereotypes—seeing Cynthia as an exception to the stereotype—and as less defenseless than a "typical female." He uses his observations of Cynthia to exceed his stereotypes. This systematic processing allows Leonard to feel OK about "playing rough" with Cynthia.

The following is an example of impression motivation:

> Jennifer's best friend, Agatha, is against abortion. Jennifer is pro-choice. In a conversation, Agatha discusses how much she looks up to a prominent anti-abortion activist, Jack Jones. Jennifer would ordinarily dismiss Jack unthinkingly as "an idiot," but, in light of her friend's feelings, Jennifer looks harder at him and discovers that, although he comes to conclusions she opposes, his underlying value system seems to be pretty similar to her own.

Although accuracy motivation tends to produce an unbiased form of systematic processing, defense and impression motivation tend to produce an intermediate form of systematic processing, one that is biased and truncated to attain the defensive or social goal sought by the perceiver. Most of the time, the application of a stereotype, which is category-based, also serves the impression former's defensive motivation to validate his or her world view (which is usually based in part on stereotypes). Thus, most of the time, defense motivation produces stereotyping, not systematic processing. On the other hand, an impression former who holds stereotypes, but who believes they are inaccurate or morally wrong, may have a defense motivation to process systematically if he or she becomes aware that he or she is likely to apply a stereotype to a situation. For example, studies show that socially egalitarian impression formers apply racial stereotypes unconsciously, just as bigots do, but rework their impressions to eliminate stereotype-based conclusions if they become aware that they might stereotype (Devine 1989).

Even if there is a strong motive to go beyond category-based processing in a particular situation, the dual-process theory predicts that category-based processing will be used, anyway, if there are insufficient resources (time, energy, attention, and the like) to devote to systematic impression formation. Why? Because, without sufficient resources to process systematically, category-based processing provides the best available prediction of what others will do. This corollary to the dual-process theory is called the *sufficiency principle.*

Characteristics of the situation or of the impression former may each contribute to a resource deficit that triggers category-based processing. Time resources may be challenged if time is short or the social interaction is an abbreviated one, whereas attention-related resources may be compromised if the impression former is stressed, if the situation is complicated, if the impression former is cognitively limited, if the impression former is ill or highly emotionally aroused, and in a host of other situations involving a high degree of "cognitive load."

In short, the sufficiency principle can be expressed as follows:

- People use systematic processing to try to understand other people only if
  - they have plenty of time and resources to devote to the task, AND
  - they are highly motivated to understand the situation accurately.
- In the absence of these two requirements, people will use categories, such as stereotypes, to draw inferences about people.

How do these theoretical principles help a conflict diagnostician? They help raise "red flags" in the search for situations in which stereotypes are likely to interfere with accurate assessment and appropriate behavior in a conflict situation. We can identify six such cautionary situations, described in the following sections and summarized in Table 14-2.

The Effect of Stress and Situational Complexity The more stressful the situation, the more likely it is that stereotyping will occur. This is because stressful situations impose a high degree of cognitive load. Involved persons are so busy coping with the stress that they don't have the internal resources to devote to systematic processing. Similarly, *complex situations promote the application of stereotypes,* again by increasing cognitive load on the perceiver.

Interpersonal conflict, *in and of itself,* tends to be an inherently stressful and complex situation that tends to impose a high degree of cognitive load. Because it involves the complicated goals and interests of two (or more) people, it is often complex. A conflict with numerous participants is still more complicated. And the simultaneous involvement of legal, financial, interpersonal, and intrapersonal issues makes conflict still more complex. A disputant who wishes to engage in integrating tactics to resolve the conflict must perform the complex mental task of keeping numerous and seemingly inconsistent personal goals in mind, as well as engaging in difficult self-reflection to keep him- or herself operating in an unbiased fashion. Coping with the complexities of interpersonal conflict is taxing and stressful. The likelihood of intense emotions further stresses the participants. The combination of stress and complexity makes the application of stereotypes in an interpersonal conflict setting highly likely because of the strain on cognitive resources.

Fatigue, Illness, Hunger, and Intense Emotion. Personal factors contributing to cognitive load also affect the propensity to stereotype—factors such as fatigue, overwork, high levels of anger or sadness, illness, and hunger. These personal stressors deprive the impression former of the mental energy and quiet contemplation needed to engage in systematic processing.

Unfamiliarity with the Other Person. Stereotyping is also more likely *if the impression former doesn't know the other person very well,* as when a disputant is negotiating with a disputant he or she has never met from another culture, race, or ethnic group.

Unfamiliarity with the Racial, Ethnic, Religious, or Other Social Group. Similarly, a conflict participant is more likely to apply a stereotype to a *member of a social group he or she has not had much experience with.*

Social Group Salience. Stereotyping is more likely if the issue of diversity is *salient* in the situation. Salience is the seeming relevance or importance of the social group membership in the conflict. *Stereotyping is more likely if the social group*

SITUATION	EXPLANATION	EXAMPLE
The situation is stressful or situationally complex.	Stress reduces the cognitive energy the impression former can devote to impression formation. Complexity adds to the cognitive load, making it harder to process information systematically.	During a highly contentious ethnic dispute, participants are likely to apply negative stereotypes based on one another's ethnicity. A disputant who really wants to use an integrating conflict style finds himself stereotyping the other disputant as a "typical police officer."
You are tired, hungry, ill or emotionally aroused.	Factors that impair clear thinking create a lack of cognitive resources.	An environmental activist engaged in a marathon negotiating session with an oil company executive finds that, the more exhausted she becomes, the more she questions the latter's proposals as untrustworthy based on stereotypes of the executive as motivated by greed.
You are unfamiliar with the other conflict participant.	You have little or no personal knowledge of this individual to counter your stereotypical assumptions. Since your stereotypes have been "activated," you may attribute the other's actions as motivated by cultural, subcultural, religious, ethnic, or professional affiliation rather than to individual differences.	You are negotiating with an individual from Japan and are having difficulty understanding his comments; instead of attributing this difficulty to your fatigue or his lack of clarity, you attribute it to his nationality.
You have dealt very little with members of the conflict participant's social group.	Since your stereotypes have been activated, and you don't have previous experience with members of this group, so that you can differentiate them as individuals, you tend to attribute the behavior of this individual to social group membership rather than individual differences.	Having never met a Jewish person, in your negotiation with a Jewish attorney, you attribute her abrasive manner to her religion, rather than to her individual personality.
The social group of conflict participants is salient under the circumstances.	Stereotypes are more likely to be activated if the conflict involves diverse social groups, or if something in the situation makes the social group membership of the individuals stand out.	You are more likely to use racial stereotypes in your diagnosis of a conflict between disputants of different races than you are to use stereotypes in your diagnosis of a conflict between two disputants of the same race. You are more likely to use sex stereotypes to judge the behavior of a female negotiator if the topic of the negotiation is a child custody battle than if the topic is a property dispute.
Strong category features are present: the social group is physically obvious or is associated with rigid social roles in society (or both).	Stereotypes are automatically "activated" by seeing or hearing the individual if his or her social group is physically obvious, or if individuals in the involved social group are traditionally restricted in their social roles.	Police and military personnel, who wear uniforms, are more likely to be stereotyped than office persons, who do not. People are more likely to stereotype African-Americans, who have a history of brutal societal oppression, than they are to stereotype Asian-Americans, whose history of societal oppression is less egregious.

memberships of the disputants are diverse. Thus, a white male disputant who is negotiating with another white male disputant is unlikely to use his stereotypes of white males in understanding the behavior of his counterpart. On the other hand, if the other disputant is an Asian-American male, the issue of diversity may become more salient, and the propensity to apply racial stereotypes is likely to increase. This point is very tricky because diversity is in the eye of the beholder. Two white males may, for example, stereotype one another if they are members of different professions (consider, for example, a college professor negotiating with a bus boy). And sometimes the stereotypes that are applied are unpredictable. An African-American female lawyer negotiating with an Asian-American male truck driver may be seen by the latter in the "black person" social group, in the "female" social group, in the "lawyer" social group, or in a combination of these social groups. Indeed, the two disputants may see themselves as "people of color" or as "Americans" and therefore in the same social group.

The *larger social context* can influence which stereotypes are salient to each impression former. For example, in our negotiation between the lawyer and truck driver, race might be more likely to be triggered as the salient social category if the negotiators are conducting their negotiation in a racially charged setting, such as a ghetto in which tensions have been running high. By comparison, if they are conducting their negotiation in India, their shared social category, "American," might be triggered instead. Moreover, social group membership may be more or less salient, depending on the configuration of the conflict. For example, in a negotiation among ten people, some of whom are white and some of whom are black, the race of one of the whites may not seem very important, whereas in a negotiation involving one white and nine black participants, race may be seen as much more important, and the white negotiator is more likely to be judged on the basis of racial stereotypes. And, if the subject matter of the conflict relates to social group membership, the propensity to stereotype is still greater. For example, imagine an Israeli and a Palestinian negotiating an interpersonal conflict. If the two disputants are negotiating as part of a team trying to resolve the Israeli-Palestinian conflict, they will be more likely to apply stereotypes to one another than if the Palestinian is a professor negotiating with an Israeli student who is applying for a student assistantship. In a dispute between an American and an Afghan, the ethnicities and religious affiliations of the disputants would be much more salient after the 11 September 2001 terrorist attacks on New York and Washington, DC, than previously.

Strong category
a social category associated with a particularly strong likelihood of stereotypes application. Strong categories tend to be those associated with obvious physical attributes and rigid social roles.

Strong Category Features: Physical Obviousness and Restricted Social Role. There are also greater propensities to stereotype people based on social groups that have two special qualities. First, *social groups that are associated with obvious physical attributes,* such as skin and hair color, size, facial features, and secondary sex characteristics, are associated with a greater propensity to stereotype. Second, *social groups associated with rigid social roles in the society* are more likely to be the targets of stereotyping. The combination of obvious physical characteristics and rigid social roles found in a given social group is called a **strong category** and shows an exceptionally strong tendency to be used by impression formers. In American society, there is evidence that sex is the strongest category and, hence, the most likely quality upon which people tend to stereotype, followed by race (particularly when an individual is categorized as African-American) and then by age if the ages of the individuals being perceived are at age extremes (Fiske & Neuberg 1990).

Processes of Stereotype Reinforcement. Individuals may hold their own unique and self-generated stereotypes, whereas cultures tend to produce stereotypes that are shared by their members. What all forms of stereotypes have in common, however, is that they are often negative, hurtful, destructive, and wrong. In interpersonal conflict, they can lead to misperception, misunderstanding, poor conflict diagnosis, and insult leading to conflict escalation. Thus, one of the most frustrating qualities of stereotypes, particularly cultural stereotypes, is their resistance to change. What makes stereotypes, which have such potential to inflict damage on their targets, so resistant to change? There are a number of reasons stereotypes are so persistent.

Processes of Stereotype Confirmation. People who hold to a particular belief system are motivated to confirm it. Nobody likes being proven wrong, and, when our beliefs are challenged, it makes us insecure about our ability to get about in the world effectively. Thus, if we hold to a stereotype, we are motivated to prove to ourselves that it's really true.[2] Seven mental processes are used unconsciously to reinforce stereotypes:

1. Ignoring
2. Explaining away
3. Memory intrusions (memories of things that didn't happen)
4. Selective weighting processes
5. Stereotype overinterpretation
6. Stereotype-consistent perception
7. Active processes that confirm stereotypes

First, people *tend not to notice* people who run modestly counter to the stereotype.

Second, an individual whose features are strongly counterstereotypical is often so noticeable that people can't ignore him or her. However, if noticed, such a person is intensively attended to and is normally *explained away* as a bizarre oddity. People tend to rationalize people who run counter to stereotypes as exceptions to the rule—that way, they continue to see the stereotype as true. (Social psychologists, in an act of levity, named this the "talking platypus" phenomenon to emphasize the idea of the target person as bizarre.) Individuals may

---

[2] That is, we want to prove our stereotypes true *unless* the motivation to be egalitarian is an important aspect of our self-concept. Even egalitarian people absorb cultural stereotypes, but they are usually motivated to disprove them.

also explain away counterstereotypical actions by *attributing* them to something special in the circumstances—for example, a female nursery-school teacher who does not show nurturant behavior might be explained away as having a bad day, a headache, or reacting to difficulties with her employer. On the other hand, stereotype-consistent behavior is attributed to innate qualities of the observed person. The phenomenon of explaining away allows the observer to filter out evidence that runs contrary to the stereotypes and to use stereotype-consistent behavior as further evidence of the truth of held beliefs.

Third, there is some limited evidence from social science research that people actually *add stereotype-consistent imaginary evidence* (called *memory intrusions*) to their long-term memories of a complex event. For example, Cantor and Mischel (1977) showed **experimental subjects** descriptions of a person described as an extrovert, an introvert, or neither (see Figure 14-1). Along with the descriptions, the subjects were shown lists of traits, some of which were consistent with the overall trait of introversion or extraversion, some of which were inconsistent, and some of which were irrelevant. Then the descriptions and lists were withdrawn. Later, the subjects were asked if they recognized trait words from the previous list in a new list, some of which had actually been presented to them and some of which had not. The subjects confidently believed that words they had not been shown, but that were consistent with the specified trait of the person they had studied, were included in the original list. This effect did not appear for trait-inconsistent or trait-irrelevant words on the list. The effect of memory intrusion is to buttress support for a stereotype-consistent inference.

Experimental subjects
people experimented upon.

◆ **FIGURE 14-1**

Cantor and Mischel's Study

Step 1: subjects were asked to study a page containing a list of characteristics of an introverted person, Jane.

Jane, an introvert
quiet
red hair
reclusive
moviegoer
stamp-collector
dislikes giving speeches

Step 2: later, subjects were given a list of words and asked which ones had been on the page they had previously studied.

Recall list: which words were on the original list?
quiet
red hair
likes blue
shy
dislikes crowds

Findings: subjects confidently remembered having seen words that had not been on the original list, such as *shy* and *dislikes crowds,* if they were consistent with the stereotype of an introvert.

People with memory intrusion phenomena believe they have encountered more evidence of the truth of a stereotype than they really have.

Fourth, there is evidence that people tend to *weight complex evidence in a way that supports their preconceptions and beliefs.* For example, readers shown unbiased scientific discussions of controversial topics tend to see the discussions as supportive of their own point of view, with advocates on all sides of an issue picking out and assigning more weight to evidence that supports their conclusions (Lord, Ross, & Lepper 1979). Remarkably, in this study, which involved the controversy over capital punishment, advocates on both sides of the debate had the intensity of their beliefs strengthened by exposure to the same materials. In the case of stereotypes, people may assign great importance to evidence that confirms their stereotypes, while discounting the importance of evidence that contradicts them (Bodenhausen & Wyer 1985).

Fifth, in *stereotype overinterpretation,* a stereotype that has a kernel of truth is taken to mean more than it does. For example, in statistical terms, women live longer than men: that is, the mean age of women at death is greater than the mean age of men—by about five years. Thus, in one sense, the stereotype of women as more long-lived than men is "true." Despite the stereotype, however, a considerable number of women die before a considerable number of men. Thus, it makes little sense to assume automatically that, between any man and woman, the man will always die first. If the stereotype is false to begin with, overinterpretation multiplies the effects of the other effects we've talked about.

Sixth, in *stereotype-consistent perception,* ambiguous events are interpreted in a way that confirms stereotypes. A classic study dramatically illustrates the point. Reseachers Sagar and Schofield (1980) showed a racially diverse group of schoolchildren pictures of stick figures. For example, one drawing showed a boy poking another boy with a pencil. The drawings were accompanied by verbal descriptions. Both the drawings and the accompanying descriptions were designed to be ambiguous as to the intent of the figures doing the poking. Two different versions of the drawings were created; each was identical to the other except that, in one, the race of the poking child was shown as white, and, in the other, the race was black. (Figure 14-2 illustrates how the drawings differed.) When asked to describe what was portrayed, the children tended to describe the poking child as significantly more mean and threatening, and significantly less playful and friendly, if the child was portrayed as black. Thus, racial stereotypes of blacks as mean and aggressive tended to influence the interpretation of the ambiguous situation in a confirmatory way. This effect was independent of the race of the child who was asked to interpret the drawing, as well as independent of the apparent race of the victim. In numerous other studies familiar to child development students, it has been demonstrated that babies dressed and identified as either girls or boys tend to be attributed physical and personality characteristics consistent with gender stereotypes. For example, in so-called Baby X research reported by Brooks-Gunn and Matthews (1979, 73–74), adults introduced to a baby dressed in a neutral outfit of shirt and pants and identified as a girl commented on her softness, sweetness, and innocence and handed it female sex-typed toys, such as dolls, whereas other adults, introduced to the baby as a

◆ **FIGURE 14-2**

Sagar and Scofield Study:
Depiction of Stimulus
Variation

"Tell a story about the boy in the light colored hat."

(Note: the race of the boy without the hat was also varied.)

boy, said "he" looked tough, active, and strong and were more likely to interact with the baby in a vigorous, active manner. Shown a videotape of a crying baby dressed in sex-neutral clothes, adults were more likely to say that the baby was "angry" if it had been identified by the researchers as a boy but as "frightened" if it had been identified as a girl.

The preceding six processes occur entirely in the mind of the observer to confirm preconceptions about people in various social categories. But people also *actively perpetuate stereotypes.* Three processes contribute to this tendency to actively confirm stereotypes:

- ◆ the fundamental attribution error,
- ◆ behavioral confirmation, and
- ◆ data collection errors.

An important variant of "explaining away," the *fundamental attribution error,* causes people to believe more strongly in the so-called strong-category stereotypes. The fundamental attribution error occurs when members of particular social groups are regimented into rigid social roles. Impression formers tend to attribute behavior to innate traits, rather than to the roles in which people have been placed. Thus, since members of strong-category social groups, whose roles have been restricted by society, are seen engaged in activities that fit the stereotypes, observers come to believe that these social groups possess innate characteristics that suit them for the roles they are playing. In other words, impression formers tend to believe that social roles are the result of innate attributes, rather than the roles themselves being responsible for the observed behavior. Thus, for example, the restriction of women into low-paying, supporting roles and men into leadership roles has led to the widespread belief that women are particularly suited for support positions and men are natural-born leaders. And the overall restriction of African Americans into less intellectual employment positions feeds the stereotype of African Americans as less intellectually capable that persists in many circles to this day.

Confederates

in experimental research, people hired by a researcher to pose in specific roles in the experiment. The experimental subjects are generally not informed of the confederates' true roles in the experiment until after it ends.

The way people treat those they are observing often tends to perpetuate stereotypes on its own. This process, known as *behavioral confirmation,* tends to create a self-fulfilling prophecy. In a classic study of this phenomenon, Word, Zanna, and Cooper (1974) first recruited white Princeton undergraduates as experimental subjects, telling them that they were being asked to serve as job interviewers. Unknown to the experimental subjects, the job candidates were, in fact, **confederates,** people hired by the researchers to play the part of someone looking for a job, and all were specially trained to respond in a uniform manner to interviewing. The subjects were randomly assigned to interview either black or white confederates. While these interviews were taking place, the researchers carefully and secretly measured the verbal and nonverbal interview tactics used by the subjects. Significant differences in interview styles were found, depending on the race of the candidate: if the candidate was black, the interviewers tended to act more nervous, ask shorter and less interesting questions, and cut off the applicants more quickly. In part 2 of the same study, a group of confederates was trained in the interview tactics seen in the experimental subjects in part 1, with one-half of the group trained to interview the way the subjects had tended to interview white candidates and the other half trained to interview the way the subjects had tended to interview black candidates. Both sets of confederates interviewed white job applicants who knew nothing of the aims of the study. A panel of experimental subjects, blind to the real purposes of the study and told to evaluate the job candidates, watched videotapes of these interviews. They rated the applicants interviewed with "white" tactics more highly than those interviewed with "black" tactics. The study suggests that the differences in the interviewers' behavior, *in and of itself,* was enough to perpetuate negative stereotypes of blacks as less well qualified for jobs, even with everything else held constant.

Finally, we tend to acquire information about our world in a manner that confirms stereotypes. This process can be thought of as the making of *data collection errors.* A sinister example, racial profiling, has been in the news of late. Many Americans hold a stereotype of drug dealing as a predominantly black crime. In accordance with the stereotype, some jurisdictions have used racial

Universal Press Syndicate

group as justification for stopping and searching automobile drivers on highways believed to carry drug traffic. Because blacks fall into the racial group in the profile, they are more likely to be stopped by the police in these jurisdictions. Because they are more likely to be stopped, if they are actually involved in crime, they are more likely to be caught. Thus, those involved in law enforcement, as well as those watching media accounts of the war on crime, come to see disproportionate numbers of blacks arrested and convicted as a result of traffic stops in these jurisdictions. Regardless of the actual relationship between race and crime rate, blacks thus are seen as proportionately more involved in criminality than they actually are, compared with other social groups.

In summary, a number of mental and social processes make stereotypes more resistant to change. These processes are summarized in Table 14-3. An individual involved in an interpersonal conflict must be on guard to prevent these processes from blinding him or her to the reality of who the other conflict participants are and what they are likely to do. Otherwise, stereotyping can introduce a "wild card" into the conflict, creating unwanted antagonism and making the participant vulnerable to costly errors of judgment. Moreover, a conflict participant should always be wary of the possibility that he or she is being stereotyped by others in the conflict and should think through the best way to deal with it.

Stereotyping is made still more resistant to change by the fact that both the application of stereotypes and the processes that confirm them are usually unconscious. We are largely unaware of the many forces at work that confirm erroneous beliefs about members of particular social groups. Thus, as we grow and develop, we come to believe that our stereotypical beliefs are the result of our rational interpretation of experience, rather than the result of biased interpretation of distorted data. These beliefs further insulate us from confronting the errors inherent in our stereotypes. The best antidote to the forces that perpetuate stereotyping is conscious awareness.

Coping With Stereotyping Issues in Interpersonal Conflict. As previously indicated, the act of stereotyping is often subconscious and can be beyond our control at times—unless we work to remain conscious of this tendency. Thus, we can get tripped up. And the bad news is that, according to scientific evidence, even well-meaning people unconsciously apply negative social stereotypes when they are triggered into thinking of a person as a member of a particular gender, race, or other social group. But the good news is that well-meaning people can work against this tendency once they're aware of it.

What should you, as a conflict diagnostician, or conflict participant, do to deal with the issue of stereotyping? *First, become well educated about the potential for stereotyping in each situation.* Analyze the conflict in light of the factors considered in this chapter. Is it likely that stereotypes will be applied? If stereotypes are likely to be activated, which social groups are likely to be involved and made salient in the situation? And what factors will tend to cause stereotyping to persist or become enhanced? Consider enlisting a negotiating agent, partner, consultant, or neutral who *shares the other negotiator's social group membership,* to help interpret behavior within the context of culture/race/ethnicity.

◆ TABLE 14-3   Processes of Stereotype Confirmation

Process	Explanation	Example
Ignoring	Stereotype-inconsistent traits are ignored, allowing the stereotype to go unchallenged.	A person who believes that "women are lousy drivers" notices only the few women he has seen driving poorly and not the vast majority who drive well.
Explaining away	Stereotype-inconsistent behavior is explained as either a fluke or a result of special circumstances, whereas stereotype-consistent behavior is attributed to innate qualities.	A professional boxer's intellectually advanced approach to negotiation is discounted as the result of "coaching"; accordingly, he is underestimated as the negotiation proceeds.
Memory intrusions	Stereotype-consistent aspects of a situation are imagined.	An American involved in a negotiation with a Japanese colleague mistakenly attributes to the colleague behavior she has seen in Japanese Kung-Fu movies.
Selective weighting processes	Stereotype-consistent events are attributed greater importance than stereotype-inconsistent events.	Both the Israelis and the Palestinians tend to discount the efforts of peaceful people on the other side, focusing instead on the efforts of the most militant factions of the enemy to prove that the other group is up to no good.
Stereotype overinterpretation	Stereotypes that are "true" in a limited sense are overextended in importance or applicability.	The fact that, statistically, men are physically stronger than women leads one man to believe that he can beat any woman in a test of strength.
Stereotype-consistent perception	Ambiguous situations are interpreted in a way that confirms stereotypes.	A negotiator who holds a stereotype of Latins as "dishonest" assumes that a Latin he is negotiating with, whose comments are confusing, is intending to be misleading, when, in fact, the other negotiator is merely having difficulty with English.
Fundamental attribution error	Behavior that is due to restricted social roles is attributed to innate characteristics.	In the nineteenth century, the style of wearing tight corsets predisposed the female wearers to fainting from lack of oxygen; accordingly, a stereotype of females as "the frail sex" was perpetuated.
Behavioral confirmation	Responses to people based on social categorization tend to create a self-fulfilling prophecy.	Law processor Carol Rose (1995) theorizes that, because women are expected to be "softer" negotiators, people negotiating against them tend to make poorer offers; women negotiators, operating in this sort of environment, often accept poorer offers in the knowledge that they are likely to have no alternative.
Data collection errors	Information available in the overall social environment is biased in favor of prevailing stereotypes.	Because African-American males are stereotyped in U.S. society as more criminal and violent than other social groups, they are more likely to be scrutinized for potential criminal behavior. Because of increased scrutiny, these men are proportionately more likely to be involved in the criminal justice system, and, hence, publicity about criminality tends to perpetuate the stereotype.

Consider how the situation could be controlled so that all conflict participants' propensities to stereotype could be minimized. To perform this analysis, review the list shown in Table 14-2. First, do your homework about the culture in question and the negotiator in particular. The better you know the other person, the less likely it is that you will stereotype. Second, lower stress. All conflict participants should be very well prepared and get lots of sleep. In a legal dispute, the importance of preparing the case, of researching the facts and the law, and getting a case file well organized cannot be overemphasized. The better prepared you are, the less stressed you will be. And, the less stress involved and the less you have to "shoot from the hip," the less you will tend to rely on stereotypes. Also consider the motivational set of the conflict participants. The use of an integrating negotiation style is most conducive to accuracy motivation—because effective integrating can't be done without the sharing of accurate information about interests. On the other hand, a competitive conflict sets the stage for the use of stereotyping: the sharing of information is minimized and the stress and emotionality of a competitive and escalating conflict add to the cognitive load of the situation. Using Table 14-2, strategize any appropriate methods that the conflict participants could use to eliminate the drive to apply stereotypes.

Be careful about attributing behavior or motivation to culture, race, ethnicity, and so on. Think through whether you have actual knowledge that a stereotype is true and what the implications of your knowledge are for this situation; don't apply stereotypes unless absolutely necessary and only in a manner that respects the dignity of the other negotiator. Remember that social group membership is but one facet of a person's identity; there are many more differences among people of the same social group than differences between different social groups taken as a whole.

If it's safe and appropriate within the context of the various relationships among conflict participants, *make the stereotyping issues part of the discussion.* Besides helping the negotiation, this act will build bridges among members of cultural groups.

If you feel that you are being stereotyped by the other negotiator, you might want to ask gently what assumptions are being made about you and find a nonthreatening way to show the other negotiator what the truth is. (This task may require creativity and diplomatic restraint.)

If you are a conflict participant in an unavoidably competitive conflict, you may find that being stereotyped creates a deception *you can take advantage of*—for example, if you are female and you find you are being stereotyped as obliging, you may be able to gain an advantage by letting the other negotiator believe it. If you are dealing with a bigot, perhaps the best revenge is success in the conflict!

Always be vigilant to your own tendencies to stereotype—the best defense is to be aware of your own tendency to stereotype and be prepared to challenge yourself consciously. Be aware of the factors in the situation that increase the likelihood of stereotyping and use them as red flags. If you find you are about to apply a stereotype, always ask yourself what impact applying the stereotype will have. If you were the person being stereotyped, how would you react? How will this reaction affect the conflict, and how does this situation comport with your ideas of moral behavior, as well as your needs in the conflict?

Is Stereotyping Ever Appropriate? You may be wondering if there are ever any situations in which it's appropriate to apply a stereotype. This is a difficult question to address.

In the next section of this chapter, we will consider the cultural differences between people, as well as the impact of this cultural diversity on the process of interpersonal conflict. In an important sense, the issues of stereotyping and of cultural difference are flip sides of the diversity coin. Stereotyping issues concern the trouble conflict participants can get into when they attribute traits and behaviors to social group membership, whereas cultural difference issues concern the trouble conflict participants can get into when they fail to recognize the influence of social group membership on traits and behaviors. Although it is inappropriate to ascribe traits and behaviors to people based on race, sex, ethnicity, nationality, and so forth, it is also insensitive not to take social context into account in dealing with others.

Thus, there is an argument that there are two appropriate uses of stereotyping if you are very careful about it. First, stereotyping may be appropriate in making initial assumptions about someone's social context, the cultural aspects of someone's background. Thus, sometimes, members of specific social groups can be predicted to have undergone characteristic experiences. For example, in negotiating with an African American, it is safe to assume that persistent, probably daily, acts of racial discrimination have been a part of the negotiator's life (although it is *not* safe to assume that he or she is comfortable acknowledging it to either him- or herself or to you). On the other hand, a white male negotiator may not have similar experiences in his background and may not be sensitive to issues related to bigotry and discrimination. If racial discrimination, or its absence, is an element of the conflict, it would be foolish, and potentially damaging to the resolution of the conflict, to fail to consider this possible element of social context.

Second, various cultures have approaches to conflict and negotiation that may differ from those you are used to, as we will see in the next section. For example, in dealing with a Chinese negotiator, it may be important to recognize that, in Chinese culture, it is traditional to devote considerable periods of time to relationship building before substantive issues are addressed (Riskin & Westbrook 1997, 292–307). If you are working with a Chinese negotiator who seems to be stalling, it is well worth it to consider the possibility that cultural differences, rather than the other person's motives to delay, are the source of your discomfort and suspiciousness. Of course, it is better to accompany any assumption based on social group membership with more systematic information gathering, to ensure that the egregious problems that stereotyping can create do not occur.

In both cases, there are three requirements for the appropriate application of stereotypes. First, they must be based on knowledge and study, rather than on preconceptions. Having consultants who share the cultural background of the conflict participant can help, as can reading up on the culture in question, taking courses in diversity, traveling to the culture in question, and so on. Second, one must always treat the stereotype as an initial hypothesis, as opposed to an ultimate truth. Depending on the nature of the relationship with the other participant, it may be appropriate to apply the stereotype overtly, checking with the person being stereotyped before applying it. In either case, stereotypes should only be applied consciously, after carefully thinking out the implications. Third, in any diversity negotiation—indeed, in all negotiations—it is crucial to use perspective taking—trying to see the situation from the other's point of view. The application of a stereotype in an effort to see things from the other person's perspective is not as likely to be offensive if you have otherwise demonstrated every effort to understand the other's point of view.

CULTURE

If stereotyping is the unwarranted attribution of difference to people based on their social group membership, cultural issues arise out of unwarranted beliefs that someone from a different culture is exactly like you. In fact, culture does create differences in background, experience, values, self-concept, communication style, and attitude toward conflict and how best to resolve it.

It is impossible, in the limited space of this book, to exhaustively examine the influences of culture on interpersonal conflict: there are just too many cultures to deal with. Instead, we will categorize these influences and discuss a few salient examples in each category.

Cultural Differences in Self-concept and Identity. You will recall from Chapter 7 that conflicts over self-concept and identity are among the hardest to manage effectively. Culture tends to contribute to identity conflicts because there are culturally originating differences that influence individual identity. Typically, these differences are completely invisible to those in the conflict, which leads to misunderstanding and conflict escalation.

A major organizing principle, one that seems to influence cultural approaches to conflict on multiple levels, is the attitude toward interpersonal harmony among members of one's in-group. The need to achieve and maintain harmony appears to differ across nations and ethnic groups, and it is closely connected to cultural differences in identity, values, communication forms, and approaches to anything that threatens harmony. Research indicates that Eastern cultures and subcultures, such as those found throughout Japan, China, and India, tend to place the most importance on the preservation of harmony with other members of one's community or social organization. Western countries tend to be the opposite and place less value on maintaining collective harmony, with the United States lying at the extreme of this continuum (Leung 1988).

The organizing principle of orientation toward harmony begins with the individual self-concept. The terms *independent self* and *interdependent self* have been coined to describe how the orientation to social context plays out in an individual. The interdependent self defines him- or herself in terms of his or her roles within social organizations, whereas the independent self sees him- or herself with clear and stable characteristics that do not depend on social context. Thus, for example, while an American man (Americans tend to be highly "independent") may define himself as twenty-five years old, with brown hair, and believing in God and social justice, an East Indian man may be more likely to define himself as a father, New Delhi resident, provider of medical services to the poor, and member of the Catholic church.

Because an interdependent self is role-dependent, this person tends to see his or her own characteristics as somewhat fluid and changeable. An independent self, in contrast, sees his or her and others' needs and wants as stable and independent of social context. Thus, when independent and interdependent selves negotiate, the interdependent self may experience the independent self as arrogant and insensitive, unwilling to bend to the vicissitudes of the situation because of "principle," whereas the independent self may experience the interdependent self's "fluidity" as dishonest and lacking in integrity.

When culture produces variations in self-concept, these variations create differences in the manner in which interests and basic needs are interpreted and expressed. Thus, although the basic needs theory of Abraham Maslow (Chapter 8) is accurate insofar as the needs that all human beings hold in common, the hierarchy may be somewhat different in different cultures. For example, the need of an interdependent self for honor and "face" can sometimes transcend deficiency needs for safety and security for a highly interdependent self.

> A young attorney provided legal representation for an Iranian-American family embroiled in a dispute over the estate of the eldest son. The family, including the son and his wife, had emigrated to the United States; after that, the son's wife filed for divorce, an act unheard of in her culture of origin. When the family objected, she explained that they were in America now and she was entitled to her autonomy. The eldest son was so dishonored by her act of disrespect that he hanged himself.
>
> The members of the legal team, none of whom were familiar with Iranian culture, were shocked and, for a time, believed that the son must have suffered from some sort of severe mental illness. However, family members explained that the suicide, although horrific, was not at all surprising, in light of the shame that the wife had brought on her husband by pursuing a divorce. The act of suicide in this situation, which would seem bizarre to most Americans, made sense in light of the close connection between social role and sense of self in the son's culture. When his honor in the context of his family and community was destroyed, he felt destroyed as well. Given his self-interdependence, it was but a small step from social to biological annihilation.

Although there are cultural dimensions to identity and self-concept, it should be remembered that these aspects of the self vary within cultures. Thus, although one can stereotype a Westerner as an independent self and an Easterner as an interdependent self, in specific instances these stereotypes will prove wrong. Thus, in conflict diagnosis, self-interdependence differences should be looked for, but not automatically assumed, in a cross-cultural conflict. Moreover, even in a conflict that appears to lack cultural diversity, self-interdependence may be an important variable.

Cultural Differences in Values. Cultural groups are also associated with commonalities in values. For example, many individuals in the United States highly value religious freedom and assume that this value is basic and transcends cultural differences. On the other hand, members of other cultures hold different values. For example, a number of countries have established governments founded on the notion that a single religion is appropriate and should be enforced across the nation.

One of the most ubiquitous of culturally influenced values is the attitude toward how to balance the rights of the individual against the needs of the collective. Cultures that influence their members to value highly the rights of the individual are known as *individualistic cultures,* whereas cultures that influence their members to value highly the needs of the collective are known as *collectivist cultures.* People who value individualism also tend to value individual rights and to be independent selves, whereas individuals who value collectivism also tend to value interpersonal harmony and tend to be interdependent selves. Disputants hailing from cultures with differences in the individualism-collectivism dimension tend to disagree not only on the substance of interpersonal conflict but also in how such conflicts should be resolved. Collectivists are, on average, more comfortable than individualists with dispute resolution mechanisms that involve an active, powerful, and personally interested intervenor, such as a village elder, whereas individualists value strictly neutral adjudicators and mediators and insist on strict due process protections during adjudication. This distinction reflects the greater propensity of collectivists to value efficient dispute resolution that seems to restore social harmony, whereas individualists value individual rights and fairness and are more willing to sacrifice harmony and efficiency to achieve such ends (Tjosvold, Leung, & Johnson 2000).

Cross-cultural differences in values can prove intractable. One reason these sorts of conflicts are so hard to deal with is that culturally determined values tend to be invisible to those raised in the culture. People absorb culturally based values from all aspects of their social environment, from their parents all the way to the media and governmental systems; as a result, they tend to see such values as obvious and beyond question. Confronted with the values of a different culture, individuals usually see them as bizarre and obviously misdirected.

A fascinating example of this phenomenon occurred during the President Clinton impeachment process in the late 1990s. There were clear racial differences in judgments about President Clinton and his personal transgressions (Connolly & Pierre 1998). These differences might have been due to a cultural difference in values. It is likely that many European Americans, particularly conservative white males, saw Clinton's sexual behavior with the young White House intern, Monica Lewinsky, as bordering on abuse. Many also may have seen his bending of the truth in the Paula Jones lawsuit as patent criminality, warranting his stepping down as president. European Americans are, by and large, accustomed to receiving benefits from the strict application of the law. On the other hand, African Americans, whose history and present circumstances feature oppressive victimization frequently clothed in the rule of law, may have been more likely than their European-American counterparts to see Clinton's sexual dalliances as "little" crimes unsuitable for impeachment ("Direct Access: Jesse Jackson" (1998)) and his behavior in the Paula Jones case as an understandable response to an oppressive effort to misuse the law to achieve immoral ends—the bloodless coup of a Democratic leader who was making an effort to overcome longstanding inequities in the social system. (For an explication of this view of the Clinton impeachment, see Hutchinson (1998)). For many African Americans,[3] looking back on a history that included legally sanctioned enslavement and patent inequality of opportunity, the concept that the strict rule of law should always prevail over what is morally right must border on the laughable. These differing values remained largely unspoken and unacknowledged during the impeachment process, with advocates seemingly talking past each other.

Cultural Differences in Frame of Reference. The Clinton example in the preceding section also illustrates a crucial issue for diversity conflicts: the importance of cultural differences in frames of reference. Individuals' experiences within certain cultural contexts color their interpretations of events and issues. For example, cultural groups that experience plenty of discrimination, such as the African-American cultural group, are more likely to interpret the ambiguous behavior of others as discriminatory. Members of a dominant cultural group—European-American males, for example—have little experience with discrimination based on race, gender, or ethnicity and are less likely to interpret the behavior of others within that framework. The reaction to the Clinton impeachment illustrates this phenomenon.

Disagreements over how to frame a conflict are particularly important and widespread in diversity-type conflicts. Consider the Ron-Stella employment discrimination dispute, first described in Chapter 7. You'll recall that Stella, a new employee, and African-American, kept to herself, seemed aloof and withdrawn, and did not improve her job skills as rapidly as expected. Ron, her white supervisor, without a personal history of experience with racial discrimination and bigotry, attributed Stella's difficulties on the job to something he's familiar with: personality conflicts and motivational problems. On the other hand, Stella, who has had to deal repeatedly with racial discrimination, easily concluded that the racism explanation fit her situation.

In the case of Ron and Stella, each is observing the same general situation from a very different frame of reference; as a result, there is a failure of the two disputants to agree even about the nature of the conflict itself. The first step in resolving such a conflict is for each disputant to become aware of the role of personal frame of reference in influencing how the conflict is perceived.

---

[3] In this textbook, when dealing with racial issues, the terms *black* and *white* are typically used to designate the perceptually apparent race of the individual being described when the principal issue is how that individual is perceived and stereotyped by someone else. The terms *African American, Asian American,* and the like are typically used to designate cultural group membership when the principal issues are cultural or ethnic beliefs, attitudes, and practices. For issues related to the treatment of Hispanics in America, the terms *Hispanic* and *Anglo* are used in accordance with common usage.

Cultural frames of reference also influence the interpretation of ambiguous behavior, leading to disputes over facts. Following is a simple illustration:

> Claire, a white female, lived two doors from her close friend, Monique, who is African-American. A young white couple moved into the house between the two. Claire found the wife to be extremely shy—indeed, many times she averted her gaze and refused to greet or acknowledge Clarie as she went by. One day, Monique and Claire were walking together when this young woman was coming out of her house. As usual, she looked down and refused to answer when Monique said, "Hello". As soon as she was out of earshot, Claire shrugged and said, carelessly, "She always does that with me." "Really?" said Monique. "I thought . . . well, you know what I thought," meaning that she had attributed the woman's behavior to racism. Obviously, being white, Claire had not given the behavior a similar attribution.

Such differences in attribution can lead to an escalation of conflict. For example, in the ongoing Israeli-Palestinian conflict, many meta-conflicts are bred by the escalating situation and the differences in frames of reference. For example, the *Baltimore Sun* on 21 August 2001, in an article by Peter Hermann, entitled "Human Rights Are Battle, Too, in Mideast: Tracking Abuses Hard with Sympathy Waning," reported a controversy over the shooting of a Palestinian, Muhammad Alwan, who was injured at an Israeli checkpoint in the summer of 2001. Alwan, a Palestinian used to the notion of Israeli oppression, framed the incident as a shooting by an Israeli soldier without provocation, whereas the Israeli army, with its history of defending Israel from constant threat, concluded that Alwan was the victim of a Palestinian gunman. In fact, as a neutral human rights group found, the shooting occurred under ambiguous circumstances, and there is no way to confirm either version of the events.[4] Each group used the incident as further evidence of the other group's evil motives and indefensible conduct.

Culturally originating differences in the framing of conflict are among the most difficult cultural impediments to a conflict's resolution. Before serious efforts to resolve such a conflict can begin, negotiators from each group *must* acknowledge the perspective of the other: "If I saw things from your point of view, I believe I would feel just the same way." Only after each frame of reference is acknowledged can negotiators move beyond statements of position and need and toward a solution that addresses the conflict from *everyone's* frame of reference.

Cultural Differences in Communication and Etiquette. As illustrated by the U.S. spy plane incident, cultural differences in communication can act as powerful barriers to the resolution of conflict. Communication issues can include outright language barriers, misunderstandings wrought by shades of meaning in terms all participants think they understand, and differences in etiquette and other elements of the "pragmatics" of communication.

---

4 The *Baltimore Sun* article indicated that it was more likely, according to the neutral rights group, that the victim was shot by another Palestinian, not by an Israeli.

Obviously, when disputants speak different languages, the lack of understanding can prevent resolution of the conflict. But, even when disputants use a common language, shades of meaning can prevent the resolution of or even escalate a dispute. Because disputants think they are talking about the same thing, these misunderstandings can lead to even more problems than an outright lack of a translation.

A somewhat comical example of this phenomenon occurred at an American Bar Association Section meeting in Washington, D.C., several years ago (some details have been changed and names have been omitted):

A panel of pre-eminent international experts in the ADR field had been chosen to lead a conference presentation on the topic of court-connected ADR programs in their respective countries. The presentation was conducted in English, which all participants spoke fluently. Professor A, from a Latin American country, described a program in which all litigants filing lawsuits in his country's court system were required to submit to mediation. He was interrupted by Professor B, hailing from Europe, who, with a concerned expression, asked whether the outcomes reached in mediation were binding. The discussion that followed went something like the following.

"Of course," replied Professor A. "If the results of mediation weren't binding, why would we do it at all?"

Professor B sat a little more upright and argued, forcefully, that, if the results of mediation were binding, litigants would be denied their day in court. "You should use conciliation instead."

"No, they aren't denied their rights to go to court," replied Professor A. "In what sense would mediating litigants be considered to have been denied their day in court? And why would we refer the litigants to a process like conciliation? That would only make the situation worse."

This disagreement became more and more heated until the panel discussants (being, after all, conflict resolution experts) were finally able to pinpoint the problem. The source of the conflict was that, in Professor A's country, *mediation* was defined as a process in which disputants were helped to reach agreement by a neutral third party. In Professor B's country, on the other hand, mediation was what in this text is called "nonbinding arbitration": each disputant argued his or her case to a neutral, who issued a decision. Had litigants been mandated to participate in such a process and then required to submit to the outcome, no lawsuit would ever be tried: since the outcome would have been binding, no such lawsuit would ever have gotten to court. On the other hand, since mediating litigants in Professor A's country had the right not to agree to any settlement, their rights to litigate were preserved. Any agreement was the result of mutual acceptance and was as binding as any other contract.

Making the language problems more confusing was the definition of *conciliation:* in Professor A's country, *conciliation* had the same definition as *mediation* in Professor B's country, whereas *conciliation* in Professor B's country meant the same thing as *mediation* in Professor A's country. Adding a further element of absurdity to the presentation was the revelation, by Professor C (who hailed from Asia), that statutes in effect in his country expressly provided that *mediation* and *conciliation* were interchangeable terms.

So-called *pragmatics,* the words and behaviors deemed to be appropriate in specific situations, can also create problems during diversity conflicts. For example, in many cultures, such as Japan, it is considered inappropriate to *express an outward disagreement,* and the language of negotiation is extremely subtle. In a negotiation that is not going well, a Japanese negotiator might thank the other party for the very interesting proposal just made and suggest a short period for the negotiator to study the details. For the Japanese negotiator, this response is a polite signal that the negotiation has ended unsuccessfully (Riskin & Westbrook 1997, 300–304). An American unfamiliar with the Japanese style of negotiation is likely to misunderstand this signal. On the other hand, an American is more likely to take an "in your face" tactic—even if a negotiation is going very well, he or she might reject a proposal outright—and, if this tactic is used with a Japanese negotiation partner, the latter may experience the communication as expressing not only the utter failure of the negotiation but outright enmity besides.

The nonverbal context of communication may also create difficulties in a diversity conflict. Some cultures (most notably, those speaking English and other Northern European languages) rely on minimal contextual factors: the language itself is sufficiently precise that nonverbal context is not needed to convey information. High-context language speakers (including those who speak Japanese, Chinese, Arabic, and Mediterranean languages) rely on the listener to infer meanings from the speaker using the surrounding social context. Low-context speakers are likely to be confused by the communication of negotiators who have been raised in cultures using a higher-context language. On the other hand, the use of a low-context language in a negotiation is likely to reduce the ability of negotiators to do the sorts of relationship building needed to create a long-term settlement (Kimmel 2000, 453–74). In a cross-cultural conflict between members of high- and low-context languages, conflict escalation is likely to result if the low-context speakers believe that the high-context speakers are being intentionally vague and if the high-context speakers feel "disrecognized"—denied the appropriate degree of recognition by the impersonality of the low-context speaker's messages.

There may also be cultural differences in the meaning attributed to nonverbal conduct. A fascinating example of this phenomenon is described by Thomas Kochman in his work *Black and White: Styles in Conflict* (Kochman 1981). Kochman, a sociology professor in New York City, noticed differences in the way in which European- and African-American undergraduates tended to engage in persuasive discussion. The middle-class European-Americans he observed tended to see a soft-spoken, unemotional delivery as indicating a commitment to the position taken. From the speaker's perspective, the content of the message was so innately correct that passion and advocacy were unnecessary. From this point of view, one didn't need to raise one's voice if the position one takes was intrinsically correct. This group saw loudness and passion as a sign of loss of objectivity—that the speaker had been taken in and had poor judgment about the argument being made. Thus, for this group, the effectiveness of advocacy depended on delivering the content of the message with scientific detachment.

For the other group Kochman observed, inner-city African Americans living in New York City, the opposite seemed to be true. Among these group members, persuasive argument was expected to be accompanied by passionate advocacy. Thus, these students were more likely to see emotionality as a sign of honest belief in the truth of an argument; further, they tended to associate the correctness of the position with the vigor of its supporting advocacy. Thus, for an argument to appear persuasive to members of this group, it was important for the speaker to advocate energetically.

Obviously, these nonverbal signals clash. An assertion made by a European-American student and accompanied by the culturally appropriate flat, unemotional delivery would likely to be devalued by an African-American listener. (Indeed, Kochman points out that, in a diversity conflict, African Americans are likely to use this sort of delivery when consciously suppressing their true beliefs.) A passionate delivery by an African-American student likely would have been interpreted by a European-American listener as "mere puffery"—speechifying by a speaker who is uncertain of the merits of his or her position and wants to cover it up.

Consider another example of differences in nonverbal pragmatics, from *gender relations* (according to psychologists who study gender). Males in a negotiation tend to use an emphatic, forceful method of getting their point across. Women are more indirect. They will typically include weakening language, such as "I could be wrong, but," "Perhaps," or "I wonder if" as they make their points. Most women understand that this use of weakening language is (paradoxically) a signal that they believe strongly in their side of an argument. If one is willing to invite others to scrutinize one's belief, then one must be really sure one is right; however, when women use these weakening phrases, many men think they are conveying doubt about their assertions. Thus, the behaviors of each gender generate misunderstanding when communicating in a mixed-gender situation.

Cultural Differences in Orientation to Conflict. There are cultural differences in the way people handle conflict that can complicate its resolution.

Because the need for interpersonal harmony varies from culture to culture, the drive to avoid open disagreement also varies. In some cultures, the custom is to avoid outward conflict, as with the Japanese. In other cultures, as in some African-American subcultures, outward disagreement is handled easily and is an expected method of discourse (Kochman 1981).

The trend toward valuing interpersonal harmony may also influence the negotiation styles seen cross-culturally. For example, a study comparing American with Taiwanese undergraduates found that, when given a hypothetical conflict involving a group project in a university course, the more collectivist Taiwanese were more likely to prefer approaching the problem using negotiation styles such as obliging and avoiding, which avoided overt disagreement, whereas the U.S. students tended to express preferences for using the dominating style, the style most likely to provoke heated confrontation (Trubisky, Ting-Toomey, & Lin 1991). Similarly, a study by Leung and Lind (1986) found that college students from the United States were more likely than those from Hong Kong to prefer the use of the adversary process to deal with a hypothetical civil tort dispute. Sometimes, these trends are tricky to define. For example, a study by Leung

(1988) comparing Chinese and American students suggests that Chinese students are more likely to be cooperative than Americans when negotiating with an acquaintance but more likely to be competitive than Americans when negotiating with a stranger.

Similarly, cultures vary in average levels of comfort with the expression of angry emotions. Even within single cultures, there are subcultural variations: for example, the expression of anger is considered more appropriate during litigation than in negotiation.

In many cultures and subcultures, the "real negotiation" takes place during social interactions outside of the negotiation. The negotiation simply formalizes what's already been agreed upon. This is true in cultures valuing social harmony and probably occurs not only because the cementing of the personal relationship between the negotiators is seen as essential to the negotiation but also to prevent loss of public face should the negotiation fail. This trend toward the use of "shadow negotiations" also occurs within subcultures and specific contexts in the United States. For example, organizational psychologist Pat Heim comments that many female executives can become baffled and feel betrayed when, prior to a meeting to negotiate a business deal, the actual negotiation has already taken place informally and behind the scenes by the males involved (*Rules of Engagement* 1996).

There are also cultural differences in people's attitudes toward the appropriateness of specific means of resolving disputes. For example, business scholar Catherine Tinsley (Tinsley 1998) studied about 400 German, Japanese, and American corporate managers. Tinsley provided the subjects with a hypothetical organizational conflict involving colleagues and asked them to identify which sorts of methods they would prefer to use to deal with the conflict. The Americans were more likely than the Germans or the Japanese to say that they would try to identify and meet the interests of everyone in the conflict. The Germans were more likely than either the Americans or the Japanese to say that they preferred to resolve the conflict by recourse to established rules and regulations. And the Japanese were more likely than the other two groups to say that they preferred to resolve the conflict by taking it to a higher-status person for a decision. If these preferences generalize beyond the business organizations context, and there is evidence that they do (Tinsley 1998), it behooves a conflict diagnostician to become aware of these and similar sorts of preferences before attempting to resolve a conflict. An American, for example, who enters into negotiation with a German and simply expects him or her to buy into an interest-based process may find unexpected obstacles to resolution.

Summary: Cultural Issues in Diversity Conflict. Paul Kimmel (2000) has coined the term *microculture* to refer to the development of a new understanding among conflict participants that recognizes and takes into account, but transcends, cultural difference. He argues that, before effective conflict resolution can take place, an effective microculture must exist, one in which individuals can depend on shared meanings, values, perceptions, and expectations. The building of such a shared context must start with the efforts of each conflict participant to understand the context of every other participant. Without this understanding, a conflict participant may have expectations that are unreasonable, given the other participants' frames of reference. When expectations are not met, effective conflict management breaks down and conflict is likely to escalate.

How can you as a conflict participant attain the goal of building a micro-culture? A necessary first step is to learn as much as possible about the typical context, attributions, goals, strategies, tactics, and communication styles used by members of the culture you are dealing with. Consider retaining a member of the other's culture on your team to help you understand the other participants' behaviors and to plan effective strategies. Also learn as much about the individual negotiators as possible to prevent the pitfalls of stereotyping. With this needed information in mind, it is useful to take frequent "times-out" to prevent egocentric thinking: "If I was in his or her shoes, what would I be thinking and feeling at this point?" is a useful question to ask. You may wish to practice your negotiation with a friend from the culture of the person you will be negotiating with, so that you can anticipate how the process might go.

Also, consider using a *mediator* to help with negotiation. A neutral third party trusted by both can help each side see the other side's point of view and help each acknowledge the other. It helps to use a mediation team consisting of members of the diverse cultures. Each mediator can help decode the meaning of what the participant from his or her shared culture is saying and can help verbalize the perspectives of the disputants.

As we move into the third millennium, the trend of encountering people from other cultures continues to grow, so understanding how to deal with cultural differences assumes greater and greater importance. However, even when we do not perceive that a conflict participant is culturally different from us, the knowledge of how cultural differences affect the response to conflict is useful. Even within single cultures, the response to conflict falls on a continuum: some people are more interdependent than others, some use more context-based communication than others, and some place more importance than others on saving face and preserving social harmony. Thus, the base of knowledge about the influence of cultural diversity on conflict resolution, and the consideration of ways to create an effective microculture, are relevant to every conflict participant and essential to the diagnosis of all conflicts.

POWER

Power issues are the "seamy underbelly" of diversity issues in interpersonal conflict. Power issues arise when cultural, racial, ethnic, or gender-based inequalities in power affect the process and outcome of a conflict. Power issues include the egregious "isms" of our time: racism, sexism, and anti-Semitism, just to name a few. A number of scholars and social scientists have detailed the ways in which dispute resolution processes in our country may disempower women and persons of color.

Chapter 13 touched upon the problems of group power imbalance. A racial, ethnic, gendered, or other cultural group that has experienced disempowerment may suffer from reduced access to resources, greater impoverishment, lessened ability to use existing social support systems (such as police and medical care systems), negative stereotyping, and lower expectations from others. These disadvantages create a vicious cycle, in which members of these groups fall further and further behind as they encounter interpersonal conflict throughout their lives.

Law professor Carol Rose, in her well-reasoned law review article "Bargaining and Gender" (Rose 1995), makes a cogent argument for why women may get worse deals than men due to stereotypes about their power and conflict behaviors. Rose starts from the prevailing stereotype of women as more obliging than men. She argues that, for her theory to work, *it is unnecessary that this stereotype be true,* only that the people in power believe it. (Other studies show that this stereotype is probably *not* true: overall, in carefully controlled studies, women are no more likely to oblige and no less likely to dominate than men. Craver & Baures, 1999.)

Rose then reasons that, since powerful people believe in the stereotype, they are less likely to give in to women. When a powerful person negotiates with an assertive woman, he or she is likely to assume that, if this woman doesn't give in to the powerful person's demands, she is simply unusual and that *he or she should hold out* for a more typical woman target. Due to the high-powered person's stereotypes about women's negotiation and conflict behaviors, he or she is likely to believe that more compliant women will be plentiful.

Rose further reasons that, since most people in powerful places are operating based on this stereotype of women as more compliant and obliging, statistically poorer offers will be made to women overall. Hence, opportunities offered to women will be poorer overall, and women will tend to get poorer offers on average than men during the negotiation of interpersonal conflicts, disputes, and transactions. Further, because women get wind of these discriminatory trends, they are more likely to take a poor offer (because they see that they have little choice). Over time, this tends to confirm the stereotype.

Rose makes an additional assertion: because women are regarded as poorer economic risks, families and employers are less willing to invest in them; therefore, women will be less likely to be offered financial support to attend college, sufficiently generous startup loans for business ventures, and mortgages for the purchase of homes. In a sense, this discriminatory regard for the economic viability of women is true, in the sense that, if women suffer widespread economic discrimination, they will operate at an economic disadvantage. The result, according to Rose, is that one could expect a widening wealth and resource gap between males and females as each progresses through the life span. Rose's thesis is impossible to verify or disconfirm, but its premise is reasonable and accords with statistical evidence of women's economic disadvantages.

Another empirical study lends support to the idea that women are disadvantaged during interpersonal conflict, but for different reasons. Coltri (1995) gave undergraduates of diverse sexes and races transcripts of child custody mediations and asked the subjects to rate the negotiation styles of each parent. Unbeknownst to the experimental subjects, the transcripts had been cobbled together from several real mediation transcripts, and the names assigned to the parents, John and Mary, had been reversed in half the experimental transcripts. (Thus, for example,

◆ **FIGURE 14-3**

Coltri's (1995) Study of Gender and Perception of Mediating Parents

If part of the media- tion transcript read...	Then half the subjects received a transcript that read...	And the other sub- jects received a tran- script that read...
Parent #1: "But, _____, you know Joan is doing better at school since she has been living with me!"	**John:** "But, Mary, you know Joan is doing better at school since she has been living with me!"	**Mary:** "But, John, you know Joan is doing better at school since she has been living with me!"
Parent #2: "You're full of it! Joan wants to live with me; she's made that clear!"	**Mary:** "You're full of it! Joan wants to live with me; she's made that clear!"	**John:** "You're full of it! Joan wants to live with me; she's made that clear!"

the parent who had the child on Saturdays was named John in half the transcripts and Mary in the other half. See Figure 14-3.) The transcript was modified to eliminate any other references to the genders of the parents. Thus, the study assessed sex-stereotype-associated differences in the interpretation of negotiation behavior.[5]

Overall, the disputant given the name Mary was, on average, rated as more dominating, more avoiding, less compromising, and less integrating than the disputant given the name John. Similarly, the parent labeled John was rated as being more concerned than the parent labeled Mary with the best interests of the child. These results reflected the underlying reaction of the students to the likeability of the target parents: regardless of which parent was given which name, the parent labeled as John was overwhelmingly rated as more likeable than the parent labeled as Mary. Although the results of this study are limited in their generalizability, they suggest that prevailing stereotypes of women as more docile and obliging can hamper the abilities of women to act assertively: men who behave assertively are liked and respected, whereas women behaving in an identical manner tend to be disliked. This attitudinal reaction may bias the interpretation of negotiation behavior so that assertive women are perceived as less cooperative. This bias in perception can place women at a disadvantage: it may be easier for men to come across as cooperative if they behave assertively during interpersonal conflict. This outcome is consistent with women's anecdotal accounts of being between a rock and a hard place in negotiations: being forceful is considered attractive in a male but is considered "uppity" and unattractive in a female. Women, therefore, may be prevented from departing from stereotypically obliging behavior by the negative reactions they receive from other conflict participants when they attempt to assert their interests. Females walk a difficult line in trying to protect themselves and their clients in interpersonal conflict.

---

[5] This sort of social psychology experiment, in which attitude toward a social group member is assessed by giving subjects a sample of an individual's behavior and manipulating the assigned gender, race, or other social group membership of the "target person" using a name, a photograph, or other information that signals social group membership, is known as the "Goldberg paradigm."

Field study

in experimental research, a study conducted in the natural setting of the behavior being examined, rather than in a laboratory or another artificial setting.

In another study, Professor Ian Ayres of the Northwestern University School of Law (Ayres 1991) and his research team conducted a **field study** to learn more about the challenges faced by both women and African Americans in a familiar interpersonal transaction context: the purchase of a car.

Ayres' team hired white and black actors of both genders to go to automobile dealerships throughout the Chicago area, posing as potential car buyers. The confederates used scripts to conduct their negotiation, so that there would be no actual differences between the behaviors of the buyers on the basis of race or gender. The study tracked the initial offers (the answer to the confederate's early question, "What would I have to pay to buy this car?"), the pattern of convergence of the offers, and the final offers made by the dealers. The scripts varied, so that the researchers could study the effects of various kinds of information on the negotiation process. Examples of these variations included whether the confederate said he or she had test-driven the car elsewhere and whether the confederate said he or she had another car. Thus, the buyers revealed different levels of personal power to the salespeople during the course of the negotiations. (For example, a buyer who did not have another car displayed lower levels of ecological power, in that he or she had less ability to shop around or to leave if the current negotiation did not go favorably.) These facts were not revealed at the outset of the contact but, instead, were revealed gradually and naturally according to the dictates of the scripts. (Results showed that these revealed facts did influence the dealers to make better deals to the buyers with better facts.)

Ayres reported a number of findings. The most pertinent relate to the amount of dealer markup initially offered by the salesperson, the amount of markup present in the dealer's final offer, and the amount of change in this markup from the beginning to the end of the negotiation. The research team found substantial differences in the pattern of offers made by salespersons based on the race and gender of the confederate. These findings are shown in Figure 14-4.

◆ **FIGURE 14-4**

Initial and Final Offer Averages from the Ayres (1991) Study

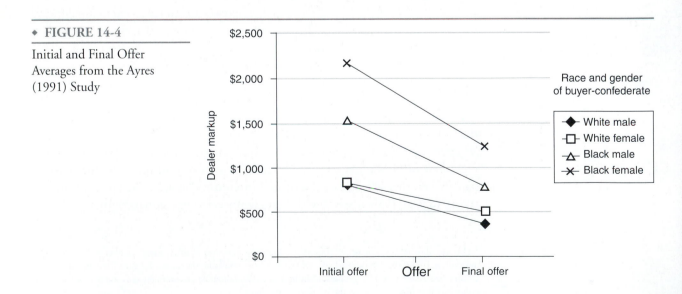

Compared with the white males, the black males started out with much worse first offers—dealer markups of about double those of the white males. And the black females were even worse off: their initial markups were around triple those of the white males. But these discrepancies decreased a bit as the negotiations progressed. (In mathematical terms, the "slope" of the line for the black buyers was steeper than that for the white males.) This pattern may exist because, initially, stereotypes of blacks as less powerful than whites influenced the initial offers (in keeping with the ideas suggested by Carol Rose, that negotiators base their behaviors on their stereotypes of how assertive the other disputant is likely to be). The convergence of the offers suggests that reality partially canceled out the stereotyping: apparently, as the dealers got to know the facts about the potential buyers, their stereotypical assumptions began to fall away—but not completely: the relative sizes of the discrepancies of the markups remained at around double and triple the white male markup for the black males and females, respectively.

For the white females, there was a different pattern. The initial offers were nearly as good as those made to the white males. But the pattern of concessions made to the white females was worse than that for any other group (in other words, their convergence line was less steep). Why? Perhaps the salespeople, relying on a stereotype about the attitudes of women toward negotiation, assumed that the women would not tolerate as much haggling and that they had to start closer to the final price to avoid the women's simply picking up and leaving. Nonetheless, the final offers made to the white women were more similar to those made to the white men than to those made to the blacks of both genders, suggesting that the dealers considered the white women more powerful in general than the black customers. Indeed, on average, the initial offers made to the white women were about the same as the average final offers made to the black men, and much better than those made to the black women.

Researcher Ian Ayres discovered patterns of racial and gender discrimination in the practices of automobile salespersons that disadvantaged black and female customers. Dana White, Photo Edit

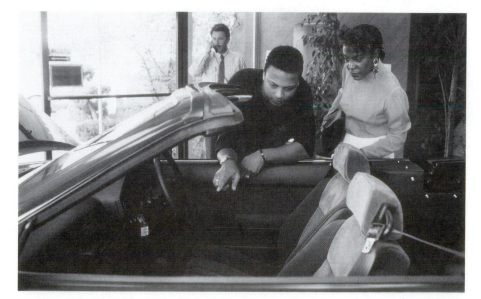

Were emotion-based attitudes toward the races and genders, such as bigotry, responsible for these results? Ayres does not think this factor was particularly important. There was evidence that the confederates were steered toward salespeople of their own race and gender.[6] When Ayres looked at the patterns of offers, he did not find that better deals were given to customers of the same race or gender. In fact, when final offers were considered, the confederates tended to receive better deals when negotiating with a salesperson of a different race and gender. Instead, Ayres concluded that the best explanation for the discrimination he found was stereotyping: stereotyping of the blacks—most egregiously, the black females—as having less bargaining power and stereotyping of the white females as less willing to bargain altogether.

Obviously, discrimination, bigotry, and sexism are not dead. Considerable work in the social sciences indicates that stereotypical beliefs about the disempowerment of particular social groups, and about the appropriateness of particular behaviors by women and minorities, affect the ability of such individuals to protect their interests during interpersonal conflicts.

As was discussed in Chapter 13, a high-power group is frequently reluctant to give up power to lower-power groups, even if power-sharing is in the long-term best interests of society as a whole. Hence, individuals committed to the ultimate achievement of effective conflict resolution must be prepared to work for equality and justice, participating effectively in the legal system and being willing to use competitive conflict resolution processes, such as litigation, where warranted. A healthy understanding of conflict diagnosis, negotiation skills, and so forth is of only limited value if the disputant hails from a disempowered social group. No matter what strategy a disempowered disputant uses, the outcome is likely to reflect the power imbalances existing within the social system at large.

It's nearly always appropriate to try the use of principled bargaining and the soft on the person/tough on the problem strategy. The principled-bargaining model, with its emphasis on self-protection and simultaneous attention to gentleness in the relationship between the conflict participants can be consistent with stereotypical expectations about behavior without requiring its user to give into unreasonable demands. A conflict diagnostician considering a diversity conflict involving power imbalance should also consider ways to partially rectify the power imbalance, such as involving advocates who share the cultural group membership of the lower-power group members, maximizing personal power, and clarifying the BATNA. It's also useful to correct stereotypical assumptions about lack of personal power where possible, and, if it appears that the other side is unbending in its bigotry, it may be useful to turn bigoted beliefs to one's advantage.

---

[6] There were no black female salespeople encountered: the black women were steered mostly to black male salespeople.

SUMMARY: DIVERSITY ISSUES IN INTERPERSONAL CONFLICT

ALL INTERPERSONAL CONFLICTS ARE DIVERSITY CONFLICTS

So-called diversity issues are a metaphor for the more general problems confronting those who are involved in interpersonal conflict. Conflict itself generates systematic distortions of perception about others that resemble stereotypes, particularly when the conflict itself is in an escalating spiral. Moreover, conflict itself is characterized by misunderstandings by participants about the context, frame of reference, and meanings of behavior of the others in the conflict. These sorts of misunderstandings are very much like the misunderstandings that occur when people of diverse cultural backgrounds attempt to communicate with one another. Finally, much conflict is marked by efforts by individual participants to use coercive power to overwhelm others, just as powerful racial, ethnic, and national groups may use their superior power to oppress people of a less powerful group. In this way, then, diversity issues complicate and increase the impediments to effective conflict resolution that otherwise exist.

CONFLICT DIAGNOSTICIANS AND DIVERSITY

Conflict diagnosis must take into account, and deal with, diversity issues. But what should be done to counter the negative impact of stereotyping, cultural misunderstanding, and oppressive action?

To begin with, those involved in the resolution of conflict must be advocates for justice and equality. Conflict diagnosticians who wish to create opportunity for constructive conflict resolution must be prepared to *work for equality and equal rights.* It's also important for society to *create safe places and forums for us to discuss these issues, so that power issues can gradually be dispelled.*

Within specific interpersonal conflicts, it may be useful to *gently correct people* who are using stereotypes and making wrong assumptions about people (or taking advantage of the mistake in the appropriate case). Sometimes, the application of stereotypes is unintended. If safe to do so, it is useful to educate the other conflict participants about the possibility that they have misapplied a stereotype. If you feel you have been the victim of bigotry or negative stereotyping, don't automatically assume that the behavior has been generated by malice: recall that diverse social contexts can lead to great differences in the interpretation of a situation. Ignorance about your social context may be operating. Similarly, be open to the likelihood that you will apply stereotypes and unwarranted assumptions to others during a diversity conflict. The best, and only, way to avoid applying stereotypes is to work at being conscious of when you tend to apply them. *It is also helpful to educate yourself* about other races, ethnicities, and cultures and to work for diversity in your work, school, and other environments. If you work for and with persons from other races/ethnicities/cultures, *take advantage of opportunities to educate and be educated.* Act as a bridge for understanding whenever you can.

Use principled-bargaining tactics. Insist on the use of objective standards for decision making. Your work at focusing on underlying interests will help lead you to an understanding of the similarities that underly differences. Be aware, however, of cultural, subcultural, and individual reluctance to adopt the principled-bargaining model of conflict resolution. Educating the other side may be an option, or you may need to bend a bit to accommodate to diverse belief systems about conflict.

If you or the disputant on your team is a member of a low-power social group, *consider how this can be turned to advantage.* Stereotyping by bigoted opponents may blind them to your motives and behaviors, allowing you to be a bit sneaky.

Most important, *do your research and maximize your expert power.* It is the best type of power to use and the one you have the most control over acquiring.

EXERCISES, PROJECTS, AND "THOUGHT EXPERIMENTS"

1. *Conflict journal.* Write about the following questions and issues in your journal:

    a. Are there any issues of stereotyping that are affecting the course of any of the conflicts you are following in the journal? Are there any issues of cultural differences that are affecting the course of any of the conflicts? Are there issues of group disempowerment connected with race, gender, social status, culture, or subculture?

    b. How is each of these diversity issues affecting the course of the conflict? Be specific and address each issue separately.

    c. What steps could you take to address each of these issues? Be specific and address each issue separately.

    d. You may choose to implement some or all of the steps you identified in question c—if you do, write about how each step you took affected the course of the conflict.

2. Identify yourself mentally with a racial, ethnic, gendered, religious, professional, or cultural group to which you belong. For example, if you are an African-American, Muslim, female attorney, you may use any of these groups as your identified group. Make as complete a list as you can of the stereotypes you believe members of the dominant social group attribute to your chosen cultural group. The stereotypes may be positive, negative, or neutral. Then find a partner in the class who has identified with a different social group. Compare your lists. Do you agree with the stereotypes of the other cultural group that he or she identified? Does he or she agree with your

list of stereotypes for your identified group? Did you learn anything from this exercise?

3. Break into groups of two people. Taking turns, each person in the pair is to talk about the following questions:

   a. Was there ever a time that you felt you were discriminated against on the basis of race, gender, religion, cultural background, ethnicity, or other social group membership? How did it feel to be discriminated against? Are you satisfied with your conduct? What would you do differently next time?

   b. Was there ever a time that you felt that you discriminated against someone else on the basis of social group membership? How did it feel to act in that way? Are you satisfied with your behavior, and, if not, what would you do differently next time?

   c. Was there ever a time that you were present when someone else suffered discrimination on the basis of social group membership? How did it feel to be involved in, or to observe, this interaction? What, if anything, did you do? Are you satisfied with what you did, and, if not, what would you do differently next time?

   d. After each person in the pair has had a chance to answer questions a through c, they should spend some time discussing how to cope with each of these situations. Then pairs of class members should share their results with the rest of the class.

4. Consider an employee who feels she has been discriminated against on the job, due to race, gender, or age, and wishes to file an Equal Employment Opportunity Office (EEO) claim against the alleged perpetrators.

   a. Is such a situation always best resolved through adversarial adjudication? Why or why not?

   b. If you are this woman's legal advisor, and don't share her membership in the social group she is claiming is the reason she has been harmed, how do you advise her accurately without giving her the impression that you are insensitive or bigoted?

   c. What would be the role of interests analysis (see Chapter 8) in assisting such a client?

   d. What would be the role of power analysis (see Chapter 13) in assisting such a client?

5. How is social perception during conflict, in general, similar to the process of stereotyping? Look back to Chapter 5 and write an essay comparing social perception during interpersonal conflict with social perception of the members of social out-groups (an out-group is a social group to which you do not see yourself belonging).

6. Consider Kimmel's idea of a microculture. Is it possible to attain good conflict resolution in a diversity conflict without creating an effective microculture among the disputants and their teams? Write an essay on this topic, or use it as the basis for discussion or debate.

7. There is some evidence that certain racial minorities within the United States place a great deal of importance on the nonmonetary aspects of dispute outcomes (LaFree and Rack 1996, 790). Read more about this issue in Chapter 16. Suppose you are a paralegal at a legal-aid clinic and that you are assisting a Hispanic man in negotiating the settlement to a dispute. Your client has done carpentry work for the other disputant, who is a wealthy white homeowner. The homeowner has unlawfully withheld much of your client's fee, contending that his work was substandard. After considerable case preparation, you are pretty sure your client could get at least $40,000 in court, but, when the homeowner offers $20,000 and an apology, your client seems eager to take it and move on. What should you do? Would your answer change if you were representing this man as his attorney?

8. Consider the situation discussed in question 7. If you were in charge of a court-based program that diverted disputes to an assisted settlement program and studies confirmed that, statistically, Hispanic disputants were settling for less money than white disputants for comparable disputes, would you be concerned? Would you advocate ending the program? Why or why not? What, if any, changes would you advocate? What, if any, additional information would you try to obtain?

RECOMMENDED READINGS

Ayres, I. 1991. Fair driving: Gender and race discrimination in retail car negotiation. *Harvard Law Review* 104:817–72.

Fiske, S. T., and S. L. Neuberg, 1990. A continuum model of impression formation from category-based to individuating processes: Influences of information and motivation on attention and interpretation. In *Advances in experimental social psychology,* edited by M. P. Zanna. San Diego, CA: Academic Press.

Gadlin, H. 1994. Conflict resolution, cultural differences, and the culture of racism. *Negotiation Journal* 10 (January):33–47.

Kimmel, P. R. 2000. Culture and conflict. In *The handbook of conflict resolution: Theory and practice,* edited by M. Deutsch and P. T. Coleman. San Francisco: Jossey-Bass.

Kochman, T. 1981. *Black and white: Styles in conflict.* Chicago: University of Chicago Press.

Leung, K. 1988. Some determinants of conflict avoidance. *Journal of Cross Cultural Psychology* 19:125–36.

Leung, K., and E. A. Lind. 1986. Procedural justice and culture: Effects of culture, gender, and investigator status on procedural preferences. *Journal of Personality and Social Psychology* 50(6):1134–40.

Riskin, L. L., and J. E. Westbrook (eds.). 1997. The roles of gender, race, and culture in negotiation. In *Dispute resolution and lawyers.* 2d ed. (pp. 270–307). St. Paul: West.

Rose, C. 1995. Bargaining and gender. *Harvard Journal of Law and Public Policy* 18:547–65.

Trubisky, P., S. Ting-Toomey, and S. L. Lin. 1991. The influence of individualism-collectivism and self-monitoring on conflict styles. *International Journal of Intercultural Relations* 15:65–84.

PART III

ALTERNATIVE DISPUTE RESOLUTION PROCESSES

Part I of this textbook introduced the concept of the invisible veil: the idea that what we think we know and observe about interpersonal conflict is frequently a small and very misleading part of what's really going on. Our human mental equipment, operating in the context of the society we grow up and live in, causes us to learn a particular way of viewing conflict, to acquire a set of skills attuned to this particular view, and to miss or reject alternate versions of what is happening. We learned why this narrow perspective is unduly restrictive and damaging. We were also introduced to conflict diagnosis: a thinking-outside-the-box technique. Conflict diagnosis is based on the premise that, by understanding the mental processes that occur during interpersonal conflict, and by using a rigorous system of understanding a specific conflict, we can transcend the invisible veil and make better decisions about how to handle the situation.

In Part II, we learned the techniques of conflict diagnosis. Through understanding sources of conflict, the conflict cycle, interests analysis, power and BATNA analysis, impediments to cooperation, negotiation theory, and the effects of stereotyping, culture, and power imbalance, we can learn to better comprehend what is going on in a conflict, why it appears to be so resistant to resolution, and how to guide it in more constructive paths.

Part III is about alternative dispute resolution (ADR). If negotiation is the basic hand tool of conflict resolution, then ADR processes are power tools. The processes you will learn about in the chapters that follow are the new power tools that belong in your toolbox of conflict resolution techniques.

Twenty years ago, most legal professionals thought there were only three alternatives when their clients had a legal dispute: litigate, negotiate, or "lump it" (live with what the other disputant wants). A decade ago, most of these professionals added a fourth option, ADR. But this acquisition was of the most rudimentary sort: ADR was recognized as an alternative to litigation, but the differences among ADR processes were not recognized or appreciated. This is a bit like saying that you are planning to use your power tool to create a fancy

303

wooden table leg without ever deciding whether the tool you will be using is your power saw, your router, your planer, or your lathe. Conflict diagnosis is the key to optimum power tool selection in the field of interpersonal conflict.

You will no doubt notice that the lion's share of Part III is devoted to mediation, seemingly a single ADR process. There are two principal reasons for this emphasis. The first, and most important, is that mediation, in its purest form, is the dispute resolution process that most radically departs from our invisible veil concept of how to resolve conflict. For this reason, a rudimentary effort to understand mediation is doomed to failure. Instead, we take it slowly—we take the time needed to understand the ins and outs of the process, its varieties and variants, its pros and cons, and its legal and practical intricacies. Relatedly, mediation is itself a highly diverse set of processes. It ranges from a proceeding virtually indistinguishable from adjudication (except that the outcome is advisory rather than binding) all the way to so-called transformative mediation, a process so radically nonadversarial that even some mediation purists have their doubts. These processes, although they are all called "mediation," are galaxies apart when viewed through the lens of conflict diagnosis. Thus, when we discuss mediation, we are really discussing a whole class of dispute resolution power tools.

As you learn about the many kinds of mediation and the other ADR processes, always keep conflict diagnosis in mind. How will a particular ADR process affect the conflict cycle? Will it lift the invisible veil or keep it firmly in place? Will using the process prevent future conflict or encourage it? How can I use this tool in a way that affirms what I now know about interpersonal conflict? If you select ADR processes with these questions in mind, you will become a sophisticated user and a master of the tools of conflict resolution.

15

Mediation:
An Introduction

"A pessimist sees the difficulty in every opportunity; an optimist sees the opportunity in every difficulty."

—Winston Churchill

In this chapter, you will learn ...

- What mediation is and how it differs from other ADR processes.
- The difference between facilitative and evaluative mediation.
- That the product of mediation, should the disputants reach agreement, is a valid, binding, and enforceable contract.
- The uses of mediation today.
- The five basic varieties of mediation and their goals, characteristics, advantages, and disadvantages.
- The roles played in mediation by mediators, disputants, disputants' lawyers, paralegals, constituents and stakeholders, and experts/consultants.

When interpersonal conflict occurs, the most common approach to resolving it is negotiation—an interplay and a dialogue between the disputants and their representatives aimed at resolving the conflict. If negotiation does not resolve the conflict, and if the conflict involves legal issues, litigation is the only option many disputants see as recourse.

It should be evident from previous chapters that negotiation offers many benefits over litigation. From the individual disputants' perspectives, negotiation offers relationship preservation, the opportunity for creative problem solving, economy, time-saving, and a greater likelihood that the settlement will not unravel over time. From the societal perspective, negotiation offers a more effective use of resources, relief of overcrowded court dockets, the likelihood of lowered relitigation rates, and the reduced need for increases in court infrastructure and personnel. Thus, negotiation is frequently the best option for addressing conflicts.

Of course, a principal drawback to negotiation is that sometimes it fails to produce a settlement. Is there any way to preserve the advantages of negotiated settlement—particularly those of collaborating—when a negotiation leads to impasse or when it is anticipated that negotiation is not likely to settle the dispute? One approach is to support negotiation with other processes to increase the likelihood that effective settlement will be the result—that is, to provide *negotiation-plus*. Many of the ADR processes described in this text have been developed to achieve just this end. And the ADR process most capable of capturing the benefits of cooperative and collaborative negotiation is the technique we will turn to next. This technique, often considered the "Cadillac" of ADR processes, is mediation.

BASIC DEFINITIONS

MEDIATION

Mediation

a form of assisted negotiation, in which a disinterested or neutral third party assists the disputants, with or without their agents and/or advocates, in negotiating a resolution of their interpersonal conflict. In mediation, the neutral is not empowered to make a decision and does not typically press for a particular alternative.

Mediation is a type of assisted negotiation that uses a third party (or panel of third parties) to help disputants negotiate their settlement. This third party, who is called the *mediator*, is typically impartial with respect to the disputants and neutral as to the settlement reached.[1]

Mediation is distinguished from other ADR processes in two principal ways:

1. In mediation, the neutral does not issue a decision in the case (unlike adjudicatory processes, such as arbitration and rent-a-judge, and unlike nonbinding evaluation processes, such as minitrial, summary jury trial, early neutral evaluation, and nonbinding arbitration).

2. In mediation, the disputants retain the power to settle, or not, at all times (unlike adjudicatory processes, such as arbitration and rent-a-judge).

In general, mediation is a process in which the disputants and/or their legal teams meet with a mediator to attempt to settle their dispute. However, beyond this very general description, it is impossible to describe how all mediation works. Mediation is not one-size-fits-all. It is conducted in a number of ways, and these differences profoundly affect the sorts of situations they are suitable for handling. To help us understand the nature of these differences, it is useful to define two other terms denoting a basic distinction among styles of mediation: the so-called *facilitative-evaluative* distinction, a concept first set forth by eminent legal scholar Leonard L. Riskin in his article "Understanding Mediators' Orientations, Strategies, and Techniques: A Grid for the Perplexed" (Riskin 1996).

---

[1] This is true, at least, for mediation as practiced in most Western nations. In many non-Western cultures, mediation is conducted by a prominent and powerful community elder or another appointee with explicit preferences and biases. Enlightening research on this topic is collected in Shapiro (1981).

What Is Mediation?

- ◆ It is an ADR process.
- ◆ It is a type of assisted negotiation.
- ◆ It uses a neutral.
- ◆ The neutral does not issue a decision.
- ◆ The disputants retain the power to settle (or not).

Facilitative mediation
mediation in which the mediator focuses on facilitating effective negotiation among the disputants and their teams.

Facilitative Mediation. In **facilitative mediation,** the mediator's primary function is to promote effective negotiation. Facilitative mediators use techniques designed to promote effective negotiation as they view it: they lay ground rules for effective communication, help participants discover their interests and those of their counterparts, guide the disputants in the steps of cooperative negotiation, and intervene at all stages of the conflict cycle to keep the conflict as noncompetitive as possible. The strictly facilitative mediator assiduously avoids any evaluation of the merits or strengths of either disputant's case.[2]

Evaluative mediation
mediation featuring an evaluation of the merits of each disputant's case by the mediator.

Evaluative Mediation. In **evaluative mediation,** the mediator works to narrow the gap between the demands of each disputant by expressly evaluating the merits, strengths, and weaknesses of each disputant's position and by strategically communicating these evaluations to the disputants.[3] In this sense, then, evaluative mediation is an intervention based on the notion that negotiation is a process of positional bargaining. The evaluative mediator attempts to minimize the effective distances between the disputants' positions and to create overlap if possible. Another way of understanding evaluative mediation is that it is a process of reducing the optimism of each disputant's BATNA assessment. With each disputant's confidence in his or her alternatives to negotiated settlement reduced, each is more likely to accept compromise settlement terms.

In extreme forms of evaluative mediation, the centerpiece of the process may be a single evaluation of the likely outcome if the dispute is taken to court.

---

[2] An effective case can be made for the proposition that a mediator who evaluates the disputants' case may be engaging in the provision of legal advice, an act that constitutes the unauthorized practice of law (for nonlawyer-mediators) and the representation of parties with conflicting interests (for lawyer-mediators). You will see more about this issue in Chapter 18.

[3] As with all other parts of the ADR field, the terminology *evaluative mediation* is the subject of some confusion. Many, if not most, scholars (e.g., Schwartz 1999) presume that *evaluative mediation* means that the mediator conducts, and issues to the parties, some sort of evaluation of the merits of the disputants' legal case. Others use the term *evaluation* in a far broader sense, to mean *any* evaluation by the mediator. Straus Institute for Dispute Resolution director L. Randolph Lowry, for example, comments that

> . . . at one level, all mediators are involved in evaluation—that sense of making judgments on the information presented. Evaluation, at least internally with the mediator, is central to the mediator's work. It is the basis on which decisions are made regarding the management of the process and the parties as well as the resolution of the problem" (Lowry 2000, 49).

This text will use the former, narrower, definition of evaluative mediation, in accordance with the predominant usage among ADR scholars.

Nonbinding evaluation

assisted negotiation featuring the provision of a case evaluation by the neutral. It is distinguished from evaluative mediation in that, generally, the neutral in a nonbinding evaluation does not make an extensive effort to settle the case beyond providing the evaluation. Forms of nonbinding evaluation, including summary jury trial, early neutral evaluation, minitrial, and nonbinding arbitration, are defined and discussed in Chapter 20.

Michigan Mediation

a form of nonbinding evaluation provided by the Michigan State Courts for certain cases filed in the court system.

Settlement conference

the process in which a judge meets with litigants and their attorneys prior to a scheduled trial. Settlement conferences are typically used to streamline and plan the trial process and to determine whether action is needed on pre-trial matters. Many judges also use a settlement conference to attempt to settle the overall dispute.

An extremely evaluative mediation may closely resemble **nonbinding evaluation** (see Chapter 20): the neutral hears all sides of the issue and then issues an opinion regarding how the case might be decided if it were to be litigated. This opinion may be virtually indistinguishable from the nonbinding decision issued by a neutral in a minitrial or another nonbinding evaluation process. The primary difference between highly evaluative mediation and nonbinding evaluation is that a neutral performing nonbinding evaluation generally stops with the evaluation, whereas an evaluative mediator proceeds to work with the disputants to reach a settlement. Nonetheless, even this distinction sometimes vanishes: for example, the so-called **Michigan Mediation** process is nothing more than court-connected nonbinding arbitration (Federal Judicial Center and CPR Institute for Dispute Resolution 1996). In short, as with any form of ADR, it obviously pays to get the details before signing on to any proposed mediation plan.

There is also much blurring in practice between facilitative and evaluative mediation. Many mediators practice midway along this continuum, and some mediators jump from facilitative to evaluative approaches based on what they think will promote the goals of the mediation.[4] Moreover, most evaluative mediators use facilitative mediation tactics (see Chapter 17) to promote cooperation and a speedy conclusion to the process. Nonetheless, the facilitative/evaluative distinction effectively explains many of the important differences among mediation programs, processes, and providers and how particular forms of mediation will respond to the unique characteristics of a particular conflict. Thus, the distinction will be used in this chapter as we explore the many varieties of mediation and the implications of these varieties for dispute resolution.

PROCESSES RELATED TO MEDIATION

It is also helpful at this juncture to define what is *not* mediation. Three dispute resolution processes have characteristics in common with mediation but are not mediation as strictly defined in this section: settlement conference, facilitation, and conciliation.

Settlement Conference. A **settlement conference** is a judicially created process presided over by a judge (or, occasionally, a master, hearing examiner, or magistrate). Settlement conferencing is used for legal disputes filed in court and headed for trial. The function of a settlement conference is typically to reach agreement as to the issues in controversy, to plan the trial so it is orderly and efficient, and to determine whether there are any extant disputes regarding witness and documentary evidence. Settlement conferences are frequently also used by the presiding court officer to attempt to settle the case in its entirety. The person

---

4 Note that different forms of mediation are associated with different goals. This issue is addressed later in the chapter.

presiding over the conference will sometimes apply mediation-style tactics to promote agreements. In fact, many judges who hold settlement conferences say that, in that role, they are actually mediating. In this text, however, mediation is not so defined.

Facilitation
a conflict resolution professional's efforts to design and organize a dispute resolution process for an interpersonal conflict involving large or multiple groups of people and/or complex interpersonal conflicts.

Facilitation. Facilitation is a term usually applied to a process in which a neutral third party, or panel of neutrals, helps prepare for a complex negotiation. Typically, facilitation is used if an interpersonal conflict involves multiple, complex parties and issues (for example, a negotiated rulemaking to create regulations for pollution control in which various municipalities, state agencies, and advocacy groups consider themselves stakeholders). The facilitator typically takes on a number of important tasks, including identifying interested participants; assisting corporate, governmental, or advocacy-group disputants in selecting representatives for the bargaining table; helping select mediators or other ADR providers to participate in the negotiation; and planning and selecting the time, place, and available amenities for the negotiation. A competent facilitator effectively sets the stage for a negotiation in which no participant feels left out and in which principled bargaining leading to effective settlement and maximal quality of consent is likely. (The term *settlement facilitation* is sometimes also used to connote mediation in which the disputants' lawyers, but not the disputants themselves, are the participants.)

Conciliation
A poorly-defined term, Sometimes, referring to mediation; other times, to relationship repair.

Conciliation. Conciliation is another term commonly applied to numerous processes conceptually related to mediation. Sometimes the term is applied to mediation itself, sometimes it is applied to facilitation, sometimes it is applied to nonbinding evaluation, and sometimes it is given other meanings. Care should be taken to clarify meaning if the use of conciliation is raised as an option.

THE PRODUCT OF MEDIATION

If the parties to mediation do settle their dispute, the settlement is usually written down. Even if the disputants are unable to settle all the elements of their dispute, frequently they are able to settle some of their issues or come to a temporary agreement. In mediation, even these interim or partial agreements are valued for their ability to advance the goals of the disputants, to reduce levels of conflict, and to build trust, so that future, more comprehensive settlements can be constructed later.

Memorandum of understanding (MOU), memorandum of settlement, memorandum of agreement
a document memorializing an agreement worked out in mediation; generally, not considered binding. Occasionally, it is called a stipulation.

If disputants reach an agreement of some sort in mediation, some mediators provide the parties with a written **memorandum of settlement, memorandum of agreement**, or **memorandum of understanding (MOU)**. This document is not intended to be binding but, instead, is "translated" by the parties' legal advocates into a contract of settlement, or stipulation; or, if the mediation is of a case filed in court, by the judge into an order or judgment. Other mediators draft a document intended for legal enforceability without rewriting. In any event, in

Contract (settlement, stipulation, agreement, settlement agreement)
a document, produced by a mediator, by a disputant's attorney, or occasionally by a disputant, memorializing an agreement reached in mediation and intended to be legally binding.

general an agreement reached in mediation has the status of a **contract**, no more and no less. Thus, a mediated agreement may be enforced in court just as any other contract may be enforced, and it may be contested based on the same defenses (fraud, duress, incapacity of a party, statute of frauds, and so on) as those applicable to other contracts. In addition, since a third party has been involved in the negotiation process, many of the usual defenses to contract enforceability may take a special form relating to the mediator's competence, ethical behavior, or personal biases. For example, a disputant who feels the mediator was biased against him or her might claim that he or she settled under duress produced by the unethical behavior of the mediator. Because mediation is typically confidential, an issue discussed later in this chapter and again in Chapter 18, there may also be special evidentiary considerations that complicate the proof of, or defense against, a mediated agreement.

USES OF MEDIATION TODAY

Mediation is actually an ancient form of conflict resolution, having been used in Eastern and African societies for thousands of years. Even today, mediation is practiced all over the world. Elsewhere, mediation-like styles of dispute resolution are much more predominant than they are in Western cultures, although mediation in non-Western nations is often quite different from its counterpart here (Shapiro 1981).

In the United States, mediation has been used for centuries in the commercial arena to maintain good ongoing business relationships. Some religious groups and traditional Native American societies have also relied on mediation-style interventions to resolve disputes among members; moreover, historically the handling of conflicts in many ethnic communities by powerful elders is very similar to mediation. In general, mediation and mediation-like practices of dispute resolution tend to flourish in subcultural groups and eras in which a homogeneous value system predominates among most disputants, making it easier to reach consensus about underlying principles, values, and interests (Auerbach 1983).

The past quarter-century marks the first time that a consensual and nonadversarial dispute resolution process such as mediation has been tried on such a broad and mainstream basis in a time and society of unprecedented social diversity. Necessity has been the mother of this invention: the modern ADR movement has been precipitated by widespread frustration with the high expense, overwhelming investment of time, and egregious social toll taken by litigation.[5] At the time ADR began to be discussed seriously, there was concern that the

---

[5] Jerold Auerbach (1983), who tracked the use of ADR processes historically, predicted this swing away from litigation as well as the demise of ADR in diverse populations. By his judgment, a society that swings toward litigation processes to cope with the problem of diversity eventually becomes fed up with the inefficiency and costliness of the litigation alternative and swings back toward ADR. By Auerbach's assessment of the situation, modern Western nations are between a rock and a hard place, striving to preserve diversity yet seeking to streamline dispute resolution.

court system, already slowed to a virtual crawl, would become completely paralyzed by the huge litigation backlog. Thus, the first efforts to adopt mediation as a mainstream process for resolving legal disputes were primarily efforts to divert cases from the legal system in order to save time and money, as well as to free up the courts, so that they could handle the cases they retained for trial more effectively (see the discussion in Chapter 3). All forms of ADR were tapped for this case-diversion goal, but the process of mediation, specifically, was also seen as a method of providing better, more appropriate dispute resolution.

After about twenty years of experience with mediation in the mainstream of American society, many observers of social events feel that this confidence in the mediation process to provide better, more effective dispute resolution has proven to be well placed. Although many issues remain controversial, and meaningful empirical research in the field is very difficult to conduct, there is overall evidence that mediation provides efficient and effective ways of handling disputes, with benefits ranging from time and cost savings to more detailed and carefully constructed settlements to better relationships among disputants who must continue to interact. More about the benefits and drawbacks of mediation appears in Chapter 16.

The 1990s saw a dramatic expansion of mediation into the legal mainstream—it is currently seen in the following areas:

- *Labor and employment relations,* particularly in federal agencies—precipitated by a host of federal statutes and regulations
- *State civil litigation,* particularly in major urban metropolitan areas such as Los Angeles, San Francisco, and the District of Columbia
- *Federal civil litigation:* as of 1996, fifty-one federal districts offered some form of court-connected mediation (Gauvey 2001)

Mediation is not a recent development. This historic lithograph by T. H. Matteson shows a youthful George Washington mediating among his squabbling companions. Library of Congress

- ◆ *Divorce and custody* cases, both private and court-connected; as of December 2000, researchers Carrie-Anne Tondo, Rinarisa Coronel, and Bethany Drucker (2001) had found some form of court-annexed family mediation practiced in all states except Indiana, New York, and Vermont
- ◆ *Special education disputes* among schools, service providers and parents of special-needs children
- ◆ *Neighborhood disputes*
- ◆ Disputes between *disputants of different countries,* in which the choice-of-law problems are too expensive or difficult to sort out in court
- ◆ Disputes involving *consumer grievances* against commercial entities
- ◆ Outside the legal arena, in *public and private schools* to resolve conflicts and prevent violence by and to students; these programs use students trained to use mediation and are called peer mediation

The past decade has seen a significant shift of mediation's acceptance by the nation's bar. Although the bench, which has been directly burdened with the consequences of a highly litigious society, has backed ADR processes for years, the bar has been slower to accept mediation. This caution can be partially attributed to mercenary concerns (fears that mediation will take business away from lawyers), but partially also attributable to concerns that the mediation process would compromise the best interests of clients. The former concerns have been seen to be largely unfounded, as many lawyers have discovered that, when their clients use mediation, they tend to be more satisfied and to place less blame for poor outcomes on the lawyer (Kichaven 1997), and, because cases settle faster, lawyers tend to get paid sooner for work done (Mosten 1997). The concern for the welfare of clients is still being sorted out by the bar and by ADR scholars and

Community mediation is used to resolve conflicts among neighbors. Bruce Ayres, Getty Images Inc., Stone Allstock

professionals.[6] Mediation, unless coercive or deceptive in some manner (see discussion later in this chapter), generally does not raise Due Process issues for disputants for the simple reason that disputants may simply walk away without settling. A more difficult issue concerns the impact of mediation on disempowered disputants. This issue will be addressed in more detail later in this chapter.

Commensurate with a growing acceptance of mediation by the bar comes a struggle over just how mediation will come to be practiced. One recent trend is for mediation to become adversarialized by lawyers who become involved in the process of creating legal and ADR policy. An example of such an adversarialization of mediation is a recent effort to allow clients to move for sanctions in court against a disputant who is accused of causing an impasse. The movement toward mediation's adversarialization is noted with dismay by prominent scholars and policymakers who view mediation as offering a way to avoid the restrictions and limitations of the invisible veil. People such as UCLA Law School's Carrie Menkel-Meadow (Menkel-Meadow 1991), Dickinson Law School's Nancy Welsh (Welsh 2001b), prominent mediator Zena Zumeta (Zumeta 2000a), and Lela Love of the Benjamin Cardozo School of Law (Love 1997) are concerned that, in building adversarial features into mediation, policymakers are threatening to kill the most important advantages of mediation as an alternative to adversarial conflict management. Kimberlee Kovach, of the University of Texas School of Law and former chair of the American Bar Association Section of Dispute Resolution, directly expresses this concern:

> The notion of mediation as a different paradigm for dispute resolution is being eroded with the lawyers now viewing the process as merely another tool within the litigation arena to be used combatively rather than for any intended purpose. Noting that mediation may be different processes when involved in the court system, the phrase "liti-mediation" is now used. Additional evidence is the remark of one lawyer telling another that he "won" the mediation. If this trend of "adversarial mediation" continues, then any opportunity for the mediation process to effect change as a novel process will be lost. (Kovach 1997, 593, citations omitted)

It is too early to tell how mediation will continue to evolve in mainstream U.S. society.

VARIETIES OF MEDIATION

To understand how mediation works, when it is effective and what its advantages and disadvantages are, it is important to understand the great diversity of mediation forms. In talking about the advantages and disadvantages of mediation, it is important to realize that each type of mediation has its own distinct characteristics, uses, strengths, and limitations. *Five fairly typical forms of mediation* are

---

[6] The assumptions of the lawyer's standard philosophical map may predispose lawyers to suspect mediation, a nonadversary process, of producing second-class justice. See Riskin (1982).

present in the United States today.[7] Each of these five forms has unique characteristics that suit it for particular sorts of disputes. Each has particular problems that make it unsuitable in certain situations.

TRIAGE MEDIATION

Triage mediation is believed to be relatively uncommon today. Formerly, it was widely seen in court systems and was developed to divert large numbers of cases away from the trial system.

This sort of mediation is typically very brief and focused. The *goal* of triage mediation is to get the dispute out of the court system as quickly as possible by seeking a quick settlement. The *focus* of triage mediation is typically narrow—it is focused in the short term on *this* dispute because that's all that's needed to get the case out of court. Because of the primacy of expediency in triage mediation, the process is typically evaluative. Evaluative mediation tends to bring cases to a quicker end. Pressure and coercion (referred to by some as "muscle mediation") are frequently used to push the disputants into a quick decision. For example, in some triage mediation programs, if an agreement is not reached, the mediator may be required to report to the court which disputant was responsible for the impasse.

> Arthur Jones sued Brenda Smith for visitation of their one-year-old son, Martin. The court sent Arthur and Brenda to court-connected mediation. After a brief orientation, a volunteer mediator was assigned. The mediator met with both parties for about twenty minutes, together, to get a flavor for the nature of their dispute. Then she met with each of them privately. She asked Arthur about whether he had been up-to-date on his child support payments ("No, not really") and suggested that he might not want to push too hard for visitation, lest Brenda get really angry about the money. To Brenda, the mediator laid out the usual policy of the court, which was to order child visitation every other weekend and overnights once a week. "Wouldn't you rather have some say in the visitation plan?" the mediator asked. Brenda finally relented and agreed to every other Saturday and overnights once a month. Arthur had wanted more time but was reluctant to alienate the mediator and risk a child support action. The entire mediation took about ninety minutes.

The main advantage of triage mediation is that it's cheap, it's quick, and it clears court dockets. However, triage mediation presents a number of significant problems (Beck & Sales 2000). Because its principal goal is to save money and avoid court, mediators are often poorly trained and poorly paid and carry overly heavy caseloads. Often, an implicit or explicit goal is to reach as many agree-

---

[7] Omitted from this discussion and this text as a whole is labor mediation. Although resembling bargaining-based mediation in some respects, labor mediation is so specialized that it is best treated as an element of labor law rather than alternative dispute resolution.

ments as possible as quickly as possible, so the mediators may feel compelled to pressure disputants into agreement. If so, the advantage of disputants' retaining control over the outcome of mediation is lost. Also, there is a due process problem with a mediator pushing disputants into an agreement, particularly if the mediation is court-ordered: the mediation process may effectively deny one or both disputants their day in court without due process of law. Moreover, the well-being of the disputants (or, in the case of disputes involving dependent persons, such as child custody mediation, their dependent constituents) may take a back seat to getting the agreement. This form of mediation is less prevalent today because it has been so resoundingly discredited.

BARGAINING-BASED MEDIATION

Bargaining-based mediation (a term coined by Elizabeth Koopman and Joan Hunt of the University of Maryland at College Park) is an extremely common form of mediation. Sometimes called concession-hunting (Young 2001), it's the predominant style used in court-connected civil dispute mediation, as well as the mediation of commercial, construction, and personal injury cases.

The primary goal of bargaining-based mediation is to attain a fair agreement through compromise.

Lawyer-mediators are more likely to use this form of mediation than any other. The focus is usually *narrow* (focused on "this dispute") and the process is typically *evaluative*. Usually, the disputants' lawyers participate in the mediation and often do the negotiating in place of their clients. Since lawyer-mediators and lawyer-advocates do most of the work, the lawyer's standard philosophical map colors how the participants frame the issues and work out a solution (Guthrie 2001; Kovach & Love 1998). Typically, bargaining-based mediators give the disputants or their representatives a chance to state their cases and follow this phase with a series of **caucuses** (separate meetings with one disputant and then the other) in which interests and positions are explored. The mediator shuttles back and forth, exploring areas of agreement and, occasionally, strategically revealing information where it would lead to compromise. Often, a compromise proposal suggests itself in the shuttle diplomacy process; then the mediator may present it to each party and solicit consent to its terms. Outcomes are usually strictly monetary and usually display a lack of creativity and innovation (Welsh 2001a). Nonetheless, litigants typically express a high degree of satisfaction when bargaining-based mediation works—and it frequently does.

> Rick Polanka, a bricklayer, sued ABC, a general contractor, over fees he alleged were due on a large construction project. Both Rick's counsel and ABC's counsel secretly admitted having some doubts about how the law would apply to the dispute. The court referred the dispute to court-connected mediation presided over by Lorinda Lattislaw, Esq., a civil attorney and volunteer mediator for the court's civil division. She asked that each lawyer state his client's case, then scheduled separate private sessions

---

Caucus

a meeting between a mediator and one disputant (with or without the disputant's representatives), out of the earshot of the other disputant and his or her representatives. A caucus is different from a joint session, which all the disputants involved in mediation, and/or their representatives, attend.

Bargaining-Based Mediation:
Bronfenbrenner's Ecological Theory in Action

The latter half of the 1990s saw a remarkable rise in the dominance of bargaining-based mediation as the primary method of handling civil disputes, such as tort and commercial litigation.

Researcher Bobbi McAdoo has presented survey results that indicate a strong preference on the part of lawyers who participate in mandatory, court-connected mediation services for lawyer-mediators who have strong backgrounds as litigators. The principal quality cited by her lawyer-respondents that they look for in a mediator is the ability to value the disputants' case effectively.

Since these lawyer-respondents are the primary customers of civil mediation services offered by the courts, their preferences control the demand for mediation services and, hence, have shaped the sorts of mediation available for civil disputes. As Bronfenbrenner (see Chapter 3) would predict, the invisible veil permeating the beliefs of those who use court-connected mediation services has influenced the sorts of mediation that are made available. Thus, although mediation has become much more popular in recent years, its adversarialization has rendered it almost unrecognizeable to those who would define mediation primarily as a process for facilitating collaboration and creative problem solving between disputants, such as Menkel-Meadow (1991), Lela Love, and Kimberlee Kovach (1998).

A number of legal scholars have documented this evolution of court-connected mediation, with its increasing emphasis on case evaluation as the predominant mediator strategy, the reduced role of disputants, the increased dominance of legal counsel in mediation sessions, the reduction or elimination of joint mediation sessions, and the lack of creativity in the settlements produced by this sort of mediation. Deborah Hensler, a prominent researcher in the mediation field, remarks that examples of facilitative mediation are fast disappearing, leaving a process that mostly resembles judicial settlement conferences (Hensler 1999). Nancy Welsh comments that "the bargaining paradigm that dominates and delivers settlements in most civil cases is capturing the mediation process" (Welsh 2001a, 789), and prominent mediation scholar John Bickerman (1999, 3–5) laments that, if mediation is treated "as glorified settlement conferences, then the value of the process may be lost."

The reader may recall the discussion of Uri Bronfenbrenner's theory of social ecology in Chapter 3. The evolution of mediation from radical alternative to the legal mainstream—and its simultaneous transformation into an adversarial process—makes sense if we recall Bronfenbrenner's concept of bidirectionality. As he would predict, the introduction of mediation has transformed the macrosystem, but the macrosystem has also transformed practitioners of mediation.

for each disputant's team. In the private meetings, Lorinda expertly attacked the basis for the attorney's confidence in the case's "winnability"—in other words, to each side she cast doubt on the strength of the BATNA estimates they had developed. In addition, she explored the bottom lines of each side and looked for some ways to trade off some monetary concessions for other issues, such as modifying the payment date, building in some interest payments, and ensuring that the dispute stayed private. Eventually, she was able to carve out a set of terms that both sides could live with. After one initial joint session, two private sessions, and several telephone conferences, Linda was able to bring the parties back into mediation to jointly confirm a compromise settlement.

Bargaining-based mediation is particularly good for cases in which there are highly divergent perceptions of fact or law—because the divergent perceptions may be the most important impediment to settlement. It's also good for cases involving highly complex legal issues, since lawyers tend to be closely involved in the mediation process. Bargaining-based mediation can also be helpful if there is not much time to obtain a settlement: because it tends to be evaluative and relies on compromising, it can be speedier than some alternative processes (Baruch-Bush 1996; Hermann, Honeyman, McAdoo and Welsh 2001; Kovach & Love 1996; Welsh 2001a, 2001b).

Because the process is evaluative, bargaining-based mediation tends to cause the disputants to become increasingly position-bound. In other words, the focus is on each disputant's position and how successful he or she is likely to be with it. Because of this focus, the outcome tends to be a compromise rather than an integrative solution, so the outcome tends to make less optimal use of resources than would occur if a more collaborative approach were used. If the lawyers participate *in place of* the disputants, they may also miss aspects of the dispute that are important to the disputants. This is both because of the influence of the lawyer's standard philosophical map (which causes the lawyers to focus on causes of action and money) and because the lawyers never know as much about the disputants as the disputants know about themselves. Usually, little is done to correct the aspects of the overall relationship that might cause problems in the future. This limited focus on the relationship is only a disadvantage if the disputants will be dealing with one other in the future. Another limitation of bargaining-based mediation is that, since it tends to be highly evaluative, only individuals with expertise in the subject matter of the dispute are appropriate mediators. Their authoritative pronouncements on the merits of the case will have the intended impact only if the disputants regard these pronouncements as legitimate.

THERAPEUTIC MEDIATION

Therapeutic mediation is generally designed to improve the relationship of the disputants, so that they are able to settle their conflicts. However, it is sometimes unclear what the goal of therapeutic mediation is, and herein lies the problem with this form of mediation.

Mediation has many similarities to therapy, and, because there are so many varieties of mediation, it can be difficult to define the difference. Sometimes, a therapist's efforts to help a couple relate more effectively involve their making agreements, and sometimes a mediator's efforts to help disputants reach agreement improve the disputants' relationship. Sometimes, a mediator with a strong mental-health background will facilitate the process of negotiation by intervening to support a disputant whose emotional or mental condition is impeding negotiation.

Gerry and Mick, married five years, had decided to separate and sought mediation with Alan Marshall, LCSW. Alan worked for several sessions with the couple to help them reduce destructive communication between them and to develop a plan for breaking the news about the separation to their four-year-old twin daughters. They then physically separated, with Gerry and the children staying in the family home and Mick moving into a nearby apartment. Alan then worked with them through the initial psychological crisis produced by the separation, and the threesome produced several agreements aimed at clarifying who would pay specific living expenses, how Gerry and Mick would communicate about the twins' well-being, and where the twins would live. As the months went by, Gerry and Mick returned to Alan to work out a property settlement. However, the resulting agreement was a general statement of principles only; Gerry and Mick ended up using lawyers to negotiate the details. They later said they felt that Alan had helped them avoid destructive behavior before, and during the height of, the separation crisis.

The problem with therapeutic mediation occurs when the neutral is unclear about what the goals are or flip-flops between basically therapeutic and basically mediative goals. Therapists who become family mediators sometimes struggle with the professional boundaries between couples therapy and mediation, and the results can be damaging to the clients. For example, if a therapist begins couples therapy with a husband and wife, finds that the marriage is irreparable, supports the wife with some individual therapy, and then attempts divorce mediation, an obvious conflict of interest is created, one that has the potential to cause deep harm to the husband.

Nonetheless, therapeutic mediation, if its goals and boundaries are very clearly defined, can be both necessary and very helpful in high-conflict situations, particularly those involving a disputant who has a mental illness or an emotional or personality disorder requiring high levels of professional support before he or she can negotiate effectively.[8] This sort of mediation is generally highly facilitative and extremely broad in terms of issues dealt with. It can be extremely empowering to both an emotionally disturbed or impaired individual and to those having to deal with them, and can get the situation to a more constructive posture.

PURE MEDIATION

Pure mediation is a facilitative process whose goal is to promote collaborative, integrative, principled bargaining. (It is very important to note that the goal of pure mediation is *not* to reach agreement but, rather, to promote the sorts of negotiation behaviors that will lead to reaching agreement.)[9]

Pure mediation is often seen in community and divorce mediation, and it is being found in other contexts in increasing numbers. This form of mediation is also becoming more accepted by the legal profession. It is highly facilitative,

---

[8] An excellent description of highly effective therapeutic mediation, and the sorts of cases to which it is best adapted, can be found in Janet Johnston and Linda Campbell's (1988) excellent book *Impasses of Divorce: The Dynamics and Resolution of Family Conflict.*

[9] The term "problem solving mediation" also applied to this form of mediation, is avoided in this text because it is also often applied to bargaining-based mediation.

and the breadth of issues dealt with is as broad or narrow as the disputants wish it to be.

"Pure" mediators work to keep the disputants in a cooperative conflict cycle and structure the process to encourage principled bargaining. The mediator sets ground rules to improve communication and often structures the mediation sessions to track through the steps of a principled negotiation. Pure mediators also work to remove impediments to settlement, such as helping disputants understand how meta-disputes occurred and referring disputants to experts so that different perceptions of fact and law can be resolved. Holding separate meetings with individual disputants (called caucusing) is seldom done, since caucusing fosters mistrust and usually does not promote collaboration.

> Sherry and Colleen had been students at the Anytown Cooking Academy, where Sherry had majored in restaurant management and Colleen had studied to become a pastry chef. Upon graduation, the two had embarked on a joint venture: a coffee and dessert café called Au Lait. Unfortunately, the two were at loggerheads over salaries to be paid to each one, over the appropriate degree to which the café should be marketed, and whether to open additional branches.
>
> They had come to the brink of dissolving their partnership when a mutual friend suggested Mort Nathan, a mediator. Mort met with the two women in a series of eight ninety-minute sessions. After introducing the mediation process, Mort asked each woman to describe her goals and hopes for the future. Each had a vision of Au Lait and articulated the wish that it remain viable. From these descriptions, Mort helped the women list a series of mutually shared goals for the venture. As they had spoken, the women had also revealed their areas of dispute, which Mort also listed. Mort had a separate list for goals that one of the disputants, but not the other, found important.
>
> The next step was to list multiple options for meeting each of the goals the women had described. Several sessions were spent fine-tuning and comparing these options. At several points in the process, one or the other disputant became so frustrated that she wanted to quit. At those times, Mort often commented on how far they had come or reminded the women of the principal goal held by each, which was to continue to nurture their joint venture. Out of the mediation, ultimately, came a new and improved joint venture agreement, one in which salaries were more clearly stated. The women also agreed to hire a marketing agent, so that neither would be responsible for a task that neither was good at. Their plan was to consult the marketing agent about expansion after a six-month period and to return to mediation if they were unable to agree on expansion.

There are many advantages to pure mediation. They mirror many of the advantages we have already noted for mediation in general. Since pure mediation facilitates principled bargaining, the agreements reached tend to be highly creative, win-win outcomes that optimize the use of resources. Pure mediation may have long-term benefits for disputants who must continue a relationship. If the mediator is able to resist the temptation to pressure the disputants into an agreement, then this sort of mediation provides a high quality of disputant consent. As a result, the disputants will psychologically "own" any resulting agreement, with the typical benefits of psychological ownership. There are long-term benefits even if agreement is not reached:

- Pure mediation narrows the issues, so that, if another dispute resolution process is required, it's likely to be easier and faster.
- There is a good chance that the disputants will be more cooperative, so other alternatives will not be as expensive, time-consuming, or traumatic.
- Pure mediation can teach principled bargaining to the disputants, so that they can use it elsewhere in their lives.

There are fewer disadvantages to pure mediation than we have seen for other varieties of mediation, but it does raise a few problems. First, if time is an important consideration and if only a narrow, short-term perspective is important, bargaining-based mediation may be a better choice. This is particularly the case if disputants enter mediation with widely divergent BATNAs. Also, pure mediation may not be appropriate for disputants with limited cognitive functioning, such as children or the mentally disabled, because of the need for higher-level thought processes involved in principled bargaining, although there may be some things the mediator can do to compensate for such problems, such as involving an advocate or referring the client to a support person for assistance. There are also marketing problems associated with pure mediation. When disputants turn to mediation, they are often desperate for a quick fix and tend to want a mediator who is pushier or more evaluative—someone who will tell the disputants what they should do. Moreover, many lawyers don't understand what pure mediation is or its advantages over bargaining-based mediation. Finally, pure mediation is also more difficult to practice than triage and bargaining-based mediation: it requires a great deal of knowledge and skill in facilitating client communication without coercion. If the mediator is ineffective, this sort of mediation can be no better than any other type.

TRANSFORMATIVE MEDIATION

Transformative mediation resembles pure mediation, except that its goals are even more completely removed from "getting an agreement." According to Robert Baruch-Bush and Joseph P. Folger, who coined the term *transformative mediation* and introduced the concept in their seminal book *The Promise of Mediation* (Baruch-Bush & Folger 1994), this form has as its goal the improvement or transformation of those who participate in the process. Specifically, there are two primary transformative goals:

- Empowerment: the improvement of the personal power of each disputant
- Recognition: the ability of each disputant to take the perspective of the other disputant and to communicate this sense of understanding to the other disputant

Note how *completely disconnected* this goal is from "reaching agreement." Generally, disputants enter mediation believing that its purpose is to resolve a conflict. In transformative mediation, the disputants are provided with the opportunity to become empowered and are encouraged to give the other disputant recognition. *Then,* if the disputants want to negotiate and reach agreement, they can.

When Baruch-Bush and Folger first proposed the concept of transformative mediation, it was regarded as entirely theoretical. However, it is being adopted and used in real-world applications, most notably by the U.S. Postal Service, apparently with substantial success (Antes, Folger, & Della Noce 2001; Bingham, Baruch-Bush, Hallberlin, & Napoli 1999).

> Next-door-neighbors Abel and Baker saw one another as nuisances—in Abel's mind, Baker played the stereo too loudly, and Baker thought Abel was way too nosy. Their animosity often erupted into loud arguments in the street. They were pressured by their frustrated neighbors into trying a storefront community mediation service, a program populated by transformative mediators. Lotta, a mediator with this service, met with Abel and Baker in two two-hour joint sessions. She helped each of them understand the perspective of the other and articulate to one another some degree of validation ("I think that, if I saw things from your point of view—which I don't—I would feel the same way you do.") She also helped each of the disputants become empowered, by referring them to legal advisors to learn more about the law of nuisance and by helping each of them understand the other. Eventually, each came to see that they would have to live with the other and that this process would be easier if each moderated his behavior. Finally, an agreement was made limiting the hours that Baker played his stereo (so that Abel could have rest time); in return, Abel agreed to stay off Baker's stoop and to stop peeking in his window.

The focus of transformative mediation is often extremely broad (the dispute isn't really the focus at all) and extremely facilitative (since case evaluations don't generally promote either empowerment or recognition). The process is much like pure mediation but less structured. The mediator encourages each disputant to tell his or her story and looks for opportunities to promote empowerment and recognition as the conversation continues.

Transformative mediation's advantages are similar to those of pure mediation. Agreements reached in transformative mediation are psychologically owned in full by the disputants, who are very likely to abide by them. However, no one really knows whether using transformative mediation instead of an alternative process would change the rate at which disputants reach agreement, either for better or for worse. The authors of *The Promise of Mediation* also assert that the use of transformative mediation will improve society at large by improving the moral development of disputants who use it. Critics counter by asserting that it is the height of arrogance for mediators to be in the business of improving their clients' characters.

The five major forms of mediation are summarized in Table 15-1.

◆ **TABLE 15-1** Forms of Mediation

FORM	TYPICAL ADHERENTS	MAJOR GOALS	TYPICAL TECHNIQUES
Triage mediation	Untrained mediators, underfunded court systems	Getting an agreement cheaply and quickly	"Muscle mediation": very directive and structured; may include elements of coercion and pressure, particularly to the disputant with the least bargaining power. Often includes nonbinding evaluation. May include "med-arb" (see Chapter 21) and/or directive to report to court which disputant was responsible for an impasse. Usually very time-limited.
Bargaining-based mediation	Lawyer-mediators, retired judges	Getting a "fair" settlement, getting a compromise	Evaluative: "instilling doubt," often in caucus format; showing each disputant that he or she has overestimated his or her chances of winning; correcting misapprehensions of the law's influence where they hamper settlement. Sometimes resembles nonbinding arbitration or judicial settlement conference.
Therapeutic mediation	Mental-health professionals	Improving the relationship between the disputants, so they can work better together and avoid present and future conflict	Broad and facilitative: encouraging listening, facilitating communication, exploring the roots of present conflicts, addressing mental-health problems that are perceived to prevent healthy relationship functioning.
Pure mediation	Some private mediators, particularly family law	Facilitating collaboration between the disputants to get a win-win outcome	Facilitative: active and reflective listening, encouragement of brainstorming, reframing and refocusing of communication, brief confirmation of feelings, refocusing on dispute, recasting positions into needs. Caucusing seldom used.
Transformative mediation	Expanding use among private mediators, used by U.S. Postal Service REDRESS program	Extremely broad, facilitative; promote empowerment of each disputant and recognition of each disputant's perspective and situation by the other; attaining settlement considered a secondary goal	Helping each disputant understand the nature of the dispute, helping each disputant understand the other's point of view, educating the disputants in effective negotiation techniques when necessary, facilitating assertive behavior by each disputant, encouraging each disputant to acknowledge the perspective of the other. Caucusing almost never used.

PARTICIPANT ROLES IN MEDIATION

Yet another set of important factors that affects the appropriateness of specific mediation processes is the set of participants. Who participates in mediation? As with other aspects of this widely varying process, the roles played by the participants are diverse.

In brief, the following individuals may participate in the process of mediation:

- ◆ The mediator (or mediators)
- ◆ The disputants (or, if a disputant is a group or corporation, the disputant's agent)

- ◆ Disputant's counsel and associated personnel, such as paralegals
- ◆ Constituents of the disputants
- ◆ Consultants and experts

MEDIATOR(S)

Of all the participants to mediation, the only party who is always present, without fail, is the mediator. The mediator is often one person, or there may be multiple individuals serving as a *panel* of mediators. Hiring one mediator to conduct mediation is, obviously, the least expensive option. However, cost aside, having multiple mediators is generally a better option. Since mediation is complex, it helps to have more than one mediator to pay attention to what is going on. For example, one can focus on legal issues, the other on relationship-building. The panel members can also role-model appropriate negotiation conduct for the disputants, such as politeness, active listening, turn-taking, and so forth; the mediators can even plan such interactions in advance. Mediators can also be chosen for their substantive expertise in the area of the law or a substantive subject-matter area, and multiple mediators can provide the opportunity for individuals whose expertise meets diverse needs. Another advantage to having multiple mediators occurs in disputes between members of distinct social groups. A mediation panel consisting of representatives of the salient disputant social groups can help each disputant feel more validated, heard, and empowered. For example, in divorce mediation, having a mixed-gender mediation team is often helpful in preventing one of the disputants from feeling intimidated. Moreover, in culturally diverse conflicts, it is often helpful for a mediation panel to be representative of all the cultural groups in the conflict. This cultural diversity enables the mediators to share their understanding of the social contexts of the disputants and to interpret communication that might otherwise lead to misunderstandings.

Since mediation is a relatively new profession in Western nations, mediators are generally career-changers or add a mediation practice to a pre-existing professional practice. There is no authoritative research documenting the professional backgrounds of mediators; however, based on anecdotal information, mediators most commonly come from the legal and mental-health professions. There is no uniform educational requirement for mediators, although individual jurisdictions impose specific qualifications on mediators working in particular fields. Mediator competency issues are considered in Chapter 18.

Impartiality and Neutrality of Mediators. A hallmark of Western-style mediation is the mediator's *impartiality* toward the disputants. In other, particularly non-Western, nations, as well as in many subcultures of the United States, persons in the role of mediator may, instead, be community elders of considerable power and authority who wield a considerable degree of influence. In some Eastern and African versions of mediation, the mediator slides back and forth between a facilitative and an adjudicative role. However, in the United States and the United Kingdom, as well as in many Latin American and European nations, the prevailing mediator model is of a disengaged professional who is impartial with respect to the disputants. Indeed, it would be considered a breach of mediator ethics in many circles for the mediator to have any sort of previous alliance with one of the disputants or an interest in the subject matter of the dispute. Mediator neutrality and impartiality are considered in more detail in Chapter 18.

Qualifications of Mediators. Mediator *qualification* has little uniformity across jurisdictions and dispute types. As a field of relatively recent formalization, there is little consistent regulation of the mediation field; hence, private mediators in most jurisdictions need not have specific qualifications except to market themselves effectively. Indeed, the recently adopted Uniform Mediation Act reflects the field's openness and diversity by providing (Section 9(f)) that

> [t]his [act] does not require that a mediator have a special qualification by background or profession.

Private mediators who operate in the civil and commercial litigation arena frequently hold themselves out as experts in the substantive field of practice or as longtime litigation specialists, in keeping with the trend for these mediators to use an evaluative style of mediation. In divorce and family mediation, there is more of a trend for interdisciplinary qualification, with legal professionals gaining training in mental-health-related knowledge bases and mental-health professionals gaining legal knowledge. In both cases, prospective mediators often take advantage of so-called forty-hour training courses available to people who want to become divorce mediators. These training courses generally provide an overview of conflict and negotiation theory, communication theory, mediation skills, legal issues, and divorce-related psychosocial issues.[10] Self-regulating professional organizations, such as the Academy of Family Mediators (now the Association for Conflict Resolution) and the American Arbitration Association also provide certification programs.

Court-connected and other program-based mediators are subject to a hodge-podge of certification and qualification requirements, such that no generalizations can be made in this textbook. An individual wishing to become a mediator must check the requirements in his or her jurisdiction for the sort of mediation he or she wishes to practice. The field is slowly becoming more unified and clear as time goes on. For example, in the state of Maryland, Maryland Rule 17-104(a), adopted in 2001, prescribes specific qualifications for mediators designated for court referral.[11] Previously, the rules allowed individual circuit courts to prescribe mediator qualifications.

---

[10] No representation is made here as to the adequacy of such courses in training people to be competent mediators.

[11] In Maryland, Rule 17-104(a) requires that court-appointed mediators be at least twenty-one years old, possess a bachelor's degree (unless this requirement is waived for good cause in a specific dispute), complete a forty-hour training course meeting requirements specified in Rule 17-106, agree to abide by a code of ethics, agree to periodic case monitoring, and agree to comply with certain case management requirements. Additional requirements are added for mediators who are dealing with parenting ("child access") issues.

DISPUTANTS AND THEIR LAWYERS

Generally, it is the norm for *disputants* to participate directly in mediation. However, both the issues involved and regional variations affect disputant involvement. In certain sorts of legal disputes (domestic relations being one important example), the disputants nearly always attend mediation sessions. Different mediators have different practices with regard to whether the disputant attends on his or her own or is accompanied by legal counsel. In some areas of practice, such as divorce mediation, whether the lawyer accompanies the client to mediation seems to vary across jurisdictions and may be a matter of local culture and the influence of respected persons in the legal or ADR communities. In other practice areas, such as the mediation of commercial disputes, it is more the norm for the attorney to attend in place of the disputant or for the attorney and disputant to attend together, with the attorney doing most of the negotiation.

It is important to appreciate the benefits of direct disputant participation from the perspective of conflict diagnosis. Disputants always know their own interests better than their lawyers do, although lawyers may be needed to explain the legal situation to disputants in order for the disputants to understand their interests better. Thus, unless the mediation is a purely evaluative process focused on positional bargaining, lawyers are poor substitutes for disputants. Also, disputants who directly and actively participate in mediation more fully psychologically own the resulting agreement and are less likely to have future conflicts over its terms. Thus, direct disputant participation is more likely to have effects that fulfill the promise of mediation in dealing effectively with interpersonal conflict.

At what point in the process of mediation do legal counsel become involved? There is no one answer to this question. The work of a lawyer for a client contemplating mediation begins *before the first contact* with a mediator. Effective

---

Lawyer Roles in Mediation

Vital
- ◆ Giving legal advice to prevent unexpected impact of settlement

Considered Extremely Important
- ◆ Giving legal advice and case preparation for empowerment and BATNA clarification

Sometimes Useful
- ◆ Giving support during negotiation
- ◆ Helping instill doubt

To Be Avoided
- ◆ Appropriating (taking over) the mediation
- ◆ Adversarial posturing
- ◆ Using mediation for trial discovery

legal counsel can explain the mediation process and its benefits to the client and can prepare the client for the process of principled bargaining in mediation. An effective lawyer can also help his or her client shop for an effective mediator.

The heart of legally representing mediation clients is empowerment and BATNA clarification through *interests analysis and case preparation*. The lawyer often helps the client clarify his or her underlying interests, values, needs, and principles by helping him or her understand how the legal issues affect these interests. The lawyer should make it clear to the client that, although the lawyer's role is to view the conflict from a legal perspective, this emphasis in no way minimizes the nonlegal aspects of the conflict. In other words, an effective legal advisor recognizes the lure of the lawyer's standard philosophical map and makes efforts to maintain an appropriate perspective. In addition to clarifying interests, the lawyer helps the client identify and increase the BATNA by preparing the case: reviewing the law, interviewing the witnesses, gathering and organizing documentary evidence, and so forth. An effective case valuation gives the client the information he or she needs to understand the BATNA, so that effective negotiation can occur during mediation. Effective case preparation also increases the client's expert power and, incidentally, moves the case closer to being ready for trial in case mediation does not result in a settlement. A continuing dilemma for lawyers and clients in mediated cases is how thoroughly to prepare: a very well-prepared case is best for effective mediation, but thorough case preparation is also very expensive.

Unfortunately, some lawyers, either for mercenary reasons or because of conceptual blinders created by the lawyer's standard philosophical map, may try to divert the client to a more adversarial method of resolving the dispute. Occasionally, mediation is, indeed, the wrong choice for the client, but a lawyer who systematically undermines his or her clients' efforts to choose mediation is doing a disservice and may even be violating the ethical obligation of effective representation (Breger 2000; Cochran 1999; see also the ABA Model Rules of Professional Conduct, Rule 2.1, comment. 5, providing that an attorney may be required ethically to advise a client of the ADR options available; the lawyer's potential obligation to advise a client of ADR options is discussed further in Chapter 22).

Lawyers may also *attend mediation sessions,* either with their clients or instead of their clients. There are advantages and disadvantages to lawyer attendance. Lawyers can help clarify legal issues for their clients as they arise during mediation. This role can be particularly helpful if the conflict presents very complex legal issues. A lawyer can also help support a frightened or intimidated client or calm down a very angry client. And, if the mediator uses an evaluative style, the lawyer can work in tandem with the mediator to help to instill doubt during the caucus. There are, however, several disadvantages to lawyer attendance at mediation sessions. The disputant may inappropriately lean on the lawyer instead of confronting the problem head on, leading to a situation in which the lawyer negotiates, instead of the disputant. This development compromises client self-determination. Some lawyers are tempted to misappropriate the mediation; that is, regardless of the disputant's desire for autonomy, the legal professional may be enticed to take over and perform the negotiation in place of the disputant. Obviously, such an appropriation will occur if the lawyer attends mediation in the client's place. If the lawyer takes over the negotiation, the client usually does not get his or her own needs and interests out on the table and usually does not psychologically own the outcome as fully as the client would have done with active participation. A lawyer may also turn the mediation into an opportunity for adversarial posturing, which pushes the mediated negotiation toward a competitive and escalating conflict cycle. The temptation to engage in adversarial posturing can be irresistible for a lawyer steeped in the adversarial system and unfamiliar with conflict and negotiation theory. Finally, a less than ethical lawyer may even use the mediation as a discovery device—to try to obtain confidential information about the other disputant.

If the lawyer does not attend the mediation sessions, he or she can play a vital role in the mediation process by *staying in touch* with the client throughout the mediation process. As we have noted elsewhere, the mediator is ethically prohibited from giving legal advice during mediation, so, if a legal issue arises, a competent mediator will frequently suggest to the client that he or she "run the issue by your attorney." Having access to legal advice can maintain client empowerment and make settlement more likely. For example, some divorce mediators find that client misunderstandings about the nature of marital property law prompt some spouses in mediation to take extreme positions on property issues. There is a cogent argument that the mediator is ethically prohibited (see Chapter 18) from correcting the client's misapprehension of the law, except to suggest the possibility of error and referring the client to the attorney. Many a mediation has been saved by the rational advice of competent attorneys.

Following mediation, the lawyer may review, or even draft, the mediated agreement. The attorney can suggest areas the clients did not consider and can point out the possibility that agreements might have unexpected or unintended consequences. This role is important, but an effective lawyer should be sensitive to the accomplishments of the disputants and take care not to use the opportunity to criticize and undermine the decisions made by the disputants in mediation.

PARALEGALS

Paralegals are becoming increasingly important members of the legal team, and many of the activities for lawyers in the mediation process are appropriate paralegal functions.[12] It is fair to say that paralegals are limited only by the proscription that they not practice law; that is, they may not give legal advice to the client and may not draft the agreement without attorney supervision. Because of the intensive involvement of the legal team with the client in preparing a case for mediation, clarifying and improving the BATNA, and speaking

---

[12] For a helpful review, see Waxler (1997), available online at *http://www.lad.org/TPJ/07/waxler.html.*

The work performed by paralegals and legal assistants can be invaluable in preparing clients for mediation. Michael Newman, PhotoEdit

with the client extensively about underlying interests, the cost savings of delegating as many of these tasks as possible to the paralegal become extremely important in a legally complex mediation. A paralegal may also have the responsibility of keeping a roster of mediators and making suggestions for referrals to the attorney and client,[13] of contacting mediators to set up initial sessions, of educating the client about the mediation process, of following and making regular contact with the mediating client, of helping create the formal settlement agreement, and even of participating in the mediation sessions to note down matters of importance.

Paralegals are also qualified to act as mediators themselves in many instances, and are becoming practitioners in increasing numbers. It is fair to say that paralegals will play an increasingly important role in the mediation profession in the years to come.

CONSTITUENTS AND DEPENDENTS

Whether constituents and dependents participate in mediation and the nature of their participation are often decided by disputants and mediators on a case-by-case basis. Dependent constituents (such as children in child custody cases) are occasionally brought into mediation for various reasons and serve as a good example of some of the complexities of involving constituents in the mediation

---

[13] The sorts of information available in this text concerning conflict and negotiation theories and the varieties of mediation can help legal professionals, such as paralegals, evaluate specific mediation processes and providers for suitability in various conflicts and disputes. A sophisticated paralegal should consider how to parlay this knowledge into a database of mediators that enables the paralegal to suggest good matches between clients and mediators.

process. There are good reasons and bad reasons to have children participate in the mediation of custody disputes. Adolescent children whose expanding autonomy and independence are facts of life may undermine or sabotage a parenting plan unless they feel heard and recognized in the process. Younger children are sometimes brought into a session with the mediator, so that the children can get a sense of the person the parents are working with and to get confirmation that their parents are working on their behalf. To foster healthy development, younger dependents should not be put in the position of feeling as if they are choosing between parents, nor should they be given the power to decide their own custody arrangements. Competent mediators sometimes use the session with the children to confirm and emphasize to the parents the need to work at keeping the children out of the middle of adult conflict.

Nondependent constituents can be important either as potential supporters or as saboteurs of agreements reached in mediation. These constituents are sometimes brought into mediation to give them a sense of greater psychological ownership of the result. Other constituents function almost as advocates: a disputant may want to bring a friend or an ally into a mediation session to reduce fear and

"I don't need time to think it over, Phillip—the answer is yes, I'll settle out of court with you."

The Cartoon Bank

increase comfort. Such constituents should be brought in only with great care, to prevent the other disputant from feeling ganged up on.

CONSULTANTS AND EXPERTS

In keeping with the general notion that a disputant negotiates more effectively if empowered, mediators frequently refer clients to experts to increase disputant knowledge and comfort level and to improve negotiation. In a commercial mediation, it may be appropriate to suggest an appraiser, an evaluator, or a marketing specialist. In divorce mediation, child psychologists, financial planners, accountants, and other professionals may be tapped to help disputants come to terms with issues raised by the divorce. In special education mediation, teachers, school psychologists, and others who have worked with the child may be consulted. Although these ancillary personnel usually remain on the sidelines to consult with disputants outside of mediation sessions, they may occasionally attend a mediation session to provide additional information to the mediator and the disputants.

EXERCISES, PROJECTS, AND "THOUGHT EXPERIMENTS"

1. *Conflict journal.* Consider your conflict and the diagnosis you have made of it. If you were to use mediation to handle the conflict, would facilitative or evaluative mediation be a better approach? Explain your answer.

2. In child custody disputes, courts often make a child custody award that perpetuates the *status quo,* on the assumption that, all other things being equal, the child will benefit from stability. If you were representing a parent in a child custody dispute, would you discourage him or her from entering into a temporary parenting plan that does not meet his or her aspirations for ultimate child custody arrangements? Why or why not? Is this a question that can be answered as a generality? Why or why not?

3. Perform an Internet search. See if you can locate websites that feature the following four kinds of mediation. For each, write down the name and location of the mediation, a description of the kind of mediation practiced, and, if you can determine it, the style of mediation practiced by each neutral:

   a. A private mediator who handles civil litigation cases

   b. An example of governmental agency mediation

   c. A mediator who handles special education cases

   d. A peer mediation program

4. Find the websites of at least three different mediators, all of whom practice in different firms, whose sites include a list of their qualifications and a description of the types of cases they accept. List the jurisdictions in which they practice, the types of cases they handle, and their qualifications. What

similarities do you see in their qualifications? What differences are there? If you do this assignment as a class project, discuss the results in class. See if you can discern patterns of qualifications among mediators specializing in the handling of particular kinds of cases.

5. Imagine yourself as a lawyer. A client enters your office with a divorce matter. She is extremely shy and reserved and seems to be intimidated by everything. The client has learned about mediation from her husband, who wants to resolve the matter out of court. She asks you to suggest a mediator and represent her during the mediation process. What do you do? Be specific and detailed.

6. Interview a mediator. Some of the questions you might pose include the following:

   a. What is your professional background?

   b. What specialized mediation training or education have you completed?

   c. Are you a member of any professional mediation or ADR associations? Which ones, and what benefits do you obtain from membership?

   d. What sorts of disputes do you mediate?

   e. How long have you been practicing mediation? How many cases have you mediated?

   f. What is your mediation style? Can you give some specific examples (while maintaining your clients' confidentiality, of course) of how you apply your style in mediating disputes?

   g. What is the most difficult aspect of the mediation profession, and what do you do to deal with it?

   h. What is the most rewarding aspect of mediation practice?

   i. Do you have any advice for people considering a career as a mediator?

7. Identify each of the following descriptions of mediation processes as one of the five varieties of mediation:

   a. Erica Sloane, a former marketing analyst turned mediator, offers disputants a chance to sit down and air out what has led them into conflict. She works to ensure that each disputant has a very clear picture of what the other's perspective is on the conflict. She also works to ensure that each disputant has enough knowledge, assistance, and strength to negotiate effectively. She tells her clients in her initial mediation session that these goals—empowerment and recognition—are the essential goals of mediation but that the most effective and lasting agreements often come from this style of mediation.

   b. Josh Bluefield is a retired hearing officer for the Workers' Compensation Commission of his state. He has now volunteered for a new program in his state aimed at settling workers' compensation claims out of the adversarial system. The disputants and their attorneys attend mediation sessions, in which he hears both sides. In separate caucus sessions with the individual disputants and their attorneys, he works to point out weaknesses in their case, the strengths in the other side's case, and reasons to settle. He works to find middle ground between the disputants, using his expertise in the workers' compensation field to give him authoritative force in his evaluations of the cases.

c. A state consumer protection agency has established a phone-in mediation clinic to handle the huge volume of grievances consumers file annually. Consumer claimants are given a list of mediators to call. A mediator takes the call, takes information from the consumer, and then tries to contact the merchant to get a settlement. Mediators are trained to be as brief as possible and to push both sides toward settlement, using threats of litigation on the merchant.

d. Social worker Francine Stein mediates divorce and child custody disputes. Her goal in mediation, stated to the clients, is to help them attain a more positive and healthy relationship, so that they can reach agreement together.

e. Social worker Inez Sykes mediates divorce and child custody disputes. Her goal in mediation, stated to the clients, is to create a setting and a structure that enable clients to negotiate effectively. She also works to educate clients about the benefits of principled bargaining and to guide clients away from behaviors that create escalated conflict.

RECOMMENDED READINGS

Baruch-Bush, R. A. B., and J. P. Folger. 1994. *The promise of mediation.* San Francisco: Jossey-Bass.

Bickerman, J. 1999. Great potential: The new federal law provides vehicle, if local courts want to move on ADR. *Dispute Resolution Magazine* (fall):3–5.

Gauvey, S. K. 2001. ADR's integration in the federal court system. *Maryland Bar Journal* 33(2):36–43.

Folberg, J., and A. Taylor, 1984. *Mediation: A comprehensive guide to resolving conflicts without litigation.* San Francisco, CA: Jossey-Bass.

Johnston, J. R., and L. E. G. Campbell. 1988. *Impasses of divorce: The dynamics and resolution of family conflict.* New York: The Free Press.

Kovach, K. K., and L. P. Love. 1996. "Evaluative" mediation is an oxymoron. *Alternatives to the High Cost of Litigation* 14(3):31–32.

Love, L. 1997. The top ten reasons why mediators should not evaluate. *Florida State University Law Review* 24 (summer):937–48.

Lowry, L. R. 2000. To evaluate or not: That is not the question! *Family and Conciliation Courts Review* 38 (January):48–58.

McIsaac, H. 2001. Confidentiality revisited: California style. *Family Court Review* 39(4):405–14.

Menkel-Meadow, C. J. 1991. Symposium: Pursuing settlement in an adversary culture: A tale of innovation co-opted or "the law of ADR." *Florida State University Law Review* 19 (summer):1–46.

Mosten, F. 1997. Checklist: Eleven questions most commonly asked about mediation. *Fairshare* 17(9):5–7.

Riskin, L. L. 1982. Mediation and lawyers. *Ohio State Law Journal* 43:29–60.

Riskin, L. L. 1996. Understanding mediators' orientations, strategies, and techniques: A grid for the perplexed. *Harvard Negotiation Law Review* 1 (spring):7–51.

Shapiro, M. 1981. *Courts: A comparative and political analysis.* Chicago: University of Chicago Press.

Tondo, C.-A., R. Coronel, and B. Drucker. 2001. Mediation trends: A survey of the states. *Family Court Review* 39 (October):431–45.

Waxler, M. E. 1997. The legal assistant's role in mediation: Some of the possibilities. *Texas Paralegal Journal* [online]. [Cited 1 July 2002]. Available from *http://www.lad.org/TPJ/07/waxler.html.*

Welsh, N. A. 2001. The thinning vision of self-determination in court-connected mediation: The inevitable price of institutionalization? *Harvard Negotiation Law Review* 6 (spring):1–96.

Zumeta, Z. 2000. A facilitative mediator responds. *Journal of Dispute Resolution* 2000:335–41.

Zumeta, Z. D. 2000. Styles of mediation: Facilitative, evaluative, and transformative mediation. In *mediate.com* [online]. [Cited 14 July 2002]. Available from *http://www.mediate.com/articles/zumeta.cfm.*

16

Advantages and Disadvantages of Mediation

"There are many occasions in life where it is possible to effect by forgiveness every object which you propose to effect by resentment."

—Sydney Smith, *Sermon: The Forgiveness of Injuries*

In this chapter, you will learn ...

- ◆ The advantages and disadvantages of mediation, as compared with other dispute resolution processes.
- ◆ The ways in which mediation can be both more and less efficient than litigation and other dispute resolution processes.
- ◆ How different varieties of mediation differ in efficiency.
- ◆ Why mediation is considered superior to other dispute resolution processes in its capacity to manage and prevent conflict.
- ◆ Why mediation is commonly regarded as the best dispute resolution process for preserving and protecting ongoing relationships.
- ◆ The capacity of mediation for flexibility and comprehensiveness in dealing with conflicts and providing remedies.
- ◆ The capacity of mediation to produce a high quality of consent and high psychological ownership of process and outcome, producing durability and compliance with a settlement.
- ◆ The controversy over whether litigation is more final than mediation.
- ◆ The reasons for choosing litigation over mediation.

If you are a disputant, is mediation appropriate to resolve your conflict? If you are an advocate or an advocate's assistant, is mediation the best option for your client? Basic to answering these questions is the issue of what mediation can offer, compared with the alternatives.

Of all the ADR techniques considered in this textbook, mediation departs most radically from the invisible veil version of what conflict resolution "should" look like. For this reason, comparing the advantages and disadvantages of mediation with those of litigation and other forms of ADR is a critical task for anyone trying to understand the field of dispute resolution. This comparison reveals the heart of how the theories we looked at in Part II of the text apply to the real world of dispute resolution.

As we have seen, mediation is a highly diverse process. The advantages and disadvantages of using mediation to resolve conflict depend on which of the many types of mediation is called into play. It is possible to talk generally about some of mediation's special qualities and possibilities. In general, in the discussion that follows it will be assumed, unless otherwise noted, that a highly facilitative form of mediation is being compared with the alternatives. As you contemplate the points raised in this chapter, try to keep in mind the differences between highly facilitative mediation and the form of mediation that more closely resembles adversarial negotiation.

ADVANTAGES OF MEDIATION

You may recall that, in Chapter 3, the idea was introduced that an evaluation of a process of conflict resolution depends on the perspective taken. Methods of resolving a conflict might be evaluated as very effective, for example, if a short-term perspective were taken but very ineffective if a long-term perspective were taken. Or a method of resolving a conflict might be very effective in meeting one person's financial goals yet very poor in settling an overall conflictual relationship. Or a settlement might effectively meet the disputant's needs, but at the expense of dependent constituents. There is no more important time to keep these considerations in mind than in our discussion of the advantages and disadvantages of mediation.

EFFICIENCY CONSIDERATIONS

Time and money considerations—the efficiency arguments (see Chapter 3)—were the original impetus for the ADR movement in the United States. Early comments on the litigation explosion and the need for alternatives prominently cite the high cost of litigation, the long delays to trial, and the burden on court systems of our litigious society. Thus, many early efforts to create ADR programs focused on considerations of immediate savings of time and money for clients and courts. When these programs were evaluated, researchers focused primarily on comparing the time required to mediate cases to settlement with that required to litigate to judgment, as well as on the money spent on moving the cases to their conclusion.

It is beyond refute that mediation is cheaper and quicker than litigation. Mediation is an informal process that does not require discovery, pleading, motions practice, hearings, or rules of evidence. As a result, even when lawyers are involved at every step of the mediation process, it is both much cheaper and much more rapid than litigation. If the disputants handle the mediation themselves, then they save additional attorney's fees as well. Resources are conserved for the court system as well as for the individual disputants when mediation is used.

The efficiency of mediation is often compared with that of litigation because it is assumed that cases that are mediated would otherwise be litigated. If mediation is compared with lawyer-assisted settlement, then the direct time and money savings of mediation are less certain. Some studies appear to indicate that mediation is still quicker and cheaper than lawyer-assisted negotiation, but others do not show such an advantage.

If mediation is compared with other ADR processes, such as arbitration and nonbinding evaluation, the picture becomes still more cloudy. Arbitration, as we will see in Chapter 19, ranges from a highly informal, inexpensive, and rapid process to something as expensive, slow, and complex as the most bureaucratically snarled lawsuit. Nonbinding evaluation (see Chapter 20) is generally designed to be more efficient than litigation (that's partially the function of nonbinding evaluation: to get a sense of what a court would do without investing time and money for a lawsuit), but, again, the amount of time and money spent is highly variable. Arbitration has the advantage that, when the procedure is over, someone will be declared the victor, and the issues submitted to arbitration (if not the overall conflict) will be ended. Mediation, in contrast, will not necessarily result in a settlement.

Another way of viewing efficiency considerations is to use the perspective of conflict theory. Litigation, arbitration, and nonbinding evaluation are dispute resolution processes that approach conflict from a *positional-bargaining paradigm.* That is, each of these processes operates on the assumption that conflict is to be resolved through the clash of inconsistent positions, with litigation and arbitration settling the conflict through the choice of one of the positions and nonbinding evaluation depending on a softening of disputant positions based on information received in the evaluation. Most mediation, on the other hand, proceeds based on either a positional bargaining model or a principled-bargaining model. When one compares positional bargaining with principled bargaining, generally the positional-bargaining process takes less upfront time and effort, because interests analysis, brainstorming, and searches for objective decisional standards are not involved in positional bargaining. Thus, if the time and money expenditures required to attain settlement—any settlement—are the only relevant considerations, a positional-bargaining process will seem like a bargain, compared with a principled-bargaining process. The evaluative and arbitration alternatives are likely to be quicker and cheaper than positional-bargaining mediation if the parties have vastly different perceptions of facts or law, because they would likely reach impasse without hard evidence to refute their extreme aspirations, with the reverse being true if the perceptions are not extremely different.

On the other hand, if a longer-term view is taken, it seems clear that mediation emphasizing the use of principled-bargaining techniques is more efficient than mediation based on a positional-bargaining model. This is because principled bargaining is more likely than positional bargaining to lead to the efficient and effective use of joint disputant resources. Moreover, principled bargaining associated with mediation is likely to resolve the conflict more permanently than positional-bargaining alternatives. Principled-bargaining mediation is associated with a high quality of settlement. It has been demonstrated that cooperative principled-bargaining processes are associated with greater quality of consent and psychological ownership of the outcome than settlements produced by more adversarial alternatives. Psychological ownership is associated with reduced levels of conflict and relitigation after settlement, thus making a cooperative principled-bargaining process more cost-effective in the long run. And research suggests that mediated agreements are complied with to a greater degree than are judicial awards (Kelly 1996, 377; King 1999, n. 331).[1]

Thus, whether mediation is more efficient than informal adjudicative and nonbinding evaluative processes depends on the perspective taken. If a short-term, narrow perspective is taken, nonbinding evaluation appears to be the most efficient choice, particularly when widely divergent perceptions of fact and law are involved. On the other hand, if a longer-term, broader perspective is taken, mediation appears to be the more efficient alternative.

CONFLICT MANAGEMENT AND CONFLICT PREVENTION

It is in the area of reducing and preventing conflict that mediation really shines, relative not only to litigation but also to arbitration and nonbinding evaluation. To understand why, it is useful to return to the cooperation-competition theory of Morton Deutsch (see Chapter 9).

We know from our consideration of conflict theory that using cooperative principled-bargaining techniques tends to short-circuit a competitive conflict cycle, promote cooperation, build mutual trust, and create solutions that better meet all disputants' most deeply seated interests. We further know that the use of consensual techniques to resolve conflict, particularly collaborative conflict resolution techniques that reject the use of positional bargaining in favor of a search to meet mutual interests, tends to create psychological ownership of the resulting settlement.

Even without mediation's special qualities, just bringing a neutral third party into the discussion often improves the quality of the negotiations by changing the dynamics of the interpersonal interactions. Neither disputant wants to lose face by looking like an irrational "bad person," and, hence, the

---

[1] This discussion omits those forms of mediation for which neither negotiation nor settlement are even goals, most notably, Transformative mediation. Transformative mediation can be expected to be even less efficient, in the short term, than other forms of facilitative mediation in leading to rapid settlement. It is theorized that Transformative mediation, however, is better at achieving conflict resolution long term than forms of mediation that emphasize negotiation or settlement as a goal. This belief is in the early stages of empirical research.

mere presence of the mediator in the discussion often improves the disputants' negotiation behavior.

More than that, however, mediation is specially designed to address the unique problems presented by interpersonal conflict. Good mediators are effective conflict diagnosticians: they use the mediation process to get a deep-seated understanding of what drives the conflict, revealing the best routes to resolution. Good mediators also involve the disputants themselves in conflict diagnosis, so that they themselves have the roots of the conflict revealed to them and are personally able to search for and understand the available solutions. Moreover, mediation is specifically targeted to interrupt a cycle of competition and encourage a cycle of cooperation to form. Mediators use a number of techniques to reframe perceptions, build mutual trust, create a sense of personal validation on the part of each disputant, and avoid and defuse meta-disputes. Mediators can also, by virtue of their neutral position in the negotiation, create communication opportunities where there were none. For example, a point or suggestion that, if made by the other disputant, would be reactively devalued can be more easily "heard" when made by the mediator.

Adjudicative and evaluative dispute resolution processes, on the other hand, do nothing to address the conflict cycle. Indeed, because they emphasize the merits of each disputant's case, these processes tend to nudge the disputants into viewing the conflict as a zero-sum game with a winner and a loser, increasing the probability of conflict escalation. Divorce mediators often hear this concept verbalized by new clients. A typical comment of such a client is "I want to try mediation and I don't want lawyers to be involved. I'm afraid that, if I or the other client goes to a lawyer, we'll end up in a war. We both want to avoid letting this thing get out of hand. Please help us." Such clients sense a truth about mediation: it is more capable than other methods of reining in the natural tendency of individuals to be swept into positional bargaining and then an escalating competitive conflict cycle.

Relatedly, mediation can have important conflict management benefits by streamlining the conflict or dispute—even if agreement isn't reached—by clarifying the conflict, narrowing the issues, and often making communication more civil. Thus, even if other methods are needed to resolve the conflict, mediation makes these other methods more efficient. As evidence of this effect of mediation, some research indicates that disputants who fail to settle during mediation are more likely to settle prior to trial than disputants who do not attend mediation (Kelly 1996, 376).

RELATIONSHIP PRESERVATION

Mediation is widely regarded as the most effective dispute resolution process for preserving ongoing disputant relationships. This advantage of mediation is particularly important in situations in which disputants will be required to deal with each other after the conflict is resolved. Examples of such situations include parents who are divorcing, disputes between neighbors, disputes between corporate shareholder groups, landlords with rental disputes with tenants, parent-teacher

Controversies About Mediation: Is Mediation "Second-Class Justice"?

The above question is certainly a hard one to answer because the term *second-class justice* is poorly defined. Moreover, the question requires a body of social science research that currently doesn't exist.

A number of scholars, including Owen Fiss (1984) and Laura Nader (1993), have criticized the ADR movement, contending that the diversion of so-called small cases to ADR relegate them to second-class justice. Although the argument takes varying forms, the gist is that the push to increase harmony in relations at the expense of the adversary process is an attempt by the powerful to pacify the less powerful—in other words, an effort at social control (Nader 1993). This argument has intrinsic logic: it seems obvious that a high-power disputant will find it easier to get his or her interests addressed in a consensual process than will a low-power disputant. Moreover, many critical reforms in the treatment of the disempowered have come from the appellate litigation process.

Underlying these arguments is an assumption that court-based adversary processes are the best way to protect the interests of the disempowered. However, empirical study to date has failed to find clear evidence that either litigation or ADR provides better outcomes for the disempowered. And we are unable to measure the impact of overall culture—the macrosystem—on empowerment or disempowerment. Are the disempowered better or worse off in a culture that promotes mediation? Will the disempowered forego the pursuit of appellate litigation because mediation is available to them? If we do this research, and see certain trends, how do we know whether they were caused by ADR? For example, if there has been a falloff in appellate litigation, could it be due to the current makeup of the Supreme Court? Presently, there is simply insufficient evidence to know one way or the other. As law professor Deborah Rhode has put it in her even-handed critique of both ADR supporters and detractors,

> critics who denounce ADR as second-class justice need to consider how often first class is available, and on what terms. The deficiencies common in alternative dispute resolution are chronic in conventional adjudication as well. Private settlements are the norm, not the exception, and procedural protections that are available in theory are often missing in practice. Imbalances of wealth, power, and information skew outcomes even in cases receiving the closest judicial oversight. As the title of Professor Marc Galanter's now classic article put it, the "Haves Come Out Ahead" in most legal settings. (Rhode, 1999, 1011)

It may make more sense to ask, "What attributes of particular ADR programs and processes would result in second-class justice?" Coercive forms of mediation, mediation that imposes burdens disproportionately on disempowered disputants (as when the fees for mediation are very high), as well as mediation conducted by individuals who are insensitive to the impact of power imbalance, could be predicted to be egregious in impact. It makes sense to assume that mediation can be damaging to disempowered disputants unable to hold their own during negotiation, or if the most important source of the conflict is a structural or personal power imbalance. On the other hand, disputants sometimes comment on the empowerment gained from dealing with the other disputant in an effective consensual process. The sense of empowerment may depend on multiple factors: some commentators note that mediation provides some disputants, particularly women, with a voice that is missing in litigation, whereas others comment that minority disputants are more comfortable in mediation and get better results if they use a mediator who shares their racial/ethnic identity. And litigation may not provide an improvement over mediation. Far more study is needed to explore the conditions under which mediation might be an improvement over litigation, and vice versa. The answers, if our current state of knowledge is any indication, are likely to be complicated. Presuming that litigation is a better option without any empirical basis for the presumption is no more logical than presuming that harmony is inherently better than contention.

Treaty between the Egyptians and Hittites, 1269 BC, is believed to be the oldest surviving peace treaty in existence. In modern times, international and interpersonal relationship preservation is often attained with the assistance of mediation. Tony Souter, Dorling Kindersley Media Library

conflicts, business partners with disputes over partnership agreements and responsibilities, employee grievance situations, and buyers and sellers in long-term supply requirements relationships. In these common situations, mediation can be invaluable, offering the chance to clarify misunderstandings, mend broken promises, set the stage for an apology to occur, and improve aspects of the relationship that have not functioned well in the past. Mediation typically provides the disputants with a communication structure in which they are required to relate to one another in a mutually respectful, amicable, clear, and self-assertive manner, and they are assisted in doing so. Communication lessons learned during mediation can have long-term benefits for the continued constructiveness of the relationship. Additionally, mediation's flexibility—its ability to offer experimental, partial, and interim settlements—allows disputants to fine-tune contractual arrangements, maximizing the likelihood that a long-term relationship will remain functional and adapt to change. Thus, mediation can have relationship-preserving qualities not available in negotiation, adjudication, and nonbinding evaluation.

COMPREHENSIVENESS

Mediation has the capacity to deal more comprehensively with interpersonal conflict than other alternatives.

Let's begin with litigation. Litigation deals only with issues that can be stated as causes of action. If you have a dispute with another individual that cannot be

Controversies About Mediation:
Does Mediation Permanently Improve Relationships?

Despite anecdotal accounts of the capacity of mediation to improve relationships, and despite clear evidence of short-term improvements, empirical study has not shown consistent long-term benefit. Early research in Denver, Colorado, indicated short-term reductions in acrimony in parents undergoing mediation (Kuhn 1984, n. 71). Moreover, there is evidence of reduced rates of relitigation among disputants who undergo mediation, suggesting that disputants who mediate learn more constructive ways to resolve future conflicts (Vestal 1999). Law professor Carol J. King, reviewing research on divorce mediation (King 1999, 433–34), comments that one study "found that children of mediated divorce seemed better-adjusted, and that their parents were less hostile to each other," compared with a group that litigated, whereas another study found "perceived improved parental relationships among the mediation participants in the year following the divorce." However, "[t]he difference between the mediation and adjudication groups did not persist at the two-year post-divorce mark." She also notes that research on relitigation rates seems to indicate that the rates for returning to court become more similar as the years go by, becoming indistinguishable after five years (King 1999, 435), although it is not clear whether this trend is primarily due to increases in relitigation by mediating disputants or to the dying out of relitigation by adversarial disputants. King comments on the brevity of mediation and the complexity of the means by which divorcing parents address their issues as reasons not to expect mediation to act as a miracle cure for escalated conflict. Indeed, Deutsch's theory (see Chapter 9) would predict that, as the mediation process became more distant in time, the potential would increase for factors that promote the escalation of conflict to "swamp" any gains made. Moreover, mediated interventions that do not feature improving negotiation skills would be predicted to have minimal, if any, effect on improving long-term relationships. Consistent with this interpretation, Joan Kelly, reviewing studies of the impact of divorce mediation on disputants, notes "small but more often short-lived" increases in cooperation and communication accompanying mediation and suggests that the inconsistencies in findings are probably due to variations in the duration of mediation, the characteristics of the clients, and the styles used by the mediators (Kelly 1996, 379). As we learned in the previous chapter, there are styles of mediation that focus on getting a quick settlement, not on facilitating effective negotiation.

set into this mold, it cannot be addressed in litigation. Consider the following anecdote, which is based on an actual lawsuit that was tried in a Maryland state trial court:

> The two litigants were neighbors who didn't get along. Their conflict had simmered along ever since litigant #2 had moved into the neighborhood nearly a decade before the trial. The conflict had started with minor affronts (such as litigant #2's children chasing balls into litigant #1's yard) and had escalated into mutual hostilities. The conflict had escalated to the point that anything negative that happened to one neighbor was automatically attributed to the other neighbor. For example, if litigant #1 found dog droppings on his lawn, he attributed it to litigant #2's intentionally allowing his dog to "do his business" on the lawn out of spite. If litigant #2 heard a car engine gun late at night, he assumed litigant #1 had instructed his teenage son to annoy him. Obviously, a great many assumptions were made by both disputants about the role of the other in creating problems, all of them negative. Finally, one of the litigants caught the other committing what constituted an actionable tort: one litigant had scratched the paint job on the other's car. The victim sued, and the defendant was able to come up with enough legally nonfrivolous grievances to file a counterclaim. The case

failed to settle, and eventually it went to trial. After two days of trial, the jury, obviously exasperated, found for the plaintiff and awarded him damages—a single dollar.[2] Clearly, the judgment the jury issued bore little relation to the issues that brought the litigants to court. Had this case been sent to mediation, the mediator could have dealt directly with the course of the disputants' relationship, assisted the disputants in effective communication, helped the neighbors untangle and understand the course of their conflict, and helped them develop an agreement to prevent mutual harassment in the future.

Another disadvantage to litigation's narrow focus on the cause of action is that it can divert participants from other important issues. For example, a patient frustrated with a physician's failure to spend enough time with her or seemingly to listen sympathetically to her concerns may be able to find (with the help of a lawyer) enough wrong with the physician's conduct to bring a malpractice case, yet this may not be what really bothers the patient. Litigation thus creates the likelihood of unnecessary legal action while diverting attention from the underlying problem, which may remain unresolved to fester.

> Jonie went to the doctor with vague intestinal complaints. The doctor made her wait three hours, then examined her for about two minutes before pronouncing her as suffering from indigestion. She prescribed antacids and told Jonie to call her if she got worse. Three days later, Jonie's appendix ruptured, and she was forced to spend a week of her summer vacation in the hospital. Jonie angrily sued the doctor, and, after the usual two-year wait, the case went to trial. Because Jonie's symptoms had been ambiguous when she saw the doctor, and because Jonie had not planned to work during the summer of her illness, the jury awarded only $20,000, enough money to pay her medical insurer for the $18,500 in medical expenses, leaving Jonie a modest sum of $1,500. Her attorney took $3,000 of the total award for legal fees, leaving Jonie with nothing. Jonie is still seething about the doctor's cavalier behavior toward her. No one has benefited from the experience, except the medical insurer. Even Jonie's lawyer did not receive enough compensation to cover her time.

In addition to issues comprehensiveness, mediation offers remedial flexibility and creativity unavailable in litigation and less likely in evaluative ADR processes. The remedies available through litigation are narrowly defined by the applicable law, and they generally involve a monetary judgment. In our example, what Jonie might really want is a sincere apology, not a lawsuit with possible money damages. In fact, even in clear cases of medical malpractice, there is evidence that taking steps to display the physician's sympathy for the patient, such as apologizing and admitting mistakes, are as important as monetary compensation. The recent experiences of one hospital indicate that, when such apologies

---

[2] It was perhaps the perversely effective function of litigation in this case that the jury, by its obvious expression of disapproval of the disputants' choice to take their dispute to court, might have ultimately shamed the neighbors into finding alternative ways to resolve their conflict.

and admissions are offered, overall malpractice expenditures are substantially re-duced (Cohen 2000). Similarly, a study of small claims court cases in New Mex-ico suggested a high degree of satisfaction in (Hispanic) litigants who mediated their cases to nonmonetary settlements (LaFree & Rack 1996, 790). These more complete remedies have the merits of satisfying the victim more fully, reducing out-of-pocket expenditures by the defendants, and allowing the defendants to express their sense of responsibility for the problems, resulting in a sense of closure for all and less defensiveness on the part of those who have done wrong. It thus becomes easier for the defendants to learn from their errors. The victim obtains the precise sort of remedy he or she sought, a sense of closure, a feeling of validation, and a sense of sustained community with those against whom he or she had a grievance.

There is empirical evidence that mediation can, in fact, lead to a high num-ber of these creative, integrative sorts of outcomes. Golann (2002, 334), study-ing the reported outcomes of private and court-based civil/commercial mediation by facilitative mediators, found that "almost two-thirds of all settle-ments in the survey were integrative," and Schepard (2000) and Kelly (1996) re-ported research indicating that mediated child custody plans tend to be more specific and detailed than those developed through lawyer-assisted negotiation.

ABILITY TO HANDLE META-DISPUTES

You may recall that one cause of escalation in interpersonal conflicts is the creation of meta-disputes, which are disputes about the way a conflict is being handled (see Chapter 11). Although it is sometimes possible for negotiators to straighten out these disputes on their own, frequently the cycle of escalating competitive conflict (see Chapter 9) prevents the disputants from reaching and addressing these sorts of problems. Mediation is uniquely able to deal directly with these disputes, un-tangling how they took place and helping disputants get past them.

> In February, Martin, a free-lance carpenter, was rear-ended by an uninsured driver, and suffered a back and neck injury that required several doctor's vis-its and physical therapy and caused him to lose work. Martin had uninsured motorist coverage, and immediately contacted his claims representative. His insurer had an automatic voice messaging system. Martin left a mes-sage, but forgot to include his policy number. Two weeks later, having not heard back, he left another message. However, the claims representative's secretary was distracted about another matter and accidentally erased the message before she got a chance to note the details. Another week later, in-censed, Martin called again and left an unfortunately rude message. Finally, a claims representative called Martin back, somewhat curtly discussed the case with him, and sent him a complicated accident report form to return. It took Martin several weeks to get a copy of the accident police report and return the form to the insurer. Then he waited again. When September rolled around without so much as a letter, Martin got even madder, hired his brother-in-law, a new and very inexperienced attorney, and filed suit

against his insurer for bad faith, seeking $2 million in punitive damages. The insurer filed a motion to have the action dismissed as frivolous.

The case was referred to court-connected mediation. After reassuring the claims representative that she would be given ample time to be heard, the mediator gave Martin a lengthy opportunity to tell his story and vent his frustration at the apparent foot-dragging of his insurer. The attending claims representative apologized (after some prodding by the mediator), and also commented that it was the insurer's practice to wait twelve months before settling personal injury claims, since some injuries take time to fully manifest. The claims representative also said that it was their usual practice to advise insureds of the waiting period, but also acknowledged that because communication had been rocky to say the least, she couldn't be absolutely sure Martin had received this critical piece of information. In no way, said the claims representative, was the delay "bad faith," indeed, it was designed to ensure that the insured's total damages were known before a case was settled. In light of Martin's mistrust of the claims representative's contention that "the twelve month waiting period is for the good of the insured," the mediator suggested that, as "homework," Martin contact some independent insurance claims representatives and/or experienced personal injury attorneys to check the contention out.

He did his homework and verified that some plaintiff's attorneys refuse to even discuss settling their clients' accident cases until a year has expired. At a follow-up mediation session, Martin, his brother in law, and the insurer agreed that Martin's complaint would be amended to a simple breach of contract action, and that the claim for punitive damages would be eliminated. A date was also set (in March) for a negotiation session to settle the insurance claim. The claims representative, knowing that the insurer would eventually be paying a substantial claim, also was able to get agreement from headquarters to advance Martin the sum of $5,000 by September 30, and an additional $5,000 by January 31. These sums would be deducted from the final settlement of the claim. The parties agreed to return to mediation if they were unable to work out an agreeable settlement on their own.

DISPUTANT QUALITY OF CONSENT, POWER, AND AUTONOMY

Unlike adjudication alternatives such as litigation and binding arbitration, mediation does not take from the disputants the power to accept or reject a possible settlement. Because of the consensual nature of mediation, there is generally (1) more satisfaction with the settlement and (2) less likelihood that the agreement will be sabotaged later.

PSYCHOLOGICAL OWNERSHIP AND QUALITY OF CONSENT

Quality of disputant consent (Lande 1997) refers to how willing the disputants are to accede to the process and outcome. Regardless of whether the outcome itself is exactly what a disputant initially sought, he or she is more likely to buy into the outcome and own it psychologically if he or she is a willing participant in the process of developing it. Psychological ownership of a settlement is likely to promote willingness to abide by the terms of the settlement and to reduce the likelihood of future disputes. The concept of quality of consent in ADR is conceptually related to the idea of *procedural justice,* introduced in Chapter 8. High-quality consent in a dispute resolution process requires that the disputants readily consent, not only to the dispute resolution process being used but also to the outcome, and that they do so from an informed and empowered position. Lande (1997) lists the following seven attributes of high-quality consent in ADR:

* Explicit identification of the principals' goals and interests—a critical step in conflict diagnosis (recall from Chapter 8)
* Explicit identification of plausible options for satisfying these interests
* Disputants' generation of options for achieving their interests
* Disputants' careful consideration of these options
* If a dispute resolution process involving an adjudicator or other third-party neutral is being used, the neutral's restraint in pressuring principals to accept particular substantive options
* Limitation on the neutral's use of time pressure
* Neutral's confirmation of principals' consent to selected options

By this definition, litigation and other adjudication processes provide the lowest quality of consent (particularly when one litigant is involved against his or her will), evaluative mediation provides moderate-quality consent, and extremely facilitative mediation provides the highest quality of consent. High-quality consent has much in common with principled negotiation, and it adds an element of restraint on the part of the ADR neutral in pushing the disputants to settle or to move in a particular direction in settling. In general, the more evaluative mediation processes are considered to have lower-quality consent, since the mediator takes the lead in structuring the range of potential settlement options and may even push the disputants toward a particular outcome. Highly facilitative mediation is thought to possess higher-quality consent under the Lande definition, and, in particular, facilitative mediation that explicitly relies on the principled negotiation model, as well as non-settlement-oriented forms, such as Transformative mediation that best meet the goals of high-quality consent. One must temper this categorization with the fact that a disputant who prefers a "head-banging" mediator (someone who pushes a compromise on the disputants), and who is not convinced otherwise by the mediator, is not likely to consent in a high-quality way to facilitative mediation. Indeed, there are people who believe that the only appropriate way of resolving legal disputes is to submit them to a court for adjudication. Unless these individuals come to be convinced otherwise, mediation will never provide a high quality of consent for them.

It is often argued that mediation is less final than litigation, and, indeed, because the disputants retain the power to agree, they also retain the power to

Controversies About Mediation: Which Is More Final, Mediation or Adjudication?

Mediation's lack of finality is often cited as a drawback to mediation in comparison with litigation (and informal processes such as arbitration). But, in fact, whether mediation is not final is a controversial issue.

Clearly, litigation is more final than mediation in the sense that, once a litigable issue is put before a court in a trial on the merits, an outcome will always result. In contrast, mediation may not achieve any settlement. This finality is often intensely seductive to disputants exhausted and frightened by protracted conflict. On the other hand, there are several ways in which mediation can be viewed as more final than adjudication.

First, not all the issues in conflict, or even the most important issues in conflict, may be before the court. Some of the issues generating the most conflict may not state causes of action, meaning that the court cannot adjudicate them. In contrast, if the parties consent, skilled mediators will help the clients sort out, through effective conflict diagnosis, which issues are most important to resolve.

Second, there are many ways that a disgruntled or dissatisfied disputant can sabotage an agreement or make its enforcement difficult. An agreement reached consensually through mediation is less likely to be sabotaged or undermined than a judgment imposed on a disputant because the mediated settlement is consented to by all parties to the agreement. Thus, if mediation results in a settlement, it is more likely than adjudication to settle the conflict permanently. Empirical research confirms that relitigation rates in disputes settled by mediation tend to be lower than those for disputes litigated to conclusion.

Third, a skilled mediator will also help the disputants co-opt important constituents who may also have the ability to sabotage or undermine the settlement, further reducing the likelihood that the settlement will fall apart.

Fourth, mediation is better than litigation at dealing with the deeply seated problems and minutae that have caused the conflict to occur and escalate in the first place, so once settled it is fair to say that the disputants are less likely to have new problems crop up if they reached their agreement in mediation.

In conclusion, if settlement does occur in a well-conducted mediation, it is likely to be more finally resolving of the disputants' conflicts than a litigated judgment. Beyond these considerations, even mediations that do not result in a settlement may reduce, narrow, and deescalate conflict to the point that adjudication results more effectively in a permanent resolution.

In sum, there are arguments in favor of both propositions. In assessing the finality of either process, one should look at all the angles.

---

prevent mediation from leading to settlement. Disputants who are very anxious to end the process with some sort of final outcome, therefore, will often avoid selecting mediation in the first place. However, the fact that the settlement is more likely to be followed if it has been the result of mediation means that, in a broader sense, mediation is often more final than adjudication. The finality of an adjudicated settlement rings hollow if it is followed by recurrent outbreaks of conflict. Disgruntled losers in litigation can do many things to make the winner miserable—they can fail to make prompt damages payments, adapt a less than polite demeanor in necessary communications, follow the letter and not the spirit of a settlement agreement calling for certain conduct, and so forth. Typical examples of post-litigation sabotage include a parent who is chronically a little late with child support payments, a civil defendant who refuses to pay a judgment until pushed into it by post-judgment proceedings, and a landlord whose promptness in responding to tenants' maintenance needs falls off.

Mediation that actively involves the disputants has a similar advantage over lawyer-assisted negotiation (King 1999, 441–42). There are three likely reasons for this advantage of mediation. The first is that the lawyers typically do not know as much about the disputants' interests as the disputants themselves. (If the dispute involves complex legal elements, then the active assistance of lawyers becomes more important to helping the disputants understand their own interests.) Second, to save time, lawyers involved in lawyer-assisted negotiations typically include so-called boilerplate clauses in their agreements, clauses that assume clients are all the same. For example, in divorce lawyering, the "custody to the mother, reasonable visitation to the father" parenting plan is frequently negotiated by the lawyers, regardless of its suitability for the individual families they are representing. Finally, active involvement of the disputants directly improves the quality of disputant consent. Thus, even if the ultimate settlements are identical, mediation in which disputants directly participate in negotiation could be expected to produce greater disputant satisfaction and greater compliance with settlement outcome.

INDIVIDUAL TRANSFORMATION

Some scholars point out that mediation can be "transformative" to individual disputants. They usually mean, in part, that mediation can be an empowering and enlightening process, helping participants see the issues more clearly, prompting them to do the research needed to prepare their case and understand their BATNA, and creating a safe environment in which to confront the other disputant.

> Private mediators were hired to handle a divorce dispute between a wealthy husband and his stay-at-home wife. After an eight-hour marathon mediation session involving this mediator, a co-mediator, and the spouses—leading to a temporary agreement—the participants took an indefinite break. About a month later, the wife called to cancel further mediation. She also thanked the mediator. She stated that mediation had helped her realize, for the first time, that she had been disempowered by her husband's conduct, that it was clearly his intention to exploit her lack of experience in negotiation, and that, to negotiate with him effectively in the future over the complex financial issues raised by the divorce, she needed to hire a competent "bomber" lawyer. Although the co-mediator lamented the failure of the mediation, the other mediator viewed the empowering effects of this mediation as a positive development, despite the lack of a permanent, comprehensive settlement of the legal issues. An argument can be made that any process that leads to the development of a more equal relationship between disputants is a positive step.

Mediation can sometimes also lead to a disputant's point of view being acknowledged by the other disputant for the first time. For many disputants, receiving this sort of acknowledgment and recognition is a profoundly empowering event. For example, in a dispute over a personnel evaluation, both the employee and the employer may, in the course of the process, come to better

Effective mediation can lead to individual and systemic transformation. Here, President Jimmy Carter presides over the Camp David accord, a good example of a process that transformed the lives of many.
Pearson Education/PH College

understand the perspective of the other. Should the employer's representative be able to communicate accurately the employer's interests to the employee, this information can enable the employee to be able to make career-enhancing moves in the future. The employer, on the other hand, will gain valuable information about how to improve employee feedback and training. Mediation can improve disputant perspective taking, encouraging disputants to see and understand the point of view of those with whom they disagree.

Additionally, mediation can educate disputants by teaching them negotiation skills they can carry into other parts of their lives. Some scholars (prominently, Baruch-Bush & Folger 1994) view these developments as positive in a broader sense and argue that mediation that leads to personal empowerment and a sense of recognition has strong benefits for society as a whole.

MINIMIZATION OF CONFLICTS OF INTEREST WITH LEGAL COUNSEL

Mediation can be very helpful to a lawyer whose client's expectations are unreasonable. This effect is particularly obvious in evaluative mediation.

Lawyers must present their client's case in the best possible light when they deal with the other disputant, his or her legal counsel, and the court. This need is created by the lawyer's ethical obligation to zealously represent the interests of the client. Clients whose lawyers are realistically pessimistic about the chances of their side's prevailing in litigation often doubt their lawyers' commitment to this zealous representation. Moreover, if a lawyer's advocacy is appropriately enthusiastic, the client often misreads the lawyer's enthusiasm as signifying that he or she has a better case than, in fact, the client really has. Thus, the duty to provide accurate advice may conflict with the duty of zealous representation. To make matters worse, some lawyers get personally caught up in the rosy picture they paint publicly about their client's case and miss or underemphasize important flaws and weaknesses.

Mediation allows a mediator to be the bearer of bad news about the lawsuit, preserving for the lawyer the zealous advocate role. Many lawyers have found this to be an unexpected benefit of mediation. Facilitative mediation is capable of fulfilling this function as well as evaluative mediation, but, in facilitative mediation, the process is more indirect, relying on reality testing that allows the disputant to reach his or her own pessimistic conclusions, in effect discovering for him- or herself the unpleasant truths about the alternatives to a negotiated agreement. In either case, the lawyer is freed from the uncomfortable position of having to give the client a pessimistic prediction of the case and risking the possibility that the client will see the lawyer as uncaring or uncommitted to the client's welfare.

ADVANTAGES OF LITIGATION OVER MEDIATION

GUARANTEED OUTCOME

If a cause of action can be stated, litigation always guarantees some sort of outcome, though it may not resolve the most important conflict. In this somewhat narrow sense, litigation is more final than mediation. Because this advantage of litigation is very obvious, it causes many disputants to reject the mediation option out of hand.

NATURE OF ENFORCEABILITY

It is also contended that mediated agreements have weaker enforceability than court judgments. Judgments are enforceable through the contempt process (in other words, a litigant who fails to comply with a court order can be threatened with fines and imprisonment), whereas mediated agreements are private contracts. Thus, mediated agreements are enforceable to the same extent as any out-of-court settlement: they must be taken to court and enforced in a contract action. If the other disputant contests the validity of a mediated agreement, this step may be an onerous one.

There may also be a psychological effect of a judge's pronouncing a decision, compared with disputants' reaching their own agreement in mediation. Some disputants may prefer having the authority of a judge behind the decision. One problem with this approach, however, is that, if the disputant chooses to litigate the issue in court, the judge may not issue the decision the disputant wants. Another problem is that, empirically, outcomes based on court judgments are *less,* rather than *more,* likely to be complied with than are mediated settlements.

LEGAL PRECEDENT

As with any out-of-court settlement, mediation does not result in a legal precedent. This feature of mediation is of particular concern if a disputant has a very large number of similar cases pending and, for some reason, these cases can't be resolved in a single comprehensive mediation (for example, when there are multiple defendants).

A public-policy argument against mediation's lack of precedential effect is also made. There are those who argue against settlement as a general matter of public policy because legal reform occurs in large part through the process of appellate review of litigated cases (see Owen Fiss' classic 1984 article, "Against Settlement"). When legal issues are taken to court and appealed, important changes in the law can ultimately result. Our legal system has an honored tradition of promulgating vitally important legal reforms—school integration, a criminal defendant's right to be given Miranda warnings, the restrictions on application of the death penalty, the right to use contraception, just to name a few—through the process of appellate review of litigation. Any system that diverts potential appellate cases to settlement can conceivably prevent this reform process from occurring. Mediation, as a form of facilitated settlement, is as vulnerable to this charge as any other form of settlement. However, it bears emphasizing that any legal dispute can be settled out of court, and, in fact, the vast majority of them do settle out of court.

Of greater concern is that mediation—or any other form of ADR—could present a serious public-policy problem if large numbers of disputants were *coerced* into settling. If an entire class of cases is forced into mediation *and* pressure is applied to these disputants to reach a settlement, it can be argued that the needed appellate litigation to create reform of the common law will not take place.

For example, in the 1980s, courts began to experiment with programs that forced all child custody cases filed in particular jurisdictions into mediation. If the mediation programs had been purely consensual—in other words, if the disputants had been required to participate, but not pressured into settling—the mandatory referral of cases into mediation would not have been much of a problem, because the cases containing issues ripe for reform would not have been likely to settle. The problem with these experimental programs was that the mediators were poorly trained, severely overloaded with cases, and evaluated based on how many cases they could clear off the dockets. As a result, they tended to practice a form of very coercive "muscle mediation" (Folberg & Taylor 1984, 135) to move cases along, so people weren't just being required to attend mediation; they were suffering negative consequences if they didn't settle. Many scholars raised concerns that, if a particular child custody issue needed to be addressed by the courts, it wasn't reaching the appellate level. In general, these coercive programs were roundly criticized. As a result, the courts have become more sophisticated about these concerns and have made court-connected mediation much less coercive (for some exceptions, see McIsaac 2001).

PRIVACY ISSUES

The intimate privacy of mediation can be good, or it can be bad. In some cases, disputants may mutually prefer the privacy and consider it a benefit of mediation over litigation. However, in some cases, the lack of public forum for mediation can benefit "bad actors" because public vindication and a public reprimand do not occur. It can be argued that this attribute of mediation applies as well to private negotiation and to other ADR processes. It can also be argued that a public outcome is possible even in a mediated setting—for example, via a press release or a mutual consent order filed in a court. The lack of a public statement thus becomes potentially harmful only if one or both disputants are coerced into mediating to settlement and if privacy is not mutually desired. It has also been argued that the private nature of mediation makes prejudiced behavior against disempowered social groups, such as women and persons of color, more likely. Again, this argument would apply equally well to other ADR processes. Research to date has been unable to document an increase in bigoted conduct in mediation as compared with litigation. The impact of mediation on racial minorities and others who might be victimized by bigoted behavior is addressed in the next section.

MEDIATION AND LOW-POWER DISPUTANTS

Although effective mediators can empower and transform disputants, incompetent or biased mediators, as well as good mediators constrained by circumstances, can do the opposite. It has been commented that mediators who are insensitive to power imbalance may unwittingly help an oppressor pressure a disempowered disputant.

However, some mediation detractors argue that *all* mediation, not just "bad mediation," is harmful to the disempowered. This issue is one of the hottest, and most controversial, in the ADR field.

A number of legal scholars, particularly some feminists and civil rights advocates, have written to attack the appropriateness of mediation, particularly for disempowered disputants, such as women and people of color. If the process of mediation is coercive—for example, when whole classes of cases are mandated to enter mediation *and* clients are pressured to reach agreement—it seems intuitive to be concerned about the impact of mediation on groups whose members are often disempowered. In court-mandated triage mediation (see Chapter 15) in which getting an agreement quickly is more important than effective negotiation, mediators may be subtly pressured by their employment situation into using whatever means they have at their disposal to get an agreement quickly. When mediators are working with disputants who are imbalanced in terms of personal power, one might imagine that the temptation to allow the more powerful disputant to coerce the less powerful disputant would be strong, indeed.

Mediation and Women. Some commentators make the argument that, because mediation may result in overreaching by powerful male disputants against disempowered female disputants, with the insensitive complicity of the mediator, no mediation should ever take place between male and female disputants. This is one argument that has been advanced by feminists who contend that women are structurally disempowered in comparison with men and are therefore endangered by mediation. Some of these scholars cite compelling (some might instead use the term *hair-raising*) anecdotal evidence that some mediation cases have been handled this way (Bruch 1992; Bryan 1992; Fineman 1988; Lefcourt 1984; Nader 1992). The classic tract supporting this point of view, Trina Grillo's article (1991) "The Mediation Alternative: Process Dangers for Women," relies on examples of mediation forced on abused women who are thereby required to reason with their physical oppressor. However, isolated anecdotes aside, these texts are largely argumentative, and many of them seem to be premised on the narrow assumptions of the lawyer's standard philosophical map. Proponents of mediation argue that eliminating mediation on this basis would be a case of "throwing the baby out with the bathwater" and that a better option would be to assess under what circumstances overreaching and oppression might occur and to reform mediation processes to address the problem.

A different arm of the feminist movement makes an argument that mediation is, instead, a gift to women, since it relies on a more "feminine" method of reaching settlement, such as the sharing of feelings and a nonhierarchical power structure (McCabe 2001; Menkel-Meadow 1985; Rifkin 1984). Empirical evidence is limited, but what is available largely supports mediation proponents (Vincent 1995, 278–82). Although the evidence is somewhat contradictory, women generally tend to express greater satisfaction than men with the mediation process. Carol J. King (1999), reviewing research results from Ohio court-mandated custody mediation programs, found that women rated mediation very positively, more positively than men on most measures. Moreover, available research indicates that there is no clear evidence that mediated agreements are either better or worse for women than litigated judgments and that, in many situations, women actually fare better than men in mediation (Gaschen 1995; Heister 1987; Kelly & Duryee 1992; LaFree & Rack 1996; Marcus, Marcus, Stilwell, & Doherty 1999; Pearson 1991; Richardson 1988). King (1999) also reports that female participants in the Ohio mediation programs reported more pressure to settle *outside* of mediation than *in* mediation. And research examining mediation between battered women and their batterers suggests that some battered women may actually experience mediation with their victimizer as an empowering event (King 1999, 443–45; Vincent 1995, 277–78).

Law professor Barbara Stark, reviewing the vigorous dialogue in the legal scholarly journals, concludes that,

> [among feminist scholars,] normative consensus with regard to mediation has evolved from early enthusiasm—and distrust—to a much more nu-

anced, contextualized, and qualified acceptance. In general, feminists view mediation as a promising alternative to the adversarial model. . . . [B]ut feminists have shown how seemingly neutral processes allow gendered norms to reassert themselves, especially in traditionally gendered contexts such as divorce. (Stark 2000, 243–44)

Before we leave the issue of gender and mediation, consider an interesting twist: one study produced evidence that mediation experience *itself* may reduce negative gender stereotyping. In a study (discussed in Chapter 14) of perceptions of undergraduates who read transcripts of a custody mediation session (Coltri 1995), the readers who reported previous personal experience with mediation displayed dramatically fewer misogynistic (antiwomen) attitudes toward the disputants than those who did not report previous mediation experience. Does mediation experience itself reduce sexist stereotyping during conflict? It is too early to tell, but this evidence is suggestive and deserves further study.

Mediation and Minorities. The argument goes that in mediation, which is not a public setting, white, particularly male, mediators handling racially diverse conflicts might subtly or even unwittingly express prejudice toward disputants of color, creating a subconscious alliance between the mediator and a white disputant and increasing the likelihood of poorer outcomes for a disputant of color.

A fair way to capsulize [the prevalent] argument goes as follows: Minorities in this country will always be the victims of oppression at one level or another. For any minority person to obtain justice, they must go to court, where the formal procedures and protections of the trial system can rebalance power. Mediation, on the other hand, will simply provide a forum for re-victimization of the minority person. Mediation services offer only second-class justice, with no safeguards for the minority victim. (Bernard 2001, 140)

Empirical evidence concerning the impact of mediation on racial and ethnic minority groups is, to date, sparse. The most widely cited research on the topic is the Metrocourt study, which examined a small claims mediation program in New Mexico (LaFree & Rack 1996; Rack 1999). The study found that Hispanic male mediation claimants (here the term *claimants* refers to people who had brought small claims actions) received poorer monetary settlements in mediation than their Anglo male counterparts and that the discrepancy was significantly larger than that which existed between Hispanic male claimants and Anglo male claimants in litigation. However, this discrepancy between discrimination in mediation and in litigation was not found for respondents (people who had been sued) or for females (in fact, Anglo females did better in mediation than any other group and did better in mediation than in litigation), and monetary differences between mediation and litigation for male claimants disappeared when the mediators were also Hispanic.

Data from research such as the Metrocourt study can be difficult to interpret. LaFree and Rack based their comparisons of mediation outcomes on the sizes of monetary outcomes compared with initial claims presented in small claims complaints. For example, a settlement in which a claimant received $500 to compensate him for a defective washing machine would have been rated as a better settlement than one in which a claimant received $400, an apology, and a day of yard work in compensation for the defect. However, racial and ethnic minorities were more likely to end up with nonmonetary elements in their mediated settlements *and to be pleased about it to a significantly greater extent than Anglos* whose settlements had nonmonetary elements.

> Compared with Anglo claimants . . . minority claimants settled twice as often for nonmonetary outcomes . . . [and] . . . compared with cases resulting in monetary outcomes, minority claimants in mediation were significantly more satisfied with cases that included substantial nonmonetary outcomes. (LaFree & Rack 1996, 790)

Moreover, the authors reported that some 37 percent of the mediated claims resulted in *strictly* nonmonetary outcomes. These cases were not considered in the statistical assessments conducted by the researchers, calling the conclusions about outcome disparity into some question. As the principles of conflict diagnosis would suggest, a monetary settlement may not fully address the underlying interests, needs, and values of the disputants (see Chapter 8). Thus, relying on the monetary part of settlement to evaluate discrepancies in mediation outcomes may not tap what is really going on, yet directly comparing the adequacy of nonmonetary outcomes is virtually impossible. The mediation field is rife with such problems in how to interpret empirical data.

Moreover, the quality of outcome may not tap the other benefits of mediation to ethnic and racial minority disputants. Depner, Cannata, and Ricci (1994) found that ethnic minority disputants—and members of other disempowered groups, such as the poor—actually rated mediation more helpful on several measures than did middle-class Anglo disputants. Generalizing from research conducted on a single mediation program also can be dangerous in the ADR field (Beck & Sales 2000), because mediation programs are characterized by wide variations in the characteristics of the disputants; the kinds of dispute sent to mediation; the qualifications and training of the mediators; the screening and referral protocols, if any, in place; the support of the bench and the bar; and the circumstances in which mediation is conducted (Kelly 1996). Each mediation program is unique, and a problem discovered in a single program can't be generalized to mediation in general.

It seems quite likely that gender, ethnicity, and race affect the experience of mediation in many ways, but much more research needs to be done to determine under what circumstances they appear and whether the differences warrant any remediation. In the meantime, avoiding coercion to settle during mediation, allowing abuse victims to opt out of mediation, allowing legal counsel to participate in mediation sessions under certain circumstances, and improving mediation training and qualification may provide protection.

MEDIATION ISN'T THE OPTION OF LAST RESORT

Perhaps the most important drawback of mediation is that disputants who could benefit most from the process typically don't choose it. By the time disputants find they are unable to negotiate an agreement on their own, their conflict has frequently entered an escalating phase with mutual hostility and recrimination. These litigants find the idea of cooperating with their "enemy" to be repugnant and would rather have an authority figure assigned to punish the opposition. There are two problems with this perspective, of course: the first is that only the winner of the litigation obtains the sought-after vindication, and the second is that adversarial conflict resolution tends to be so costly, time-consuming, and ineffective that even the vindicated litigant typically loses as much as he or she gains. Research indicates that many of the most angry and hostile disputants, when forced to participate in mediation, often become its biggest fans (McEwen & Milburn 1993).

ADVANTAGES OF NEGOTIATION OVER MEDIATION

The advantages of mediation over negotiation have already been previously discussed. Primarily the benefits of negotiation over mediation involve an "if it ain't broke, don't fix it" premise. Mediation is more expensive than face-to-face negotiation since a mediator must be retained. If negotiation is going very well already, there is no need to hire a mediator, and adding a third party to a well-functioning negotiation may be counterproductive.

SUMMARY: ADVANTAGES AND DISADVANTAGES OF MEDIATION

Table 16-1 summarizes, for your convenience, the advantages and disadvantages of mediation, compared to litigation and negotiation.

◆ TABLE 16-1   Advantages and Disadvantages of Mediation

ADVANTAGES OF MEDIATION, COMPARED WITH LITIGATION	DISADVANTAGES OF MEDIATION, COMPARED WITH LITIGATION
Mediation is quicker and less expensive.	Mediation does not always result in settlement.
Mediation is more likely to encourage collaboration and cooperation.	Litigation guarantees some kind of outcome.
Resolution is more efficient and makes better use of parties' resources.	Unlike litigation, mediation does not create legal precedent, which might prevent legal reform through the appellate litigation process if mediation is coercive.
Mediation can address all issues, not just those for which a cause of action can be stated.	
More creative remedies are possible.	Incompetent mediators or mediators pressed for time may unwittingly contribute to the exploitation of a weak disputant by a strong one.
The WHOLE conflict can be dealt with, including linkages and conflicts with nondisputants.	
Mediation is likely to reduce meta-disputes, whereas litigation often creates more of them.	Because mediation is private, vindication and public reprimand may not be available remedies. This aspect of mediation makes it unpalatable for some disputants.
Mediation promotes greater quality of consent and psychological ownership, leading to greater satisfaction and voluntary compliance.	
Relationship advantages: "competent" mediators help defuse anger, improve communication, and specifically work on trust-building.	Because mediation is private, say some scholars, bigoted disputants, and mediators might be more likely to act on their prejudices than litigants and judges.
Mediation can "transform" disputants by empowering them, teaching them negotiation skills, and helping them see the other disputant's point of view.	
Mediation that does not result in agreement can streamline the dispute, clarifying and narrowing issues and making future resolution easier, quicker, and cheaper.	

ADVANTAGES OF MEDIATION, COMPARED WITH NEGOTIATION	DISADVANTAGES OF MEDIATION, COMPARED WITH NEGOTIATION
Mediation is better able to move disputants past impasse because it is better able to handle people problems, meta-disputes, and emotional factors.	Mediation is more expensive because it includes another professional.
The presence of a third party often alters the relationship dynamics that led disputants to impasse in the first place.	If negotiation is proceeding very well, it may be counterproductive to introduce a third person (the mediator).
Mediators can say things to the disputants that the disputants would reactively devalue if they had come from one another.	
Mediation is better at teaching disputants how to negotiate effectively.	
Mediators can usually address issues of trust, anger, and communication more effectively than simple negotiation or lawyer-assisted negotiation can.	
"Good" mediators are usually more effective at diagnosing the conflict and choosing appropriate methods of addressing it than disputants and their lawyers.	
Compared with lawyer-assisted negotiation, mediation usually results in more creative resolutions better tailored to the interests of all disputants.	

EXERCISES, PROJECTS, AND "THOUGHT EXPERIMENTS"

1. One possibility raised in this chapter is that mediation can permanently improve the relationships between some disputants by encouraging them to interact in a cooperative manner. How can a short-term intervention, such as mediation, result in long-term improvements in cooperation? Using Deutsch's theory, provide a theoretical explanation.

2. *Conflict journal.* Now that you have reviewed the distinctions between mediation and other forms of dispute resolution, what ADR process would you apply to your conflict to best resolve it? Why?

3. Could mediation be used to resolve the Israeli-Palestinian conflict? Write an essay exploring this issue. How would it be used? Who would need to be at the bargaining table? How should the mediator be chosen? Should the mediator use a facilitative style, an evaluative style, or a combination of these? How would the stakeholders be encouraged to come to the mediation table?

4. Should you encourage trying mediation or litigation first in the following disputes? Explain your answer. If mediation is your answer, be sure to comment on how you would encourage the other side to enter mediation. There are no absolute right or wrong answers.

   a. A state consumer agency has had numerous complaints from aggrieved college students who say they have been ripped off by a stereo equipment store next to the college that allegedly provides inferior equipment packed in an ambiguously labeled box. The receipts provided by this seller do not specify the exact model being sold. For example, one student says that he bought a high-end receiver and paid $900. When the box was opened, the student says he found an older, discontinued model worth much less. The seller says that he has never misrepresented stereo equipment to buyers. Assume that state laws allow the consumer agency to file a lawsuit against the seller and that, if successful, the agency can obtain a court order requiring the seller to compensate the buyers.

   b. Melody works as a legal assistant at a private law firm, Nip and Tuck, P.A. She has just been reassigned to a new attorney-associate, Mr. Tuck's daughter, Amazonia Tuck. Amazonia is impossible to work with—she's arrogant, she's intolerant, she doesn't listen, and she gives Melody an unreasonable amount of work. Melody does not want to leave the firm—she has worked there ten years and has accumulated lots of perks. Also, she has never had problems before. Melody has tried informally complaining to the human relations department, to no avail. Melody doesn't feel she can go to the partners—after all, Mordecai Tuck is the father of the person she can't stand. Assume Melody has a cause of action against Nip and Tuck and that she has a 50:50 chance of winning a month's wages if she litigates. Also assume that Nip and Tuck would not be allowed to fire Melody in retaliation for bringing legal action.

c. You live in a rental condo. Your next-door neighbor has started playing loud music late at night for hours and hours. You can't sleep at all. Moving would be an extreme hardship for you, and the neighbor owns his condo, so eviction isn't an option. You have gone to this neighbor to ask him nicely to turn down the music, and the neighbor completely lost it—screaming, pacing up and down, and flailing his arms—you think he may even have been crying. This guy is really scaring you. A civil action for nuisance could be brought and you might win. The small claims court doesn't have the jurisdiction to provide injunctive relief (such as a court order prohibiting him from playing music after a set hour), so you would have to use the regular trial court.

d. You are a paralegal. Your boss's new client is the chief financial officer of a failing dot-com. Your client says that she used a creative approach to representing earnings on the past three years' financial statements. She says she talked to the CPA firm that audits the books, Snidely, Whiplash, & Co., about her reporting methods and that the accountant "blessed" (approved) the accounting method, saying "all the dot-coms are doing it this way." Whiplash is now serving fifteen years in the federal penitentiary for accounting fraud—the same creative approach to stating earnings, as well as other dubious practices, occurred with frequency among all his clients. Your client was investigated by the SEC. She was found not to be criminally negligent. However, this does not mean she is not civilly negligent: she has been sued by an investor group that wants big bucks to compensate it for its losses in the stock market as a result of her negligent misrepresentation.

5. Imagine you work in a law office that handles general tort, contract, and business litigation. Prepare the text for a brochure that explains the advantages and disadvantages of mediation to clients.

6. Support or critique the following statement, in debate or in a written essay: "Courts should never require women to mediate disputes with male disputants—unless they have legal counsel present during mediation sessions—because the probability of harm to the woman is too great."

7. Your client is a businessman who owns a restaurant. His partner and head chef is claiming that he is not receiving his fair share of the profits—he and your client have a difference of opinion about the ownership of revenues from a catering business run out of the restaurant premises by your client and a different chef. Your client is quite anxious to retain the restaurant, which will be vulnerable to failure if he loses the chef, so you have suggested taking the dispute to a mediator, and your client is all for it. However, the chef's attorney is balking because the chef "doesn't want to throw money down a dark hole"—in other words, he doesn't like the idea that mediation won't promise a resolution. Develop a strategy to assist this client in meeting his underlying interests and needs. Is there a way to improve the chances of reaching agreement while retaining all the relationship-protection benefits of mediation?

RECOMMENDED READINGS

Baruch-Bush, R. A., and J. P. Folger. 1994. *The promise of mediation: Responding to conflict through empowerment and recognition.* San Francisco: Jossey-Bass.

Depner, C. E., K. Cannata, and I. Ricci. 1994. Client evaluations of mediation services: The impact of case characteristics and mediation service models. *Family and Conciliation Courts Review* 32 (July):306–25.

Gaschen, D. E. 1995. Mandatory custody mediation: The debate over its usefulness continues. *Ohio State Journal on Dispute Resolution* 10:469–90.

Grillo, T. 1991. The mediation alternative: Process dangers for women. *Yale Law Journal 100* (April):1545–1610.

Heister, J. W. 1987. Appendix. Property allocation in mediation: An examination of distribution relative to equality and to gender. *Mediation Quarterly* 1987 (17, fall):97–98.

Kelly, J. B. 1996. A decade of divorce mediation research. *Family and Conciliation Courts Review* 34(3):373–85.

Kelly, J. B., and M. A. Duryee. 1992. Women's and men's views of mediation in voluntary and mandatory mediation settings. *Family and Conciliation Courts Review* 30(1):34–49.

LaFree, G., and C. Rack. 1996. The effects of participants' ethnicity and gender on monetary outcomes in mediated and adjudicated cases. *Law and Society Review* 30(4):767–91.

Lande, J. 1997. How will lawyering and mediation practices transform each other? *Florida State University Law Review* 24 (summer):839–901.

Marcus, M. G., W. Marcus, N. A. Stilwell, and N. Doherty. 1999. To mediate or not to mediate: Financial outcomes in mediated versus adversarial divorces. *Mediation Quarterly* 7 (winter):143–52.

McCabe, K. 2001. A forum for women's voices: Mediation through a feminist jurisprudential lens. *Northern Illinois University Law Review* 21:459–82.

McIsaac, H. 2001. Confidentiality revisited: California style. *Family Court Review* 39(4):405–14.

Menkel-Meadow, C. J. 1985. Portia in a different voice: Speculations on a women's lawyering process. *Berkeley Women's Law Journal* 1:39–63.

Pearson, J. 1991. The equity of mediated divorce agreements. *Mediation Quarterly* 9(2):179–97.

Rhode, D. L. 1999. Too much law, too little justice: Too much rhetoric, too little reform. *Georgetown Journal of Legal Ethics* 11:989–1017.

Rifkin, J. 1984. Mediation from a feminist perspective: Promise and problems. *Law and Inequality* 2:21–31.

17

The Process of Mediation

*"Focus 90% of your time on solutions and
only 10% of your time on problems."*

—Anthony J. D'Angelo, *The College Blue Book*

In this chapter, you will learn …

- The stages of mediation.
  - Initial client contact.
  - Introduction.
  - Issues clarification/communication.
  - Productive stage.
  - Agreement consummation.
  - Debriefing and referral.
- Facilitative mediation tactics.
  - Education.
  - Structuring the negotiation.
  - Improving communication.
  - Handling emotions.
  - Maintaining motivation.
- Evaluative mediation tactics.
  - Instilling doubt.
  - Case evaluation.
  - Caucusing.

What is mediation actually like? Of course, we have seen that mediation is a highly variable process, difficult to describe with specificity. However, it is reasonable to make a few overall generalizations about the mediation process and how it works.

Mediation generally takes place in a series of one or more sessions. Most mediators set the length of the sessions at between one and two hours, although some mediation sessions are much longer.[1] A typical mediation begins and ends with a joint session, at which the mediator and all the disputants (and/or their lawyers) are in attendance. The prevalent model for civil and personal injury mediation is for the initial joint session to be followed by several sessions in caucus, followed eventually by more joint sessions to tie down agreements. In divorce and family mediation, there is less likelihood of caucus sessions, and much if not all of the mediation occurs in joint sessions.

STAGES OF MEDIATION

Although mediation is a highly fluid process, it is possible to conceptualize mediation as occurring in a series of stages. Table 17-1 shows one such stage model.

INITIAL CLIENT CONTACT

Mediation begins when one or both disputants make contact with a mediation provider. Although clients may be referred to mediation by a court or their lawyers, often one of the two disputants contacts the mediator directly to inquire about services. The mediator must inform the person making contact of the nature of the services, answer relevant questions, and at the same time avoid discussing substantive details about the dispute (the mediator will appear biased if one disputant has been allowed to state his or her side of the dispute before the other disputant becomes involved). The mediator will also try to motivate the client to choose mediation, not only for marketing reasons but also because, since mediation is a consensual process, some level of trust in the process is essential to its success. The mediator will frequently send informative brochures that provide specific facts about mediation and demonstrate its advantages. During the initial client contact, the mediator will often also need to provide guidance to the disputant on how to coax the other disputant into the mediation process. This task can require much tactical skill. Although some disputants will be making contact with the mediator with the knowledge and consent of the other disputant, others will be making contact independently. Almost inevitably, if the disputants are hostile, the move to contact a mediator will be reactively devalued by the other disputant. The other disputant will, moreover, regard as a hostile invasion of privacy any effort made by the mediator to contact him or her directly. Some mediators find that offering a free initial consultation can help overcome this barrier to involvement.

---

[1] In labor and international mediation, so-called marathon sessions are held. These sometimes depend on fatigue factors to move the disputants closer to agreement.

STAGE	DETAILS: FACILITATIVE MEDIATION	DETAILS: EVALUATIVE MEDIATION
Initial client contact	Basic information taken without compromising future impartiality or appearance of impartiality. Basic marketing of process. If one disputant team has contacted mediator, development of strategy for involving other disputant.	Basic information taken without compromising future impartiality or appearance of impartiality. Basic marketing of process. If one disputant team has contacted mediator, development of strategy for involving other disputant.
Introductory stage	Describe ground rules, rights, and responsibilities; break the ice; educate about the mediation; process. Review and sign any contractual documents. Begin reframing of issues from contentions to joint problems to be solved.	Describe ground rules, rights, and responsibilities; break the ice; educate about the mediation process. Sign any needed contractual documents.
Issues clarification and communication	Use active listening to obtain information about disputants' shared and divergent interests and their goals in mediation. Develop list of areas of agreement and disagreement. Develop list of disputants' interests in a working document. Reframe contentions as goals, joint problems to be solved, and deep-seated interests, values, and needs. Address "people problems." Seek understanding of meta-disputes and linkages. Seek mutual recognition on the part of each disputant ("If I saw things as you do, I'd feel the same way").	Ask parties to state cases or positions or describe the nature of the conflict. (Some facilitative techniques may also be used.) Develop lists of areas of agreement and areas of nonagreement.
Productive stage	Using list of principles, brainstorm multiple joint options for mutual gain. Develop objective standards for assessing options. Fine-tune and select options, using the objective standards. Compromise often used to select between candidate options. Write down draft agreement and get feedback.	Instill doubt and provide evaluation in an effort to reduce differing perceptions of facts and law and to move disputants' aspirations closer together. Explore whether aspirations overlap using backwater techniques applied during caucus. In joint session, compromise may be used to finalize settlement. Write down agreement and get feedback.
Agreement consummation	Develop formal agreement and execute agreement; may occur within or outside of mediation.	Develop formal agreement and execute agreement; may occur within or outside of mediation.
Debriefing and referral	Assess whether tasks of mediation are complete and, if not, what else needs to be done. Refer to other professionals as necessary. Assess successes and failures of process.	Assess whether tasks of mediation are complete and, if not, what else needs to be done. Refer to other professionals as necessary. Assess successes and failures of process.

Note: These stages are not strictly chronological: participants will repeatedly loop back through earlier stages on their way to completing mediation. Most mediations are neither purely facilitative or purely evaluative, although it is safe to say that evaluative mediators are much more likely to incorporate facilitative techniques than facilitative mediators are likely to incorporate evaluative techniques. Transformative mediation is considered facilitative, but is staged differently.

INTRODUCTORY STAGE

The purposes of the introductory stage of mediation are to break the ice and get comfortable, to introduce and clarify the mediation process, to establish the ground rules and policies of mediation, to clarify and establish the legal basis of mediation, and to begin to orient the disputants toward productivity in mediation.

Assuming that both disputants decide to give mediation a try, an appointment for an initial session is scheduled. Mediators usually seat their clients around a conference table. The table may be round to eliminate symbolic power distinctions between mediator and clients, emphasizing the critical role the disputants have in fashioning the settlement. After introductions, the mediator may allow the clients to talk about what brought them to mediation, but typically this phase is very short because of the tendency for disputants to become caught up in arguments and statements of positions. A competent mediator will balance the need of each client to talk about what is upsetting him or her with the need to avoid conduct that escalates the conflict.

Once a certain comfort level is established, the mediator will typically spend a substantial amount of time talking to and at the disputants. Usually, it is at this stage of the mediation process that the mediator will appear most "active" to the clients. The mediator must ensure that the clients know exactly what mediation is all about. The mediator must communicate his or her style of mediation, the goals of mediation, and the typical techniques the mediator uses to help the participants strive toward these goals. The mediator will also discuss the ground rules for behavior in mediation, such as the need for turn-taking, the need to curtail name-calling, the need for promptness, and so forth. The mediator will typically also present contractual documents that participants must sign in order to create a mediator-client relationship, protect the confidentiality of the mediation process, and so forth. Additionally, most mediators will present information on the many benefits of this ADR technique in order to further co-opt the disputants to trust the process and motivate them to negotiate in good faith.

Because disputants entering mediation have been unable to achieve a settlement of their differences on their own, it is typical for them to enter mediation caught up in a competitive conflict cycle. The mediator will often experience immediate and continuous pressure from the disputants to get swept up in mutual blame games and recriminations. For this reason, from the first moments, mediators will work actively to interrupt this cycle and replace it with a cycle of cooperation. This aspect of the art of mediation is most important in facilitative mediation and is emphasized less in evaluative mediation.

Numerous techniques are used to subtly reorient the disputants away from conceptualizing the conflict as a win-lose contest and replacing it with the idea that the disputants have a joint problem to be solved together. The mediator will choose his or her words with extreme care to reflect this noncompetitive perspective on the conflict. For example, given parents disputing over where a child will live after divorce, instead of saying, "So, you have come to mediation to settle your dispute over child custody," the mediator might instead say, "So, you have come to mediation to create a parenting plan that will be healthy for your child."

Another technique used by mediators to interrupt the competition cycle is to emphasize the cooperative elements of the disputants' relationship and to deemphasize the competitive elements. For example, if during the introduction to mediation one disputant, a longtime business partner of the other disputant, says, "I have no confidence that Joe will ever stop his abusive name-calling of me! Good luck with your so-called ground rules," the mediator might respond, "You are showing a lot of optimism by being willing to come into mediation, and I am impressed that you and Joe have been able to keep your business relationship so profitable for so long despite the hard feelings. You must both be very hard workers. Let's work together to get the relationship onto an easier plane." The point is that the work of the mediator in reframing the disputant's perceptions away from a competitive conflict cycle begins from the first moment of contact and is continuous throughout the mediation process.

ISSUES CLARIFICATION AND COMMUNICATION

Following the introductory stage of mediation, the mediation will move into a stage of actively *communicating and clarifying issues.* It is here that the details of the dispute, and the nature of whatever impasses are preventing settlement, become most explicit.

Facilitative and evaluative mediators generally handle the issues clarification and communication stage quite differently. An evaluative mediator's goal at this stage is to get a sense of the positions and aspirations of each disputant. The evaluative mediator is apt to begin by asking each disputant to state the case, or to describe the disagreement. What follows will typically be each disputant's efforts to convince the mediator of the merits of his or her case. Although the mediator is not the person who must be persuaded (after all, the mediator does not decide the dispute), it is almost inevitable that aggrieved disputants will want to win over the sympathies of the mediator. Moreover, the persuasiveness of each side's contentions may alter the evaluations the mediator gives to each side. The mediator will sometimes use information gained in the other side's presentation in an effort to lower the expectations of each disputant. The mediator will typically become actively involved in filling in the details of the disputants' contentions and to get up to speed on important details of the dispute. The National Institute for Trial Advocacy's text *The Art of Mediation* (Bennett & Hermann 1996) contains an excellent description of the art of mediator information-gathering questioning.

Following this joint session, the evaluative mediator will typically meet each disputant separately to gain further information about the disputant's real aspirations. The disputant has been posturing in front of the other disputant, but, without him or her present, the disputant is free to reveal more about what he or

Mediators often act as organizers of information provided by the disputants. Michael Newman, PhotoEdit

she really thinks. Additionally, the mediator will use the caucus sessions to determine whether there are secrets in the dispute that are impeding successful negotiation but that the disputant is unwilling to share with the other disputant.

Issues clarification and communication in a facilitative mediation usually occurs entirely in a joint session. The reason for this emphasis is that, in a facilitative mediation, the primary goal at this stage is to facilitate the disputant's clarification of issues and underlying interests *with each other.* This goal cannot be accomplished if the disputants are not communicating with each other.

A typical facilitative mediation that has reached the stage of issues clarification and communication is focused on developing an interests analysis for each disputant. Most disputants enter mediation without a carefully conceived notion of their interests but, instead, with a list of positions and aspirations. Disputants also typically have a negatively biased belief about the motivations of the other disputant. For this reason, the facilitative mediator will begin this phase with specific tactics designed to deflect the disputants away from positional bargaining and set the stage for interests analysis. For example, in a dispute between the parents of a special-needs child and the school system, a facilitative mediator is apt to ask each disputant to tell about the child, an initiating gambit that usually elicits child-centered goals from all the participants.

As each disputant speaks about the conflict, the facilitative mediator reframes and refocuses the communication to defuse personal attacks directed at the other disputant and to clarify the interests, needs, principles, and values connoted by the speakers' statements. *Active listening* is a critical skill the mediator uses at this juncture to help speakers feel they have been heard while reconstructing the message, so that it can be absorbed and accepted with less defensiveness by the other disputant. Active listening also helps the mediator reframe the disputant's communication from statements of position into statements about underlying principles.

Active Listening

Active listening is a skill vital to effective mediators. It is also a skill that proves useful to all effective negotiators.

Active listening serves several vital purposes: it helps the speaker feel heard by the listener, helps the listener understand more fully the interests that underlie the speaker's position, and helps both speaker and listener become more "legitimized" in one another's eyes. Because each feels the other is taking him or her seriously, active listening improves trust and communication. Active listening is also a powerful tool in the process of principled bargaining.

To engage in active listening, simply listen very carefully to what a speaker has said. Then repeat, in your own words, what was stated. Do not say that you either agree or disagree with what the speaker has said. A key aspect of active listening is that, when you repeat the speaker's statement, you must reframe it to remove any aspects of the comment that are designed to make the listener feel angry or hurt (some negotiators like to call these "zingers"). Following the restating, you then draw the speaker out, so that he or she will say more.

For example, suppose you are having a conversation with a member of the opposite political party, and this person says the following:

I just think that _____ is the best presidential candidate out there. He seems to be in favor of everything I think is important. Anyone who thinks otherwise is a real idiot!

You oppose this candidate vigorously, and detest him. To engage in active listening, you would say something like the following:

So you feel that _____ would make the best president of all the candidates out there right now. Tell me more about why you hold that opinion.

The response reframes the speaker's statement, omits the aspect of the communication that functioned as a personal attack, and asks for further information. Repeat this cycle of reframing and drawing the other person out as long as he or she seems willing to share his or her opinion. The act of actively listening did not require you to engage in any dishonesty—it did not require you to agree with the other speaker's opinion (though it may have required a degree of emotional restraint).

Mediators of all persuasions often act as organizers of information. An evaluative mediator will often summarize the conflictual issues in a single document or will write a list on a white board or poster. Facilitative mediators will also make a list of the issues that need to be resolved but will also typically list the deep-seated interests, needs, values, and principles with which the disputants agree. The agreed-upon interests are used as a sort of map, or "constitution," to guide the disputants in the next stage, the productive stage, of their negotiation.

PRODUCTIVE STAGE

As issues are clarified, communicated, and organized, the mediation enters the third stage, the productive stage. In the productive stage, issues are resolved and the agreement is written down.

In an evaluative mediation, it is in the productive stage that the evaluation occurs. During caucus, the evaluative mediator expertly probes the situation, pointing out weaknesses in the case of the disputant before him/her and suggesting strengths in the opponent's case that the disputant might have missed or

During the productive phase of mediation, any agreements generated will usually be recorded by the mediator. Dorling Kindersley Media Library

discounted. Occasionally, an evaluative mediator will, instead, perform an evaluation in front of the two disputants together, indicating that "if this case were to go to court, it seems to me it would come out about this way." The evaluative mediator will tactfully probe each disputant for bottom lines, looking for integrative opportunities and mutually beneficial concession trades. If the mediator can help the two disputants get to the point at which their bottom lines overlap, the mediator will often bring the parties back together and allow them to conduct the final act of reaching agreement themselves. The mediator will gently coach the disputants in how to bring this final agreement about, avoiding telling either disputant what the other's bottom line is but suggesting appropriate directions to go in.

In a facilitative mediation, the productive stage often involves a period of brainstorming for possible options to address the list of interests that the disputants generated previously. These possible options are then examined and reality-tested. At some point in this process, some amount of compromising, or haggling, is generally required to reach ultimate agreement. The mediator may suggest selecting "objective standards" to guide this final selection process if the disputants are unable to make this final decision themselves. More often, the disputants will readily agree to some final minor compromising once they are very close to full settlement.

Both facilitative and evaluative mediators will write down any settlements that the disputants reach, either in an informal memorandum of agreement or in a formal contract. Mediators will typically ask disputants for feedback on this written product and make revisions as needed. If the disputants' attorneys participated in the mediation sessions, they will sometimes do the agreement drafting instead of the mediator.

A Sample List of Shared Principles for a Child Custody Mediation

We, John Jones and Mary Smith, the loving parents of Margaret Jones, agree to the following shared principles:

1. We agree to keep our daughter's needs and interests at the forefront of our negotiations.
2. We agree that our daughter should have the opportunity to spend lots of time with each of us.
3. We agree that we should find a way to structure our parenting agreement so that our daughter's present school system, after-school activities, church, and so on are not disrupted very much.
4. We agree that our daughter should have permission to love and care about both of us and that neither of us should put the other parent down in front of her.
5. We agree that our daughter should be kept safe, so neither of us should do risky things, such as drinking and driving when she is with us.
6. We agree that it is important for us to have effective and friendly communication, so we demonstrate good problem-solving techniques for our daughter.
7. We agree that our daughter needs for each of us to support the discipline of the other parent as long as it isn't damaging to her.

Michael Newman, PhotoEdit

AGREEMENT CONSUMMATION

Agreement consummation can occur inside or outside of mediation. If the mediator has drafted a formal contract, sometimes the disputants will execute this contract at a mediation session. More commonly, a written account of the settlement is transformed into a formal written contract outside of mediation, after the disputants have had a chance to discuss the settlement with legal counsel. (See the discussion in Chapter 18 regarding the ethical issues involved in mediators' drafting the settlement agreement.)

DEBRIEFING AND REFERRAL

The last stage of mediation is *debriefing and referral*. This stage may occur before or after the agreement consummation stage. The mediator and disputants review what has been decided in mediation and what remains to be done. The mediator may provide guidance as to the appropriate next steps and as to the appropriate professional assistance needed for these next steps. If the disputants have reached a temporary agreement, plans may be made for a return to mediation in the future. The disputants and the mediator may also discuss and confirm the successes and drawbacks of the mediation process.

The process of mediation is typically nonlinear. The stages presented in this section and, indeed, in any description of mediation are not fixed in sequence. Often, mediation backtracks to an earlier stage. For example, during the agreement consummation stage, the participants may realize that they have forgotten to deal with an issue, which will require a return to the issues clarification and communication stage. Or communication in mediation may break down, necessitating a return to the ground-rules phase of the introductory stage of mediation.

WHAT DO MEDIATORS DO?

Mediation is both a science and an art. Although some sense of the mediator's toolbox of strategies and tactics can be gained, you should be aware that each mediator and each mediation is different. For a better idea of how mediators work, any one of a number of helpful descriptions of real mediations are available. For an even better idea of what mediation is like, you should find a way to attend some actual mediation sessions.

FACILITATIVE TACTICS IN MEDIATION

Even highly evaluative mediators have as a goal the facilitation of a negotiated settlement. For this reason, nearly every mediator uses a number of facilitative tactics.

What Is Mediation Like? Some Ways to Find Out

Some descriptions that offer a taste of how mediation really works can be found in the following sources:

Riskin and Westbrook's (1997) law school text, *Dispute Resolution and Lawyers* (2nd ed.), contains a section, entitled "Brief Takes on Real Mediations," that contains accounts of the use of mediation in professional malpractice disputes, personal injury claims, corporate shareholder management disputing, environmental disputing, and Native American fishing rights disputing.

On the Internet, the mediate.com website, *www.mediate.com,* contains a number of descriptions of mediation. They include "With No Lawyers in Sight, Landlords and Tenants Talk Out Disputes," by Gustav Spohn (*http://www.mediate.com/articles/landlord.cfm*); David Gage, Dawn Martin, and John Gromala, "Mediation During Business Formation or Reorganization" (*http://www.mediate.com/articles/formation.cfm*); and Forrest Mosten, "What Happens in Mediation" (family mediation) (*http://www.mediate.com/articles/mosch3.cfm*).

In addition, many of the Online Dispute Resolution websites (see Chapter 21 for more details) describe actual or simulated mediation sessions. SquareTrade offers three case studies in commercial and consumer mediation (*http://www.squaretrade.com/cnt/jsp/knw/fraud.jsp*). Resolution Forum (*http://www.resolutionforum.org/s_demo.html*), contains a transcript of a simulated mediation session dealing with a contracting dispute.

It is helpful to an understanding of mediator behavior to place facilitative mediator tactics in the following categories:

- ◆ Educating
- ◆ Structuring the negotiation
- ◆ Improving communication
- ◆ Handling emotions
- ◆ Maintaining disputant motivation

Educating. Mediators *educate* their clients in numerous ways. Much of this educational process occurs in the introductory stage of mediation but continues throughout the mediation process. Mediators provide information about the benefits and appropriate uses of mediation. This information allows the disputants to make informed choices about whether mediation is right for them, and it persuades disputants to make an emotional commitment to trying mediation. Mediators also educate their clients about the process of mediation. This information enables disputants to anticipate what they will experience and minimizes surprises. For example, mediators will often anticipate the likelihood that an impasse will be encountered in mediation by warning the disputants of this possibility and reassuring clients that impasse is both expected and manageable. Mediators also educate clients about the ground rules of mediation. In this fashion, the mediator begins to control and structure the mediation process in a way that promotes effective negotiation. For example, a mediator will typically begin a mediator-client relationship by distributing and discussing one or more written documents containing ground rules—such as the need to take turns without interruption, the need not to use abusive language, and the need to attend all sessions promptly. By this means, the mediator tells the clients how to conduct themselves in mediation, further increasing the likelihood that the mediation will meet the goals set for it. Many mediators also teach clients the value of, and the steps of, principled bargaining. This educative function helps clients buy into the premises of mediation, helps clients negotiate effectively, and, as a side benefit, may help clients in negotiations that occur outside mediation.

Mediators educate didactically—in other words, by direct lecture to the clients. They also teach indirectly in a number of ways. One of the most important educative techniques is *role-modeling*. The nonconfrontational active listening techniques and other communication tactics engaged in by mediators not only serve as a direct intervention in the conflict but also educate clients as to the behavior expected of them during the mediation. Mediators acting in panels also frequently role-model cooperative behavior in front of the clients. This is the reason that some mediators insist on all communication regarding the substance of mediation take place in a joint session: any communication can be of positive educational value. Mediators also role-model appropriate behavior: staying calm, listening actively, avoiding name-calling, staying positive, and so forth. In addition to role-modeling, mediators may educate by giving outside activities— "homework"—and by referring clients to other professionals, such as therapists, appraisers, and financial planners.

Structuring the Negotiation. The "meat" of what a mediator does is to *structure the negotiation.* The clients have presumably come to the mediator specifically to get help in negotiating effectively. Thus, the mediator's efforts to structure the negotiation are designed specifically to address this need of the clients.

The precise structure imposed or promoted by the mediator depends on the mediator's chosen style, on the preferences of the clients, and on the demands imposed by the situation. Nearly all mediators impose basic ground rules related to the number and length of sessions and the behavior required of both the clients (e.g., the use of respectful language) and the mediator (e.g., lack of bias in favor of either client). Beyond these nearly universal truths about mediation, the structure varies. Pure mediators frequently impose a structure following the principled-bargaining model: they encourage a period of interests analysis, followed by brainstorming sessions, a period of reality-testing of options, and, throughout mediation in general, guidance in staying "soft on the person, tough on the problem." Bargaining-based mediators, on the other hand, often call for an initial statement of the case in an initial session, followed by an examination of interests and aspirations in caucus, followed by an evaluation and then an exploration of opportunities for compromise. Other structuring by the mediator is determined by the specific situation the mediator finds the parties to be involved in. For example, a facilitative mediator may conclude that a mutual acknowledgment and recognition may further settlement, and, based on this conclusion, the mediator may structure a mutual active listening session.

Improving Communication. At all times, a competent mediator *improves communication* between the disputants. Effective communication has the following goals:

- Developing a complete and accurate interests analysis (particularly for pure mediation)

- Encouraging a perception of cooperation among the disputants, thus interrupting or preventing a competitive conflict cycle

- Airing misunderstandings and meta-disputes, so that mutual trust-building can begin

- Recognizing and acknowledging the perspectives of the individual disputants ("If I had seen things from your point of view, I probably would have felt the same way") if possible by one disputant to the other and, if not, by the mediator to each disputant

- Avoiding conflict escalation brought on by inflammatory communication

- Performing effective conflict diagnosis

- Engaging in effective principled bargaining and collaboration, which is built on complete, open, and honest communication

Handling Emotions. Mediation inevitably gives rise to strong emotion, and *handling emotions* is an important aspect of the mediator's craft. One of the things that distinguishes the mediation process from what goes on in a therapy session is the manner in which emotions are dealt with. A mental-health professional, such as a psychotherapist, often works on the assumption that, by unblocking difficult emotions, the patient can make strides in healthy functioning. Thus, providing emotional catharsis for patients is frequently a direct goal of mental-health professionals. On the contrary, getting emotions out and on the table is *not* a primary goal of mediation.

The primary goals of mediation typically revolve around setting the stage for effective negotiation.[2] A disputant's emotional state sometimes prevents the disputant from dealing rationally with substantive issues in the negotiation. And sometimes the client's emotional state points the way to an important issue in the conflict that was buried or not acknowledged. To get past such issues, to address them appropriately, and to reach a lasting agreement acceptable to all disputants, these emotions must be out on the table. Moreover, for a disputant to feel heard and cared for in the negotiation process and by the settlement, the emotions raised by the conflict must be validated. Ideally, the best person to validate a disputant's emotion is the other disputant, because the recognition conferred by the other disputant promotes positive feelings and cooperation. However, sometimes the hot and hurtful emotions around the conflict prevent the other disputant from conferring this element of recognition, and in such a case the mediator is often forced to provide the recognition in the disputant's place.

On the other hand, there are problems with *unfettered emotional expression* in mediation. Encouraging a disputant to vent feelings can scare and anger the other disputant and can cause the conflict to enter a period of destructive escalation. Moreover, if the mediator validates a disputant's emotions based on a grievance aired against the other disputant, the mediator runs the risk of appearing to agree with the aggrieved disputant's version of the story. If the mediator is to validate the disputant's feelings, he or she must do so without seeming to agree with the disputant's account of the underlying facts. A mediator does not act as a factfinder: if he or she did, the process would be nonbinding evaluation, not mediation.

How are disputants' emotions validated as necessary without creating problems of conflict escalation and mediator bias? The solution is to find a way to validate feelings in a depersonalized way. Professor Elizabeth Koopman, formerly of the University of Maryland, College Park, developed the *confirm and focus* technique to create respectful, distancing, and bias-free responses to emotionality in mediation.

Here is how confirm and focus works. Imagine an emotion-laden comment made by a client in mediation. For example, suppose a fifty-year-old wife in a divorce case says, "My husband's a total jerk. In our entire twenty-five years of marriage, he never lifted a finger to help with the kids!" First, the mediator attempts to determine what feelings are being expressed. To do this, the mediator has to "listen with the third ear," looking for the feelings that lie

---

[2] This, of course, is a generalization. The specific goals of mediation depend on the variety of mediation being practiced. Refer to the section on the varieties of mediation for the specific goals of each of the five types of mediation (Chapter 15, "Varieties of Mediation").

beneath the words spoken. It helps for the mediator to have expert knowledge of the typical experience of individuals in the position of the disputant. Sometimes, active listening is helpful in developing an accurate picture of the emotions being expressed. In our example, the mediator might hear anger, frustration, and possibly some underlying fear of having insufficient support in the future. Second, the mediator confirms the expressed feeling, but *uses the third-person voice,* not first-person. This impersonal voice validates the feelings but does not encourage the speaker to ventilate more. Additionally, the response does not validate the underlying factual allegation; instead, it presumes that the version of the facts is an opinion held by the speaker. This point of view avoids putting the mediator in the position of expressing agreement with the factual component of a disputant's statement. Thus, an *improper* response might be the following:

> *Wrong:* "I can see how angry, scared, and frustrated you are that he was so uncooperative and unreliable."

A *better* response takes care not to confirm the factual underpinnings of the statement:

> *Better:* "I can understand that, if you felt you didn't get support for your parenting, you would react with anger, fear, and frustration."

An even better response uses the third-person instead of the first-person voice. Using the third-person voice does not encourage further expression of emotion as much as the first person voice:

> *Better yet:* "People who feel they didn't get support for their parenting often feel angry, scared, and frustrated."

Dealing with heated emotions during mediation can prevent conflict from escalating. Christopher Bissell, Getty Images Inc. Stone Allstock

Transformative Mediator Tactics— Facilitating, But With a Difference

The predominant form of facilitative mediation practiced today is "pure mediation," but "transformative mediation" is another important form—one that is experiencing a great rise in popularity today.

Researchers Dorothy Della Noce, James R. Antes, and Judith A. Saul (Antes, Della Noce, & Saul 2002) have explored some of the differences between pure (referred to in the research as "problem-solving") mediators and transformative mediators. To do this work, the researchers selected four mediators, two of each type, and all of whom were recognized as pre-eminent practitioners in the field. Studying mediator-client discourse during videotapes of these mediators in action, they found several important differences between the facilitative behavior of pure mediators and that of transformative mediators:

- While pure mediators often structure the mediation process to encourage effective negotiation, transformative mediators are careful to leave the structuring of the process to the disputants themselves. For example, a pure mediator typically sets ground rules for mediation, such as "the disputants will take turns speaking," but a transformative mediator more often asks the disputants themselves whether any ground rules would be helpful and what those rules should be. The "hands-off" approach is grounded in the transformative goal of granting the disputants the opportunity to empower themselves.
- Transformative mediators "orient the parties to each other," while pure mediators orient the disputants toward the problem they need to solve. Moreover, transformative mediators are trained to "open" the parties' verbal conflict; that is, to follow the "hot buttons" in the conflict and encourage the disputants to expand on them. Thus, the common pure-mediation strategy of refocusing disputants away from hot emotion and back on solving the substantive problem, as is seen in the tactic "confirm and focus," would be rejected by transformative mediators, who would be more likely to confirm a point of view and then invite further comment. This encouragement of emotional expression is an effort to give disputants opportunities to give one another recognition.

Note how this response allows the mediator to validate the wife's feelings without agreeing with her assessment of the facts and without encouraging a lot of additional ventilation. Next, the mediator couples the validating statement with a direction to *refocus* the speaker on the mediation issues raised by the statement:

> *Even better:* "People who feel they didn't get support for their parenting often feel angry, scared, and frustrated. Let's work on setting up some clear parenting responsibilities, so that you won't be so likely to feel let down. What promises do you need from John about future parenting?"

This response validates the wife, obviates the need for the mediator to become entangled in an argument over whether the husband was a good spouse (which is irrelevant to the task at hand), and directs the couple back to the substantive task of mediation.

Sometimes, the mediation reaches a point at which the disputants, as well as the mediator, gain the capacity to provide "recognition" to one another. Whether the clients have attained this capacity is a judgment call for the mediator, and, if the mediator incorrectly guesses that a disputant is ready to communicate empathically with the other disputant, the results can wreak havoc on the mediation (such as when a disputant who, when called upon to say "I understand your feelings" responds "No way," creating a sense of betrayal and probably escalating the conflict). On the other hand, disputants who are able to communicate a sense of recognition of the other's perspective are often well on their way to leaving emotional baggage behind and achieving a rationally negotiated settlement.

Maintaining Disputant Motivation. The final group of facilitative mediator tactics relate to *maintaining disputant motivation.* Conflict is usually an unpleasant experience, and mediation confers only limited protection from this unpleasantness. Disputants are confronting difficult issues, issues they have not been able to deal with without help. Moreover, interpersonal conflict frequently presents difficult issues of ego and identity repugnant to the disputants. When mediation hits a snag, disputant pessimism often takes over. When enthusiasm flags, a good mediator intervenes to raise the disputants' motivation to continue.

Numerous tactics are used by mediators to maintain or improve disputant motivation. Mediators frequently remind disputants of how far they have come already. If confidence seems to be flagging, many mediators will review the list of partial agreements already made. Mediators will make a practice of praising agreements as they are reached, no matter how minor they seem, mining the discussion for small victories to celebrate. For example, one mediator half-jokingly says that, if confidence seems low, the mediator can suggest an outrageous settlement and, when both disputants attack the mediator's suggestion, the mediator can point out that at least they agree on the idiocy of that option. Mediators frequently remind the disputants of the dismal alternatives to settlement, as well as, in an appropriate case, the potential benefits of being able to keep their relationship going. Mediators will frequently remind the disputants of how far they've come, demonstrating that giving up now would abandon important work they've already done.

EVALUATIVE TACTICS IN MEDIATION

Even evaluative mediators use many of the facilitative tactics we've just discussed. However there are some techniques that are unique to evaluative mediators and some that are used more frequently in this style of mediation:

- Instilling doubt
- Offering opinions about the case (Case Evaluation)
- Caucusing

Instilling doubt
an evaluative mediator tactic, in which the mediator casts doubt on each side's assessment of the merits of its case, in an effort to reduce aspirations and move positions toward a compromise.

Instilling Doubt. An extremely powerful tool in the evaluative mediator's arsenal is known as **instilling doubt.** This tactic consists of identifying overly optimistic BATNA assessments and providing strategic information to lower expectations. (You may recall that BATNA stands for Best Alternative to a Negotiated Agreement, a concept discussed in Chapter 13.) This technique is used heavily in the mediation of many civil and contract legal disputes.

As an example of the technique of instilling doubt, imagine a mediated dispute over a medical malpractice case. Typically, both patient and physician will use case valuation to assess the BATNA. Therefore, the mediator will attack each side's valuation of the case, trying to make each less optimistic. In our imaginary medical malpractice mediation, the mediator might take the patient, and the patient's lawyer, into a private caucus session and question the merits of their case. Perhaps there is an issue of whether the doctor's provision of care did or did not meet the "reasonable physician" standard for physicians in the community. The mediator will place the physician's version of the case in the best possible light in an effort to reduce the patient's expectations about how the litigated case will come out. Subsequently, the mediator will meet with the physician and the lawyer, also in caucus. The mediator might instill doubt by emphasizing the patient's sympathetic demeanor and the horrible disability he was left with. Emphasizing the best aspects of the plaintiff's case, the mediator might argue to the physician and her lawyer that there is a substantial chance of the plaintiff's prevailing on the law and that the typical jury would bend over backward to give this plaintiff a huge judgment to compensate him for his awful injuries.

The technique of instilling doubt makes compromising more likely by reducing the confidence of each disputant in his or her BATNA. If the disputants are bargaining positionally, reducing disputant expectations is essential to overcoming impasse. Instilling doubt can be helpful in dealing with disputants afflicted with the Jackpot Syndrome—in other words, disputants whose highly inflated idea of possible recovery is blinding them to the likelihood that they will lose in court. It is also helpful to lawyers whose clients want them to "gladiate" on their behalf: it allows the lawyer to delegate to the mediator the task of reality-

TWO KINDS OF MEDIATORS

EVALUATIVE   FACILITATIVE

Laurie S. Coltri 2003

testing the merits of the case. Unlike more facilitative techniques, in a case of overly optimistic BATNA evaluations, the instilling doubt tactic is highly efficient at creating quick settlements.

Instilling doubt has some drawbacks as a mediation technique. Because it focuses on the disputant's case and treats the conflict as a zero-sum game, it tends to draw the disputants into a cycle of positional bargaining and competition. And, because it focuses on positions rather than on interests, it draws disputants away from the sort of introspection that creative problem solving requires. Many times, a more facilitative mediator can accomplish the same BATNA-clarification goal by reality-testing, assigning homework in which the disputant gathers information about the case, or referring the disputant to experts.

Obviously, the technique of instilling doubt requires the use of caucusing. If instilling doubt is used in joint session, more often than not the reduction in one disputant's BATNA will produce more optimism on the part of the other disputant. Also, to use this technique effectively, a mediator must be able to claim substantive expertise in the subject matter of the legal dispute. For example, the mediator in our medical malpractice example would have a legitimate claim of being able to instill doubt if she were a trial judge with extensive experience trying medical malpractice cases. A nonlawyer-mediator with terrific credentials in conflict resolution, but no experience with medical malpractice litigation, would have a difficult time convincing the disputants to believe her assessment of their BATNAs.

Offering Opinions About the Case (Case Evaluation). Highly evaluative mediators may go beyond instilling doubt and actually offer an opinion about the likely outcome of the case, were it litigated. Such a mediator may listen to both sides present their cases—almost as if they were presenting opening statements at trial—and then offer an opinion. The opinion may represent a range—"I think it's likely the plaintiff would recover between $25,000 and $35,000"—or be more specific—"I think the case is worth around $30,000." Specific evaluation is often followed with more facilitative tactics: the mediator might then try to help the disputants reach a compromise based on the evaluation. As with the tactic of instilling doubt, the offering of opinions is best done by a mediator who can hold him- or herself out as a substantive authority in the type of case presented by the disputants. This sort of evaluation is frequently offered by mediators who are retired judges.

The function of offering opinions is to narrow the distance between the positions of the disputants by providing a specific estimate of what the litigation alternative would yield. In some cases, the opinion would moderate both disputants' BATNAs; in others, the opinion might be very close to the demands of one of the disputants but distant from the demands of the other. In either case, the goal, similar to that of instilling doubt, is to narrow the distance between BATNAs and to prompt compromising. Unlike instilling doubt, this sort of opinion need not be given in caucus. If presented in caucus, the opinion can be combined with instilling doubt to create a stronger impetus to moderate the BATNA. Such an opinion is also quite useful if both disputants have a strong desire to settle the case, are not particular about the exact nature of the settlement, but are reluctant to lose face by making voluntary concessions. Such disputants can justify their concessions by rationalizing that it was the mediator's idea.

As with instilling doubt, the offering of opinions about case value focuses the disputants on their positions and on the likelihood that their position will prevail, diverting attention away from underlying interests and integrating tactics. As such, pure and transformative mediators argue that this tactic creates a suboptimal mediation process.

Additionally, providing a specific opinion, or range of opinions, may create the appearance of bias if the opinion is substantially closer to the contentions of one disputant than the other:

> Peter has filed an action for medical malpractice against Dinah, an anesthesiologist. They are involved in evaluative mediation before the Honorable Minnie Mediator, a retired judge. Peter presents his contention that his case is worth $1,500,000, and Dinah presents her contention that the case is worthless. Minnie listens to the two statements, discusses the case with each legal team, and reviews documentary evidence prepared by both sides. Minnie comes to the conclusion that Peter's case is extremely weak. She brings the parties back together and conveys her honest opinion, that Peter has a very poor case and will be lucky if he recovers anything in court. She follows her comments with an invitation to both legal teams to engage in some further compromising, so that the disputants can avoid the cost and trauma of litigation.

In such a dispute, when the mediator's opinion is much more in line with the contentions of one disputant, the mediator will have difficulty avoiding the appearance of favoring that disputant, and the mediator, by expressing her opinion about the merits of the case, will appear to be pressuring the party whose contention is further from the mediator's opinion. Such pressure is inconsistent with the primary tenet that mediation be purely voluntary and free of coercion.

Another problem with issuing an opinion, according to business law professor Murray S. Levin of the University of Kansas (Levin 2001), is that such evaluations have little likelihood of accuracy. Professor Levin canvassed the rather sparse research regarding the valuation of legal disputes and found vast discrepancies in valuations even among experienced litigators with objective perspectives on the disputes in question. For example, in one study, a personal injury case that settled for $25,000 was evaluated by five experienced personal injury lawyers for values of $2,500, $3,000, $7,500, $12,000, and $25,000; another personal injury case, which settled for $2,500, was valued by the experts at $7,500, $17,500, $20,000, $22,500, and $40,000 (Levin 2001, 290). Thus, the estimate of a mediator, whose familiarity with the issues is typically less thorough than that of the disputant's legal team (Levin 2001, 295), is not likely to represent an accurate prediction of what would happen if the dispute went to court.

Caucusing. The technique of *caucusing,* or meeting with one side individually and out of earshot of the other side, is used by both evaluative and facilitative mediators. However, since virtually all evaluative mediators caucus,[3] and a significant number of facilitative mediators reject caucusing out of hand, it is considered an evaluative tactic.

It has already been mentioned that caucusing is necessary if the mediator instills doubt. The caucus can also be used to confront disputants about issues that would cause loss of face if dealt with in joint session. Additionally, mediators can use the caucus to perform "backwater" negotiation—that is, informal exploration for information about positions that the disputants do not wish to share with one another or with the general public. For example, in international mediation, the mediator will often meet with world leaders, or their representatives, in caucus to discuss elements of the negotiation (such as concessions of land) that these leaders cannot articulate publicly without loss of face or authority. Caucusing is also used by both facilitative and evaluative mediators to uncover client secrets he or she is uncomfortable articulating in joint session with the other disputant.

Generally, to promote open communication in caucus sessions, the mediator will hold all utterances in caucus confidential unless the disputant explicitly consents to the mediator's sharing the information with the other disputant. Most mediators try to preserve as much perceived impartiality as possible by offering equal time in caucus to each of the disputants.

The reason that many facilitative mediators avoid caucusing is that caucusing does not advance the cause of principled bargaining, which requires honest and open communication between the disputants. Additionally, the caucus process raises trust and mediator bias problems. There is a strong temptation for the individual disputants to try to use the caucus to convince the mediator that his or her side is "right." When trust is low between the disputants (which is typically the case with clients in mediation), disputants, who are aware of their own temptation to co-opt mediator sympathy and assume the other disputant is similarly motivated, will frequently suspect that the other disputant is telling the mediator lies, exaggerations, or half-truths in the caucus. This suspicion undermines the perception of mediator impartiality, further eroding trust between the disputants, and may create meta-disputes. Thus, if the facilitation of principled bargaining, rather than the attainment of settlement, is the principal goal of mediation (as with many pure mediators), the caucus can be counterproductive. These mediators often conclude that the risks of caucusing outweigh the benefits.

---

[3] The technique is so widespread among particular subgroups of mediators that many accounts of the "stages of mediation" include the caucus as a necessary component of the mediation process, yet other mediators never caucus.

EXERCISES, PROJECTS, AND "THOUGHT EXPERIMENTS"

1. *Try active listening.* Choose a partner, preferably someone you don't know. Select a controversial topic you intensely disagree about. (Some examples are abortion, capital punishment, and corporal punishment of children.) Take turns actively listening to one another's opinions on the topic. Take about five to ten minutes for each of you. Then answer the following questions:

   a. How did it feel to be actively listened to? Did you feel that the other person was really listening to you?

   b. Did the experience change your attitude toward the other person? In what way?

   c. Did you get more information about the other person's reasons for feeling the way he or she does? How could this information help you if you were a disputant in negotiation or mediation?

   d. Did the experience change your mind at all about the topic or about the motives of people who disagree with you on that topic?

   e. How could the use of active listening help a mediator?

2. Ronnell, who has an R.N. degree and worked in hospital and physician settings before changing careers, has been working as a paralegal for a number of years and has developed extensive expertise in medical malpractice cases. Ronnell now wishes to change careers again. She obtains the necessary qualifications in her jurisdiction to practice medical malpractice mediation. Reviewing the facilitative and evaluative mediator strategies and tactics presented in this chapter, do you think she should practice facilitative mediation, evaluative mediation, or a mix of the two? Justify your answer.

3. Imagine that you are a paralegal working for a law firm specializing in tort cases. You have decades of experience preparing and assisting in tort litigation. You have volunteered with the local court system to mediate civil actions coming before the court. A case has been referred to you, as mediator, involving a grocery store owner and a woman who slipped and fell in the aisles, breaking a hip. The woman has sued the store for $300,000. Although the case was referred to you by the court system, each side was willing to try to use mediation to resolve the issue. Neither side has legal counsel, and both are begging you to tell how the case would come out if it were sent to court. Is there any harm in your performing this evaluative function? Discuss.

4. Would your answer to question 3 be different if you were an attorney? Why or why not?

5. You are mediating a divorce. In caucus, the husband launches into what promises to be a long tirade against his wife, accusing her of everything from having repeated affairs to picking her nose in public. What do you do?

   a. What are the advantages of allowing the husband to vent these feelings in caucus? (After all, the wife is not there to hear them.) What are the disadvantages? (Hint: if you allow him to ventilate in this way, what would he think about what might transpire in a caucus session between the mediator and the wife?)

b. If you felt the husband's comments should be reined in, how would you do this? What are the advantages of your approach and what are the disadvantages?

c. Is there anything a mediator can do in a joint session to prevent this sort of quandary from arising in the caucus?

6. Many battered-spouse advocates assert that abuse victims should never be required to mediate with their abuser. They cite evidence that victims have been systematically disempowered by the abuser and worry that victims may be threatened with violence if they do not cooperate with the wishes of the abuser during a negotiation. In fact, some abuse victims are assaulted—and killed—in the parking lots of courts where their hearings have been held. On the other hand, there is research to suggest that many former abuse victims are very satisfied with the mediation process and find it to be personally empowering. Discuss the following questions, either orally or in essays:

a. In light of these concerns, how can mediators address the needs of abuse victims?

b. What sort of screening process might be useful in these cases? (Is it likely that a victim, coerced into mediating by an abuser and/or the court system, would reveal this sort of information in a joint session with the abuser looking on?)

c. If the mediator uses a private intervention, such as a caucus session, to gather abuse information and then terminates the mediation upon learning of a history of battering, does the abrupt termination endanger the victim?

d. If an abuse victim asserts that he or she would like to mediate in spite of the history of abuse, should he or she be able to do so? How would the mediator know that this expressed wish to mediate is not the result of coercion or pressure?

e. Should disputants be able to have settlements set aside on the basis of coercion into mediation by abusers, and should mediators be held responsible if this sort of coercion occurs?

7. Choose a kind of legal dispute (for example, medical malpractice or child custody). Write an introduction that you might give clients if you were acting as a mediator in this sort of dispute.

8. Read each of the following descriptions of mediator tactics. For each one, (1) state what is wrong with what the mediator did and (2) propose an improvement:

a. After introductions, the mediator says, "First, let's hear the plaintiff's case."

b. The disputant says, "Harold is worse than a criminal. He lied to me at every turn. He should be prosecuted for criminal fraud." The mediator answers, "I can understand your being mad because he lied to you. But your childish language is totally uncalled for."

c. The mediator in a child custody case says, "We are here to decide who should have custody of Greta."

d. In response to a disputant's comment that the disputants have been able to agree on a settlement amount but not the terms of payment, the mediator says, "So you have a dispute about the terms of payment."

e. Disputants are at impasse. The mediator says, "Let's caucus!"

RECOMMENDED READINGS

Bennett, M. D., and M. S. G. Hermann. 1996. *The art of mediation.* Notre Dame Law School.

Coogler, O. J. 1978. *Structured mediation in divorce settlement.* Lexington, MA: Lexington Books.

Gage, D., D. Martin, and J. Gromala. 1999. Mediation during business formation or reorganization. *Family Business.* (spring). Available from *http://www.mediate.com/articles/formation.cfm.*

Haynes, J. M. 1981. *Divorce mediation.* New York: Springer.

Mosten, F. S. 2003. What happens in mediation? Available from http://www.mediate.com/articles/mosch3.cfm.

Riskin, L. L., and J. E. Westbrook (eds.). 1997. Brief takes on real mediations. In *Dispute resolution and lawyers.* 2d ed. St. Paul, MN: West.

18

The Law and Ethics of Mediation

"In civilized life, law floats in a sea of ethics."

—Earl Warren

In this chapter, you will learn …

- The reasons for the regulation of mediation: to preserve the essence of mediation, to preserve the effectiveness of mediation, and to protect rights that otherwise might be compromised in mediation.
- Why confidentiality is considered an important element of mediation.
- Some of the ways that confidentiality is protected in mediation.
- The circumstances in which confidentiality is often waived or suspended.
- The reasons that mediation is sometimes made mandatory.
- The ways in which disputants are sometimes pressured or coerced to participate in mediation.
- The legal, constitutional, and ethical dilemmas posed by mandatory mediation.
- About the regulation of the unauthorized practice of law by nonlawyer-mediators.
- The ethical dilemmas posed by the provision of legal services by lawyer-mediators.
- About the regulation of the behavior of lawyer-advocates in mediation.
- About the need for mediator impartiality, and about some of the ways that impartiality is currently regulated.
- The kinds of mediator neutrality and their implications for the mediation process.
- About the regulation of mediator qualifications.
- About the legal standing of a mediated agreement and the complications posed by the confidentiality of the mediation process for proof and disproof of a mediated agreement.

INTRODUCTION: WHY REGULATE MEDIATION?

As many mediators often advise their new clients, mediation is a legal event. Although mediation technique is influenced by psychological considerations and sometimes resembles psychotherapy, the endpoint of mediation is usually a legally binding settlement. Moreover, there is a need to protect participants from illegal or unconstitutional effects of mediation that is sponsored by a court or administrative agency.

Early mediation pioneers operated largely in a legal vacuum. The laws of contract were virtually the only legal scaffold on which to build a viable process. But this situation is slowly changing as mediation becomes more widespread and institutionalized. An evolving regulatory structure is developing, primarily from statutory law (including regulations and rules of court and interpreted by decisional authority) and from rules of mediator ethics. Some commentators question whether the direction this evolution is taking is really in the best interests of users of mediation, or whether mediation is being inappropriately adversarialized, depleting it of its advantages in resolving conflict effectively.[1]

The regulation of mediation can be best understood as a series of efforts designed to protect and preserve the essence of the process, to ensure its effectiveness, and to ensure that, as it is used, other legal rights and obligations are not damaged. As we have seen, however, there is much disagreement over the essence of mediation and the definition of good mediation. Moreover, there are differences of opinion over the extent to which society should promote nonadversarial forms of dispute resolution. The more radical wing of the ADR movement argues that the presence of the invisible veil keeps us from truly realizing the promise of mediation. But more traditional elements assert that pushing nonadversarial dispute resolution threatens important individual rights. Because of these diverse voices affecting the mediation movement, the law and ethics of mediation are characterized by a lack of consensus, as well as by a series of tensions between conflicting goals.

Why Is Mediation Regulated?

- ◆ To preserve the essence of mediation
- ◆ To ensure the effectiveness of mediation
- ◆ To protect other legal rights

---

[1] See, for example, Professor Carrie Menkel-Meadow's (1991) excellent discussion in "Pursuing Settlement in an Adversary Culture: A Tale of Innovation Co-opted or 'the Law of ADR,'" *Florida State University Law Review* 19: 1–46 and Professor Kimberlee Kovach's (2001) intriguing "New Wine Requires New Wineskins . . . , *Fordham Urban Law Journal* 28: 935–977.

PRESERVING THE ESSENCE OF MEDIATION

As we have already noted, mediation is such a diverse process that what one practitioner calls "mediation" can be almost unrecognizable to a colleague (Kovach & Love 1996; Riskin 1994).[2] Nonetheless, practitioners, users, and scholars of ADR have been able to agree on the following two essential characteristics of mediation:

1. A third-party mediator must be involved.
2. Mediation is characterized by disputant self-determination.

It is easy to determine whether there is a third-party intermediary involved in a dispute resolution process, although whether a given intermediary is correct to refer to his or her services as mediation is sometimes controversial. Little regulation exists—as yet—to control mediator "truth in advertising," although some glimmerings of this sort of regulation are beginning to appear.[3]

The second element of the essence of mediation, the need for self-determination, has been the topic of far more controversy among both mediation scholars and policymakers. Self-determination is the right of disputants to control the mediation and/or the outcome of the mediation. Self-determination is generally regarded as "the fundamental principle of mediation" (ABA/SPIDR Model Standards of Conduct for Mediators, Section I A; Welsh 2001b).

Essence-of-Mediation Issues

Participation of Mediator
- Impartiality and neutrality
- Truth in advertising and client-informed consent to the process

Client Self-determination
- Compulsion to mediate
- Need for informed consent
- Sources of legal advice
- Distinguishing of mediation from evaluative ADR

Preservation of Mediation as a Nonadversarial Process
- Confidentiality in mediation

---

[2] For example, the professional literature contains discussions by prominent scholars in the field over whether to call evaluative mediation "mediation" at all (Kovach & Love 1996, Riskin 1994, and Zumeta 2000). Some processes labeled *mediation* are, in fact, nonbinding arbitration.

[3] For example, in a recent state mediator ethics case (Florida Mediator Qualifications Advisory Board, Ethics Op. 95-007, 1995), a mediator was chastised for advertising that the client could obtain a dispassionate case evaluation by using the service.

It is generally agreed that forcing an outcome on disputants is inimicable to self-determination and results in a process of adjudication, not mediation. However, more controversial is whether penalizing the disputants for failing to come to a settlement violates the essence of informed consent. Still more difficult is the issue of whether, and to what extent, disputants can be compelled to participate in mediation and pressured to come to a settlement (Welsh 2001b). These incursions into self-determination are commonly justified by considerations of short-term efficacy and efficiency in resolving disputes and conserving judicial resources.

An additional problem with disputant self-determination is the extent to which it requires that disputants understand the legal consequences of their actions. The legal field interprets the concept of self-determination to mean "informed consent." Informed consent means, essentially, having all the information one needs to consent to an action. In practice, informed consent in mediation may refer to many things, including the need for the client to understand the nature of the dispute resolution process in which he or she is involved, as well as the consequences of various process and outcome choices.

There is an important difference between informed consent as understood by the legal community, and self-determination as understood by the mediation community. In the domain of legal ethics, *informed consent* refers to being informed about the likely success of one's claim, should it be litigated. Although there is little argument between lawyers and mediators that disputants should understand the legal *consequences* of their agreements in order to make effective choices about their settlement, making a *prediction about the outcome* of litigation involving the legal dispute goes a step further—it is information critical to the analysis of the BATNA (see Chapter 13). Is knowing one's BATNA essential to self-determination, or is it merely useful in negotiating effectively? Many lawyers and law professors, such as Professor Jacqueline Nolan-Haley (1999), assert that knowledge of the likely outcome of litigation is synonymous with informed consent, and, to the extent that mediation fails to provide such information, unjust results are likely. However, others argue that knowing the litigation alternative is not relevant to self-determination unless the disputants wish to adopt legal norms and practices as their index of fairness. As many mediators are aware, there are disputants who don't wish to use legal principles to guide them in making a fair agreement, nor are they concerned about knowing the litigation alternative to clarify their BATNA, even after these uses of the information are explained to them. Are such disputants negotiating without informed consent, or are they exercising their right to self-determination? Consider the following example:

> An unmarried couple, John and Barbara, entered mediation because they were breaking up and wished to settle issues of jointly held property. Both were articulate, sophisticated, and well-read clients in their late forties and had grown children from previous marriages. The couple decided that property held in their joint names should be divided 50 percent to Barbara and 40 percent to John, with 10 percent donated to a respected charity. This decision was a compromise between Barbara's assertion that John had wasted

their money during the relationship and John's position that assets should be divided equally. The mediator, aware of the developing law in his jurisdiction regarding property held by unmarried couples, suggested that each of them get legal advice about how the property dispute might be resolved in court. To persuade the clients of the usefulness of getting legal advice, the mediator commented on the litigation alternative as useful information as to the ideas of fairness expounded in the law. The mediator commented that the disputants were free to adopt this notion of fairness but were not required to do so. The mediator also explained the concept of the BATNA to them and posed the following hypothetical: "How would you feel if you made the agreement you're leaning toward now but later learned, that if you had gone to court, you could have gotten 80 percent of the property instead?" For both John and Barbara, the response was immediate and unhesitating. "We don't care," both exclaimed. "We think our agreement is fair."

Some would argue that John and Barbara lacked the informed consent necessary to make a fair agreement. But others would respond that, although John and Barbara didn't know their BATNA, they exercised self-determination in developing shared norms and principles (Welsh 2001b) for arriving at settlement and in deciding that knowing their respective BATNAs was irrelevant to them (see Waldman 1997). Critics might also argue that disputants who lacked John and Barbara's sophistication might not appreciate the merits of knowing one's BATNA and the relationship of the BATNA to receiving legal advice.

The tension between informed consent and the larger concept of self-determination is articulated in the regulation of how legal advice is provided to mediating clients. This regulation occurs through limitations placed on evaluative mediation and the regulation of conduct considered the practice of law by mediators. More will be said about this issue later in the chapter.

Another self-determination issue relates to the provision of evaluative mediation services under the "mediation" name. It seems self-evident that, the more options are provided to clients, the greater is their the ability to exercise self-determination. On the other hand, given the prevalence of the invisible veil, a strong counterargument can be made: unless mediation is defined in the public arena as a clear alternative to the more position-bound process that evaluative mediation represents, potential disputants will reflexively choose evaluative mediation and never reach the point of choosing the alternative. According to this argument, evaluative mediation should be recognized as the oxymoron that it is (Kovach & Love 1996), that such processes be given a name to distinguish them from "actual" mediation, and evaluative tactics be prohibited from the practice of "actual" mediation. In the words of Kimberly Kovach,

> to allow a number of different activities to be called "mediation" only confuses the issue. If this practice is continued, lawyers will never distinguish between the processes, and mediation will lose all potential to establish a different paradigm for resolving disputes. (Kovach 1997, 583, n. 50)

Many other issues addressed in this chapter are tied in with the goal of preserving self-determination in mediation, such as the need for the mediator to act impartially and the extent of lawyer participation in mediation. The role of self-determination in guiding the regulation of mediation in these areas is unclear. Consider, for example, the issue of lawyer participation in mediation. A policymaker who interprets the principle of self-determination to mean that disputants should autonomously develop their own norms, principles, and agreement terms would likely advocate minimizing, or even prohibiting, the participation of lawyers in mediation sessions. A different policymaker, who equates self-determination with informed consent, might make the opposite decision and require that parties be represented by lawyers during sessions.

The issue of mediation's confidentiality, although appropriately considered necessary for a mediation effectiveness, may also be seen as central to the preservation of mediation's essence. Confidentiality is often seen as a precondition for open, honest, and free communication between the disputants. If mediation is viewed as a nonadversarial alternative to competitive processes of conflict resolution, then confidentiality is critical: it ensures that such communication will not be used later as part of an adversarial strategy. Additionally, if mediation is viewed as a process for facilitating principled bargaining or collaboration between the disputants, confidentiality is essential to mediation's goals, since collaboration is impossible without open and honest communication about interests.

Ensuring the Effectiveness of Mediation

Mediation is also regulated to ensure its effectiveness; however, here also controversy and uncertainty abound. One area of controversy concerns the nature of "effectiveness." You may recall the discussion of good conflict and bad conflict in Chapter 3. Assessing mediation's effectiveness in producing good conflict depends on your point of view. One common approach to this question is to consider whether settlement has been reached and how much time and money it has taken to reach it. This short-term, "efficiency" approach suggests a much different set of regulations than an approach that considers the long-term impact of mediation on the overall interactions of the disputants and their overall abilities to deal with conflicts. Indeed, regulating mediation to promote short-term efficiency leads to a much different regulatory structure than regulating mediation to promote long-term social change. For example, a policymaker wishing to promote short-term efficiency goals would be tempted to promote evaluative and coercive mediation practices, which are regarded as taking less time, whereas one trying to promote a more nonadversarial approach to disputes in general might outlaw evaluative mediation altogether, or at least strongly promote more facilitative practices.

Perhaps the most important regulatory issue that springs from the motivation to ensure effectiveness relates to the confidentiality of mediation. It is the

> ### *Mediation Effectiveness Issues*
>
> ◆ Perspectives on effectiveness: short- vs. long-term and broad vs. narrow
> ◆ Confidentiality
> ◆ Enforceability of settlement
> ◆ Construing settlement agreement
> ◆ Good-faith participation
> ◆ Ensuring competent mediators:
>   ◆ Regulating credentialing, competence, behavior
>   ◆ Suspending confidentiality to deal with malpractice issues

consensus of most mediation scholars and practitioners that, for mediation to work well, it must be confidential, for reasons that will be discussed later in this chapter. However, to ensure that disputants are participating in mediation in good faith, to ensure that the mediator is behaving competently and ethically, to ensure that any agreements reached in mediation are being enforced appropriately and are not the result of fraud or duress, and to ensure that violations of the law are not occurring during the mediation process, various efforts have been made to limit confidentiality in mediation. For example some jurisdictions have considered enacting rules that would require or permit sanctions against mediation participants, who fail to mediate in good faith. To make such rules work, it would be necessary to compel or permit participants to testify about what has transpired during mediation in (see "The Duty to Participate In Good Faith"). Confidentiality is one of the most unsettled areas of mediation law.

Effectiveness in mediation is also promoted through the regulation of mediator credentialing, competence, and conduct. This effort is largely via ethical rules developed by professional ADR societies, although the ethical precepts of associated professions and a developing body of statutory law also affect the area. The behavior of others who participate in mediation, such as attorneys, is also subject to regulation, although it is primarily through pre-existing professional ethical precepts, such as attorney codes of ethics, not specifically applicable to mediation. These codes are beginning to evolve to accommodate the special needs of clients involved in mediation.

PROTECTING OTHER RIGHTS

The third major reason for the regulation of mediation is to protect the rights held by the participants in mediation and others affected by the process. For example, advocates for battered women worry that compelling them to participate

---

Protecting Other Rights

Due Process Considerations
- ◆ Limitations on coercion in mediation
- ◆ Informed consent
- ◆ Lifting of confidentiality to protect the right to give evidence in other proceedings

Safety Issues
- ◆ Mediation in abuse situations

Conflict with Other Rights
- ◆ Confidentiality of mediation involving the government: effects of laws rendering proceedings open to the public

---

in mediation with their abusers (for example, to resolve assault cases) may create physical dangers to the victims as they confront those who may have assaulted them.

There is a tension between mediation effectiveness concerns and the desire to protect other legal rights. For example, if mediation is made compulsory for certain kinds of disputes, the risk exists that certain due process rights—most notably, the right to have one's civil claims adjudicated pursuant to an adversary procedure—may be inappropriately compromised.

LEGAL ISSUES IN MEDIATION

The need to preserve essential aspects of the mediation process, and to preserve and promote the effectiveness of mediation, has led to efforts to regulate mediation in a number of areas. These include confidentiality; coercive or mandatory aspects of mediation; the regulation of conduct regarded as the practice of law performed by mediators; conduct of legal advocates during mediation; mediator impartiality, neutrality, and competency; and the enforceability of mediated agreements.

CONFIDENTIALITY

Most kinds of mediation are held in a confidential setting; that is, secrets revealed or communications made in mediation can't be shared with others or used in litigation.[4] Confidentiality is invoked because it is believed that disputants won't feel as free to communicate openly with one another if they believe that what they say or reveal might be used against them. Moreover, the

---

[4] A notable exception occurs in some governmental and administrative hearings subject to mediation. In these disputes, so-called sunshine laws mandate that the sessions are public. See "Conflict with Another Explicit Law."

quality of mediation as a cooperative process could be compromised if disputants believed that communications in mediation would be the subject of discovery or trial tactics later on. Additionally, confidentiality is needed to preserve the neutrality of the mediator: disputants participating in mediation need to be reassured that the mediator will not testify against them later. Additionally, some disputants, such as large corporations with goodwill and an image to protect, choose mediation over a more public dispute resolution process, so that their privacy can be protected.

Many relationships between professionals and their clients are confidential. These include the physician-patient relationship, the lawyer-client relationship, the priest-penitent relationship, and the therapist-client relationship, just to name a few. These relationships are confidential by law: typically, a common-law rule enhanced by statutes confirming or clarifying the common law establish the confidentiality of these relationships and protect parties to the relationship from being required to reveal the substance of communications.[5] The mediator-client relationship, by contrast, has no common-law basis of confidentiality, and there is a growing, but spotty and inconsistent, statutory confidentiality law. Something that distinguishes the mediation situation from that of other confidential relationships is the fact that there are two clients, with diverse interests, involved. In other confidential relationships, the client is typically free to waive confidentiality (for example, when a patient requests copies of his or her medical records and chooses to make them public). In mediation, one client's wish to end secrecy may be opposed by the other. Moreover, even if both clients consent to waiving confidentiality, many mediators assert that confidentiality should nonetheless continue. They argue that it would compromise the integrity of the overall profession if disputants knew, upon entering mediation, that, if the clients were later involved in litigation, they could, by mutual consent, compel the mediator to serve as a weapon.

Early in the mediation movement, there were two principal sources of confidentiality in mediation: law providing for the inadmissibility of compromise negotiations and specific contracts specifying that mediation be confidential. The law of inadmissibility of settlement negotiations has both statutory and common-law sources. In legal disputes before federal court, Rule 408 of the Federal Rules of Evidence, which has been used as a model for similar statutes in many states,[6] makes evidence of conduct or statements made in the course of settlement negotiations inadmissible for the purpose of proving the validity or invalidity of the claim sought to be settled:

> Rule 408. Compromise and Offers to Compromise. Evidence of (1) furnishing or offering or promising to furnish, or (2) accepting or offering or promising to accept, a valuable consideration in compromising or attempting to compromise a claim which was disputed as to either validity

---

[5] Typically, there are exceptions to confidentiality based on the need to protect children and other possible victims from harm, such as when parents admit in confidence that they have been abusing their children.
[6] See, for example, North Dakota Rules of Evidence, Rule 408; Texas Rules of Civil Evidence 408; Pennsylvania Rules of Evidence, Rule 408.

or amount, is not admissible to prove liability for or invalidity of the claim or its amount. Evidence of conduct or statements made in compromise negotiations is likewise not admissible. This rule does not require the exclusion of any evidence otherwise discoverable merely because it is presented in the course of compromise negotiations. This rule also does not require exclusion when the evidence is offered for another purpose, such as proving bias or prejudice of a witness, negativing a contention of undue delay, or proving an effort to obstruct a criminal investigation or prosecution.

This statute codifies the general common law rule (Fed. R. Ev. 408, Notes of Advisory Committee). Since mediation is a form of assisted settlement negotiation, such rules provide some confidentiality protection for mediation. However, there are four significant limitations to this protection. First, the rule is confined to the exclusion of offers of compromise, not to all communications made during settlement discussion. Thus, other communications, such as assertions of fact and claims, are not considered confidential. Second, the protection afforded by settlement discussion rules is limited to preventing admissibility in litigation and does not make the communication confidential—that is, protected against any disclosure. Third, such a rule does not specify who possesses the privilege to claim confidentiality of a communication (Rogers & McEwen 1989, §8.4). Fourth, the rule specifically allows the admission of such communications if for a purpose other than to prove or disprove a claim—such as the impeachment of a witness at trial.

Because of the uncertainty in the law of confidentiality in mediation, many mediators have required their clients to sign contracts making the mediation process confidential. It is important to be aware that these contracts do not bind third parties if they decide to subpoena disputants or mediators to testify in court. For example, if a mediating disputant reveals evidence relevant to a non-participant's lawsuit, a contract binding the mediating participants to confidentiality would not prevent the non-participant's attorney from subpoenaing the mediator or another mediating participant to testify. These contracts may also be limited beyond their explicit terms by social policy considerations—for example, if a disputant wishes to admit the statement of another participant to help him or her defend against a criminal charge.[7]

The absence of confidentiality protection of mediation is gradually being rectified: more focused efforts to codify confidentiality for mediation are underway. Kentra (1997) reported that, by the year 1997, statutes or court rules mandating some sort of confidentiality or privilege for statements made during mediation were in effect in all fifty states and all federal agencies with ADR processes.[8] Many of these statutes, however, protect communication only in the mediation of certain varieties of disputes (Kentra 1997, app.), meaning that

---

[7] See, for example *Rinaker v. Superior Court,* 62 Cal. App. 4th 155 (1998), relating to juvenile proceedings. See "To Uphold the Administration of Justice."

[8] The federal government can now be included among these jurisdictions. The Federal Administrative Dispute Resolution Act of 1996 (5 U.S.C.A. §§571 *et seq.*) does contain a provision guaranteeing confidentiality for mediation occurring under its auspices in federal agencies.

A Sample of a Mediator's Confidentiality Contract

To protect the integrity of the mediation process and promote full and complete disclosure between us, we, the mediator and the mediation participants, agree that communications made during mediation are to be considered "privileged" ("confidential") and will not be shared or used outside of mediation. Although it is understood that certain matters may be wished to be shared with lawyers, counselors, and so on, it is the responsibility of the individual sharing the information to assure that the communication or its contents not be shared outside the scope of the confidential relationship between the person and the helping professional.

It is a breach of this contract to disclose, or to require disclosure, either directly or indirectly through third persons such as attorneys, any communication or information that is subject to the privilege. It is intended that this agreement can be enforced by court injunction, including expedited process, where the legal requirements for relief are otherwise met.

Information that was not private before mediation does not become so simply because it is also shared in mediation. Also, the privilege for a given communication is lost in the following circumstances:

- Where all the persons signing this Confidentiality Agreement agree that a particular communication should not be privileged and confidential;
- Where disclosure is necessary in a court action presenting a nonfrivolous claim of mediator misconduct. In such case, loss of confidentiality shall be limited to evidence actually relevant or necessary either to prove the claim or to defend it. In the event that such an action is filed, the plaintiff shall immediately notify the other parties to this agreement, who shall be entitled to intervene in the action for the purpose of protecting their rights under this agreement.
- Where the mediator learns of possible abuse or risk of abuse of a child. Pursuant to Maryland law, professionals dealing with families are required to notify appropriate public authorities (such as Child Protective Services) in such an instance. If this issue presents itself, the mediator's policy is to first give the mediation participant an opportunity to contact public authorities themselves if it would not place the child/ren involved at increased risk.

Waiver of the privilege of confidentiality with respect to a given communication does not create a waiver of the privilege for any other communication.

Caution: Under current law, this agreement may not protect its signers from attempts to compel the disclosure of privileged information by a person other than a signer or his or her legal representative. For example, a governmental organization, such as a district or state's attorney, is not legally prevented by this agreement from compelling evidence of criminal behavior disclosed by a mediation client. No representation is intended regarding the effects of procedural rules intended to apply to court-connected mediation on this private mediation process.

Nothing in this agreement shall be construed to limit or narrow the rights of the mediator or of either party to confidentiality in mediation as otherwise prescribed by law.

We, the mediation participants and the mediator, have read and understand the provisions of this agreement. We agree to abide by it and to protect the confidentiality of the mediation process in which we will be involved.

(signatures and dates follow)

other kinds of cases are left unregulated. A disputant, a mediator, or an advocate must therefore research the availability and applicability of these statutes to specific cases and must work to keep abreast of a fluid and constantly evolving area of law. In addition to statutory and other regulatory sources of confidentiality rules, mediator ethical standards also provide for the confidentiality of the mediation process. Moreover, certain statutes and court rules allow courts to create a common-law privilege for certain relationships. One such rule, which has been used to develop a common-law mediation privilege, is the Federal Rules of Evidence, Rule 501. This rule has been used by the federal court to create a federal common law mediation privilege. (See *Folb v. Motion Picture Industry Pension & Health Plans,* 16 F. Supp. 2d 1164, D.C. Cal., 1998.)

Waiver of Confidentiality. Statutes and court rules, as interpreted by decisional law, provide for waiver of confidentiality in particular circumstances. Professor Carol Izumi of George Washington University Law School summarized waiver situations as follows (Feerick et al. 1995):

- Consent of the participants
- Mediator malpractice or malfeasance claim or defense
- Protection of the mediation process
- Matter to be revealed not confidential to begin with
- Evidence of a crime or child abuse/neglect
- To uphold the administration of justice
- Confidentiality in conflict with another explicit law

Consent of the Participants. Most, if not all, rules regarding confidentiality allow the secrecy to be lifted if the participants in mediation consent. However, confidentiality rules differ as to who possesses the *privilege* of raising a defense of confidentiality. In the federal district court case of *Olam v. Congress Mortgage Company,* 68 F. Supp. 2d 1110 (N.D. Cal., 1999),[9] in which both parties, but not the mediator, waived confidentiality; the mediator was compelled to testify to mediation communications that were considered relevant to proving whether the settlement was made under duress. In contrast, in the Model Uniform Mediation Act, adopted in August 2001, the mediator is explicitly required to provide a separate waiver before he or she can be compelled to testify in such circumstances. Rules of ethics, such as the Model Standards of Conduct for Mediators, often speak of the mediator's need to respect the other participants' expectations concerning confidentiality. The Society for Professionals in Dispute Resolution (SPIDR, an organization now merged into the Association for Conflict Resolution) Ethical Standards of Professional Responsibility provides, in relevant part, the following:

> Maintaining confidentiality is critical to the dispute resolution process. Confidentiality encourages candor, a full exploration of the issues, and a neutral's acceptability. There may be some types of cases, however, in which

---

[9] Although a trial court case, *Olam* is considered particularly important because its author, the Honorable Wayne Brazil, is a notable proponent and scholar of mediation; hence, his decision to lift confidentiality in these circumstances has been regarded as particularly noteworthy.

confidentiality is not protected. In such cases, the neutral must advise the parties, when appropriate in the dispute resolution process, that the confidentiality of the proceedings cannot necessarily be maintained. Except in such instances, the neutral must resist all attempts to cause him or her to reveal any information outside the process. A commitment by the neutral to hold information in confidence within the process also must be honored. (SPIDR Ethics Committee 1986, section 3).

Ethical standards impose on the mediator the obligation to clarify and protect confidentiality to mediation participants, but they do not empower the mediator to claim it as a privilege.

Malpractice or Malfeasance Claim or Defense. Confidentiality in mediation, and in other ADR processes that feature intervention by a third-party neutral, is generally suspended in situations in which disclosure is required either to prove or to defend against an action against the mediator for malpractice or other misconduct. This exception appears to have been widely accepted in the legal and mediation community, and, due to the lack of mediator malpractice cases, it has not yet come under significant judicial scrutiny.

Protection of the Mediation Process. Revelation that is needed "to protect the mediation process" has proven to be a very problematic exception to confidentiality, since many ADR professionals would contend that airtight confidentiality is, in itself, essential to the protection of the mediation process.

Confidentiality is sometimes waived to ensure that those participating in mediation do so in good faith. ADR commentators note that, if disputants fail to mediate in good faith, the essence of the process is corrupted. However, confidentiality is endangered by attempts to enforce such a duty. To enforce the duty of good faith participation, the substance of the mediation must often be revealed in a subsequent adversary proceeding to determine whether the duty was breached.

The following is an example of how such an exception to confidentiality could inflict lasting damage on a mediation program:

> Fred, a federal worker, and Barry, his supervisor, enter agency-sponsored mediation to resolve their workplace dispute. Fred contends that Barry has had it in for him and is subjecting him to harassment based on his sexual preference. Barry asserts that Fred is a "hothead" and that, in addition to doing his work poorly, he has alienated everyone else in the office. It is obvious to the mediator that these disputants frame the conflict completely differently and that their mutual hostility is extreme. After three hours of mediation, no progress is made, and the mediation ends.
>
> Thereafter, Fred files an Equal Employment Opportunity Commission (EEOC) grievance proceeding. The case enters an adjudication phase. Barry seeks sanctions for Fred's failure to participate meaningfully in mediation and seeks to introduce various mediation communications into the proceeding to support his claim. Barry claims that Fred took very extreme

positions, which he knew Barry could never agree to, and that, hence, his participation in mediation was a sham. The court allows the information to enter the proceeding, commenting that Fred had a legal duty to mediate in good faith, which was violated, and awards Barry attorney's fees for the failed mediation.

Others at the agency get wind of the adjudication pending between Barry and Fred, and employment lawyers begin to counsel their clients about the option of threatening to assert failure to participate in good faith as leverage in mediation. They begin to counsel their clients to be careful about what they reveal during mediation, since what they say may be used against them in a later adjudication. Agency mediators become less facilitative, since their attention is taken up more with determining which disputants are mediating in bad faith. As a result, mediation at this agency becomes less and less successful in resolving employment disputes. As the situation continues to evolve, it becomes common knowledge among employment attorneys that mediation at this agency is simply another useless bureaucratic impediment to getting to an EEOC adjudication.[10]

In practice, states have come out both ways in their attempts to resolve this issue. In *Foxgate Homeowner's Association, Inc., v. Bramalea,* 26 Cal. 4th 1 (2001), the California Supreme Court held that the mediator could not be called upon to recount communications uttered during mediation to prove, or disprove, the good faith participation of one of the parties. (The court commented that the mediator could be called upon to testify to "conduct," such as whether parties with settlement authority had attended the mediation sessions.) On the other hand, in *Olam vs. Congress Mortgage Company,* confidentiality was deemed lifted in a situation in which one disputant claimed that the other had committed fraud during the mediation session in inducing her to settle. (It may have been determinative that the disputants in the *Olam* court had both consented to waiver and that the mediator was the only person opposing admission of the evidence in question.) Both decisions were purportedly based on the same confidentiality statute.

The California confidentiality statute upon which both the *Foxgate* and *Olam* decisions were based did not explicitly recognize a "protect the mediation process" exception to confidentiality, but many other state statutes do. Arizona has a statute that allows confidentiality to be waived if necessary to enforce the agreement to mediate, Wyoming allows waiver if necessary to enforce a mediated agreement, and North Dakota allows waiver to prove the validity of the settlement (Feerick et al. 1995).

Matter to Be Revealed Not Confidential to Begin With. Most mediation confidentiality rules provide that one cannot make something a secret merely by bringing it into mediation. Such an exception is universal: virtually everyone agrees that one should not be able to render something a secret merely by bringing it into

---

[10] An excellent discussion of this issue is found in Alfini and McCabe (2001).

A Powerful Confidentiality Provision

The State of Texas is considered to have a relatively powerful confidentiality rule with relatively few exceptions. Following are some relevant excerpts from the Texas Alternative Dispute Resolution Act, Tex. Civ. Prac. & Remedies C., §§154.001 *et seq.*:

§154.053:

(b) Unless expressly authorized by the disclosing party, the impartial third party may not disclose to either party information given in confidence by the other and shall at all times maintain confidentiality with respect to communications relating to the subject matter of the dispute.

(c) Unless the parties agree otherwise, all matters, including the conduct and demeanor of the parties and their counsel during the settlement process, are confidential and may never be disclosed to anyone, including the appointing court.

§154.073:

(a) Except as provided by Subsections (c) and (d), a communication relating to the subject matter of any civil or criminal dispute made by a participant in an alternative dispute resolution procedure, whether before or after the institution of formal judicial proceedings, is confidential, is not subject to disclosure, and may not be used as evidence against the participant in any judicial or administrative proceeding.

(b) Any record made at an alternative dispute resolution procedure is confidential, and the participants or the third party facilitating the procedure may not be required to testify in any proceedings relating to or arising out of the matter in dispute or be subject to process requiring disclosure of confidential information or data relating to or arising out of the matter in dispute.

(c) An oral communication or written material used in or made a part of an alternative dispute resolution procedure is admissible or discoverable if it is admissible or discoverable independent of the procedure.

(d) If this section conflicts with other legal requirements for disclosure of communications or materials, the issue of confidentiality may be presented to the court having jurisdiction of the proceedings to determine, in camera, whether the facts, circumstances, and context of the communications or materials sought to be disclosed warrant a protective order of the court or whether the communications or materials are subject to disclosure.

The limited scope of the exceptions to confidentiality in this statute is typical of "expansive" confidentiality rules. Most notably, there is an absence of exceptions that allow a wide degree of judicial discretion, such as exceptions to prevent injustice.

---

mediation. Thus, originally nonconfidential documents, provided to the other participants as part of the mediation process, are generally admissible in court.

Evidence of a Crime or Child Abuse/Neglect. In general, many states have statutes that explicitly require professionals in confidential relationships to suspend confidentiality when a party has indicated that he or she intends to commit a crime, or when a party has indicated a likelihood of ongoing abuse or neglect of a child, warranting intervention.

To Uphold the Administration of Justice. Occasionally, the need for confidentiality in mediation is deemed overcome by a more critical need for its disclosure. For example, in *Rinaker v. Superior Court.* 62 Cal. App. 4th 155 (1998), a juvenile defendant wanted to admit into his trial a confidential communication made in mediation that he contended was exculpatory (that is, it tended to prove his innocence). The appellate court ruled that the communication was admissible. The court ruled that due process considerations required the juvenile to be able to introduce exculpatory communications.[11] In contrast, in *Williams v. State,* 770 S. W. 2d 948 (Tex. App. 1989), the government was prevented from having *in*culpatory evidence from an ADR proceeding admitted to *support* a criminal conviction.

Confidentiality has also been held to have been waived where necessary to prove or disprove the enforceability of a mediated settlement, as in *Olam*. A contrary result was reached under Texas law in *Smith v. Smith,* 154 F.R.D. 661 (N.D. Texas, 1994), but the *Olam* case concerned a mediator who claimed the privilege despite waiver by both disputants, whereas the *Smith* case concerned a dispute in which only some of the disputants wanted the privilege waived.

Considerations of justice might also be deemed to require that confidentiality be lifted if fraud occurred during the mediation session. Consider the following example:

> Erica is mediating a dispute over the dissolution of a live-in relationship. During one session, one of the partners, Amelia, a chief executive officer at a medium-sized real estate holding company, states that she put all of her wages into the couple's joint checking account, which was used for household expenses. On the basis of that assertion, the other partner, Jessica, a graduate student, who also contributed half her wages to the joint account, agrees to a dissolution agreement that specifies that one-half of the couple's monetary assets would go to each of them. After mediation, Jessica learns that Amelia secretly banked one-third of her wages in a separate account.

There's a compelling argument that Jessica should be able to get the agreement they reached in mediation set aside on the basis of fraud by Amelia. To prove the fraud, Jessica would have to be allowed to lift confidentiality to show how the fraud occurred. However, arguments over the enforceability of contracts are seldom this clear-cut. When one disputant's allegation of fraud is met by a counterassertion that "I didn't lie; you just didn't hear what I said," the argument that confidentiality should be waived is more difficult to sustain. In the final analysis, many disputes over the meaning of a contract can be framed as a misrepresentation by one of the disputants. Mediation advocates are concerned that allowing into court evidence about what went on in mediation in order to prove whether one of the disputants misled the other would swamp mediation as a confidential process.

A very difficult situation arises when a mediator presiding over an attorney-assisted mediation witnesses attorney misconduct. If a mediator reveals the behavior, confidentiality is violated and the mediator may lose neutrality in the case; however, if the mediator maintains confidentiality, the unethical behavior may wreak havoc. For example, in *In Re Waller,* 573 A .2d 780 (D.C. 1990), Waller, the attorney for a malpractice plaintiff, had filed suit against a hospital, but not the surgeon who had performed an allegedly negligent procedure. In mediation, Waller revealed to the mediator that he represented the surgeon as well as the plaintiff. Recognizing the significant disadvantage in which Waller had placed the

---

[11] The court did rule that the defendant was required to make an in camera (out of the public eye) proffer to the court so that relevance and admissibility could be predetermined.

plaintiff, the mediator tried to convince the attorney to name the surgeon in the complaint and, failing that, to self-report his conflict of interest to the court. When Waller failed to do either, the mediator revealed the communication to the judge himself, despite the fact that the revelation violated a court order in the case:

> that no statements of any party or counsel shall be disclosed to the court or admissible as evidence for any purpose at the trial of this case . . . *Waller, supra,* 573 A.2d at 781.

If the mediator is also an attorney (as was the mediator in the *Waller* case), the duty to maintain confidentiality may clash directly with the lawyer's ethical duty to report the misconduct (Kentra 1997). The DC court handling the *Waller* incident chose not to discipline the mediator, despite the absence of legal rules allowing the mediator to violate confidentiality. A few states expressly exempt such communications from confidentiality in mediation. For example, Minnesota Statutes, §595.02(n)(1a) provides

> Alternative dispute resolution privilege. No person presiding at any alternative dispute resolution proceeding established pursuant to law, court rule, or by an agreement to mediate, shall be competent to testify, in any subsequent civil proceeding or administrative hearing, as to any statement, conduct, decision, or ruling, occurring at or in conjunction with the prior proceeding, except as to any statement or conduct that could:
> (1) constitute a crime;
> (2) give rise to disqualification proceedings under the rules of professional conduct for attorneys; or
> (3) constitute professional misconduct.

However, Minnesota is the exception: by and large, this situation is not dealt with directly by mediation laws.

Conflict with Another Explicit Law. Mediation confidentiality sometimes conflicts with another explicit law, and in such a case, an exception to confidentiality is often carved out. This sort of exception is important in mediation involving the government as a party, as in the mediation of environmental disputes and the mediation of antitrust violations, where so-called "sunshine laws" may mandate that the proceedings be public. Such a rule may ultimately prove troublesome in cases in which there is no obvious or express intent to supersede confidentiality provisions (as in the attorney misconduct situation previously mentioned).

No thorough review of the confidentiality of the mediation process is possible in a text of this nature: this discussion is intended merely to provide an idea of the nature and scope of the law of confidentiality as it is presently evolving and how existing law is attempting to address tensions among the diverse goals of practitioners and users of mediation. Every professional involved in mediation must stay abreast of legal developments in his or her jurisdiction and field to remain current about the state of mediation confidentiality.

A Modest Confidentiality Provision

The Administrative Dispute Resolution Act of 1996, 5 U.S.C.A. §§571 *et seq.,* requires that each federal agency adopt ADR processes to resolve disputes with employees, clients, and the public. The act, which applies to *all* forms of ADR, contains a relatively modest confidentiality provision, §574. Following are subsections (a) and (b):

(a) Except as provided in subsections (d) and (e), a neutral in a dispute resolution proceeding shall not voluntarily disclose or through discovery or compulsory process be required to disclose any dispute resolution communication or any communication provided in confidence to the neutral, unless—

(1) all parties to the dispute resolution proceeding and the neutral consent in writing, and, if the dispute resolution communication was provided by a nonparty participant, that participant also consents in writing;

(2) the dispute resolution communication has already been made public;

(3) the dispute resolution communication is required by statute to be made public, but a neutral should make such communication public only if no other person is reasonably available to disclose the communication; or

(4) a court determines that such testimony or disclosure is necessary to—

(A) prevent a manifest injustice;

(B) help establish a violation of law; or

(C) prevent harm to the public health or safety, of sufficient magnitude in the particular case to outweigh the integrity of dispute resolution proceedings in general by reducing the confidence of parties in future cases that their communications will remain confidential.

(b) A party to a dispute resolution proceeding shall not voluntarily disclose or through discovery or compulsory process be required to disclose any dispute resolution communication, unless—

(1) the communication was prepared by the party seeking disclosure;

(2) all parties to the dispute resolution proceeding consent in writing;

(3) the dispute resolution communication has already been made public;

(4) the dispute resolution communication is required by statute to be made public;

(5) a court determines that such testimony or disclosure is necessary to—

(A) prevent a manifest injustice;

(B) help establish a violation of law; or

(C) prevent harm to the public health and safety, of sufficient magnitude in the particular case to outweigh the integrity of dispute resolution proceedings in general by reducing the confidence of parties in future cases that their communications will remain confidential;

(6) the dispute resolution communication is relevant to determining the existence or meaning of an agreement or award that resulted from the dispute resolution proceeding or to the enforcement of such an agreement or award;

(7) except for dispute resolution communications generated by the neutral, the dispute resolution communication was provided to or was available to all parties to the dispute resolution proceeding.

This statute is typical of limited confidentiality rules. Note that confidentiality may be lifted for various public-policy reasons, such as the prevention of "manifest injustice" and the prevention of harm to public safety. Since such provisions allow a wide degree of judicial discretion, some might argue that they result in a chilling effect on disputants' willingness to be open and honest during mediation.

What makes this particular statute unusual is subsection (b)(7), which exempts from confidentiality any communication, except one made by the neutral, that occurs during a joint session. Essentially, in a two-party dispute, this single exception makes all disputant and advocate communications nonconfidential unless made in a caucus. Thus, unless the disputants make an agreement before the inception of mediation (§574(d)), allowing confidentiality during joint session, they would have no confidentiality there.

Implications for Conflict Diagnosis. Overall, the role of mediation in the constructive resolution of conflict is better served by strong confidentiality protections. Because our society operates within the blinders and distortions created by the invisible veil (see Chapter 3), disputants tend to play their negotiations close to the vest. Confidentiality is needed to coax disputants into the kind of open information sharing needed for effective collaborating during mediation. Otherwise, disputants may fear that what they say in mediation might be used against them later in court. Additionally, the mediator's neutrality is an important component of trust-building during the mediation process. If the parties feel that the mediator is taking note of their actions for later revelation to a court or others, the relationship with the mediator may become adversarialized. On the other hand, if, regardless of what happens in mediation, the mediator has promised to refrain from being sucked into an escalation of the conflict, disputants are less likely to behave in ways that emphasize the competitive aspects of their conflict.

Vague exceptions to confidentiality such as the interests of justice exception may have a chilling effect on disputant communication, since it is hard to predict what will and won't be protected. On the other hand, exemptions to confidentiality to protect disputants (such as reporting the attorney who represented adverse disputants in *In Re Waller*) may serve the long-term viability of mediation as a nonadversarial alternative by reassuring potential participants that mediation won't be a forum for misbehavior. Perhaps conflict diagnosticians would be most comfortable with confidentiality exemptions that relate to matters not directly associated with the conflict itself, as when confidentiality is waived to report an instance of professional misconduct.

The issue of how to raise defenses to settlements reached in mediation presents a similar dilemma for those promoting effective and constructive conflict resolution and the lifting of the invisible veil. On one hand, the viability of the mediation process requires that disputants act in good faith; hence, misconduct such as fraud during mediation shouldn't be allowed to subvert the mediation process. On the other hand, such defenses are vulnerable to tactical misuse by sharp advocates: for example, there is a fine line between "puffery" and fraud, and there will likely be many instances in which an adversary can make a weak but nonfrivolous claim that his or her client was misled by the other disputant or his or her legal counsel during mediation. Allowing the free use of litigation to deal with such claims could eviscerate mediation as a means of constructive conflict resolution. The mere ability of disputants to raise the contents of the mediation in an adversary proceeding may be argued by some to poison the environment and make the mediation itself more adversarial.

Another issue for conflict diagnosticians is whether the mediator should have an independent privilege. On one hand, helping professionals generally don't have the independent right to withhold information if their clients want it produced. It can be argued that allowing the clients to mutually decide whether information can be made public supports the goal of disputant self-determination. On the other hand, mediators have the right and obligation to protect the profession. There is an argument that, in a society permeated by the invisible veil, there is constant pressure on disputants to use whatever means they can (including exemptions to mediation confidentiality) to adversarialize their conflict. Those seeking to preserve mediation as a true alternative to competitive conflict resolution are likely to err in favor of a strong confidentiality rule, so that the disputants are less likely to misuse the mediation process in this fashion. Allowing the mediator to retain an independent privilege to refuse to participate in the adversarialization of a mediated conflict promotes this overall goal.

MANDATING OF MEDIATION

Many mediation scholars believe that disputant self-determination is the essence of mediation. Thus, the mediation process is generally interpreted to require the right of the disputant to refrain from settlement unless the settlement is of his or her choosing. But can disputants be forced to try mediation, even if they can't be forced to settle? If so, how far can disputants be forced to mediate? And should disputants suffer negative consequences if they don't reach a settlement? When does such pressure violate disputant self-determination? And when does such coercion create such a deprivation of rights that it can be considered a violation of due process of law?

A preliminary question one might pose is this: why would an element of coercion ever be considered for a voluntary process such as mediation? There are two reasons, each of which leads to a different sort of coercion. First, it has been found that, when mediation is offered, Americans don't typically choose it (the experts in ADR term this an "underuse" phenomenon). Second, policymakers comparing mediation with litigation often wish to increase the "settlement rate" of mediation.

The underuse of mediation has been well documented by researchers. There are probably five major reasons for this underuse of mediation. First, interpersonal conflict breeds meta-conflicts. Sociologists Craig McEwen and T. Milburn (McEwen & Milburn 1993) argue that mediation is not usually considered by disputants unless they have been unable to reach settlement on their own. Disputants who negotiate unsuccessfully characteristically experience conflict escalation during the negotiation. The escalation breeds meta-conflicts that heighten anger, frustration, hostility, and vengefulness. By the time the disputants acknowledge that they need help from a third party, they are too angry to consider a cooperative intervention, such as mediation. Ironically, studies show that, when these vengeful disputants are forced to attend mediation, they are on average highly satisfied, despite not having wanted to attend in the first place, and quite pleased that they were forced to undergo mediation (Kressel & Pruitt 1989; McEwen & Maiman 1982).

Second, reactive devaluation can interfere with the decision to mediate. Voluntary mediation must start with a proposal from one of the disputants to try it. If the relationship between the disputants has entered a competitive cycle, the decision by the first disputant to suggest mediation as an option is viewed with suspicion by the other disputant. Hence, since voluntary mediation requires consent by both disputants, often it is difficult to get the mutual consent necessary to begin mediation.

Third, disputants in an unpleasant conflict often feel overwhelmed and repulsed by the conflict and want quick finality. Since mediation can't advertise itself as guaranteeing settlement, disputants can be afraid of wasting time and money. They either don't understand the ways in which mediation can lead to more final and permanent solutions or simply fear the possibility that the dispute will still be there after mediation has been tried.

Fourth, mediation usually requires facing the other disputant across a bargaining table. Disputants involved in a conflict are upset with each other and may fear or abhor having to be in the same room with one another. They may feel better about a process, such as litigation, in which a powerful advocate acts as a buffer during the process.

Fifth, legal subculture and the invisible veil probably contribute to the underuse of mediation. Anecdotal evidence from legal and ADR professionals suggests that, as the legal community in a particular court jurisdiction becomes familiar with mediation, and comes to accept it as an expected part of the process of resolving disputes, it is selected, and accepted, much more readily.[12]

The problems of mediation's underuse have been noted with great concern in the scholarly mediation literature for two decades. Because of the consensus about the many advantages of using mediation as an approach to interpersonal conflict, numerous attempts have been made to persuade, or even force, disputants to participate.

In addition to underuse problems, some legal policymakers would like to reduce or eliminate the problem of mediation's lack of finality. Thus, there is pressure in some circles to make mediation more likely to result in agreement. To further this objective, some mediation programs have been the subjects of experiments with methods of making the settlement outcome of mediation more likely.

Coercion in Private Mediation. In practice, how have the desires for greater use and greater finality of mediation played out? In addressing this question, purely private mediation should be distinguished from mediation under the auspices of a court. Private mediators often take cases of disputants who are simply trying to get help for a conflict they have not been able to resolve on their own. In most of these situations, one disputant contacts the mediator and, somehow, the other disputant is also convinced to try mediation. Other than the time and money invested in the mediation process, no coercion is involved.[13]

Sometimes, individuals contract in advance to require that disputes be submitted to mediation before any litigation is attempted (sometimes referred to as

---

[12] It may also be that the invisible veil contributes to the legal culture's aversion to mediation. As mediation becomes more popular among legal communities, it also tends to become more adversarial. See Menkel-Meadow (1991) and Alfini (1991).

[13] Mediators have a variety of techniques for encouraging full participation. Some mediators require a substantial deposit—an advance equivalent to up to ten hours of mediation, for example—to begin work. This fee is refundable only to the extent that agreement results in less time than charged. These mediators are of the opinion that the monetary investment keeps the disputants motivated to reach agreement. To this extent that the arrangement is coercive, it should be kept in mind that the parties to mediation have a choice of whether to accept the terms of mediation in the first place.

an "executory contract to mediate"). Although both disputants may have willingly agreed to the clause originally, mediation may not be the first choice of one disputant at the time the clause is invoked by the other. Generally, this sort of recalcitrance is not considered a matter of coercion, provided that both disputants acted of their own free and informed will at the time they made the executory contract.

However, enforcing such a contract presents some problems. It might be inferred that the parties to such an agreement have implicitly contracted to mediate in good faith, opening the recalcitrant disputant to the possibility of legal sanctions if he or she refuses to mediate. As we have seen elsewhere in this chapter, enforcement of the duty to mediate in good faith often raises difficult confidentiality problems. Even looking beyond confidentiality considerations, defining the duty to participate in good faith in a process that is, by definition, voluntary can be problematic. To apply the perfect colloquialism to this situation, "you can lead a horse to water, but you can't make it drink." What does *good faith participation* mean in the context of a process supposedly designed with disputant self-determination in mind? Does a disputant who attends, listens, but informs the other participants that he or she does not intend to settle and thereafter remains silent meet this criterion? What about a disputant who attends and answers questions but refuses to make any proposals? What about a disputant who makes very extreme offers, which the other disputant cannot be expected to consider seriously? Should *self-determination* mean that disputants must sit in mediation and seem to listen to the proceedings, so that they can make up their own minds whether to negotiate, or do disputants have a duty to negotiate affirmatively? And, if the latter, is the making of concessions required? It seems clear that the duty to participate in good faith has no simple, straightforward meaning.

An additional problem can occur if the contract has been foisted on a consumer by a large commercial entity. In certain instances, the contract may be considered one of "adhesion." A contract of adhesion is one that is considered to be involuntary in the eyes of the law because the consumer has had no real choice in negotiating terms. Such clauses could also coerce the consumer by specifying the mediator, requiring one disputant but not the other to submit to mediation, specifying the location of mediation, and so forth. No mediation clause of this sort has been contested in published litigation, although contracts of adhesion requiring dispute *arbitration* are now being subject to appellate review (see

---

Coercive Elements in Purely Private Mediation

- ◆ Contract clauses requiring disputants to attempt mediation before taking a dispute to litigation
- ◆ Contracts of adhesion in consumer contracts requiring the submission of disputes to mediation

Chapter 19).[14] Commercial entities are far more likely to specify mandatory arbitration than mandatory mediation.

Coercion in Court-Connected Mediation. Court-connected mediation raises somewhat different issues. There are numerous ways that courts can, and do, coerce disputants into mediating. Some of these methods of pressure may raise important constitutional issues by burdening or impeding the right to bring an action to court.

A fully voluntary court-connected mediation program would be one offered to disputants as an alternative to litigation. To minimize fully the impact on the disputants, the mediation would be offered free of charge and would not create delays in the schedule of the disputants' pending litigation, unless both disputants consented to such delays. Court-connected "mandatory" mediation applies coercion by varying these indicia of voluntariness.

Required Attendance. To persuade disputants to mediate, one approach that is taken by some courts is to *require some degree of participation.* The degree of coercion depends on what level of participation is required. For example, a very noncoercive program might require only attendance at an orientation session. (See, for example, Idaho R.C.P. 16(j).) A somewhat more coercive alternative might require attending at least one mediation session. The more participation required, the more coercive the program. At the extreme in this sort of coercion would be a program that required disputants to attend "so many sessions as the mediator directs." The state of Maryland (Md. Rules of Court 9-205) requires attendance as directed by the mediator, but not more than two sessions "unless good cause is shown and upon the recommendation of the mediator," in which

---

> ### *Coercive Elements in Court-Connected Mediation*
>
> - Extent to which attendance is required
> - Sanctioning lack of participation in good faith
> - Limits on ability to opt out of mediation
> - Regulation of payment of the mediation fee
> - Delay of litigation
> - Case evaluation by the mediator

---

[14] See *Wells v. Chevy Chase Bank,* 363 Md 232 (2001) for an example of a possible consumer contract of adhesion involving mediation. This litigation involved a credit card agreement which specified that, at the request of the claimant, any claim arising out of the credit agreement had to be submitted to mediation, and, if mediation did not result in settlement, binding arbitration would necessarily follow (this sort of arrangement is known in the ADR industry as "med-arb-different," see Chapter 21, meaning that mediation is followed by arbitration if no settlement results and that the arbitrator is a different person from the mediator). In the *Wells* case, the borrower contended that the ADR provision was never legally amended into the credit agreement. The court never reached the issue, ruling that, since the cardholder had never requested mediation, the issue was moot.

case up to two additional sessions can be ordered.[15] Further extensions are allowed only if the parties consent.

Sanctioning Lack of Participation in Good Faith. If a disputant attends mediation, but does not participate actively, an issue is raised as to whether he or she has attended in any *meaningful* sense. Hence, a corollary to requiring disputants to attend multiple mediation sessions is often a need to define whether a disputant "*participated in good faith.*" The disputant failing to do so can be found in contempt of a court order and sanctioned, by imposing responsibility for the other party's attorney's fees, by preventing the disputant from going forward with his or her part of the litigation, or by proceeding otherwise as provided by applicable statute.

There are compelling policy arguments both for and against the imposition of a duty to mediate in good faith. On one hand, mediation's fundamental principle of self-determination suggests a hands-off approach, so that disputants aren't compelled to settle against their will. Additionally, an expansive reading of a duty to participate in good faith would require the court to inquire into the process of mediation itself, compromising confidentiality. And allowing parties to engage in so-called ancillary litigation (Cole, Rogers, & McEwen 2001, §7:6) over the issue of whether each disputant negotiated in good faith during the mediation sessions undermines the special nonadversarial quality of mediation. It also compromises the mediator's special role as a neutral if he or she is required to assess whether participation was in good faith or not. On the other hand, law professor Kimberly Kovach (1997) asserts that, because the legal community and its clientele operate within the confines of the invisible veil, a duty to participate in good faith must be imposed in order to protect the process against adversarial conduct that might destroy its essence, such as adversarial posturing, misuse of the process to obtain discovery information, or use of the process to gather information for trial strategy.

Courts and legislatures have imposed a variety of legal requirements of good-faith participation to court- and agency-connected ADR.[16] Legal rules of good-faith participation in mediation, and the court cases that interpret them, are hard to summarize, because each has characteristics that make it unique. However, it may be generalized that they run from the very narrow to the very broad (Cole, Rogers, & McEwen 2001, §7:6). Rules of narrow scope limit the application of the good-faith participation requirement to clear conduct, which prevents the possibility of the mediation's resulting in settlement—such as the failure to attend mediation, the failure to provide information or witnesses considered essential for the process to go forward, and the failure to bring a representative with the authority to settle (Weston 2001). It requires no breach of confidentiality to

---

[15] This provision raises potential confidentiality problems by requiring both "good cause"—a factual showing—and the recommendation of the mediator.

[16] Many of these rules do not distinguish mediation from nonbinding evaluation processes that courts and agencies refer disputants to. Also, processes that are named "mediation" are often nonbinding evaluation processes. The effects of a good-faith participation requirement on purely facilitative mediation are likely to be different from the effects on an evaluative process.

Requiring the mediator to report disputant conduct to the court can jeopardize the impartiality of the mediator and confidentiality of the mediation process. John Neubauer, PhotoEdit

assess whether participants have contravened a duty to participate in good faith if limited to such conduct.

Other rules, however, are broader in scope. In extreme cases, it is left to the parties to argue over whether negotiation has been in good faith or to the mediator to make such a judgment in a report to the court. These broader rules raise numerous problems. As previously discussed, these rules often require a violation of confidentiality.

Moreover, requiring the mediator to "finger" the person at fault in a process that has not gone anywhere is inconsistent with the mediator's role as an impartial third party: it requires the mediator to, in effect, adjudicate an important issue in the case. If the disputants are not informed, at the commencement of mediation, of this adjudicatory role of the mediator, they will not be able to participate in mediation as fully informed participants, whereas, if they do begin mediation with this information, they will be likely to treat the mediator as if he or she were a sort of judge or jury. As we have seen in earlier chapters, Deutsch's Crude Axiom provides that a disputant's perceptions of the conflict tend to create a situation consistent with the perception. If the disputants perceive the mediation process as involving the possibility of future adjudication over who has done the better job of negotiating, they are more likely to be adversarial in their conduct. Finally, if a penalty attaches to a determination of failure to mediate in good faith, the disputant can be effectively prevented from litigating the issue. A disputant thus obstructed may have a valid claim that he or she has been denied due process of law. Thus, a court-connected mediation program that requires "meaningful" participation in mediation is bound to run into problems.

Ability to Opt Out of Mediation. As a corollary to requiring attendance in mediation, a court-connected mediation program can be made more or less mandatory, depending on the *ease of a disputant's opting out* of mediation. It may not take much coercion to produce participation. For example, anecdotal accounts circulating at some professional conferences on ADR suggest that participation in voluntary court-connected mediation shoots up when all litigants are automatically referred to mediation and then allowed to opt out simply by submitting a letter of request to the court. And studies indicate that court-connected mediation programs that allow litigants to opt out of the process are as well attended as those for which participation is mandatory (Bingham 2002).

A more coercive program would require additional effort to opt out. For example, in jurisdictions such as Nevada's Douglas County (Nev. N.J.D.C.R. 26), a disputant who is ordered into mediation of a child custody dispute may make a motion to opt out of mediation on the basis that mediation would be "inappropriate." Coercion in these sorts of jurisdictions varies, depending on the level of proof required. Within this category of "mandatory mediation," a relatively noncoercive program might accept a letter, whereas a more coercive alternative would be to require a declaration under penalty of perjury. A still more coercive alternative would require an evidentiary hearing, at which the opting-out disputant had to satisfy the burden of providing admissible and relevant evidence on the issue of qualification to opt out. A still more coercive alternative would require the opting-out disputant to have the burden of persuasion as well as the burden of producing relevant supporting evidence.

Coercion may also be manipulated by specifying that only certain disputants and disputes are exempt from mandatory participation. For example, many court-connected child custody mediation programs allow opting out by a parent who has been physically abused by the other parent (on the theory that the balance of power required for effective negotiation probably does not exist). Most programs allow this opt-out to be automatic if the abuse victim refuses to mediate, and they allow such disputes to be ordered into mediation in certain limited circumstances. New Mexico has a typical provision:

> B. When custody is contested, the court:
> (1) shall refer that issue to mediation if feasible unless a party asserts or it appears to the court that domestic violence or child abuse has occurred, in which event the court shall halt or suspend mediation unless the court specifically finds that:
> (a) the following three conditions are satisfied: 1) the mediator has substantial training concerning the effects of domestic violence or child abuse on victims; 2) a party who is or alleges to be the victim of domestic violence is capable of negotiating with the other party in mediation, either alone or with assistance, without suffering from an imbalance of power as a result of the alleged domestic violence; and 3) the mediation process contains appropriate provisions and conditions to protect against an imbalance of power between the parties resulting from the alleged domestic violence or child abuse; or

(b) in the case of domestic violence involving parents, the parent who is or alleges to be the victim requests mediation and the mediator is informed of the alleged domestic violence. . . . (N.M. Stat. Ann. §40-4-8)

Coerciveness of such an opt-out provision depends on the level of proof that the court requires in meeting the evidentiary threshold of demonstrating the history of domestic violence.

Regulation of Payment of the Mediation Fees. Another means by which the coerciveness of court-connected mediation is manipulated is by means of the *regulation of payment of the mediation fee.* The least coercive court-connected programs are free or require only a token fee payment. Other programs establish a set fee, typically with a sliding scale based on ability to pay. These commonly used programs often set their fees at the lower end of the market rate for private mediators. In a somewhat more coercive variation, the court takes a hands-off attitude toward fees: disputants choose their mediators from a court-approved panel of private mediators and pay the rate the mediator specifies. Still more coercive programs split the fee if settlement is reached but assess the fee in total to the disputant who is judged to have created an impasse in mediation. As with the issue of good-faith participation, this last method of fee assessment requires breach of confidentiality and threatens the mediator's impartial role, since it requires him or her to pass judgment on which disputant should have been more accommodating. Other forms of court-connected mediation split the fee if settlement is reached but assess the mediation fee as a court cost to the losing party if the case must be litigated. This rule serves as pressure on the disputants to settle the case for close to what they think the court would decide. Although this pressure may promote settlement, it may also promote the sort of unidimensional, zero-sum-game perspective on the dispute that mediation is used to transcend.

Other monetary penalties are sometimes assessed to pressure disputants into settling during mediation. An example sometimes cited to support this proposition is so-called Michigan Mediation, which is actually a form of nonbinding evaluation.[17] In this process, the "mediator" holds a hearing and issues a nonbinding evaluation of the case. If the valuation is rejected and the case is brought to trial, a party rejecting the valuation must pay costs and attorney's fees if he or she does not do at least 10 percent better at trial than the valuation (Plapinger & Steinstra 1996, part II).

Delay of Litigation. Court-connected mediation programs may also apply coercion by instituting *delays in the litigation process.* Some amount of delay in the process of discovery and trial preparation is often necessary to allow the mediation to proceed. When adversary pre-trial processes are proceeding apace, they can often interfere with the cooperative tone being worked toward in the

---

[17] Michigan Mediation is one example of the loose terminology applied to ADR processes.

mediation. Moreover, if a trial date is imminent, mediation may make no sense unless trial is put on hold for a time. However, an overly lengthy delay of litigation may put litigation so far out of reach that it effectively denies litigants the right to their trial, in which event it can be a denial of due process of law.

Case Evaluation by the Mediator. A final means of coercion in mediation is *evaluation of the case by the mediator.* This is a very coercive feature. Some court-connected programs have instituted processes in which the mediator either provides the court with a case evaluation (as when the mediator is a mental-health professional who provides a custody evaluation) or even issues a nonbinding decision in the dispute.[18] This sort of variation on coercion in mediation is designed not to pressure disputants into participation but, rather, to increase the likelihood of mediation's leading to settlement. Some California jurisdictions—most notably, Alameda County—have a history of using this sort of mediation program for child custody matters (McIsaac 2001).

Mediation programs that require the mediator to evaluate the dispute, or to recommend possible resolutions to the court, raise difficult and problematic issues, both of mediator role confusion and violation of confidentiality. Some commentators remark that using evaluation to pressure disputants into settling their cases is contrary to the spirit and purpose of mediation. The idea of punishing disputants who fail to settle may be seen as an adversarialization of the mediation process, which detracts from its role as a process of moving conflict into a cycle of cooperation. Indeed, one scholar, Hugh McIsaac, reviewing California's experience with nonconfidential evaluations used in court-connected child custody mediation, finds that the counties that use recommendations are actually less efficient at promoting settlement than those that retain a purely facilitative form of mediation, suggesting that the adversarialization of such dispute processes is actually counterproductive (McIsaac 2001). Moreover, court programs that prevent participation in the litigation process potentially raise constitutional problems for all litigants. In particular, the availability of a nonconfidential evaluation by the mediator has been criticized by many legal scholars as opening up the system to systematic discrimination. For example, Trina Grillo, in her classic article "The Mediation Alternative: Process Dangers for Women" (Grillo 1991), asserts that, when mediators use threats of nonconfidential evaluation to pressure parties into settlement, more pressure is placed on women, whose appropriate social role is to protect relationships and to be accommodating, to make the lion's share of concessions.[19] Court systems are

---

[18] Even the requirement that the mediator act as a binding arbitrator if the case does not reach agreement, known as "med-arb-same" (see Chapter 21), has been tried. In addition to raising problems of confidentiality and mediator role disruption, if the arbitration is binding and the referral to mediation is mandatory, this sort of arrangement effectively denies the disputants the right to a hearing in court and clearly raises constitutional problems.

[19] It can be argued that, regardless of the availability of nonconfidential evaluation, any mediation program that rewards mediators for short mediations and high settlement rates will result in a system that pressures lower-power litigants to make concessions in the name of getting an agreement, since such litigants are thought to be more vulnerable to pressure.

wrestling with these difficult issues, and the next decades promise to be eventful ones in the evolution of court-connected mediation.[20]

Implications for Conflict Diagnosis. Policymakers, mediators, and court personnel alike express frustration at the continuing underuse of purely voluntary mediation. As might be expected, efforts to counter this underuse problem have been marked by the invisible veil: mandatory mediation is characterized by coercive elements that detract from the special qualities of mediation as a paradigm departure from typical adversary processes.

After conducting careful conflict diagnosis, a conflict diagnostician should learn about the sort of mandatory mediation program in which the conflict participants would be required to participate. To what extent might the characteristics inherent in the available mandatory processes subvert the important interests and needs of the conflict participants? How important is creative problem solving? To what extent are there long-term interests at stake? How important are emotional, as opposed to financial, considerations? To some extent, an awareness of the limitations of a mandatory process, and the education of the conflict participants, can be effective in counteracting such limitations. However, in some cases, the conflict diagnostician might serve the participants more effectively by pushing for an alternative, such as voluntary private mediation, that fulfills the participants' needs better. Conflict diagnosticians whose field is policymaking, rather than the support and representation of individual disputants, may need to go further and consider the long-term implications of adversarializing the mediation process.

PROVISION OF LEGAL SERVICES BY MEDIATORS

Many disputants enter mediation with the hope and expectation that the mediator will tell them what the law is, as well as helping them resolve their dispute. These disputants conceptualize mediation as an alternative legal service in which the lawyer acts on behalf of both disputants instead of a single disputant. It is a considerable frustration to these potential clients when they discover that mediation is not a form of "one-stop shopping."

How mediators deal with legal issues during the mediation process can be problematic. If a mediator activity is considered the "practice of law," and the mediator is a nonlawyer, the practitioner can be liable under civil or criminal statutes that prohibit the unauthorized practice of law (UPL). On the other hand, attorney-mediators who hold themselves out as providing legal services during mediation may be accused of representing clients whose interests are in conflict (see, for example, the ABA Code of Professional Responsibility, DR5-105). If an attorney-mediator clarifies that he or she is providing mediation services, rather

---

[20] McIsaac notes that, as of the year 2001, California was the only state remaining that allowed such recommendations in child custody mediation. No statistics are available as to the use of nonconfidential evaluation in nonfamily law court-connected mediation.

than legal services, then, if the services provided are determined to constitute the practice of law, he or she may be accused of advertising improprieties.

What constitutes the practice of law in the context of mediation? Generally, the trend is to focus on two major activities, the offering of legal advice and the drafting of settlement agreements (Cole, Rogers, & McEwen 2001, §10.2; Guidelines on Mediation and UPL Advisory Committee 2000). The offering of legal advice is generally considered to include either of the following activities:

- The application of legal rules to the specific facts of one's case; or
- The urging of a particular legal action (Guidelines on Mediation and UPL Advisory Committee 2000)

Some mediation scholars argue that a new set of ethical standards need to be developed to govern the mediation process. They propose to make mediation an activity distinguished from the practice of law and subject to a different set of ethical precepts based on the notions of neutrality, client autonomy, holistic consideration of client interests, and protection of the mediation process. This work has begun in earnest: in an article entitled "ABA Task Force Agrees Mediation Not Practice of Law," published in *ADRWorld.com,* 27 June 2003, it was reported that the American Bar Association Task Force on the Model Definition of the Practice of Law decided to include language in its final report stating flatly that mediation does not constitute the practice of law. However, the proposed language has no legal impact. For now, the ethics of providing legal and quasi-legal services during mediation are still a no-man's land.

BEHAVIOR OF LEGAL ADVOCATES DURING MEDIATION

Another issue that puts legal ethics in the center of controversy involves the conduct of legal advocates during the mediation process. Legal advocates are traditionally obligated by their codes of ethics to provide zealous advocacy for their clients. In practice, this ethical obligation translates into a duty to compete vigorously on the client's behalf. Lawyers are trained to use any advantage to their client, including the use of hard bargaining tactics, threats, and coercion, to achieve this zealous representation. Judge Wayne Brazil of the United States District Court lists some of the conduct commonly associated with the adversarial role of the attorney during mediation:

> Advancing arguments known or suspected to be specious, concealing significant information, obscuring weaknesses, attempting to divert the attention of other parties away from the main analytical or evidentiary chance, misleading others about the existence or persuasive power of evidence not yet formally presented, . . . resisting well-made suggestions, intentionally injecting hostility or friction into the process, remaining rigidly attached to positions not sincerely held, delaying other parties' access to information, or needlessly protracting the proceedings—simply to gain time, or to wear down the other parties or to increase their cost burdens. (Brazil 2000, 29)

Such behavior is recognized (e.g., Browe 1994) as antithetical to the use of mediation to overcome conflict escalation and promote collaboration, and knowledgeable conflict diagnosticians will recognize each of the actions listed by Judge Brazil as characteristic of the competition cycle (see Figure 9-2 in Chapter 9). As you may recall from Chapter 9, Deutsch's Crude Axiom teaches that competitive behavior by a disputant's team promotes the escalation of a conflict into a destructive cycle. Thus, the lawyer's traditional adversarial role is in direct conflict with the needs of a client who wishes to take full advantage of mediation to prevent conflict escalation and promote cooperative, collaborative settlement.

In its extreme form, adversarial representation deteriorates into "Rambo" litigation tactics that involve winning at all costs—such as threatening to go to trial on a case known to be frivolous. Pre-existing legal ethical requirements can be used to discipline attorneys who engage in such tactics, although the need for confidentiality in mediation can often make enforcement problematic. However, many remain convinced that the skills and conduct that work well in adversarial dispute resolution, even those that are unassailable by current ethical standards, are antithetical to mediation (for example, Love 2000). Proponents of mediation have made a variety of recommendations to modify legal ethical requirements to allow lawyers to represent clients effectively during a non-adversary process. These range from the rather extreme suggestion that an impartial "advisory attorney," representing all disputants to the process, be hired to accommodate the needs of the clients in mediation (Coogler 1978, 85–92) to more modest proposals for the development of codes of ethics providing for "settlement attorneys," similar to British solicitors (Coyne 1999). Scholars and practitioners of mediation have also proposed (for example, Kovach 2001) that specific ethical codes applicable to lawyers representing clients in mediation be developed. One variant, known as "collaborative lawyering" (see Chapter 22), proposes that lawyers involved in collaborative negotiation processes contract with their clients that they be held to standards of cooperativeness, good faith, open and honest communication, and openness to the other side's point of view (Tesler 2001). Such lawyers, who are required to withdraw from representing their clients should their cases go to litigation, are held to traditional adversarial ethical precepts only to the extent that they are consistent with their contractual agreement to engage in collaborative representation (Kovach 2001; Rack 1998). Lawyers who contract with their clients to act in such a capacity are now available, but more time is needed to determine whether such services will prove either marketable or safe from the perspective of traditional legal ethics.

Internet Note—Collaborative Law

Additional information about collaborative lawyers and legal organizations is available on the Internet. Most websites devoted to collaborative law focus on divorce and family law disputes. A useful resource is posted by HALT, an organization of Americans for legal reform. The Internet address is *http://www.halt.org/FLIP/CLP.cfm.*

MEDIATOR IMPARTIALITY AND NEUTRALITY

Since one hallmark of mediation is disputant self-determination, the mediator must not pressure or coerce either disputant into accepting a particular solution to the conflict they are negotiating. Accordingly, the mediator must not be seen to favor or impose his or her will on one disputant. This feature of the mediator is known as **impartiality** and **neutrality**.[21] Mediator impartiality and neutrality are important for a conflict diagnosis reason. One critical role of the mediator is to help the disputants develop trust in the mediation process, so that disputants feel they can safely abandon the defensive tactics that lead to conflict escalation. If the disputants cannot trust the mediator to be even-handed, then this trust in the mediation process becomes impossible to establish.

Impartiality and neutrality are not easy to define. Impartiality is generally taken to refer to the **pecuniary disinterest** of the mediator in the claim or to the lack of bias for or against any mediation participant. For example, a mediator who formerly represented a particular disputant as legal counsel might be said to lack the requisite impartiality to act as a mediator. Neutrality, on the other hand, usually denotes a mediator's attitude toward the substantive dispute. This definitional distinction is the one adopted by the National Conference of Commissioners on Uniform State Laws, in its comments to the November 2000 draft of the Uniform Mediation Act.

Impartiality. Ethical mediators usually avoid outright conflicts of interest. For example, a mediator should never be a member of the law firm representing either client: this would be an overt conflict of interest. A difficult controversy arises when the mediator's firm represented both disputants in a previous controversy (as when the lawyer formerly represented two members of a corporate board of directors and a dispute has developed between board members). The best answer is to avoid acting as the mediator altogether, or to act as a mediator only if the conflict of interest is carefully explained and all disputants consent to using the mediator anyway. The AAA/ABA/SPIDR Model Standards of Conduct for Mediators[22] takes the approach that mediators who have a conflict of interest should avoid serving except upon the consent of the parties and upon full disclosure of the interest and, further, provides that the mediator may not establish a professional relationship with one of the disputants after mediation except upon the parties' consent (Standard III). The Uniform Mediation Act (§§8(d) and (e)) requires that, before the commencement of mediation, the mediator make reasonable inquiries to determine whether there might be conflicts

Impartiality
a mediator's refusal to favor any one mediation participant.

Neutrality
the mediator's refusal to express opinions, feelings, beliefs, or values concerning the subject matter of the interpersonal conflict or to allow such opinions, feelings, beliefs, or values to color his or her conduct during mediation.

Pecuniary disinterest
the absence, on the part of the mediator, of a financial stake in the dispute or in other matters in which the disputants are involved.

---

[21] Mediators are not impartial in all versions of mediation. For example, in Imperial China, where mediation was a traditional and widely used form of dispute resolution, the mediator's role was quite coercive, and it was common for the mediator to be a widely respected, opinionated, and often pecuniarily involved elder of the community in which the dispute has occurred (Shapiro 1981).

[22] AAA stands for American Arbitration Association, ABA for American Bar Association, and SPIDR for Society of Professionals In Dispute Resolution. The last organization is now defunct, having been merged into the Association for Conflict Resolution, ACR.

of interest and to disclose such conflicts to the participants. Optional Section 8(f) requires that the mediator act with impartiality, unless the participants consent otherwise.

Relatedly, a line of decisions beginning with *Poly Software International, Inc. v. Su,* 880 F. Supp. 1487 (D. Utah 1995) have held that, if mediation does not fully resolve a dispute, a lawyer-mediator may not be retained as counsel by one of the mediation participants in the same or a related dispute. Courts reason that, because of the likelihood of confidential information's being revealed to the mediator during mediation, the litigant retaining the former mediator would obtain an unfair advantage. From a conflict diagnosis perspective, if disputants entering mediation were aware of the possibility that the mediator could, in essence, abandon his or her impartial stance and use confidential communication made during mediation for an adversarial purpose, the requisite trust needed to maintain collaborative negotiation would be hard to establish.

Under virtually every mandatory and voluntary code of ethics applicable to mediators, the mediator has the obligation to disclose all potential sources of conflict of interest, as well as any issues about which he or she is nonneutral. Mediators who have an obvious conflict of interest with their clients often require the clients to sign a clear written acknowledgment of disclosure and consent to proceed with mediation.

The Uniform Mediation Act (National Conference 2001) does not include mandatory language requiring impartiality from the mediator. The reporter for the draft Uniform Mediation Act commented that requiring a bias-free mediator might encourage "meta-litigation over whether the mediator was in fact free from bias." Instead, the act (at §9) requires only full disclosure of potential biases by the mediator and leaves it up to the disputants whether to proceed with mediation involving an "interested" mediator:

> (a) Before commencing a mediation, an individual who is requested to serve as a mediator shall (1) make an inquiry that is reasonable under the circumstances to determine whether there are any known facts that a reasonable person would consider likely to affect the impartiality of the mediator, including a financial or personal interest in the outcome of the mediation and any existing or past relationship with a party or foreseeable participant in the mediation; and (2) disclose any such known fact to the mediation parties as soon as is practical before accepting a mediation.
> (b) If a mediator learns any fact described in subsection (a)(1) after accepting a mediation, the mediator shall disclose it as soon as is practicable.

An optional section of the Uniform Mediation Act, §9(g), allows states to adopt a rule requiring the mediator to act impartially unless the parties agree otherwise.

Neutrality. Good and ethical mediators don't have or show favoritism toward any one disputant. However, mediators have feelings, values, and ethics, which don't go away just because they are involved in mediation. Moreover, it can be argued that some situations demand extra support for some disputants to allow them to negotiate effectively. It can also be argued that constituents not participating in mediation—particularly dependents, such as children—may have interests that should be promoted directly by the mediator.

The National Conference on Uniform State Laws specifically advocates against requiring mediator neutrality (National Conference 2001, comments to section 9(g)). Mediators sometimes find themselves in the middle of a dispute that challenges their set of values, and there are variations in how a mediator handles this event. Some mediators are primarily advocates for disputant autonomy. These mediators take a completely hands-off position in the mediation process to protect the disputants' right to make any agreement, however repugnant to the mediator.

When disputants apparently lack equality of bargaining power, however, this stance becomes more problematic. Thus, some mediators are advocates for "non-exploitative" agreements. In practice, no two people ever have exactly equal bargaining power (indeed, usually one disputant has the edge in one power arena and the other has an edge in another), and it is often hard to be sure whether an agreement is based on substantially equal bargaining power or not. The mediator in these situations must do the requisite probing and reality-testing to determine whether an agreement is being reached under duress without undermining the hard work the disputants have done to reach the agreement. Even highly experienced mediators find this to be a hard line to walk. Mediators also often refer disempowered clients to helpers, such as lawyers, tax professionals, therapists, and the like, in order to help the client improve his or her power. Occasionally, a mediator will respond to this sort of situation by declaring his or her concerns in a letter to the clients. Mediators will sometimes withdraw altogether from mediation if it becomes clear that one party is overreaching and the other party can't be empowered to cope with the situation.

These difficult ethical dilemmas have led to diverse practices in mediator neutrality. Some mediators are *completely disengaged*—disputants can make any agreement they come to. The underlying ethic for such mediators is the disputants' overriding need for autonomy and freedom, using any value system each disputant is comfortable with.

Some mediators take a step back from this rather extreme position. As experts in conflict diagnosis and conflict resolution, these mediators are *advocates for agreements that are workable and avoid future conflict escalation.* These mediators often use reality-testing—"Let's imagine how it will play out if John's workday ends at 5 P.M. and he is required to pick up the children across town at 5:05"— to help guide disputants in developing agreements that will work for them.

Other mediators are *advocates for nonexploitive agreements.* These practitioners, recognizing the prevalence of power imbalances between disputants in mediation, wish to preserve the ethic of self-determination but also recognize that some disputants may not be able to hold their own in a negotiation. Often, a blatantly unfair agreement is the only clear evidence of power imbalance and overreaching (in fact, a perennial problem for mediators who wish to prevent exploitation by a disputant is determining whether exploitation is, in fact, occurring). Thus, such mediators conclude that complete disengagement does not serve the ethic of self-determination as well as a more active role. There are a variety of mediator responses to possible overreaching on the part of a disputant. Some mediators use reality-testing to gently raise the issue of whether the less powerful disputant has considered all possible options or suggest to the disputants that other experts who can increase expert power be consulted. A more direct, but still mild, tactic is for the mediator to raise the possibility of unfairness during the mediation or to write a letter expressing his or her concern to the disputants during or at the close of mediation. A more active response is for the mediator to withdraw from a process that appears to be moving in an unfair direction.

A different interventionist stance is taken by mediators who see themselves as *advocates for unrepresented constituents.* For example, many child custody mediators with backgrounds in child development hold themselves out as advocates for the best interests of children—and warn the parents against a clearly inappropriate plan. These mediators are concerned that disputants may not always protect vulnerable people who are relying on them.

It could be argued that *evaluative mediators* are representative of a still more interventionist position on the neutrality continuum. Evaluative mediators do not show partiality toward any disputant, but they do not hesitate to communicate what they believe to be the strengths and weaknesses of each disputant's claims—even if it means telling one disputant that his or her case is weak. Moreover, evaluative mediators, in performing an evaluation based on the legal merits of the dispute, implicitly endorse the use of the rule of law, as opposed to any other shared or compatible beliefs or values held by the disputants, as the "correct" standard to use in developing a settlement.

In the least neutral version of mediation common in Western countries, the mediator becomes a *factfinder or arbitrator* if the mediation does not lead to an agreement. These mediators are neither impartial nor neutral in any true sense. The change of role of the mediator into an adjudicator is a clear breach of mediator ethics, unless the disputants have explicitly agreed to this type of process. If the mediation has been made mandatory by governmental statute or rule, the adjudication of a dispute by the mediator deprives the disputants of the power to engage in litigation of their dispute; in doing so, it arguably deprives the disputants of due process of law.

Given the broad diversity of mediator approaches to neutrality, it has proven difficult—and by some reckonings, unwise—to regulate this area of mediator conduct. As a general rule, mediators are usually given the freedom to operate anywhere within the range of neutrality discussed in this section, provided that their stance is disclosed to the disputants before mediation begins and the disputants give their informed consent.

REGULATION OF MEDIATOR COMPETENCY

The development of standards of competency, and the regulation of mediator education, training, and experience, has proven to be another difficult and unsettled area of law and ethics. A commonly advanced reason for this difficulty is that mediation is a new and evolving field requiring flexibility and experimentation. Perhaps equally responsible for the lack of consensus about mediator competency is the diversity of perspectives about ADR in general. "Efficiency" proponents of ADR are most interested in inexpensive service providers and expeditious mediation, and they are more likely to support evaluative mediators with modest credentials, or lawyer-mediators with strong backgrounds and experience in the legal basis of the disputes they are mediating, who volunteer their time. Proponents of evaluative mediation—and this, according to the available research, includes most attorneys (Hermann, Honeyman, McAdoo, & Welsh. 2001)—value substantive legal knowledge above all other competencies among mediators. On the other hand, "radical" ADR proponents are more likely to endorse mediators with strong backgrounds and skills in conflict diagnosis, conflict management and resolution, and communication skills. Certain specialties also demand specialized training; for example, many court systems demand that court-connected child custody mediators have educational backgrounds in divorce, child development, and psychology.

The rule for anyone wishing to go into business as a mediator is to research the requirements carefully. The legal requirements for education and training are quite specific to both the jurisdiction and to the type of dispute being mediated; thus, there is no substitute for focused legal research to determine the applicable requirements. Court-connected mediators are far more likely to be subject to competency and licensure requirements than private mediators. For example, in many jurisdictions offering court-referred mediation of contract and tort litigation, the mediator must be an attorney, and, in many of these jurisdictions, the prospective mediator must also have completed a forty-hour mediation training program.

It is one thing to ask whether one's qualifications to mediate comport with legal requirements and another to ask whether one's qualifications make one marketable as a mediator. In the world of commercial and tort mediation, where highly evaluative bargaining-based mediation is the norm, private mediators tend to be more marketable if they are experienced attorneys or retired judges. It is extremely difficult to obtain clients in that substantive area if one cannot hold oneself out as having handled such cases as a litigator or judge. The most marketable mediators in the area of tort and contract litigation tend to be retired judges who can perform evaluations based on their long experience on the bench.

More facilitative mediation is the norm in divorce and family mediation and in employment mediation. Divorce and family mediators often find that a dual expertise in psychology and the law, with specialized mediation training, is helpful to being marketable, whereas employment mediators typically have training in mediation and in human resources.

Membership in professional organizations devoted to mediation, such as the American Arbitration Association and the Association for Conflict Resolution, add to mediator marketability, allow the practitioner access to resources that im-

To become effective mediators, substantial training is required. Here, a group of prospective mediators converse in small groups during a training workshop. McLaughlin, The Image Works

prove competency, and may even provide voluntary certification. The Academy of Family Mediators (AFM, which merged into the Association for Conflict Resolution in 2001) had multiple membership levels; the highest level, Advanced Practitioner, required the completion of specific educational requirements, plus a period of mentored practice under particular AFM members. A number of court-connected mediation programs require their court-connected mediators to be certified by such organizations. On the other hand, the codes of ethics of many mediator organizations require merely that the mediator be educated, trained, and experienced in a manner that is adaptive to the cases taken. For example, the AAA/ABA/SPIDR Model Standards of Conduct for Mediators (Standard IV) provides the following:

> Any person may be selected as a mediator, provided that the parties are satisfied with the mediator's qualifications. Training and experience in mediation, however, are often necessary for effective mediation. A person who offers herself or himself as available to serve as a mediator gives parties and the public the expectation that she or he has the competency to mediate effectively. In court-connected or other forms of mandated mediation, it is essential that mediators assigned to the parties have the requisite training and experience.

Such standards provide little guidance, beyond requiring the mediator to use his or her judgment in developing competence, in providing full disclosure to potential clients, and in following whatever applicable legal requirements are in effect.

ENFORCEABILITY OF MEDIATED AGREEMENTS

The final event in mediation is often the finalization of a mediated agreement. What is the legal significance of this occurrence?

In general, since the mediation itself is an assisted negotiation, the mediated agreement is considered enforceable to the same extent as any other negotiated agreement. This simple statement belies the complexity of reconciling the confidential mediation process with the written outcome.

If the mediation process is handled carefully, a clear demarcation between the mediation process itself and the mediated agreement will exist. To prevent unauthorized practice of law and conflict of interest problems, many mediators issue a written memorandum of agreement, which, by its explicit terms, is not an enforceable document until reduced to a legal writing by the disputants' attorneys. Other mediators may be more bold, offering a document that, by its terms, becomes intended for enforceability when signed. If, however, the function of the document memorializing the mediated agreement is not made clear, trouble can result.

> Smith and Jones mediated their dispute over an automobile accident in which Smith was injured. The outcome of mediation was a written document providing that Jones would pay Smith $5,000 and Smith would dismiss his complaint filed in the state court. Smith signed the document but Jones refused. Smith contends that Jones clearly agreed to the settlement during mediation and he wants to enforce it.

The problem is, how can Smith enforce the agreement reached in mediation without breaching confidentiality? If the unsigned agreement is deemed unenforceable, doesn't this result seem unfair to Smith? The best answer is probably to consider a mediated negotiation as similar to any other negotiation. The common law, codified in statutes such as the Federal Rules of Evidence, Rule 408, makes offers and acceptances made during compromise negotiations inadmissible to enforce a settlement agreement.

A closely related problem is the extent to which mediation confidentiality will be suspended either to prevent enforcement of the mediated agreement (due to typical contract defenses, such as fraud, duress, incompetency of a disputant, or undue influence) or to interpret the meaning of ambiguous provisions. This area of the law is unsettled at this time. As with other aspects of mediation law and ethics, the struggle between the desire to protect the enormous potential of mediation to pierce the invisible veil and provide nonadversarial conflict resolution, and the desire to preserve the adversarial rights of individual disputants, will make the resolution of these issues a tough challenge.

EXERCISES, PROJECTS, AND "THOUGHT EXPERIMENTS"

1. Refer back to exercise 2 in Chapter 17, featuring Ronnell, the paralegal who chose to become a medical malpractice mediator. In Ronnell's first case, she met in caucus with both the plaintiff, who did not have legal counsel, and the defendant physician. The plaintiff begged Ronnell to tell her how a court would decide the case. "You advertised yourself as having had twenty years of experience handling malpractice cases, and you've worked in a hospital. Just tell me how a court would deal with the case. I want to know what's fair, so that the other side doesn't steal me blind." Ronnell can't help but have opinions about what a court would do—for twenty years, she prepared cases like this one for trial and watched courts decide them. What should Ronnell do, and why?

2. Would your answer to question 1 differ if Ronnell were a qualified attorney, rather than a paralegal? Why or why not? Do any regulations or ethical rules address this situation? Is Ronnell prohibited from evaluating the case at all? If so, how do you square this conclusion with the fact that there are many mediators comfortably practicing an evaluative style of mediation?

3. Sanjay is mediating a marital breakup between Edna and Marve. As the mediation proceeds, Sanjay begins to suspect that Marve is hiding assets from Edna—he tends to be vague when asked where all the money he made has gone, and his family owns a very closely held used car business. He "has lost" all the tax returns from the past five years, and his bank account statements are very incomplete. Edna does not seem to be aware of Marve's possible deception. What should Sanjay do? How can he handle this situation in a manner that preserves the mediation process (so that if, in fact, Marve has done nothing wrong, both parties can benefit), empowers Edna, yet preserves mediator impartiality? Or is Sanjay required to terminate mediation? Is ending the mediation relationship enough to satisfy Sanjay's ethical obligations? Justify your response.

4. Imagine that the two students described in Chapters 1 and 3, Jeff and Marsha, with the software development dispute had developed their revenue-sharing agreement during mediation with a particularly poor mediator, who didn't help them clarify the ambiguities in their agreement. Suppose they were unable to resolve their dispute amicably, and one of them sued the other. Should either Jeff or Marsha be allowed to introduce evidence of what went on during mediation as a way of showing what their intent was in reaching the agreement they did? Why or why not? Use the concepts listed in the box entitled "Why Is Mediation Regulated?" If both of them concur that confidentiality should be waived, should they be allowed to subpoena the mediator to testify about the proceedings? Why or why not?

5. What is your opinion in the confidentiality versus good-faith requirement controversy? Consider the following situations involving court mediators. Should the mediator be required to advise the court that one of the

disputants failed to participate in good faith? What should the mediator reveal and what should he or she advise the court?

a. A judge orders the parties to mediation. One party shows up but the other does not. The mediator calls the absent disputant, who apologizes and states that he forgot about the session. The mediator schedules a second session two weeks later and mails and telephones appointment reminders to both parties. Again, the second disputant fails to attend.

b. A judge orders the parties to mediation. One party shows up promptly. The other shows up twenty minutes late and says she was held up in heavy traffic. After the mediator's introduction, when asked whether she has any questions, the tardy disputant says no. When asked about the situation that led her to court and mediation, she simply says that the other party sued her and that she was ordered to mediation. After the other party discusses the conflict from his point of view, the recalcitrant disputant, when asked, says she has nothing to add or respond to. After two hours, the mediator is forced to terminate mediation, because it is obvious that the recalcitrant disputant is failing to participate actively.

c. A judge orders the parties to mediation. Both parties appear to participate in discussions in good faith. However, Party B refuses to make any concrete proposals for resolving the dispute, even after Party A makes several. Party B makes no constructive suggestions about the proposals made by Party A—she simply says, "That's not a good enough offer for me to accept," each time a proposal is made. The mediator feels that Party A's last proposal was extremely generous in light of the facts.

d. A judge orders the parties into mediation. One of the parties is a corporate entity. The executive vice president attends for the corporate party. After three hours of hard bargaining, the exhausted parties reach a settlement, only to have the executive vice president say, "I'll have to take this issue to the CEO and legal department. I don't have authority to sign off on any settlement."

e. A judge orders the parties into mediation. Three hours of hard work produces lots of discussion of options but no final settlement. The mediator is flabbergasted when Party B says no to what the mediator feels is a terrific settlement of the dispute. Later, Party A petitions the court for "sanctions"—a fine for misconduct—alleging that Party B failed to mediate in good faith. Party A asks the mediator to back him up by telling the court what a good deal Party B refused.

f. Would your reaction to fact situation e be different if the mediator were less certain about the fairness of the rejected settlement offer? If the mediator felt that none of Party A's offers had any merit? In general, when one disputant claims the other did not mediate in good faith, should the mediator have the authority to decide whether an offer is good enough to suspend confidentiality? How would such a rule affect the strategic (mis)use of mediation for adversarial purposes during litigation?

6. Read and summarize the following appellate decisions. (If you have been trained to brief an opinion, brief rather than summarize.) How do you reconcile these decisions—or are they irreconcilable?

   a. *Olam v. Congress Mortgage Company,* 68 F. Supp. 2d 1110 (N.D. Cal., 1999)

   b. *Foxgate Homeowners' Association, Inc., v. Bramalea,* 26 Cal. 4th 1 (2001)

7. Research the state of mediator qualification law in your state.

   a. Is there one statute or regulation that covers all mediators, or are different specialties required to meet different qualification standards? Does your state describe explicit requirements or defer to a professional organization to set standards? Do court mediators have one set of qualifications and private mediators another?

   b. Choose one kind of mediator qualification law within your state and look at the standards in detail. Does the law require a particular professional background (for example, do the mediators have to be lawyers, therapists, or social workers)? What is the nature and scope of any required mediation-specific training or education? Are prospective mediators required to apprentice to a mentor and, if so, for how long? Are qualified mediators required to fulfill mediation-specific continuing education requirements? If so, how much?

RECOMMENDED READINGS

Alfini, J. J., and C. G. McCabe. 2001. Mediating in the shadow of the courts: A survey of the emerging case law. *Arkansas Law Review* 54:171–206.

Brazil, W. D. 2000. Continuing the conversation about the current status and the future of ADR: A view from the courts. *Journal of Dispute Resolution* 2000:11–39.

Cole, S. H., N. H. Rogers, and C. A. McEwen. 2001. *Mediation: Law, policy and practice.* 2d ed. St. Paul, MN: West.

Foxgate Homeowner's Association, Inc., v. Bramalea, 26 Cal. 4th 1 (2001).

Kovach, K. K. 2001. New wine requires new wineskins: Transforming lawyer ethics for effective representation in a non-adversarial approach to problem-solving: Mediation. *Fordham Urban Law Journal* 28:935–77.

McEwen, C. A., and T. W. Milburn. 1993. Explaining a paradox of mediation. *Negotiation Journal* 9(1):23–36.

Menkel-Meadow, C. 1991. Pursuing settlement in an adversary culture: A tale of innovation co-opted or "the Law of ADR." *Florida State University Law Review* 19 (summer):1–46.

National Conference on Uniform State Laws. 2000. *Uniform Mediation Act with prefatory note and reporter's notes.* [Online.] November. [Cited 15 July 2002.] Available on the National Conference of Commissioners on Uniform State Laws website, *http://www.law.upenn.edu/bll/ulc/mediat/med300.htm.*

Nolan-Haley, J. M. 1999. Informed consent in mediation: A guiding principle for truly educated decisionmaking. *Notre Dame Law Review* 74 (March):775–840.

Nolan-Haley, J. M. 2001. Mediation. In *Alternative dispute resolution in a nutshell* (pp. 60–137). St. Paul, MN: West.

Olam vs. Congress Mortgage Company, 68 F. Supp. 2d 1110 (N.D. Cal., 1999).

Plapinger, E., and D. Steinstra. 1996. *ADR and settlement programs in the federal district courts: A sourcebook for judges and lawyers.* Federal Judicial Center and CPR Institute for Dispute Resolution. [Online.] [Cited 15 July 2002.] Available from Federal Judicial Center website, *http://www.fjc.gov/ALTDISRES/adrsource/adrblurb.html.*

Weston, M. A. 2001. Checks on participant conduct in compulsory ADR: Reconciling the tension in the need for good-faith participation, autonomy, and confidentiality. *Indiana Law Journal* 76 (Summer):591–645.

19

Arbitration

"Law and settled authority is seldom resisted when it is well employed."

—Dr. Johnson, *The Rambler,* 1750–52

In this chapter, you will learn ...

- About arbitration, an ADR process that can closely resemble litigation.
- About the tension between providing informality and legalistic protections in arbitration.
- The advantages and disadvantages of arbitration compared with litigation and other ADR processes and how this information can be useful to conflict diagnosticians.
- How the arbitration process works.
- The situations in which courts intervene to enforce, modify, or eliminate the process or outcome of arbitration.
- The many ways in which the law supports a deferential attitude toward the arbitration process.
- The principal "front-end" and "back-end" arbitration issues.
- The thorny controversies created when contracts require arbitration of civil rights claims and public-safety matters.
- The reviewability of arbitration awards.
- The problems of choice of law in interstate, international, and multinational arbitration.

Three-year-old Adam and his twin brother, Ron, are playing with Adam's football. Their rambunctious but good-natured game is threatened when Ron refuses to give Adam a turn. "I'm not finished!" shouts Ron when Adam tries to take matters into his own hands. "You had it a long time already!" counters Adam. A literal sort of "focus on positions" develops: they both grab the ball, dig in their heels, and start pulling.

Enter big sister Sonia. "Help, sissie! He's taking my ball!" "It's my turn!" "No it's my turn!" "You're a big doo doo head!" "No, you are!" Ron starts to cry.

Taking these remarks as a mutual request for assistance, Sonia gets involved. "Who had it first?" she asks. "He did," admits Adam. "But it's my turn now. He's had it for a year!" "Well," says Sonia, "Ron will have the ball for another five minutes. When the big hand on my watch is on the 12, then Adam will have his turn."

Arbitration award
the binding decision issued by an arbitrator.

Adam and Ron are having perhaps their first, but not their last, experience with arbitration. By seeking Sonia's assistance to decide how to handle their dispute over who gets to play with the football, the boys implement a basic, ancient, and natural process: they are having a disagreement and they agree to let someone else make the decision for them. Arbitration is simply a process of adjudication in which the power to decide the outcome is conferred upon a decision maker by the agreement of the disputants.[1] The binding decision made by the arbitrator is referred to as the **arbitration award.**

FROM "PEOPLE'S COURT" TO "CREEPING LEGALISM": THE DILEMMA OF MODERN ARBITRATION

For many years, arbitration was the principal form of ADR (other than negotiation) available in the United States. Arbitration fits the American culture particularly well: it involves a competitive process of dispute resolution, yet it allows disputants to resolve their differences outside the legal system.

Arbitration today is very different from a century or two ago. Originally a sort of "people's court," a hallmark of populism, arbitration has now evolved into something quite different, in many ways antithetical to its original purposes. This new characteristic of arbitration raises a dilemma for those who want to use it. To understand the essential dilemma of modern arbitration, it is useful to trace its history.

A BRIEF HISTORY OF ARBITRATION IN THE UNITED STATES

According to various commentators, arbitration can be traced back to biblical times. In pre-twentieth-century America, arbitration was largely a reaction against the restrictiveness, formality, and authoritarianism of the courtroom

---

[1] We're assuming here that the words of the two boys constituted a mutual request for Sonia to intervene and make the decision. Were we to conclude that she intervened because of her status as older sister, rather than because the boys requested her help, then this incident would be more like litigation.

(Auerbach 1983). Arbitration in colonial times was a populist movement. It flourished in homogeneous communities, such as communities of faith and commerce, and in ethnic groups insulated by language or ghettoization. This form of arbitration reflected the communitarian spirit and stood in opposition to legalization and lawyers. Arbitration was an informal process conducted by respected elders of the community in which the dispute arose. For example, a dispute between families might be arbitrated by the local religious leader, whereas a dispute over a commercial transaction might be arbitrated by a prominent and respected businessman in the community. The informality of arbitration and choice of the arbitrator assured that community norms, rather than the sterile rules of prevailing law, would be applied and that the outcomes of arbitration would reflect local standards of fairness and propriety. Traditional arbitration was also marked by facilitative efforts and by compromise and integrative solutions imposed by the arbitrator, who often knew the disputants intimately and could therefore intervene in this manner.

In a sense, early arbitration law reciprocated arbitration's populist and anti-legal origins, for early English law was hostile to arbitration. Although awards of an arbitrator were generally enforceable under a theory of agency, the "Ouster Doctrine" (*Vynior's Case,* 8 Coke Rep. 81b [1609]) provided that **"executory" agreements to arbitrate**—that is, agreements to submit future disputes not yet in existence to arbitration—were not enforceable because the arbitration would "oust the jurisdiction" of the courts (Cole 2001; Reuben 2000). There were also concerns that agreements to arbitrate violated the right to trial by jury (Hursh 2001) and some concerns by judges who feared loss of salary or job (Cole 2001). The rule against executory agreements to arbitrate meant that any party who entered into such an arrangement could refuse to participate in arbitration and could withdraw from the process at any time before the award was made. These rules were imported to the United States during the colonial period, where they persisted into the twentieth century. Thus, the courts left arbitration alone, and arbitrating parties left the courts alone. Because of the law hostile to arbitration, parties who willingly submitted to arbitration could gain its benefits, whereas parties who did not consent to arbitration—or who decided midstream not to continue with arbitration—did not have to. This legal situation left arbitration in a posture in which willing mutual consent was needed to use it. Thus, early arbitration was a flexible process that accommodated to mutual disputant needs. People who did not embrace it wholeheartedly were unlikely to use it.

The early twentieth century saw a softening of attitudes toward the enforcement of arbitration agreements, in the United States and worldwide. The most important development in the United States was the 1925 adoption of the United States Arbitration Act, the forerunner of the Federal Arbitration Act (FAA, 9 USCS § 1 *et seq.*). The purpose of the act was to place executory contracts to arbitrate in the same position as other contracts and to remove the historical judicial hostility toward the process, as specified in Section 2 of the FAA:

Section 2. Validity, irrevocability, and enforcement of agreements to arbitrate.
A written provision in any maritime transaction or a contract evidencing a

Executory agreements to arbitrate
agreements to submit future disputes, not currently in existence, to arbitration.

"Then it's agreed. Watson, Smith, Teller, and Wilson go to Heaven; Jones, Paducci,
and Horner go to Hell; and Fenton and Miller go to arbitration."

The Cartoon Bank

transaction involving commerce to settle by arbitration a controversy thereafter arising out of such contract or transaction, or the refusal to perform
the whole or any part thereof, or an agreement in writing to submit to arbitration an existing controversy arising out of such a contract, transaction,
or refusal, shall be valid, irrevocable, and enforceable, save upon such
grounds as exist at law or in equity for the revocation of any contract.

By the terms of this provision, an executory agreement to arbitrate is made
no less enforceable than any other contractual promise to do something at a future date. Moreover, Section 3 of the Act provides that a disputant who is involved in the litigation of an arbitrable issue can ask that the litigation be
"stayed," or suspended, to permit arbitration to be completed; and Section 4 establishes a federal court procedure for compelling disputants to participate in arbitration pursuant to a pre-existing arbitration agreement.

The adoption of the FAA triggered profound changes in the law of arbitration in the United States. Arbitration was subsequently adopted in 1947 in the
Taft-Hartley Act, 29 USCS § 141 *et seq.,* as a principal mechanism for further-
ing collective bargaining negotiations and resolving unfair labor practice complaints. Moreover, a series of Supreme Court cases cemented a policy of
deferential treatment to the arbitrator in the determination of whether an issue
could be arbitrated, in how the arbitrator chose to proceed with the procedure,
and in court review of an arbitration award.

Flourishing in the more favorable legal climate, arbitration, formerly a strictly
voluntary process used primarily by arms-length disputants, began to be adopted
wholesale by large organizations to deal with disputes involving consumers, employees, and other "little guys". The National Arbitration Forum (NAF), a commercial association of arbitrators, reported at its website in January 2002 that the

courts have upheld contracts binding consumers to arbitrate their disputes with credit card companies, residential services providers, mail order merchants, mortgage lenders, lenders of consumer loans, auto sales merchants, and warrantors of consumer goods.[2] Such arbitration agreements require the consumer to waive any right to litigate issues, should the other party elect binding arbitration. Following is a typical provision, excerpted from a Visa cardmember agreement[3]:

> Any claim or dispute . . . by either you or us against the other, or against the employees, agents, or assigns of the other arising from or relating in any way to the Cardmember Agreement, any prior Cardmember Agreement, your credit card Account or the advertising, application or approval of your Account, will, at the election of either you or us, be resolved by binding arbitration. . . . As used in this Arbitration Agreement, the term "Claim" is to be given the broadest possible meaning . . . [An exception for small claims follows.] (Chase Manhattan Bank 2002)

In February 2003, the private-sector U.S. Payment Card Information Network reported that virtually all the major credit card issuers have incorporated mandatory, binding arbitration provisions into their cardholder agreements (CardWeb.com 2003).

Arbitration has also become quite common in employment contexts: it has become common for prospective employees to be required to sign promises to arbitrate, rather than litigate, any dispute arising out of employment. Internationally, the adoption of the New York, or UNCITRAL[4], convention by participating nations made it possible for multinational disputes to be submitted to arbitration with reasonable certainty that they would be enforced by local courts and with some degree of clarity concerning the standards of enforcement that would be used.

Because of the balance shift in favor of executory agreements to arbitrate and because of the shift to imposing arbitration on disputants with inferior bargaining power, it was recognized that additional protections were needed to protect those who were being pulled along unwillingly. Moreover, because it was no longer possible simply to withdraw from an arbitration prior to completion, disputants who had initially agreed to an executory arbitration provision, but regretting the decision, began to use legal process to find the means to be relieved

---

[2] An indication of the fast-evolving nature of ADR is that, between the time this book was written and the time it was first edited for publication, the NAF revised its website to account for recent developments in the area of consumer arbitration law and no longer contains the expansive language it originally contained concerning the willingness of courts to uphold consumer arbitration contracts. According to the NAF, the courts are more closely scrutinizing consumer arbitration contracts to ensure their fairness. Nonetheless, the NAF site contains the following comment: "Given the state of the current law, consumer arbitration is not only allowed, but courts seem to be encouraging it as a means for dealing with burgeoning lawsuits" (*http://www.arb-forum.com/arbitration/NAF/file1.asp*).

[3] A Google search of the Internet in January 2002 using the search terms *arbitration, cardholder,* and *agreement* returned 1,160 results. Contained in the results were numerous credit cardholder agreements requiring consumers to submit to binding arbitration of all disputes with card issuers, requiring consumers to waive their right to a jury trial, and, in most cases, requiring cardholders to waive any right to participate in class actions against the issuers.

[4] UNCITRAL is the acronym of the United Nations Commission on International Trade Law.

of the responsibility to arbitrate. In response, of course, the disputants wishing to enforce executory agreements litigated their claims as well. In many situations, arbitration became yet another opportunity for adversarial maneuvering. In response to, and because of, these developments, a sort of "creeping legalism" (Zirkel & Krahmal 2001) began to infuse arbitration: in many contexts, it became more formalized, more procedurally rigorous, and more vulnerable to legal attack. Although arms-length disputants can sometimes plan for, and use, the traditional model of arbitration, they no longer can guarantee that the law of arbitration won't have some unexpected impact on the process. Moreover, traditional arbitration, which is embraced as quick, simple, and efficient, has in many settings been replaced with a legalistic morass even more baffling, expensive, and time-consuming than litigation. And rules respecting the degree to which courts can become involved in disputes subject to arbitration often lead to seemingly unpredictable and illogical outcomes, undercutting the original purpose of arbitration as dispute resolution "for the people" and eliminating the original reason to use arbitration in the first place.

Arbitration Between a Rock and a Hard Place

In short, modern arbitration presents a dichotomy and a dilemma. The dichotomy is between the dream of arbitration as an informal people's court, in which the disputants themselves can control the adjudicatory process, and the increasing reality of a process encrusted with complex, formalized, and often counterintuitive legalisms. The dilemma is how to promote the benefits of traditional arbitration, avoiding ancient judicial hostilities toward arms-length executory agreements to arbitrate, avoiding the intractable problems caused by overly legalistic arbitration, and yet still protect the rights of individuals who might be taken advantage of.

VARIETIES OF ARBITRATION

Beyond the dichotomy between traditional and legalistic arbitration, there are other variants commonly seen in today's arbitration practice. Table 19-1 summarizes some of these varieties.

Executory and Ad-Hoc Arbitration

Executory arbitration is arbitration provided according to an executory agreement. Thus, for example, if a consumer opens a bank account with a bank that imposes a duty of arbitration on the consumer, and later a dispute arises over a bank fee, the arbitration is of the executory type. *Ad-hoc arbitration* is arbitration agreed to after the fact of a dispute. For example, if an auto accident victim agrees to arbitrate his or her claim for damages with the other driver's insurance company, the proceeding is considered ad-hoc arbitration.

◆ **TABLE 19-1**   Varieties of Arbitration

CHARACTERISTIC	VARIATIONS		
Formality and rigidity of the process	*Informal arbitration: arbitration* characterized by minimal participation by lawyers, minimal discovery, procedural rules, or rules of evidence. Arbitrator may act in a facilitative manner.	*Formal arbitration:* arbitration marked by intensive participation by lawyers and by the same sorts of formalized and rigid procedural and evidentiary rules as are characteristic of litigation. In its extreme form, this sort of arbitration is almost identical to litigation.	
When a contract to arbitrate is formed	*Executory arbitration:* agreement to arbitrate predates dispute	*Ad-hoc arbitration:* agreement to arbitrate made after a dispute arises	
Types of labor arbitration	*Interest arbitration:* arbitration to determine terms of collective bargaining agreement	*Rights arbitration:* arbitration to adjudicate an unfair labor practices claim or another grievance	
Private or public sector	*Private arbitration:* arbitration not under auspices of public sector	*Court-connected "arbitration":* nonbinding evaluation process under court auspices	*Private judging,* or *rent-a-judge:* privately hired judge or referee provides arbitration with a legal impact identical to that of litigation
Varieties that restrict the nature of the arbitrator's award	*High-low arbitration:* arbitrator's decision is restricted to a range of possible outcomes by prior agreement of the disputants	*Final-offer or baseball arbitration:* arbitrator must choose between the final settlement offers propounded by the disputants	*Night baseball arbitration:* variant of final-offer arbitration in which the arbitrator renders a decision without knowing the final offers; the award is the final offer closest to the decision.
Bindingness of the outcome	*Binding arbitration:* arbitration in which the outcome is binding on all disputants ("true" arbitration)	*Incentive arbitration:* nonbinding evaluation in which the disputant who rejects the evaluator's decision is subject to a penalty	*Nonbinding "arbitration":* nonbinding evaluation process in which the evaluator renders a decision, which may be rejected without penalty by either disputant

ADMINISTERED AND NONADMINISTERED ARBITRATION

Another way to distinguish forms of arbitration is to consider whether the arbitration is *administered* or *nonadministered*. A number of organizations provide arbitration services to the public, the most well known of which is the American Arbitration Association (AAA, *www.adr.org*). Such organizations may be hired to provide a full range of support services, such as calendaring, hearing site, and the provision of procedural rules. Such a full-service arbitration is known as administered arbitration. Arbitration in which such administrative support is not provided by an arbitration organization is known as nonadministered arbitration. The AAA and other arbitration organizations have published model procedural rules, which can be used by disputants who wish to engage in nonadministered arbitration but who do not wish to create a set of rules from scratch.

INTEREST AND RIGHTS ARBITRATION

Labor arbitration is divided into *interest arbitration* and *rights arbitration* according to the sorts of issues being arbitrated. Put simply, interest arbitration settles collective bargaining *transactions,* whereas rights arbitration deals with *disputes* such as unfair labor practices complaints.

OTHER ARBITRATION VARIETIES

De novo

Latin, meaning "anew." In the law, a retrial of a previously decided dispute, in which all of the legal and factual issues may be relitigated and redecided. A trial *de novo* is in contrast to an appeal, in which only errors of law can be the basis for a change in the outcome.

One can distinguish between *private arbitration* and *court-based* (or court-connected) *arbitration.* However, court-based arbitration is not arbitration in the conceptual sense: it is nonbinding. In court-connected arbitration, disputants have a right to a trial **de novo.** This makes court-based arbitration a form of nonbinding evaluation: it is an assisted negotiation process, rather than an adjudicatory process, thus, court-based arbitration is discussed in Chapter 20. Another variant of arbitration, known as *incentive arbitration,* is midway between arbitration and nonbinding evaluation. In incentive arbitration, the arbitrator's decision is nonbinding, but penalties are assessed against the disputant who refuses to go along. This sort of process is a hybrid ADR process and is discussed in Chapter 21.

Several other arbitration variants are common. In *high-low arbitration,* disputants select a range of arbitration awards and the arbitrator is allowed to select only an award within that range. A special form of high-low arbitration called *final-offer* or *baseball arbitration*—so-called because it is often used to resolve baseball player contract disputes (Neuhauser & Swezey 1999)—requires the disputants to submit their final and best offers to the arbitrator, who may only select between them. The purpose of this form of arbitration is to give the disputants incentive to negotiate in good faith and to present a less extreme case to the arbitrator. In a subvariant of this sort of arbitration, referred to colorfully as *night baseball arbitration,* the final offers are submitted in secret, the arbitrator renders a decision without knowing them, and the final award is deemed to be the submitted offer that is closest to the arbitrator's decision. Finally, *rent-a-judge,* or *private judging,* is a form of judicial privatization in which the disputants hire a referee or an adjudicator pursuant to a statutory scheme (Kim 1994). In rent-a-judge, although the dispute is submitted by agreement to the neutral, defining the process conceptually as arbitration, the process and outcome of the proceeding are, in many respects, identical to that of litigation: the judge or referee may empanel juries, rules of evidence apply, and the result is appealable and of precedential impact.

ARBITRATION AND THE CONFLICT DIAGNOSTICIAN

How does arbitration fit into the arsenal of dispute resolution processes? The answer to this question is not a simple one, because there are so many varieties of arbitration.

Whatever the variety, arbitration is an adversary process, although some kinds of informal arbitration are less adversarial and more facilitative than other, more formal varieties. For this reason, arbitration fails to have many of the advantages of mediation for de-escalating conflict, protecting disputant relationships, and promoting integrative and creative solutions to conflict. Arbitration tends to create position-boundedness in the disputants. As each disputant, or advocate, presents his or her side of the dispute, the human tendency is to become ego-invested in the position that is taken. Unless the arbitrator is intimately familiar with the disputants and can look beyond positions to underlying interests, the arbitrator is likely merely to choose between the positions taken or to issue some sort of compromise.[5] Arbitration may also be less capable than facilitative mediation at producing the sorts of flexible remedies that deal best with interpersonal conflict. The arbitrator's ability to conceive of innovative, creative remedies will depend on his or her appreciation of the disputants' underlying interests, but, even if the arbitrator is an intimate of both disputants, his or her ability to perceive creative solutions may be blinded by the adversarial setting, and his or her ability to issue flexible solutions may be limited by the contract to arbitrate. Arbitration awards are, therefore, less likely than mediated agreements to result in a win-win accommodation for all concerned. Upon issuance of the award, one disputant is very likely to be unhappy with the result. This effect is important if the disputants will have any sort of continuing relationship after the conclusion of arbitration. Moreover, because the solution is unlikely to have integrative properties, it is typically less efficient in using the disputants' resources than are outcomes reached in mediation.

On the other hand, the extent to which arbitration harms relationships and promotes conflict escalation depends on the attitudes of the disputants and the form of the arbitration. For example, a consumer with a credit card dispute who is forced into arbitration by an executory agreement obscured in fine print in his cardholder agreement will likely be hostile about the result if he or she doesn't win, and his or her attitude toward other aspects of the relationship with the lender is likely to deteriorate. Even if the outcome is a compromise, the cardholder may see it as a defeat because of his or her perception that the process itself was tainted. On the other hand, imagine two business partners who are unable to resolve a dispute over business profits. If they mutually and willingly enter into ad-hoc arbitration under flexible and informal rules of engagement, the process is likely to reduce hostility and promote the continuance of the relationship. This is doubly the case if having recourse to arbitration is a familiar element of "industry culture." It should be borne in mind that the mediation of such a dispute might also promote the disputants' relationship and deescalate the conflict. But, if mediation has been tried and has failed to produce a settlement, informal arbitration is probably less escalating than litigating the issue.

---

[5] An arbitrator in the United States today is unlikely to have such familiarity with the disputants because of the demand for the arbitrator to be neutral and disinterested. In other parts of the world, arbitrators sometimes sacrifice their objectivity in favor of familiarity with the dispute and the disputants.

In some contexts and subcultures, arbitration is recognized as an alternative to litigation and a welcome respite from an even more adversary process. As such, it is less likely than litigation to generate conflict escalation. Also, if the arbitrator is an expert in the field being arbitrated (for example, in a software intellectual property context if the arbitrator is a software developer), the disputants may emphasize the arbitrator's expert power, rather than the adversarial context: the experience may be more like receiving parental advice than like going to battle. In some informal arbitration, fairness and industry culture are emphasized over legalisms, and the outcomes of these arbitrations are likely to be less escalating than those of highly legalistic arbitrations in which the major issue is who wins.

Besides the issues of relationship preservation and outcome creativity, another important conflict diagnosis issue is that of psychological ownership of the outcome. You may recall that psychological ownership is the sense that one has chosen, and can live with, the outcome of a dispute. Any process in which the outcome is imposed on the disputants by a third party, as opposed to being agreed to voluntarily, raises the possibility that one or both disputants will not psychologically own the outcome. Lack of psychological ownership increases the likelihood of legal challenge to the outcome, sabotage of the outcome, and outright lack of compliance.

A disputant's psychological ownership of an arbitration award depends, in part, on the extent to which the decision to arbitrate was the result of an arms-length transaction between the disputants, as opposed to something imposed by one disputant on the other. An arbitration award with which a disputant is unhappy is more likely to be psychologically owned if the disputant perceives the process itself as procedurally just. If the disputant willingly goes along with the arbitration, and feels that the process is fair and just, then he or she will have a greater sense of psychological ownership of the outcome than if he or she feels the process is imposed or unfair. Perceptions about procedural justice of the process, in turn, depend on the context of the dispute resolution process and the unique characteristics of the disputant. For example, in a community setting involving a neighborhood dispute, a highly formalized process involving rigid rules of evidence and other legalisms might not be understandable to the disputant and, therefore, would not be perceived as particularly fair. On the other hand, a highly informal process might be perceived as unfair and unjust to a disputant who is an experienced trial attorney or a business executive familiar with the litigation process. When arbitration between very different disputants occurs, it may be difficult to achieve a process that all parties feel is procedurally just.

In considering whether arbitration is an appropriate process to use, a conflict diagnostician should consider some basic advantages and disadvantages of the arbitration process. These advantages and disadvantages are summarized in Table 19-2 and discussed later.

◆ TABLE 19-2   Advantages and Disadvantages of Arbitration

COMPARISON WITH	PROS	CONS
Litigation	Informal arbitration is usually much less time-consuming, less expensive, easier to handle	Informal arbitration may create due process problems
	Informal arbitration: arbitrator may not be limited by "cause of action" perspective and narrow remedy options	Arbitration imposed on consumers or others with inferior bargaining power may violate constitutional guarantees of the right to civil trial by jury
	Some types of arbitration act as precedent	Some arbitrators' decisions are arbitrary; limited appealability may lead to bad outcome
	Particularly useful when there are intractible choice-of-law or choice-of-forum issues, as in international commercial conflicts	Most arbitration does not result in the creation of legal precedent; if large numbers of particular types of cases are forced into arbitration, the need for legal reform will not be communicated to judges and legislators
	If litigants want adjudication, hiring an arbitrator can take less time than waiting for a trial date	
	Not reviewable to the same extent as litigation; disputants may wish to have this greater degree of finality	Arbitrators may contribute to the exploitation of a weak disputant by a strong one; of particular concern when binding arbitration is mandated in contracts of adhesion
	Disputants can choose an adjudicator with a specific background and expertise	Privacy may make it easier for bigoted disputants and arbitrators to act on their prejudices than it is for litigants and judges
	Assuming that the agreement to arbitrate is a voluntary, arms-length transaction and perceived as procedurally "just," disputants are more likely to psychologically own the result because it is the result of their voluntary action	Formalized arbitration designed to protect disputant due process rights can be at least as expensive, time-consuming, and complex as litigation
Negotiation	Particularly effective when the principal source of the conflict is a differing perception about facts or law	More harmful to relationships: an adversary process; may settle a short-term dispute but set the stage for a long-term adversarial relationship
	More final in that a final decision is definitely rendered	Disputants must surrender control over the outcome to a third party
	Because the decision is rendered by a third party, loss-of-face problems in making concessions are avoided	Less likely to generate creative, optimal solutions
		More expensive, time-consuming
		Rules of reviewability, choice of law, and arbitrability are highly complex; results are often counterintuitive and/or hard to predict; more likely to be vulnerable to legal maneuvering
Mediation	Particularly effective when the principal source of the conflict is a differing perception about facts or law (but skilled mediators can deal effectively with this issue)	More harmful to relationships: an adversary process; may settle a short-term dispute but set the stage for a long-term adversarial relationship
	More final in that the final decision is definitely rendered	Disputants must surrender control over the outcome to a third party
	"Informal arbitration" may be quicker than facilitative mediation	Less likely to generate creative, optimal solutions
	Because a decision is rendered by a third party, loss-of-face problems in making concessions are avoided (but mediators are often skilled at dealing with such impediments, anyway)	More likely to impair due process rights because the outcome is binding
		"Formal" arbitration is far more expensive and time-consuming
		Rules of reviewability, choice of law, and arbitrability are highly complex; results are often counterintuitive and/or hard to predict; more likely to be vulnerable to legal maneuvering

ADVANTAGES OF ARBITRATION, COMPARED TO LITIGATION

The advantages of arbitration over litigation depend, in part, on the type of arbitration that is used. Arbitration almost always takes less time—from the inception of a claim to the outcome—than litigation, because it isn't necessary to wade through the usual backlog of court cases. The disputants simply hire an arbitrator and move directly into the process. Whether the arbitration process itself is more efficient than the litigation process depends on the kind of arbitration and on the existence of any legal challenges to arbitration. Informal, mutually chosen arbitration is much simpler, quicker, less expensive, and more efficient than litigation. Very formalized arbitration can be at least as time-consuming and may be even more expensive because of the arbitrator's fees.

Informal arbitration also offers flexibility that litigation cannot. The arbitration can, with mutual consent, be structured to permit the arbitrator to make his or her ruling on fairness grounds, rather than on a strictly legal basis. Arbitrators may also be empowered to engage in a certain amount of facilitation prior to entering a ruling—which may allow the arbitrator to learn more about the disputants' underlying interests before making the award and may enable the arbitrator to increase the disputants' psychological ownership of the outcome. The arbitrator may also be given a degree of remedial flexibility that is not available in litigation because the outcome of any lawsuit is strictly limited by the applicable law. On the other hand, arbitrator flexibility, especially flexibility and informality of process, can backfire. If one of the disputants feels that the arbitrator is biased against him or her, a flexible process can undermine the sense of psychological ownership of the outcome and can even lead to a legal challenge to the award in some cases. A disinterested, rigid, and legalistic arbitration process can protect the process from the appearance or fact of bias or injustice—after all, that is the reason for procedural rigor in the litigation process.

Like mediation, another advantage to arbitration over litigation is that disputants can mutually choose whether to make the proceeding public or private. Arbitration offers a choice of private or public forum, whereas litigation is always, with limited exceptions, public. On the other hand, if public-policy considerations would favor publicizing the outcome, or if one disputant imposes privacy or publicity on a disputant with inferior bargaining power, this feature of arbitration can be detrimental. Imagine, for example, a credit card agreement affecting millions of consumers in which private arbitration is mandated.

Arbitration may also offer a degree of finality that litigation cannot. As we shall see later in the chapter, arbitration awards are not, with the exception of decisions reached by rent-a-judges, reviewable by a court to the same extent as litigated judgments. This feature of arbitration can be of substantial benefit to disputants who simply need the matter settled once and for all. On the other hand, if the outcome is extremely adverse to one of the disputants, and appears to be clearly erroneous, this feature of arbitration can be a detriment.

Choice of law
the determination of which
jurisdiction's laws should apply.

Arbitration also has advantages in situations in which, for whatever reason, an adjudication is desired but litigation is impractical. For example, the litigation of a dispute between multinational disputants can raise nasty **choice-of-law** issues. Litigating these issues, perhaps in multiple courts, can be time-consuming, can be expensive, and can raise the potential of unpredictable results. Moreover, the citizens of one nation may fear biased treatment if the matter is litigated in the court of a different nation. If the disputants are able to specify choice of law and forum in the agreement to arbitrate, these intractable issues can be avoided simply, expediently, and cheaply.

Another area in which arbitration shines, compared with litigation, is in the participants' ability to select the arbitrator. If the dispute involves a highly technical area, an expert in the field can be chosen to be arbitrator. For example, in a dispute involving the determination of responsibility of one of several contractors for the failure of a building under construction, the disputants could select a panel of arbitrators that includes an experienced construction lawyer and a structural engineer. Such selection will reduce the amount of hearing preparation required by the disputants, will help to ensure that the outcome reflects fairness in the context of industry culture, and may help to reassure the parties that the decision is based on sound wisdom. In the arbitration of a child-custody matter, the disputants can select an arbitrator with a professional background in child development, ensuring that the outcome reflects a real consideration of the health and welfare of the child.

DISADVANTAGES OF ARBITRATION, COMPARED WITH LITIGATION

What weaknesses does arbitration have, relative to litigation? When arbitration is between arms-length disputants and is wholeheartedly embraced by all concerned, there aren't many weaknesses. But, when arbitration is forced on disputants, the situation is different. Arbitration, particularly the informal variety, into which disputants are pressured or coerced, raises due process issues. The lack of procedural protections may mean that the arbitrator is not presented with an effectively balanced case to decide. The arbitration itself may be so lacking in the basic elements of fairness that the process is egregious. For example, in *Hooters of America v. Phillips,* 173 F. 3d 933 (C.A. 4 1999), an employee was required by her employment contract to participate in arbitration determined by the court to be "so egregiously unfair as to constitute a complete default of [the employer's] contractual obligation to draft arbitration rules and to do so in good faith" (173 F.3d at 938). The *Hooters* agreement to arbitrate provided that the employee, but not the employer, was required to provide written notice of claim and a list of all prospective witnesses; that the employer, but not the employee, was allowed to cancel the agreement to arbitrate; that the panel of arbitrators had to be selected from a list promulgated by the employer; that the employer, but not the employee, was allowed to raise additional claims at the hearing; that the employer, but not the employee, could seek summary judgment; and that the employer, but not the employee, could seek review of the award (173 F.3d at 939). In addition to procedural due process issues associated with the procedural details of arbitration, it has been asserted (Sternlight 2001) that executory agreements to arbitrate between disputants of unequal bargaining power impermissibly take away the weaker disputant's right to a jury trial. Even if a jury trial right is not of concern, it has been argued that executory agreements to arbitrate foisted on low-power individuals by large organizations are unfair because the large organizations are "repeat players": they have numerous such agreements, and thus far more experience with the entire process, and with how to get the best possible result, and they are likely to have developed cozy relationships with the arbitrators. The low-power individuals, primarily employees and consumers, are not likely to have this sort of knowledge and experience. Commentators such as law professor Sarah Rudolph Cole (1996) assert, for these reasons, that executory agreements to arbitrate imposed on employees and consumers by employers and large commercial entities should not be enforced.

Other problems with arbitration concern its privacy. As with coercive forms of mediation, if large numbers of particular sorts of cases are pushed into an arbitration process, the need for legal reforms might not be communicated to the level of the appellate courts or legislatures, as they would if the matter were litigated. For example, if banks required their patrons to arbitrate according to a scheme adopted by the entire industry, then prevailing problems in the law of consumer banking would not reach the appellate courts. A second problem connected to privacy involves disempowerment and bigotry. As with other private ADR processes, private arbitration allows for the increased possibility of oppression of weaker disputants by stronger ones. Similarly, commentators have worried that private ADR will lead to more openly bigoted behavior by the participants. Privacy may make it easier for bigoted disputants and arbitrators to act on their prejudices than it is for litigants and judges. And, unlike mediation and other forms of negotiation, arbitration is more dangerous, because the disputant has no power to reject the outcome.

ADVANTAGES OF ARBITRATION, COMPARED WITH NEGOTIATION

Arbitration offers some major advantages when compared with negotiation not involving a neutral. Arbitration is particularly effective in overcoming a conflict whose principal source is a divergence of perception over facts or law. Nonbinding evaluation (see Chapter 20) offers similar benefits, but arbitration is also more final, in that a final decision is definitely rendered. Often, if disputants are going to be involved in an adversary process before a neutral, it will seem nonsensical to stop with an evaluation when a final decision can be made by the neutral, settling the entire matter.

Additionally, because the arbitration decision is rendered by a third party, loss-of-face problems in making concessions can sometimes be avoided. The arbitrator can take on the possible loss of face by issuing what is clear to the disputants to be the "fair" decision, while allowing the disputant who risks loss of face to retain his or her position. This facet of arbitration can also be desirable to attorneys who wish to retain their "gladiator" image during the proceedings. Finally, as with mediation, arbitration may be advantageous simply because it exists as an option. Often, disputants who enter arbitration have already tried negotiation, and it has failed to resolve the conflict.

DISADVANTAGES OF ARBITRATION, COMPARED WITH NEGOTIATION

There are several disadvantages of arbitration, compared with negotiation without a neutral. Arbitration is likely to be more harmful to relationships because it is an adversary process. Thus, arbitration may settle a short-term dispute but set the stage for a long-term adversarial relationship. Since it is adversarial, arbitration is more likely to result in a choice between extreme positions, rather than win-win, optimal solutions for both parties. Obviously, this is a particular problem in final-offer arbitration. Moreover, disputants in arbitration must surrender their control over the outcome of their dispute to the arbitrator, making it likely that one or both disputants will lack psychological ownership of the outcome. It is likely to be more expensive and time-consuming than negotiation, and, since an outcome is imposed on the disputants, it is more likely than consensual processes to be subject to legal maneuvering.

ADVANTAGES OF ARBITRATION, COMPARED WITH MEDIATION

Arbitration's advantages over mediation are similar to those of arbitration over other forms of negotiation. It can be useful in overcoming divergent perceptions of fact or law. Many disputants and their advocates also appreciate the binding quality of arbitration and its ability to overcome the loss-of-face issues associated with negotiation. Arbitration may simply have a more familiar feel to many attorneys, who are used to trial work, and feel like fish out of water in the mediation setting. Thus, many attorneys may choose arbitration for their clients on the basis that they believe they can provide more effective representation in such a context.

Although both arbitration and mediation are noted for their efficiency, some informal varieties of arbitration are probably quicker, in theory, than highly facilitative forms of mediation. The reason for this advantage of arbitration is that it takes less time and effort to state a position than to explore the sources of a conflict, conduct an interests analysis, invent multiple options for disputants' mutual gains, and choose among the options. On the other hand, facilitative mediation may be more efficient in the long run in resolving the wider conflict and supporting a more effective disputant relationship.

DISADVANTAGES OF ARBITRATION, COMPARED WITH MEDIATION

A recent trend has been for commentators, including scholars and practitioners of arbitration, to advocate the use of mediation over arbitration as a process of "first resort" (Barnes 1997; Sander & Goldberg 1994, 59–60). The principal reason for this development is probably that the apparent usefulness of arbitration in overcoming loss of face and divergent perception may be more illusory than real: skilled mediators have specific tools and expertise in dealing with face-saving and perceptual challenges. Moreover, in many instances, a dispute that looks, at first glance, like a simple case of individual greed or divergent perception turns out to be something different and more amenable to mediation. In such cases, creative problem solving will produce much more satisfied disputants and a more optimal use of resources. Also, as discussed in Chapter 15, mediation is better able than adjudication to handle the entire landscape of an interpersonal conflict in a way that creates psychological ownership of the outcome. But, without trying mediation first, the disputants will often be blinded by the invisible veil to the complexities of such a conflict, and the benefits of using mediation will never become evident. Moreover, since arbitration is an adversary process, it is more likely to generate conflict escalation, whereas mediation (particularly the facilitative type) is specifically designed to de-escalate conflict. Finally, if arbitration is in any way coercive, or imposed unwillingly on one of the disputants, issues of fairness and due process may be raised. Mediation, a consensual process, is less likely to run afoul of these considerations, simply because the disputants have the option of rejecting any proposed settlement.

PROCESS OF ARBITRATION

Arbitration consists of eight basic steps:

1. Creating the arbitration contract
2. Demanding, choosing, or opting for arbitration
3. Selecting the arbitrator or arbitrator panel
4. Selecting a set of procedural rules
5. Preparing for arbitration
6. Participating in the arbitration hearing
7. Issuing the arbitration award
8. Enforcing the award

CREATING THE ARBITRATION CONTRACT

Arbitration always begins with a *contract to arbitrate*. The arbitration contract may be executory—that is, developed prior to the development of a dispute—or ad-hoc—that is, developed in an effort to resolve an existing dispute.

As with any other contract, the arbitration contract should be designed to minimize the likelihood of dispute escalation. For this reason, it should be as clear and simple as possible, should anticipate future developments, and should be appropriately fair and equitable. Gary H. Barnes (1997) of Downs Rachlin & Martin makes the following additional recommendations:

1. The matters to be arbitrated should be set out explicitly. Ambiguity in the arbitration contract as to what matters are arbitrable can open up the outcome to court challenge later. As we shall see later in our discussion, arbitrators are generally given the benefit of the doubt in such matters, but not before the time and expense of litigation are added to the process.

2. The expenses of arbitration, such as the cost of the arbitrator's fee, the cost of any transcript, and the cost of renting a hearing room, should be shared equitably by the disputants.

3. Arbitrator selection and qualification should be considered carefully. It's important to have a selection process that is appropriately tailored to the dispute, that is perceived as fair by all concerned, and that minimizes the possibility of deadlock (for example, never use an even number of arbitrators).

4. The agreement should specify whether discovery is to be permitted, and, if so, the permissible forms and extent of discovery and due dates should be specified clearly.

5. The hearing or hearings, and their duration, may be explicitly scheduled. Or this matter may be left to the arbitrator or administrating organization.

6. Privacy and confidentiality should be addressed, as should the preparation of transcripts.

7. The arbitrators' roles in the process should be clarified. For example, some disputants may want to create a hybrid process in which mediation occurs before or after an arbitration hearing. Arbitrators run the gamut from strictly judicial to informal and facilitative; if the disputants have a preference, the nature of the arbitrator's intervention should be clarified.

8. If specific rules of evidence are desired, and mutually agreed upon, they should be specified. Otherwise, the hearing will generally be informal, without rigid rules of evidence.

9. The disputants should specify whether briefs, points and authorities, and other ancillary documentation will be accepted in arbitration; if so, they should set out a schedule for their submission.

10. The agreement should specify the nature of the arbitrator's award. For example, some arbitration awards simply state the outcome, whereas others are accompanied by detailed explanatory opinions.

11. Reviewability and enforcement of the award may be spelled out. However, the prevailing law should be consulted before launching into the drafting of such a provision. There are situations in which

the arbitration contract will override prevailing law, other situations in which the prevailing law will override the contract, and situations in which the law is unsettled. (For more on this subject, a useful review is found in Curtin 2000.)

12. Choice of law may be spelled out in the agreement if the disputants come from different states or nations, or the subject matter of the dispute may occur in a state or nation different from the residence of one of or both of the disputants. However, including such a provision can open the award to attack in the courts unless the provision is very clear or explicitly vests the power to determine choice of law in the arbitrator. Choices of law sometimes lead to counterintuitive results because of local differences in procedure and substantive practice and because of the influence of the FAA and other supervening law.

13. If provisional remedies, such as preliminary or temporary injunctions, may be needed while arbitration is pending, they must be explicitly provided for in arbitration. The arbitrator's powers are limited to those specified in the arbitration contract.

14. Finally, disputants should consider including a clause providing for mediation as a first resort in any executory agreement to arbitrate. Mediation is less adversarial and can protect ongoing business relationships more effectively than arbitration.

A Sample Executory Arbitration Clause

United States Arbitration and Mediation (USA&M), a private ADR service provider, posts the following sample arbitration clause on the World Wide Web for use by individuals who wish to use its arbitration services:

In the event a dispute shall arise between the parties to this [contract, lease, etc.], it is hereby agreed that the dispute shall be referred to [one of the following choices:

(1) designate a specific USA&M office or alternate service by agreement of the parties

(2) provide a method of selecting the arbitrator and sites of the hearing, such as "from the county wherein the manufacturing plant is located"; or for multijurisdictional disputes

(3) insert "a USA&M office to be designated by USA&M National Headquarters"]

for arbitration in accordance with the applicable United States Arbitration and Mediation Rules of Arbitration. The arbitrator's decision shall be final and legally binding and judgment may be entered thereon.

Each party shall be responsible for its share of the arbitration fees in accordance with the applicable Rules of Arbitration. In the event a party fails to proceed with arbitration, unsuccessfully challenges the arbitrator's award, or fails to comply with the arbitrator's award, the other party is entitled to costs of suit, including a reasonable attorney's fee for having to compel arbitration or defend or enforce the award.

THIS CONTRACT CONTAINS A BINDING ARBITRATION PROVISION WHICH AFFECTS YOUR LEGAL RIGHTS AND MAY BE ENFORCED BY THE PARTIES.

The authors note that many issues related to the conduct of the arbitration, such as the selection of the arbitrator and the adoption of specific procedural rules, are handled by the firm's administered arbitration rules; if nonadministered arbitration is chosen, these matters must be explicitly covered in the arbitration clause. (*http://www.usam.com/services/arb_clause.shtml*, 23 January 2002.)

DEMANDING, CHOOSING, OR OPTING FOR ARBITRATION

Assuming an executory agreement to arbitrate is in effect, arbitration is triggered by a *demand to institute arbitration*. This demand can be as informal as a telephone call, but more often it is made in writing. Professional associations such as the AAA provide forms for formally instituting arbitration. If the dispute arises in the absence of an executory agreement to arbitrate, an ad-hoc agreement to arbitrate will substitute for a demand to arbitrate.

A Sample Notice of Arbitration

Following is the American Film Marketing Association's sample notice of arbitration, provided to the public on its website, *http://www.afma.com/Arbitration/sample_arbit_notice.asp*:

[Date]
[Respondent Company Name]
[Address]
Attention: [Name]
Via [fax] and/or [mail]
Re: Notice of Arbitration

In accordance with the requirements of Rule 2 of the AFMA Rules for International Arbitration, Claimant hereby notifies Respondent and AFMA of the following:

Pursuant to Rule 2.4.1., demand is hereby made that the dispute between [Claimant Name] and [Respondent Name] be referred to arbitration.

Pursuant to Rules 2.4.2. and Rule 2.4.3., the names, addresses, telephone, and fax numbers, if available, of the parties to this dispute and the names, addresses, telephone, and fax numbers, if available, of the respective legal counsel are as follows:

[List information]

Pursuant to Rule 2.4.4., a copy of the arbitration clause contained in the attached contract(s) located [List the page or paragraph number of each contract where the arbitration clause is located] is referenced as follows:

[Copy the entire arbitration clause language]

Pursuant to Rule 2.4.5., a copy of the relevant contract(s) are attached hereto.

Pursuant to Rule 2.4.6., [Claimant Name] sets forth a statement of the nature of the dispute and the amount involved, if any, as follows:

[Describe dispute]

Pursuant to Rule 2.4.7., the relief or remedy sought by [Claimant Name] is as follows:

[Describe relief or remedy sought]

The foregoing is not intended nor shall it be construed as a complete recitation of the facts and events concerning the above-referenced matter, nor shall it be construed as a waiver of any rights, remedies or claims, legal or equitable, which [Claimant Name] may have.

Sincerely,
[Claimant Name]

_____
[Name of Signatory]
[Title]
cc: AFMA Arbitral Agent

SELECTING THE ARBITRATOR OR ARBITRATION PANEL

The third step in the arbitration process is *selecting the arbitrator*. In many cases, this step will have begun with the executory agreement to arbitrate. Deciding who will serve as the arbitrator should be determined by a multitude of factors. If the dispute is highly technical, it is useful to choose an arbitrator who is an expert in the subject matter of the dispute. If emotions are running high, it may be helpful to ask a disinterested party to choose the arbitrator; for example, a professional association such as the AAA can assign a member arbitrator to the dispute. Or a common approach to a low-trust, high-conflict situation is for each of the disputants to select an arbitrator and for the two selected persons to pick a third arbitrator. Of course, a multiple-arbitrator panel is usually more costly than a single arbitrator. The arbitrator selection process is limited only by the nature of the agreement to arbitrate, the creativity of the disputants and their advocates, and the participants' shared notions of fairness.

SELECTING THE PROCEDURAL RULES

Next, the parties to arbitration should *select procedural rules* to govern the arbitration. The general guidelines for this decision are the following:

- If the arbitration agreement doesn't empower the arbitrator to do something, the arbitrator won't be able to do it. For example, if the arbitration agreement doesn't specify that the arbitrator can provide provisional relief, the granting of provisional relief will be beyond the scope of the arbitration.
- In the absence of procedural rules, the arbitrator is empowered to run an informal arbitration proceeding and probably will do so.

Whether arbitration is administered or nonadministered, disputants may choose to arbitrate under the auspices of a particular professional arbitration organization's procedural rules. For example, the AAA provides rules and procedures that are intended to govern a wide range of disputes, including employment, health-care, real estate, commercial, estate, intellectual property, and online disputes. (These rules and procedures are available online at *http://www. adr.org.*) Disputants and advocates can benefit from the adoption of such model rules because it avoids the need to reinvent the wheel and helps the disputants cover all the necessary procedural issues. Disputants can agree to waive any or all of the specific rules in a set of model rules in preference for their own version. For example, disputants might agree to modify a discovery provision in a set of procedural rules to allow interrogatories, but not depositions, to streamline the process and save time and money.

PREPARING FOR ARBITRATION

Assuming that a dispute is pending, arbitration has been demanded, and neither disputant is contesting arbitrability of the dispute, the next step is to *prepare for arbitration.*

The sort of preparation necessary will depend on the arbitration agreement. Preparing for an arbitration hearing is similar to preparing for litigation, except that arbitration is usually less formal. There are arbitration processes, however, that are virtually indistinguishable from litigation except for the identity of the neutral and the source of the neutral's authority. As with any ADR process, effective preparation for arbitration requires maximizing one's expert power: getting up to speed on facts and law, organizing the evidence to be presented, and planning a presentation strategy that complies with the procedural rules in effect. If discovery and/or brief submission are permitted, the team should take advantage of these opportunities. Additionally, the team must make strategic decisions about how to ensure that the appropriate witnesses will appear at the hearing. Many arbitration statutes confer subpoena power on the arbitrator to help the legal team ensure that witnesses attend.

As with mediation and other assisted negotiation processes, an effective conflict diagnosis, including a careful interests analysis and BATNA analysis, can be critical in preparing for arbitration. Many times, arbitration will have a facilitative component, and the disputant and his or her legal team should be prepared to take advantage of such an opportunity to maximize underlying interests, values, and needs. In any event, a careful conflict diagnosis should precede the effort to prepare a case for any sort of adjudication, because it will guide the team in determining how best to present the case in view of the disputant's overall best interests. Since arbitration is more flexible than litigation in procedure and potential outcomes, it may be possible to do more in arbitration to see that underlying interests are addressed.

PARTICIPATING IN THE ARBITRATION HEARING

The next step is to *participate in the arbitration hearing.* Generally, the disputants and their attorneys attend, and the disputants give evidence, usually on an informal basis. Some arbitration hearings are transcribed by a court reporter, if so specified in the procedural rules the disputants have adopted. The attorneys may present opening and closing statements, and they may conduct direct and cross-examination, as with litigation. The arbitrator may also ask questions, and the disputants may be free to add their own remarks. The arbitrator may also receive (or reject, if deemed appropriate) documentary and other evidence. It is likely to be received on a less formal basis than in litigation, and the arbitrator is likely to accept a wider range of evidence than a court would.

For example, the arbitrator may allow hearsay evidence, with the understanding that he or she will duly consider the possibility that it is untrustworthy. In some expedited forms of arbitration, there may not be an actual hearing; instead, the arbitrator will decide the case based on documentary arguments and evidence.

The arbitration hearing typically has an adversarial, adjudicatory flavor, but it may also look a little like mediation as well. Traditionally, some arbitrators have seen their role as going beyond the rigid restrictions of legal determination and are motivated to make a decision that all parties can live with. Hence, some arbitrators facilitate negotiations between the disputants and may even encourage the disputants to settle the matter instead of waiting for the arbitration decision. Or the arbitrator may try to get a sense of what the disputants can accept, then issue a compromise decision on that basis.

ISSUING THE ARBITRATION AWARD

Following the hearing, the arbitrator, or arbitration panel, *issues a decision.* The decision may be issued on the spot, or, as is more common, after a period of deliberation the outcome may be communicated by mail. (The Uniform Arbitration Act, which is a model arbitration statute adopted by a majority of the states, requires that the award be in writing.) Depending on the rules of procedure chosen, an explanatory opinion may accompany the award.

ENFORCING THE AWARD

If the arbitrator's award requires action by one of the disputants, it may become necessary to engage in legal action to *enforce the arbitrator's award.* A refusal to comply with an arbitrator's award can be considered a breach of the original contract to arbitrate, so an action can be filed in an appropriate court for confirmation of and enforcement of the award. (Arbitrators are hired hands, not arms of the government, so they do not have direct power to enforce their own awards. Rent-a-judges are exceptions.) Since a breach-of-contract case can be cumbersome and time-consuming, many jurisdictions have adopted streamlined procedures that allow the confirmation and enforcement of arbitration awards.[6]

LAW OF ARBITRATION

Arbitration would be an extremely simple process if everyone involved in every arbitration proceeding accepted it with enthusiasm. However, arbitration, being an adjudicatory process, frequently leads to at least one dissatisfied customer. And, when a disputant is dragged, kicking and screaming, into an arbitration he considers loathsome, the disputant is likely to search for ways to avoid the process or its outcome. From these obvious facts about human motivation, and the legal community's response to making arbitration a process with "teeth", a complex, often difficult, and occasionally bizarre law of arbitration has arisen. As with mediation, the field of arbitration is rapidly evolving, and a legal or dispute professional involved in an arbitration issue must constantly update his or her understanding of arbitration law. Figure 19-1 displays the legal issues in arbitration law. "Front-end" and "back-end" issues are those specific to arbitration law, affecting when the court system will become involved with an arbitration proceeding. The law during arbitration is generally determined by the arbitrator and relates to the substantive and procedural law the participants will use and apply. Finally, choice-of-law issues affect the arbitration process before, during, and after the arbitration ends.

BEFORE ARBITRATION

When Should a Dispute Be Arbitrated? Enforceability and Arbitrability. If disputants make an executory agreement to arbitrate, but one disputant subsequently drags his or her feet, should the agreement be enforced? The FAA seemingly answered this question by providing (Section 2) that arbitration agreements are enforceable, as is any contract, and by providing for a federal court procedure for enforcing arbitration agreements (Section 4). This seemingly simple approach belies a level of complexity in determining the **enforceability** and arbitrability of disputes.

Enforceability. Like any contract, some arbitration agreements can be successfully challenged as unenforceable, due to a defect, such as fraud in the inducement or

Enforceability
whether the contract to arbitrate is valid and can be enforced against the party seeking to avoid arbitration.

---

[6] For example, the Uniform Arbitration Act provides for such expedited procedure.

◆ **FIGURE 19-1**

Arbitration Law

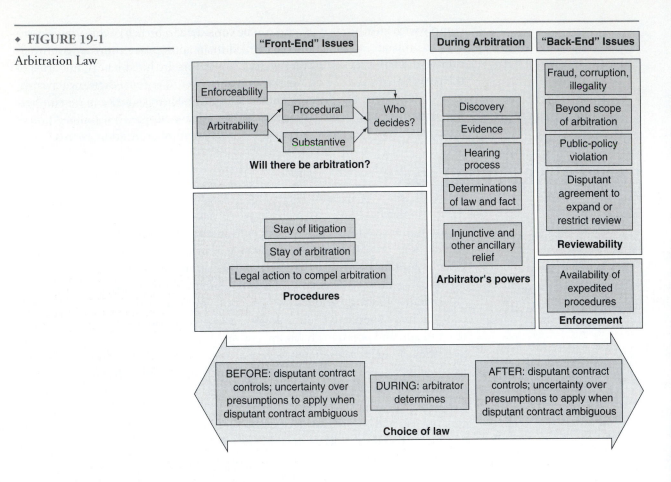

illegality. For example, in the *Hooters* case, the court held that the rules of arbitration propounded by the employer-disputant in an employment arbitration were so one-sided and unfair that they merited recission (undoing) of the arbitration agreement. In *Prima Paint Corp. v. Flood & Conklin Mfg. Corp.,* 388 U.S. 395 (1967), the claim was fraud in the inducement of one of the parties to enter into the contract of which the arbitration agreement was a part.

One increasingly controversial issue in the arbitration field is whether arbitration clauses that are imposed on consumers, or other disputants lacking bargaining power, by large commercial enterprises or other powerful entities should be enforceable. Of particular concern are arbitration agreements that are offered on a take-it-or-leave-it basis to consumers who do not have the power to negotiate an alternative. Although many commentators express a concern that such contracts are unfair to consumers (Carrington 1998; Haagen 1998; Schwartz 1997; Smith 2001; Speidel 1998), the courts have uniformly held that such contracts are valid and enforceable, even against a consumer who does not wish to arbitrate, unless something about the arbitration scheme itself is grossly unfair, as in the *Hooters* litigation.[7] Moreover, the Supreme Court has held that state laws that attempt to restrict the abilities of commercial entities to impose such contracts on consumers are invalid because they conflict with the FAA. See, for instance, *Doctor's Associates, Inc. v. Casarotto,* 517 U.S. 681 (1996), discussed in the context of substantive arbitrability below. Courts have generally required some additional impediment to the contract in order to deny enforcement (Smith 2001).

Arbitrability
whether a particular dispute is subject to an agreement to arbitrate.

Arbitrability. **Arbitrability** refers to whether the dispute in question is legally subject to arbitration under an otherwise valid arbitration agreement. Arbitrability can be of two varieties, substantive and procedural. *Substantive arbitrability* refers to whether the contract to arbitrate does, or can, cover the interpersonal conflict between the disputants. *Procedural arbitrability* refers to whether there are procedural impediments to arbitration.

Substantive arbitrability, in turn, is usually thought of as including two subissues. The first is whether the language of the contract to arbitrate should be interpreted to include the dispute, as in whether an agreement to arbitrate "all disputes arising out of John Doe's employment with ABC Corporation" would cover a dispute over ABC Corporation's contracting out work to a subcontractor, thereby lessening the amount of work available for the employee.[8] Although principles that apply to all contracts are used to determine whether a claim is arbitrable, agreements to arbitrate are liberally interpreted to require arbitration. The reason for this deferential treatment is to close a potential loophole in the scheme providing for arbitration. A disputant who wants to make an end run around arbitration may argue that the other disputant's claims for relief are so frivolous that they, in effect, are not contemplated by the arbitration agreement. By this means, the resisting disputant can bring the "merits" of the case—that is, who would win on the underlying claim—into the courtroom, short-circuiting the efficiency of the arbitration scheme. This is the sort of problem presented in *International Ass'n of Machinists, Local Number 402 v. Cutler-Hammer, Inc.,* 74 N.E.2d 464 (N.Y. 1947). To avoid this sort of result, the Supreme Court has ruled that, in determining whether a dispute falls within an arbitration agreement, a court is confined to ascertaining whether the party seeking arbitration is making a claim which on its face is governed by the contract *(United Steelworkers of America v. American Mfg. Co.,* 363 U.S. 564, 568 [1960] *(Steelworkers I)).*

Although *Steelworkers I* involves labor law, and, thus, a different statutory scheme than nonlabor cases, this rule of presumptive arbitrability has been

---

[7] *Circuit City Stores v. Adams,* 279 F.3d 889 (C.A. 9 2002) reached a similar result. Although the fact that a contract to arbitrate is one of adhesion is not enough to allow a disputant to escape having it enforced on him or her, the contract will often be set aside if it provides for an unfair or one-sided process. In the *Circuit City* case, the United States Court of Appeals refused to enforce an arbitration agreement against an employee when the employer, but not the employee, had the choice of going directly to court and when the employee was disallowed from pursuing certain statutory remedies under the arbitration process.

[8] These are substantially the facts in *United Steelworkers of America v. Warrior & Gulf Navigation Co.,* 363 U.S. 574 (1960), commonly known as *Steelworkers II.*

extended to matters of commercial arbitration governed by the FAA (Hayford 2000; *Moses H. Cone Memorial Hospital v. Mercury Construction Corp.,* 460 U.S. 1, 1983). In general, in determining arbitrability, a court can't go beyond looking at the plain language of the arbitration provision to determine whether the claim, on its face, could be considered within the agreement. Modern arbitration provisions in contracts are so broad that this sort of challenge to arbitrability is seldom successful.

The second issue of substantive arbitrability concerns whether a particular matter is legally excluded from arbitration. One such arbitrability question arises when a statute seems to disallow arbitration of the dispute in question or provides for a process that excludes the arbitration alternative.[9] For example, in *Wilko v. Swan,* 346 U.S. 427 (1953), subsequently overruled by *Rodriguez de Quijas v. Shearson/American Express,* 490 U.S. 477 (1989), the Supreme Court held that claims by a consumer against a securities broker for fraud arising under the Securities Act of 1933 are not arbitrable because the act provided a specific adjudicatory process and prevented "stipulations" allowing waiver of the act's benefits.

Under present law, a dispute is considered arbitrable unless a statute clearly disallows arbitration.[10] Moreover, *state* statutes, even those that clearly and explicitly require disputants to use the courts, rather than arbitration, to address disputes are typically held to be *pre-empted* by the FAA. In other words, such state statutes prohibiting arbitration are held to be improperly in conflict with the FAA's overriding rule favoring providing for the disputants' ability to contract for arbitration. That's substantially what happened in *Southland Corp. v. Keating,* 465 U.S. 1 (1984). In *Southland,* a group of Seven-Eleven franchise owners in California claimed that Southland, the franchisor, had defrauded them and had breached their franchise agreements. The franchise agreements contained arbitration clauses, but the California Franchise Investment Law contained an explicit court procedure for deciding such issues and disallowed any effort to circumvent the judicial remedy. The United States Supreme Court, holding that the franchisees could not seek a remedy in court, ruled that the statute purporting to invalidate arbitration in such cases was void under the FAA.

This rule has been extended to encompass even modest statutory efforts to restrict arbitration. For example, in an effort to make arbitration agreements consumer-friendly, a Montana statute provided that "notice that a contract is subject to arbitration . . . shall be typed in underlined capital letters on the first page of the contract; and unless such notice is displayed thereon, the contract may not be subject to arbitration" (Mont. Code Ann. § 27-5-114(4)). In 1996, the Supreme Court struck down this statutory provision *(Doctor's Associates, Inc.*

---

[9] If a statute specifies the situations in which arbitration agreements are considered unenforceable, then in those situations *arbitrability* is indistinguishable from *enforceability*. See, for example, *Doctor's Associates, Inc. v. Casarotto,* 517 U.S. 681 (1996).

[10] The leading cases that are considered as representing this rule of law are *Gilmer v. Interstate/Johnson Lane Corp.,* 500 U.S. 20 (1991) in the employment arena and *Mitsubishi v. Soler,* 473 U.S. 614 (1984) in the commercial context.

v. Casarotto), holding that an arbitration provision that did not comply with this requirement was nonetheless valid and enforceable. The court reasoned that any restriction in arbitrability was in conflict with the liberal arbitration provisions of the FAA. It appears likely that, unless a statute limiting arbitrability is both explicit and federally promulgated, it will be deemed ineffective.

Procedural arbitrability, the other type of arbitrability issue, concerns procedural matters that prevent arbitration, such as the failure to seek arbitration in a timely manner or the failure to fulfill conditions necessary before arbitration can take place. An issue of procedural arbitrability was, arguably, presented to the high court of Maryland in *Wells v. Chevy Chase Bank,* 363 Md. 232 (2001). In *Wells,* a group of credit cardholders took Chevy Chase Bank to court, contending that their interest and fee charges were illegal. The cardholder agreements contained the following provision:

> *Mediation and Arbitration*—Any controversy or claim ("Claim") between or among you and us or our agents, employees and affiliates, including but not limited to those arising out of or relating to this Agreement or any related agreements, including without limitation any Claim based on or arising from an alleged tort, shall, at the request and expense of the claiming party, be submitted to mediation, using the rules of the American Arbitration Association ("AAA").
>
> If mediation fails to resolve the Claim within 30 days from the date of engagement, then the Claim shall be determined by binding arbitration. (Mediation or Arbitration, as appropriate, are sometimes referred to below as the "Proceeding".) Arbitration shall be conducted in accordance with the United States Arbitration Act (Title 9, U.S. Code), notwithstanding any choice of law provision in this Agreement, and under the rules of the AAA. Either you or we may, by summary proceedings (e.g., a plea in abatement or motion to stay further proceedings), bring an action in any court having jurisdiction for the sole purpose of compelling compliance with these mediation and arbitration provisions. (363 Md. at 236–237)

Chevy Chase Bank tried to avoid the pending litigation by moving to arbitrate. The cardholders responded that the arbitration clause had been illegally inserted into the cardholder agreement and was unenforceable. The Court of Appeals of Maryland (Maryland's highest appellate court) instead ruled on the basis of procedural arbitrability. It held that the proper procedure to institute arbitration had not been followed in this case, because the first step was for a "claimant" to request mediation. Since the "claimants" in this case were the cardholders, and since they had not requested mediation, the dispute was not ripe for arbitration under the agreement. By the plain language of the arbitration provision, only a "claimant" could trigger the arbitration process, by first requesting mediation.

Who decides whether a case will be arbitrated? Unless the parties otherwise agree, courts decide issues of substantive arbitrability. The arbitrator is in charge of deciding procedural arbitrability, unless, as in the *Wells* case, when the issue is whether to stay or dismiss pending litigation (Heinsz 2001, 39; *John Wiley & Sons v. Livingston,* 376 U.S. 543, [1964]). However, determining the enforceability of an arbitration agreement takes a middle ground. In *Prima Paint Corp. v. Flood & Conklin Mfg. Co.,* 388 U.S. 395 (1967) the Supreme Court held that a disputant's fraud challenge to the enforceability of a contract that included an executory agreement to arbitrate was a matter to be determined by the arbitrator, not the court. However, ***dicta*** in the opinion suggest that, if the agreement to arbitrate were the only part of the contract challenged as unenforceable, determining the validity of the agreement would fall to the court. The basis for this distinction appears to be that, if the arbitration agreement itself were procured improperly, the requisite mutuality and voluntariness of the arbitration contract would itself fail; hence, the arbitrator would never have been vested with the power to make any determination at all.

Suspending Court Proceedings and Compelling Arbitration. If one disputant has taken an interpersonal conflict to court and the conflict is subject to an arbitration agreement, another disputant may wish to suspend or terminate the litigation. Otherwise, the usefulness of the arbitration process could be sabotaged by the time and expense of litigation.

The FAA provides (Section 3) that a litigant can apply to a district court in which litigation is pending to stay the litigation to permit the completion of arbitration:

> If any suit or proceeding be brought in any of the courts of the United States upon any issue referable to arbitration under an agreement in writing for such arbitration, the court in which such suit is pending, upon being satisfied that the issue involved in such suit or proceeding is referable to arbitration under such an agreement, shall on application of one of the parties stay the trial of the action until such arbitration has been had in accordance with the terms of the agreement, providing the applicant for the stay is not in default in proceeding with such arbitration.

Under Section 4 of the FAA, a disputant in a dispute over which a federal court would otherwise have jurisdiction can bring an action to compel the other disputant to arbitrate, provided that enforceability and arbitrability are established. Similarly, Section 7 of the Uniform Arbitration Act contains provisions similar to Sections 3 and 4 of the FAA, allowing a court to stay litigation to permit arbitration to proceed and to compel a party to comply with an arbitration agreement.

AFTER ARBITRATION

The issues of enforceability, arbitrability, compelling arbitration, and stays of pending litigation are sometimes referred to as front-end issues, since they are issues that bring people into court before the arbitration gets underway. Once these issues are resolved, and arbitration begins, legal issues that arise during the arbitration process, such as discovery problems and the admissibility of evidence,

---

Dicta

plural of *dictum,* Latin; language in a court's opinion that is not essential to the reasoning for the court's ruling.

are generally handled by the arbitrator. Thus, courts don't typically deal with mid-arbitration problems.[11] Litigation is more likely to begin again when the arbitration ends and the arbitrator has issued an award.

Enforcement of Arbitration Awards. The FAA (Section 9) and Revised Uniform Arbitration Act (Section 22) set forth the processes for the judicial enforcement of arbitration awards. These rules provide that, upon application by a disputant, the court will reduce the award of the arbitrator to a court judgment, thus allowing the party seeking enforcement to use judicial remedies, such as garnishment of monies and the seizure and sale of property, to pay a monetary award.

Review of Arbitration Awards. Once an arbitrator has issued an arbitration award, it is considered final. In contrast to a litigated judgment, which may be overturned on appeal if the trial court made an error of law or lacked evidence to support a necessary finding of fact, parties to arbitration are presumed to have bargained for a nonappealable decision by the arbitrator. The rationale for this difference in treatment is that litigation is often not chosen by one of the litigants, so there must be adequate process of law for the handling of errors. In contrast, arbitration involves the presumably voluntary submission of the dispute by all disputants to the arbitrator.

Issues of arbitrator review were almost unheard of before the FAA, because disputants, having willingly submitted to arbitration, were almost always comfortable with the process. With the huge rise in the enforcement of executory agreements to arbitrate against unwilling participants, challenges to arbitrators' decisions became more prevalent.

Vacatur
the overturning of an arbitration award by a court.

Vacatur. The FAA (Section 10) provides for the **vacatur** (overturning) of an arbitration award by a court in cases

1. Where the award was procured by corruption, fraud, or undue means.
2. Where there was evident partiality or corruption in the arbitrators, or either of them.
3. Where the arbitrators were guilty of misconduct in refusing to postpone the hearing, upon sufficient cause shown, or in refusing to hear evidence pertinent and material to the controversy; or of any other misbehavior by which the rights of any party have been prejudiced.
4. Where the arbitrators exceeded their powers, or so imperfectly executed them that a mutual, final, and definite award upon the subject matter submitted was not made.

A similar provision is contained in the Revised Uniform Arbitration Act (Section 23).

---

[11] The Revised Uniform Arbitration Act (RUAA) does allow for the issuance, by a court, of provisional remedies (such as preliminary injunctions) and for the enforcement of pre-award remedies issued by the arbitrator. See the RUAA, Sections 8 and 18.

In addition to these somewhat narrow statutory grounds for overturning an arbitrator's award, the courts have also been willing to vacate an arbitrator's award if it appears that the arbitrator decided an issue that was not substantively arbitrable under any plausible interpretation of the agreement to arbitrate. The general rule in this regard is that the arbitrator must have made a ruling that reflects the "essence of the agreement" to arbitrate. *United Steelworkers of America v. Enterprise Wheel and Car Corp.,* 363 U.S. 593 (1960) (commonly referred to as "*Steelworkers III*"). In practice, the federal courts have sometimes found it difficult to apply this standard without intruding into the arbitrator's domain of contract interpretation (Hayford 2000). This area of law is a fruitful one for adversaries who wish to use the arbitration process for strategic posturing.

Courts will also refuse to enforce an arbitration award if the award reflects a violation of public policy. This rule comes from basic contract law: no contract that violates public policy is considered enforceable. For example, a court faced with a contract to engage in prostitution, practice income tax evasion, or defraud someone would likely refuse to enforce such an agreement.

As with other aspects of arbitration law, the public-policy exception to enforcing arbitration awards reflects a difficult balance between the strong deference shown to arbitration awards and the need to effectuate countervailing policies, here, important public policies. Such cases frequently arise in the labor field. The seminal case was *W.R. Grace & Company v. International Union of the United Rubber, Cork, Linoleum and Plastic Workers of America,* 461 U.S. 757 (1983). W.R. Grace & Company, the employer, and the union had entered into a collective bargaining agreement that contained a seniority system. Later, the Equal Employment Opportunity Commission (EEOC) determined that the company had discriminated against blacks and women in their hiring and promotional practices and that the seniority system was perpetuating the problem. While the discrimination matter was in litigation, Grace hired some female workers and promoted them over some existing male employees. The male employees filed grievances, which ultimately went to arbitration on the issue of back pay. The issue ultimately before the Court was whether an arbitrator's award of back pay violated the public policy against discrimination enunciated by the EEOC and then-existing caselaw. To simplify the outcome, the Supreme Court determined that the mere award of back pay to the male employees did not, in and of itself, violate public policy, since it did not require the employer to also countervene any nondiscrimination practices adopted by the employer. Thus, the Court ruled that the arbitration award could stand.

Recently, the public policy vacatur of arbitration awards has been clarified somewhat in the case of *Eastern Associated Coal Corporation v. United Mine Workers of America,* 531 U.S. 57 (2000). This case is the culmination of a line of often confusing labor litigation concerning the reinstatement, by arbitrators, of employees who have engaged in unsafe practices on the job. Employers who fire these claimants typically contend that the discharges were motivated by public safety determinations, whereas the employees argue that the public policies involved don't prevent their reinstatement. In *Eastern Associated,* the employee was fired after a random drug test turned up marijuana in his system, a second such infraction. The employee opted for arbitration, and the arbitrator reinstated the employee, imposing instead a suspension and other conditions of continued employment. The Supreme Court ruled that, although the employee's behavior—being on the job while intoxicated—violated public safety policies, the arbitrator's decision should not be vacated because the award itself did not violate public policy. An arbitrator's award must be treated as an agreement between the parties to the arbitration, stated the Court. Hence,

> the question to be answered is not whether Smith's drug use itself violates public policy, but whether the agreement to reinstate him does so. (531 U.S. at 62–63)

The rule is that an arbitration agreement may not be vacated as against public policy unless

> such public policy [is] "explicit," "well defined," and "dominant." [Citing the *W.R. Grace* case.] It must be "ascertained by reference to the laws and legal precedents and not from general considerations of supposed public interests." (531 U.S. at 62)

The Court explained that the statutory scheme providing for public safety also provided for employee rehabilitation; hence, it could not be said that the arbitrator's award itself contravened explicit public policy.

The *Eastern Associated* case may, or may not, resolve uncertainty in the area of public-policy review of arbitration awards. Other, similar cases exist in which similar reinstatements have been vacated by reviewing courts, including cases decided after *Eastern Associated*.[12] In the words of one commentator,

> Parties who have agreed to arbitrate their contractual disputes should remain aware of the ever changing and expanding body of statutes, regulations, and even common law on which public policy may be based, because awards resolving their disputes may be successfully challenged on these grounds. Like a "Hail Mary" pass such challenges will occasionally, though very infrequently, succeed. (Glanstein 2001, 334)

Arbitration Agreements That Specify Reviewability. The final wrinkle in the issue of reviewability and vacatur of arbitration agreements is that occasionally parties to an arbitration agreement will try to spell out the circumstances and conditions under which an arbitration agreement may be reviewed by the court. The arbitration agreement may represent an effort to restrict arbitrability, or it may represent an effort to expand it.

---

[12] For example, see *Chicago Fire Fighters Union Local No. 2 v. City of Chicago,* 323 Ill. App. 3d 168 (2001). A helpful review is available in Glanstein 2001.

The law in this area is both difficult and inconsistent. Some courts hold that the parties to an arbitration agreement should be allowed to expand or limit judicial review of arbitration awards on the basis of "freedom of contract," whereas other courts hold that efforts to expand judicial review may either impair the arbitration process or even exceed the jurisdiction of the reviewing court[13]. (Curtin 2000 contains a cogent discussion of the caselaw.) Thus, the legal professional should be aware that any effort to alter judicial reviewability of an arbitrator's decision may have unanticipated effects. Agreements to restrict arbitrability are more likely to be given effect than agreements to expand it.

CHOICE OF LAW

Choice of law refers to the problem of which state or nation's laws should apply if disputants come from differing jurisdictions, if the dispute or transaction is multijurisdictional or international, or if for some other reason there is a disagreement over whose law should apply. Choice of law can come into play at any point in the arbitration process, from the enforcement of an agreement to arbitrate and stays of pending litigation to reviewability and vacatur of an arbitration award.

Choice of Law During Arbitration. Generally, choice of law during the arbitration process itself presents little difficulty. Because the arbitrator is in charge of making decisions concerning the arbitration itself, he or she is also in charge of making decisions about which law to apply, and these decisions will not be second-guessed unless they constitute the sort of action that is subject to vacatur. An example of such a situation is an ADR neutral, who, upon being conferred the status of arbitrator under an agreement providing that "the law of California shall apply," exceeds the powers conferred by the arbitration agreement by expressly deciding to apply the law of Arizona instead. Except in this sort of extreme error, the arbitrator's application of choice of law generally prevails. A disputant, an advocate, or a conflict diagnostician should become educated in the laws of the jurisdictions involved before drafting the agreement to arbitrate, so that the arbitrator applies the desired body of law. If the disputants are at odds on this point and don't specify the law, the arbitrator decides what law applies, and his or her judgment is generally given deference.

---

[13] The jurisdictional argument was applied recently by the California Court of Appeals in *Crowell v. Downey Community Hospital Foundation,* 95 Cal. App. 4th 730 (2002). In *Downey,* the parties signed an arbitration agreement that provided for the judicial review of an arbitration award based on grounds similar to those that are applied to civil lawsuits. The court held, on the grounds of the limited review jurisdiction conferred to the court, that the parties themselves could not expand reviewability. In reaching its conclusion, the court also emphasized the public policy advantages to retaining a highly limited scope of arbitration. A contrary result was reached by the Court of Appeals for the Ninth Circuit (which includes California) in *LaPine Technology v. Kyocera,* 130 F.3d 884 (C.A. 9 1997) and other appellate decisions of state and federal courts.

Choice of Law in Matters of Enforceability, Arbitrability, and Reviewability.
Choice of law becomes a problem when the arbitration and litigation process
make contact—that is, when issues of enforceability, arbitrability, and reviewability are raised. Choice-of-law issues represent an extremely difficult area in arbitration law and may impose an unfortunate lack of clarity and unpredictability
into the arbitration process. The murkiness results from a lack of consensus
among appellate courts about how to choose which laws should be applicable.

In disputes arising within the United States, an arbitration agreement without a choice-of-law provision is generally interpreted with reference to the FAA.
On the other hand, if the parties to an arbitration clearly spell out the law to be
applied, then their intent is given effect, according to the United States Supreme
Court in its two leading cases on the matter, *Volt Information Sciences, Inc. v.
Board of Trustees,* 489 U.S. 468 (1989) and *Mastrobuono v. Shearson Lehman
Hutton,* 514 U.S. 52 (1995). The problem, however, is that it is often unclear
whether the contract is ambiguous as to the appropriate law. For example, the
Volt and *Mastrobuono* cases involved executory agreements to arbitrate that were
part of overall contracts between the disputants. There were clauses in both contracts clearly spelling out which state's law was to apply to the contract as a
whole, but the clauses did not relate explicitly to arbitration. In this sort of circumstance, an agreement to arbitrate is considered ambiguous as to the choice
of law.

In *Volt,* the dispute between the parties to arbitration was linked to a larger
dispute with other disputants who were not a direct party to the arbitration
agreement, and the Supreme Court held that it was appropriate to apply a state
law requiring the postponement of arbitration while the linked conflict was litigated. (The FAA would have required the litigation to be stayed, pending the
completion of the arbitration.) On the other hand, in *Mastrobuono,* the Court
held that a state law limiting the authority of an arbitrator to award punitive
damages was not applicable because the FAA applied, instead. Given the similar
settings and situations of these two cases, commentators have made numerous
efforts to harmonize them. For example, law professor Thomas A. Diamond suggests that the cases stand for the proposition that, if applying the state law would
limit the scope of arbitration or the authority of the arbitrator, there must be a
presumption against the state law's application, whereas, if applying the state law
affects only arbitration procedure, no such presumption should be imposed (Diamond 1997). Professor Diamond's rationale is both commonsense and based
on careful and well-reasoned research; nonetheless, it does not have the status of
a court decision. Confusing language in *Volt* and *Mastrobuono* has produced numerous disparities in lower court rulings, with at least four different rationales
and results (Diamond 1997, 58–60). The scene is made still muddier by the fact
that different states have different choice-of-law rules; hence, one must decide
not only whose substantive rules should be applied but also whose choice-of-law
rules should apply to decide the choice-of-law issues.

In the international arena, choice-of-law considerations relating to arbitrability, enforceablity, and reviewability depend in part on the choice of a forum for the arbitration (in other words, the nation where the arbitration is physically held) (Holland 2000). Many nations have adopted international treaties, such as the New York and Panama Conventions, to make these rules more uniform. As in wholly domestic disputes, usually disputants who explicitly and unambiguously specify the law to be applied have their intent respected. In international transactions, given the wide variety of legal and judicial systems, it is extremely important to make explicit the law to be applied. An arbitrator who is confronted with an international dispute and no guidelines for what law to apply has several choices, including applying the law of the forum, resolving the conflicts-of-law issues using the forum's conflicts rules, or acting as an "amiable compositeur," which means using good conscience and a sense of equity (Holland 2000).

In summary, any ambiguity in the choice-of-law provisions of an arbitration agreement can produce substantial uncertainty. Since one of the major advantages of arbitration is the ability to give effect to the desires of the disputants in designing a "custom" dispute resolution process, choice-of-law problems can be ruinous, eroding disputant autonomy, perception of procedural justness, and psychological ownership of the outcome. Moreover, arbitration conducted in an atmosphere of great uncertainty is more likely to feature a high level of formality and legalism as participants try to protect themselves, driving up the cost and time investment needed. Conflict diagnosticians should make sure that choice of law is clearly addressed in any agreement to arbitrate.

EXERCISES, PROJECTS, AND "THOUGHT EXPERIMENTS"

1. *Internet or library research.* Study the arbitration rules in the American Arbitration Association (AAA) Commercial Dispute Resolution Procedures. Also study the AAA's Supplementary Procedures for Consumer-Related Disputes. (The Association's website is located at *www.adr.org*. Click on "Rules" and follow the links to the specific procedures.) Clearly describe the differences between the two procedures. It may be useful to use a time line or flow chart to organize the information.

2. Find the websites of at least three arbitrators, all of whom practice in different firms, whose sites include a list of their qualifications and a description of the types of cases the arbitrators accept. If you do not have access to the Internet, briefly interview at least three practicing arbitrators from three firms. Ask the arbitrators to recite their qualifications as an arbitrator and the types of cases they arbitrate. What similarities do you see in their qualifications? What differences do you see? If you do this assignment as a class project, discuss the results in class. See if you can discern patterns of qualifications among arbitrators specializing in the handling of particular kinds of cases.

3. Interview an arbitrator in depth. Some of the questions you might pose include the following:

    a. What is your professional background? If you are a lawyer, how long did you practice law before becoming an arbitrator?

    b. What, if any, specialized arbitration training or education have you completed?

    c. Are you a member of any professional arbitration or ADR associations? If so, which ones, and what benefits do you obtain from membership?

    d. What sorts of disputes do you arbitrate?

    e. How long have you been arbitrating? How many cases have you arbitrated?

    f. Do you prefer to use any particular set of procedures? Which ones, and why? Do you commonly practice in an administered or a nonadministered context?

    g. What is the most difficult aspect of the arbitration profession, and what do you do to deal with it?

    h. What is the most rewarding aspect of arbitration practice?

    i. Do you have any advice to people considering a career as an arbitrator?

4. Read and summarize (or brief, if you have been taught to brief opinions) *Hooters of America v. Phillips,* 173 F. 3d 933 (C.A. 4 1999). How can employees be protected against such egregious misuses of executory agreements to arbitrate? Consider the following examples. Try to draft a single statute that would protect Clarke, Amanda, and Bankco.

    a. Clarke applies for a job as a sanitation engineer (a position formerly termed "janitor") with an enormous petroleum company. The jobsite is not unionized. The employment contract specifies that any dispute arising out of Clarke's employment be submitted to mandatory arbitration. The arbitrator is to be chosen from a panel provided by the employer, and the employer, but not the employee, may opt out of arbitration. Clarke has a vague idea of what arbitration is and doesn't like it, but he feels he has no alternative in supporting his family.

    b. Amanda, the chief executive officer of a major dot-com company, is courted by a financial firm, Bankco. The potential position would pay seven figures and would be accompanied by numerous perks and benefits. Amanda retains a renowned business lawyer to assist her in developing a top-flight employment contract. After hours of tough negotiation, they reach an agreement. The negotiated contract includes a mandatory arbitration provision. If a dispute arises, each disputant is to select an arbitrator, and the two selected arbitrators are to select a third arbitrator by mutual consent. The AAA rules of commercial arbitration apply to the arbitration process.

5. The *Hooters* case shows how harmful mandatory arbitration can be. Is there any risk to individuals with limited bargaining power—consumers and employees—of *prohibiting* mandatory arbitration provisions in employment and consumer contracts? Discuss this issue.

6. Brief or summarize the following appellate decisions: (1) *Crowell v. Downey Community Hospital Foundation,* 95 Cal. App. 4th 730 (2002) and (2) *LaPine Technology v. Kyocera,* 130 F.3d 884 (C.A. 9 1997). Are these decisions capable of being harmonized, or are they in conflict? What do you think would be the appropriate rule regarding the contractual expansion of reviewability of arbitration awards?

7. Imagine that you are a legal assistant or an attorney. All of the following new clients have specified that they want to use an ADR procedure to resolve their disputes. Would you recommend mediation or arbitration? If arbitration, would you recommend an informal procedure or a formal, litigation-like procedure? Why would you make these recommendations?

   a. The client slipped and fell in a local supermarket. She had $10,000 in medical expenses and lost a month of job income. Medical insurance covered the medical bills. The client is a secretary at a dental office and earns $2,000 a month. The owner of the supermarket has denied liability but it is unclear why.

   b. The client purchased a golden retriever from the other disputant, paying $500. The disputants had an oral agreement that the seller would forward the dog's pedigree papers to the client within three months after sale. The seller now refuses to do so.

   c. The client is a business partner of the person with whom she is disputing. The dispute is over the interpretation of a provision in the partnership agreement that specifies who is responsible for the payment of accounting expenses.

   d. The client is a tenant. He claims that the landlord has failed to provide the signage specified in the lease for the tenant's restaurant business. The lease specifies that the rent be calculated as $2,000 per month plus a share of the profits. No mention is made of an adjustment if a party to the lease breaches the lease. The landlord contends that he is not required to provide the signage because the tenant failed to open the business in a prompt and timely manner, thus depriving the landlord of expected rentals.

   e. The disputants are ex-spouses. The conflict is over the interpretation of a provision in the marital settlement agreement that specifies how, and when, the residence owned by the two ex-spouses is to be allocated between them. There is an agreement in principle that the residence is to be refinanced in the sole name of the client, that the other ex-spouse is to sign over title to the client, and that an amount equal to one-half the value of the increase in the value of the residence over the original purchase price is to be paid by the client to the other ex-spouse. When the agreement was reached, interest rates for mortgages were hovering around 6 percent. Now the due date for the transfer is approaching, the interest rates have doubled to around 12 percent, and your client no longer qualifies for refinancing the mortgage.

RECOMMENDED READINGS

Barnes, G. H. 1997. Drafting an arbitration clause—a checklist. *Hieros Gamos— Alternative Dispute Resolution Law.* [Online.] [Cited 15 July 2002.] Available from *http://www.hg.org/adradd1.html.*

Cole, S. R. 2001. Uniform arbitration: "One size fits all" does not fit. *Ohio State Journal on Dispute Resolution* 16(3):759–89.

Convention on the Recognition and Enforcement of Foreign Arbitral Awards, 1959 [online]. [Cited 16 July 2002.] Available on the United Nations Commission on International Trade Law website, *http://www.uncitral.org/english/texts/* arbitration/NY-conv.htm. Convention adopted by USA at 9 USCS §201.

Curtin, K. M. 2000. An examination of contractual expansion and limitation of judicial reviews of arbitral awards. *Ohio State Journal on Dispute Resolution* 15(2):337–71.

Federal Arbitration Act, 9 USCS §1 *et seq.*

Glanstein, D. M. 2001. A Hail Mary pass: Public policy review of arbitration awards. *Ohio State Journal on Dispute Resolution* 16:297–334.

Kim, A. S. 1994. Rent-a-judges and the cost of selling justice. *Duke Law Journal* 44 (October):166–99.

National Conference of Commissioners on Uniform State Laws. 2000. *Uniform Arbitration Act* [online]. [Cited 4 July 2003.] Available from *http://www.law.upenn.edu/bll/ulc/uarba/arbitrat1213.htm.*

Nolan-Haley, J. M. 2001. Arbitration. In *Alternative dispute resolution in a nutshell* (pp. 138–96). St. Paul, MN: West.

Riskin, L. L., and J. E. Westbrook (eds.). 1997. Arbitration. In *Dispute resolution and lawyers* (2nd ed., pp. 502–88). St. Paul, MN: West.

Smith, S. 2001. Mandatory arbitration clauses in consumer contracts: Consumer protection and the circumvention of the judicial system. *DePaul Law Review* 50:1191–251.

Steelworkers trilogy: *United Steelworkers of America v. American Mfg. Co.,* 363 U.S. 564, 568 (1960); *United Steelworkers of America v. Enterprise Wheel and Car Corp.,* 363 U.S. 593 (1960); *United Steelworkers of America v. Warrior & Gulf Navigation Co.,* 363 U.S. 574 (1960).

Zirkel, P. A., and A. Krahmal. 2001. Creeping legalism in grievance arbitration: Fact or fiction? *Ohio State Journal on Dispute Resolution* 16:243–65.

20

Nonbinding Evaluation

"A little inaccuracy sometimes saves a ton of explanation."

—H. H. Munro

In this chapter, you will learn …

◆ About nonbinding evaluation: a class of dispute resolution processes that features evaluation of the merits of the dispute.

◆ The advantages and disadvantages of nonbinding evaluation, compared with litigation and other forms of dispute resolution.

◆ The appropriate uses of nonbinding evaluation.

◆ Some of the legal issues presented by the use of nonbinding evaluation.

◆ Some of the interesting and innovative nonbinding evaluation processes, including nonbinding arbitration, summary jury trial, minitrial, neutral evaluation, and dispute review boards.

Nonbinding evaluation is a group of processes used in legal disputes to evaluate the likely outcome of the dispute being taken to court. The processes that comprise this type of ADR are sometimes referred to as "mixed" or "hybrid" forms of ADR, since they contain elements of both adjudication and negotiation.[1] Conceptually, however, nonbinding evaluation is a form of assisted negotiation. It consists of a hearing phase followed by the neutral's issuance of an evaluation, which is advisory only. The evaluation may be a specific decision, a range of likely outcomes, or an assessment of the strengths and weaknesses of each side's case. The issuance of the evaluation is followed by negotiation, which may occur within the nonbinding evaluation process or later on.

Within the confines of the adversarial legal system, nonbinding evaluation can be viewed as the best of all worlds: it provides disputants and their legal teams

---

[1] In this book, the terms *mixed* and *hybrid* ADR will be reserved for the processes that, in fact, combine two or more of the basic ADR processes—mediation, arbitration, and nonbinding evaluation. These processes are discussed in Chapter 21.

with a preview of what might happen in litigation without going all the way to trial. Viewed from the perspective of conflict diagnosis, however, it might instead be seen as the worst of all worlds: it encourages an adversarial perspective on the conflict without providing the certainty of an adjudicated outcome. Perhaps the most useful way to look at nonbinding evaluation is that it is very useful to achieve certain goals and should be considered in light of both its strengths and its weaknesses.

Nonbinding evaluation can take a number of forms. A variety of approaches to selecting the neutral are taken: the decision maker may be an expert in the merits of the case; an expert in the law, such as a retired judge, a lawyer, or even a respected paralegal; a panel chosen from prospective jurors in the community; or even a panel consisting of representatives of the disputants. The complexity and formality of the process is also variable: the process may be brief and informal or lengthy and detailed, and it may or may not include discovery, the taking of testimony, and the submission of other evidence. And the outcome may be a single decision, a range of decisions, or a detailed assessment. The details of the process depend on the jurisdiction in which it is held (if it is provided by a court or another governmental entity) and on the mutual decision of the disputants and their legal teams. In any event, the hallmark of nonbinding evaluation, and the thing that makes it a process distinct from the ADR processes we have discussed so far, is that the neutral renders a decision or an opinion on the merits of the case, but the decision is not binding on the disputants.[2]

Because the result of nonbinding evaluation is an assessment of what would happen if the case went to court, and because court is always one way of dealing with a legal dispute, a primary function of nonbinding evaluation is BATNA clarification. You may recall from Chapter 13 that the BATNA is the Best Alternative To a Negotiated Agreement—a concept used to help negotiators realize when to settle, when to keep negotiating, and when to use other forms of dispute resolution. Nonbinding evaluation gives an estimate of what would happen if the case were litigated. Varieties of nonbinding evaluation are tailored to the specific kind of litigation anticipated by the advocates: some processes use "juries" chosen from the available jury pool, whereas others use neutral adjudication professionals, such as retired judges. Still other forms of nonbinding evaluation use disputant representatives, such as chief executive officers, as the neutrals, in an effort to bring the BATNA clarification process to those most likely to be in charge of the ultimate settlement decision. If the nonbinding evaluation process results in an advisory decision, the result places a case value on the legal dispute. If the nonbinding evaluation results not in an advisory decision but, rather, an assessment of the strengths and weaknesses of each side's case, then each

---

[2] This description is an oversimplification. Some forms of *evaluative mediation* involve the rendering of one or more opinions by the mediator about the strengths and weaknesses of the disputants' legal cases. It is, in fact, difficult to distinguish highly evaluative mediation from nonbinding evaluation, and this problem has led a number of commentators to recommend giving evaluative mediation a different name to distinguish it from classic facilitative mediation. Moreover, some forms of "incentive arbitration" involve nonbinding evaluation with penalties attached to rejecting the decision of the neutral.

disputant's team can use the information to increase the accuracy of its case valuation process (Connolly 1999). In either event, the additional information is used to hone each side's BATNA assessment, increasing the disputants' willingness to agree to a settlement that improves on their respective BATNAs.

Attorney-advocates who choose nonbinding evaluation also often look to it to serve two additional functions. First, they hope that the outcome will show the other side that its BATNA assessment is overblown. If nonbinding evaluation can minimize *the other disputant's* BATNA assessment, it can improve the other side's offers. In this way, nonbinding evaluation serves the same function that instilling doubt does in the process of evaluative mediation. Second, if, on the other hand, the nonbinding evaluation demonstrates that one's own client has a weak case, the attorney can use this result to reality-test with a client who expects too much. Thus, an overly optimistic client can be sobered up without the attorney's appearing to be unenthusiastic. Generally, the neutral in a nonbinding evaluation helps support each attorney's appearance in the eyes of his or her client. This support helps the attorney demonstrate that the case itself seems to be a "loser" without compromising his or her image as a zealous and enthusiastic advocate.

VARIETIES OF NONBINDING EVALUATION

You may recall that, in Chapter 3, the twin metaphors of the invisible veil and the lawyer's standard philosophical map were introduced to describe the societal perception of conflict as competitive and the legal profession's conceptualization of dispute resolution as adversarial. The basic skeleton of the nonbinding evaluation process is reflective of these frameworks. Nonbinding evaluation operates on the assumption that disputes are either settled through a competitive process of positional bargaining or adjudicated through an adversary process of litigation. Within this overall framework, there are a number of varieties of nonbinding evaluation. Nonbinding evaluation is intended to give each disputant's legal team a preview at a litigation future, in an effort to give both sides enough information that their positions will overlap, enabling settlement to take place. The basic forms of nonbinding evaluation are summarized in Table 20-1, and discussed in the sections that follow.

NONBINDING ARBITRATION

Nonbinding arbitration is the most basic form of nonbinding evaluation. Nonbinding arbitration simply consists of an adjudication process in which the outcome is not binding. Sometimes, nonbinding arbitration is a process chosen by private parties, but often it is a mandatory process ordered by the court. (Courts ordinarily cannot mandate *binding* arbitration without violating the constitutional rights of litigants.) In court-connected mandatory arbitration, arbitrators are often lawyers empanelled as arbitrators by the court system. The arbitrator is-

◆ **TABLE 20-1**   Nonbinding Evaluation Processes

PROCESS	WHO IS TYPICALLY THE NEUTRAL?	WHAT IS TYPICALLY PRESENTED?	NATURE OF OUTCOME	WHAT IS THE PROCESS USEFUL FOR?
Nonbinding arbitration	Arbitrator, who may be an attorney, a retired judge, or an ADR neutral	Oral arguments; occasionally exhibits and informal testimony (as in arbitration)	Arbitration award, advisory only; may be oral, written, or both	General BATNA clarification
Minitrial	Corporate executives with authority to settle; may also be a neutral moderator	Typically, oral arguments; may also be some evidentiary showing	Typically, no outcome *per se;* observations of hearing provide BATNA clarification to those with authority to negotiate settlement; advisory award may be issued by neutral if no settlement reached	BATNA clarification for those in a position to settle
Summary jury trial	Members of the jury pool as adjudicators; judge or retired judge as moderator	Abbreviated version of litigated case	Nonbinding verdict	Teasing out of complicated factual issues (as in class actions/products liability); BATNA if jury trial expected; "day in court" for litigants
Neutral evaluation	Experts in technical area of dispute, or lawyers with expertise in the sort of dispute being litigated	Typically, oral arguments	Assessment of the strengths and weaknesses of each side's case; may include advisory award	BATNA clarification; expert empowerment
Dispute review board	A panel of leaders or other experts in the field involved, empanelled by the owner and contractor in a construction project	A summary of a dispute that threatens to delay or derail a complex construction project	An advisory decision	Overcoming of costly impasses and delays created by disputes that occur during complex construction projects

sues a decision, which the disputants are free to disregard if they wish to.[3] Most jurisdictions treat the proceedings as settlement negotiations and, hence, preserve the privacy and confidentiality of the process and outcome.

MINITRIAL

In this text, the term *nonbinding evaluation* will include a process known as minitrial. In minitrial, the time and expense of case presentation is mimimized through the presentation of a summary version of the dispute. Minitrials are usually attended by representatives of the disputants who have the authority to settle the case (such as corporate officers or board members). After case presentation, the neutral will either issue a nonbinding decision or will discuss strengths and weaknesses with disputant representatives and their advocates.

---

[3]In some court-connected arbitration programs, the choice is to accept the arbitrator's award, or undergo a trial *de novo.* A few jurisdictions employ incentive arbitration.

Sometimes, the neutral then proceeds to facilitate settlement negotiations, much as a mediator does.[4]

SUMMARY JURY TRIAL

Summary jury trial is a form of nonbinding evaluation intended to promote settlement by demonstrating to the disputants and their legal teams what would be likely to happen if a jury decided the case. Invented and introduced by federal court judge Thomas Lambros in 1980 (Lambros 1984), the summary jury trial started as a court-mandated and court-supervised process intended to give disputants "their day in court" and to approximate the results of a full-blown jury trial in complex cases, such as products liability cases (Ponte 1995). Judge Lambros described the sort of dispute amenable to summmary jury trial:

> There is a certain class of cases in which the only bar to settlement among parties is the difference in opinion of how a jury will perceive evidence adduced at trial. These cases involve issues, like that of "the reasonable man" in negligence litigation, where no amount of jurisprudential refinement and clarification of the applicable law can aid in the resolution of the case. (Lambros 1984, app. A)

In summary jury trial, an advisory jury is selected from the pool of jurors in the community and an abbreviated version (usually lasting one day or less) of the

---

[4] Another variant of the minitrial, in which disputant representatives serve as the decision makers and the neutral simply presides over the hearing and facilitates, is considered in Chapter 21.

case is tried. The trial may include the calling of witnesses and the taking of testimony, and the neutral presiding over the trial may be a hired ADR professional, a lawyer, or an active judge (as in *In re Telectronics Pacing Sys.,* 137 F. Supp. 2d 985, S.D. Ohio, 2001). At the termination of the case, the jury deliberates and issues a decision, which is used by the parties as a basis for settlement discussions. The jury is often unaware of the nonbinding quality of their deliberations (Woodley 1997, 552). Summary jury trials are popular devices for narrowing the factual issues that bedevil complex products-liability class action litigation and are mandated in a number of jurisdictions for complex civil litigation (Libbey 1999).

NEUTRAL EVALUATION

Neutral evaluation is a process in which an expert in the subject matter of the dispute, or a legal expert, is hired to give an assessment of the strengths and weaknesses of each side's case. Neutral evaluation has many variations and is known by a variety of terms, used in often inconsistent fashion. As a court-connected process, and known as *early neutral evaluation,* it is often used to circumvent the prohibitively high costs of conducting discovery prior to trial. Frequently made available under the auspices of a court system, early neutral evaluation involves the assignment of an expert, such as a retired judge or lawyer, who hears or receives oral or written statements of each disputant's case. The neutral then issues an evaluation, which may be either oral or written, detailing a likely outcome or a range of likely outcomes, as well as reasons for the evaluation. The disputants use the information to conduct settlement negotiations. The process is also known as *case evaluation* and may occur at any point prior to trial. Case evaluation can be particularly advantageous in highly technical disputes in which an expert in the substance of the dispute can do a more capable job of understanding and assessing the situation. In such cases, as with the arbitration of similar cases, the neutral evaluator can be selected for his or her expertise.

DISPUTE REVIEW BOARDS

Dispute review boards (also known as dispute resolution boards) are entities created by contract to resolve disputes as they arise during construction projects. Boards are generally made up of three members empanelled by the owner and contractor. As disputes arise during construction, they are submitted by informal hearing process to the dispute review board, which issues an advisory decision in the matter. According to the Dispute Resolution Board Foundation, only 2 percent of construction projects using dispute review boards end with outstanding disputes (Harmon 2002).

The dispute review board process is designed to facilitate the complex relationships among owners, contractors, and others involved in large construction projects. The construction of an office tower, a freeway, or a stadium is an enormously complicated process, and disputes are inevitable. If unsettled conflict is

In neutral evaluation and many other forms of nonbinding evaluation, the neutral issues an authoritative, but nonbinding, opinion about the likely outcome of the dispute. Identikal, Getty Images Inc.—Artville LLC

For More Information. . .

You can read more about dispute review boards at the Dispute Resolution Board Foundation, *http://www.drb.org/*.

allowed to halt or slow the work, the entire project can fail. Thus, dispute review boards are designed to provide on-the-fly dispute resolution that keeps the project moving and on-schedule. In this way, dispute review boards are designed to prevent conflict escalation and damage, serving a preventive function not unlike that of dispute resolution systems (see Chapter 21).

ADVANTAGES AND DISADVANTAGES OF NONBINDING EVALUATION

Nonbinding evaluation represents an effort to obtain the benefits of both negotiation and adjudication. Does it, in fact, do so? The conflict diagnostician should consider the evidence.

COMPARED WITH LITIGATION

How does nonbinding evaluation compare with litigation? The most important advantage of nonbinding evaluation is probably also its greatest disadvantage: its nonbinding quality. Nonbinding evaluation allows the disputants to retain a measure of their autonomy. A settlement reached after nonbinding evaluation is more likely to be accompanied by psychological ownership than a judgment imposed by the court, because the disputants have freely chosen the outcome themselves. For this reason, nonbinding evaluation is often recommended for disputants who are engaged in a continuing relationship. An example in which such processes are considered useful is in multimillion-dollar construction projects, in which costly disputes may develop among contractors and subcontractors who must continue to deal with one another until the project is completed. Although nonbinding evaluation is more adversarial than facilitative ADR processes, it is kinder on relationships than all-out litigation. And, many times, parties and their lawyers have a strong interest in avoiding court: what they really want is BATNA clarification, so that they can get a better idea of the appropriate settlement range. Nonbinding evaluation is tailored to provide this information. On the other hand, nonbinding evaluation may not result in a settlement at all, in which case litigation occurs, anyway, creating all the problems of litigation with an additional layer of cost and delay, though some argue that nonbinding evaluation may narrow issues, making litigation less damaging, even if settlement does not result (see Libbey 1999). Moreover, attorneys bent on adversarial behavior could misuse the process by participating without any intention of ever settling, in order to acquire otherwise discoverable information and get a preview of the other side's planned litigation tactics (Woodley 1997).

Nonbinding evaluation is also chosen by disputants because it is potentially cheaper and faster than litigation. Nonbinding evaluation can be done with less prehearing preparation than trial, and the hearings themselves are typically informal condensations of what would occur at trial. Summary jury trials are ordered by judges for class actions to achieve such time and cost savings, and those who are involved in these proceedings are beginning to see nonbinding evaluation as the rule rather than the exception.

However, nonbinding evaluation is sometimes touted as an efficiency measure without due regard for whether, in fact, the presumed cost and time savings will be realized (Posner 1986). It is not entirely clear that the wholesale referral of cases to nonbinding evaluation actually saves time and money. The Honorable John Connolly and a committee of researchers studied court-connected ADR processes in Minnesota in the mid-1990s, comparing summary jury trial with arbitration, mediation, and litigation in a scientifically controlled manner (Connolly 1999). Judge Connolly's research committee controlled for variations in the kinds of cases that undergo various dispute resolution processes by randomly assigning approximately 100 civil cases each to non-ADR, summary jury trial, and mediation with a possibility of subsequent arbitration. He tracked the cases, collecting data, and sought the opinions of both litigants and lawyers about the experiences. Although summary jury trial reduced the percentage of cases that ended in trial, the average time it took for cases to be disposed of was higher for this group than for either litigated or mediated/arbitrated cases. Moreover, an analysis of the number of court appearances that were required for each case (a measure of the court resources needed) indicated that, although summary jury trial reduced the average number of court hearings per case from .99 to .94, the cases that were referred to mediation or arbitration did far better, with an average per-case hearing rate of only .54. More mediating litigants than litigants participating in summary jury trial reported that participating in ADR saved them money, and, whereas about one-third of the litigants thought that use of summary jury trial decreased the amount of time their attorneys had to spend on their case, almost 60 percent of the litigants thought that it increased the needed time. Attorneys felt that both ADR processes were more likely to save time than increase time, but there was no substantial difference between mediation and summary jury trial on this measure. These findings call into some question the prevailing belief that nonbinding evaluation processes are time and money savers, at least when applied indiscriminately to all legal disputes. Some courts, in reviewing cases sent to nonbinding evaluation for a determination of counsel fees in subsequent litigation, have commented on the considerable time and money the process often requires. For example, in *Brotherton v. Cleveland,* 141 F. Supp. 2d 907, 911 (S.D. Ohio, 2001) the judge in charge of awarding plaintiff attorney's fees in a class action commented that,

> [a]lthough the case had not yet proceeded to trial at the time of settlement, Class Counsel's participation in the Summary Jury Trial required almost as much preparation as the actual trial would have.

Another potential advantage of nonbinding evaluation is the parties' ability to choose the qualifications of the neutral. In a highly technical scientific dispute or a dispute over an arcane element of law or commerce, the choice of an expert neutral can save time and effort and can increase both disputants' expert power. When a factual question is in doubt, the summary jury trial method can provide BATNA clarification by the choice of a neutral panel that resembles a typical jury. Nonbinding evaluation is frequently used in complex products liability cases and class action litigation—it's a "natural" in factually complex situations in which a hired factfinder can efficiently and expediently deal with the principal impasses to resolution. Generally, judges do not possess this sort of expertise.

Finally, like other forms of ADR, nonbinding evaluation is typically a private process. Privacy can have both advantages and disadvantages. Some disputants may benefit from the privacy, whereas others prefer that the public be informed of the process and outcome. Moreover, public policy considerations may be affected. Although there has been a tendency to turn to nonbinding evaluation in complex products liability cases and class action litigation, these are often the very cases in which the general public has an important stake in knowing about the process and outcome of the dispute. It can be argued that they are precisely the situations that cry out for public scrutiny. As previously mentioned when mediation was discussed, privacy may also increase the chances that the parties and the neutral will engage in bigoted or prejudiced behavior.

COMPARED WITH ARBITRATION

In many ways, nonbinding evaluation is similar to arbitration: in fact, it can seem indistinguishable from arbitration until the moment when one disputant decides not to accept the decision of the neutral. It should not be surprising, then, that nonbinding evaluation has many of the same advantages and disadvantages of arbitration. Like arbitration, it has a tendency to promote an adversarial, competitive perspective on the conflict and to promote positional bargaining. Unlike arbitration, the decision itself is not finalized in the outcome of the neutral's evaluation. Because the ultimate outcome depends on the disputants' reaching consensus, it may be argued that the ultimate settlement will achieve greater psychological ownership in a nonbinding evaluation and that, because the ultimate outcome is a negotiated settlement, nonbinding evaluation may be better at protecting relationships. On the other hand, settlement is less certain, and, on balance, since the conflict may not be resolved and the process tends to lead to a positional-bargaining focus, the relationship-protection aspect of nonbinding evaluation may be illusory.

COMPARED WITH MEDIATION

The comparison of nonbinding evaluation with facilitative varieties of mediation raises the most interesting questions for conflict diagnosticians. Nonbinding evaluation is considered effective in dealing with extreme differences of fact or law, and it is useful for BATNA clarification: it functions as a dry run at litigation, enabling attorneys and their clients to get a reasonable estimate of what would happen if the case went to trial. If BATNA clarification is important to the disputant or his or her advocates, this aspect of nonbinding evaluation may be very important. Judges experienced in handling one such process, the summary jury trial, characterize it as producing very reliable estimates of what a jury would have decided had the case gone to trial, and others comment that such processes give the disputants a dose of litigation reality, giving them a taste of the nonmonetary costs of actually litigating their case and the effects of the uncertainties in their case before a factfinder (Woodley 1997). If the legal dispute is extremely complicated or difficult to understand, a neutral evaluation process that improves expert power may be very helpful in promoting an effective settlement.

Moreover, nonbinding evaluation may be a more comfortable process for some disputants and many lawyers. Trial attorneys may be more comfortable with the trial-like nonbinding evaluation process than with a facilitative mediation process (Connolly 1999). (Indeed, one possible reason advanced by some scholars for the widespread acceptance of mediation by lawyers over the past decade is that mediation has been recast and reconfigured to closely resemble nonbinding evaluation (Sabatino 1998).) Like lawyers, many disputants may be more comfortable with a process consistent with the invisible veil version of disputing. Such disputants, as well as those who wish for a "day in court" for reasons of vengeance or vindication, may prefer nonbinding evaluation as a way to provide this experience without submitting to the problems of litigation.[5]

---

[5] A number of judges experienced with summary jury trial believe that the process has special qualities to offer in allowing disputants to ventilate their feelings and express their positions before a trial-like body (Libbey 1999; Woodley 1997).

Lawyer and Litigant Attitudes Toward Summary Jury Trial

As part of the Ramsey County, Minnesota Summary Jury Trial study, Judge Connolly's research group asked attorneys and litigants questions that tapped their attitudes toward the processes they had used. Most revealing of the resulting data was the overall satisfaction each group expressed. The litigants reported about a 55 to 60 percent satisfaction rate for both SJT and mediation, with only a very slight 4 percent preference for summary jury trial (SJT). The attorneys, on the other hand, were far more likely to be satisfied with SJT, with 68 percent reporting being "satisfied" or "very satisfied," compared with only 42 percent satisfaction with mediation (Connolly 1999).

The disadvantages of nonbinding evaluation spring from its status as an adversary process. It tends to promote the narrowed focus of positional bargaining and the lawyer's standard philosophical map, making it harder to hammer out creative, efficient, problem-solving settlements. It tends to be less protective of relationships and more likely to lead to conflict escalation. Mediation proponents often argue that good mediation can deal effectively with extreme disputes of fact, anyway. In fact, there may be other, less expensive, less damaging, and equally effective methods of BATNA clarification available if the parties can think creatively about the situation.

Nonbinding evaluation and facilitative mediation need not be mutually exclusive processes. Nonbinding evaluation can be used by the disputants as an adjunct to facilitative mediation for BATNA clarification and expert empowerment. If the disputants are working collaboratively under the guidance of a good facilitative mediator, they can design a nonbinding evaluation process that addresses and promotes their needs most effectively without causing undue collateral damage.

CONCLUSIONS: ADVANTAGES AND DISADVANTAGES OF NONBINDING EVALUATION

Trying to determine which ADR process is best in all cases would certainly be a fool's errand. The better approach is suggested by conflict diagnosis: to determine whether, in a given situation, nonbinding evaluation would be the best dispute resolution process to use and, if so, what form of nonbinding evaluation would be best suited to the situation.

One might appropriately generalize that nonbinding evaluation is likely to be most helpful in situations in which a negotiated settlement is the best option, but the disputants' litigation ATNAs are difficult to determine, as in complicated fact situations and technically challenging disputes. If time is of the essence and repair of the disputants' relationship is of secondary importance, nonbinding evaluation might be the dispute resolution process of choice. On the other hand, if the disputants can afford investing a little time in the dispute resolution process, facilitative mediation within which the disputants use nonbinding evaluation to help with BATNA clarification is a

Conflict diagnosis principles suggest that nonbinding evaluation processes are more likely than mediation to promote positional bargaining, and the trouble it brings. Eric Meola, Getty Images Inc.—Image Bank

better option. Nonbinding evaluation has a tendency to produce position-boundedness: using it within the confines of facilitative mediation can protect the disputants against falling into pure positional bargaining, ensuring that the disputants' relationship is preserved and the outcome truly meets the needs of all involved.

LEGAL ISSUES IN NONBINDING EVALUATION

Nonbinding evaluation processes are, essentially, forms of assisted negotiation. Conducted privately, nonbinding evaluation is subject to the legal principles that apply to negotiation in general (such as the inadmissibility of negotiation communications under Federal Rules of Evidence, Rule 408, and similar provisions protecting settlement negotiations[6]). In one study of construction law attorneys conducted by the ABA Forum, respondents who had participated in minitrials reported that some 63 percent were conducted pursuant to procedural rules developed by the parties and their attorneys themselves, with the remaining procedures conducted according to rules promulgated by ADR organizations such as the American Arbitration Association and the Center for Public Resources Institute (Henderson 1995). Although these agreed-to procedures constitute contracts and could theoretically be the subject of litigation if disagreements arose

---

[6] For example, in *Gunter v. Ridgewood Energy Corp.,* 32 F. Supp. 2d 162 (D. NJ 1998), a district court judge ruled that early neutral evaluation proceedings were confidential and privileged under Federal Rules of Civil Procedure, Rule 408.

about how they operate, in practice there is very little reported litigation arising out of nonbinding evaluation in the private sector.

Public-sector nonbinding evaluation, the processes conducted under court and agency auspices, is subject to specific implementing statutes, rules, and regulations and varies widely. Matters such as eligibility, opting out, rules of procedure, pre-hearing discovery, confidentiality, costs, and duty to participate in good faith are controlled by whatever statutory law undergirds the process, and these rules are widely varying. Although flexibility in the rules that govern nonbinding evaluation are considered by some to be desirable as a way to promote innovation, at least one scholar (Woodley 1997) argues that the lack of uniformity is a threat to the long-term usefulness of public-sector nonbinding evaluation as a dispute resolution process, and it is advocated that more consistency among courts, agencies, and other public arenas would promote the long-term success of nonbinding evaluation as an effective technique. As this area of law becomes more mature, it will become easier to characterize and understand. Meanwhile, anyone who is going to become involved in nonbinding evaluation must check the law applicable to the jurisdiction, type of dispute, and court or agency under whose auspices the dispute is being processed.

EXERCISES, PROJECTS, AND "THOUGHT EXPERIMENTS"

1. Research the law and rules for the United States District Court for the district in which you live. If you don't reside in the United States, choose any jurisdiction's court system. Find the rules or statutes, if any, providing for a nonbinding evaluation process to be used as ADR in litigated cases. If you cannot find any, choose a different jurisdiction. Attach a copy of the statutes or rules to your answers to the following questions:

   a. What sorts of cases can be referred to nonbinding evaluation?

   b. Is referral mandatory? If so, under what circumstances?

   c. What kind or kinds of nonbinding evaluation are available under these rules or statutes? (Remember to consider the format of the process, not just the name of the process, in answering this question.)

   d. Are the ADR neutrals private entrepreneurs, court employees, or something else?

   e. Who pays for the process, and how?

   f. Is litigation postponed to accommodate the ADR process? If so, for how long?

   g. Do you think this statutory scheme is a good one? Identify the strengths and weaknesses of the statutes or rules. What would you do to improve this system's ADR program?

2. Look at the fact situations in exercise 7 of Chapter 19. Knowing what you now know about nonbinding evaluation processes, would you recommend one of these instead of either mediation or arbitration for any of these

clients? Why or why not? If so, which kind of nonbinding evaluation process would you recommend, and why?

3. Nonbinding evaluation (including nonbinding arbitration) is the most widely used form of ADR in civil (nonfamily-law) court-connected programs. Why do you think this is so? Is it the best choice, or would you recommend something else for these sorts of disputes? Justify your response.

4. Should early neutral evaluators be required to be qualified attorneys or judges? Why or why not? Are there some circumstances under which evaluators should be attorneys and some not? If you think so, what are these circumstances, and why the distinction?

5. In general, would you expect nonlawyer litigants to prefer medition or nonbinding evaluation? Why? Justify your opinion.

6. Is confidentiality more, less, or equally important in nonbinding evaluation, compared with mediation? Justify your opinion. Under what circumstances (if any) would it be appropriate for a judge in a litigated case referred to a nonbinding evaluation process to be informed of the outcome of the procedure? Justify your opinion.

7. In a court-connected nonbinding evaluation program, should incentives to settle be built into the program? For example, some jurisdictions provide that, if the case does not settle and if litigation does not improve a litigant's outcome over the evaluator's assessment by a specified percentage, the litigant is assessed monetary penalties, such as being required to foot the entire bill for the evaluator's services or being required to pay court costs for litigation. Is this an appropriate policy for courts to adopt? Why or why not?

RECOMMENDED READINGS

Henderson, D. A. 1995. Avoiding litigation with the mini-trial: The corporate bottom line as dispute resolution technique. *South Carolina Law Review* 46 (winter):237–62.

Lambros, T. D. 1984. *The summary jury trial and other methods of dispute resolution.* 103 F.R.D. 465–477.

Nolan-Haley, J. M. 2001. Dispute resolution in the court system. In *Alternative dispute resolution in a nutshell* (pp. 197–219). St. Paul, MN: West.

Posner, R. A. 1986. The summary jury trial and other methods of alternate dispute resolution: Some cautionary observations. *University of Chicago Law Review* 53 (spring):366–93.

Riskin, L. L., and J. E. Westbrook (eds.). 1997. *Dispute resolution and lawyers* (2nd ed., pp. 589–657). St. Paul, MN: West.

Sabatino, J. M. 1998. ADR as "litigation lite": Procedural and evidentiary norms embedded within alternative dispute resolution. *Emory Law Journal* 47:1289–349.

21

Mixed (Hybrid) and Multimodal Dispute Resolution Processes

"Necessity is the mother of invention."

—Proverb

"A camel is a horse designed by a committee."

—Anonymous

In this chapter, you will learn …

- How the basic forms of dispute resolution have been combined and modified to produce a panoply of mixed (hybrid) and multimodal forms.
- The uses, benefits, and drawbacks of dispute resolution forms that combine mediation and arbitration, mediation and nonbinding evaluation, and arbitration and nonbinding evaluation.
- About ombuds, a powerful means of addressing and resolving conflict within large organizations.
- The uses of dispute resolution systems design for preventing escalating, destructive conflict within organizations.
- The history, typical features, and effects of court-connected alternative dispute resolution programs.
- The dizzying panoply of ADR processes available in the online environment.

In chapters 15 through 20, we considered three basic forms of alternative dispute resolution: mediation, arbitration, and nonbinding evaluation. Mediation and nonbinding evaluation are both forms of assisted negotiation, in which the decision to settle rests with the disputants, whereas in arbitration the power to determine the outcome rests with the neutral. The two forms of assisted negotiation differ as to the basics of the process. At the crux of nonbinding evaluation is the neutral's assessment of the merits of the case, whereas mediation is the facilitation of the disputants' negotiation.

Mediation, arbitration, and nonbinding evaluation are basic ADR forms. Each of the "basic three" has characteristic strengths and weaknesses. What if we could go further and develop processes that combine the best of each? That's the idea behind mixed, or hybrid, and multimodal dispute resolution processes—they are efforts to gain the best of the attributes of each and to tailor dispute resolution more precisely to the unique situation presented. To use a metaphor, if ADR were clothing, then mediation, arbitration, and nonbinding evaluation would be off-the-rack styles, and mixed, or hybrid, processes would be the hand-tailored versions. The concept of the multidoor courthouse introduced by law professor Frank E. A. Sander (Chapter 4), in which a broad variety of dispute resolution processes are available for the choosing, is the prototype multimodal ADR program. If ADR processes were clothing, multimodal processes would be an entire department store, offering a broad range of styles and sizes.

In considering a mixed (hybrid) or multimodal dispute resolution process, a conflict diagnostician should never lose sight of the fact that disputes, and their resolution, occur within a social and cultural context. In the United States, this context invariably includes the blinders of the invisible veil and its cousin, the lawyer's standard philosophical map. This context is critical when considering dispute resolution methods that combine facilitative processes, such as mediation, with processes that presume bargaining will be adversarial and positional. Culturally, we are predisposed to see the adversary process as the best, or only, method. If a new process hybridizes a facilitative dispute resolution process with an adversary or positional-bargaining process, disputants are likely to see the conflict, and the opportunities for resolution, within the cultural context of the invisible veil. Because of this focus, mixing facilitative and evaluative/adversary processes can impair the facilitative elements.

VARIETIES OF MIXED, OR HYBRID, PROCESSES

Mixed, or hybrid, dispute resolution processes combine elements of mediation, arbitration, and/or nonbinding evaluation into a new process. Some of these processes, such as med-arb, arb-med, and mediation windowing, link mediation and arbitration. Others, such as incentive arbitration, blend nonbinding evaluation with arbitration. Still others, such as ombuds, are a fluid and flexible effort to provide basic or combination ADR processes on an as-needed basis.

MED-ARB

One of the most widely used and well-known of the mixed, hybrid processes is *med-arb*. In med-arb, the disputants agree that an attempt to mediate will be followed by arbitration if the mediation fails to result in a full settlement. There are a number of important subvarieties of med-arb. In *med-arb-same,* the arbitrator and mediator are the same person (sometimes, this person is referred to as the "med-arbitrator"), whereas in *med-arb-different,* the roles are served by different people. In *co-med-arb,* the mediator and arbitrator are different people, but both attend the mediation, so that time can be saved presenting evidence only once. *Opt-out med-arb* is a variation in which med-arb-same is initially specified, but, upon the election of either disputant, the process changes into med-arb-different. Finally, *MEDALOA* is a variant in which mediation is followed by final-offer arbitration (see Chapter 19). Med-arb processes (except MEDALOA) may incorporate nonbinding (Chapter 20) instead of binding arbitration: the nonbinding version is more common in court-connected settings, where mandatory binding arbitration raises constitutional problems (Chapter 19).

Benefits of Med-Arb. Med-arb is attractive to disputants and their lawyers for several reasons. Disputants and lawyers worried about the possibility that mediation won't produce settlement can choose med-arb, knowing that they will get some of the benefits of mediation yet will ensure an ultimate outcome. Since they are opting for arbitration as a back-up, they are less likely to feel as if they were signaling weakness to an opponent. Some proponents of med-arb also believe that, because arbitration is hanging over disputants' heads, they will be more motivated to settle in mediation. Some also believe that, with med-arb-same, the disputants will make less extreme demands (they'll "behave") because they know the mediator will be adjudicating their case and the failure to cooperate and negotiate in good faith may cast them in a negative light. Anecdotal information coming to light in the 1980s suggested very high settlement rates in the mediation component of med-arb.

Drawbacks of Med-Arb. Despite the lure of a process that takes advantage of mediation and arbitration's unique features, it is now considered the collective consensus of ADR scholars and professionals that combining mediation and arbitration does not create a process with desirable characteristics (Stulberg 2002).

Med-arb-same suffers from a number of fairness, neutrality, and conflict diagnosis problems (Peter 1997). During mediation, the med-arbitrator may become privy to confidential information, particularly if he or she uses the caucus heavily. He or she can't help but consider this information in making an arbitration award, which can compromise impartiality in the arbitration process. For example, information and communication relevant to the disputants in their discussion of the conflict (such as personal feelings of hostility, a sense of guilt or remorse, or a willingness to apologize) will be irrelevant and may be prejudicial to an adjudicator dealing with explicit legal issues. An additional issue of partiality arises if the mediation is evaluative: in that case, the med-arbitrator will have conducted an evaluation even before arbitration begins, further compromising partiality. In making an evaluation during evaluative mediation, the med-arbitrator is predicting how the case would come out if litigated, whereas, during the arbitration, he or she has to decide the case based on law and equitable principles. These are not necessarily the same, and it may be tough for the med-arbitrator to let go of the prediction and focus on the appropriate basis for decision. Moreover, if the med-arbitrator relies heavily on caucusing during the mediation phase, issues of fairness and due process arise. The disputants aren't able to hear and deal with comments raised by the other disputants in their mediation caucuses, yet the med-arbitrator will invariably have to rely on this material when wearing the hat of the arbitrator.

Trouble can also result from the incorporation of an adversary process (arbitration) into a facilitative one, particularly in med-arb-same. The fact that the mediator may ultimately arbitrate the case creates coercion to settle (this is one of the justifications for using med-arb: to pressure disputants to settle), and this feature impairs the quality of consent, decreasing the psychological ownership of the outcome. A disputant who says no to a course of action explicitly recommended, or implicitly suggested, by the med-arbitrator may fear that the mediator will retaliate by ruling against him or her in arbitration, and, if the med-arbitrator makes a suggestion during the mediation phase, he or she may become ego-invested in the suggestion, which will impede independent judgment during the arbitration phase. Moreover, since the disputants must protect their positions in case arbitration occurs, interest-based, principled negotiation is likely to be curtailed: the disputants have an incentive to play things close to the belt, trading concessions from an initially extreme demand. Some commentators have also worried that mediators and arbitrators require different sorts of skills (only a problem if the med-arbitrator is not trained in both disciplines).

Med-arb-different presents fewer problems than med-arb-same. Most of the role-confusion problems of med-arb-same are absent, since the mediator and arbitrator are different people. In a sense, med-arb-different is two separate processes, except that the disputants enter mediation knowing that arbitration will definitely occur if settlement doesn't result.

There are conflict diagnosis problems with med-arb-different, but they are subtle. They relate to the disputants' knowledge of the ready availability of the adjudication alternative. Mediation requires the attainment of mutual consensus, which may be difficult and requires commitment and energy. In mediation without arbitration, there is no fall-back to adjudication, except that litigation is a possibility. The major difference between such a situation and med-arb-different is that, in the latter, disputants commit in advance to adjudication. This knowledge that adjudication is around the corner may create a heightened awareness of the positional-bargaining aspects of the dispute that may infuse mediation and prevent creative problem solving. Moreover, since there's already an agreement to arbitrate in place, the disputants know that, if they can't reach a consensus, there will definitely be an end to their dispute. Because of this feature of med-arb-different, disputants may be less committed to putting energy into the consensus-building phase of their ADR process. The pressures to abandon mediation in favor of arbitration are likely to be especially acute when the mediation process reaches an impasse, which probably occurs in the vast majority of mediated disputes. Finally, since the egregious litigation alternative is

Consensus

We are so accustomed to life within the invisible veil that we often don't see its effects. Does the availability of adversarial dispute resolution processes reinforce the reliance of individuals on such processes?

Some subcultures that value the rights of the individual also reject decisional processes that produce a winner and a loser. According to Richard H. Pildes and Elizabeth S. Anderson, a team consisting of a law professor and a philosophy professor, the Quaker ("Society of Friends") and Shaker societies rely solely on consensus—the agreement of all community members—before decisions are made. Why isn't voting an option in these communities? Pildes and Anderson note that it's believed that voting would harm the will of the collective, and, from a spiritual perspective, the will of the collective is believed to represent the will of God (Pildes & Anderson 1990, 2198).

Consensus can be difficult to attain, as noted by environmentalist Marc Reisner, who notes his experience with the Friends faith from his college days and exalts democratic process over consensus for many disputes (Reisner 2000, 12). A Quaker colleague of the author of this textbook has commented that Quaker meetings sometimes go on for hours, even days, while the congregation tries to persuade a single holdout to come around to the viewpoint of the other members in an effort to reach consensus. If individuals knew that they could short-circuit the often time-consuming and difficult process of consensus-building by invoking majority rule, wouldn't they be likely to do it?

Does this logic apply to the analogous situation in which a facilitative dispute resolution process is paired with an adversary process, as in med-arb? What do you think?

---

eliminated as a possibility, the disputants can afford to be less committed to the process of mediation.[1]

In addition to the more theoretical conflict diagnosis issues associated with med-arb-different, the process has the simple and practical problem of requiring two different neutrals, which costs additional time and money if mediation doesn't settle the matter. Co-med-arb, in which the arbitrator sits in on the mediation phase, saves time but can be even more expensive, and it presents some of the partiality problems of med-arb-same. Additionally, since the arbitrator is observing the mediation process in co-med-arb, there is strong incentive for the disputants to couch their dispute in adversarial terms during mediation in order to maximize their chances of winning, should arbitration be needed. Like med-arb-same, co-med-arb can be expected to produce adversarial posturing and positional bargaining, making it harder to achieve principled negotiation and cooperative settlement during the mediation phase.

ARB-MED

Arb-med is a less commonly used process. It begins with the case being presented to an arbitrator, who issues a decision but keeps the decision secret. In a subsequent phase, the disputants attempt to mediate a settlement. (The arbitrator may

---

[1] The most radical supporters of pure and transformative mediation might apply this argument to litigation as well as to med-arb. They might say that the ready availability of litigation as the "default" dispute resolution process causes disputants to short-circuit their commitment to the processes, such as mediation and negotiation, that depend on consensus. Unfortunately, although this argument has merit, our species has not yet come up with a better last resort than litigation.

be the same person as, or a different person than, the mediator.) The arbitration award is revealed and used if, and only if, mediation does not settle the matter. It is thought that disputants' knowledge that there is already an arbitration award and that the award may affect the disputant adversely will increase incentives to come to a reasonable, voluntary agreement in mediation.

Benefits of Arb-Med. Arb-med is grounded in a positional-bargaining paradigm of conflict resolution, and it is based on incentives very similar to final-offer arbitration. Arb-med assumes that negotiation will be adversarial, with each disputant's team having an incentive to make the most extreme offers they can get away with. It is believed that, since the disputants know that there is an arbitration award hanging over their heads, there will be counterincentives to make compromises that offset the usual motive to make extreme offers during negotiation.

Drawbacks of Arb-Med. Arb-med is beset with several problems. The fact that arbitration, which is an adversary process, precedes mediation makes it more likely that disputants will be caught up in escalated conflict. Deutsch's Crude Axiom (Chapter 9) cautions that a conflict will tend to become what the disputants believe and perceive it to be: thus, the imposition of an adversarial framework onto the conflict is likely to create the perception, and then the reality, that the dispute is competitive. Deutsch has also postulated that, the more competitive the perception and reality of the conflict, the more likely the conflict is to escalate destructively and that it is harder to move from an escalated, competitive conflict to a cooperative one than vice versa. Thus, one might expect arb-med to be associated with conflict escalation. This development would be especially likely if the mediator and the arbitrator were the same person—because both disputants will fear losing face and appearing to be weak in front of the neutral and the other disputant.

Arb-med also presents subtle motivational pressures similar to those of med-arb. If the disputants reach impasse during mediation, they know that an arbitration award is available to bail them out. Given the investment of time and money in the arbitration phase and the fact that an arbitrated outcome is already ready and waiting, it's likely the disputants will simply prefer to go with the arbitration award, rather than investing great time, energy, and emotional risk in mediation.

Arb-med-same also presents a problem of arb-mediator neutrality. Once the arb-mediator has conducted the arbitration, he or she will have preconceptions about how the mediation "should" go (since he or she has already adjudicated the case) and may have an ego investment in a particular outcome. Hence, the arb-mediator may be in danger of pressuring the disputants to produce an outcome similar to the one he or she has arbitrated.

Finally, there is a practical cost-effectiveness problem with arb-med: it could be perceived as a waste of time and money (Peter 1997, 99–100). If mediation turns out to be a sufficient process, then arb-med will have imposed an unnecessary layer of time and cost.

MEDIATION WINDOWING

The concept of providing "mediation windows" (Peter 1997, 102) formalizes a practice that often occurs informally during arbitration hearings: that of informal ad-hoc facilitation by the arbitrator. Many arbitrators periodically move into a more facilitative role in an effort to get a consensual settlement instead of an arbitrated award. In a conceptual sense, it's as if the disputants make an ad-hoc agreement to mediate all or part of the conflict midstream during arbitration. Mediation windowing makes this informal practice explicit. Mediation windows may occur on an ad-hoc basis, or they may be built into the process in predetermined ways (for example, as each new issue is raised or once every two hours). In the (fairly unusual) case in which the arbitrating disputants are clearly receptive to principled negotiation,[2] this technique can improve process and outcome, and, if the mediator is different from the arbitrator, the impartiality problems of med-arb can be minimized. On the other hand, this technique is unlikely to succeed unless both disputants are enthusiastic about it: if conflict escalation is occurring, one or both disputants are likely to perceive mediation windowing as a waste of time or worse.

INCENTIVE ARBITRATION

Incentive arbitration is a hybrid process falling midway between nonbinding evaluation and arbitration. The case is submitted to arbitration and an award is issued. The arbitration award is nonbinding, but there are penalties for not accepting it. For example, in one common form, a party rejecting the arbitration award must do better in litigation by a predetermined percentage or face a penalty, such as paying the other side's attorney's fees and court costs. Incentive arbitration is used in the private sector; however, additionally it is becoming a choice of court policymakers who wish to impose mandatory, binding arbitration on disputants to cut the burden on the system while retaining the finality of a binding adjudication. For example, such a process is being offered by the state courts of Idaho for cases with monetary claims of under $25,000 under the name "neutral evaluation" (Cahill 2002).

Benefits of Incentive Arbitration. Disputants frequently turn to incentive arbitration in an effort to obtain the certainty of adjudication without giving up the autonomy and control of a consensual process. A party is free to reject the arbitrated outcome but must be prepared to pay for it if he or she turns out to be unreasonable in his or her actions. This sort of process allows more autonomy and control than a straight adjudication—but not very much, since each disputant is vulnerable to the other disputant's decision to relitigate the dispute.

---

[2] Arbitrating disputants who are receptive to principled bargaining can be expected to be uncommon, because conflict theory predicts that the use of arbitration, an adversary process, will promote a competitive orientation on the part of the disputants.

Drawbacks of Incentive Arbitration. Incentive arbitration is based on a strictly adversarial model and is therefore unlikely to encourage principled bargaining, cooperation, or creative problem solving. As such, it is suitable for disputants to reject a cooperative-bargaining model out of hand, as with the resolution of disputes in competitive sports, such as salary and bonus disputes involving professional players. Whether such a process is more or less efficient than straight adjudication is unknown, because it is unknown how many evaluations are rejected in favor of adjudication.

MINITRIAL

Minitrial was discussed in Chapter 20 in its incarnation as a nonbinding evaluation process. In this chapter, we will discuss it in its hybrid version. A minitrial is an abbreviated version of a litigated dispute, attended by the disputants or their officers or directors who have the authority to settle. Typically, there is also a neutral third party present to moderate the proceeding. A summary version of the evidence is put on, so that the representatives themselves can get a sense of the strengths and weaknesses of their respective cases. Whether the presentations consist solely of statements by counsel or include some sort of witness or documentary evidence submission is up to the disputants. Following the minitrial, the disputants' representatives meet to negotiate, often without their lawyers present. There may or may not also be a mediation-like settlement facilitation or an advisory evaluation presented by the neutral.

Minitrial is a very effective process to provide information about the litigation option for BATNA clarification. The disputants themselves (or the representatives of the disputants with the authority to settle) get a significant dose of reality-testing. This litigation dry-run can be particularly effective when there are significant uncertainties in fact or law or a human dimension that might affect outcome (such as a particularly effective or ineffective witness). And some believe that the trial-like atmosphere of minitrial can provide some of the emotional catharsis and sense of vindication that a trial can. On the other hand, since the presentation is adversarial, minitrial tends to promote competition and conflict escalation to a greater degree than facilitative mediation. If the neutral avoids evaluation and sticks to moderating the process, mintrial tends to promote a higher quality of consent than purer forms of nonbinding evaluation. It can be highly effective as a process used within a facilitative framework for BATNA clarification.

OMBUDS

An ombuds is a person, not a process.[3] The ombuds concept originated in Scandinavia several hundred years ago as a way to deal with governmental complaints

---

[3] Many professionals in the field recognize the original, gender-nonneutral version of the term *ombudsman* as the technically correct name of this ADR neutral. Others have adopted the term *ombudsperson.* This book uses the popular, gender-neutral *ombuds* as the term that appears to be most likely to supplant *ombudsman.*

Ombuds-Additional Resources

An international organization, The Ombudsman Association (TOA), provides information, networking, training opportunities, ethical and substantive guidance, and a forum for ombuds. You can view more information about TOA and ombuds at *http://www.ombuds-toa.org/*.

by the populace.[4] It was recognized that, to keep government responsive to the people, a human face needed to be put on the government. The ombuds was an individual who handled the concerns of the citizenry in an informal, flexible manner. The ombuds had connections to people in power and had the authority to cut through bureaucratic red tape to resolve issues.

The ombuds concept has gained a widespread reputation and use as a means of personalizing the dispute resolution processes of large organizations, such as corporations, municipalities, and governmental agencies. Ombuds' popularity over the past twenty to thirty years has been the result of systemic problems that accompany the formalism and bureaucracy of very large organizations: the idea of ombuds is to provide people with the sort of individualized and flexible attention that is an attribute of well-functioning small organizations, yet in a large-organizational context. Numerous large organizations that have employed ombuds are thought to have realized clear gains in terms of internal morale, operating efficiency, and corporate image.

What Is an Ombuds? An ombuds is a sort of dispute resolution jack of all trades—an informal complaint and dispute manager. An ombuds (or office of ombuds) is always associated with a specific large organization, such as a particular corporation, municipality, or agency. Ombuds may deal with internal, workplace issues (workplace ombuds), issues involving complaints from individuals outside an organization (client ombuds), or occasionally a combination of both.

An ombuds serves as a human factor to counterbalance all the size and formalism of a large organization—someone who can help individuals communicate their concerns and effect helpful change in a large organization. Ombuds are generally high-ranking employees of the organizations they serve but are outside the regular chain of command to ensure that they are not perceived as a tool of management or leadership. Ombuds makes themselves available to hear and counsel individuals with conflicts and disputes (sometimes these individuals are referred to as "inquirers"). For example, a corporate ombuds may be available to hear concerns raised by disgruntled, demoralized employees or employees who feel harassed. Equal Employment Opportunity (EEO) departments and Em-

---

[4] The term *ombudsman* originally meant "collector of the bribe" in medieval Germanic cultures. In these cultures, a neutral agent was often appointed to collect a bribe, or fine, from the family of a wrongdoer to pay to a victim. This informal adjustment of a dispute avoided the retaliatory killing of the wrongdoer by the victim or his family. A more modern version of the ombuds was developed by the Swedish parliament in 1809, but the concept was not adopted in large scale in the United States until the last quarter of the twentieth century (Wiegand 1996, 97–98).

ployee Assistance Program (EAP) offices also handle such problems in the workplace, but ombuds can deal with such issues in a less formal, less adversarial manner and can deal with problems that lie outside the jurisdiction of these specialized offices.

Ombuds enter some conflicts because concerned persons come to them for help. Ombuds generally have lockable offices with secure telephone lines to ensure the confidentiality of communications with persons accessing the service. Effective publicity and outreach efforts by ombuds are needed to make their availability and function known to potential clients and employees. Workplace ombuds also prowl the hallways and lunchrooms of offices, and client ombuds research in front offices and public hearings, in an effort to learn what is bothering people or disrupting the office or public culture.

Ombuds use a variety of techniques to address and deal with conflict. An ombuds acts as sympathetic ear for the inquirer and may serve as a confidant, as a conduit for facilitating communication between the complainant and those with whom he or she needs to make contact, and as a recommender and persuader. An ombuds may occasionally serve a mediator's role, facilitating the resolution of conflicts. An ombuds can also make referrals to more formalized dispute resolution processes, such as mediation, arbitration, grievance adjudication, or nonbinding evaluation, and may refer appropriate cases to EEO and EAP offices.

Basic Features of Ombuds: Neutrality and Confidentiality. Neutrality and confidentiality are virtually universally recognized as essential characteristics of the ombuds role. A workplace ombuds does not serve management, nor does he or she advocate on behalf of inquirers, although meeting the needs of both is always a goal of a person in the ombuds role. In order to encourage people to come forward with problems and issues of concern to them, inquirers need to know that the ombuds won't turn against them, and, in order to be effective conflict resolvers, the ombuds must not appear to be acting as advocates of the inquirer. The fact that the ombuds is hired by and can be fired by management makes this neutrality fragile. Leadership must publicly lend strict and unwavering support to ombuds' neutrality to render them effective. Mistrust of this neutrality can arise easily, leading to ombuds whose client bases refuse to consult them. For this reason, organizations that have established successful ombuds programs typically take pains to protect the perceived and actual neutrality of the ombuds. Many ombuds occupy a high-level position in the corporation or agency, outside the normal chain of command. It also appears to help for the individual ombuds (or directors of the ombuds office) to be well regarded by the representatives of various stakeholder groups, such as unions, management, and/or consumer groups (Meltzer 1998).

Confidentiality is the second cornerstone of the ombuds role. The personal and informal process of handling difficult and sometimes private or embarrassing conflicts is impossible to do effectively unless inquirers feel free to share private, and sometimes unpleasant or embarrassing, information with the ombuds. The Ombudsman Association Standards of Practice require the ombuds to have a clearly delineated document-destruction policy to avoid the possibility of confidential documents' getting into the wrong hands (TOA Std. of Prac., §3.3) and provides that the ombuds is to protect the anonymity of the inquirer while conducting investigations and exploring possible resolutions to conflicts (TOA Std. of Prac., §§2.1 and 2.2).

Generally, in the workplace context, confidentiality is conferred by job description and workplace policy. However, despite the fact that ombuds who are members of The Ombudsman Association (TOA) pledge to resist any efforts to get them to testify (TOA Std. of Prac. §3), there is no statutory right to confidentiality of an ombuds in most jurisdictions. Standards of practice, such as those of TOA, rendering communications confidential and privileged will generally not protect the communications from being subpoenaed if the dispute escalates into litigation. For example, in *Carman v. McDonnell Douglas Corp.,* 114 F. 3d 790 (C.A. 8 1997), an employment dispute originally taken to the ombuds escalated into litigation. In this dispute, the employee sought to produce damaging evidence collected by the ombuds in court, and the employer contended that there should be a common-law right privilege against testimony for ombuds. The court held that no such common-law right existed in the federal system and allowed the information to come in. This ruling does not represent the universal opinion of judges: several district courts have recognized a privilege for communications made to ombuds, and several state courts have done the same. Additionally, many governmental ADR statutes provide for the confidentiality of communications made during proceedings, including ombuds. For example, the Federal Administrative Dispute Resolution Act (5 U.S.C. §§571 *et seq.*), governing dispute resolution processes in federal agencies, includes the ombuds process in its definition of alternative dispute resolution (ADRA, §571(3)) and specifies the confidentiality of ADR proceedings in general (ADRA, §574).

Ombuds assists elderly resident at a long-term care facility. Michael Heron, Pearson Education/ PH College

Critical Features of Competent Ombuds. Ombuds are unique in the ADR world in that an explicit process, or set of processes, is not specified in the role of the ombuds. Rather, being an ombuds is a personal role. For this reason, the personal qualities of the ombuds are particularly important to effective functioning. A competent ombuds must be able to navigate between sometimes mistrustful sides without becoming caught up in polarizing influences and must be able to convey a sense of integrity and neutrality to all concerned. The effective ombuds should be compassionate, be an effective listener and communicator, have a high degree of integrity, have mediation skills, and have an in-depth understanding of organizational structure, culture, and politics. Because the ombuds approaches each conflict flexibly and must custom-design strategies for resolving them or referring inquirers appropriately, it's also extremely important for an ombuds to be an effective conflict diagnostician and to have an in-depth understanding of how each of the strategies and processes available to bring to bear on the conflict will affect its course and outcome. Since the ombuds' role is to help resolve conflict constructively and to prevent future destructive conflict, an understanding of the cycles of cooperation, competition, and conflict escalation is a must, as is an ability to engage in nonescalating, emotionally validating forms of communication.

The ombuds must also be capable of garnering respect from all sides, and this aspect of the role is particularly important at the inception of an ombuds program. When the ombuds office, program, or job description is first implemented, there must be psychological ownership of the concept by all the interested stakeholders: management, employees, unions, and so on. Otherwise, the office may be mistrusted, underused, or fail outright. When D. Leah Meltzer, ADR specialist at the Securities and Exchange Commission, investigated federal ombuds offices (Meltzer 1998), she found resistance to the appointment of ombuds from stakeholders who had been left out of the decision-making process. For example, when the U.S. Information Agency implemented an ombuds program in 1985, the employees' union had not been consulted. The union executive board members felt that the ombuds program endangered the system of grievances and remedies that had been developed in the collective bargaining process. This effort at establishing an ombuds program failed. Then, in 1988, a second effort by the agency secretary to create an ombuds program almost failed again when the unions were again omitted from the decision-making process. Meltzer reports that, after an ombuds had been appointed, the union, in turn, left the ombuds out of important meetings and told their members to steer clear of him. She also reports that some employees at the Smithsonion Institution have expressed fear that the ombuds there is a tool of management, while at the Secret Service there was initial concern that the ombuds would be infringing on management's responsibilities. Meltzer found the most successful ombuds programs in agencies where all stakeholder groups were involved in program development from the outset and where the ombuds selected were trusted and respected by both union and management.

Additionally, there must be adequate publicity, outreach, and education to acquaint an organization and its management, the union, EEO and EAP members, employees, and clients with the office, its neutrality, and its confidentiality and with what the ombuds can do. In a dysfunctional organization, an ombuds put in place without adequate prior informational outreach is likely to be mistrusted as just another gimmick and will probably go unused.

Benefits of Ombuds. Ombuds can be a particularly effective tool for the constructive resolution of conflict. Because ombuds can persuade, but have no power to impose decisions and must remain neutral (and, hence, are unlikely to be in the business of giving nonbinding evaluations), a well-trained and talented ombuds can be highly effective in constructively managing conflict and in making recommendations to improve the overall functioning of an organization. Decisions reached through an ombuds process are likely to have a high quality of disputant consent and therefore to be psychologically owned and adhered to by the participants. Because the ombuds may receive confidential information from potentially numerous sources, he or she has a finger on the pulse on the organization and can be a valuable resource in diagnosing the more systemic problems within the organization that generate interpersonal conflict. As such, ombuds are an important source of information for designers of dispute resolution systems for the organizations in which they operate.

It's hard to study the impact of ombuds. Many ombuds comment that the mere fact of their availability as a listener and change agent for employees creates improvements in morale, organizational culture, and functioning (Meltzer 1998). It would be hard to assess such changes and trace them back to specific programs or processes, but the explosion in the use of ombuds by organizations that must financially justify such initiatives suggests that they are perceived by many as great successes.

MULTIMODAL ADR PROGRAMS AND PROCESSES

Mixed, or hybrid, ADR processes are specific processes that combine elements of the three basic ADR forms—mediation, arbitration, and nonbinding evaluation. Multimodal ADR programs, on the other hand, are programs and systems that integrate multiple distinct ADR processes. We will discuss three such types of programs in this section: ADR systems, court-connected ADR, and online ADR. Of these, online ADR doesn't really fit our conceptual definition, since the online environment isn't a single ADR program. However, its characteristic of offering numerous options for dispute resolution makes it most useful to include it here.

DISPUTE RESOLUTION SYSTEMS

Within the past decade or so, large organizations, such as private corporations and governmental agencies, have paid closer attention to ADR as it has become mainstreamed within the legal community and the courthouse. Dispute resolution systems design, like ombuds programs, is an effort to gain the benefits of alternative dispute resolution processes for organizations (Lynch & German

2002). In the past ten years, several helpful works on dispute resolution systems design have been published,[5] and the profession of dispute resolution systems design consultant has flourished. With statistics indicating almost half of managerial time being spent handling interpersonal conflicts (Hicks 2002), this new attention makes financial sense to cost-conscious organizations.

The new focus on organizational conflict management may also reflect a growing understanding that conflict within organizations, rather than simply representing an annoyance or a source of friction or damage, allows organizations to discover opportunities for reform and innovation. Consider the following example:

> Belinda Marshall works as a chief managing paralegal, and Cory Logan works as an office manager at Doms and Jason, a large and growing law firm in Anytown, USA. Belinda and Cory are at parallel levels within the firm's nonattorney hierarchy, and they frequently butt heads over a variety of issues. Right now, they are involved in a simmering dispute over the firm's efforts to adopt a new information system. Belinda is strongly in favor of adopting MicroLegal, a system that integrates a timeslip system for tracking staff billable hours with automated billing, office inventory, resource management, and other office management systems. Cory prefers LawyerTrak, a system that he feels is much better at all the management processes he has to handle. A partnership meeting is planned two months from now for making the decision. The firm does not have an established communication system for making the managing partners aware of such disputes, but, as office manager, Cory submits bimonthly reports to the partners, and he has advised them of the merits of LawyerTrak. Belinda is left out of the formal communication loop, even though the partners have reassured her that "their doors are open." She is fearful that, if LawyerTrak is adopted, it will make her job of managing her paralegal staff much more difficult. Belinda is increasingly angry that the firm seems to ignore her department's needs, and she is beginning to attribute her problems to gender discrimination.

If the firm treats Cory and Belinda's dispute as merely a problem, positive opportunities will be lost. The two have different perspectives on the problem of how to choose office management software. If the conflict is treated as an opportunity to make an effective decision about the software, the existence of the diverse perspectives will help the firm make a better choice. Moreover, dealing with the ongoing conflict between Belinda and Cory could lead to better lines of communication being established within the firm. On the other hand, if Belinda is left out of the decisional process, she is likely to feel disempowered. She is very likely to use a resource such as the EEO office to express her concerns, and this could easily result in a displaced conflict over gender discrimination. If Belinda

---

[5] The best known include Costatino and Merchant (1996) and Ury, Brett, and Goldberg (1988). A fine bibliography is available online at *http://www.peacemakers.ca/bibliography/bib8design.html* and a set of valuable articles on the subject are available full-text at the *mediate.com* website, *www.mediate.com*, by selecting "Systems Design" in the topic search.

pursues an EEO grievance, it will likely produce hostility among the male employees and partners, leading to additional meta-disputes and impairing, rather than improving, gender relations. Developing a process for allowing this conflict to be aired and discussed in a meaningful fashion may prevent destructive conflict escalation and lead to a better communication process for the firm, as well as a better decision about office management software. Thus, treating Cory and Belinda's dispute as an opportunity to improve the firm, rather than as a problem to be eliminated, can have numerous advantages for Cory, Belinda, and the firm in general.

Dispute resolution systems design requires the application of conflict diagnosis principles on a macro, organizational level, rather than on an individual level. System designers must understand not only conflict, conflict escalation, negotiation, power, and so on as presented in this text, but also organizational structures, systems, processes, and functions. Dispute resolution systems designers integrate systems and organizational development knowledge with conflict diagnosis concepts to create effective dispute systems designs. Aimee Gourlay and Jenelle Soderquist, law professors and ADR professionals, writing in the *Hamline Law Review* (Gourlay & Soderquist 1998), note that an effective dispute system resolution should encourage interest-based conflict resolution to ensure that resolution is constructive for the organization as a whole and preserves relationships within the organization. They further note that beginning a dispute resolution process after a conflict has reached the stage of a formal grievance misses a valuable opportunity to prevent the conflict from becoming destructive. Thus, these as well as other professionals in the field argue for a preventive function for dispute resolution systems.

How do systems designers accomplish their objectives? Peter Woodrow (1998), a dispute resolution systems designer in South Africa, explains,

> While every situation is unique, the typical steps involved in dispute resolution systems are the following:
>
> - Establish a process for making decisions about new or enhanced dispute resolution processes.
> - Identify and diagnose the causes of recurring organisational conflicts and the effectiveness of existing dispute handling procedures.
> - Examine the range of options for additional procedures or revisions of existing procedures.
> - Select or revise conflict resolution procedures, considering the corporate culture and the kinds of disputes that arise.
> - Organise the selected procedures in a comprehensive conflict management system.
> - Seek support from key organisational constituencies and secure approval for the proposed new system.
> - Develop a plan for implementing the new system and promoting its use. Train personnel to administer the system and to provide specific services, such as mediation.
> - Create a process for quality control, feedback and refinement of the system.

There are three areas systems professionals seem to agree are vital to the effective practice of dispute resolution systems design. First, experts in the field comment on the need for the dispute resolution system to be tailored to the structure and culture unique to the organization in question. A one-size-fits-all mentality, it is believed, is doomed to failure, because each organization has a unique structure and culture. The temptation to adopt someone else's version of a dispute resolution system should be resisted (Gourlay & Soderquist 1998). Thus, the experts in the field consider it vital to apply conflict diagnosis and organizational systems concepts to the specific situation in an individualized fashion. Moreover, the resultant system should be consistent with corporate values and goals, so that there is greater impetus for it to succeed (Hicks 2002). Second, many experts in dispute resolution systems design comment on the need to involve stakeholders at all stages of system design and implementation, from initial planning onward. Psychological ownership of the resulting system by all potential users is essential. This is particularly true in a situation in which stakeholder groups have been at loggerheads with one another: any effort by one group to adopt a dispute resolution system will be reactively devalued by other groups, who will likely believe it to be merely a tool of "the enemy." Such suspicious stakeholders will be motivated to sabotage the new design (Gourlay & Soderquist 1998). As a part of the process of stakeholder involvement, commentators further urge commitment and care in providing education, training, publicity, and outreach. Third, experts note the need for continuing evaluation of the system (Hicks 2002; Woodrow 1998). Organizations are extremely complex systems, and conflict resolution is a tricky business. A system that seems appropriate in theory may not work in practice. Moreover, the imposition of a new dispute resolution system invariably alters organizational structure and culture, so that a system that was ideally suited to the organization initially carries within itself the seeds of its own obsolescence.

In our example, what might a fully implemented dispute resolution systems design for Doms and Jason look like? Without knowing the corporate culture, recurring dispute situations, organizational structure, and stakeholder interests, it would be impossible to predict the details. However, a dispute resolution system generally combines multiple options for dispute resolution within a coherent whole. The Doms and Jason plan might have a reparative element, for handling overt disputes such as the one between Belinda and Cory, as well as a plan for preventing destructive conflict escalation by altering the organizational communication and governance system to give greater voice to stakeholders. Figure 21-1 shows one possible way of structuring a reparative dispute resolution system for Doms and Jason.

The advantages and disadvantages of a particular dispute resolution system design depend on how well its designers are able to understand the organization and diagnose the conflictual situations being addressed, on how effectively the needed stakeholders are included in the design and implementation process, on how effectively the organization as a whole can be educated and trained in its use, and on how effectively the system is evaluated and improved. Judging by the

◆ **FIGURE 21-1**

A Possible Model for a Reparative Dispute Resolution System for the Doms & Jason Law Firm

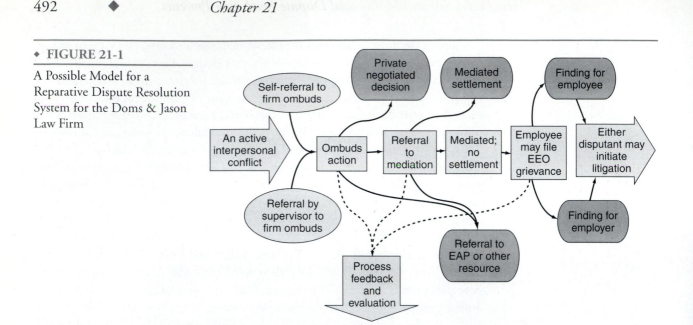

![Flowchart: An active interpersonal conflict leads to Ombuds action (via Self-referral to firm ombuds or Referral by supervisor to firm ombuds), then to Referral to mediation, leading to Private negotiated decision or Mediated settlement or Mediated; no settlement, then Employee may file EEO grievance, then Either disputant may initiate litigation; outcomes Finding for employee and Finding for employer; Referral to EAP or other resource; Process feedback and evaluation]

Systems Design for Federal Agencies

In 1996, the U.S. Congress passed the Administrative Dispute Resolution Act of 1996 (ADRA, PL 104-320), mandating the implementation of ADR processes to handle both client and internal disputes involving federal agencies. This mandate has prompted efforts by each agency to design and implement dispute resolution systems.

A comprehensive and periodically updated description of each federal agency's dispute resolution system is available on the Internet from the Office of Personnel Management. It is called "Alternative Dispute Resolution: A Resource Guide" and is available at *http://www.opm.gov/er/adrguide/toc.htm.*

---

increasing ubiquity of dispute resolution systems design in large organizations and its adoption for the federal government, it appears that these systems are achieving a degree of success in improving the operation of corporations, agencies, and others that use them.

COURT-CONNECTED ADR

One of the most common multimodal applications of ADR today occurs in state and federal court systems across the United States. The idea began with Frank E. A. Sander's conception of the multidoor courthouse in 1976. Sander's idea (Sander 1976, 130–33) was for courts to offer one-stop shopping to meet a variety of disputant and societal needs:

> What I am advocating is a flexible and diverse panoply of dispute resolution processes, with particular types of cases being assigned to differing processes (or combinations of processes). . . . [O]ne might envision . . . not simply a courthouse but a Dispute Resolution Center, where the grievant would first be channeled through a screening clerk who would then direct him to the

process (or sequence of processes) most appropriate to his type of case. The room directory in the lobby of such a Center might look as follows:

- Screening Clerk   Room 1
- Mediation   Room 2
- Arbitration   Room 3
- Fact Finding   Room 4
- Malpractice Screening Panel   Room 5
- Superior Court   Room 6
- Ombudsman   Room 7

History of Court-Connected ADR. By 1980, a number of courts, spurred on by visionaries such as Sander (1976) and federal judge Thomas Lambros (1984), had begun to implement experimental ADR processes as a way to divert cases from the overcrowded court system and resolve legal disputes more effectively.

Ad-hoc experimentation with ADR in the 1970s and 1980s, as well as visible and vocal support from influential leaders such as Chief Justice Warren Burger (1982) of the United States Supreme Court, led to increased federal congressional support for such programs. In 1988, Congress authorized twenty federal district courts to implement pilot arbitration programs, ten voluntary programs and ten mandatory programs (Judicial Improvements and Access to Justice Act, PL 100-702). This initial foray into court-connected ADR was followed by the landmark Civil Justice Reform Act of 1990 (CJRA, 28 U.S.C. §§471–482), which mandated that the federal district courts implement plans to make courts speedier and more efficient. ADR was recommended as one of the cornerstones of this process.

§471 of the CJRA provides

Requirement for a district court civil justice expense and delay reduction plan. There shall be implemented by each United States district court, in accordance with this chapter, a civil justice expense and delay reduction plan. The plan may be a plan developed by such district court or a model plan developed by the Judicial Conference of the United States. The purposes of each plan are to facilitate deliberate adjudication of civil cases on the merits, monitor discovery, improve litigation management, and ensure just, speedy, and inexpensive resolutions of civil disputes.

Because the CJRA was intended principally to make courts more speedy, efficient, and inexpensive, it has primarily focused on diverting cases out of the trial and hearing process and making their resolution more speedy. As a result of the CJRA and the efforts of numerous individuals committed to the development of ADR in the federal courts, as of 1996 nearly all federal district courts engaged in some sort of court-connected ADR. A report published by the Federal Judicial Center in 1996 (Plapinger & Seinstra 1996) reported that 83 percent of the ninety-four district courts were engaging in, or referring litigants to, some sort of ADR, with fifty-two districts using mediation, forty-eight using summary jury trial, twenty-two using arbitration, thirteen using early neutral evaluation, three using "settlement week" proceedings (a process in which volunteer attorneys get together with litigants and their attorneys to try to hammer out settlement to pending litigation), and two using case valuation.

Congress next passed the Alternative Dispute Resolution Act of 1998, mandating the provision of ADR in all federal district courts, including the bankruptcy courts. In particular, Section 652 provides in part (subsection a) that

> each district court *shall,* by local rule adopted under section 2071(a), require that litigants in all civil cases consider the use of an alternative dispute resolution process at an appropriate stage in the litigation. Each district court *shall provide* litigants in all civil cases with at least one alternative dispute resolution process, including, but not limited to, mediation, early neutral evaluation, minitrial, and arbitration as authorized in sections 654 through 658. Any district court that elects to require the use of alternative dispute resolution in certain cases may do so only with respect to mediation, early neutral evaluation, and, if the parties consent, arbitration. (emphasis added)

This provision has three important components:

1. It mandates that all district courts require litigants to consider using ADR.
2. It requires all district courts to make available to litigants at least one ADR process.
3. It authorizes, but does not require, district courts to mandate participation in either mediation or early neutral evaluation.

Individual district courts are permitted, within this broad statutory mandate, to create and implement whatever ADR program is felt to be appropriate. As of 2002, at least eleven of the federal district courts that had not reported having a court-connected program in 1996 had subsequently adopted explicit ADR rules or implemented ADR programs, leaving fewer than five without an explicit ADR program.

The trend to providing for court-connected ADR has spread to the state courts as well (Streeter-Schaefer 2001). Initially, the impetus to provide ADR on the state court level was driven by the divorce field. In the late 1970s, lawyer O. J. Coogler voiced a popular concern that the use of the adversarial system to handle divorce matters burdened family members in crisis with unnecessary financial and psychological stress. His ground-breaking book, *Structured Mediation in Divorce Settlement,* published in 1978, recommended a less adversarial alternative, built on a carefully structured system of facilitated negotiation. His work was followed some three years later by *Divorce Mediation,* authored by social work professor and divorce mediator John M. Haynes, which proposed an alternative, and more therapeutic, model for mediating divorces (Haynes 1981). The notion of turning to mediation to create a more humane and less damaging alternative to the divorce courts was supported by developmental psychology research indicating that children exposed to destructive conflict between their parents suffered developmental setbacks, compared with their counterparts whose parents dealt with conflict constructively (Camara & Resnick, 1988, 1989). The implementation of mediation to handle divorce issues, and particularly to protect the best interests of the children of divorce, was therefore a natural step for the state court systems, which were responsible for handling family law matters. Mediation also meshed nicely with the revolution in custody law away from sole custody and toward joint custody.

Initially, a few pioneering states, such as California, Florida, and Michigan, implemented court-connected programs to mediate child custody disputes, and a scattering of pilot programs in other states began to pop up.[6] In contrast to the federal efforts, which were primarily spurred by efficiency considerations, the child custody programs were more commonly implemented because of the awareness of many legal and mental-health professionals that using an adversary process to deal with parenting issues was likely to inflame and escalate conflict and to impair healthy child development. Despite this initial reason for implementing mediation, some of the first custody mediation programs were of the triage type, particularly in some California districts, such as Alameda County. These programs tended to be coercive, to be nonconfidential, and to focus on quick settlement rather than healthy postdivorce family functioning (McIsaac 2001). The worst travesties created by these programs were horribilized in the professional journals by the scathing attacks of feminist law professors such as Trina Grillo, whose classic article "The Mediation Alternative: Process Dangers for Women" (1991) raised a considerable uproar in the legal and ADR communities. Grillo and others claimed that child custody mediation that included coercive and nonconfidential features disproportionately pressured women into giving in to their male opponents. (This contention, and the controversy it generated, is discussed in more detail in Chapter 16.) For a time, it appeared that feminist opposition to all mediation between male and female disputants would stop court-connected divorce and custody mediation dead in its tracks. However, by and large, jurisdictions adopting mediation as a way to deal with child custody and visitation disputes were able to avoid the mistakes made in California, and subsequent research, although not consistently positive, by and large suggested that women were not systematically disadvantaged by mediation (Emery, Matthews, & Wyer 1991; Gaschen 1995; Heister 1987; Kelly & Duryee 1992; Marcus, Marcus, Stilwell, & Doherty 1999; Pearson 1991; Richardson 1988). By the late 1990s, mediation was widely implemented as the court-connected ADR process of choice for family law disputes, according to Connie J. A. Beck and Bruce D. Sales of the University of Arizona (Beck & Sales 2000).

In a parallel development, ADR in state civil disputes took hold during the 1990s. Both mediation and nonbinding evaluation processes were adopted in state court-connected programs and processes, to deal with commercial, contract, and tort cases. In contrast with court-connected ADR in the divorce field,

---

[6] For example, in 1984 and 1986, the first court-connected child custody disputes in two Maryland counties were mediated as part of pilot programs developed by these jurisdictions in collaboration with the University of Maryland, College Park.

which often took the form of mediation and eschewed attorney involvement in sessions, court-connected civil mediation was marked by attorney participation, often in place of the disputants themselves, and by a process that closely resembled a judicial settlement conference. These court programs began in major metropolitan areas, such as Los Angeles; achieved success in diverting cases from litigation; caught fire; and began to spread widely in the mid to latter part of the decade. In addition to mediation, nonbinding arbitration, early neutral evaluation, factfinding, and summary jury trial became popular court-connected processes.

Court-connected ADR in tort, commercial, and contract disputes is typically a highly evaluative, lawyer-controlled process. As mediation has become mainstreamed into civil litigation, it has been transformed far from its original radical roots as a facilitative, nonadversary process into something fundamentally reflective of the adversarial system and invisible veil culture in which it operates. As previously mentioned, a number of commentators have lamented that the original promise of ADR to radically transform our somewhat pathological methods of resolving disputes has been subverted by its gaining mainstream status (Menkel-Meadow 1991; Sabatino 1998). However, empirical research indicates that attorneys, particularly those who do *not* specialize in family law, strongly prefer evaluative ADR to more facilitative processes and believe "head-banging" neutrals who profess expertise in case valuation to be more effective than neutrals who help disputants negotiate (Deja 1999; Hermann, Honeyman, McAdoo, & Welsh 2001).

Typical Features of Court-Connected ADR. Today, several varieties of court-connected ADR are common in the United States. Highly evaluative ADR processes are available to address civil disputes, such as commercial and tort cases. Mediation, early neutral evaluation, minitrial, and summary jury trial, as well as voluntary forms of arbitration and incentive arbitration, are all used by state and federal courts. In particular, summary jury trial and forms of neutral evaluation have become popular methods of dealing with very large and factually complex disputes, such as class action litigation, in which it is impractical to resolve every issue in the formal courtroom. In addition, mediation continues to be used widely in the state courts to address child custody and visitation disputes.

ADR is also used widely to dispose of matters in small claims court—indeed, it may be most accurate to state that ADR has been adopted most consistently in very large civil cases and in very small ones.[7] Additionally, criminal and juvenile courts often apply facilitative forms of mediation to the development of restitution agreements between offenders and the victims they have harmed. Although the idea of applying ADR to criminal matters seems inappropriate at first glance (guilt of a crime against society, it may be argued, should not be subject

---

[7] The fact that mediation has been singled out as an appropriate method of disposing of small claims, plus the fact that the mediators used in these court systems are sometimes undertrained and underpaid, prompts some commentators to identify mediation as second-class justice. See the discussion in Chapter 15.

Victim-Offender Mediation—Additional Resources

Additional information regarding victim-offender mediation is available on the World Wide Web. See the website of the Victim Offender Mediation Association, *http://www.voma.org/index.html*, the Victim-Offender Reconciliation Program (VORP), *http://www.vorp.com/*, and the U.S. Department of Justice roster of programs, *http://www.ojp. usdoj.gov/ovc/publications/infores/restorative_justice/96521-dir_victim-offender/welcome.html*.

to private negotiation), victim-offender mediation is not typically used to determine guilt. Victims often comment that the experience of confronting the offender, letting him or her know the impact the offense has had and receiving an apology and restitution, can be quite healing.

Court-connected ADR of civil matters varies widely and differs by court system. It can include all or some of the following: mediation, nonbinding arbitration, voluntary binding arbitration, summary jury trial, early or other neutral evaluation, as well as settlement week. Apart from mediation in family courts and victim-offender mediation, court-connected ADR processes tend to be highly evaluative, with some court systems offering a single process and others more closely resembling the multidoor courthouse model envisioned by Sander. Within the varieties offered by each court, the specific ADR processes used in each lawsuit are usually chosen by the settlement judge, with input from the litigants. It's typical for the ADR referral to be preceded by a series of supporting documents submitted by the attorneys, including statements of position, estimates of discovery and trial time, and other information, including recommendations for the most appropriate ADR procedure to be used.

Family law is still marked by a more facilitative form of mediation offered to deal with child custody disputes, though even in this domain, there are pending issues over how much ADR should look like an adversarial legal negotiation versus a facilitative, collaborative process. Many state courts refer all child custody disputes to mediation unless the dispute is exempt due to extraordinary circumstances, such as a history of spousal or child abuse.

Conflict Diagnosis Issues in Court-Connected ADR. For Frank Sander's vision of a multidoor courthouse to attain its full promise, two things must happen: (1) each court system must offer a full panoply of dispute resolution processes from which disputants may select, including both facilitative and a range of evaluative processes, and (2) those in charge of deciding, or helping to decide, on the best process to use must be skilled conflict diagnosticians. Neither of these goals has been fully realized in most court systems.

For example, many court systems offer only one or two ADR processes. In many court systems, only nonbinding evaluation is offered, even though multiple forms are available. In court systems offering mediation, it often resembles nonbinding evaluation so closely that the option is merely illusory. For example, in the state of Michigan, the original mediation process offered, Michigan Mediation, is none other than early neutral evaluation. When policymakers recognized the absence of a mediation process, they added it, calling it "facilitative mediation," but even this process is highly evaluative. In jurisdictions that provide limited ADR options, there is often little for the conflict diagnostician to choose from unless both sides can be convinced to voluntarily use a private practitioner whose specialty matches the needs of the disputants.

Court-connected ADR is the front line of the struggle between the radical wing of the ADR movement and the entrenched macrosystem with its invisible veil. As Bronfenbrenner's ecological theory might have predicted (see Chapter 3), ADR has transformed the macrosystem, and the macrosystem has simultaneously transformed ADR. Three decades ago, most lawyers could not have even distinguished mediation from arbitration. The few who practiced mediation outside the specialized arena of the collective-bargaining field were members of the radical wing, practicing in either the divorce or the community mediation movement. These early ADR professionals practiced a pure form of mediation. The advent of mass referrals to ADR through the court system has substantially transformed the practice of ADR from a process operating at odds with the prevailing culture into a process that in many ways resembles litigation (Alfini 1991; Guthrie 2001; Kovach & Love 1998; Welsh 2001a). At the same time, however, the legal profession has begun to transform law school and continuing legal education to recognize and teach the principles of conflict diagnosis and the unique advantages of facilitative ADR processes. Movements in "collaborative law;" lawyers who practice holistic, interest-based client counseling (see Chapter 22); and the adoption of transformative mediation practices and ombuds by large organizations are a testament to the bidirectional influence between the radical ADR movement and the invisible veil culture.

ONLINE ADR

The electronic superhighway has made possible exciting innovations in the provision of dispute resolution services. At the same time, the Internet has created problems in interpersonal conflict that have never been encountered before. Thus, the Internet is responsible for both problems and promise in conflict diagnosis and alternative dispute resolution.

Online dispute resolution (ODR)
ADR processes that use the Internet as a platform.

ADR of cyber-disputes
the use of ADR to resolve disputes that occur in the online environment.

ADR that specifically uses the online environment as a forum, or platform, is referred to as **online dispute resolution (ODR)**. ODR processes can be used for any sort of interpersonal conflict, those occurring both online and off. The term **ADR of cyber-disputes** refers to the use of ADR to deal with disputes occurring in the online environment. Common cyber-disputes include

- ◆ Intellectual property disputes, such as disputes over the ownership of domain names and over the fair use of material posted on the Internet
- ◆ Speech-related disputes, such as complaints over defamatory communication, offensive and hateful communication, and the right to free speech in the Internet environment

◆ E-commerce disputes, especially e-commerce involving business-to-consumer and consumer-to-consumer sales and barters that occur over the Internet

Cyber-disputes can be addressed using ODR or traditional ADR. In some cases, an ADR form may be mandated by a governing entity, and, in increasing numbers of cases, the vendor or service provider requires a particular form of ADR as a condition of making the sale or contract for services. This chapter will deal primarily with ODR, rather than with cyber-disputes, although some conflict diagnosis aspects of cyber-disputing will be considered along the way.[8]

Varieties of ODR. The Internet offers a wide variety of dispute resolution processes. The typical ADR forms are available: mediation, arbitration, and non-binding evaluation, including case evaluation and summary jury trial. Many ODR providers also provide hybrid dispute resolution forms, such as med-arb. Additionally, the Internet is home to specialized automated dispute resolution services made possible by computer technology.

Face-to-face ADR occurs in real time and involves verbal interchange, as well as the exchange and review of written documentation and supporting evidence. ODR is characterized by flexibility and variety in communication methods. Real-time interaction is possible in the ODR environment and is known as **synchronous communication.** It most commonly occurs as exchanges of text. Internet software can enable disputants and neutrals to communicate in writing using instant messaging and similar technology. A few providers also offer computer-facilitated audio- or even videoconferencing, which allows the participants to hear, and even see one another as they speak. The Internet, like the telephone, enables disputants to communicate over long distances.

ODR also offers disputants the opportunity to communicate at a time that is convenient to them individually. This form of communication is known as **asynchronous communication.** The most common form of Internet-based asynchronous communication platform is e-mail. Some ODR providers supply a secure chat room, grist, or threaded-discussion platform for the ODR process or provide a combination of these platforms. Asynchronous communication can also include the transmission of graphical materials, audio, or video communication. For example, an ODR process could offer streaming video of a witness's testimony, recorded earlier, or include transmission of the results of a brainstorming session conducted with a white board.

Synchronous communication
Communication that occurs in real time, such as face-to-face discussion, telephone conversation, instant messaging, and videoconferencing.

Asynchronous communication
Communication that occurs at the convenience of the participants rather than in real time, such as communication by letter, by e-mail, or by computer asynchronous conferencing.

---

8 Some ADR professionals and scholars also include two other processes as ODR. The first are traditional complaint resolution processes in which the aggrieved party submits the claim online (Hang 2001, 848–49). The second is the so-called trustmark. Similar to the Good Housekeeping Seal of Approval, a trustmark is an approval certification provided by a watchdog agency, such as the Better Business Bureau. To obtain a trustmark, a business operating online is generally required to undergo an examination process specified by the watchdog agency, to abide by a code of ethics and fair practices, and to agree in advance to submit to a particular dispute resolution system (Teitz 2001, 995–96).

Tracking Down Online Dispute Resolution Providers

Online Dispute Resolution is evolving at breakneck speed, but it's easy to research ODR providers, since they maintain an Internet presence. Here are some places to start. First, the Center for Information Technology and Dispute Resolution (CITDR), co-sponsored by the University of Massachusetts and the Hewlett Foundation, posts an online list of links to ODR providers. The list can be found at *http://www.ombuds.org/center/onlineadr.html.* You may also want to keep an eye out for providers who haven't made it onto the CITDR list. This is easy using a search engine such as Google.com. Simply use "online dispute resolution," or variants of other ADR terminology, as search terms. Also, a journal tracking the progress of this evolving field, *ODR News,* is available to the public at *http://www. odrnews.com.* There are a number of links at this site to useful articles about innovative providers of ODR.

ODR is a rapid-growth industry, so describing it in a textbook is a bit dangerous, since the account is likely to become out of date quickly. However, in the early twenty-first century, it is possible to classify ODR into the following predominant types:

Traditional ADR Conducted by E-mail Communication. An example of traditional ADR conducted by e-mail communication was the (now defunct) IntelliCourt, *http://www.intellicourt.com/index.html.* IntelliCourt provided three levels of service, all of which used an email platform. The express service was a document-based arbitration. The two more comprehensive service levels were med-arb processes. The arbitration component was binding or nonbinding, according to the mutual agreement of the parties. All cases were heard and decided by a retired judge from the California state trial court system, the Honorable Roderic Duncan.

Traditional ADR Conducted in a Web-Based Conferencing Format. A slightly more technologically sophisticated variant uses web-based asynchronous virtual rooms—threaded discussion sites in which disputants can post their communications and review the results of past exchanges. Entries by each participant are visible to others having access to the room but are inaccessible to members of the public. This sort of ODR process is exemplified by Virtual Magistrate, *http://www.vmag.org/* (affiliated with Chicago-Kent College of Law). "Vmag" provides a format identified by the service provider as a "listserv" or "grist," in which disputants can post their conversations. Virtual Magistrate offers nonbinding arbitration of cyber-disputes only (Kentra 2002). A similar service is offered by SquareTrade, *http://www.squaretrade.com/cnt/jsp/index.jsp/,* the ODR provider of eBay, the online auction provider. SquareTrade offers a virtual room for negotiation between the disputants and offers e-mail-based mediation in a caucus-only format if negotiation does not produce a settlement (Leone 2002).

Traditional ADR Conducted Using Technologically Sophisticated Multimodal Platforms. Multimodal ADR platforms are often designed and provided by separate technology firms known as ODR application service providers (ASPs). A typical such ODR service is Online Resolution, *http://www.onlineresolution.com/index. html,* a comprehensive online ADR service offering negotiation, mediation, ar-

Modern technology allows effective conflict resolution despite impediments of time, inconvenience, and distance. Here, a business executive negotiates with his counterparts using computer-based video conferencing. B. Busco, Getty Images Inc.—Image Bank

bitration, and evaluation. Documentation, audio, video, and graphical supporting information are submitted online. This service uses an ASP known as Reso-lutionRoom, *http://www.resolutionroom.com/*, a sophisticated suite of online platforms including instant messaging, white boarding, a list-serv-like threaded discussion virtual room, collaborative documents, private virtual rooms for cau-cusing, and so on. Other similar ODR providers include Nova Forum, *http:// www.novaforum.com/index.html* (Canadian); Internet Neutral, *http://www. internetneutral.com/index.htm*; WebMediate, *http://www.webmediate.com/*; and Resolution Forum, Inc., *http://www.resolutionforum.org/s_demo.html.*

Technologically Sophisticated ADR with Analytical Tools. Several ODR providers offer an even more sophisticated option than those previously described. In addition to providing multimodally sophisticated communication platforms, these providers also offer accessory tools designed to assist disputant teams in assessing their interests and fashioning appropriate proposals. An example is SmartSettle, *http://www.smartsettle.com/flash.html.* This ADR provider offers face-to-face, teleconferencing, and online exchange or a combination of communication formats. Using a facilitator, the parties communicate to generate a list of the terms that have to be addressed (such as price, delivery date, and so forth). Then, privately, each side identifies a range of expectations for each term, an optimal resolution of the term, and optionally a function or graph that represents how satisfied they would be along the range of potential outcomes for the term. They also generate numbers that correspond to how important each issue is to them. (For example, time of payment may be worth 500 to the claimant but only 50 to the respondent.) Parties can even identify "even exchanges" to denote how the terms measure up for example, "my getting $500 now is equal to my getting $1,000 next Friday." Thus, the disputants' interests are reduced to mathematical equations, and these are kept confidential and stored in the ODR computer.

After this initial analysis, the parties issue proposals. The software can generate possible concessions for each disputant, and parties can register secret proposals on terms—if the computer verifies an agreement on an individual term, they are added to a tentative settlement. After a tentative agreement is reached on all terms, the software uses the confidential information regarding interests and weights provided by each team to generate alternative proposals that improve both disputants' expressed interests as much as possible without reducing anyone's outcome.

Blind-Bidding Sites. Very popular and inexpensive, blind-bidding sites operate on the assumption that bargaining will be positional and that money is the only term in dispute. Many blind-bidding ODR providers seem to direct their marketing specifically to insurance claim representatives, who may be bound by corporate policy to use positional bargaining but want to avoid the ego investment and reactive devaluation that comes from making offers directly to the other disputant's negotiating team. Blind-bidding ODR is completely automated; no human intermediator is involved; as a result, the service tends to be very rapid and inexpensive. The process may be either binding or advisory, as determined by the disputants.

In a blind-bidding process, each disputant's negotiating team places a bid, which is kept secret from the other disputant's team. If the bids are within a prescribed "distance" from each other, the computer computes a settlement, usually at the midpoint of the two bids. If the respondent's offer exceeds the claimant's demand, the claim usually is settled at the amount of the offer. At some sites, distance is a flat figure (such as $5,000); at other sites, it's a percentage of the offer or the demand; at other sites, the disputants mutually choose the distance. Most blind-bidding sites allow repeated bidding; some provide three bids at a flat rate, whereas others charge for each bid process.[9]

Online Summary Jury Trial. As of March, 2003, the Internet also boasted one site that provided online summary jury trial. Icourthouse, *http://www.icourthouse. com,* is unique in harnessing the universal-access characteristic of the Internet as a tool, by soliciting the casual web browser to serve as a volunteer juror. Disputants register and then submit material to an online "trial book," which may include written text and graphics. In the online environment, jurors may browse both disputants' trial books, ask questions of disputants, and receive answers. The jurors post individual "verdicts" (and may comment as well), and these ver-

---

[9] Examples include We Can Settle, *https://www.wecansettle.com/pages/* (United Kingdom); US Settle.Com, *http://www.ussettle.com/howworks2.htm* (which offers traditional mediation as an alternative if blind bidding fails to settle the matter); SettleSmart, *http://www.settlesmart.com/how.htm;* Settlement OnLine, *http://www.settlementonline.com/About.html* (a software package, rather than a provider); ResolveItNow, *http://www.resolveitnow.com/;* Mediation Arbitration Resolution Services (MARS) SuperSettle, *http://www. resolvemydispute.com/;* Cybersettle, *http://www.cybersettle.com/;* WebMediate, *http://www.webmediate.com/* (which also provides traditional mediation and arbitration as ODR); 1-2-3-Settle, *http://www.123settle.com/* (which also provides arbitration); AllSettle, *http://www.allsettle.com/;* and SettleX, *http://www.settlex.com/ Default.htm.*

dicts are communicated to the disputants. The verdicts are anonymous, but data are kept concerning the demographics of each juror rendering each verdict. If the verdict involves a monetary outcome, the mean of the jurors' assessments is reported. An innovation called JurySmart allows attorneys to download the information about their client's Icourthouse case, including demographic information about jurors and each juror's verdict and comments.

Special Considerations in ODR. ODR raises interesting, and difficult, issues, as well as opportunities, for conflict diagnosticians and legal professionals. A number of psychological considerations make the ODR process different from the face-to-face process, and these differences are examined in light of the principles of conflict diagnosis. In addition, ODR—and cyber-disputes—raise tough legal issues that are only now being faced by governments and legal policymakers.

Advantages of Using the Internet to Resolve Disputes. We naturally use spoken language and communicate face to face. The communication used in ODR is very different from face to face communication and raises both special problems and special opportunities.

Many of the psychological benefits and problems associated with ODR are also seen when therapeutic interventions are provided over a distance, such as by telephone. As with telephone communication (Ranan & Blodgett 1983; Springer 1991), the Internet can enable individuals to get access to services who could not otherwise get help due to geographical distance and separation. This feature of ODR is particularly important in this age of borderless transactions. The asynchronous features of some Internet platforms can take disputants a step further than the telephone can: it enables communication to take place at the leisure of the participants and between participants in disparate time zones. Imagine the problems, for example, negotiating or mediating between a disputant in Kansas City and one in Sydney, Australia. Communication is similar in this respect to regular mail communication, but its increased informality and immediacy may allow a freer flow of communication that more closely resembles actual conversation. It may also be possible to facilitate communication between people who would otherwise be unable to communicate—for example, by interposing a translator for disputants who speak different languages. Translation services that would be cumbersome by telephone, or impossibly drawn out using "snail mail," could be easier to offer online and with asynchronous communication.

The asynchronous nature of some ODR platforms has other potential benefits. ODR participants can consider the statements of others in repose and contemplation, whereas in a synchronous, face-to-face interaction there is an irresistible urge to respond instantaneously, to avoid long silences. An ODR participant who receives communication from another involved party can carefully review what has been said and consider the possible meanings and implications at his or her leisure, seeking further clarification if it's needed. If the participant is a knowledgeable conflict diagnostician, he or she can avoid overreacting to the other participant in the heat of the moment and can gain time to apply conflict diagnosis to the ongoing interaction. When the ODR participant does reply, he or she can write several drafts of a contemplated response and review it to make certain that it conveys the substantive, emotional, and relational content that he or she intends and that the communication will not have unintended negative side effects. Thus, an effective writer with experience and skill communicating online can masterfully overcome the perils of engaging the mouth before the brain is in gear.

Distance forms of communication can also help individuals who would be resistant in a traditional office setting, as when disputants are enraged by meeting face to face. Studies by Springer (1991) and Ranan and Blodgett (1983) make this point for telephone intervention, but the point is even more pertinent in text-based Internet communication, where the element of voice inflection is lost. Additionally, processes that allow participation from the disputant's home or office can make help available to individuals who are unable to attend office appointments due to physical disability (Evans, Fox, Pritzl, & Halar 1984; Springer 1991), physical illness, phobia, depression and other disabling mental problems, or inclement weather (Ranan and Blodgett 1983). Moreover, the flexibility of the Internet allows participation by all interested stakeholders, their agents and advocates, and important witnesses, as long as they have a personal computer and access to the World Wide Web. The increased accessibility of services and service providers has been one aim of those seeking to provide ODR (Teitz 2001).

Like telephone-based intervention, the use of Internet-based dispute resolution processes can help equalize power imbalances based on the intimidation of physical proximity: an intimidated client can remain in his or her own home or office (Ranan & Blodgett 1983; Springer 1991), the object of fear is not physically present (Springer 1991), and the client can maintain a degree of privacy and anonymity (Evans, Fox, Pritzl, & Halar 1984). For example, Springer (1991) described a case in which a divorced mother and father were able to communicate effectively for the first time by teleconference because the mother was freed from seeing nonverbal cues from the father that she found intimidating. Like telephone-based therapeutic interventions (Evans, Fox, Pritzl, & Halar 1984; Springer 1991), ADR conducted in an Internet setting can save money and increase efficiency as well (Teitz 2001); as long as both disputants have access to the Internet, the cost savings can help equalize power between financial unequals. Power can be equalized in other ways as well. The anonymity of the Internet can mean that disputants may never know the race, gender, age, or physical appearance of those they are dealing with; thus, prejudices that might come into play in face-to-face interaction may not be activated. One commentator has additionally noted that the anonymity of the ODR environment is often a prized commodity for disputants who have become comfortable operating in cyberspace and that this feature of ODR may be valued in its own right by cyber-disputants (Hang 2001).

ODR's flexibility and multimodality give it a substantial potential advantage over traditional distance communication, such as mail and telephone. Platforms such as ResolutionRoom allow participants to choose from among synchronous and asynchronous methods and from among graphical and textual communication; as technology develops, it is quite likely that the use of audio- and videoconferencing over the Internet will become more common as well. Thus, participants with an understanding of conflict diagnosis can use the flexibility of ODR platforms to tailor the communication process to the needs of the people and the situation. Moreover, resources made possible by the technological power of web-based resources (as with the interests analysis components of SmartSettle) allow disputants and their teams to refine their conflict diagnosis before and during the dispute resolution process.[10] It is likely that, as experience is gained and technology advances, ODR ASPs will continue to become increasingly powerful and flexible.

Disadvantages of Using the Internet to Resolve Disputes. The use of ODR, in contrast to face-to-face ADR, has some clear drawbacks. Many of these drawbacks are psychological, some are legal, and some relate to the specific process being used.

For example, scholars studying telephone-based therapeutic intervention report that the lack of nonverbal cues can block effective communication and can inhibit helpers from assessing the emotional status of clients (Ranan & Blodgett 1983). Although the use of the Internet frees the interaction from the emotional "loading" present in body language and tonal voice inflection, it also denies the participants the ability to obtain the meanings present in these nonverbal signals. In other words, the lack of nonverbal cues adds to the ambiguity of communication.

Deutsch's conflict theory (see Chapter 9) predicts that, as communication becomes more ambiguous, disputants will be more likely to project onto one another motives consistent with their beliefs about the nature of the conflict. Disputants caught up in an escalating and competitive conflict cycle are likely to assume the worst about the other disputant in any such interaction. Thus, using a remote and nonvisual communication method might contribute to conflict escalation in hot conflicts unless special care is used to counteract this limitation.

Asynchronous communication formats heighten the problem of misattribution of motive. Because there is no immediate reply to communication, there is no immediate opportunity for a disputant to correct a mistaken impression. The receiver of a communication may have hours, even days or weeks, to brood on and potentially act on his or her negative misimpressions. Thus, using an asynchronous remote communication method may produce meta-disputes, as each disputant defensively acts on inaccurately negative impressions about the other.

Meta-disputes can also be generated by the technology itself and by confusion over how the technology is functioning:

> Matt Randall, a Wyoming bank teller with an interest in first editions, purchased a used book from a woman living in Hawaii, Ruth Smithe-Lovell. They used an Internet auction site to conduct the transaction. The book arrived in very poor condition, and Matt, who has never met the seller, doesn't trust her. Matt and Ruth consent to the use of the auction site's

---

[10] For example, JavaScript, a software language used to automate Internet documents, can be used to streamline some elements of the conflict diagnosis process.

E-mail server

a large computer that receives e-mail from users and directs it to other e-mail servers, which, in turn, send the e-mail to its recipients.

in-house ODR service, which involves e-mail-based negotiation, followed by mediation. During negotiation, an angry Matt makes a proposal that Ruth reduce her price by 60 percent and refund him the money right away. He demands that Ruth issue a response within forty-eight hours to show good faith. Matt sends the e-mail to Ruth at 3:30 P.M. on Tuesday. Unbenownst to Matt, his **e-mail server** holds his communication for twenty-four hours before sending it to Ruth. It arrives in Ruth's e-mail inbox at 3:30 P.M. Wednesday, just after she has checked her e-mail for the last time that day. By the time Ruth comes in the following morning, it has already been forty-two hours since Matt sent his missive. Ruth makes an immediate e-mail response, which is to state with indignation that she did not send the book in bad condition. She wants to know exactly what the problem is with the book. She suspects that the book was damaged in transit. Actually, she plans to give him a discount, anyway, to show good faith, but she doesn't want to give away the farm by knuckling under right away. She mistypes Matt's e-mail address and sends the message. Then, she signs off the computer and attends a day of meetings. At 5 P.M. that afternoon, after Ruth has left, the message is returned undelivered by the server. Ruth discovers the undelivered message, and her error, on Friday morning. By this time, Matt is hopping mad. His mistrust in Ruth has been confirmed: in his mind, she's clearly a flake and a con artist. No matter what Ruth does at this point, there's little she can do to restore trust, and the assigned mediator will face a daunting task.

Anyone who relies on e-mail will recognize this exchange as familiar in many respects. Those who do a lot of communicating online are used to technology glitches. The problem is that, in an escalated conflict, angry disputants are likely to attribute problems to evil behavior by the other disputant, rather than to malfunctioning technology.

Another problem with ODR has to do with the lack of a human face. In an ODR communication, disputants may not be able to see their counterpart's emotional reactions or to hear their voice inflections.[11] Thus, the empowerment that comes from observing the nonverbal aspects of communication, and the recognition that comes from having one's emotional state validated, is lost (Hang 2001). For this reason, disputants may not experience the same emotional closure and reconciliation when settlement occurs, and the element of psychological ownership of the outcome may be compromised. And because the nonverbal element is missing, disputants are likely to fill in the missing information with their suspicions about the other's evil motives.

The lack of nonverbal information also presents difficulties for ODR providers. Facilitative neutrals, such as mediators, may be denied the nonverbal data they need to assess accurately the clients' meaning, attitude, and emotional state. This is information the client is unlikely to provide the mediator verbally, even when asked, and, without seeing the person face to face, the neutral may

---

[11] This problem may lessen as computer-mediated videoconferencing becomes more widely available.

have difficulty interpreting the force of emotion behind a written communication. Mediators and others who deal with hot emotions in their clients confront the challenge of assessing, and affirming, the emotional states of people who are frequently unaware of their feelings, have forgotten about the feelings they had when they issued the communication, or are ashamed of the feelings they are having. Therefore, direct verbal inquiry to confirm an emotional state (as in "I'm wondering if you felt angry as you wrote your last e-mail") may be ineffective and may shame the disputant if made in the presence of the other, whereas making an incorrect assumption about an emotional state is very dangerous to effective dispute resolution—it can be extremely alienating to be the subject of mistaken assumptions about feelings. Therefore, it may be very difficult for the neutral to engage in interventions that affirm and recognize an online disputant's perspective and emotional state.

Commentators have also noted concerns with the anonymous nature of the Internet. Some believe that it is easy for disputants to disconnect from an anonymous interaction. Thus, ODR participants may be more likely to abandon the process when the negotiation gets tough. It is easy for people to overlook a pending ODR process when they are busy with other things: the computer doesn't call them on the phone or require them to keep an appointment. Thus, experienced ODR service providers find that they must make a special effort to keep participants engaged. When asynchronous methods are used, it is often necessary to include special incentives, such as schedules or deadlines, to keep the process from slowing so much that communication ceases to be effective. Moreover, there is some evidence that cyberspace anonymity is associated with loosened inhibitions on offensive or impolite communication (Bordone 1998, 180–81); however, there is no specific research to determine whether there is a greater incidence of such language, which is likely to escalate conflict, in ODR, as compared with face-to-face ADR.

Although ODR can equalize power, it can also produce power imbalances. ODR can severely disempower those who are uncomfortable using the written word or who express themselves poorly in writing. These individuals will be less able to communicate ideas, interests, concerns, proposals, and reactions. As with other written forms of communication, poor writing used in an ODR process can also disempower the writer by projecting a less intelligent, less able persona to the other participants. Additionally, ODR can disempower those who rely heavily on nonverbal communication to express themselves or to read the communication of others. The advent of videoconferenced ODR should allay this problem somewhat.

ODR also disempowers those with poor or limited access to technology. For example, a disputant with outdated hardware or software or a poor Internet service provider has to work harder and spend more time engaging in ODR than someone who has up-to-date technology. Similarly, a disputant who must take public transportation to a public library to gain access to the Internet is impaired, relative to someone with a high-quality system at home. A lack of proficiency or comfort with using the computer and the Internet is likely to create similar impediments to empowerment. For disputants who are consumers in the Internet marketplace, these power considerations are often magnified. To use ODR in dealing with a dispute in the online marketplace, the consumer is likely a "first user" of an ODR process, whereas the merchant is likely a repeat customer, more familiar with the hardware, software, rules of the process, and ODR providers.

It should not be forgotten that, although ODR can disempower, it can empower as well. Many individuals have disempowering qualities, such as physical appearance, problems expressing themselves orally, or an inability to travel to the site of a face-to-face negotiation, which are eliminated by ODR.

Legal Issues in ODR. ODR presents vexing legal issues that are being grappled with by a number of organizations, including the American Bar Association (ABA.[12]), the Federal Trade Commission (FTC Workshop Comments 2000), the Center for Public Resources (CPR Institute, 2001), the Hague (Hague Conference on Private International Law, 2002), and the European Union (ECLIP Workshop, 2000–2002) Conflict diagnosticians should become familiar with the issues facing the development of ODR, so that they can follow the developments in this interesting and complex field as they happen.

Transactions conducted in cyberspace raise a basic philosophical and practical issue: does it make sense to consider the transaction as having occurred within one or more physical territories, or should cyber-transactions be considered borderless? Consider the following example:

> Kawamoto and Moreau engage in a barter transaction using an online auction site. Later, they have a dispute about their transaction and agree to use an ODR service. The service markets itself as exclusively online, uses servers (the computers that hold its software) in several countries, and offers web pages and communications platforms in English, Spanish, French, Danish, and Japanese. Mediators from anywhere may register to provide services, and the ODR service requires them to post resumes, so that the participants can select the most qualified candidate.

Does it make sense to consider this potential mediation as "occurring in a specific country or jurisdiction" in any meaningful sense? When an ADR provider offers ODR services, one way of thinking about the service is that it occurs in the nonterritorial environment of cyberspace—or, as Robert C. Bordone (1998, 180–81) creatively calls it, "Cyberia." Thus, beyond the choice of law questions posed by the dispute itself, it is important to ask the question "Is the ODR process governed by the law of any specific territory or territories, and how can we tell which ones?" This question is important because legal considerations—such as confidentiality during ODR, the ODR provider's liability for malpractice, the enforceability of a decision to engage in ODR, and the enforceability of the outcome—may turn on the answer. Even if a particular nation's laws are

---

[12] The ABA has convened a task force on e-commerce and ADR to study the matter.

referred to as being binding on the process, if legal action is brought in a different forum, that national court may not have an obligation to recognize the provision. The problem is particularly acute for consumer transactions, because consumers are not sophisticated in the world of international commerce and may be unaware of the pitfalls of transacting in the absence of universally applicable consumer protection.

No one has an easy answer to this question. Some legal experts have argued that the cyberspace world should have its own law—some are advocating a "world government," others an international cyber-court, others a treaty or convention. However, without international consensus on the development of a world government, it would be impossible to ensure the adoption or enforcement of such laws. Individuals in cyberspace can voluntarily agree to abide by a set of rules, but there is no universally applicable enforcement process, although international treaties and conventions developed to facilitate international commerce and the enforceability of international arbitration awards can help. One group of ODR experts points to the fact that consensual processes are more likely to be used in cyber-disputing because of the legal vacuum: although it may be difficult to enforce an arbitration award against a recalcitrant loser, it is more likely that a mediated agreement will be followed, because both disputants consented to the settlement (Katsh, Rifkin, & Gaitenby 2000).

Voluntary and consensual mechanisms are enforced primarily by the threat of publicity that inappropriate or dishonest behavior can inflict. There are some other processes that make the Internet a slightly less dangerous place to transact business:

- The trustmark process, in which Internet providers promise to abide by a code of ethics and a dispute resolution process developed by a watchdog organization. Transgression can mean loss of the trustmark, with a consequent loss of business.

- Escrowing or bonding, requiring the disputants temporarily to post assets sufficient to cover anticipated future disputes with a neutral and trusted third party. Should a dispute arise and one disputant refuse to abide by the result of an ODR process, the escrowed amount can be released to the aggrieved disputant.

- The use of credit cards in online consumer purchasing. This technique is useful mainly in the United States, where consumer-protection laws limit monetary losses to the purchaser if he or she notifies the card issuer in writing of a problem within a certain period of time.

Until a universal convention is adopted to regulate ODR, it helps to specify choice of law and choice of forum before an online dispute resolution process is begun. Indeed, the ideal transaction will specify choice of law for the transaction itself and will have a separate provision regulating the resolution of disputes.

EXERCISES, PROJECTS, AND "THOUGHT EXPERIMENTS"

1. Identify the following ADR processes offered by retired judges—as mediation, arbitration, nonbinding evaluation, or a mixed (hybrid) process:

   a. Gordon Gould is a retired judge. He offers disputants an opportunity to present their case before him. He then uses his extensive background on the bench as he gives his opinion about what the case is worth. Afterwards, he sits with the disputants and tries to help them work out a settlement. If the case does not settle, he issues a binding written decision, which he promises is based on fairness as well as the law.

   b. Eileen Einhorn is a retired judge. She offers disputants the chance to present their case to her. Afterwards, she meets with each disputant and his or her lawyer separately, where she uses her extensive experience on the bench to assist the teams in exploring the strengths and weaknesses of their individual cases. Einhorn also looks for any overlap in the positions of the two sides. If there is an overlap, she uses shuttle diplomacy to help the disputants reach a settlement.

   c. Norton Nelson is a retired judge. He offers disputants the chance to present their case to him. Afterwards, he uses his extensive experience on the bench to give the disputants an idea of what he thinks would happen if they took the case to court. He generally gives a range of likely outcomes.

   d. George Garrettson is a retired judge. He offers the disputants a chance to present their case to him. Afterwards, he uses his extensive experience on the bench to give the disputants a decision in the matter. The decision is considered binding. He advertises that he provides as fair and effective a decision as a court of law, but at a fraction of the time and expense.

2. *Internet or library research.* Study the American Arbitration Association's Commercial Dispute Resolution Procedures (the association's website is located at *www.adr.org.*). Find the provision that allows for mediation windowing. Cite the provision. Do you think this is a good provision to include in an arbitration agreement? Why or why not?

3. Frank, a buyer, and Michelle, a seller, are disputing over the sale of a baby grand piano. Frank says that Michelle misrepresented the condition of the piano when he agreed to pay $9,500 for it and that they agreed she would be responsible for transporting the piano to Frank's residence. Michelle contends that she made no misrepresentations, that she offered to allow Frank to have an appraiser inspect the piano before finalizing the sales price, and that they agreed the piano would be Frank's responsibility to move. Their written contract specifies only the transaction date, the names of the parties, and the price. Michelle has recently taken a course in alternative dispute resolution and wants to submit the dispute to a mediator. Frank is absolutely opposed to any process that will not result in a final settlement. However,

he is receptive to using med-arb. Is med-arb a good option for these individuals? Why or why not? In responding, consider what alternatives the disputants have if med-arb is not used.

4. Frank Sander's vision of the multidoor courthouse embodies a system that offers the full panoply of civil dispute resolution mechanisms, including litigation, arbitration, mediation, and the numerous forms of nonbinding evaluation. Who should decide what process should be used? What referral process should be used? What are the benefits and drawbacks of each referral mechanism? To start you thinking about some of the options, here are a few:

   a. A judge could be responsible for deciding which dispute resolution method is used for a particular case.

   b. An "ADR case manager" or a similar specialist could screen cases as they are filed and then make the referrals.

   c. All filed cases of a particular type could automatically go to a particular method (as, for example, all child custody disputes are routinely referred to mediation).

   d. The litigants might be required to reach a consensus to use particular methods, with a "default" dispute resolution process if they fail to reach consensus. Traditionally, this default mechanism has been formal litigation—is that the best choice?

   e. Some processes could be initiated by an individual litigant's unilateral choice, with others initiated only by consensus of the litigants.

5. Most court-connected and other multimodal ADR programs provide for a single confidentiality rule that applies across the board to all the processes involved. For example, look at Section 574 of the Administrative Dispute Resolution Act of 1996, page 641, cited in the context of mediation. This provision applies to any ADR process, including facilitative and evaluative forms of mediation, arbitration, and any nonbinding evaluation form. Are the reasons that confidentiality is important or useful the same for all these types of ADR processes? Should the rules be different for different processes? If so, why? If not, why not? If different rules are adopted for different sorts of ADR, will the law of confidentiality become unnecessarily complicated or unpredictable? Isn't that the case, anyway, since there are exceptions to confidentiality that vest discretion to determine confidentiality in a judge?

6. *Term project.* Start by reading Cathy A. Costatino and Christina Sickles Merchant, *Designing conflict management systems: A guide to creating productive and healthy organizations* (San Francisco: Jossey-Bass, 1996). Then, if you work in an office, consider the sorts of interpersonal conflicts that arise between members of the office, between employees and their managers and supervisors, and between members of the organization and members of the public. If you do not work in an office, consider the sorts of conflicts or disputes that arise at the college or university you attend. Using the principles of conflict diagnosis, write a paper (1) evaluating the state of conflict

resolution at this organization and (2) proposing a dispute resolution system that you believe would effectively address the issues you see. Be sure to justify the proposal in part 2 using your evaluation in part 1.

7. *Research project.* Research the court-connected ADR program in effect in the federal district court that serves your area. Answer the following questions in a research paper:

   a. What forms of dispute resolution are used in this court system? What do they call each of these processes?

   b. Summarize the history of court-connected ADR in this district court. How long has ADR been used?

   c. Obtain statistics on the number and types of disputes sent to this program. What are the trends?

   d. Does it appear that this program is resulting in a reduction of backlog in this court? Discuss any evidence that supports your assertion.

   e. Are statistics available that track client and advocate satisfaction with this program? If so, summarize the results.

   f. Examine the rules that apply to this program. They may appear in the rules of the court, as well as in the Federal Rules of Civil Procedure. Summarize the procedural rules with respect to this program.

   g. Evaluate the program yourself. Is this a good program? Is it merely better than nothing? Could it be improved? If so, how? Is there more information the court would need to collect to make an evaluation more meaningful? Be sure to justify your answers to these questions.

RECOMMENDED READINGS

Alfini, J. J. 1991. Trashing, bashing and hashing it out: Is this the end of "good mediation"? *Florida State University Law Review* 19 (summer):47–75.

Burger, W. W. 1982. *Isn't there a better way?* Annual Report on the State of the Judiciary, presented at the 1982 midyear meeting of the American Bar Association, Chicago, January 24. Reprinted as Burger, W.W. 1982. Isn't there a better way? *ABA Journal* 68 (March):274.

Costatino, C. A., and C. S. Merchant. 1996. *Designing conflict management systems: A guide to creating productive and healthy organizations.* San Francisco: Jossey-Bass.

Hang, L. Q. 2001. Online dispute resolution systems: The future of cyberspace law. *Santa Clara Law Review* 41:837–66.

Meltzer, D. L. 1998. The federal workplace ombuds. *Ohio State Journal on Dispute Resolution* 13:549–609.

Nolan-Haley, J. M. 2001. Hybrid dispute resolution procedures. In *Alternative dispute resolution in a nutshell* (pp. 220–35). St. Paul, MN: West.

Plapinger, E., and D. Steinstra. 1996. *ADR and settlement programs in the federal district courts: A sourcebook for judges and lawyers.* Federal Judicial Center and CPR Institute for Dispute Resolution [online]. Available on the Federal Judicial

Center website, *http://www.fjc.gov/ALTDISRES/adrsource/adrblurb.html* [cited 15 July 2002].

Riskin, L. L., and J. E. Westbrook. (eds.). 1997. *Dispute resolution and lawyers* (2nd ed., pp. 657–92). St. Paul, MN: West.

Sander, F. E. A. 1976. *Varieties of dispute processing.* 70 FRD 111.

Streeter-Schaefer, H. A. 2001. A look at court mandated civil mediation. *Drake Law Review* 49:367–89.

Teitz, L. E. 2001. Providing legal services for the middle class in cyberspace: The promise and challenge of on-line dispute resolution. *Fordham Law Review* 70 (December):985–1016.

Ury, W., J. M. Brett, and S. B. Goldberg. 1988. *Getting disputes resolved: Designing systems to cut the costs of conflict.* San Francisco: Jossey-Bass.

PART IV

PUTTING IT ALL TOGETHER

As we've seen throughout this textbook, resolving interpersonal conflict is far more complex than the simplistic winner-loser portrayal we usually see in movies and on TV. In fact, interpersonal conflict is very often not what it first appears to be. Part I introduced the notion of the invisible veil, a cultural predisposition to see interpersonal conflict as a battle between enemies, only one of whom will emerge victorious. We saw how this blueprint for conflict and its adversarial toolbox unduly limit us in our efforts to develop effective means of resolving and preventing conflict, and we explored the need to find better blueprints to improve our handling of conflict. Part I also introduced the concept of conflict diagnosis as a powerful tool for understanding conflict, for seeing past the invisible veil, and for determining what steps we can take to resolve conflict most effectively. In Part II, we looked at the steps of conflict diagnosis in more detail. Conflict diagnosis emerges as a fundamental tool to keep handy in our new and improved conflict resolution toolbox, the one we use to understand conflict accurately and in-depth. But conflict diagnosis also serves another important function: it gives us a conceptual framework for understanding how other conflict resolution tools work.

In Part III, we examined the power tools of the conflict resolution toolbox, the processes of alternative dispute resolution. We looked at the principal alternatives to litigation: mediation, arbitration, nonbinding evaluation, and the mixed and multimodal processes. Each of these processes, examined through the lens of conflict diagnosis, was revealed to respond in unique ways to the diverse characteristics of conflicts and disputants.

Where do we go from here? Let's put together what we've learned. How do we use conflict diagnosis to choose strategies and processes for resolving interpersonal conflict?

22

Power Tools and Magic Keys: Using Conflict Diagnosis to Manage Legal Disputes and Select ADR Processes

"There is one thing stronger than all the armies in the world, and that is an idea whose time has come."

—Victor Hugo

In this chapter, you will learn …

+ The potential for conflict diagnosis to improve the delivery of legal services.
+ The ethical and practical issues that complicate the use of conflict diagnosis by lawyers and legal assistants.
+ The ethical obligation of lawyers to advise their clients of ADR options and the scope of this obligation.
+ Approaches to lawyering that incorporate the ideas advanced in this textbook, including client-centered lawyering and collaborative law.
+ How to use conflict diagnosis to develop effective strategies and tactics for representing legal disputants.
+ A leading approach to selecting a dispute resolution process and provider, known as Fitting the Forum to the Fuss.
+ An alternative approach to selecting a dispute resolution process and provider, suggested by the principles of conflict diagnosis.

In Part II of this textbook, you were introduced to conflict diagnosis, a theory-based set of skills that have several uses. As a stand-alone technique, conflict diagnosis is a practical method of understanding and analyzing interpersonal conflict, particularly legal disputes. If you've tried to use conflict diagnosis in your everyday conflicts, you may have found that it opens your eyes to important aspects of these situations that you may not have previously recognized. These realizations can lead to new, less destructive, and more creative approaches to resolving conflicts. Additionally, conflict diagnosis illuminates the world of alternative dispute resolution, helping explain the uses, strengths, and weaknesses of the ADR processes we looked at in Part III. In this chapter, we'll put it all together, examining the use of conflict diagnosis in evaluating legal disputes and selecting ADR. We can think of this practical application of conflict diagnosis as the *practice* of conflict diagnosis in the legal and ADR professions.

IS CONFLICT DIAGNOSIS NECESSARY?

It's fair to ask whether conflict diagnosis is really necessary. After all, it's mentally challenging and often time-consuming. Most lawyers would say no, such an analysis is not necessary or that the efforts to develop an understanding of underlying interests, sources of conflict, personal power, and the need to preserve relationships and trust are in the domain of the client alone. However, a small but increasing number of voices would answer yes, if you want to resolve conflict in an optimal manner. The reason is that the invisible veil always hides many important aspects of interpersonal conflict from those involved in it. Most of the time, one enters a conflict aware of the resource disputes, preferences and nuisances problems, and perhaps the disputes over facts or law, but little else. The hidden information will be critical to assessing the hidden reasons the conflict has appeared, the participant's most important interests, the opportunities presented by the other disputant's interests, and the best routes around impediments to getting the situation resolved. Even if the conflict is patently about money (for example, a simple fender-bender), emotional issues and hidden interests may complicate or impede resolution, and unrecognized nonmonetary aspects of the dispute (for example, a desire for an apology, an issue over the time of payment, or a concern over insurance coverage) may need to come out before an optimal resolution can be developed. Because of the way people perceive and evaluate information about conflict, they generally aren't aware of these sorts of complications without performing a conflict diagnosis. And, once adversarial negotiation or litigation starts, it is extremely hard to find out about them. Conflict escalation, identified by Deutsch and discussed in Chapter 9, creates strong forces that distort perception in favor of the invisible veil interpretation of reality. Unfortunately, a person caught up in an escalated conflict inevitably acquires perceptual biases and distortions about the conflict, about his or her own interests, and about the other disputant. These biases and distortions are significantly disempowering: they impair the ability to think clearly about the conflict and resolve it effectively. Thus, there are some very distinct advantages in diagnosing conflict and, if possible, in doing so at an early point, before the conflict has escalated.

Frequently, of course, the situation will preclude comprehensive conflict diagnosis. Consider the following example:

> Martha LaRue is an assistant county counsel for the town of Marburry. Her job is to negotiate fender-benders and other minor legal disputes brought by members of the public against the municipality. (Marburry has lifted its sovereign immunity laws to allow tort claims against the municipality for traffic accidents, slip-and-falls, and other similar cases.) In a typical week, she receives thirty new claims to resolve. Martha has no investigational staff: she has one secretary and a paralegal working under her. She must rely on the municipality's claims adjuster to provide her with factual data concerning claims, although she sometimes follows up on investigations on her own time. A typical claimant hires an attorney, who submits official documentation and follows it up with a telephone call. Given Martha's resources and caseload, she can afford to spend, on average, about thirty minutes total handling each dispute. If the claim cannot be settled, it is sent to outside counsel to be litigated.

Martha cannot hope to engage in any significant conflict diagnosis unless somehow her employment situation is altered—either her caseload is dramatically reduced or her support staff is dramatically expanded. In cases like Martha's, it is often necessary to focus on an aspect of conflict diagnosis that is likely to prove most enlightening or effective. Martha, for example, focuses on establishing collaborative relationships with the town's attorneys by exploring their communication styles. One of the attorneys, Bill, typically comes on with a highly adversarial opening—he usually starts out by saying that his client won't settle the case and that he's already got a complaint prepared. A careful diagnosis of what Bill generally does later in the negotiation has led her to conclude that this bluster is simply window dressing meant to portray zealous advocacy. Now, Martha and Bill have a working partnership: she allows him to bluster for a few minutes, she takes her usual tough stand in opposition, and then they "talk turkey". Both lawyers have come to understand that the adversarial opening positions are merely the first moves in a cooperative negotiation dance. Now that Martha has developed these comfortable relationships with Bill, and the other repeat players in the system, she has been able to begin a process of mutual interests analysis with some of the lawyers she works with. She is even beginning to see a creative settlement here and there.

Some interpersonal conflicts cry out for full-blown conflict diagnosis. For example, it's fair to say that the longstanding Israeli-Palestinian conflict will never be resolved merely by applying invisible veil tactics, such as war, terrorism, or a world court, unless one considers extinction, genocide, or world war to be a form of resolution. Any conflict that features immense complexity or that has become highly escalated will be poorly resolved, or not resolved at all, unless the effort to resolve it is preceded by thorough conflict diagnosis.

Somewhere between Martha's assembly-line negotiation practice and the Middle East situation lie most interpersonal conflicts. In these settings, conflict diagnosis opens a window of opportunity for better, more effective, and more lasting solutions to difficult issues. From one perspective, in our invisible veil culture, it would help many conflicted situations immeasurably if those involved performed more conflict diagnosis.

As previously emphasized, some consider the analyses that constitute conflict diagnosis to be vital for effectively choosing an ADR process. As demonstrated in Part III, each dispute resolution process is unique in how effectively it prevents conflict escalation, enhances trust, makes it possible to generate creative options for maximizing available resources, prevents future conflict, reveals each participant's true interests, empowers disputants, and affects the likelihood of compliance. As a society, we appear to have made a choice to offer alternatives to litigation. If we wish to realize the promise of ADR to become a vehicle of *better dispute resolution,* rather than merely *quicker or cheaper dispute processing,* those referring clients to ADR must conduct conflict diagnosis to refer clients to the right process.

Lawyers have historically been our society's dispute experts. Shouldn't lawyers therefore be experts in the diagnosis of conflict? That has not been the state of affairs up to the present time. The lawyering that dominated the United States throughout the latter half of the twentieth century operated from deep within the invisible veil. Although the lawyer of a century ago was also considered a *counselor* at law, the typical lawyer of the late twentieth century United States was considered an adversarial specialist, not a conflict resolution specialist. As we saw in Chapter 3, this emphasis on adversary justice begins with legal education. Law school did, and does now, focus primarily on litigation and appellate decisions. Clinical courses in negotiation and alternative dispute resolution began to appear only in the last decade or so of the century. Thus, lawyers traditionally were not taught how to diagnose a conflict. And early efforts to educate lawyers in negotiation and ADR often used an invisible veil perspective.

Two additional forces kept lawyers from engaging in conflict diagnosis, at least until quite recently. These forces were economics and ethics. Experts in the lawyering process point out that the invisible veil lawyers were trained to hone their information-acquisition and analytic skills to determine whether legal claims or defenses were available to the client and what steps were needed to prepare a case in support of these claims or defenses (Menkel-Meadow 1996; Riskin 1982; Schneider 2000). This strict focusing of attention had some of its roots in the economics of law practice. The rising costs of legal fees and the need to strictly document **billable hours** contributed to a narrow focus on what would be likely to happen if the case were litigated and on how to maximize this outcome for the client. Spending time and resources to consider other aspects of the client's conflict could not be justified as appropriate billable client hours. Legal negotiation reflected this emphasis on litigation. Settlement negotiation has consisted, by and large, of a series of positional statements intended to display an inflated belief about the merits of one's case. This posture is taken to convince the other side that the members of one's team are ready and willing to litigate, and believe they were likely to win. It is hoped that such tactics will cause the other side to sweeten its counteroffer (Bellow & Moulton 1981, 27–35; Goodpastor 1996). Many legal professionals believe that an adversarial, position-bound posture is imposed on the attorney by the ethical duty of zealous advocacy. The economics of law practice, the emphasis on positional bargaining in negotiation, the

Billable hours

the time a lawyer or, in some states, a certified paralegal spends or documents spending on a given client's case. A lawyer cannot contractually charge a client on an hourly basis unless he or she can document how the hours are spent. Legal professionals typically document their time in tenths of an hour (six-minute segments).

ethical underpinnings of advocacy, and the steeping of legal education in the adversary process all have precluded lawyers from spending the time, effort, and resources needed to diagnose a conflict effectively.

This situation may be beginning to change. A rising chorus of scholars (Menkel-Meadow 1996; Riskin 1982; Schneider 2000) is now expressing concern that the narrow focus on adversarial approaches to resolving disputes is compromising the quality of dispute resolution. Additionally, a movement has begun to ethically require lawyers to advise their clients of the option to resolve their dispute via ADR (Breger 2000; Cochran 1999; Sander & Prigoff 1990; Warmbrod 1997). ABA Model Rules of Professional Conduct, Rule 2.1, comment 5, states that there "may" be a duty on the part of an attorney to advise the client of ADR options (American Bar Association 2003). This area of legal ethics is an evolving one. According to Marshall J. Breger of the Columbia School of Law, Catholic University (Breger 2000), an obligation to advise of, and explain, ADR can be implicitly derived from the ABA Model Rules of Professional Conduct. Model Rule 1.2(a) requires a lawyer to consult with the client about the means by which he or she will fulfill the duty of legal representation, Model Rule 1.2(b) requires that the lawyer provide enough information to the client to make informed decision possible, and Model Rule 3.2 requires the lawyer to expedite the client's matter to a reasonable extent. Considering these rules together, an argument can be made that the lawyer is under an obligation to inform the client of the possible means by which his or her case can be handled (including ADR), so that the client can make an informed decision about the process he or she wishes to use. Moreover, the lawyer is particularly obligated to help the client seek an expeditious process, and ADR is noted for its time efficiency. Since ADR is now within the mainstream of the law, the duty to advise the client of ADR can be implied as part of the duty to discuss these options with the client (Breger 2000). The Virginia Rules of Professional Conduct, 1.4, Comment 1a, provides that the duty to keep a client reasonably informed about the status of a pending matter, an ethical duty ubiquitous to American legal practice, includes

> a duty to advise the client about the availability of dispute resolution processes that might be more appropriate to the client's goals than the initial process chosen. For example, information obtained during a lawyer-to-lawyer negotiation may give rise to consideration of a process, such as mediation, where the parties themselves could be more directly involved in resolving the dispute.

If other states interpret this general ethical obligation to provide informed consent in similar fashion, one could expect the duty to advise of ADR options to become widely recognized.[1] Beyond this implicit duty, the state bar association ethical bodies of Kansas, Michigan, and Pennsylvania have ruled explicitly that, if an ADR process has been suggested by the court or by opposing counsel, a duty

---

[1] This movement is not without its detractors: some legal scholars—most notably, Michael L. Prigoff (1990)—worry that imposing a duty to advise clients of ADR would drive up legal fees unnecessarily.

arises to discuss ADR with the client. Kansas further requires that the lawyer raise the issue of ADR with the client if the lawyer deems it to be appropriate, even if no one else has raised it (Breger 2000). As of the year 2000, courts in Arkansas, Colorado, Delaware, Hawaii, Louisiana, Massachusetts, New Jersey, and New Mexico had adopted "precatory" (in other words, aspirational, nonbinding) clauses encouraging lawyers to advise clients of ADR options, whereas courts in California, Connecticut, Georgia, Minnesota, Missouri, New Hampshire, Ohio, Texas, and Virginia had adopted rules requiring lawyers to advise their clients of ADR (Breger 2000, app. A). Additionally, the ADR alternative is being introduced to litigants in pre-trial educational programs operating in a number of court systems or during pre-trial or status conferences (Breger 2000).

Breger points out that, even if there is no ethical duty to inform the client of ADR options, the failure to do so, or the failure to suggest ADR in appropriate cases, may constitute attorney malpractice. An attorney failing to advise a client of ADR in an age in which ADR has entered the legal mainstream may be seen as failing to exercise the requisite degree of professional expertise needed to represent a client effectively. Breger warns,

> It should be pointed out that the question may no longer turn on the existence of express "ethical" language mandating ADR disclosure. The increased application of ADR as a method of dispute resolution may place an attorney at risk if he is not familiar with ADR methods, following a standard which requires him to exercise "the degree of skill, knowledge and judgment ordinarily possessed by members of the legal profession." As more state professional codes require ADR disclosure implicitly or otherwise, an attorney's failure to instruct a client regarding ADR options could therefore result in [professional malpractice] liability. (Breger 2000, 450)

But does it follow that conflict diagnosis is required? There is no explicit duty to engage in conflict diagnosis. However, some legal scholars have also pointed out that the ethical duty to advise the client of ADR is of little value unless the legal advisor can intelligently advise the client which ADR alternative is best for that client (Sander & Goldberg 1994; Schneider 2000). Attorney and ADR practitioner Patricia Gearity, of Silver Spring, Maryland, comments that attorneys whose clients are involved in mediation must also re-orient their consultations, going beyond the short-term results of the dispute under consideration and helping them focus on long-term goals and needs (Gearity 2002). Although Gearity specializes in family law, this holistic approach to serving the client has been reported in other practitioners. For example, the June 2001 issue of the *ABA Journal* reported a business lawyer, Arnie Herz, whose practice involves helping clients unblock fearful or angry feelings that are impeding their rational judgment; assisting clients in recognizing their long-term interests, values, needs, and goals; and empowering clients to select the best way to attain these goals (Keeva 2001). For example, a client might enter Herz's office wanting to litigate with a former business partner, and this might be the ultimate decision the client makes, but not until he has explored with Herz the reasons he has come into the office wanting to sue. Or the client might, after the meeting

The Ethics of Law Practice: Who Chooses, Attorney or Client?

Rita has a dispute with her neighbor over the boundary line between their houses. The neighbor wants to place a fence on a part of the property that Rita thinks is hers, but the neighbor contends it is his. Rita thinks the fence will be ugly and fears property values will plummet. Rita's lawyer mentions mediation as one possible option but then files a lawsuit against the neighbor without inviting Rita to consider an alternative process. Was it proper for the lawyer to choose the dispute resolution process, or should this have been Rita's decision?

On the legal end of the debate whether attorneys must advise clients about ADR lies an underlying ethical issue: how much should lawyers control the course of a client's dispute? The classic ethical "bright line" has traditionally been that the client controls the "goals" aspects of the case, such as whether to settle the case for a particular sum, whereas the lawyer controls the "means" aspects, such as whether to demand a jury or a court trial or whether to pursue particular forms of discovery. This rule has its roots in a characterization of the practice of law as "craft," in which the lawyer is considered the best expert in how to execute the craftsmanship required. If a lawyer develops a particular legal strategy for litigating a dispute, it is considered counterproductive to have a client acting as a back-seat driver, second-guessing tactics and trying to control parts of the lawyer's behavior.

ADR raises a difficult complexity. While one might regard the decision whether to use ADR as merely a decision about the means of dealing with a dispute, it may also be argued that the client should remain in control of such basic decisions as whether to pursue litigation and, hence, should control whether alternatives to litigation are used. Moreover, since the client often has more of an interest in pursuing low-cost alternatives to court than the lawyer, allowing the client to make this choice creates less likelihood of a conflict of interest damaging the client. Finally, proponents of "client-centered lawyering," a legal reform movement that argues that the traditional control of the client's situation by the lawyer is wrong-headed, would assert that vesting as much control as possible over the handling of the dispute in the client is an intrinsically positive development. For a detailed discussion of the issue of lawyer-client control over the ADR decision, see Cochran (1999).

In Rita's case, the court system made up for what her lawyer failed to do: the judge referred Rita and her neighbor to mediation. Together, they determined where the property lines were, and they stipulated to a fencing and landscaping plan that gave the neighbor the fencing he needed for his privacy without compromising the appearance of the neighborhood.

Collaborative law
a form of lawyering, currently seen primarily in family law and based on a contractual relationship between a lawyer and a client. This contract generally specifies the lawyer's duty to seek collaborative and interest-based settlement with the other disputant. If litigation commences, the lawyer is required to withdraw from representing the client.

with the lawyer, decide that reconciliation with the partner, with a better-drawn contract, would better serve his long-term interests. The article reports a number of clients who made choices other than the one they entered the law office with and their sense that the experience has transformed their lives for the better. Not only are the clients satisfied, but the article reports that Herz himself is commanding considerable financial success with this approach.

Other winds of change are in the air. A new movement called **collaborative law** hinges on the notion that the duty of zealous representation should, in appropriate situations, be tempered with a corresponding duty to establish a collaborative relationship with the other disputant and his or her counsel. Practitioners of collaborative law enter into retainer agreements with their clients providing that the lawyer must withdraw from representation if litigation begins. The clients also retain experts for the negotiation jointly, and these experts are similarly disqualified from participating in any subsequent litigation. The retainer agreement further provides that the lawyer will use his or her skills to seek a collaborative settlement with the other disputant and his or her team using an interest-based negotiation strategy. Collaborative lawyers are permitted—indeed, they are expected—to help the client consider his or her long-term and nonmonetary interests, values, and needs. Thus, although a traditional adversarial lawyer who foregoes an opportunity to obtain a high monetary settlement—at the cost of alienating an ex-spouse or a business partner—might be accused of failing to represent the client zealously, a collaborative lawyer who advises the client to make this choice to preserve long-term relationship interests rests on firmer ethical ground. Although collaborative law is practiced primarily in the family law field, there is no reason its ideas could not be extended to other forms of disputes, such as disputes between employees and their supervisors or disputes between commercial entities with continuing relationships. Many lawyers with extensive negotiation practices would point out that they already take this sort of collaborative approach in client representation.

Although there are still numerous legal practitioners who reject the concept of nonadversarial dispute resolution out of hand, a growing number of lawyers are being schooled in at least some of the ideas of conflict diagnosis. Dual-concern conflict theory, interest-based bargaining, and the lawyer's standard philosophical map (and its impediments to clear thinking) are becoming mainstream elements of law school negotiation courses, which are, in turn, becoming ubiquitous elements of legal education. Moreover, ADR is becoming a common continuing legal education focus. It is fair to expect that, if collaborative law becomes integrated into the legal mainstream, and as attorneys continue to explore the reasons for ADR, some degree of conflict diagnosis will be increasingly seen as necessary for effective legal practice.

Do you need to be a psychologist to diagnose a conflict? No, but it certainly helps to understand theories of human motivation and development. And counseling skills can help you listen effectively to a client, to compose effective questions, and to understand the subtext of a client's communications, yet many legal

The advantages of using Conflict Diagnosis in law practice, and the ethical obligation to discuss ADR with legal clients, suggest a need for lawyers to adopt a role closer to that of the traditional Counselor-at-Law. Jeff Greenberg, PhotoEdit

████ *Making It as a Cooperative Lawyer* ████

Ronald J. Gilson and Robert H. Mnookin (1994) examined the practice of law in the context of the classic prisoner's dilemma and concluded that lawyers with reputations for sharing information are more able to obtain win-win resolutions of their clients' disputes than are those with reputations for "hiding the ball." On this basis, Gilson and Mnookin predict that there will be a market in the community for lawyers who advertise themselves as cooperative negotiators and whose reputations as cooperators are well established. Gilson and Mnookin explored some of the impediments to making and keeping a cooperative reputation, and considered some methods for becoming well-known as a cooperator.

professionals have some of these skills already. For example, adversarial litigators are often experts at human motivation: they use such knowledge to determine how best to threaten and intimidate the opposition. It requires an attitudinal shift, but not that much knowledge acquisition, to convert this knowledge from adversarial to diagnostic service. Moreover, any legal or dispute professional who can understand the material in this textbook and can muster up the time and discipline to follow its recommendations can diagnose conflict. That having been said, it may be impossible or very difficult for some legal advocates to change their stripes. Some lawyers, by temperament, experience, or training, are probably unsuited to a practice involving a great deal of conflict diagnosis. This possibility has led one scholar, lawyer-mediator William F. Coyne, to recommend that lawyers specialize as either litigators or settlement counsel (Coyne 1999). Like the barrister/solicitor distinction common in the United Kingdom, a distinction between litigators and settlement counsel would allow dyed-in-the-wool gladiators to keep to their warrior path but also would allow knowledgeable clients to choose attorneys with temperaments more suited to conflict diagnosis and collaborative advocacy.

USING CONFLICT DIAGNOSIS

The *practice* of conflict diagnosis has two major uses in dealing with legal disputes and transactions: it assists the disputant or conflict professional in (1) choosing strategies and tactics for handling conflict and (2) choosing a dispute resolution process and provider.

CHOOSING STRATEGIES AND TACTICS FOR HANDLING CONFLICT

In real-world interpersonal conflict, the practice of conflict diagnosis can reap benefits if applied early, before ADR is even a consideration. A disputant or conflict professional who regularly engages in conflict diagnosis can maximize gain for clients, prevent conflict escalation and dispute recurrence, ensure optimal resource use, and, for disputes that involve ongoing relationships, protect the viability of these relationships. The application of conflict diagnosis to a pending interpersonal conflict allows one to better understand the conflict itself, why it arose, the underlying interests and needs of the stakeholders, the forces impeding its resolution, and the best practices for dealing with it.

Disputants or stakeholders applying the principles of conflict diagnosis, early and often, can help prevent the thought distortions that come from being involved in an escalating conflict. Being able to think clearly and objectively about a conflict confers enormous power. With the power of clear thinking and observation, a participant may be better able to make planful and intelligent choices about the most important goals he or she has for the process and outcome of the conflict, as well as the strategies that would best address those goals.

Legal professionals and other advocates can enhance their advocacy role by applying conflict diagnosis as early as possible. Conflict diagnosis can help advocates serve the true interests of their client, rather than merely the "presenting problem" he or she walked into the office verbalizing. The client's presenting problem and how he or she describes the other participants are likely to be distorted by conflict escalation as well as incomplete. Conflict diagnosis is useful to get a more accurate and complete picture of the conflict, so that advocate and client can *both* gain a conscious awareness of the client's most important goals and can develop an effective strategy for reaching them.

Client Interviewing and Counseling. Lawyers, legal assistants, and paralegals begin their process of understanding a conflict with effective client interviewing and counseling techniques. The kind of interviewing technique used sets the stage for the kind of process chosen by the legal professional and client.

The starting point for invisible veil lawyering is an interviewing process narrowly focused on the existence and strength of legal causes of action and defenses. The interviewing technique features close professional control of the conversation and narrowly drawn questions designed to confine the substance of the response to the identification of legal issues and the evidence relevant to their proof or disproof.[2] For a legal professional who uses conflict diagnosis, the process is quite different. Although the legal issues on which invisible veil lawyers focus are important in ensuring that the client's expert power is maximized and the client's BATNA is clarified, legal professionals using conflict diagnosis must take a broader perspective on the client and his or her situation. Jumping too quickly to the legal issues will distract legal professional and client from these additional considerations and impose the invisible veil on the conversation.

---

[2] For example, lawyers attending law school in the 1970s were often criticized by their professors if, during exercises meant to simulate client interviewing, their line of questioning strayed from the search for causes of action and legal defenses. The examination and grading process for law school courses further reinforced the narrow focus of lawyering by grading students primarily on the extent to which they were able to review a fact situation and pull out the causes of action and affirmative defenses that could be argued from the facts. Adding other information to an essay was grounds for a reduction in one's grade.

Leonard Riskin and James Westbrook, noted ADR authorities from the University of Missouri School of Law, describe a much broader purpose of the lawyer-client interview. They conceive of this purpose as having three components (Riskin and Westbrook 1997, 89):

1. Understand the client's situation and interests and . . . situation (and, generally, the situations and interests of others who are involved in the matter). This is accomplished principally through interviewing.
2. Help the client define the problem or problems to be addressed and the client's goals. This requires interviewing and counseling.
3. Help the client choose a course of action to address the problems defined, in ways that serve the client's interests and, perhaps, the interests of others. This involves counseling.

Riskin and Westbrook point out that the narrow, cause-of-action-based interrogation of traditional, invisible veil lawyering often causes the legal professional to miss important client goals and appropriate vehicles for reaching these goals. For example, taking the client's presenting problem at face value can cause the lawyer to miss out on the really important interests underlying that problem. Riskin and Westbrook recommend a more open-ended and client-centered interviewing and counseling technique. Like holistic and client-centered lawyering advocates, they advocate the liberal use of *open-ended questions, active listening,* and *the limited use of narrower or leading questions* to encourage the client to tell his or her version of the facts and to gather information on what is really important (Riskin & Westbrook 1997, 92–94). An example follows to illustrate the distinction between invisible-veil interviewing and the more open-ended alternative.

An Invisible Veil Interview. Mr. Sawyer enters a law office for an initial consultation. Invisible veil lawyering might include a sequence like the following very early in the interview:

Legal Professional: Good morning, Mr. Sawyer. It's good to meet you.

Client: Good morning, Mr. Johnson.

Legal Professional: I understand you have been in an auto accident. On what date did the accident take place?

Client: August 26 of this year.

Legal Professional: What street were you driving on, and in what direction were you going?

Client: I was driving, I believe, south, on Main Street.

Legal Professional: And you were hit? Were you hit at an intersection?

Client: Not really. I was close to a corner.

Legal Professional: What was the nearest cross-street?

Client: Maple Avenue.

Legal Professional: In what direction was the other car traveling?

Client: I'm not sure. I think they had just come out of a driveway somewhere.

Legal Professional: And were the police called to the scene?

Client: Yes.

Legal Professional: Do you have a copy of the accident report with you?

Client (searching among his papers): Oh, I forgot it. Can I send it to you?

Legal Professional: Yes. Were you injured?

Client: I did have some neck pain and I saw a doctor.

Legal Professional: What is the doctor's name and telephone number?

Client (searching among his papers): Here's the receipt I got from the emergency room.

Legal Professional: Have you seen anyone else for your injuries? [etc.]

Notice how, from the very outset of the conversation, the invisible veil lawyer narrowly casts his questioning to keep the client focused on information relevant to the client's cause of action.

A Client Interview to Promote Conflict Diagnosis. Contrast the preceding example of invisible veil client interviewing with the following example of interviewing by a legal professional who takes a more holistic approach:

Legal Professional: Good morning, Mr. Sawyer. It's good to meet you.

Client: Good morning, Ms. Robinson.

Legal Professional: I understand you've come to see me about an auto accident.

Client: Yes, I was in an accident last week and I need to know what I should do.

Legal Professional: What do you hope to have come out of my work with you?

Client: Well, first, I want to know what my legal rights are.

Legal Professional: We'll be sure to go over those rights today, to the extent that I can without doing research and investigation. Anything else?

Client: Well, I had a neck injury and a friend of mine told me that, unless I try to recover from the other party, I'll have to pay some of my medical expenses.

Legal Professional: So you've had some expenses from this accident.

Client: To tell you the truth, I feel really derailed by this entire incident. The day of the accident, I had a major meeting at the office. I was so rattled that I couldn't concentrate at all. I don't know if it is going to affect my job performance review. That's coming up soon.

Legal Professional: You're really worried about the effect this experience is having on your work.

Client: Well, I was finally starting to feel a little more confident about my job performance and my ability to get ahead in the company. To tell you the truth, a lot is going on at the office. I just don't need this on top of everything else!

Legal Professional: OK, so your office environment has been challenging, and you seem to be saying that the accident sort of derailed you.

Client: Yes, and I'm really angry about it. The other driver was some young punk. I bet he's never had a real job in his life!

Legal Professional: There are some things a lawyer can do and some things she can't. Unfortunately, one of the things a lawyer can't do is choose the guy her client gets hit by!

Client: Yeah, I see your point.

Legal Professional: What do you hope will happen here?

Client: Well, I think this punk needs to know how he's hurt me and my family. I bet he doesn't even know I have a teenager about his age! If I can't make a living, my son won't be able to have a car like this jerk does. This guy needs to give our whole family an apology!

Legal Professional: So meeting with this driver and his family might give you the opportunity to let them know how this accident has affected you.

Client: Yeah, they have no idea how it's thrown me off.

Legal Professional: I hear you saying that your equilibrium was really affected by this accident. Has your job performance really suffered since the accident?

Client: I've been able to cope pretty well. My director knows what happened and has cut me some slack. It's just the principle of the thing!

Legal Professional: So it's important to you as a matter of principle to let this driver and his family know how the accident has affected you. We could accomplish that through a settlement meeting or through a process called mediation, which is where a neutral third party helps you and the other side negotiate. We can consider whether these would be effective options after we have a little more information on the table. You also mentioned money. What are you hoping for economically?

Client: A million bucks. Just kidding!! To tell you the truth, I wasn't really hurt badly; this happened about a week ago and I've seen a doctor for a little neck strain, but he says it's minor.

Legal Professional: If you want a million bucks, you should go next door and buy a lottery ticket! Seriously, though, we usually give these neck injuries about six months to see if something more serious develops. The law will generally provide for you to get compensated for medical expenses if the other driver is considered legally at fault. It also sounds as if you're pretty busy at work. You should know that, although the lawyer takes on the lion's share of the work in a lawsuit, you would get tied up, too. I am more than willing to go to bat for you, but I just wanted you to know what you would be getting into. Lawsuits take time and effort for the client as well as the lawyer.

Client: I need to teach that punk a lesson, but I really don't have the time to screw around in court.

Legal Professional: So getting the other driver to see how he's inconvenienced you seems to be a pretty important goal for you, but you'd prefer to avoid sinking a lot of time into it.

Client: Yes! Absolutely.

Legal Professional: I wonder if a meeting with "the punk" and his family might serve the purpose better than litigation. Why don't you spend some time thinking about it?

Client: OK.

Legal Professional: We'll put that thought in our back pocket. Now, to get a better idea of how a lawsuit might go, if that becomes your choice, and to have a better idea of how a monetary settlement might play out if we negotiate, I need some details about the accident. When did this accident occur? [What follows is similar to the invisible veil interview.]

Notice that the holistic legal professional begins by inviting the client to frame the conflict in his own "voice." She does this by keeping her early questioning open-ended and by reflecting the client's comments about his goals in a way that avoids assigning blame. The legal professional is careful to avoid leading the client into a discussion of causes of action until she thinks she has obtained a clear picture of the client's goals and priorities. In our invisible veil society, it is important that the professional not begin with a purely adversarial interpretation of the conflict, because emphasis on this element of the conflict will readily foreclose all consideration of alternative ways of looking at the situation. In the initial interview, the legal professional should aim to allow the client to tell his or her own story and should further aim to get a sense of the client's legal and nonlegal interests and goals. The interviewer should be prepared to encounter a person already in the throes of the thought distortions that accompany escalated conflict: for this reason, the interviewer should gently guide the client away from "what a bad guy the other disputant is" and toward his or her hopes, dreams, and goals for how the conflict will end.

Client Counseling and Referral. A skilled legal interviewer can accomplish a number of goals in a client interview: he or she can help the client feel heard and understood, which is also an effective marketing technique; appreciate the client's interests; get a sense of what, if any, legal and nonlegal issues are afoot; and get a sense of what needs to be done next. The interview will likely yield lists of tasks for the legal professional to accomplish, to be delegated to assistants or secretaries, or to be assigned to investigators. Additionally, the interview may suggest the need for client referrals—to therapists, accountants, or educators. The result may even be a realization that legal assistance isn't what the client actually needs at this point. If so, the legal professional can part with the client on a positive note, secure in the knowledge that he or she may not have secured a client at the present but has successfully marketed his or her services for the future.

Case Preparation. If the client does retain the professional's services, conflict diagnosis provides a useful framework in which to elaborate on and specify the details of the client's conflict in a manner that will be most helpful in counseling the client and recommending strategies and tactics for managing the conflict. At this point in the process, the legal professional should take a first pass at diagnosing the conflict. It helps to organize the components of conflict diagnosis on separate pages or in separate sections and to keep a working draft on the computer. The initial draft of the conflict diagnosis should contain, in addition to basic identifying information about the client, the following information:

- ◆ A summary of the client interview
- ◆ A description of the client's presenting problem(s) and goals
- ◆ A description of the likely sources of the conflict
- ◆ A sociogram (see Chapter 6), showing the participants and their roles
- ◆ An exploration of the client's underlying interests and goals, as well as the other disputant's likely goals and interests (it is helpful analytically to use interest trees)
- ◆ An analysis of how the other participants' interests may play into exacerbating or resolving the conflict
- ◆ A sense of how escalated the conflict has become and the state of trust between the parties
- ◆ An initial list of the apparent impediments to cooperative resolution
- ◆ An assessment of the various sources of power held by the client and the other disputant
- ◆ An analysis of the client's BATNA, including a case valuation, and the same for the other disputant
- ◆ A list of the information needed to prepare the case, including an analysis of the legal and factual issues
- ◆ An analysis of what strategy would best help the client meet his or her underlying goals, interests, and needs, with a discussion of the tactics that might be useful
- ◆ A section discussing "next steps"—further interviews, investigation, legal research, referrals, and so forth

These entries should be dated. As information is gathered and the case progresses, the conflict diagnosis working document should be updated as needed. Conflict diagnosis is always a work in progress.

Like any other legal professional, one who diagnoses a conflict usually also spends a great deal of time preparing the case—conducting legal and factual research and organizing the results into a case file and/or trial notebook. Case preparation has four major purposes, apart from preparing the case for trial, if it becomes necessary:

- ◆ Case preparation empowers the client and the legal team. Gaining an understanding of the facts and the law behind the conflict—and getting an idea of the state of the evidence in support of, and in opposition to, the client—provides the team with expert power, coercive power, and reward power.

- ◆ Case preparation is needed for BATNA maximization and clarification. Knowing the likelihood of prevailing in court provides the information the client will need to make an appropriate decision regarding out-of-court options.

- ◆ Case preparation furthers the understanding of the conflict itself. Factual investigation may uncover hitherto hidden sources of conflict and impediments to settlement. Better understanding of the legal and factual aspects of the conflict will also help the team create a more detailed and informative interest tree. Sometimes, a factual investigation will uncover inconsistencies between a client's stated goals and the supporting information. Such inconsistencies may point out omissions or errors in the pending interest tree and can lead to a better understanding of client motivation.

- ◆ Case preparation furthers a better understanding of the other disputant and other stakeholders. Knowing more about the other team and about bystanders can help the legal team appreciate the likely motives of these other people, to make a better guess at the contents of their interest tree, and to better predict and understand their behavior. The more that is known about the other participants in the conflict, the less the legal professional and client are likely to draw (probably erroneous) inferences about motive from the behavior of the other team during the conflict. Thorough familiarity with the case will also help give the team a clearer sense of whether the other team is seeking an exploitative outcome, enabling fine-tuning of strategies and tactics.

Deciding how fully to prepare the case depends on the resources the client has, and wants, to expend. Frequently, preparing a case for trial costs a large fraction of the amount in dispute. Moreover, fully preparing a case for trial often leads to overcommitment—a sense, on the part of lawyer and client, that one must therefore proceed to trial to avoid wasting all that time and money. Thus, conflict diagnosis and case preparation inevitably occur in tandem, with each process informing the team how to proceed with the other process. Early conflict diagnosis can uncover deeply seated interests on the part of the client or the other disputant, impediments to cooperation, and opportunities for cooperation-building that short-circuit the need to prepare fully for litigation. Consider the following example, which reflects recent findings concerning the role of apologies in medical malpractice disputes.[3]

> Harvey Franks, a fifty-five-year-old father of two, entered Anytown Hospital for a routine cardiac catheterization. During the procedure, something went wrong: the contrast dye used in the process led to permanent kidney impairment and Harvey was forced to go on dialysis. Although this sometimes happens in such procedures, there was a factual issue concerning whether Harvey was adequately informed of the risks and a mixed factual and legal issue concerning whether hospital protocol had allowed inadequate risk screening. As a hypertension sufferer, there was some question whether he may have had some pre-existing kidney damage predisposing him to harm from the dye, a fact that might have made the procedure medically inadvisable; however, the same condition may have caused the lion's share of the damage prior to the catheterization. Moreover, the procedure uncovered an arterial blockage, which was corrected with a stent; had it not been done, Harvey would have been at risk for a heart attack.
>
> Harvey and his family consulted a medical malpractice attorney, Bernice Jensen. In her interview with the Franks, Bernice allowed them to express their grief and anger at the event. She also explored the legal issues with them. Bernice neither encouraged nor discouraged the option of litigation but spent time in the initial interview asking the Franks to discuss their hopes and dreams for how this matter would play out. The Franks expressed interest in settling out of court: Harvey is weak and sick much of the time, and the Franks felt it would be in the family's best interests to avoid litigation if possible. Additionally, the Franks have few other options for medical care because they live in a very small town. Their trust in the hospital has been severely tested, but not shattered. All other things being equal, they prefer that their status as users of the hospital not be irrevocably terminated. However, they want visible evidence that the hospital and doctor are more trustworthy than their recent experience has indicated. It also troubles them to consider the possibility that others might suffer as they have.
>
> Bernice then contacted the hospital by letter and telephone, stating that, although litigation might be considered at a later time, the Franks were interested in discussing the matter with the doctor and hospital. In response, the hospital legal staff called a meeting with the Franks; Bernice; hospital counsel; the attending physician, Dr. Trenton; the hospital vice president; and the head of the hospital's nephrology department, Dr. Kim.
>
> At the meeting, Harvey and his wife described how difficult it had been to discover that Harvey's kidneys had failed and his pain and discomfort with tri-weekly dialysis treatments. Dr. Kim broke down in tears. Consumed with remorse, he apologized to the Franks for their pain and difficulties. "I see myself as a healer, not as a giver of pain," he said.
>
> The Franks then asked what the hospital could do to "make them whole." In response, and over the course of three additional working set-

---

[3] A number of scholars (e.g., Cohen 2000; Shuman 1994, 68) have cited research indicating that medical malpractice victims are much less likely to litigate if they receive an apology from the persons responsible.

tlement meetings, the hospital's vice president signed a stipulation stating that Harvey would be considered for a kidney transplant at the hospital's expense. All the costs of the transplant, plus the costs of supportive care and medication, would be taken care of by the hospital; in addition, the hospital offered the Franks a structured settlement to compensate for Harvey's pain and suffering. In addition, the hospital agreed in writing to conduct a review of its informed-consent and risk-assessment procedures for cardiac catheterization and associated processes, so that others would not experience the same outcome as Harvey. The settlement with the Franks led to a hospitalwide review of screenings for cardiac catheterization procedures, which in turn led to publicized reforms that made the procedure safer in hospitals everywhere. The Franks still obtain their medical care at Anytown Hospital. Because of the savings in legal fees, the hospital was able to make a liberal settlement with the Franks, and, although its reputation was harmed by news of the pending dispute, the hospital used the subsequent reforms to rebuild goodwill with the community. The entire process was completed in under three months, and Harvey Franks was placed on the transplant list the day after the first settlement meeting.

The case of Harvey Franks illustrates how conflict diagnosis, used early, can sometimes short-circuit the need to prepare fully for litigation. The key in the Franks case was the attorney's willingness to spend the time upfront exploring her client's interests, both short-term and long-term, financial and otherwise. An invisible veil approach to this dispute probably would have involved an intensive factual and legal investigation, the hiring of a number of expensive experts, plus a grueling and costly phase of discovery about hospital policies, Harvey's preexisting condition, and the procedure in question. This alternative would have cost everyone a lot more money and might have led to a poorer process and outcome for Harvey and his family. Rubin, Pruitt, and Kim (1994, 114–16) suggest four ways to avoid this sort of overcommitment:

1. Setting limits to involvement
2. "Chunking"—that is, building periodic reappraisals of strategy into the process of pursuing a resolution of the dispute
3. Making sure that the costs of continuing to pursue case preparation are always in mind
4. Keeping in mind that the effort to save face can create a strong impetus to pursue adversarial dispute resolution beyond the point at which it is appropriate

Conflict diagnosis processes can assist a legal team in implementing all four of these strategies. First, continuing conflict diagnosis can enable the team to set and maintain intelligent limits to involvement by making clear what the underlying participant goals are—in other words, keeping one eye on conflict diagnosis helps the legal team see the big picture, and seeing the big picture prevents overcommitment. For example, the interests and BATNA analyses will help team members assess when they are better off accepting a negotiated settlement, even if emotions are urging participants not to give in. Without conflict diagnosis, team members will be flying blindly: they will be unable to assess accurately when it would be in the best interests of the client to pursue a given strategy and goal. Second, conflict diagnosis can be used to assist the team in making intelligent reappraisals. As the dispute proceeds, the parameters, benefits, and risks of potential strategies and tactics will change. Continuing conflict diagnosis will enable the team to engage in rational reassessment based on the new information. Third, conflict diagnosis is useful in developing a truly comprehensive cost-benefit analysis of strategies and tactics. Because conflict diagnosis requires the team to examine the conflict closely and rigorously, it provides a comprehensive assessment of benefits and costs. As a result, disputants and their teams are less likely to rush blindly into counterproductive and costly behaviors. Finally, the process of conflict diagnosis can often help team members get past loss-of-face issues by forcing the team to look dispassionately at underlying interests, conflict-escalation effects, and the BATNA. Paradoxically, although conflict diagnosis requires a headlong look at the emotional aspects of the conflict, it frees participants from the restraints that unrecognized emotions often place on disputants.

Mediators, particularly those with backgrounds in the mental-health professions, often use a journaling process to keep track of and analyze their pending cases. The journaling process can be enhanced by incorporating conflict diagnosis principles into the observations and analysis. One divorce mediator comments that each new case she takes on benefits from the conflict diagnosis process in a different manner. Most often, an in-depth interests analysis using theories of human motivation, or an examination of the sources of conflict or impediments to resolution, suggests creative ways to address the conflict. She also remarks that conflict diagnosis makes it very clear that each case must be addressed uniquely. One divorcing family may primarily need to clarify and get past meta-disputes, whereas another may need mostly help in organizing and appraising their estate; another may need power balancing through referrals to lawyers and other experts. Conflict diagnosis allows the professional to respond to each set of disputants in a manner that respects and acknowledges their unique situation.

CHOOSING A DISPUTE RESOLUTION PROCESS AND PROVIDER

The use of conflict diagnosis for selecting ADR processes is a field still in its earliest infancy.[4] This lack of maturity makes conflict diagnosis very exciting to study and practice: you might someday be one of the pioneers in a growing field.

Fitting the Forum to the Fuss. The most well-known effort to describe how to select ADR processes was published by eminent law professors Frank E. A.

---

[4] Although the idea of diagnosing a conflict is well established, the term *diagnosis,* applied to interpersonal conflict, means different things to different people.

Sander, of Harvard Law School, and Stephen B. Goldberg, of Northwestern University Law School. Their ground-breaking article "Fitting the Forum to the Fuss: A User-Friendly Guide to Selecting an ADR Forum" (1994) is an attempt to create a systematic ADR selection process based on matching the qualities of each process to the characteristics of the clients and the conflict. Sander and Goldberg assert that the client's interests and the setting and situation of the conflict should control the choice of a dispute resolution process. Guided by their own knowledge and concerns, they created a simple grid system to represent the various strengths of the available processes. For example, they rated mediation and early neutral evaluation best at minimizing costs and maximizing speed, whereas they rated litigation best at obtaining a binding precedent. For each dispute resolution process and each client objective, they assigned a numeric score to represent, roughly, the relative utility of that process in meeting that objective. The idea advanced by Sander and Goldberg was that the legal professional would then assign an importance to the client of each objective. For example, a client might rate minimizing costs as very important—a 10—but getting a binding precedent as only moderately important—a 5. The relative merits of a given dispute resolution process for the client is determined by multiplying the utility factor by the user's importance factor and summing the products over all the client's objectives. One then compares the scores for each dispute resolution process, with the highest score representing the best fit between the client's goals and the process. Sander and Goldberg presented one table to represent the utility of processes for meeting various client objectives (see Table 22-1) and another to represent the utility of ADR processes for overcoming impediments to settlement.

◆ **TABLE 22-1** Sander and Goldberg's Grid to Assess the Best Dispute Resolution Process to Meet Various Client Objectives (Modified)

CLIENT OBJECTIVES	MEDIATION Utility Times Importance (User Defined)	MINITRIAL Utility Times Importance (User Defined)	SUMMARY JURY TRIAL Utility Times Importance (User Defined)	EARLY NEUTRAL EVALUATION Utility Times Importance (User Defined)	ARBITRATION Utility Times Importance (User Defined)	LITIGATION Utility Times Importance (User Defined)
Minimize costs	$3 \times \_\_ = \_\_$	$2 \times \_\_ = \_\_$	$2 \times \_\_ = \_\_$	$3 \times \_\_ = \_\_$	$1 \times \_\_ = \_\_$	$0 \times \_\_ = 0$
Speed	$3 \times \_\_ = \_\_$	$2 \times \_\_ = \_\_$	$2 \times \_\_ = \_\_$	$3 \times \_\_ = \_\_$	$1 \times \_\_ = \_\_$	$0 \times \_\_ = 0$
Privacy	$3 \times \_\_ = \_\_$	$3 \times \_\_ = \_\_$	$2 \times \_\_ = \_\_$	$2 \times \_\_ = \_\_$	$3 \times \_\_ = \_\_$	$0 \times \_\_ = 0$
Maintain/improve relationships	$3 \times \_\_ = \_\_$	$2 \times \_\_ = \_\_$	$2 \times \_\_ = \_\_$	$1 \times \_\_ = \_\_$	$1 \times \_\_ = \_\_$	$0 \times \_\_ = 0$
Vindication	$0 \times \_\_ = 0$	$1 \times \_\_ = \_\_$	$1 \times \_\_ = \_\_$	$1 \times \_\_ = \_\_$	$2 \times \_\_ = \_\_$	$3 \times \_\_ = \_\_$
Neutral opinion	$0 \times \_\_ = 0$	$3 \times \_\_ = \_\_$	$3 \times \_\_ = \_\_$	$3 \times \_\_ = \_\_$	$3 \times \_\_ = \_\_$	$3 \times \_\_ = \_\_$
Precedent	$0 \times \_\_ = 0$	$0 \times \_\_ = 0$	$0 \times \_\_ = 0$	$0 \times \_\_ = 0$	$2 \times \_\_ = \_\_$	$3 \times \_\_ = \_\_$
Maximize/minimize recovery	$0 \times \_\_ = 0$	$1 \times \_\_ = \_\_$	$1 \times \_\_ = \_\_$	$1 \times \_\_ = \_\_$	$2 \times \_\_ = \_\_$	$3 \times \_\_ = \_\_$
Total[*]						

[*]Sum the products in each column to obtain relative usefulness in meeting client objectives.

Let's see how this process might work in a conflict. Imagine that an initial negotiation in the Franks medical malpractice case did not result in an agreement, and suppose further that Harvey Franks' attorney, Bernice Jensen, worked with Mark to fill out the grid shown in Table 22-1. Step 1 is for attorney and client to identify how important each of the client objectives are to the client. Bernice asks Harvey to rate each of the eight objectives on a scale from 1 to 10, with 10 being most important. The following are Harvey's responses:

Minimize costs	7
Speed	8
Privacy	4
Maintain/improve relationships	9
Vindication	6
Neutral opinion	2
Precedent	1
Maximize/minimize recovery	7

Bernice inserts these weights into the grid. Note that each of Harvey's chosen weights are inserted under "Importance (User Defined)" and are the same across each row. Inserting these numbers into the table yields the results shown in Table 22-2. Applying the objectives grid to Harvey's situation indicates that mediation would narrowly beat out early neutral evaluation and other assisted negotiation processes in satisfying Harvey's objectives and that litigation would be least likely to satisfy Harvey, at least until ADR were tried.

Sander and Goldberg characterized their grids as merely a beginning to an ongoing discussion about fitting the forum to the fuss and commented that they are useful primarily in illustrating that different processes have different strengths and weaknesses in specific settings. Many ADR practitioners would probably argue that using these grids in practice would oversimplify the process of choosing a dispute resolution process and provider. Do the grids proposed by Sander and Goldberg contain the correct client objectives and impediments to settlement? What about other client goals? For example, Harvey Franks is motivated to reform or improve the system, so that others won't have to suffer, a motive that many tort litigants express.[5] This client objective is not among the choices on the grid. And how do we account for the overlap among goals? Is it appropriate, for example, to have "vindication," "neutral opinion," and "maximize/minimize recovery" as separate client goals in the grid if a client's sense of anger and betrayal

---

[5] Frances H. Miller, professor of law at Boston University, reports (Miller 1986, 434) the results of a British study, which found that "Action for the Victims of Medical Accidents, a charity established to aid people injured through medical treatment, stated in 1984 that in approximately 70 percent of its almost 2000 cases, medical malpractice victims: '. . . are interested in financial compensation only as a secondary matter or not at all. What they invariably seek is an honest explanation of what went wrong and why, an apology if that is appropriate, and an assurance that steps will be . . . taken, to ensure that an accident of that kind does not happen to anyone else'."

◆ **TABLE 22-2**   Mark Farley's Client Objectives analysis

MARK FARLEY'S RATINGS OF HIS OBJECTIVES (1 = LEAST IMPORTANT TO 10 = MOST IMPORTANT):	
• Minimize costs	7
• Speed	8
• Privacy	4
• Maintain/improve relationships	9
• Vindication	6
• Neutral opinion	2
• Precedent	1
• Maximize/minimize recovery	7

CLIENT OBJECTIVES	MEDIATION: UTILITY TIMES *Importance (User Defined)*	MINITRIAL: UTILITY TIMES *Importance (User Defined)*	SUMMARY JURY TRIAL: UTILITY TIMES *Importance (User Defined)*	EARLY NEUTRAL EVALUATION: UTILITY TIMES *Importance (User Defined)*	ARBITRATION: UTILITY TIMES *Importance (User Defined)*	LITIGATION: UTILITY TIMES *Importance (User Defined)*
Minimize costs	3 × 7 = **21**	2 × 7 = **14**	2 × 7 = **14**	3 × 7 = **21**	1 × 7 = **7**	0 × 7 = **0**
Speed	3 × 8 = **24**	2 × 8 = **16**	2 × 8 = **16**	3 × 8 = **24**	1 × 8 = **8**	0 × 8 = **0**
Privacy	3 × 4 = **12**	3 × 4 = **12**	2 × 4 = **8**	2 × 4 = **8**	3 × 4 = **12**	0 × 4 = **0**
Maintain/improve relationships	3 × 9 = **27**	2 × 9 = **18**	2 × 9 = **18**	1 × 9 = **9**	1 × 9 = **9**	0 × 9 = **0**
Vindication	0 × 6 = **0**	1 × 6 = **6**	1 × 6 = **6**	1 × 6 = **6**	2 × 6 = **12**	3 × 6 = **18**
Neutral opinion	0 × 2 = **0**	3 × 2 = **6**	3 × 2 = **6**	3 × 2 = **6**	3 × 2 = **6**	3 × 2 = **6**
Precedent	0 × 1 = **0**	0 × 1 = **0**	0 × 1 = **0**	0 × 1 = **0**	2 × 1 = **2**	3 × 1 = **3**
Maximize/minimize recovery	0 × 7 = **0**	1 × 7 = **7**	1 × 7 = **7**	1 × 7 = **7**	2 × 7 = **14**	3 × 7 = **21**
Total[*]	**84**	**79**	**75**	**81**	**70**	**48**

[*]Sum the products in each column to obtain relative usefulness in meeting client objectives.

motivate her to want all three? Or does this constitute triple-weighting—counting the same motive three times? Another thing that makes the grid system problematic is that the utilities of the processes vary with the situation. For example, the "maximize/minimize recovery" goal is met well by litigation only if the client has an airtight case. If the client's case is very weak, a consensual process is likely to do a much better job of giving the client a good monetary outcome. And, finally, it is unclear whether the real world supports the weightings that the authors assigned to the different dispute-resolution processes. The authors themselves acknowledge that these weightings are based on their own experiences and those of professionals they had worked with and are not (at least, not yet) supported by empirical research (Sander & Goldberg 1994, 52).

Toward a Conflict Diagnosis Approach. It's unlikely a simple grid will ever provide an appropriate substitute for the information provided in Parts II and III of this textbook. Moreover, Sander and Goldberg caution that they did not intend for the grid to serve as an all-purpose ADR selection tool. However, the basic concept illustrated by the Sander and Goldberg grids, that ADR processes should be chosen to respond to client objectives and the characteristics of the conflict, is a valid one. In considering how to select dispute resolution processes, it is helpful to recap what we've learned about the unique qualities of each process. These qualities are summarized in Table 22-3 (pages 539–543). The listed qualities are primarily hypothetical and based on application of the theories that constitute conflict diagnosis, although some are widely recognized in the scholarly literature, as discussed in Parts II and III.

Sander and a number of other legal and ADR scholars express a "rule of presumptive mediation"—that mediation should be tried first (Sander & Goldberg 1994, 59–60; see also Barnes 1997). Sander and Goldberg point out that mediation excels over alternative dispute resolution methods in overcoming most impediments to settlement (impediments to settlement are discussed in Chapter 11). The exceptions, say Sander and Goldberg, are disparate views of fact and law, and the Jackpot Syndrome—and mediators often have ways to help disputants settle that don't require the disputants to resolve disparate views of fact or law (Sander and Goldberg 1997, 59). There are a number of other reasons to begin with mediation, as well. First, "it can't hurt." Unless time is of the essence and one of the disputants is likely to harm the other irreparably unless immediately restrained, good mediation is, even at worst, helpful in reducing conflict escalation. Mediation may help even if agreement is not reached—if well done, it will strengthen relationships and may narrow the issues in dispute (making subsequent litigation faster and less costly), may clarify BATNAs, may help each disputant understand the other's perspective, and may help each team prepare for whatever other process they'll be involved in, whether litigation or arbitration. Mediation can also result in partial agreements that can reduce the cost and trauma of any adversary processes that may be needed later. Other processes, such as nonbinding evaluation, arbitration, and even litigation, can be used within a facilitative mediation framework to provide answers to questions that are more appropriately handled that way—in this way, the facilitative framework can help minimize conflict escalation and cope with the natural weaknesses of the other processes.

Conflict diagnosis principles suggest three important reasons to choose *facilitative* mediation first. First, facilitative mediation is a highly consensual process. Obviously, consensual processes can provide a high quality of consent—that is, the disputants are the ones who psychologically own the decision and are more likely to make it work enthusiastically. The highest quality of consent is attained using a process in which the disputants themselves generate the settlement, rather than settling on an outcome because someone else has told them it's what they'd get if they went to court. Hence, well-done facilitative mediation, and negotiation without evaluation, can yield the highest quality of consent. Theoretically, of the facilitative mediation processes, transformative mediation, which vests complete control over settlement in the disputants, yields the very highest quality of consent. A highly facilitative process also has the potential to do the best job of counteracting the damaging effects of conflict escalation. Additionally, evaluative processes tend to promote invisible veil thinking, and this

	FACILITATIVE MEDIATION	NONBINDING EVALUATION AND EVALUATIVE MEDIATION	INFORMAL ARBITRATION	FORMAL ARBITRATION	LITIGATION
Cost	Less expensive than litigation and formal arbitration; usually comparable to informal arbitration	Usually less expensive than formal arbitration and litigation; cost compared to other forms depends on the nature of the evaluation process	Generally the least expensive of all the ADR forms	Can be extremely expensive, sometimes even exceeds expense of litigation	Extremely expensive
Time	Quicker than litigation and formal arbitration; slower than informal arbitration	Quicker than facilitative mediation, but more vulnerable to the creation of impasse (which increases the time needed to resolve the conflict)	Extremely quick	Can be as time-consuming as litigation	Extremely time-consuming
Finality	Disputants may not settle; however, settlement likely to resolve entire conflict	No final outcome, but final recommendation may result; disputants may not settle; because evaluation is generally one-dimensional, settlement less likely to resolve entire conflict than settlement reached through facilitative mediation	Final outcome always reached, but may not resolve entire conflict	Final outcome always reached, but may not resolve entire conflict	Final outcome always reached, but may not resolve entire conflict; law restricts issues and remedies that court can address and provide
Psychological ownership and quality of consent	Best at creating psychological ownership of process and outcome, leading to high satisfaction rates and low rates of post-settlement disputing	No imposed outcome, but often there is a recommended outcome: moderately good at creating psychological ownership of process and outcome, leading to moderate satisfaction rates and moderate rates of post-settlement disputing	Worse at creating psychological ownership of process and outcome than assisted negotiation processes, but better than litigation; satisfaction rates and rates of post-settlement disputing tend to be worse than for assisted negotiation processes	Worse at creating psychological ownership of process and outcome than assisted negotiation processes, but better than litigation; satisfaction rates and rates of post-settlement disputing tend to be worse than for assisted negotiation processes	Poor at creating psychological ownership in the losing party; victor tends to be highly satisfied but rates of post-settlement disputing are worse than for assisted negotiation processes. Due process protections may enhance quality of consent, however.

(Continued)

◆ TABLE 22-3 Comparing the Major Dispute Resolution Forms (*continued*)

	FACILITATIVE MEDIATION	NONBINDING EVALUATION AND EVALUATIVE MEDIATION	INFORMAL ARBITRATION	FORMAL ARBITRATION	LITIGATION
Outcome creativity and Pareto-optimality	Settlements reached are often creative and meet underlying interests of all concerned	Tends to produce positional bargaining mentality and one-dimensional outcomes	Tends to produce invisible-veil mentality and one-dimensional outcomes	Tends to produce invisible-veil mentality and one-dimensional outcomes	Outcome strictly prescribed by law; reinforces invisible-veil mentality
Conflict containment and escalation	Nonadversarial; best at containing and de-escalating conflict and preserving/improving relationships	Non-coercive but based on a positional-bargaining paradigm: not as harmful to relationships as adjudication, but not as good at containing conflict and preserving relationships as facilitative mediation	Participation is voluntary but process is adversarial; not as harmful to relationships as litigation, but not as good at containing conflict and preserving relationships as assisted negotiation processes	Participation is voluntary but process is adversarial; not as harmful to relationships as litigation, but not as good at containing conflict and preserving relationships as assisted negotiation processes	Highly adversarial, coercive process; considered harmful to relationships and promotive of conflict escalation
Invisible-veil thinking	Discourages invisible-veil thinking; its use constitutes a paradigm shift in cultural beliefs and attitudes	Perpetuates invisible-veil thinking	Perpetuates invisible-veil thinking	Perpetuates invisible-veil thinking	Perpetuates invisible-veil thinking
Sense of procedural justice	If done well, disputants control process and therefore consider it to be procedurally just; but poor mediators may produce a sense of injustice by allowing one disputant to oppress the other	Voluntary quality of process allows the potential for sense of procedural justice; however, neutral vulnerable to being seen as biased	Most vulnerable to being perceived as unjust because outcome is not voluntary and process contains few procedural protections; generally no appeal is possible even if outcome is at variance with law	Involuntary outcome, but high levels of procedural protections, will create a perception of procedural justice; however, if neutral seems biased and proceeding is private, sense of justice will be undermined; generally no appeal is possible even if outcome is at variance with law	High perception of procedural justice brought about by built-in procedural protections, public nature of process, cultural beliefs

Bigoted or prejudiced behavior: dangers	Some believe that private nature of process makes it vulnerable to prejudiced or bigoted behavior; however, focus on meeting interests and needs of all disputants may counteract this tendency	Some believe that private nature of process makes it vulnerable to prejudiced or bigoted behavior	Some believe that private nature of process makes it vulnerable to prejudiced or bigoted behavior; involuntary nature of outcome makes any such behavior more damaging	If process is public, some believe participants less likely to engage in prejudiced or bigoted behavior; however, involuntary nature of outcome makes any such behavior more damaging	Process is public and officials are held accountable, leading some to believe that participants less likely to engage in prejudiced or bigoted behavior; however, involuntary nature of outcome and power of judge makes any such behavior more damaging
Dealing with disparities in bargaining power	Because these mediators often facilitate collaborating/integrating negotiation, moderately effective in minimizing damage from unequal bargaining power; good facilitative mediators work directly at empowering disputants; bad mediators may reinforce existing inequalities of bargaining power	May enlighten disputant as to the value of his or her case; otherwise, no real impact on bargaining power	Good for dealing with disparities of bargaining power that result from unequal access to justice system; however, large commercial entities and other so-called "repeat players" often do better than consumers and other one-time participants	Large commercial entities and other so-called "repeat players" often do better in these processes than consumers and other one-time participants; otherwise these processes generally don't affect bargaining power	In special cases, can equalize bargaining power; large commercial entities and other so-called "repeat players" often do better in litigation than consumers and other one-time participants
Disputant transformation	Can improve negotiation skills, empower, encourage perspective-taking, help achieve psychological closure	Assists disputants in knowing their cases better	Generally, no effect on disputant transformation apart from that provided by the outcome	Generally, no effect on disputant transformation apart from that provided by the outcome	Generally, no effect on disputant transformation apart from that provided by the outcome; in special cases, disputants may be participating in historic legal reform; occasionally victory over a "bad actor" may result in disputant transformation

(Continued)

◆ TABLE 22-3   Comparing the Major Dispute Resolution Forms *(continued)*

	FACILITATIVE MEDIATION	NONBINDING EVALUATION AND EVALUATIVE MEDIATION	INFORMAL ARBITRATION	FORMAL ARBITRATION	LITIGATION
Where it's often found	Community mediation; divorce mediation; child custody mediation; peer mediation; increasingly in employment dispute resolution (example, United States Postal Service REDRESS program); increasingly in other types of legal disputes	Court-connected ADR; factfinding use in complex cases, such as class action litigation	Private sector civil dispute resolution	Private sector civil dispute resolution; used with cases in which much is at stake financially	The "default" process, always available if the aggrieved party can state a cause of action even if other party does not accede to process
Usefulness in conjunction with other processes	Can be used as the root resolution process, with evaluative or adjudicative processes used to clarify BATNAs or resolve sub-issues; disputants engaged in litigation may be referred to these processes to resolve issues that are better dealt with facilitatively	Disputants engaged in a facilitative process can be referred to these processes to provide information such as BATNA clarification; disputants in complex litigation may be referred to these processes to resolve complicated factual or legal issues that the court is ill-suited to address	Disputants engaged in a facilitative process can be referred to these processes to resolve isolated issues that they are unable to settle voluntarily	Disputants engaged in a facilitative process can be referred to these processes to resolve isolated issues that they are unable to settle voluntarily	Disputants engaged in a facilitative process can be referred to these processes to resolve isolated issues that they are unable to settle voluntarily; disputants in litigation are often referred to mediation or nonbinding evaluation as part of a court-connected ADR program

Misconduct by neutral	Private nature of process makes it difficult to make neutral accountable for misconduct; voluntary nature of process lowers potential for harm	Private nature of process makes it difficult to make neutral accountable for misconduct; however, ability to reject outcome lowers potential for harm	Private nature of process makes it difficult to make neutral accountable for misconduct; potentially more harmful than assisted negotiation processes since disputant is bound by outcome	If process is private, difficult to make neutral accountable for misconduct; potentially more harmful than assisted negotiation processes since disputant is bound by outcome	Disputant is bound by outcome, which has imprimatur of governmental action; however, danger is ameliorated by public nature of process and right to seek relief through motions and appeals
Special qualities	Particularly good at dealing with angry or vengeful disputants; ironically, these are the disputants who are the least likely to choose this process	Particularly good at clarifying BATNAs for negotiating disputants; effective for large differences in perceptions of fact or law; comfortable for lawyers who want a process that "feels like" the litigation process; useful where an expert in subject matter is needed or the dispute presents complex legal issues	Very palatable to disputants who are very angry but don't want the time and expense of litigation	Very useful if disputants wish to litigate, but choice of a forum is problematic (as in international or cyberspace disputing); useful if disputants want to litigate but delay in getting to trial is unacceptable; if public, may create precedent	Needed if legal reform is sought (but it may not result); may provide precedent (particularly if case is appealed); provides rapid enforcement mechanism if there is a factual showing of potentially irreparable harm and a likelihood of prevailing on the merits of the case; good for containing dangerous or sociopathic behavior

Facilitative and Evaluative Mediation: The Civil Litigator's Perspective

Conflict diagnosis concepts lead to the hypothesis that facilitative mediation will, all other things being equal, lead to better conflict resolution than evaluative mediation. This is because facilitative mediation promotes a higher quality of consent—the disputants have more say in whether and how the conflict gets resolved—and the facilitative process leads to more creative problem solving and less conflict escalation.

Despite the theoretical advantages of facilitative mediation, the available empirical research indicates that lawyers involved in mediation overwhelmingly prefer evaluative mediation. In a series of studies of attitudes toward court-connected mediation (Harmann, Honeyman, McAdoo & Welsh 2001), lawyers participating in Minnesota and Missouri civil mediation identified "provided needed reality check for my client" and "provided needed reality check for opposing counsel or party" as principal reasons for choosing mediation. Almost 70 percent of the Missouri attorneys identified "helps everyone to value the case" as an important reason they chose mediation. And, of the Missouri attorneys, 87 percent stated that "knowing how to value a case" was an important mediator qualification, more than any other criterion listed. The runner up, at 83 percent, was "mediator should be a litigator," followed by "mediator should be a lawyer," at 77 percent. In contrast, only 35 percent felt that it was important for the mediator to "know how to find creative solutions."

> ### *Advantages of Facilitative Mediation- The Conflict Diagnosis Perspective*
>
> - ◆ It maximizes quality of consent.
> - ◆ It avoids invisible veil thinking.
> - ◆ It preserves relationships.
> - ◆ It optimizes resources.
> - ◆ It promotes voluntary compliance.
> - ◆ It promotes cooperation.
> - ◆ It prevents oppressive outcomes.

thinking can lead to less creative problem solving and poorer settlements. Once invisible veil thinking begins, it tends to self-promote. Invisible veil thinkers tend to see the conflict more and more as a zero-sum contest requiring competitive approaches to resolution. The actions of invisible-veil thinkers tend to trigger competitive behavior in the other disputant, causing the conflict to begin to escalate, and the escalating conflict seemingly proves that it was correct to perceive the conflict from an invisible veil perspective. Theories of conflict, cooperation, and competition, and negotiation style, suggest that the best processes for promoting constructive, equitable, and efficacious dispute resolution are those in which the participants are persistently guided away from invisible veil, zero-sum thinking and toward collaborative, integrative problem solving. These processes include (1) pure mediation geared directly toward promoting collaborative problem solving and (2) transformative mediation. Lying slightly beneath these consensual, collaborative processes are the consensual processes that avoid providing evaluations but that promote compromising. These include facilitative mediation processes that focus on compromising rather than collaborating.

These purely facilitative, consensual ADR forms are followed in usefulness by consensual forms of dispute resolution that add an element of evaluation to an otherwise facilitative process. They include evaluative mediation that features large amounts of facilitation as well as minitrial without neutral evaluation. These minimally evaluative forms add a dimension of BATNA clarification, although many facilitative mediators would argue that BATNA clarification is just as attainable in facilitative mediation. The more evaluative the process, the lower the quality of consent and the more invisible-veil thinking is promoted. Thus, evaluative mediation—and minitrial without an evaluation—can be expected to be less effective in this regard than facilitative mediation in meeting these goals.

ADR featuring nonbinding evaluation as the process centerpiece—early neutral evaluation, nonbinding evaluation, minitrial with neutral evaluation, and summary jury trial—can be expected to fall below evaluative mediation and minitrial without neutral evaluation in promoting a high quality of consent and in making optimal dispute resolution possible. Although these processes falter in setting the stage for creative problem solving, and create the risk of conflict escalation if they fail to produce a settlement, they are good for situations in which rapid, low-cost determinations are needed and in which it is clear that both parties are willing to abide by the evaluation.

Nonconsensual processes bring up the rear of this hierarchy. Arbitration processes are often more consensual than litigation, because the disputants have contracted that they take place. (In the case of consumer contracts of adhesion, this is usually not the case.) One can expect med-arb to be slightly more effective than straight arbitration for achieving quality of consent. Litigation is the least consensual process unless both litigants have enthusiastically chosen it. Litigation is also generally the poorest option for reducing conflict escalation, resolving the entire landscape of the conflict, developing creative and flexible outcomes, and promoting disputant relationships. Figure 22-1 shows this relationship among dispute resolution forms, quality of consent, and ability to minimize invisible-veil thinking.

Thus, in considering quality of consent and ability to resolve conflict in an optimal manner—and assuming that there is a specific reason the dispute can't be resolved through collaborative, face-to-face negotiation—the highest and best form of dispute resolution is facilitative mediation that actively involves the disputants themselves and promotes collaborative, integrative forms of problem solving. Such a process is optimal in terms of quality of consent, control of conflict escalation, and capacity to optimize resources and interests creatively. Both transformative and pure mediation typically satisfy this description.

When the Presumption Doesn't Apply. There are a number of reasons, however, that disputants and their teams don't, or shouldn't, jump directly into facilitative mediation. Some of these reasons are best dealt with by laying a more careful groundwork for using mediation. Others are better dealt with by incorporating

◆ **FIGURE 22-1**

How the Dispute Resolution Forms Rate on Two Important Dimensions—Ability to Reduce Invisible-Veil Thinking and Quality of Consent

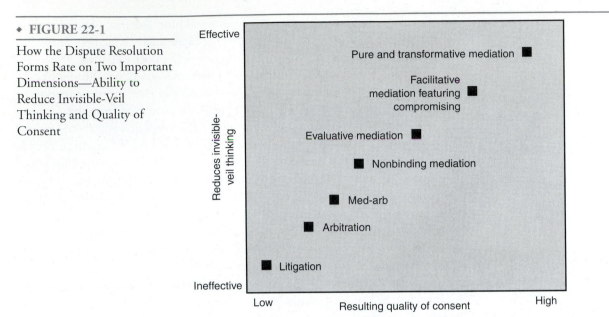

other processes into an overall facilitative framework. Still others are best handled by jumping right to evaluative or even adjudicative processes. A summary of these reasons is presented in Table 22-4.

Reason 1: The Other Side Won't Play.   Frequently, a disputant—or his or her legal advocate—resists getting involved in a facilitative process.[6] There are many possible reasons for such a reaction. Sometimes, this reticence is due to a lack of understanding of the process; other times, it is due to the influence of the invisible veil—a belief that it can't possibly work. Sometimes, the opposition occurs as a reactive devaluation to a suggestion by the other disputant that such a process be tried, and occasionally it is because the other disputant's team feels disempowered by a facilitative process—it is unfamiliar and therefore frightening. Or the disputant's advocate, rather than the disputant, may have these reservations and therefore recommends an evaluative or adjudicative process. It is also possible that the other team has diagnosed the conflict and has concluded that, for various appropriate reasons, an evaluative or a nonconsensual process would be preferable. If the other team is dragged into a facilitative process unwillingly, and cannot be sold on the process by the mediator or the other process neutral, quality of consent will be impaired.

To gain the advantages of facilitative approaches, a disputant can sometimes use persuasion. An individual who balks due to lack of knowledge can be educated. A competent mediator, for example, will always begin the mediation process by educating the participants about the nature of the process and its advantages. If the problem is reactive devaluation, sometimes the process can be ordered by a court rather than suggested by "the enemy." Sometimes, a facilitative

---

[6] One construction lawyer, asked whether federal construction ADR would be likely to become more facilitative or remain evaluative, responded, "My clients don't want to sit in no [sic] hot tub with the enemy!"

◆ **TABLE 22-4**   Factors Thought to Impede the Usefulness of Facilitative Mediation

FACTOR	EFFECTS	COMMENTS
Other disputant/ team refusing to participate	May not be possible to use facilitative mediation. Even if other team's participation can be coerced, quality of consent may be impaired.	Persuasion and "flashing the BATNA" can sometimes convince the other team to give the process a try. Many disputants are "won over" once they become involved.
Unfamiliar format disturbing to other disputant/team	Quality of consent may be impaired.	Facilitative mediation may sometimes be designed to include more familiar features.
One or both disputants or their teams unsure of their BATNAs	Quality of consent may be impaired.	Facilitative mediation can also produce BATNA clarification. An evaluative dispute resolution process may also be used to supplement mediation.
Large differences in perceptions of fact or law	Impasse may result unless BATNAs are clarified.	Facilitative mediation can also produce BATNA clarification. An evaluative dispute resolution process may also be used to supplement mediation.
Immediate enforcement needed	Irreparable harm may result from failure to act decisively.	Escalated conflict can produce an illusion that the other disputant is untrustworthy or that immediate unilateral action is the only solution. The phenomenon may prevent use of facilitative mediation when, in fact, it would be the best option.
Untrustworthy disputant	Irreparable harm may result from failure to act decisively.	Escalated conflict can produce an illusion that the other disputant is untrustworthy or that immediate unilateral action is the only solution. The phenomenon may prevent use of facilitative mediation when, in fact, it would be the best option.
Underlying interest in legal reform	Consensual processes may not address underlying interests.	Litigation and legislative reform are often the only appropriate recourse.
Disempowered disputant	Exploitation of disempowered disputant may occur in any dispute resolution process. Decisions will reflect poor quality of consent unless disputant acquires more power.	Many facilitative mediators use techniques that create empowerment. Disputant empowerment is a primary goal of transformative mediation. Involvement of legal counsel in the mediation process can also mitigate power imbalance and promote higher quality of consent.
Time and/or money very limited	Facilitative mediation can take longer than more evaluative, informal processes.	Evaluative processes are more likely to create impasse. If impasse occurs, the efficiency of the evaluative process will be very low. Adjudicatory, formal processes, such as formal arbitration and litigation, are the most expensive and lengthy of all the alternatives.

approach can be designed to seem more familiar: for example, a mediator can structure a facilitative process to feel more like a business meeting featuring brainstorming sessions than (what many lawyers dread, usually needlessly) a therapy session. Or a mediator may be chosen who will offer a free introductory session, at which he or she can sell the benefits of a collaborative process to the participants without requiring an up-front commitment. But it may not be possible to tempt the other side into a facilitative dispute resolution process, or consent may be obtained only begrudgingly. In that case, the benefits of collaborative, integrative

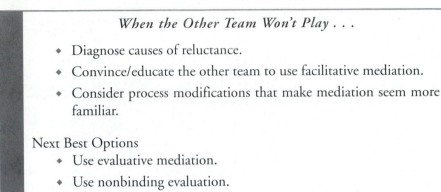

When the Other Team Won't Play . . .

- ◆ Diagnose causes of reluctance.
- ◆ Convince/educate the other team to use facilitative mediation.
- ◆ Consider process modifications that make mediation seem more familiar.

Next Best Options
- ◆ Use evaluative mediation.
- ◆ Use nonbinding evaluation.
- ◆ Use arbitration.

bargaining will have to be traded off against the quality of consent. In order to have psychological buy-in by a disputant who is uncomfortable with a facilitative process, one may need to abandon principled bargaining in favor of a more evaluative process that features a zero-sum characterization of the dispute. In other cases, the other disputant will have started litigation, and the first team will have no choice but to respond; or the other team will absolutely refuse any contact with the first team unless they file suit. If litigation does begin, it doesn't hurt to suggest settlement negotiations, with or without a mediator, frequently during the course of litigation.

Reason 2: Choosing a Facilitative Process Seems to Signal Weakness to the Other Side.   Some disputants and their teams avoid suggesting mediation, or other facilitative approaches, because they believe it will imply they have a weak case. But, if a facilitative process would be beneficial, choosing another process to avoid seeming weak is not an optimal choice. Indeed, although disputants with weak cases can potentially benefit from a collaborative negotiation process, they are more likely to be "taken to the cleaners" if they try to bang heads with a stronger opponent. Thus, this is a false consideration: the choice of mediation or another process featuring cooperation, although sometimes seen as a sign of weakness, isn't really a sign of a poor case.

What can a disputant or his or her team do to counter this problem? One option is to signal strength along with the suggestion for mediation or other facilitative or cooperative processes. One can "flash one's BATNA"—clearly indicate willingness to use adversarial tactics. One lawyer tells the story of attempting

If You're Afraid You'll Signal Weakness . . .

- ◆ Explain and educate the other team about the benefits of facilitative mediation.
- ◆ Flash your BATNA: signal strength to the other team.
- ◆ Relax: you'll have plenty of opportunity to correct this impression.

The Cartoon Bank   *"Norman won't collaborate."*

to negotiate collaboratively with her son's middle school for special accommodations for his learning disability. Upon encountering resistance, she wrote to the assistant principal, stating that she emphatically believed it to be in everyone's interests to work collaboratively to support effective learning and that she felt an adversarial approach would not promote her son's interests. "On the other hand," she wrote, "you should know that I have been trained as an attorney and am willing to use my training to advocate on behalf of my son if it becomes necessary." This display of a powerful BATNA promptly brought the school representative to the bargaining table for some amicable and constructive negotiation. Once in a facilitative setting, one can directly communicate one's commitment to a fair settlement that takes advantage of no one. If it is the other disputant who is afraid to signal weakness, it may be possible to educate the disputant's team that acceding to facilitation doesn't signal weakness and that mediation is not a cake walk.

Reason 3: One or Both Disputants Don't Know Their BATNAs.   Unless a disputant is crystal clear about his or her deeply seated interests and knows they can't be met outside of negotiation, the lack of a clear BATNA can prevent settlement from occurring. A disputant often has difficulty deciding whether to accept a settlement if he or she is uncertain whether there are better options. A disputant lacking knowledge of the BATNA may back into litigation accidentally.

There are at least three important reasons legal professionals often gravitate toward evaluative processes, which feature case valuation and BATNA clarification as the centerpiece. First, the lawyer's standard philosophical map causes

---

When the BATNA Is Unknown or Uncertain . . .

- Use BATNA analysis.
- Prepare the case.
- Use a facilitative mediator who uses reality-testing techniques.
- Use outside consultants who can clarify the BATNA.
- Encourage the use of outside consultants by the other team.

Next Best Options
- Agree to nonbinding evaluation within facilitative mediation.
- Use evaluative mediation.
- Use nonbinding evaluation.
- Use arbitration.

---

many lawyers, and their clients, to perceive impasses in the resolution of legal disputes as a mere matter of BATNA analysis. ("I think the case is worth only $5,000 at most, and he won't go below $30,000. If he just realized his case is chopped liver, we could settle it tonight.") Lawyers who believe the impasse to settlement is caused by an opponent's unrealistic BATNA estimate will often choose a process that drives home the reality of reduced expectations. Second, lawyers can't lose with this tactic. Sometimes, in their zeal to play the gladiator role, lawyers himself themselves inflate the BATNA, or clients may have developed unrealistic expectations as a result of the thought distortions that accompany conflict escalation. If the case evaluation seems to indicate that one's own BATNA is inflated, the client will be able to settle at close to the case evaluation without the lawyer's appearing weak or apathetic. Thus, consensual processes featuring evaluation solve a number of problems for lawyers. Third, most evaluative processes feel like processes lawyers are familiar with—trials, motions hearings,

---

If Widely Divergent BATNAs Seem to Be the Problem . . .

- The invisible veil may be distorting perception. Good conflict diagnosis can correct distorted perception.
- A good facilitative mediator can minimize invisible veil effects.
- Use a reality-testing mediator.

Next Best Options
- Agree to nonbinding evaluation within facilitative mediation.
- Use evaluative mediation.
- Use nonbinding evaluation.
- Use arbitration.

and settlement conferences. For all these reasons, evaluative processes have quite a lure for attorneys and clients.

Since facilitative processes have better potential than evaluative processes for reversing conflict escalation, promoting effective and creative resource allocation, and maximizing quality of consent, the team should consider whether there are ways to achieve BATNA clarification without abandoning facilitative negotiation or mediation. If the disputant and his or her team are uncertain of the BATNA, careful case preparation can help clarify it. If a large data-type conflict—a discrepancy between perceived BATNAs—seems to be occurring, a helpful approach is to *use evaluative approaches within a facilitative negotiation or mediation framework*— to design a multimodal process. For example, within the context of a facilitative mediation or negotiation, the disputants can agree to submit an issue to summary jury trial, to conduct a minitrial, or even to submit an issue to arbitration. The facilitative framework helps maintain the cooperative and creative approach, control any conflict escalation that seems to be resulting from the evaluation, and ensure that the disputants' decisions are purely autonomous and voluntary.

Reason 4: Limited Time and Money.   Although mediation of all sorts is usually touted as a time and money saver, in some situations evaluative processes are faster and cheaper. If, after the conflict is diagnosed, it appears that the reasons for preferring a facilitative process are relatively unimportant, using an evaluative process can sometimes be a shortcut.

There are occasions when both disputants are enthusiastic about reaching a quick settlement, see the issue as simply one of money, and are unlikely ever to see one another again. In these sorts of situations, an evaluation to clarify the BATNA can lead to prompt and efficient settlement. The online dispute resolution providers that feature blind bidding, detailed in Chapter 21, owe their market primarily to these sorts of cases. However, if there are hard feelings on either side, or an escalated conflict is involved, the evaluative process can promote positional bargaining, which can lead to lines drawn in the sand and then to

---

If Limits on Time and Money Are a Problem . . .

- ◆ Facilitative mediation takes longer than nonbinding evaluation, but nonbinding evaluation is more likely to result in impasse.

- ◆ Carefully diagnose conflict to determine motivation to settle and level of hostility. Use nonbinding evaluation if disputants are highly motivated to reach quick settlement *and* conflict is *not* escalated. Otherwise, stick to evaluative mediation.

Next Best Option

- ◆ If adjudication is used, stick to less formal options, which are quicker and cheaper.

impasse. If impasse occurs, the time and money savings will not take place. If quality of consent is truly unimportant and a quick, cheap result is paramount, informal arbitration, which offers a final outcome with minimal investment in preparation and hearing, may be the best option.

Reason 5: Need for a Rapid Enforcement Mechanism.   There are times when immediate recourse to the court system is necessary. For example, in a marital separation a spouse may need to stop the other spouse from abusing him or her. Or, in a consumer action against a business, the court may be needed to guard against dissipation of assets. To avoid irreparable harm, such cases need to be taken to court. After interim relief is obtained, the disputant and team can think carefully about whether it is possible to build enough protections into a facilitative settlement process that advantage can be gained from using one.

> Lester, a fifty-year-old concert violinist, went to Charlie's law office to file for divorce. He and Melanie had been married twenty-five years and had no children. Lester entered the marriage with a $600,000 inheritance from an uncle; however, over the course of the marriage, the inheritance slowly dissipated and there was nothing left. Melanie, a successful real estate broker, had been responsible for keeping track of the family finances during the marriage. When he had asked her where the money was going, she had responded that home repairs had been expensive, she had needed additional money to pay a large bill, or that they had needed an extra little bit to finance a vacation. Lester now suspected that Melanie had been planning to leave him for some time and had been gradually hiding assets, so that he could no longer find or get to them. He'd had his suspicions confirmed when Melanie decided to move a jointly owned $100,000 certificate of deposit to a bank in Florida, near her family of origin, in her sole name: the old bank had called their home about the transaction and had spoken to him to get some identifying information. Melanie's computer records did not indicate that they had owned this sort of asset, or anything else except their home and cars and a small checking account. Lester went to Charlie without first confronting Melanie; he was in terror that there were other assets and that, if Melanie became aware of his suspicions, she would systematically dispose of them.

If Immediate Enforcement Is Needed . . .

- Be ready to protect yourself and your team: *expect the best, but be ready for the worst.*
- The invisible veil, and resulting mistrust, can create the erroneous impression that immediate enforcement is necessary. Diagnose the conflict thoroughly to prevent perceptual distortion.
- Consider creative protection options, such as escrowing the amount in controversy.
- If protection options aren't available, use litigation.

In Lester's case, there isn't time for thorough conflict diagnosis to determine whether it is appropriate to use a facilitative process. Lester needs his legal advocate to protect the marital assets. After the immediate crisis has been taken care of, conflict diagnosis can take place, and appropriate strategies and tactics for meeting Lester's long-term interests can be developed.

Escalated conflict leads to a dramatic erosion of trust between disputants. A disputant in an escalated conflict may therefore perceive the situation as one requiring immediate interim relief, when, in fact, such is not the case. Moreover, at the outset of legal representation, attorneys are often forced into acting as if the other disputant were maliciously motivated, because they have insufficient information to conclude otherwise. Attorneys' ethical obligation to protect the client often requires them to behave as if a worst-case scenario were occurring, until an investigation can occur. Initial protective moves by just-hired attorneys often include heavy-handed, aggressive tactics such as filing lawsuits, initiating burdensome discovery, moving for protective orders, freezing or sequestering assets, and so forth. Thus, the very conduct designed to keep the client from being harmed, if it turns out to have been unnecessary, can escalate the conflict, damage the client's long-term interests, and demonize the other disputant in the eyes of the team, creating a self-fulfilling prophecy.

Thus, it behooves members of a disputant's legal team to think carefully before applying heavy-handed protective tactics, and to accompany the use of such tactics with communication designed to signal willingness to use facilitative strategies for resolving the dispute, provided that it is safe to do so. Conflict diagnosis should follow, to determine whether the initially defensive approach turns out to have been necessary. It is also helpful for the attorney to explain frankly to the other team why a heavy-handed tactic was used. Experienced attorneys on the other team will usually understand opposing counsel's protective strategy, and not hold it against him or her, but less experienced or emotionally involved lawyers may need the additional information. It's also important to avoid using any tactic that creates an irreparable rift with the other disputant's team unless absolutely unavoidable.

Sometimes, creative problem solving by the disputants' teams can defuse a tense situation, allowing a more facilitative approach to settlement.

Iris went to Bernie's law office to file for divorce. She and Forrest had no children and the couple had a house, but few other valuable assets. Iris said she and Forrest had been in a couple of physical altercations within the past two months as their marriage deteriorated but that, in general, they had simply drifted apart. Forrest emphatically did not want the divorce, but Iris had thought about it for two years, had thrashed the decision out with a therapist, and was very sure this was what she wanted.

Iris was frantic because Forrest had taken some very sexually explicit photographs of his wife, and, about a month ago during a heated argument, he had threatened to make them public if she left him. Bernie contacted Forrest's lawyer, who stated that Forrest had no intention of making the pictures public and would be amenable to settlement negotiations. But Forrest balked at having them destroyed—he felt they were his sole source of power over his wife. The two lawyers worked out a deal in which the negatives and all copies of the pictures would be placed in the hands of a close and trusted friend of the family. The materials were sealed, and the friend was asked never to break the seal. Forrest and Iris signed a stipulation requesting that, if settlement negotiations had not produced an agreement after ten months, the friend was to return the sealed package to Forrest; however, if negotiations were successful, they would instruct the friend to destroy all traces of the photos. Six months later, after difficult but productive negotiations, that's what happened.

Reason 6: Dishonest or Sociopathic Disputant or Legal Professional.   A consensual process will work only if the participants can be trusted to play reasonably fairly. Participants who are so lacking in a conscience, and confident of their ability to evade discovery, that they have no difficulty committing fraud during the course of the process usually must be dealt with in litigation. Some disputants, either sociopathic or very desperate, will agree to anything in order to delay the inevitable, or in the hope that the other party will eventually give up and go away. (That's not to say that litigation will invariably succeed when other processes fail—it's just easier to obtain enforcement if the disputant cheats.)

As with the need for immediate enforcement, conflict escalation often causes disputants to come to an erroneous conclusion that the other disputant is dishonest, sociopathic, or outright evil. For this reason, careful conflict diagnosis, performed as soon as possible, is warranted to ensure that the perception of the other side is accurate. Although litigation is often the only option when dealing with people who have no conscience, it is a very poor remedy compared with facilitative processes in other situations. If, after careful diagnosis, this issue cannot be clarified, it may be useful to secure basic protections, using litigation if necessary, but to accompany the filing of the lawsuit with explanatory communication inviting the possibility of a facilitative, consensual process with protections built in. If the situation permits, the disputant should go ahead with facilitative mediation and raise his or her concerns explicitly with the other disputant and the mediator.

If the Other Disputant Appears Untrustworthy . . .

- ◆ Be ready to protect yourself and your team: *expect the best, but be ready for the worst.*
- ◆ Recall that conflict escalation can create the false impression that the other disputant can't be trusted. Diagnose the conflict and try to discover the truth. Mistrusting the other disputant in error can be harmful and costly.
- ◆ Consider creative protection options. Explore protection issues explicitly during negotiation or mediation.
- ◆ Use litigation if you can't otherwise protect yourself and your team.

Reason 7: Underlying Interest in Legal Reform.   Litigation should be considered if, after careful conflict diagnosis, one concludes that an important source of the conflict is a structural or an interpersonal power imbalance that must be rectified through legal reform. Typically, only litigation, culminating in the pronouncement of an appellate court, can yield this sort of result.

It is often asserted that litigation should be used anytime a disputant suffers from disempowerment relative to the other disputant. This assertion is probably based on an assumption that the court will protect the disempowered litigant. But that's only true if the law is on his or her side. If so, then the disempowered disputant should seek out competent legal representation to maximize the effectiveness of his or her situation. The advocate may want to flash the BATNA to persuade the other side of the advantages of consensual settlement and to prepare for litigation in case the other disputant is unwilling to bend. If the law is *not* on the side of the disempowered person, then litigation is likely to be fruitless, unless social evolution makes overturning the existing law in the courts likely. A disputant who is disempowered because of a weak case, regardless of the morality of the situation, is unlikely to do well regardless of the setting. People usually bargain in the shadow of the law[7]—that is, people usually are constrained by their litigation ATNAs—and what a disputant might obtain in court is often reflected in what the disputant is able to obtain in an ADR process. Indeed, using a competent, collaboration-focused mediator can sometimes net the disempowered disputant a better outcome than an expensive, and fruitless, court case. A disputant who goes to a legal professional's office seemingly disempowered will benefit from the power analysis phase of conflict diagnosis: there may be hidden areas of power that could be mobilized during whatever dispute resolution process is selected. The specific nature of the disputant's power will affect the selection of a dispute resolution process as well. For example, a highly articulate disputant who is a mental-health professional is likely to be able to use his or her communication skills most effectively in a process such as mediation, whereas a professional athlete's agent is more likely to be proficient in the sort of communication that takes place during arbitration.

Litigation may be an effective option if the social climate is ripe for legal reform. For example, consider the parents whose children were legally prevented from attending white schools in Topeka, Kansas, in the late 1940s because of their race. To change the law allowing segregation in the public schools, these parents had to take their case to court. They eventually achieved the groundbreaking legal reform that culminated in the Supreme Court decision *Brown v. Board of Education*.[8] The families involved in the *Brown* litigation might have obtained better individual results (in a material sense) by seeking private settlements with the school board; however, it is unlikely that any amount of money or school placement could have undone the psychological damage done by living in a system in which a state law excluded one from going to school with

---

[7] See footnote 3 in Chapter 3.

[8] *Brown v. Board of Education,* 347 U.S. 483 (1954). In the *Brown* case, it was determined that having separate school systems for white and black children was inherently a denial of equal protection of the law under the Fourteenth Amendment of the Constitution, even if the facilities of such school systems were equivalent.

> ### *If You Have an Underlying Interest in Legal Reform . . .*
>
> ◆ Carefully conduct an interests analysis: balance the interest in legal reform against other important interests, values, and needs.
>
> ◆ Consider going ahead with facilitative mediation anyway if the legal climate is not ripe for reform.
>
> ◆ Consider the intangible advantages of social activism, even if victory in litigation seems unlikely.
>
> ◆ If the need for legal reform is paramount, and the time is ripe, litigate with the expectation of taking the case to the appellate level.

members of the dominant race. The *Brown* plaintiffs may also have benefited psychologically and even materially by their having been so instrumental in changing the course of the history of the civil rights movement.

In considering whether to litigate a matter for its legal reform potential, one must, of course, consider the downsides. *Brown v. Board of Education* had to be taken all the way to the United States Supreme Court. This is not a short or an inexpensive path, although in many cases volunteer attorneys are willing to help out in pathbreaking litigation with important consequences for social reform. Moreover, there is no guarantee that the position one is advocating will prevail. In fact, such cases are usually lost—they go against the prevailing law of the land. The disputant and legal team must balance the likelihood of losing against the intangible benefits of participating in legal pioneering, even if unsatisfying in its immediate outcome.

Reason 8: All the Alternatives Have Been Tried.   Consensual processes, mediation and nonbinding evaluation, are good at achieving a high quality of consent, because no disputant is forced to come to agreement. If these consensual processes fail to produce a settlement, obviously another process must be used. Quality of consent is not an issue if consent itself is unattainable.

If there is a strong interest in saving time and money, and if the parties can agree, a variant of arbitration may be useful. Informal arbitration is best if the need for efficiency outweighs the need for procedural protections, whereas a more formal version is better for situations in which achieving procedural justice is a highly valued interest. If the right to appeal is important, litigation should be considered in lieu of formal arbitration, although it will usually take longer to complete.

IN SEARCH OF MAGIC KEYS TO RESOLVING CONFLICT

Although conflict is as old as humankind itself, the scientific discipline of conflict resolution, with its implications for conflict diagnosis and ADR, is still in its earliest infancy. Within this discipline, the magic keys to reaching the goals of

Lawyers who successfully argued before the U.S. Supreme Court for abolition of segregation in public schools congratulate one another as they leave the court May 17, 1954, after announcement of the court's decision. They are (from left), George E. C. Hayes, Washington; Thurgood Marshall, New York; and James M. Nabrit. AP/Wide World Photos

If a Facilitative Process Has Been Tried and Settlement Did Not Result . . .

- Engage in careful interests and power analyses to determine what sort of evaluative process would be best.
- Consider nonbinding evaluation if motivation to settle is high and the conflict is not escalated.

Next Best Options
- Consider some form of informal arbitration to save time and money.
- Consider litigation or formal arbitration if procedural protections are important.

---

effective conflict diagnosis, masterful ADR selection, and constructive conflict resolution may be waiting. The student of these fields may find that the paths to finding these keys seem to shimmer: sometimes they appear clear, but at other times the ways fade into obscurity. The invisible veil is a strong and seductive influence on the handling of conflicts and disputes. Nonetheless, a cogent argument can be made that the lure of oversimplifying the messy business of human conflict into simple win-lose paradigms must no longer be surrendered to—we lose too much time, money, security, and human capital.

"Never, ever, think outside the box."

The Cartoon Bank

The advent of the twenty-first century, with its new and frightening challenges to peace and stability in the United States and throughout the world, creates a pressing crisis of need: we must strive to lift the veil and to understand the best ways to understand and handle conflict—in families, neighborhoods, business relationships, schools, and societies, as well as internationally. With the world becoming a smaller and more vulnerable place, we have no choice but to continue to engineer an increasingly effective array of alternative tools for dealing with interpersonal conflict and to develop proficiency in choosing the right tools to handle each dispute as it occurs. Our ability to meet the challenge this crisis presents is becoming more and more critical to our survival as a species. As a student of this messy business, you are in the forefront of a critical human mission. May you gain the clarity of vision to find the magic keys we all seek.

EXERCISES, PROJECTS, AND "THOUGHT EXPERIMENTS"

1. Raymond is a senior paralegal for Jordana DeLancie PC, attorney at law. Jordana takes on a new client, Ari Kaufman, who is seeking compensation due to allegedly fraudulent behavior by a business partner, Mort McLarty. Ari is anxious to litigate the issue and take his partner to the cleaners. Raymond

wonders whether litigation is the right option for Ari—Ari's feelings are clearly hurt, he seems out of control emotionally when he talks about the dispute, and he seems to have overly optimistic ideas of what will happen in court. Raymond suspects that the most important issues—in terms of what would best meet Ari's underlying goals, needs, and interests—are emotional, not monetary. Raymond feels that conflict diagnosis is important to clarify Ari's interests, values, and needs and to develop an appropriate strategy for addressing the dispute. But Ari is so angry that he will only talk about how evil and underhanded Mort has been to him and how he's going to give him what he really deserves. Raymond's time is billed to the client. What should Raymond do?

2. Suppose Raymond's firm decides to resolve issues such as that posed in question 1 by revealing upfront that the lawyers and legal assistants will use conflict diagnosis to develop effective strategies for client representation. Are there any problems with this approach?

   a. Consider the ABA's Model Rules of Professional Conduct, Rule 1.1: *"A lawyer shall provide competent representation to a client. Competent representation requires the legal knowledge, skill, thoroughness and preparation reasonably necessary for the representation."* What would a lawyer need to do to avoid transgressing this rule if he or she tried to diagnose a client's dispute?

   b. Is there a practical problem in marketing this lawyering approach to potential clients? If so, how could it be circumvented?

3. Select an ADR process appropriate to the following situations, and justify your selections:

   a. The Digi-Date dispute over revenues from its new computer game, presented in Chapters 1, 2, and 5

   b. The five legal disputes described in exercise 6, Chapter 2

   c. The alleged sexual harassment situation described in Chapters 1 and 5

4. Return to your conflict journal. If your conflict has ended, think back to a time prior to the resolution of your conflict.

   a. Using the conflict diagnosis approach described in this chapter, assess which form of dispute resolution would be best to resolve the conflict. Be sure to document, in writing, the process you used to reach your conclusion.

   b. Make the same assessment using the forum to the fuss grid (Table 22-1). Again, be sure to document your work.

   c. Compare the two methods referred to in exercises a and b. Discuss the benefits and drawbacks of each approach.

5. If you work in a law office, design a set of forms or a procedural manual that you can use to guide and streamline your use of conflict diagnosis principles in your work.

6. Your law firm represents Markus Maloney in a dispute brought by a subcontractor against Maloney and a general contractor for monies allegedly due and payable after maintenance work performed on his large residence.

The subcontractor and its general contractor are regular service providers for Maloney; accordingly, all parties decide to attempt to negotiate a settlement of the dispute. As a further protection of the parties' relationships, it has been decided that collaborative law would be used. The contract provided, *inter alia* ("among other things"), that "all documents expressly identified and entitled 'for settlement only in the Collaborative Law Process' shall be inadmissible for any purpose in any subsequent proceedings except as otherwise agreed between the parties."[9] The subcontractor, who is a Latino immigrant of modest means, says in negotiation that he heard that Maloney admitted he owed the money to his private secretary. In an effort to fulfill his obligation to negotiate in good faith, Maloney provided a copy of a memo that he wrote to his private secretary, in which he appears to admit full liability. Maloney has the document marked "for settlement only in the collaborative law process" and explains that the document refers only to his past belief that he was morally obligated to pay the money and that, after gaining a better understanding of the law from your firm, he now realizes that his belief was in error. The collaborative law negotiation breaks down, and the plaintiff subcontractor petitions the court to allow the document to be entered into evidence at trial. The plaintiff asserts that he is of limited financial means, that the document is highly probative, and that he should be entitled in the interests of justice to allow the factfinder at trial to assess its meaning. He cites *Olam v. Congress Mortgage Company,* 68 F. Supp. 2d 1110 (N.D. Cal., 1999) in support of his assertion, maintaining that the confidentiality of a collaborative negotiation should, like that of mediation, be waived if the interests of justice cannot otherwise be served. How would you counter this argument? If you were the judge hearing the issue, how would you decide it?

7. Emily Parrington files a grievance against her former attorney, Mike Snakeoil, in your state. She contends that Mike had a duty to advise her of ADR options and completely failed to do so. As a result, Emily chose to endure a two-year litigation trauma and paid $20,000 in legal fees, only to lose her slip-and-fall case against the assisted living facility in which she used to live. Emily has now learned about mediation and believes it would have been cheaper and quicker and might have enabled her to remain at her former home.

    a. Research the laws and legal ethics of your state. Would the legal ethics or grievance commission have a good case against Mike?

    b. Research the laws pertaining to attorney malpractice. Would Emily have a good valid cause of action against Mike? Is she likely to win? Why or why not?

---

[9] This provision is from the form *Stipulation and Order re. Collaborative Law* set forth in Tesler 2001, 146–51.

c. Do you think the general law concerning the liability of attorneys who fail to meaningfully advise their clients about ADR should change or at least be clarified? What change or clarification would you recommend, and why?

d. Is punishing attorneys who fail to advise their clients about ADR the best way to encourage them to do so? Design an optimum process for meeting the goal of having the duty to advise about ADR a necessary part of legal representation. Consider including elements that rely on the principles you learned in Part II of this text.

RECOMMENDED READINGS

Breger, M. J. 2000. Should an attorney be required to advise a client of ADR options? *Georgetown Journal of Legal Ethics* 13 (spring):427–76.

Cochran, R. F., Jr. 1999. ADR, the ABA, and client control: A proposal that the Model Rules require lawyers to present ADR options to clients. *South Texas Law Review* 41 (winter):183–201.

Coyne, W. F., Jr. 1999. The case for settlement counsel. *Ohio State Journal on Dispute Resolution* 14:367–413.

Mnookin, R., and L. Kornhauser. 1979. Bargaining in the shadow of the law: The case of divorce. *Yale Law Journal* 88:950–97.

Riskin, L. L., and J. E. Westbrook. 1997. Choosing and building dispute resolution processes. In *Dispute resolution and lawyers* (2nd ed., pp. 693–800). St. Paul, MN: West.

Sander, F. E. A., and S. Goldberg. 1994. Fitting the forum to the fuss: A user-friendly guide to selecting an ADR process. *Negotiation Journal* 10 (January): 49–68.

Schneider, A. K. 2000. Building a pedagogy of problem-solving: Learning to choose among ADR processes. *Harvard Negotiation Law Review* 5 (spring):113–35.

Tesler, P. H. 2001. *Collaborative law: Achieving effective resolution in divorce without litigation.* Chicago: American Bar Association, Section of Family Law.

Appendix A

Alternative Dispute Resolution Act of 1998

28 USC §§651 *ET SEQ.*

SECTION 1. SHORT TITLE.

This Act may be cited as the Alternative Dispute Resolution Act of 1998.

SEC. 2. FINDINGS AND DECLARATION OF POLICY.

Congress finds that—

1. alternative dispute resolution, when supported by the bench and bar, and utilizing properly trained neutrals in a program adequately administered by the court, has the potential to provide a variety of benefits, including greater satisfaction of the parties, innovative methods of resolving disputes, and greater efficiency in achieving settlements;
2. certain forms of alternative dispute resolution, including mediation, early neutral evaluation, minitrials, and voluntary arbitration, may have potential to reduce the large backlog of cases now pending in some Federal courts throughout the United States, thereby allowing the courts to process their remaining cases more efficiently; and
3. the continued growth of Federal appellate court-annexed mediation programs suggests that this form of alternative dispute resolution can be equally effective in resolving disputes in the Federal trial courts; therefore, the

district courts should consider including mediation in their local alternative dispute resolution programs.

28 USC §651. AUTHORIZATION OF ALTERNATIVE DISPUTE RESOLUTION

a. *Definition*   For purposes of this chapter, an alternative dispute resolution process includes any process or procedure, other than an adjudication by a presiding judge, in which a neutral third party participates to assist in the resolution of issues in controversy, through processes such as early neutral evaluation, mediation, minitrial, and arbitration as provided in sections 654 through 658.
b. *Authority*   Each United States district court shall authorize, by local rule adopted under section 2071(a), the use of alternative dispute resolution processes in all civil actions, including adversary proceedings in bankruptcy, in accordance with this chapter, except that the use of arbitration may be authorized only as provided in section 654. Each United States district court shall devise and implement its own alternative dispute resolution program, by local rule adopted under section 2071(a), to encourage and promote the use of alternative dispute resolution in its district.
c. *Existing Alternative Dispute Resolution Programs*   In those courts where an alternative

dispute resolution program is in place on the date of the enactment of the Alternative Dispute Resolution Act of 1998, the court shall examine the effectiveness of that program and adopt such improvements to the program as are consistent with the provisions and purposes of this chapter.

d. *Administration of Alternative Dispute Resolution Programs* Each United States district court shall designate an employee, or a judicial officer, who is knowledgeable in alternative dispute resolution practices and processes to implement, administer, oversee, and evaluate the court's alternative dispute resolution program. Such person may also be responsible for recruiting, screening, and training attorneys to serve as neutrals and arbitrators in the court's alternative dispute resolution program.

e. *Title 9 Not Affected* This chapter shall not affect title 9, United States Code.

f. *Program Support* The Federal Judicial Center and the Administrative Office of the United States Courts are authorized to assist the district courts in the establishment and improvement of alternative dispute resolution programs by identifying particular practices employed in successful programs and providing additional assistance as needed and appropriate.

28 USC §652. JURISDICTION

a. *Consideration of Alternative Dispute Resolution in Appropriate Cases* Notwithstanding any provision of law to the contrary and except as provided in subsections (b) and (c), each district court shall, by local rule adopted under section 2071(a), require that litigants in all civil cases consider the use of an alternative dispute resolution process at an appropriate stage in the litigation. Each district court shall provide litigants in all civil cases with at least one alternative dispute resolution process, including, but not limited to, mediation, early

neutral evaluation, minitrial, and arbitration as authorized in sections 654 through 658. Any district court that elects to require the use of alternative dispute resolution in certain cases may do so only with respect to mediation, early neutral evaluation, and, if the parties consent, arbitration.

b. *Actions Exempted from Consideration of Alternative Dispute Resolution* Each district court may exempt from the requirements of this section specific cases or categories of cases in which use of alternative dispute resolution would not be appropriate. In defining these exemptions, each district court shall consult with members of the bar, including the United States Attorney for that district.

c. *Authority of the Attorney General* Nothing in this section shall alter or conflict with the authority of the Attorney General to conduct litigation on behalf of the United States, with the authority of any Federal agency authorized to conduct litigation in the United States courts, or with any delegation of litigation authority by the Attorney General.

d. *Confidentiality Provisions* Until such time as rules are adopted under chapter 131 of this title providing for the confidentiality of alternative dispute resolution processes under this chapter, each district court shall, by local rule adopted under section 2071(a), provide for the confidentiality of the alternative dispute resolution processes and to prohibit disclosure of confidential dispute resolution communications.

28 USC §653. NEUTRALS

a. *Panel of Neutrals* Each district court that authorizes the use of alternative dispute resolution processes shall adopt appropriate processes for making neutrals available for use by the parties for each category of process offered. Each district court shall promulgate its own procedures and criteria for the selection of neutrals on its panels.

b. *Qualifications and Training*   Each person serving as a neutral in an alternative dispute resolution process should be qualified and trained to serve as a neutral in the appropriate alternative dispute resolution process. For this purpose, the district court may use, among others, magistrate judges who have been trained to serve as neutrals in alternative dispute resolution processes, professional neutrals from the private sector, and persons who have been trained to serve as neutrals in alternative dispute resolution processes. Until such time as rules are adopted under chapter 131 of this title relating to the disqualification of neutrals, each district court shall issue rules under section 2071(a) relating to the disqualification of neutrals (including, where appropriate, disqualification under section 455 of this title, other applicable law, and professional responsibility standards).

28 USC §654. ARBITRATION

a. *Referral of Actions to Arbitration*   Notwithstanding any provision of law to the contrary and except as provided in subsections (a), (b), and (c) of section 652 and subsection (d) of this section, a district court may allow the referral to arbitration of any civil action (including any adversary proceeding in bankruptcy) pending before it when the parties consent, except that referral to arbitration may not be made where—

   1. the action is based on an alleged violation of a right secured by the Constitution of the United States;
   2. jurisdiction is based in whole or in part on section 1343 of this title; or
   3. the relief sought consists of money damages in an amount greater than $150,000.

b. *Safeguards in Consent Cases*   Until such time as rules are adopted under chapter 131 of this title relating to procedures described in this subsection, the district court shall, by local rule adopted under section 2071(a), establish procedures to ensure that any civil action in

which arbitration by consent is allowed under subsection (a)—

   1. consent to arbitration is freely and knowingly obtained; and
   2. no party or attorney is prejudiced for refusing to participate in arbitration.

c. *Presumptions*   For purposes of subsection (a)(3), a district court may presume damages are not in excess of $150,000 unless counsel certifies that damages exceed such amount.

d. *Existing Programs*   Nothing in this chapter is deemed to affect any program in which arbitration is conducted pursuant to section title IX of the Judicial Improvements and Access to Justice Act (Public Law 100–702), as amended by section 1 of Public Law 105–53.

28 USC §655. ARBITRATORS

a. *Powers of Arbitrators*   An arbitrator to whom an action is referred under section 654 shall have the power, within the judicial district of the district court which referred the action to arbitration—

   1. to conduct arbitration hearings;
   2. to administer oaths and affirmations; and
   3. to make awards.

b. *Standards for Certification*   Each district court that authorizes arbitration shall establish standards for the certification of arbitrators and shall certify arbitrators to perform services in accordance with such standards and this chapter. The standards shall include provisions requiring that any arbitrator—

   1. shall take the oath or affirmation described in section 453; and
   2. shall be subject to the disqualification rules under section 455.

c. *Immunity*   All individuals serving as arbitrators in an alternative dispute resolution program under this chapter are performing quasi-judicial functions and are entitled to the immunities and protections that the law accords to persons serving in such capacity.

28 USC §656. SUBPOENAS

Rule 45 of the Federal Rules of Civil Procedure (relating to subpoenas) applies to subpoenas for the attendance of witnesses and the production of documentary evidence at an arbitration hearing under this chapter.

28 USC §657. ARBITRATION AWARD AND JUDGMENT

a. *Filing and Effect of Arbitration Award* An arbitration award made by an arbitrator under this chapter, along with proof of service of such award on the other party by the prevailing party or by the plaintiff, shall be filed promptly after the arbitration hearing is concluded with the clerk of the district court that referred the case to arbitration. Such award shall be entered as the judgment of the court after the time has expired for requesting a trial *de novo.* The judgment so entered shall be subject to the same provisions of law and shall have the same force and effect as a judgment of the court in a civil action, except that the judgment shall not be subject to review in any other court by appeal or otherwise.

b. *Sealing of Arbitration Award* The district court shall provide, by local rule adopted under section 2071(a), that the contents of any arbitration award made under this chapter shall not be made known to any judge who might be assigned to the case until the district court has entered final judgment in the action or the action has otherwise terminated.

c. *Trial De Novo of Arbitration Awards*

  1. *Time for Filing Demand* Within 30 days after the filing of an arbitration award with a district court under subsection (a), any party may file a written demand for a trial *de novo* in the district court.

  2. *Action Restored to Court Docket* Upon a demand for a trial *de novo,* the action shall be restored to the docket of the court and treated for all purposes as if it had not been referred to arbitration.

  3. *Exclusion of Evidence of Arbitration* The court shall not admit at the trial *de novo* any evidence that there has been an arbitration proceeding, the nature or amount of any award, or any other matter concerning the conduct of the arbitration proceeding, unless

     (A) the evidence would otherwise be admissible in the court under the Federal Rules of Evidence; or

     (B) the parties have otherwise stipulated.

28 USC §658. COMPENSATION OF ARBITRATORS AND NEUTRALS

a. *Compensation* The district court shall, subject to regulations approved by the Judicial Conference of the United States, establish the amount of compensation, if any, that each arbitrator or neutral shall receive for services rendered in each case under this chapter.

b. *Transportation Allowances* Under regulations prescribed by the Director of the Administrative Office of the United States Courts, a district court may reimburse arbitrators and other neutrals for actual transportation expenses necessarily incurred in the performance of duties under this chapter.

Appendix B

Administrative Dispute Resolution Act of 1996
Selected Provisions

SEC. 1. SHORT TITLE

This Act may be cited as the "Administrative Dispute Resolution Act of 1996."

SEC. 2. FINDINGS

The Congress finds that—

1. administrative procedure, as embodied in chapter 5 of title 5, United States Code, and other statutes, is intended to offer a prompt, expert, and inexpensive means of resolving disputes as an alternative to litigation in the Federal courts;

2. administrative proceedings have become increasingly formal, costly, and lengthy resulting in unnecessary expenditures of time and in a decreased likelihood of achieving consensual resolution of disputes;

3. alternative means of dispute resolution have been used in the private sector for many years and, in appropriate circumstances, have yielded decisions that are faster, less expensive, and less contentious;

4. such alternative means can lead to more creative, efficient, and sensible outcomes;

5. such alternative means may be used advantageously in a wide variety of administrative programs;

6. explicit authorization of the use of well-tested dispute resolution techniques will

eliminate ambiguity of agency authority under existing law;

7. Federal agencies may not only receive the benefit of techniques that were developed in the private sector, but may also take the lead in the further development and refinement of such techniques; and

8. the availability of a wide range of dispute resolution procedures, and an increased understanding of the most effective use of such procedures, will enhance the operation of the Government and better serve the public.

SEC. 3. PROMOTION OF ALTERNATIVE MEANS OF DISPUTE RESOLUTION

a. *Promulgation of Agency Policy*   Each agency shall adopt a policy that addresses the use of alternative means of dispute resolution and case management. In developing such a policy, each agency shall—

1. consult with the agency designated by, or the interagency committee designated or established by, the President under section 573 of title 5, United States Code, to facilitate and encourage agency use of alternative dispute resolution under subchapter IV of chapter 5 of such title; and

2. examine alternative means of resolving disputes in connection with

(A) formal and informal adjudications;

(B) rulemakings;

(C) enforcement actions;

(D) issuing and revoking licenses or permits;

(E) contract administration;

(F) litigation brought by or against the agency; and

(G) other agency actions.

b. *Dispute Resolution Specialists* The head of each agency shall designate a senior official to be the dispute resolution specialist of the agency. Such official shall be responsible for the implementation of

1. the provisions of this Act and the amendments made by this Act; and

2. the agency policy developed under subsection (a)

c. *Training* Each agency shall provide for training on a regular basis for the dispute resolution specialist of the agency and other employees involved in implementing the policy of the agency developed under subsection (a). Such training should encompass the theory and practice of negotiation, mediation, arbitration, or related techniques. The dispute resolution specialist shall periodically recommend to the agency head agency employees who would benefit from similar training.

5 USC §571. DEFINITIONS

For the purposes of this subchapter, the term—

1. "agency" has the same meaning as in section 551(1) of this title;

2. "administrative program" includes a Federal function which involves protection of the public interest and the determination of rights, privileges, and obligations of private persons through rule making, adjudication, licensing, or investigation, as those terms are used in subchapter II of this chapter;

3. "alternative means of dispute resolution" means any procedure that is used to resolve issues in controversy, including, but not limited to, conciliation, facilitation, mediation, factfinding, minitrials, arbitration, and use of ombuds, or any combination thereof;

4. "award" means any decision by an arbitrator resolving the issues in controversy;

5. "dispute resolution communication" means any oral or written communication prepared for the purposes of a dispute resolution proceeding, including any memoranda, notes or work product of the neutral, parties or nonparty participant; except that a written agreement to enter into a dispute resolution proceeding, or final written agreement or arbitral award reached as a result of a dispute resolution proceeding, is not a dispute resolution communication;

6. "dispute resolution proceeding" means any process in which an alternative means of dispute resolution is used to resolve an issue in controversy in which a neutral is appointed and specified parties participate;

7. "in confidence" means, with respect to information, that the information is provided—

A. with the expressed intent of the source that it not be disclosed; or

B. under circumstances that would create the reasonable expectation on behalf of the source that the information will not be disclosed;

8. "issue in controversy" means an issue which is material to a decision concerning an administrative program of an agency, and with which there is disagreement—

A. between an agency and persons who would be substantially affected by the decision; or

B. between persons who would be substantially affected by the decision;

9. "neutral" means an individual who, with respect to an issue in controversy, functions specifically to aid the parties in resolving the controversy;

10. "party" means—
    A. for a proceeding with named parties, the same as in section 551(3) of this title; and
    B. for a proceeding without named parties, a person who will be significantly affected by the decision in the proceeding and who participates in the proceeding;
11. "person" has the same meaning as in section 551(2) of this title; and
12. "roster" means a list of persons qualified to provide services as neutrals.

5 USC §572. GENERAL AUTHORITY

a. An agency may use a dispute resolution proceeding for the resolution of an issue in controversy that relates to an administrative program, if the parties agree to such proceeding.
b. An agency shall consider not using a dispute resolution proceeding if—
    1. a definitive or authoritative resolution of the matter is required for precedential value, and such a proceeding is not likely to be accepted generally as an authoritative precedent;
    2. the matter involves or may bear upon significant questions of Government policy that require additional procedures before a final resolution may be made, and such a proceeding would not likely serve to develop a recommended policy for the agency;
    3. maintaining established policies is of special importance, so that variations among individual decisions are not increased and such a proceeding would not likely reach consistent results among individual decisions;
    4. the matter significantly affects persons or organizations who are not parties to the proceeding;
    5. a full public record of the proceeding is important, and a dispute resolution proceeding cannot provide such a record; and
    6. the agency must maintain continuing jurisdiction over the matter with authority to alter the disposition of the matter in the light of changed circumstances, and a dispute resolution proceeding would interfere with the agency's fulfilling that requirement.
c. Alternative means of dispute resolution authorized under this subchapter are voluntary procedures which supplement rather than limit other available agency dispute resolution techniques.

5 USC §573. NEUTRALS

a. A neutral may be a permanent or temporary officer or employee of the Federal Government or any other individual who is acceptable to the parties to a dispute resolution proceeding. A neutral shall have no official, financial, or personal conflict of interest with respect to the issues in controversy, unless such interest is fully disclosed in writing to all parties and all parties agree that the neutral may serve.
b. A neutral who serves as a conciliator, facilitator, or mediator serves at the will of the parties.
c. The President shall designate an agency or designate or establish an interagency committee to facilitate and encourage agency use of dispute resolution under this subchapter. Such agency or interagency committee, in consultation with other appropriate Federal agencies and professional organizations experienced in matters concerning dispute resolution, shall
    1. encourage and facilitate agency use of alternative means of dispute resolution; and
    2. develop procedures that permit agencies to obtain the services of neutrals on an expedited basis.

d. An agency may use the services of one or more employees of other agencies to serve as neutrals in dispute resolution proceedings. The agencies may enter into an interagency agreement that provides for the reimbursement by the user agency or the parties of the full or partial cost of the services of such an employee.

e. Any agency may enter into a contract with any person for services as a neutral, or for training in connection with alternative means of dispute resolution. The parties in a dispute resolution proceeding shall agree on compensation for the neutral that is fair and reasonable to the Government.

5 USC §574.
CONFIDENTIALITY

a. Except as provided in subsections (d) and (e), a neutral in a dispute resolution proceeding shall not voluntarily disclose or through discovery or compulsory process be required to disclose any dispute resolution communication or any communication provided in confidence to the neutral, unless

1. all parties to the dispute resolution proceeding and the neutral consent in writing, and, if the dispute resolution communication was provided by a nonparty participant, that participant also consents in writing;

2. the dispute resolution communication has already been made public;

3. the dispute resolution communication is required by statute to be made public, but a neutral should make such communication public only if no other person is reasonably available to disclose the communication; or

4. a court determines that such testimony or disclosure is necessary to—

   (A) prevent a manifest injustice;

   (B) help establish a violation of law; or

   (C) prevent harm to the public health or safety, of sufficient magnitude in the particular case to outweigh the integrity of dispute resolution proceedings in general by reducing the confidence of parties in future cases that their communications will remain confidential.

b. A party to a dispute resolution proceeding shall not voluntarily disclose or through discovery or compulsory process be required to disclose any dispute resolution communication, unless

1. the communication was prepared by the party seeking disclosure;

2. all parties to the dispute resolution proceeding consent in writing;

3. the dispute resolution communication has already been made public;

4. the dispute resolution communication is required by statute to be made public;

5. a court determines that such testimony or disclosure is necessary to

   (A) prevent a manifest injustice;

   (B) help establish a violation of law; or

   (C) prevent harm to the public health and safety, of sufficient magnitude in the particular case to outweigh the integrity of dispute resolution proceedings in general by reducing the confidence of parties in future cases that their communications will remain confidential;

6. the dispute resolution communication is relevant to determining the existence or meaning of an agreement or award that resulted from the dispute resolution proceeding or to the enforcement of such an agreement or award; or

7. except for dispute resolution communications generated by the neutral, the dispute resolution communication was provided to or was available to all parties to the dispute resolution proceeding.

c. Any dispute resolution communication that is disclosed in violation of subsection (a) or (b), shall not be admissible in any proceeding relating to the issues in controversy with respect to which the communication was made.

d. 1. The parties may agree to alternative confidential procedures for disclosures by a neutral. Upon such agreement the parties shall inform the neutral before the commencement of the dispute resolution proceeding of any modifications to the provisions of subsection (a) that will govern the confidentiality of the dispute resolution proceeding. If the parties do not so inform the neutral, subsection (a) shall apply.

2. To qualify for the exemption established under subsection (j), an alternative confidential procedure under this subsection may not provide for less disclosure than the confidential procedures otherwise provided under this section.

e. If a demand for disclosure, by way of discovery request or other legal process, is made upon a neutral regarding a dispute resolution communication, the neutral shall make reasonable efforts to notify the parties and any affected nonparty participants of the demand. Any party or affected nonparty participant who receives such notice and within 15 calendar days does not offer to defend a refusal of the neutral to disclose the requested information shall have waived any objection to such disclosure.

f. Nothing in this section shall prevent the discovery or admissibility of any evidence that is otherwise discoverable, merely because the evidence was presented in the course of a dispute resolution proceeding.

g. Subsections (a) and (b) shall have no effect on the information and data that are necessary to document an agreement reached or order issued pursuant to a dispute resolution proceeding.

h. Subsections (a) and (b) shall not prevent the gathering of information for research or educational purposes, in cooperation with other agencies, governmental entities, or dispute resolution programs, so long as the parties and the specific issues in controversy are not identifiable.

i. Subsections (a) and (b) shall not prevent use of a dispute resolution communication to resolve a dispute between the neutral in a dispute resolution proceeding and a party to or participant in such proceeding, so long as such dispute resolution communication is disclosed only to the extent necessary to resolve such dispute.

j. A dispute resolution communication which is between a neutral and a party and which may not be disclosed under this section shall also be exempt from disclosure under section 552(b)(3).

5 USC §575. AUTHORIZATION OF ARBITRATION

a. 1. Arbitration may be used as an alternative means of dispute resolution whenever all parties consent. Consent may be obtained either before or after an issue in controversy has arisen. A party may agree to—

   (A) submit only certain issues in controversy to arbitration; or

   (B) arbitration on the condition that the award must be within a range of possible outcomes.

2. The arbitration agreement that sets forth the subject matter submitted to the arbitrator shall be in writing. Each such arbitration agreement shall specify a maximum award that may be issued by the arbitrator and may specify other conditions limiting the range of possible outcomes.

3. An agency may not require any person to consent to arbitration as a condition of entering into a contract or obtaining a benefit.

b. An officer or employee of an agency shall not offer to use arbitration for the resolution of issues in controversy unless such officer or employee—

1. would otherwise have authority to enter into a settlement concerning the matter; or
2. is otherwise specifically authorized by the agency to consent to the use of arbitration.

c. Prior to using binding arbitration under this subchapter, the head of an agency, in consultation with the Attorney General and after taking into account the factors in section 572(b), shall issue guidance on the appropriate use of binding arbitration and when an officer or employee of the agency has authority to settle an issue in controversy through binding arbitration.

5 USC §576. ENFORCEMENT OF ARBITRATION AGREEMENTS

An agreement to arbitrate a matter to which this subchapter applies is enforceable pursuant to section 4 of title 9, and no action brought to enforce such an agreement shall be dismissed nor shall relief therein be denied on the grounds that it is against the United States or that the United States is an indispensable party.

5 USC §577. ARBITRATORS

a. The parties to an arbitration proceeding shall be entitled to participate in the selection of the arbitrator.
b. The arbitrator shall be a neutral who meets the criteria of section 573 of this title.

5 USC §578. AUTHORITY OF THE ARBITRATOR

An arbitrator to whom a dispute is referred under this subchapter may—

1. regulate the course of and conduct arbitral hearings;
2. administer oaths and affirmations;
3. compel the attendance of witnesses and production of evidence at the hearing under the provisions of section 7 of title 9 only to the extent the agency involved is otherwise authorized by law to do so; and
4. make awards.

5 USC §579. ARBITRATION PROCEEDINGS

a. The arbitrator shall set a time and place for the hearing on the dispute and shall notify the parties not less than 5 days before the hearing.
b. Any party wishing a record of the hearing shall

1. be responsible for the preparation of such record;
2. notify the other parties and the arbitrator of the preparation of such record;
3. furnish copies to all identified parties and the arbitrator; and
4. pay all costs for such record, unless the parties agree otherwise or the arbitrator determines that the costs should be apportioned.

c. 1. The parties to the arbitration are entitled to be heard, to present evidence material to the controversy, and to cross-examine witnesses appearing at the hearing.
2. The arbitrator may, with the consent of the parties, conduct all or part of the hearing by telephone, television, computer, or other electronic means, if each party has an opportunity to participate.
3. The hearing shall be conducted expeditiously and in an informal manner.
4. The arbitrator may receive any oral or documentary evidence, except that irrelevant, immaterial, unduly repetitious, or privileged evidence may be excluded by the arbitrator.

5. The arbitrator shall interpret and apply relevant statutory and regulatory requirements, legal precedents, and policy directives.

d. No interested person shall make or knowingly cause to be made to the arbitrator an unauthorized ex parte communication relevant to the merits of the proceeding, unless the parties agree otherwise. If a communication is made in violation of this subsection, the arbitrator shall ensure that a memorandum of the communication is prepared and made a part of the record, and that an opportunity for rebuttal is allowed. Upon receipt of a communication made in violation of this subsection, the arbitrator may, to the extent consistent with the interests of justice and the policies underlying this subchapter, require the offending party to show cause why the claim of such party should not be resolved against such party as a result of the improper conduct.

e. The arbitrator shall make the award within 30 days after the close of the hearing, or the date of the filing of any briefs authorized by the arbitrator, whichever date is later, unless

1. the parties agree to some other time limit; or
2. the agency provides by rule for some other time limit.

5 USC §580. ARBITRATION AWARDS

a. 1. Unless the agency provides otherwise by rule, the award in an arbitration proceeding under this subchapter shall include a brief, informal discussion of the factual and legal basis for the award, but formal findings of fact or conclusions of law shall not be required.

2. The prevailing parties shall file the award with all relevant agencies, along with proof of service on all parties.

b. The award in an arbitration proceeding shall become final 30 days after it is served on all parties. Any agency that is a party to the proceeding may extend this 30-day period for an additional 30-day period by serving a notice of such extension on all other parties before the end of the first 30-day period.

c. A final award is binding on the parties to the arbitration proceeding, and may be enforced pursuant to sections 9 through 13 of title 9. No action brought to enforce such an award shall be dismissed nor shall relief therein be denied on the grounds that it is against the United States or that the United States is an indispensable party.

d. An award entered under this subchapter in an arbitration proceeding may not serve as an estoppel in any other proceeding for any issue that was resolved in the proceeding. Such an award also may not be used as precedent or otherwise be considered in any factually unrelated proceeding, whether conducted under this subchapter, by an agency, or in a court, or in any other arbitration proceeding.

5 USC §581. JUDICIAL REVIEW

a. Notwithstanding any other provision of law, any person adversely affected or aggrieved by an award made in an arbitration proceeding conducted under this subchapter may bring an action for review of such award only pursuant to the provisions of sections 9 through 13 of title 9.

b. A decision by an agency to use or not to use a dispute resolution proceeding under this subchapter shall be committed to the discretion of the agency and shall not be subject to judicial review, except that arbitration shall be subject to judicial review under section 10(b) of title 9.

Uniform Mediation Act

Selected Provisions

National Conference of Commissioners on Uniform State Laws
Approved and Recommended August 10–17, 2001
Copyright © 2001 By National Conference
of Commissioners on Uniform State Laws
www.nccusl.org
Author's Note: Bracketed material contains text adopted by the Commissioners as optional.

SECTION 1. TITLE.

This [Act] may be cited as the Uniform Mediation Act.

SECTION 2. DEFINITIONS.

In this [Act]:

1. "Mediation" means a process in which a mediator facilitates communication and negotiation between parties to assist them in reaching a voluntary agreement regarding their dispute.

2. "Mediation communication" means a statement, whether oral or in a record or verbal or nonverbal, that occurs during a mediation or is made for purposes of considering, conducting, participating in, initiating, continuing, or reconvening a mediation or retaining a mediator.

3. "Mediator" means an individual who conducts a mediation.

4. "Nonparty participant" means a person, other than a party or mediator, that participates in a mediation.

5. "Mediation party" means a person that participates in a mediation and whose agreement is necessary to resolve the dispute.

6. "Person" means an individual, corporation, business trust, estate, trust, partnership, limited liability company, association, joint venture, government; governmental subdivision, agency, or instrumentality; public corporation, or any other legal or commercial entity.

7. "Proceeding" means:

   a. a judicial, administrative, arbitral, or other adjudicative process, including related pre-hearing and post-hearing motions, conferences, and discovery; or

   b. a legislative hearing or similar process.

8. "Record" means information that is inscribed on a tangible medium or that is stored in an electronic or other medium and is retrievable in perceivable form.

9. "Sign" means:

   a. to execute or adopt a tangible symbol with the present intent to authenticate a record; or

   b. to attach or logically associate an electronic symbol, sound, or process to or with a record with the present intent to authenticate a record.

SECTION 3. SCOPE.

a. Except as otherwise provided in subsection (b) or (c), this [Act] applies to a mediation in which:

   1. the mediation parties are required to mediate by statute or court or administrative agency rule or referred to mediation by a court, administrative agency, or arbitrator;

   2. the mediation parties and the mediator agree to mediate in a record that demonstrates an expectation that mediation communications will be privileged against disclosure; or

   3. the mediation parties use as a mediator an individual who holds himself or herself out as a mediator or the mediation is provided by a person that holds itself out as providing mediation.

b. The [Act] does not apply to a mediation:

   1. relating to the establishment, negotiation, administration, or termination of a collective bargaining relationship;

   2. relating to a dispute that is pending under or is part of the processes established by a collective bargaining agreement, except that the [Act] applies to a mediation arising out of a dispute that has been filed with an administrative agency or court;

   3. conducted by a judge who might make a ruling on the case; or

   4. conducted under the auspices of:

     (A) a primary or secondary school if all the parties are students or

     (B) a correctional institution for youths if all the parties are residents of that institution.

c. If the parties agree in advance in a signed record, or a record of proceeding reflects agreement by the parties, that all or part of a mediation is not privileged, the privileges under Sections 4 through 6 do not apply to the mediation or part agreed upon. However, Sections 4 through 6 apply to a mediation communication made by a person that has not received actual notice of the agreement before the communication is made.

SECTION 4. PRIVILEGE AGAINST DISCLOSURE; ADMISSIBILITY; DISCOVERY.

a. Except as otherwise provided in Section 6, a mediation communication is privileged as provided in subsection (b) and is not subject to discovery or admissible in evidence in a proceeding unless waived or precluded as provided by Section 5.

b. In a proceeding, the following privileges apply:

   1. A mediation party may refuse to disclose, and may prevent any other person from disclosing, a mediation communication.

   2. A mediator may refuse to disclose a mediation communication, and may prevent any other person from disclosing a mediation communication of the mediator.

   3. A nonparty participant may refuse to disclose, and may prevent any other person from disclosing, a mediation communication of the nonparty participant.

c. Evidence or information that is otherwise admissible or subject to discovery does not become inadmissible or protected from discovery solely by reason of its disclosure or use in a mediation.

SECTION 5. WAIVER AND PRECLUSION OF PRIVILEGE.

a. A privilege under Section 4 may be waived in a record or orally during a proceeding if it is expressly waived by all parties to the mediation and:

1. in the case of the privilege of a mediator, it is expressly waived by the mediator; and
2. in the case of the privilege of a nonparty participant, it is expressly waived by the nonparty participant.

b. A person that discloses or makes a representation about a mediation communication which prejudices another person in a proceeding is precluded from asserting a privilege under Section 4, but only to the extent necessary for the person prejudiced to respond to the representation or disclosure.

c. A person that intentionally uses a mediation to plan, attempt to commit or commit a crime, or to conceal an ongoing crime or ongoing criminal activity is precluded from asserting a privilege under Section 4.

SECTION 6. EXCEPTIONS TO PRIVILEGE.

a. There is no privilege under Section 4 for a mediation communication that is:

1. in an agreement evidenced by a record signed by all parties to the agreement;
2. available to the public under or made during a session of a mediation which is open, or is required by law to be open, to the public;
3. a threat or statement of a plan to inflict bodily injury or commit a crime of violence;
4. intentionally used to plan a crime, attempt to commit or commit a crime, or to conceal an ongoing crime or ongoing criminal activity;
5. sought or offered to prove or disprove a claim or complaint of professional misconduct or malpractice filed against a mediator;
6. except as otherwise provided in subsection (c), sought or offered to prove or disprove a claim or complaint of professional misconduct or malpractice filed against a

mediation party, nonparty participant, or representative of a party based on conduct occurring during a mediation; or
7. sought or offered to prove or disprove abuse, neglect, abandonment, or exploitation in a proceeding in which a child or adult protective services agency is a party, unless the

[Alternative A: [State to insert, for example, child or adult protection] case is referred by a court to mediation and a public agency participates.]

[Alternative B: public agency participates in the [State to insert, for example, child or adult protection] mediation].

b. There is no privilege under Section 4 if a court, administrative agency, or arbitrator finds, after a hearing in camera, that the party seeking discovery or the proponent of the evidence has shown that the evidence is not otherwise available, that there is a need for the evidence that substantially outweighs the interest in protecting confidentiality, and that the mediation communication is sought or offered in:

1. a court proceeding involving a felony [or misdemeanor]; or
2. except as otherwise provided in subsection (c), a proceeding to prove a claim to rescind or reform or a defense to avoid liability on a contract arising out of the mediation.

c. A mediator may not be compelled to provide evidence of a mediation communication referred to in subsection (a)(6) or (b)(2).

d. If a mediation communication is not privileged under subsection (a) or (b), only the portion of the communication necessary for the application of the exception from nondisclosure may be admitted. Admission of evidence under subsection (a) or (b) does not render the evidence, or any other mediation communication, discoverable or admissible for any other purpose.

SECTION 7. PROHIBITED MEDIATOR REPORTS.

a. Except as required in subsection (b), a mediator may not make a report, assessment, evaluation, recommendation, finding, or other communication regarding a mediation to a court, administrative agency, or other authority that may make a ruling on the dispute that is the subject of the mediation.

b. A mediator may disclose:

   1. whether the mediation occurred or has terminated, whether a settlement was reached, and attendance;

   2. a mediation communication as permitted under Section 6; or

   3. a mediation communication evidencing abuse, neglect, abandonment, or exploitation of an individual to a public agency responsible for protecting individuals against such mistreatment.

c. A communication made in violation of subsection (a) may not be considered by a court, administrative agency, or arbitrator.

SECTION 8. CONFIDENTIALITY.

Unless subject to the [insert statutory references to open meetings act and open records act], mediation communications are confidential to the extent agreed by the parties or provided by other law or rule of this State.

SECTION 9. MEDIATOR'S DISCLOSURE OF CONFLICTS OF INTEREST; BACKGROUND.

a. Before accepting a mediation, an individual who is requested to serve as a mediator shall:

   1. make an inquiry that is reasonable under the circumstances to determine whether there are any known facts that a reasonable individual would consider likely to affect the impartiality of the mediator, including a financial or personal interest in the outcome of the mediation and an existing or past relationship with a mediation party or foreseeable participant in the mediation; and

   2. disclose any such known fact to the mediation parties as soon as is practical before accepting a mediation.

b. If a mediator learns any fact described in subsection (a)(1) after accepting a mediation, the mediator shall disclose it as soon as is practicable.

c. At the request of a mediation party, an individual who is requested to serve as a mediator shall disclose the mediator's qualifications to mediate a dispute.

d. A person that violates subsection [(a) or (b)][(a), (b), or (g)] is precluded by the violation from asserting a privilege under Section 4.

e. Subsections (a), (b), [and] (c), [and] [(g)] do not apply to an individual acting as a judge.

f. This [Act] does not require that a mediator have a special qualification by background or profession.

g. [A mediator must be impartial, unless after disclosure of the facts required in subsections (a) and (b) to be disclosed, the parties agree otherwise.]

SECTION 10. PARTICIPATION IN MEDIATION.

An attorney or other individual designated by a party may accompany the party to and participate in a mediation. A waiver of participation given before the mediation may be rescinded.

Federal Arbitration Act

Selected Provisions
9 USC §§1 *et seq.*

9 USC §2. VALIDITY, IRREVOCABILITY, AND ENFORCEMENT OF AGREEMENTS TO ARBITRATE

A written provision in any maritime transaction or a contract evidencing a transaction involving commerce to settle by arbitration a controversy thereafter arising out of such contract or transaction, or the refusal to perform the whole or any part thereof, or an agreement in writing to submit to arbitration an existing controversy arising out of such a contract, transaction, or refusal, shall be valid, irrevocable, and enforceable, save upon such grounds as exist at law or in equity for the revocation of any contract.

9 USC §3. STAY OF PROCEEDINGS WHERE ISSUE THEREIN REFERABLE TO ARBITRATION

If any suit or proceeding be brought in any of the courts of the United States upon any issue referable to arbitration under an agreement in writing for such arbitration, the court in which such suit is pending, upon being satisfied that the issue involved in such suit or proceeding is referable to arbitration under such an agreement, shall on application of one of the parties stay the trial of the action until such arbitration has been had in accordance with the terms of the agreement, providing the applicant for the stay is not in default in proceeding with such arbitration.

9 USC §4. FAILURE TO ARBITRATE UNDER AGREEMENT; PETITION TO UNITED STATES COURT HAVING JURISDICTION FOR ORDER TO COMPEL ARBITRATION; NOTICE AND SERVICE THEREOF; HEARING AND DETERMINATION

A party aggrieved by the alleged failure, neglect, or refusal of another to arbitrate under a written agreement for arbitration may petition any United States district court which, save for such agreement, would have jurisdiction under title 28, in a civil action or in admiralty of the subject matter of a suit arising out of the controversy between the parties, for an order directing that such arbitration proceed in the manner provided for in such agreement. Five days' notice in writing of such application shall be served upon the party in default. Service thereof shall be made in the manner provided by the Federal Rules of Civil Procedure. The court shall hear the parties, and upon being satisfied that the making of the agreement for arbitration or the failure to comply therewith is not in issue, the court shall make an order directing the parties to proceed to arbitration in accordance with the terms of the agreement. The hearing and proceedings, under such agreement, shall be within the district in which the petition for an order directing such arbitration is filed. If the making of the arbitration agreement or the failure, neglect, or refusal to perform the same be in issue, the court shall proceed summarily to the trial thereof. If no jury trial be demanded by the party alleged to be in default, or if the matter in dispute is within admiralty jurisdiction, the court shall hear and determine such issue. Where such an issue is raised, the party alleged to be in default may, except in cases of admiralty, on or before the return day of the notice of application, demand a jury trial of such issue, and upon such demand the court shall make an order referring the issue or issues to a jury in the manner provided by the Federal Rules of Civil Procedure, or may specially call a jury for that purpose. If the jury find that no agreement in writing for arbitration was made or that there is no default in proceeding thereunder, the proceeding shall be dismissed. If the jury find that an agreement for arbitration was made in writing and that there is a default in proceeding thereunder, the court shall make an order summarily directing the parties to proceed with the arbitration in accordance with the terms thereof.

9 USC §5. APPOINTMENT OF ARBITRATORS OR UMPIRE

If in the agreement provision be made for a method of naming or appointing an arbitrator or arbitrators or an umpire, such method shall be followed; but if no method be provided therein, or if a method be

provided and any party thereto shall fail to avail himself of such method, or if for any other reason there shall be a lapse in the naming of an arbitrator or arbitrators or umpire, or in filling a vacancy, then upon the application of either party to the controversy the court shall designate and appoint an arbitrator or arbitrators or umpire, as the case may require, who shall act under the said agreement with the same force and effect as if he or they had been specifically named therein; and unless otherwise provided in the agreement the arbitration shall be by a single arbitrator.

9 USC §7. WITNESSES BEFORE ARBITRATORS; FEES; COMPELLING ATTENDANCE

The arbitrators selected either as prescribed in this title or otherwise, or a majority of them, may summon in writing any person to attend before them or any of them as a witness and in a proper case to bring with him or them any book, record, document, or paper which may be deemed material as evidence in the case. The fees for such attendance shall be the same as the fees of witnesses before masters of the United States courts. Said summons shall issue in the name of the arbitrator or arbitrators, or a majority of them, and shall be signed by the arbitrators, or a majority of them, and shall be directed to the said person and shall be served in the same manner as subpoenas to appear and testify before the court; if any person or persons so summoned to testify shall refuse or neglect to obey said summons, upon petition the United States district court for the district in which such arbitrators, or a majority of them, are sitting may compel the attendance of such person or persons before said arbitrator or arbitrators, or punish said person or persons for contempt in the same manner provided by law for securing the attendance of witnesses or their punishment for neglect or refusal to attend in the courts of the United States.

9 USC §9. AWARD OF ARBITRATORS; CONFIRMATION; JURISDICTION; PROCEDURE

If the parties in their agreement have agreed that a judgment of the court shall be entered upon the award made pursuant to the arbitration, and shall specify the court, then at any time within one year after the award is made any party to the arbitration may apply to the court so specified for an order confirming the award, and thereupon the court must grant such an order unless the award is vacated, modified, or corrected as prescribed in sections 10 and 11 of this title. If no court is specified in the agreement of the parties, then such application may be made to the United States court in and for the district within which such award was made. Notice of the application shall be served upon the adverse party, and thereupon the court shall have jurisdiction of such party as though he had appeared generally in the proceeding. If the adverse party is a resident of the district within which the award was made, such service shall be made upon the adverse party or his attorney as prescribed by law for service of notice of motion in an action in the same court. If the adverse party shall be a nonresident, then the notice of the application shall be served by the marshal of any district within which the adverse party may be found in like manner as other process of the court.

9 USC §10. SAME; VACATION; GROUNDS; REHEARING

a. In any of the following cases the United States court in and for the district wherein the award was made may make an order vacating the award upon the application of any party to the arbitration—

 1. Where the award was procured by corruption, fraud, or undue means.

 2. Where there was evident partiality or corruption in the arbitrators, or either of them.

 3. Where the arbitrators were guilty of misconduct in refusing to postpone the hearing, upon sufficient cause shown, or in refusing to hear evidence pertinent and material to the controversy; or of any other misbehavior by which the rights of any party have been prejudiced.

 4. Where the arbitrators exceeded their powers, or so imperfectly executed them that a mutual, final, and definite award upon the subject matter submitted was not made.

 5. Where an award is vacated and the time within which the agreement required the award to be made has not expired the court may, in its discretion, direct a rehearing by the arbitrators. . . .

9 USC §11. SAME; MODIFICATION OR CORRECTION; GROUNDS; ORDER

In either of the following cases the United States court in and for the district wherein the award was made may make an order modifying or correcting the award upon the application of any party to the arbitration—

a. Where there was an evident material miscalculation of figures or an evident material mistake in the description of any person, thing, or property referred to in the award.

b. Where the arbitrators have awarded upon a matter not submitted to them, unless it is a matter not affecting the merits of the decision upon the matter submitted.

c. Where the award is imperfect in matter of form not affecting the merits of the controversy.

The order may modify and correct the award, so as to effect the intent thereof and promote justice between the parties.

Federal Statute concerning the Convention on the Recognition and Enforcement of Foreign Arbitral Awards

Selected Provisions
9 USC §§201 *et seq.*

USC §201. ENFORCEMENT OF CONVENTION.

The Convention on the Recognition and Enforcement of Foreign Arbitral Awards of June 10, 1958, shall be enforced in United States courts in accordance with this chapter.

9 USC §202. AGREEMENT OR AWARD FALLING UNDER THE CONVENTION.

An arbitration agreement or arbitral award arising out of a legal relationship, whether contractual or not, which is considered as commercial, including a transaction, contract, or agreement described in section 2 of this title, falls under the Convention. An agreement or award arising out of such a relationship which is entirely between citizens of the United States shall be deemed not to fall under the Convention unless that relationship involves property located abroad, envisages performance or enforcement abroad, or has some other reasonable relation with one or more foreign states. For the purpose of this section a corporation is a citizen of the United States if it is incorporated or has its principal place of business in the United States.

9 USC §203. JURISDICTION; AMOUNT IN CONTROVERSY.

An action or proceeding falling under the Convention shall be deemed to arise under the laws and treaties of the United States. The district courts of the United States . . . shall have original jurisdiction over such an action or proceeding, regardless of the amount in controversy.

9 USC §204. VENUE.

An action or proceeding over which the district courts have jurisdiction pursuant to section 203 of this title may be brought in any such court in which save for the arbitration agreement an action or proceeding with respect to the controversy between the parties could be brought, or in such court for the district and division which embraces the place designated in the agreement as the place of arbitration if such place is within the United States.

9 USC §205. REMOVAL OF CASES FROM STATE COURTS.

Where the subject matter of an action or proceeding pending in a State court relates to an arbitration agreement or award falling under the Convention, the defendant or the defendants may, at any time before the trial thereof, remove such action or proceeding to the district court of the United States for the district and division embracing the place where the action or proceeding is pending. The procedure for removal of causes otherwise provided by law shall apply, except that the ground for removal provided in this section need not appear on the face of the complaint but may be shown in the petition for removal. For the purposes of Chapter 1 of this title any action or proceeding removed under this section shall be deemed to have been brought in the district court to which it is removed.

9 USC §206. ORDER TO COMPEL ARBITRATION; APPOINTMENT OF ARBITRATORS.

A court having jurisdiction under this chapter may direct that arbitration be held in accordance with the agreement at any place therein provided for, whether that place is within or without the United States. Such court may also appoint arbitrators in accordance with the provisions of the agreement.

9 USC §207. AWARD OF ARBITRATORS; CONFIRMATION; JURISDICTION; PROCEEDING.

Within three years after an arbitral award falling under the Convention is made, any party to the arbitration may apply to any court having jurisdiction under this chapter for an order confirming the award as against any other party to the arbitration. The court shall confirm the award unless it finds one of the grounds for refusal or deferral of recognition or enforcement of the award specified in the said Convention.

9 USC §208. CHAPTER 1; RESIDUAL APPLICATION.

Chapter 1 [the Federal Arbitration Act] applies to actions and proceedings brought under this chapter to the extent that chapter is not in conflict with this chapter or the Convention as ratified by the United States.

AUTHOR'S NOTE:

The Convention on the Recognition and Enforcement of Foreign Arbitral Awards, adopted by the United Nations on 10 June 1958, can be viewed at the website of the World Intellectual Property Organization (WIPO), *http://arbiter.wipo.int/arbitration/ny-convention/text.html* [cited 11 November 2002].

References

A Class Divided. 1987. Part of the FRONTLINE video series, available through the Public Broadcasting Service.

Alfini, J. J. 1991. Trashing, bashing and hashing it out: Is this the end of "good mediation"? *Florida State University Law Review* 19 (summer):47–75.

Alfini, J. J., and C. G. McCabe. 2001. Mediating in the shadow of the courts: A survey of the emerging case law. *Arkansas Law Review* 54:171–206.

Antes, J. R., D. J. Della Noce, and J. Saul. 2002. *Toward intentionally theory-based instruments and approaches.* Paper presented at the 2002 symposium, Assuring Mediator Quality: What Are the Alternatives? Presented by the Institute for Conflict Transformation, Inc., and co-sponsored by the Center for Dispute Resolution at the University of Maryland Law School and the Maryland Judiciary's Mediation and Conflict Resolution Office (Maryland MACRO), 9 December at the University of Maryland School of Law, Baltimore.

Antes, J. R., J. P. Folger, and D. J. Della Noce. 2001. Transforming conflict interactions in the workplace: Documented effects of the USPS REDRESS™ program. *Hofstra Labor and Employment Law Journal* 18:429–67.

Auerbach, J. S. 1983. *Justice without law: Resolving disputes without lawyers.* New York: Oxford University Press.

Ayres, I. 1991. Fair driving: Gender and race discrimination in retail car negotiation. *Harvard Law Review* 104:817–72.

Bandura, A. 1971. *Social learning theory.* Morristown, NJ: General Learning Press.

Bandura, A. 1977. *Social learning theory.* Englewood Cliffs, NJ: Prentice-Hall.

Barnes, G. H. 1997. Drafting an arbitration clause—a checklist. *Hieros Gamos—Alternative Dispute Resolution Law* [online]. [Cited 15 July 2002]. Available from *http://www.hg.org/adradd1.html.*

Baruch-Bush, R. A. 1996. "What do we need a mediator for?:" Mediator's "value-added" for negotiators. *Ohio State Journal on Dispute Resolution* 12:1–36.

Baruch-Bush, R. A., and J. P. Folger. 1994. *The promise of mediation: Responding to conflict through empowerment and recognition.* San Francisco: Jossey-Bass.

Beck, C. J. A., and B. D. Sales. 2000. A critical reappraisal of divorce mediation research and policy. *Psychology Public Policy and Law* 6 (December):989–1056.

Bellow, G., and B. Moulton. 1978. *The lawyering process.* Mineola, NY: Foundation Press.

Benhamin, R.W. 1975. Images of conflict resolution and social control. *Journal of Conflict Resolution* 19(1):123–37.

Bennett, M. D., and M.S.G. Hermann. 1996. *The art of mediation.* Notre Dame, IN: National Institute for Trial Advocacy.

Berk, L. E. 1997. *Child development* (4th ed.). Needham Heights, MA: Allyn & Bacon.

Bernard, P. E. 2001. Only Nixon could go to China: Third thoughts on the Uniform Mediation Act. *Marquette Law Review* 85 (fall):113–46.

Bickerman, J. 1999. Great potential: The new federal law provides vehicle, if local courts want to move on ADR. *Dispute Resolution Magazine* (fall):3–5.

Bingham, L. 2002. Why suppose? Let's find out: A public policy research program on dispute resolution. *Journal of Dispute Resolution* 2002:101–26.

Bingham, L., R. Baruch-Bush, C. Hallberlin, and L. M. Napoli. 1999. *Changing workplace culture: Lessons learned from mediation of employment disputes at the United States Postal Service.* Paper presented at the 27th annual conference of the Society of Professionals in Dispute Resolution, 23–25 September, Baltimore, Maryland.

Blake, R. R., and J. S. Mouton. 1964. *The managerial grid.* Houston, TX: Gulf.

Blake, R. R., and J. S. Mouton. 1970. The fifth achievement. *Journal of Applied Behavioral Science* 6:413–26.

Bodenhausen, G. V., and R. S. Wyer, Jr. 1985. Effects of stereotypes on decision making and information-processing strategies. *Journal of Personality and Social Psychology* 48(2):267–82.

Bordone, R. C. 1998. Electronic online dispute resolution: A systems approach—potential, problems, and a proposal. *Harvard Negotiation Law Review* 3 (spring):175–211.

Brazil, W. D. 2000. Symposium: Continuing the conversation about the current status and the future of ADR:

A view from the courts. *Journal of Dispute Resolution* 2000:11–39.

Breger, M. J. 2000. Should an attorney be required to advise a client of ADR options? *Georgetown Journal of Legal Ethics* 13 (spring):427–76.

Bronfenbrenner, U. 1979. *The ecology of human development.* Cambridge, MA: Harvard University Press.

Brooks-Gunn, J., and W. S. Matthews. 1979. *He and she: How children develop their sex role identity.* Englewood Cliffs, NJ: Prentice-Hall.

Browe, K. P. 1994. A critique of the civility movement: Why Rambo will not go away. *Marquette Law Review* 77 (summer):751–84.

Bruch, C. S. 1992. And how are the children? The effects of ideology and mediation on child custody law and children's well-being in the United States. *Family and Conciliation Courts Review* 30(1):112–34.

Bryan, P. 1992. Killing us softly: Divorce mediation and the politics of power. *Buffalo Law Review* 40:441–523.

Bunker, B. B., J. Z. Rubin, and Associates. 1995. *Conflict, cooperation and justice: Essays inspired by the work of Morton Deutsch.* San Francisco: Jossey-Bass.

Burger, W. W. 1982. *Isn't there a better way?* Annual Report on the State of the Judiciary, presented at the 1982 midyear meeting of the American Bar Association, Chicago, 24 January. Reprinted as Burger, W.W. 1982. Isn't there a better way? *ABA Journal* 68 (March):274.

Cahill, S. F. 2002. Idaho law eases dispute resolution: Measure gets backing of tort reformers and plaintiffs lawyers [online]. *ABA Journal E-Report* (29 March). Available from http://www.abanet.org/journal/ereport/m29arb.html. [Cited 1 April 2002]. Also available online at the website of the Nederlands Mediation Instituut, *http://www.mediation.nl/nieuws0402.htm#1.* Idaho law eases dispute resolution. [Cited 17 July 2002.]

Camara, K. A., and Resnick, G. 1988. Interparental conflict and cooperation: Factors moderating children's post-divorce adjustment. In *The impact of divorce, single parenting, and stepparenting on children,* edited by E.M. Heatherington and J.D. Arasteh. Hillsdale, NJ: Lawrence Erlbaum.

Camara, K. A., and G. Resnick, G. 1989. Styles of conflict resolution and cooperation between divorced parents: Effects on child behavior and adjustment. *American Journal of Orthopsychiatry* 59(4):560–75.

Cantor, N., and W. Mischel. 1977. Traits as prototypes: Effects on recognition memory. *Journal of Personality and Social Psychology* 35:38–48.

CardWeb.com. 2003. "Short stick." *Card Trak* [online], February. Available at *http://www.cardweb.com/cardtrak/pastissues/feb03.html.*

Carrington, P. D. 1998. Regulating dispute resolution provisions in adhesion contracts. *Harvard Journal on Legislation* 35:225–32.

Chaiken, S. L., D. H. Gruenfeld, and C. M. Judd. 2000. Persuasion in negotiations and conflict situations. In *The handbook of conflict resolution: Theory and practice,* edited by M. Deutsch and P.T. Coleman. San Francisco: Jossey-Bass.

Chase Manhattan Bank, USA, N. A. 2002. *Arbitration agreement and change in terms of notice.* Wilmington, DE: Chase Manhattan Bank, N.A.

Coben, J. R. 1998. Summer musings on curricular innovations to change the lawyer's standard philosophical map. *Florida Law Review* 1998:735–51.

Cochran, R. F., Jr. 1999. ADR, the ABA, and client control: A proposal that the Model Rules require lawyers to present ADR options to clients. *South Texas Law Review* 41 (winter):183–201.

Cohen, J. R. 2000. Apology and organizations: Exploring an example from medical practice. *Fordham Urban Law Journal* 27 (June):1447–82.

Cole, S. H., N. H. Rogers, and C. A. McEwen. 2001. *Mediation: Law, policy and practice.* 2nd ed. St. Paul, MN: West.

Cole, S. R. 1996. Incentives and arbitration: The case against enforcement of executory arbitration agreements between employers and employees. *University of Missouri at Kansas City Law Review* 64 (spring):449–83.

Cole, S. R. 2001. Uniform arbitration: "One size fits all" does not fit. *Ohio State Journal on Dispute Resolution* 16(3):759–89.

Coleman, P. T. 2000. Power and conflict. In *The handbook of conflict resolution: Theory and practice,* edited by M. Deutsch and P.T. Coleman. San Francisco: Jossey-Bass.

Coltri, L. S. 1993. *Development and pilot testing of an instrument to measure conflict style in mediation disputants.* Unpublished.

Coltri, L. S. 1995. *The impact of sex stereotypes on the perception of disputant conflict style by undergraduates.* Ph.D. dissertation, University of Maryland.

Conflict: The Rules of Engagement. 1997. Videocassette featuring Pat Heim. 41 min. Buffalo Grove, IL: CorVision.

Connolly, C., and R. Pierre. 1998. African American voters standing by Clinton. *The Washington Post* [online]. 17 September. [Cited 22 July 2002]. Available from *http://www.washingtonpost.com/wp-srv/politics/special/clinton/stories/blacks091798.htm.*

Connolly, J. S. 1999. A dose of social science: Support for the use of summary jury trials as a form of alternative dispute resolution. *William Mitchell Law Review* 25:1419–60.

Coogler, O. J. 1978. *Structured mediation in divorce settlements.* Lexington, MA: Lexington Books.

Corben, J. R. 1998. Summer mussing on curricular innovations to change the Lawyer's Standard Philosophical Map. *Florida Law Review,* 1998: 735–51.

Costantino, C. A., and C. S. Merchant. 1996. *Designing conflict management systems: A guide to creating productive and healthy organizations.* San Francisco: Jossey-Bass.

Coyne, W. F., Jr. 1999. The case for settlement counsel. *Ohio State Journal on Dispute Resolution* 14:367–413.

CPR Institute. 2001. *CPR business-to-business e-commerce initiative.* At CPR Institute for Dispute Resolution [online]. 9 March. [Cited 18 July 2002.] Available from *http://www.cpradr.org/ecommerce.htm.*

Curtin, K. M. 2000. An examination of contractual expansion and limitation of judicial reviews of arbitral awards. *Ohio State Journal on Dispute Resolution* 15(2):337–71.

Darley, J. M., and R. H. Fazio. 1980. Expectancy confirmation processes arising in the social interaction sequence. *American Psychologist* 35(10):867–81.

Deja, D. R. 1999. The required submission of an ADR joint settlement plan in civil cases in the Berrien County, Michigan trial court: An evaluation of its impact on case disposition time. *Ohio State Journal on Dispute Resolution* 15(1):173–99.

Depner, C. E., K. Cannata, and I. Ricci. 1994. Client evaluations of mediation services: The impact of case characteristics and mediation service models. *Family and Conciliation Courts Review* 32 (July):306–25.

Deutsch, M. 1973. *The resolution of conflict: Constructive and destructive processes.* New Haven, CT: Yale University Press.

Devine, P. G. 1989. Stereotypes and prejudice: Their automatic and controlled components. *Journal of Personality and Social Psychology* 56(1):5–18.

Dezalay, Y., and B. Garth. 1996. Fussing about the forum: Categories and definitions as stakes in a professional competition. *Law and Social Inquiry* 21:285.

Diamond, T. A. 1997. Choice of law clauses and their presumptive effect upon the Federal Arbitration Act: Reconciling the Supreme Court with itself. *Arizona Law Review* 39 (spring):35–65.

Eisler, R. 1988. *The chalice and the blade: Our history, our future.* San Francisco: Harper & Row.

Emery, R. E., S. G. Matthews, and M. M. Wyer. 1991. Child custody mediation and litigation: Further evidence on the differing views of mothers and fathers. *Journal of Consulting and Clinical Psychology* 59(3):410–18.

Epstein, S. 1973. The self-concept revisited or a theory of a theory. *American Psychologist,* 28:405–16.

Erikson, E. 1950. *Childhood and society.* New York: W.W. Norton.

Evans, R. L., H. R. Fox, D. O. Pritzl, and E. M. Halar. 1984. Group treatment of physically disabled adults by telephone. *Social Work in Health Care* 9(3):77–84.

Federal Judicial Center and CPR Institute for Dispute Resolution. 1996. *Eastern District of Michigan: In Brief.* Excerpted from *ADR and settlement in the federal district courts: A sourcebook for judges & lawyers.* Federal Judicial Center and CPR Institute for Dispute Resolution.

[Online]. [Cited 12 July 2002.] Available from Federal Judicial Center website, *http://earth.fjc.gov/ALTDISRES/adrsource/miched.html.*

Feerick, J., C. Izumi, K. K. Kovach, L. Love, R. Moberly, L. Riskin, and E. Sherman. 1995. Symposium: Standards of professional conduct in alternative dispute resolution. *Journal of Dispute Resolution* 1995:95–128.

Fineman, M. 1988. Dominant discourse, professional language, and legal change in child custody decisionmaking. *Harvard Law Review* 101(4):727–74.

Fisher, R., and W. Ury. 1981. *Getting to yes: Negotiating agreement without giving in.* New York: Penguin Books.

Fisher, R., W. Ury, and B. Patton. 1991. *Getting to yes: Negotiating agreement without giving in.* 2nd ed. New York: Penguin Books.

Fiske, S. T., and S. L. Neuberg. 1990. A continuum model of impression formation from category-based to individuating processes: Influences of information and motivation on attention and interpretation. In Vol. 23 of *Advances in experimental social psychology,* edited by M.P. Zanna. San Diego, CA: Academic Press.

Fiss, O. 1984. Against settlement. *Yale Law Journal* 93:1073–90.

Flowers, R. K. 1996. A code of their own: Updating the ethics codes to include the non-adversarial roles of federal prosecutors. *Boston College Law Review* 37 (September): 923–74.

Folberg, J. and A. Taylor. 1984. *Mediation: A comprehensive guide to resolving conflicts without litigation.* San Francisco: Jossey-Bass.

FTC Workshop Comments. 2000. In *Joint Workshop on Alternative Dispute Resolution for Online Consumer Transactions* [online]. 6-7 June 2000. [cited 18 July 2002]. Available on *http://www.ftc.gov/bcp/altdisresolution/comments/index.htm.*

Fuller, L. L., and J. D. Randall. 1958. Professional responsibility: Report of the Joint Conference. *ABA Journal* 44:1159–61.

Gadlin, H. 1994. Conflict resolution, cultural differences, and the culture of racism. *Negotiation Journal* 10 (January):33–47.

Gage, D., D. Martin, and J. Gromala. 1999. Mediation during business formation or reorganization. *Family Business* [online]. (Spring). [Cited 12 July 2002.] Available from *http://www.mediate.com/articles/formation.cfm.*

Gaschen, D. E. 1995. Mandatory custody mediation: The debate over its usefulness continues. *Ohio State Journal on Dispute Resolution* 10:469–90.

Gauvey, S. K. 2001. ADR's integration in the federal court system. *Maryland Bar Journal* 33(2):36–43.

Gearity, P. 2002. ADR and collaborative lawyering in family law. *Maryland Bar Journal* 35(3): 2, 4.

Gilligan, C. 1982. *In a different voice.* Cambridge, MA: Harvard University Press.

Gilson, R. J., and R. H. Mnookin. 1994. Disputing through agents: Cooperation and conflict between lawyers in litigation. *Columbia Law Review* 94 (March):509–66.

Glanstein, D. M. 2001. A Hail Mary Pass: Public policy review of arbitration awards. *Ohio State Journal on Dispute Resolution* 16:297–334.

Goble, F. G. 1970. *The third force: The psychology of Abraham Maslow.* New York: Pocket Books.

Golann, D. 2002. Is legal mediation a process of repair—or separation? An empirical study, and its implications. *Harvard Negotiation Law Review* 7 (spring):301–36.

Goldberg, S. H. 1997. Wait a minute. This is where I came in. A trial lawyer's search for alternative dispute resolution. *Brigham Young University Law Review* 1997:653–82.

Goodpastor, G. 1996. A primer on competitive bargaining. *Journal of Dispute Resolution* 1996:325–77.

Gourlay, A., and J. Soderquist. 1998. Mediation in employment cases is too little too late: An organizational conflict management perspective on resolving disputes. *Hamline Law Review* 21 (winter):261–86.

Gray, J. 1992. *Men are from Mars, women are from Venus.* New York: HarperCollins.

Grillo, T. 1991. The mediation alternative: Process dangers for women. *Yale Law Journal* 100 (April):1545–1610.

Gross, J. (ed.). *The Oxford book of aphorisms.* Oxford, England: Oxford University Press.

Guthrie, C. 2001. The lawyer's philosophical map and the disputant's perceptual map: Impediments to facilitative mediation and lawyering. *Harvard Negotiation Law Review* 6 (spring):145–88.

Haagen, P. H. 1998. New wineskins for new wine: The need to encourage fairness in mandatory arbitration. *Arizona Law Review* 40:1039–68.

Hague Conference On Private International Law (Conférence De La Haye De Droit International Privé). n.d. *Electronic commerce* [online]. [Cited 18 July 2002.] Available from *http://hcch.net/e/workprog/e-comm.html.*

Hamilton, D. L., and T. K. Trolier. 1986. Stereotypes and stereotyping: An overview of the cognitive approach. In *Prejudice, discrimination, and racism,* edited by J.F. Dovidio and S. L. Gaertner. Orlando, FL: Academic Press.

Hammock, G. S., D. R. Richardson, C. J. Pilkington, and M. Utley. 1990. Measurement of conflict in social relationships. *Personality and Individual Differences* 11(6):577–83.

Hang, L.Q. 2001. Online dispute resolution systems: The future of cyberspace law. *Santa Clara Law Review* 41:837–66.

Harmon, K. M. J. 2002. The role of attorneys and dispute review boards. *ADR Currents* 2002 (March-May):6.

Hayford, S. L. 2000. Unification of the law of labor arbitration and commercial arbitration: An idea whose time has come. *Baylor Law Review* 52 (fall):781–927.

Haynes, J. M. 1981. *Divorce mediation.* New York: Springer.

Heinsz, T .J. 2001. The Revised Uniform Arbitration Act: Modernizing, revising, and clarifying arbitration law. *Journal of Dispute Resolution* 2001:1–66.

Heister, J. W. 1987. Appendix. Property allocation in mediation: An examination of distribution relative to equality and to gender. *Mediation Quarterly* 1987 (fall):97–98.

Henderson, D. A. 1995. Avoiding litigation with the mini-trial: The corporate bottom line as dispute resolution technique. *South Carolina Law Review* 46 (winter):237–62.

Hensler, D. R. 1999. A research agenda: What we need to know about court-connected ADR. *Dispute Resolution Magazine* (fall):15.

Hermann, H., C. Honeyman, B. McAdoo, and N. Welsh. 2001. *Judges, attorneys, clients, mediators: What do they want from mediation? Are they all after the same thing?* Seminar presented at the first annual international conference of the Association for Conflict Resolution, Toronto, Ontario, Canada, 12 October.

Hicks, T. 2000. Steps for setting up an effective conflict management system [online]. Available on the mediate.com website at *http://www.mediate.com/ workplace/hicksT4.cfm,* citing Watson, C., and L. R. Hoffman. 1996. Managers as negotiators. *Leadership Quarterly* 7(1):63–85.

Hochman, T. 1981. *Black and white: Styles in conflict.* Chicago: University of Chicago Press.

Holland, D. L. 2000. Drafting a dispute resolution provision in international commercial contracts. *Tulsa Journal of Comparative and International Law* 7:451–79.

Hunt, E. J., E. J. Koopman, L. S. Coltri, and F. G. Favretto. 1989. Incorporating idiosyncratic family system characteristics in the development of agreements: Toward an expanded understanding of "success" in the mediation of child custody disputes. In *Managing conflict: An interdisciplinary approach* edited by M. A. Rahim. New York: Praeger.

Hursh, R. D. 2001. *Annotation: Constitutionality of arbitration statutes.* 55 *A.L.R.2d* 432.

Hutchinson, E. F. 1998. GOP in south sees a war it can win. *Los Angeles Times,* 21 (pp. 231–43), December.

Hutchinson, E. O. 1998. Impeachment is punishment for Clinton's civil rights support. *Afrocentric News* [online]. 18 December. [Cited 22 July 2002.] Available from *http://www.afrocentricnews.com/html/ofariclinton.html.*

Indiana Conflict Resolution Institute. 2001. *Mediation at work: The report of the National REDRESS ™ evaluation project of the United States Postal Service.* Paper presented at the American Bar Association Section on Dispute Resolution Section Meeting, Washington, DC, April.

Invisible rules: Men, women, and teams. 1996. Videocassette featuring Pat Heim. 34 min. Buffalo Grove, IL: CorVision.

Jhally, N. n.d. Bill Cosby, Willie Horton & O. J. Simpson: Why most blacks think O. J. is innocent. [Online]. [Cited 15 November 2002.] Available from *http://www.sutjhally.com/onlinepubs/oj.html.*

Johnston, J. R., and L. E. G. Campbell. 1988. *Impasses of divorce: The dynamics and resolution of family conflict.* New York: The Free Press.

Katsh, E., J. Rifkin, and A. Gaitenby. 2000. E-commerce, e-disputes, and e-dispute resolution: In the shadow of "ebay law." *Ohio State Journal on Dispute Resolution* 15(3):705–34.

Keeva, S. 2001. What clients want. *ABA Journal,* 87 (June):48–52.

Kelly, J. B. 1996. A decade of divorce mediation research. *Family and Conciliation Courts Review* 34(3):373–85.

Kelly, J. B., and M. A. Duryee. 1992. Women's and men's views of mediation in voluntary and mandatory mediation settings. *Family and Conciliation Courts Review* 30(1):34–49.

Kentra, P. A. 1997. Hear no evil, see no evil, speak no evil: The intolerable conflict for attorney-mediators between the duty to maintain mediation confidentiality and the duty to report fellow attorney misconduct. *Brigham Young University Law Review* 3:715–56.

Kentra, P. A. 2002. Personal e-mail communication (1 April).

Kichaven, J. G. 1997. The real benefit of ADR. *Los Angeles Lawyer* (September).

Kim, A. S. 1994. Rent-a-judges and the cost of selling justice. *Duke Law Journal* 44 (October):166–99.

Kim, S. H., and R. H. Smith. 1993. Revenge and conflict escalation. *Negotiation Journal* 9(1):37–43.

Kimmel, P. R. 2000. Culture and conflict. In *The handbook of conflict resolution: Theory and practice,* edited by M. Deutsch and P. T. Coleman. San Francisco: Jossey-Bass.

King, C. J. 1999. Burdening access to justice: The cost of divorce mediation on the cheap. *St. John's Law Review* 73 (spring):375–475.

Kochman, T. 1981. *Black and white: Styles in conflict.* Chicago: University of Chicago Press.

Koopman, E. J. 1983. Personal communication, College Park, Maryland.

Koopman, E. J. 1985. Personal communication, College Park, Maryland.

Koopman, E. J., and E. J. Hunt. 1984. Personal communication. College Park, Maryland.

Kovach, K. K. 1997. Good faith in mediation—requested, recommended, or required? A new ethic. *South Texas Law Review* 38 (May):575–622.

Kovach, K. K. 2001. New wine requires new wineskins: Transforming lawyer ethics for effective representation in a non-adversarial approach to problem-solving: Mediation. *Fordham Urban Law Journal* 28:935–77.

Kovach, K. K., and L. P. Love. 1996. "Evaluative" mediation is an oxymoron. *Alternatives to the High Cost of Litigation* 14(3):31–32.

Kovach, K. K., and L. P. Love. 1998. Mapping mediation: The risks of Riskin's grid. *Harvard Negotiation Law Review* 3 (spring):71–92.

Krauss, R. M., and E. Morella. 2000. Communication and conflict. In *The handbook of conflict resolution: Theory and practice,* edited by M. Deutsch and P.T. Coleman. San Francisco: Jossey-Bass.

Kressel, K., and D. G. Pruitt. 1989. Conclusion: A research perspective on the mediation of social conflict. In *Mediation research: The process and effectiveness of third-party intervention,* edited by K. Kressel and D. Pruitt. San Francisco: Jossey-Bass.

Kuhn, S. C. 1984. Mandatory mediation: California Civil Code Section 4607. *Emory Law Journal* 33 (summer):733–78.

LaFree, G., and C. Rack. 1996. The effects of participants' ethnicity and gender on monetary outcomes in mediated and adjudicated cases. *Law and Society Review* 30(4):767–91.

Lambros, T. D. 1984. *The summary jury trial and other alternative methods of dispute resolution.* 103 F.R.D. 465–77.

Lande, J. 1997. How will lawyering and mediation practices transform each other? *Florida State University Law Review* 24 (summer):839–901.

Lande, J. 1998. Failing faith in litigation? A survey of business lawyers' and executives' opinions. *Harvard Negotiation Law Review* 3 (spring):1–70.

Lefcourt, C. 1984. Women, mediation, and family law. *Clearinghouse Review* 18(3):266–69.

Leone, G. 2002. Settling e-commerce disputes [online]. *ODR News* (31 March) [Cited 17 July 2002]. Available from *http://www.odrnews.com/leone.htm.*

Lester, P. E., and L. K. Bishop. 2001. *Handbook of tests and measurement in education and the social sciences.* 2nd ed. Lancaster, PA: Technomic.

Leung, K. 1988. Some determinants of conflict avoidance. *Journal of Cross-Cultural Psychology* 19(1):125–38.

Leung, K., and E. A. Lind. 1986. Procedural justice and culture: Effects of culture, gender, and investigator status on procedural preferences. *Journal of Personality and Social Psychology* 50(6):1134–40.

Levin, M. S. 2001. The propriety of evaluative mediation. *Ohio State Journal on Dispute Resolution* 16(2):267–96.

Lewicki, R. J., and B. B. Bunker. 1995. Trust in relationships: A model of development and decline. In *Conflict, cooperation and justice: Essays inspired by the works of Morton Deutsch,* edited by B.B. Bunker, J.Z. Rubin, and Associates. San Francisco: Jossey-Bass.

Lewicki, R. J., and C. Wiethoff. 2000. Trust, trust development, and trust repair. In *The handbook of conflict resolution: Theory and practice* (pp. 86–107), edited by M. Deutsch and P. T. Coleman. San Francisco: Jossey-Bass.

Libbey, D. E. 1999. Avoiding a civil action: Mandatory summary jury trial in the settlement of products liability design defect cases in light of the Restatement (Third) of Torts. *Ohio State Journal on Dispute Resolution* 15:285–309.

Lord, C. G., L. Ross, and M. R. Lepper. 1979. Biased assimilation and attitude polarization: The effects of prior theories on subsequently considered evidence. *Journal of Personality and Social Psychology* 37(11):2098–109.

Love, L. P. 1997. The top ten reasons why mediators should not evaluate. *Florida State University Law Review* 24 (summer):937–48.

Love, L. P. 2000. Teaching a new paradigm: Must knights shed their swords and armor to enter certain ADR arenas? *Cardozo Online Journal of Conflict Resolution* [online], 1:3–21. [Cited 15 July 2002.] Available from *http://www.cojcr.org/*.

Love, L. P., and K. K. Kovach. 2000. ADR: An eclectic array of processes, rather than one eclectic process. *Journal of Dispute Resolution* 2000:295–307.

Lowry, L. R. 2000. To evaluate or not: That is *not* the question! *Family and Conciliation Courts Review* 38 (January): 48–58.

Luban, D. 1998. Rediscovering Fuller's legal ethics. *Georgetown Journal of Legal Ethics* 11 (summer):801–29.

Lynch, J., and P. German. (2003, forthcoming). The emergence of integrated conflict management systems as an organizational development strategy. In *The shifting culture of conflict: Perspectives on conflict prevention, management and resolution,* ed. S. Sutherland. Toronto: University of Toronto Press.

Marcus, M. G., W. Marcus, N. A. Stilwell, and N. Doherty. 1999. To mediate or not to mediate: Financial outcomes in mediated versus adversarial divorces. *Mediation Quarterly* 7 (winter):143–52.

McCabe, K. 2001. A forum for women's voices: Mediation through a feminist jurisprudential lens. *Northern Illinois University Law Review* 21:459–82.

McEwen, C. A., and R. M. Maiman. 1982. Arbitration and mediation as alternatives to court. *Policy Studies Journal* 10:712–26.

McEwen, C. A., and T. W. Milburn. 1993. Explaining a paradox of mediation. *Negotiation Journal* 9(1):23–36.

McIsaac, H. 2001. Confidentiality revisited: California style. *Family Court Review* 39(4):405–14.

Meltzer, D. L. 1998. The federal workplace ombuds. *Ohio State Journal on Dispute Resolution* 13:549–609.

Menkel-Meadow, C. J. 1985. Portia in a different voice: Speculations on a women's lawyering process. *Berkeley Women's Law Journal* 1:39–63.

Menkel-Meadow, C. J. 1991. Symposium: Pursuing settlement in an adversary culture: A tale of innovation co-opted or "the law of ADR." *Florida State University Law Review* 19 (summer):1–46.

Menkel-Meadow, C. J. 1996. The trouble with the adversary system in a post-modern, multi-cultural world. *Journal of the Institute for the Study of Legal Ethics* 1:49–77.

Menkel-Meadow, C. J. 2000. Mothers and fathers of invention: The intellectual founders of ADR. *The Ohio State Journal on Dispute Resolution* 16(1):1–37.

Miller, F. H. 1986. Medical malpractice litigation: Do the British have a better remedy?" *American Journal of Law & Medicine* 11:433–63.

Mnooken, R., and L. Kornhauser. 1979. Bargaining in the shadow of the law: The case of divorce. *Yale Law Journal* 88:950–97.

Moore, C. 1996. *The mediation process.* San Francisco: Jossey-Bass.

Morris, C. n.d. Dispute resolution systems and organizational conflict resolution. In *Conflict resolution and peacebuilding: A selected bibliography* [Online.] [Cited 18 July 2002.] Available from *http://www.peacemakers.ca/bibliography/bib8design.html.*

Mosten, F. S. 1997. Checklist: Eleven questions most commonly asked about mediation. *Fairshare* 17(9):5–7.

Mosten, F. S. n.d. What happens in mediation? [online]. [Cited 12 July 2002.] Available from *http://www.mediate.com/articles/mosch3.cfm.*

Murphy, B. S., M. Gout, J. M. Abascal, G. Horlick, A. Parra, and A. Ponieman. 1998. *Trade pacts, regional agreements, organizations and dispute resolution systems.* Panel presented at the section meeting of the Section on Dispute Resolution of the American Bar Association, "Resolving Disputes in the Global Marketplace," Washington, DC, 3 April.

Nader, L. 1992. From legal processing to mind processing. *Family and Conciliation Courts Review* 30(4):468–73.

Nader, L. 1993. Controlling processes in the practice of law; Hierarchy and pacification in the movement to re-form dispute ideology. *Ohio State Journal on Dispute Resolution* 9(1):1–25.

National Conference of Commissioners on Uniform State Laws. 2000. *Uniform Arbitration Act.* [Online.] [Cited 15 July 2002.] Available from *http://www.law.upenn.edu/bll/ulc/uarba/arbitrat1213.htm.*

National Conference of Commissioners on Uniform State Laws. 2001. *The Uniform Mediation Act.* [Online]. August. [Cited 15 July 2002.] Available from *http://www.law.upenn.edu/bll/ulc/mediat/UMA_Final_Styled_Draft-01.htm.*

National Conference of Commissioners on Uniform State Laws. 2001. *Uniform Mediation Act with prefatory note and reporter's notes.* [Online.] November. [Cited 15 July 2002.] Available from *http://www.law.upenn.edu/bll/ulc/mediat/UMA2001.htm.*

National Federation of Paralegal Associations. 1996, updated 2001. Litigation. [Online.] 14 February. [Cited 2 August 2002.] Available from *http://www.paralegals.org/Development/Handbook/litigate.htm#1.*

Neuhauser, F., and C. L. Swezey. 1999. *Preliminary evidence on the implementation of "baseball arbitration" in workers' compensation.* Report prepared for the California Commission on Health and Safety and Workers' Compensation. [Online.] [Cited 15 July 2002.] Available from *http://www.dir.ca.gov/CHSWC/Baseballarbfinal'rptcover.htm.*

Nolan-Haley, J. M. 1999. Informed consent in mediation: A guiding principle for truly educated decisionmaking. *Notre Dame Law Review* 74 (March):775–840.

Nolan-Haley, J. M. 2001. *Alternative dispute resolution in a nutshell.* 2d ed. St. Paul, MN: West.

Pearson, J. 1991. The equity of mediated divorce agreements. *Mediation Quarterly* 9(2):179–97.

Peter, J.T. 1997. Med-arb in international arbitration. *The American Review of International Arbitration* 8:83–116.

Pildes, R. H., and E. S. Anderson. 1990. Slinging arrows at democracy: Social choice theory, value pluralism, and democratic politics. *Columbia Law Review* 90 (December):2121–2214.

Plapinger, E., and D. Steinstra. 1996. *ADR and settlement programs in the federal district courts: A sourcebook for judges and lawyers.* Federal Judicial Center and CPR Institute for Dispute Resolution. [Online.] [Cited 15 July 2002.] Available from the Federal Judicial Center website, *http://www.fjc.gov/ALTDISRES/adrsource/adrblurb.html.*

Ponte, L. M. 1995. Putting mandatory summary jury trial back on the docket: Recommendations on the exercise of judicial authority. *Fordham Law Review* 63:1069–98.

Posner, R. A. 1986. The summary jury trial and other methods of alternate dispute resolution: Some cautionary observations. *University of Chicago Law Review* 53 (spring):366–93.

Prigoff, M. L. 1990. At issue; Professional responsibility: Should there be a duty to advise of ADR options? *ABA Journal* 76 (November):50.

Prueher, J. 2001. *Letter from Ambassador Joseph W. Prueher to Chinese Foreign Minister Tang Jiaxuan.* [Online.] 11 April. [Cited 18 July 2002.] Available from *BBC Online, http://news.bbc.co.uk/hi/english/world/asia-pacific/newsid_1272000/1272279.stm.*

Pruitt, D. G., and P. V. Olczak. 1995. Beyond hope: Approaches to resolving seemingly intractable conflict. In *Conflict, cooperation and justice: Essays inspired by the work of Morton Deutsch,* edited by B.B. Bunker, J.Z. Rubin, and Associates. San Francisco: Jossey-Bass.

Psenicka, C. and M. A. Rahim. 1988. Integrative and distributive dimensions of styles of handling interpersonal conflict and bargaining outcome. In M.A. Rahim, ed., *Managing conflict: An interdisciplinary approach.* New York: Praeger.

Putnam, L. L. (ed.). 1988. Special issue: Communication and conflict styles in organizations. *Management Communication Quarterly* 1(3):357.

Rack, C. 1999. Negotiated justice: Gender and ethnic minority bargaining patterns in the Metro Court Study. *Hamline Journal of Law and Public Policy* 20:211–98.

Rack, R. R., Jr. 1998. Settle or withdraw: Collaborative lawyering provides incentive to avoid costly litigation. *Dispute Resolution Magazine* 4 (summer):8–9. Reprinted and available from The Collaborative Law Center website, *http://www.collaborativelaw.com/Documents/settleor.htm.* [Cited 15 July 2002.]

Rahim, M. A.1983. A measure of styles of handling interpersonal conflict. *Academy of Management Journal* 26(2):368–76.

Ranan, W., and A. Blodgett. 1983. Using telephone therapy for "unreachable" clients. *Social Casework* 1:39–44.

Reisner, M. 2000. The new water agenda: Restoration, deconstruction, and the limits to consensus. *Journal of Land, Resources, and Environmental Law* 20:1–13.

Reuben, R. C. 2000. Constitutional gravity: A unitary theory of alternative dispute resolution and public civil justice. *UCLA Law Review* 47 (April):949–1104.

Rhode, D. L. 1999. Too much law, too little justice: Too much rhetoric, too little reform. *Georgetown Journal of Legal Ethics* 11:989–1017.

Ricci, I. 1980. *Mom's house, dad's house: Making shared custody work.* New York: Collier Books.

Richardson, J. C. 1988. *Court-based mediation in four Canadian cities: An overview of research results.* Ottowa: Department of Justice Canada.

Rifkin, J. 1984. Mediation from a feminist perspective: Promise and problems. *Law and Inequality* 2:21–31.

Riskin, L. L. 1982. Mediation and lawyers. *Ohio State Law Journal* 43:29–60.

Riskin, L. L. 1994. Mediator orientations, strategies, and techniques. *Alternatives to the High Cost of Litigation* 12(9):111–14.

Riskin, L. L. 1996. Understanding mediator orientations, strategies, and techniques: A grid for the perplexed. *Harvard Negotiation Law Review* 1 (spring):7–51.

Riskin, L. L., and J. E. Westbrook. 1997. *Dispute resolution and lawyers.* 2nd ed. St. Paul, MN: West.

Rogers, N. H., and C. A. McEwen. 1989. *Mediation: Law, policy, and practice.* Deerfield, IL: Clark, Boardman, Callaghan.

Rose, C. 1995. Bargaining and gender. *Harvard Journal of Law and Public Policy* 18:547–65.

Rothbart, M., and W. Hallmark. 1988. In-group–outgroup differences in the perceived efficacy of coercion and conciliation in resolving social conflict. *Journal of Personality and Social Psychology* 55(2):248–57 .

Rubin, J. Z., D. G. Pruitt, and S. H. Kim. 1994. *Social conflict: Escalation, stalemate, and settlement.* 2nd ed. New York: McGraw-Hill.

Sabatino, J. M. 1998. ADR as "litigation lite": Procedural and evidentiary norms embedded within alternative dispute resolution. *Emory Law Journal* 47:1289–349.

Sagar, H. A., and J. W. Schofield. 1980. Racial and behavioral cues in black and white children's perceptions of ambiguously aggressive behavior. *Journal of Personality and Social Psychology* 39(4):590–98.

Sander, F. E. A. 1976. *Varieties of dispute processing.* 70 FRD 111.

Sander, F. E. A., and M. Prigoff. 1990. Professional responsibility: Should there be a duty to advise of ADR options? *ABA Journal* 76 (November):50.

Sander, F. E. A., and S. Goldberg. 1994. Fitting the forum to the fuss: A user-friendly guide to selecting an ADR process. *Negotiation Journal* 10 (January):49–68.

Schepard, A. 2000. The evolving judicial role in child custody disputes: From fault finder to conflict manager to differential case management. *University of Arkansas at Little Rock Law Review* 22 (spring):395–428.

Schneider, A. K. 2000. Building a pedagogy of problem-solving: Learning to choose among ADR processes. *Harvard Negotiation Law Review* 5 (spring):113–35.

Schwartz, D. S. 1997. Enforcing small print to protect big business: Employee and consumer rights claims in an age of compelled arbitration. *Wisconsin Law Review* 1997:33–132.

Schwartz, J. R. 1999. Note: laymen cannot lawyer, but is mediation the practice of law? *Cardozo Law Review* 20 (May/June):1715–45.

Shapiro, D. L., B. H. Sheppard, and L. Cheraskin. 1992. In Theory: Business on a handshake. *Negotiation Journal* 8(4):365–77.

Shapiro, M. 1981. *Courts: A comparative and political analysis.* Chicago: University of Chicago Press.

Shonholtz, R. 2002. Personal Correspondence.

Shubik, M. 1971. The Dollar Auction Game: A paradox in noncooperative behavior and escalation. *Journal of Conflict Resolution* 15:109–11.

Shuman, D. W. 1994. The psychology of compensation in tort law. *Kansas Law Review* 43 (fall):39–77.

Smith, S. 2001. Mandatory arbitration clauses in consumer contracts: Consumer protection and the circumvention of the judicial system. *DePaul Law Review* 50:1191–251.

Speidel, R. E. 1998. Consumer arbitration of statutory claims: Has pre-dispute mandatory arbitration outlived its welcome? *Arizona Law Review* 40:1069–94.

Spohn, G. 1998. With no lawyers in sight, landlords and tenants talk out disputes. American News Service. [Online.] [Cited 12 July 2002.] Available from *http://www.mediate.com/articles/landlord.cfm.*

Springer, A. K. 1991. Telephone family therapy: An untapped resource. *Family Therapy* 18(2):123–28.

Stark, B. 2000. Bottom line feminist theory: The dream of a common language. *Harvard Women's Law Journal* 23 (spring):227–46.

Sternlight, J. R. 2001. Mandatory binding arbitration and the demise of the Seventh Amendment right to a jury trial. *Ohio State Journal on Dispute Resolution* 16(3):669–733.

Streeter-Schaefer, H. A. 2001. A look at court mandated civil mediation. *Drake Law Review* 49:367–89.

Stulberg, J. B. 2002. Symposium on the impact of mediation: 25 years after the pound conference: Questions. *Ohio State Journal on Dispute Resolution* 17(3):532–34.

Taslitz, A. E. 1998. An African-American sense of fact: The O. J. trial and black judges on justice. *The Boston Public Interest Law Journal* 7 (spring):219–49.

Teitz, L. E. 2001. Providing legal services for the middle class in cyberspace: The promise and challenge of on-line dispute resolution. *Fordham Law Review* 70 (December):985–1016.

Tesler, P. H. 1999. Family law: Collaborative law: A new paradigm for divorce lawyers. *Psychology, Public Policy and Law* 5 (December):967–1000.

Tesler, P. H. 2001. *Collaborative law: Achieving effective resolution in divorce without litigation.* Chicago: American Bar Association, Section of Family Law.

Ting-Toomey, S. 1988. Intercultural conflict styles: A face-negotiation theory. In *Theories in intercultural communication,* edited by Y. Kim and W. Gudykunst. Newbury Park, CA: Sage.

Tinsley, C. 1998. Models of conflict resolution in Japanese, German, and American cultures. *Journal of Applied Psychology* 83(2):316–23.

Tondo, C-A., R. Coronel, and B. Drucker. 2001. Mediation trends: A survey of the states. *Family Court Review* 39 (October):431–45.

Trope, J. 1986. Identification and inferential processes in dispositional attribution. *Psychological Review* 93(3):239–57.

Trubisky, P., S. Ting-Toomey, and S.-L. Lin. 1991. The influence of individualism-collectivism and self-monitoring on conflict styles. *International Journal of Intercultural Relations* 15:65–84.

Ury, W., J. M. Brett, and S. B. Goldberg. 1988. *Getting disputes resolved: Designing systems to cut the costs of conflict.* San Francisco: Jossey-Bass.

van de Vliert, E., and B. Kabanoff. 1990. Toward theory-based measures of conflict management. *Academy of Management Journal* 33(1):199–209.

van de Vliert, E., and H. C. M. Prein. 1989. The difference in the meaning of forcing in the conflict management of actors and observers. In *Managing conflict: An interdisciplinary approach,* edited by M.A. Rahim. New York: Praeger.

Vestal, A. 1999. Mediation and parental alienation syndrome: Considerations for an intervention model. *Family and Conciliation Courts Review* 38 (October):487–502.

Vidmar, N., and N. M. Laird. 1983. Adversary social roles: Their effects on witnesses' communication of evidence and the assessments of adjudicators. *Journal of Personality and Social Psychology* 44(5):888–98.

Vincent, M. 1995. Mandatory mediation of custody disputes: Criticism, legislation, and support. *Vermont Law Review* 20:255–97.

Wade, J. 2001. Don't waste my time on negotiation and mediation: This dispute needs a judge. *Mediation Quarterly* 18 (spring):259–80.

Waldman, E. A. 1997. Identifying the role of social norms in mediation: A multiple model approach. *Hastings Law Journal* 48 (April):703–69.

Wallerstein, J. S., and J. B. Kelly. 1980. *Surviving the breakup: How children and parents cope with divorce.* New York: Basic Books.

Warmbrod, M. L. 1997. Could an attorney face disciplinary actions or even legal malpractice liability for failure to inform clients of alternative dispute resolution? *Cumberland Law Review* 27:791–819.

Washington Post. 1998. *Direct access: Jesse Jackson.* Washingtonpost.com. [Online interview of Jesse Jackson.] 16 December. [Cited 22 July 2002.] Available from *http://www.washingtonpost.com/wp-srv/politics/talk/zforum/jackson121698.htm.*

Waxler, M.E. 1997. The legal assistant's role in mediation: Some of the possibilities. *Texas Paralegal Journal.* [Online.] [Cited 1 July 2002.] Available from *http://www.lad.org/TPJ/07/waxler.html.*

Weider-Hatfield, D. 1988. Assessing the Rahim Organizational Conflict Inventory–II (ROCI–II). *Management Communication Quarterly* 1(3):350–56.

Welsh, N. A. 2001a. Making deals in court-connected mediation: What's justice got to do with it? *Washington University Law Quarterly* 79:787–861.

Welsh, N. A. 2001b. The thinning vision of self-determination in court-connected mediation: The inevitable price of institutionalization? *Harvard Negotiation Law Review* 6 (spring):1–96.

Weston, M. A. 2001. Checks on participant conduct in compulsory ADR: Reconciling the tension in the need for good-faith participation, autonomy, and confidentiality. *Indiana Law Journal* 76 (summer):591–645.

Wiegand, S. A. 1996. A just and lasting peace: Supplanting mediation with the ombuds model. *Ohio State Journal on Dispute Resolution* 12:95–145.

Wilder, D. A. 1981. Perceiving persons as a group: Categorization and intergroup relations. In *Cognitive processes and intergroup behavior*, edited by D.L. Hamilton. Hillsdale, NJ: Lawrence Erlbaum.

Williams, G. R. 1983. *Legal negotiation and settlement.* St. Paul, MN: West.

Williams, G. R. 1996. Negotiation as a healing process. *Journal of Dispute Resolution* 1996:1–66.

Wolfe, J. S. 2001. Alternative dispute resolution in the twenty-first century: Across the ripple of time: The future of alternative (or, is it "appropriate?") dispute resolution. *Tulsa Law Journal* 36 (summer):785–812.

Woodley, A. E. 1997. Strengthening the summary jury trial: A proposal to increase its effectiveness and encourage uniformity in its use. *Ohio State Journal on Dispute Resolution* 12:541–620.

Woodrow, P. 1998. *Reducing the costs of conflict through dispute resolution systems design* [online]. August. [Cited 2 April 2002.] Available from *http://www.mediate.com/workplace/woodrow.cfm.* Reprinted from *Track Two* (Vol. 7, No. 2, August 1998), a quarterly publication of the Centre for Conflict Resolution and the Media Peace Centre (South Africa).

Word, C. O., M. P. Zanna, and J. Cooper. 1974. The nonverbal mediation of self-fulfilling prophecies in interracial interaction. *Journal of Experimental Social Psychology* 10:109–20.

Workshop on Alternative Dispute Resolution. 2000–2002. In ECLIP, Electronic Commerce Legal Issues Platform. [Online.] January. [Cited 18 July 2002.] Available from *http://www.eclip.org/workshop/7th/ADR.htm.*

Young, P. M. 2001. One-text mediation process: Clinton's Christmas 2000 proposal to the Israelis and Palestinians. [Online.] [Cited 12 July 2002.] First published by the *St. Louis Lawyer* (February 2001). Available from *http://www.mediate.com/articles/young1.cfm.*

Zirkel, P. A., and A. Krahmal. 2001. Creeping legalism in grievance arbitration: Fact or fiction? *Ohio State Journal on Dispute Resolution* 16:243–65.

Zumeta, Z. D. 2000a. A facilitative mediator responds. *Journal of Dispute Resolution* 2000:335–41.

Zumeta, Z. D. 2000b. Styles of mediation: Facilitative, evaluative, and transformative mediation. [Online.] [Cited 14 July 2002.] Available from *http://www.mediate.com/articles/zumeta.cfm.*

Table of Legal References

CASES

Brotherton v. Cleveland, 141 F. Supp. 2d 907, 911 (S.D. Ohio, 2001)

Brown v. Board of Education, 347 U.S. 483 (1954)

Carman v. McDonnell Douglas Corp., 114 F. 3d 790 (C.A. 8 1997)

Chicago Fire Fighters Union Local No. 2 v. City of Chicago, 323 Ill. App. 3d 168 (2001)

Circuit City Stores v. Adams, 279 F.3d 889 (C.A. 9 2002)

Crowell v. Downey Community Hospital Foundation, 95 Cal. App. 4th 730 (2002)

Doctor's Associates, Inc. v. Casarotto, 517 U.S. 681 (1996)

Eastern Associated Coal Corporation v. United Mine Workers of America, 531 U.S. 57 (2000)

Florida Mediator Qualifications Advisory Board, Ethics Op. 95-007, 1995

Folb v. Motion Picture Industry Pension & Health Plans, 16 F. Supp. 2d 1164, D.C. Cal., 1998, *aff'd* 216 F.3d 1082 (C.A. 9 2000).

Foxgate Homeowners' Association, Inc., v. Bramalea, 26 Cal. 4th 1 (2001) 621, 622

Gardner v. Florida, 430 U.S. 349 (1977)

Gilmer v. Interstate/Johnson Lane Corp., 500 U.S. 20 (1991)

Gunter v. Ridgewood Energy Corp., 32 F. Supp. 2d 162 (D. NJ 1998)

Hooters of America v. Phillips, 173 F. 3d 933 (C.A. 4 1999)

In re Telectronics Pacing Sys. 137 F. Supp. 2d 985 (S.D. Ohio, 2001)

In Re Waller, 573 A .2d 780 (D.C. 1990)

International Ass'n of Machinists, Local Number 402 v. Cutler-Hammer, Inc., 297 N.Y. 519 (1947)

John Wiley & Sons v. Livingston. 376 U.S. 543 (1964)

LaPine Technology v. Kyocera, 130 F.3d 884 (C.A. 9 1997)

Mackey v. Montrym, 443 U.S. 1 (1979)

Mastrobuono v. Shearson Lehman Hutton, 514 U.S. 52 (1995)

Mitsubishi v. Soler, 473 U.S. 614 (1985)

Moses H. Cone Memorial Hospital v. Mercury Construction Corp., 460 U.S. 1 (1983)

Olam v. Congress Mortgage Company, 68 F. Supp. 2d 1110 (N.D. Cal., 1999)

Plessey v. Ferguson, 163 U.S. 537 (1896)

Polk County v. Dodson, 454 U.S. 312 (1981)

Poly Software International, Inc. v. Su, 880 F. Supp. 1487 (D. Utah 1995)

Prima Paint Corp. v. Flood & Conklin Mfg. Corp., 388 U.S. 395 (1967)

Rinaker v. Superior Court, 62 Cal. App. 4th 155 (1998)

Rodriguez de Quijas v. Shearson/American Express, 490 U.S. 477 (1989)

Smith v. Smith, 154 F.R.D. 661 (N.D. Texas, 1994)

Southland Corp. v. Keating, 465 U.S. 1 (1984)

United Steelworkers of America v. American Mfg. Co., 363 U.S. 564 (1960)

United Steelworkers of America v. Enterprise Wheel and Car Corp., 363 U.S. 593 (1960)

United Steelworkers of America v. Warrior & Gulf Navigation Co., 363 U.S. 574 (1960)

Volt Information Sciences, Inc. v. Board of Trustees, 489 U.S. 468 (1989)

Vynior's Case, 8 Coke Rep. 81b (1609)

W. R. Grace & Company v. International Union of the United Rubber, Cork, Linoleum and Plastic Workers of America, 461 U.S. 757 (1983)

Wells v. Chevy Chase Bank, 363 Md. 232 (2001)

Wilko v. Swan, 346 U.S. 427 (1953)

Williams v. State, 770 S. W. 2d 948 (Tex. App. 1989)

CONSTITUTIONAL PROVISIONS, STATUTES, RULES, REGULATIONS

Administrative Dispute Resolution Act, 5 U.S.C. §§571 *et seq.*

Alternative Dispute Resolution Act of 1998, 28 U.S.C. §§651 *et seq.*

Civil Justice Reform Act of 1990 (CJRA), 28 U.S.C. §§471-482

Federal Arbitration Act, 9 USCS §§ 1 *et seq.*

Federal Rules of Evidence, Rule 408.

Idaho R.C.P. 16(j).

Judicial Improvements and Access to Justice Act, PL 100-702

Minnesota Statutes, § 595.02.

Mont. Code Ann. § 27-5-114(4).

N.M. Stat. Ann. § 40-4-8.

Nev. N.J.D.C.R. 26.
North Dakota Rules of Evidence, Rule 408.
Pennsylvania Rules of Evidence, Rule 408.
Securities Act of 1933, 15 U.S.C. §§77a *et seq.*
Taft-Hartley Act, 29 USCS §§141 *et seq.*
Tex. Civ. Prac. & Remedies C. §§154.001 *et seq.*
Texas Rules of Civil Evidence 408.
Va R. Prof. C. 1.4

TREATIES AND CONVENTIONS

Convention on the Recognition and Enforcement of Foreign Arbitral Awards. 1959. Available on the United Nations Commission on International Trade Law website, *http://www.uncitral.org/english/texts/arbitration/ NY-conv.htm* [cited July 16, 2002]. Convention adopted by USA at 9 USCS § 201.

CODES OF ETHICS

AAA/ABA/SPIDR. 1998. *Model Standards of Conduct For Mediators*, available from *www.abanet.org/dispute/ modelstandardardsofconduct.doc* [cited 22 March 2003].

American Bar Association. 1983, amended 2002. *Model Rules of Professional Conduct.* Available from the American Bar Association website at: *http://www.abanet.org/cpr/mrpc/ mrpc_home.html* [cited 22 March 2003].

Guidelines on Mediation and UPL Advisory Committee. 2000. Legal and ethical prohibitions against legal advice. *Unauthorized Practice of Law.* Available from: Virginia State Court website, *http://www.courts.state.va.us/text/drs/upl/ legal_advice.html* [cited 15 July 2002].

SPIDR Ethical Standards of Professional Responsibility, Responsibilities to the Parties, Section 3. 2001. Available from the website of the Association For Conflict Resolution at: *http://www.acresolution.org/research.nsf/ key-print/Eth-Sta?OpenDocument* [cited 2 September 2003].

The Ombudsman Assn. Stds. Of Prac. Available online on The Ombudsman Association website, *http://www. ombuds-toa.org/code_of_ethics.htm* [cited July 17, 2002].

American Arbitration Association. 2002. *American Arbitration Association website.* Available from: *http://www.adr.org* [cited 8 August 2002.].

American Film Marketing Association website, http://www.afma.com/ [cited 8 August 2002].

Daniels, M. 2002. *The Prisoner's Dilemma.* Available from *http://www.princeton.edu/~mdaniels/PD/PD.html* [cited 2 August 2002].

Dispute Resolution Board Foundation website, http://www.drb.org/ [cited 22 March 2003],

HALT website. Available at: *http://www.halt.org/FLIP/CLP.cfm* [cited 19 July 2002].

Helfrich, S. 2002. *Serge Helfrich's Prisoner's Dilemma.* Available from *http://www.xs4all.nl/~helfrich/prisoner/index.html* [cited 2 August 2002].

Icourthouse, http://www.i-courthouse.com [cited 22 March 2003].

IntelliCourt, http://www.intellicourt.com/index.html [cited 17 July 2002].

Internet Neutral, http://www.internetneutral.com/index.htm [cited 17 July 2002].

LIFL – UPRESA. 1999. *Iterated Prisoner's Dilemma Game.* Laboratoire de Recherche en Informatique de l'Université des Sciences et Technologies de Lille. 2 February. Available from *http://www.lifl.fr/IPD/applet-tournament.html* [cited 2 August 2002].

National Arbitration Forum website, http://www.arb-forum.com/arbitration/NAF/financialclauses.asp [cited 18 January 2002].

Nova Forum, http://www.novaforum.com/index.html [cited 17 July 2002].

Online Resolution, http://www.onlineresolution.com/index.html [cited 17 July 2002].

Parent's Club, http://www.activeparenting.com/parents.htm [cited 2 July 2002].

Resolution Forum, http://www.resolutionforum.org [cited 11 June 2002].

ResolutionRoom, http://www.resolutionroom.com/ [cited 17 July 2002].

Resources for the Study of Communication, http://www.uwec.edu/Sampsow/Resources/Measures.htm [cited 17 July 2002].

Shor, M. 2002. *Repeated Prisoner's Dilemma Applet.* Available from *http://www.gametheory.net/Web/PDilemma/default.htm* [cited 2 August 2002].

SmartSettle, http://www.smartsettle.com/flash.html [cited 17 July 2002].

SquareTrade, http://www.squaretrade.com/cnt/jsp/index.jsp [cited 17 July 2002].

Testing Materials Resource Book Online, http://www.psychtest.com/curr01/CATLG003.HTM [cited 17 July 2002].

United States Arbitration and Mediation website, http://www.usam.com/services/arb_clause.shtml [cited 23 January 2002].

Virtual Magistrate, http://www.vmag.org/ [cited 17 July 2002].

WebMediate, http://www.webmediate.com/ [cited 17 July 2002].

Glossary

A

Accommodating   see **Obliging**.

Actionable   a term that describes a claim that can be expressed as a *cause of action,* and which is, therefore, subject to action by a court.

Active Listening   generally, a form of communication in which the listener actively takes part in facilitating the communication of the speaker. In mediation and negotiation, active listening generally includes an effort by the listener to reframe the speaker's comments to eliminate rude, incendiary, or provocative content; to refrain from responding judgmentally to statements by the speaker; and to encourage the speaker to elaborate on his or her remarks.

Actual Self-Efficacy   a person's actual ability to carry out a contemplated action.

Adhesion   see **Contract of Adhesion**.

Ad-Hoc Arbitration   arbitration in which the agreement to submit to arbitration is made after the specific dispute arises.

Adjudication   any form of dispute resolution in which the disputants submit their interpersonal conflict to a third party and in which the third party has the power to issue a decision binding on the disputants.

Adjudicator   the neutral third party that decides the outcome of an adjudicated case. For example, in litigation, the judge and, if there is one, the jury act as adjudicators.

Administered Arbitration   arbitration that takes place under the established procedural rubrics of a known dispute resolution association, such as the American Arbitration Association.

ADR   see **Alternative Dispute Resolution**.

ADR of Cyber-Disputes   the use of ADR to resolve disputes that occur in the online environment.

Adversarial   a quality of some interpersonal conflicts, in which participants treat one another as enemies or adversaries.

Adversary Process   an approach to handling interpersonal conflict in which each person presses for an advantage at the expense of the other's interests—in other words, competition is used in an effort to resolve the conflict.

Advisory   the nonbinding quality of an opinion or a decision issued by an ADR neutral in a nonbinding evaluation process.

Advocate   someone who acts as an agent for a disputant during an interpersonal conflict and who is ethically obligated to represent the interests of the disputant zealously and competently.

Advocate-Assisted Negotiation   see **Agent- or Advocate-Assisted Negotiation**.

Agency   in *Dual-Concern Theory,* concern-for-self; in *negotiation,* the type of role played by an agent.

Agency adjudication   an *adjudication* process that proceeds under the auspices of agency law or regulation and features an adjudicator and adjudicatory procedures specific to that agency.

Agent   someone who "stands in the shoes" of a disputant during an interpersonal conflict, acting in the disputant's behalf.

Agent- or Advocate-Assisted Negotiation   negotiation in which one or both disputants are represented in the negotiation by an individual who acts on the disputant's behalf. The disputants retain the ultimate authority to accept or reject a settlement.

Agreement   see **Contract**.

Alienation   the extent to which a person becomes mistrustful of, hateful toward, and unwilling to assist another. Alienation is usually accompanied by a disbelief in the legitimacy of the actions and motives of the other.

594

Alternative Dispute Resolution (ADR) generally, the dispute resolution processes used in the resolution of legal, business/commercial, and other interpersonal conflicts, other than litigation, other than doing nothing, and other than illegal or violent approaches such as extortion or assault.

Answer a written document, filed with the court, containing a formal response to a document initiating a lawsuit. Sometimes also called a *response.*

Appellate pertaining to the appeal of a legal dispute.

Appellate Review the review of the outcome of a lawsuit by a higher court. Appellate review is generally confined to determining whether the lower court committed legal or procedural errors and not to whether the lower court interpreted the factual evidence correctly.

Application Service Provider (ASP) In *online dispute resolution (ODR),* a firm that supplies online software, such as Virtual Room, Instant Messaging, Online Conferencing, case analysis software, or, most commonly, more than one of these modalities in combination to an ODR provider.

Arbitrability whether a particular dispute is legally subject to an arbitration under an otherwise valid arbitration agreement.

Arbitration a form of adjudication in which the decision to adjudicate is made by contract between the disputants. The agreement to arbitrate may be made either in advance of any dispute arising (see also **Executory Arbitration Agreement**) or after the dispute arises (see also **Ad-Hoc Arbitration**).

Arbitration Award the binding decision issued by an arbitrator.

Arbitrator the adjudicator that hears and decides an arbitrated dispute.

Arb-Med a *hybrid dispute resolution* process. The disputants present their case to a neutral third party who is empowered to issue a binding decision. The neutral makes a decision, but this decision is not initially shared with the disputants. Subsequently, the disputants enter mediation, either with the neutral already appointed in the matter or with a different mediator. The adjudicated decision becomes an arbitration award if, and only if, mediation does not result in a settlement.

ASP see **Application Service Provider.**

Aspiration a concrete goal to which a disputant aspires during an interpersonal conflict. For example, an auto accident victim may aspire to receiving at least $50,000 in damages from the perpetrator's insurer.

Assisted Negotiation also known as *facilitated negotiation,* any form of negotiation in which the disputants are assisted by nondisputants. There are three major kinds of assisted negotiation: (1) negotiation assisted by agents or advocates for one or more disputants; (2) mediation in which negotiation is facilitated by a neutral third party; and (3) nonbinding evaluation, in which negotiation is assisted by a neutral third party's advisory decision or opinion about how to resolve the interpersonal conflict.

Asynchronous Communication communication that occurs at the convenience of the participants rather than in real time, such as communication by letter, by e-mail, or by computer-based conferencing.

Asynchronous Platform in computing, a software-hardware combination that allows users to communicate in an *asynchronous* manner, as with *Virtual Rooms* that allow participants to post messages and to read messages previously posted by other participants.

Attribution the causal explanation given for a phenomenon whose cause is ambiguous or not ascertainable. For example, a negotiator might *attribute* puzzling behavior by a negotiator from an unfamiliar culture to the latter's culture.

Autistic Hostility a phenomenon that sometimes occurs during escalated conflict. The disputants, out of aversion to one another, disengage from communicating. Rather than hot and angry interaction, there is little or no interaction. Because of the lack of contact, distorted negative beliefs and attitudes held by each disputant cannot be corrected.

Avoiding one of the five negotiation styles posited by the *Dual-Concern Theory.* The avoiding style is characterized by a low level of engagement in conflict resolution and by low levels of concern for both one's own interests and the interests of the other disputants.

B

Back-End Issue in arbitration, a legal issue, such as reviewability, that arises after the issuance of an arbitration award.

Bargaining-Based Mediation a form of mediation in which the primary goal is to reach a fair agreement.

Baseball Arbitration see **Final-Offer Arbitration.**

Best Alternative to a Negotiated Agreement (BATNA) Before or during negotiation, a disputant's best recourse if negotiation does not settle the interpersonal conflict. A BATNA is used to help a disputant determine whether he or she should accept a proposed settlement, whether to pursue a negotiation that appears to be bogging down, or whether to seek other methods of dealing with the conflict. Knowing one's BATNA can also reduce stress and anxiety during negotiation.

Billable Hours the time a lawyer or, in some states, a certified paralegal spends or documents spending on a given client's case. Often a lawyer cannot contractually charge a client on an hourly basis unless he or she can document how the hours are spent. Legal professionals typically document their time in tenths of an hour (six-minute segments).

Binding in alternative dispute resolution, an outcome that is imposed on the disputants. Pronouncements by an *adjudicator* are binding, but not those of a neutral in *nonbinding evaluation* or *mediation*. Participants in a nonbinding process, such as *mediation* or other *assisted negotiation*, may mutually agree to make a proposed settlement binding.

Blind-Bidding a form of nonbinding or binding dispute resolution in which each disputant makes an offer that is transmitted privately to a neutral intermediary. Using a previously agreed-to rubric, the intermediary determines whether the two bids are within a specified "distance" and, if so, computes an outcome based on a calculation specified in the rubric. Blind-bidding is a particularly popular online dispute resolution process, and in that context often the intermediary is a computer loaded with software that performs the agreed-to rubrics.

C

Calculus-Based Trust a form of trust based on knowledge of the consequences of breaching trust. For example, a disputant may trust that the other disputant will pay a court judgment because he or she knows that the other party will be punished for nonpayment.

Case Evaluation a process in which an expert in the subject matter of a dispute evaluates the dispute as a potential court case, providing an assessment of the strengths and weaknesses of each side's legal case, a range of probable court outcomes, or a specific estimation of the probable court outcome. Case evaluation is featured in *evaluative*

mediation and is the centerpiece of all varieties of *nonbinding evaluation*.

Case Valuation a mathematical method of assessing the value of a case if it were to be taken to court. Using estimates of the probabilities of prevailing at steps along the litigation path and estimates of the most likely outcomes of prevailing or not prevailing, the case valuation is a computation of the *expected value*— the value with uncertainty taken into account. Case valuation is used to assess whether a sure settlement is a better "bet" than litigating with an uncertain chance of obtaining a range of outcomes.

Caucus a meeting between the neutral and one disputant (with or without the disputant's representatives) and out of the earshot of the other disputant and his or her representatives. A caucus is to be distinguished from a *joint session,* in which all disputants involved in the dispute resolution process, and/or their representatives, attend.

Cause of Action a group of operative facts giving rise to one or more bases for suing; a factual situation that entitles one person to obtain a remedy in court from another person (*Black's Law Dictionary,* 7th ed, s.v. "cause of action").

Choice of Law a legal term denoting the search for the correct body of law to apply to a legal dispute when the cause of action arose in more than one jurisdiction, the disputants reside in different jurisdictions, the disputants reside in a jurisdiction other than the one where the cause of action arose, the cause of action arose in cyberspace, or some combination thereof.

Client-Centered Lawyering a style of law practice that invests considerable power in the client to control and dictate the process and goals of legal representation. Client-centered lawyers focus on understanding the client's underlying interests, whether legal or not; allow the client considerable latitude in goal-setting; and give considerable power to the client to control the course of legal representation.

Coercive Power a form of relationship power that comes from the ability to inflict punishment, harm, pain, or other unpleasantness.

Collaborating see **Integrating.**

Collaborative Law a form of lawyering, currently seen mostly in the field of divorce law. Attorneys who practice collaborative law enter into contracts with their clients and with attorneys for the opposing client that collaborative negotiation practices will be used to address the clients' disputes. The contracts specify that an integrating/collaborating negotiation style will be used in dealing with the disputes. The contracts further specify that, if settlement is not reached through the collaborative process, if a participant refuses to use collaborative processes, or if a disputant wishes to resolve the case through contested litigation, the collaborative lawyers must withdraw from representation and never again represent that client in the pending matter.

Communion in Dual-Concern Theory, the concern-for-other dimension of negotiation orientation.

Competing see **Dominating.**

Competition an orientation to interpersonal conflict, described in *Deutsch's Theory of Constructive and Destructive Conflict.* It is characterized by a belief on the part of each disputant that, if he or she helps the other disputant, it will impair his or her own interests and vice versa (in other words, a belief that the disputants are contriently interdependent). Thus, disputants in a competitive conflict view the conflict as a contest over whose needs will be met and whose interests will be addressed. Competition is characterized by predictable changes in behavior, attitude, and perception; these increase the likelihood that the conflict will escalate, spread, and become destructive.

Complaint a formal legal document that is filed by a disputant (or a disputant's attorney) in a court. The filing of a *complaint* initiates a lawsuit. It is called a *petition* in some jurisdictions and for some causes of action.

Complementary Interests in an interpersonal conflict, the interests of one disputant that, if addressed, will also promote the interests of another disputant. For example, in a child custody case, granting a father's wish to spend time with the children on a weeknight may also address the mother's need to have time to run errands without the children present.

Compromising one of the five negotiation styles posited by the *Dual-Concern Theory.* In compromising, the disputants assume that their interests are mutually incompatible but make an effort to equitably address the interests of each disputant partially. The process of compromising is often referred to as *splitting the difference.*

Conciliation a poorly defined term, sometimes referring to mediation, other times to various processes that focus on relationship repair.

Confederate in experimental research, people hired by a researcher to play specific roles in the experiment. The experimental subjects are generally not informed of the confederates' true identity in the experiment until after it ends.

Confidentiality in mediation and other helping professions, the quality of the process as private: in a confidential process, no participant may share, reveal, or publish information about what went on in the process to a third party or in public. See also **Privilege.**

Conflict see **Interpersonal Conflict.**

Conflict Diagnosis the rigorous, step-by-step, theory-based analysis of an *interpersonal conflict* to determine its features and characteristics. Conflict diagnosis enables the user to plan an approach to dealing effectively with interpersonal conflict.

Conflicts of Law a situation in which the laws of different jurisdictions governing a legal dispute differ and are in conflict. See also **Choice of Law.**

Constituent a party whose interests, goals, or needs will be affected by the process or outcome of a conflict.

Contract of Adhesion a legal term that refers to a contract offered to a consumer or other relatively low-power disputant by a large and powerful disputant (such as a commercial vendor or employer), on a take-it-or-leave-it basis. The contract typically has provisions very friendly to the disputant who offers the contract, and often there are no alternatives available to the consumer. A contract of adhesion is sometimes considered "involuntary" in the eyes of the law because the lower-power disputant has had no real choice in negotiating terms.

Contract (also called a Settlement, Stipulation, Agreement, Settlement Agreement) a document, produced by a mediator, by a disputant's attorney, or occasionally by a disputant, memorializing an agreement and intended to be legally binding.

Contriently Interdependent a state of interdependence such that one party's efforts to satisfy needs, interests, or goals adversely affects those of the other.

Convergent Interests see **Complementary Interests.**

Cooperation An orientation to interpersonal conflict, described in *Deutsch's Theory of Constructive and Destructive Conflict.* It is characterized by a belief on the part of each disputant that, if he or she helps the other disputant, it will promote his or her own interests and vice versa (in other words, a belief that the disputants are *promotively interdependent*). Thus, disputants in a cooperative conflict view the conflict as a joint problem to be resolved through joint effort. Cooperation is characterized by predictable changes in behavior, attitude, and perception; these increase the likelihood that the conflict will remain contained, will de-escalate, and will be resolved efficiently.

Cooperative Conflict   a conflict in which the disputants believe that, when one disputant helps him- or herself, the other disputant is also helped.

Culture   the set of customary beliefs, social forms, traits, and characteristics of a particular social group. In the context of conflict diagnosis, culture includes issues of language difference, culture-specific values and frames of reference, and culture-specific attitudes toward conflict, negotiation, and conflict resolution.

Cyber-Dispute   a dispute over an interaction that occurs in cyberspace. An example is a dispute over the sale of goods by an online merchant. Contrast *online dispute resolution* (ODR), which refers to online processes of dispute resolution applied to interpersonal conflict, wherever the conflict occurs.

D

De Novo   the retrial of a cause of action in a higher court. Unlike *appellate review,* in adjudication *de novo* the adjudicator starts fresh and may assess the facts of the case, the believability of witnesses, and so forth.

Decedent   one who has died.

Defendant   the person or entity against whom a lawsuit has been brought.

Deficiency Needs   in Maslow's needs theory, the most basic of needs: the fulfillment of these needs, without which survival is not possible. These include food, air, shelter, and sleep.

Deutsch's Crude Axiom   a corollary to *Deutsch's Theory of Constructive and Destructive Conflict.* Deutsch's Crude Axiom proposes that, to the extent disputants perceive their interpersonal conflict as cooperative, it will tend to become more cooperative in fact; to the extent the conflict is perceived as competitive, it will become more competitive in fact. A corollary to the axiom is that an intermediary, such as a mediator, can alter the course of conflict by manipulating the perceptions of the disputants (for example, making the conflict more cooperative by emphasizing the cooperative aspects of the situation to the disputants).

Deutsch's Theory of Constructive and Destructive Conflict   a set of assumptions and theories, proposed by Morton Deutsch, explaining the conditions under which interpersonal conflict is likely to lead to either constructive or destructive processes and outcomes.

Dicta   plural of *dictum,* Latin; language in a court's opinion that is not essential to the reasoning for the court's ruling.

Disputants   participants in a conflict who have actual or perceived incompatibilities of goals, needs, and/or interests with one another. Although non-disputants may have such incompatibilities, disputants are those parties whose incompatibilities define the interpersonal conflict that is the focus of the conflict diagnostician.

Dispute   non-latent *interpersonal conflict* characterized by the disputants' emphasis and concentration on incompatible needs, goals, and interests.

Dispute Resolution   the methods that people use in an effort to resolve interpersonal conflicts.

Distributive Justice   the perceived fairness, justness, and equity of the outcome of a dispute resolution process. Contrast **Procedural Justice.**

Divergent Interests   see **Incompatible Interests.**

Dominating   in **Dual-Concern Theory,** one of the five negotiation styles, characterized by a high concern for self and a low concern for other. The dominating style is characterized by a coercive, competitive approach; assertiveness; and an attempt to force one's own solution on the other disputant.

Dual-Concern Theory   the theory that proposes that negotiation strategies vary according to the levels of concern for one's own interests (also known as *agency*), as well as the levels of concern for the interests of the other disputant (also known as *communion*), and that these two dimensions can vary independently. Dual-Concern Theory proposes that there are five negotiation styles, which correspond to varying degrees of concern for self and concern for other.

E

Early Neutral Evaluation   a form of *nonbinding evaluation,* applied to legal disputes, in which a neutral evaluator hears a summary of, and gives an assessment of the strengths and weaknesses of, each disputant's legal case.

Ecological Power   a form of power in which the disputant's ability to affect his or her environment, either through changing locations or altering of the physical surroundings, provides choices and options for the improvement of his or her situation. Ecological power may also be used to create and exercise relationship power, as when a disputing country embargos the port of its enemy to exercise coercive power.

E-Mail Server   a large computer that receives e-mail from users and directs it to other e-mail servers, which, in turn, send the e-mail to recipients.

Enforceability   in nonbinding processes such as mediation, the term refers to whether the settlement reached by the disputants is considered a legally binding contract. In arbitration, the term refers to whether the contract to arbitrate is valid and can be enforced against the party seeking to avoid arbitration.

Entrapment   a feature of escalated conflict, created by *overcommitment.* The disputant who incrementally overcommits time and resources to contesting a conflict may come to feel that withdrawing from the contest will constitute a waste of time and money. Accordingly, the disputant may persevere in competitive conflict behavior long after it has ceased to be productive. See also **Overcommitment.**

Environmental Power   the use of power to affect one's situation, other than by using relationship power; the exertion of nonsocial influence.

Erikson's Psychosocial Theory   the theory of human development, developed by Erik Erikson, that proposes that throughout the life span there are age-characteristic life challenges or preoccupations that motivate human behavior.

Evaluative Mediation   mediation in which the mediator issues one or more opinions or evaluations about the likely outcome of the conflict, should it be taken to court, or about the strengths and weaknesses of each disputant's case. It is distinguished from nonbinding evaluation in that the evaluation is not the centerpiece, or endpoint, of the process.

Exchange Power   see **Reward Power.**

Executory Arbitration Agreements   agreements to submit future disputes, not currently in existence, to arbitration.

Expectancy of Reinforcement   a person's belief about the likely personal rewards and drawbacks of an action he or she is contemplating.

Expected Value   a mathematical term referring to the value of an event of uncertain outcome. For example, if a single die is rolled and the player would receive $100 if he or she rolled a 6, but nothing otherwise, the expected value of the event is $100 divided by 6, or about $16.67. The concept of expected value is used in *case valuation* to determine whether taking a settlement is worth foregoing the uncertainty of litigation.

Experimental Subjects   people experimented upon.

Expert Power   the ability to exert purposive influence over another person because of one's superior knowledge. For example, a very well-prepared attorney may be better able to convince a judge that his or her interpretation of the relevant law is correct than is a poorly prepared opponent.

F

Facilitated Negotiation   see **Assisted Negotiation.**

Facilitation   a conflict resolution professional's efforts to design and organize a dispute resolution process for an interpersonal conflict involving large or multiple groups of people and/or complex interpersonal conflicts.

Facilitative Mediation   mediation in which the mediator focuses on facilitating effective negotiation among the disputants and their teams.

Facilitator   an ADR neutral responsible for conducting *facilitation.*

False Conflict   a conflict situation in which the incompatibilities of goals, needs, and interests are perceived, but not real.

Field Study   in experimental research, a study conducted in the natural setting of the behavior being examined, rather than in a laboratory or another artificial setting.

Final-Offer Arbitration   a variant of *high-low arbitration.* The disputants agree to submit their "final offers" to one another. If they are not able to thereby negotiate a settlement, the case goes to arbitration. The arbitrator is required to select between these offers.

Front-End Issue   in *arbitration,* a legal issue that arises before the commencement of the arbitration hearing (such as *enforceability* of the agreement to arbitrate or *stay* of pending litigation).

Fundamental Attribution Error   the mistaken belief, by observers of people in stereotypical social roles, that the behavior within those roles is created by an inherited suitability for the role. For example, the fundamental attribution error might lead observers of female nurses, who are required by their job descriptions to defer to physicians and nurture patients, to conclude that females are inherently subservient and nurturing.

H

Hearing Examiner one who acts as an adjudicator before a governmental agency.

Heuristics generally, rules of thumb; in social psychology, mental shortcuts that people use to make quick assessments of other people during social interactions.

High-Low Arbitration a form of arbitration in which the disputants predefine a range of (monetary) arbitration awards. The arbitrator is empowered only to issue an award that falls within that range.

Holistic Law Practice the practice of legal counseling in which the broader needs of the client, rather than simply his or her narrow monetary legal interests, are addressed. See also **Client-Centered Lawyering.**

Hybrid Dispute Resolution Process any one of a number of *ADR* processes that feature a combination of two or more basic dispute resolution processes. Also called *mixed dispute resolution processes.*

I

Iatrogenic treatment that inflicts damage on those meant to be helped.

Identification-Based Trust a form of trust that occurs when individuals become so emotionally bonded that each knows the other will want to act in the former's best interests.

Impartiality an ADR neutral's refusal to favor any one disputant.

Incentive Arbitration a hybrid process in which non-binding arbitration occurs, but a disputant refusing to go along with the arbitrator's decision is penalized under certain circumstances. For example, such a disputant might be required to pay his or her opponent's attorney's fees and court costs if he or she files a lawsuit but fails to significantly better the outcome thereby.

Incompatible Interests interests of two or more disputants are said to be *incompatible* if attainment of the interests by one disputant would impair the attainment of interests by the other.

Inquirer *ombud's* client.

Instilling Doubt an evaluative mediator tactic, in which the mediator casts doubt on each side's assessment of the merits of its case, in an effort to reduce aspirations and move positions toward a compromise.

Integrating one of the five negotiation tactics posited by the *Dual-Concern theory,* characterized by a mutual search on the part of disputants for a resolution that meets everyone's underlying interests to the extent possible. Integrating is thought to combine a very high degree of concern for self (self-assertiveness) with a very high degree of concern for the other disputant.

Integrating Tactic one of several tactics that promote the *Pareto-superior* allocation of resources, thus resulting in a win-win settlement.

Interdependence a state of relationship between persons or entities such that what happens to one is likely to affect the state, attributes, resources, or well-being of the other.

Interest Arbitration in labor relations, the use of arbitration to determine the outcome of a collective-bargaining transaction. Contrast **Rights Arbitration.**

Interests the considerations that motivate people in a conflict, or the reasons underlying the positions that people take in a conflict. For purposes of this book, the term *interests* also includes principles, values, and needs.

Interpersonal Conflict the perceived and/or actual incompatibility of needs, interests, and/or goals between two or more interdependent parties.

Interrogatories written questions sent to a litigant, asking him or her to answer questions relevant to a pending lawsuit. Lawyers use them to gather information about the facts of a case.

J

Jackpot Syndrome an emotional/motivational state held by some disputants, in which they refuse to settle a dispute in which they have a miniscule chance of being awarded a very large sum of money if they pursue litigation. Such disputants either thrive on risk or fail to appreciate the implications of the improbability of the jackpot result.

Joint Session in *alternative dispute resolution,* a meeting attended by the ADR neutral and all sides in the conflict.

K

Knowledge-Based Trust a situation in which a person grows to trust another person based on the former's knowledge of the values, beliefs, or habits of the latter. For example, John may trust his buddy, Tim, to meet him at a bar after work because John knows that Tim goes to this bar after work every day.

L

Latent Conflict an interpersonal conflict of which no participant in the conflict is aware.

Legal Dispute an interpersonal conflict that can be expressed as one or more *causes of action.*

Legal Remedy see **Remedy.**

Litigant a disputant who is involved in *litigation.*

Litigation an *adjudication* process that proceeds under the auspices of state or federal law in a court.

Logrolling an *integrating tactic* in which something that Disputant A has that is highly valued by Disputant B is traded for something that is highly valued by Disputant A and in the possession of Disputant B.

M

Macrosystem the part of a person's environment consisting of overall societal social structures, including the government, the mass media, cultural attitudes, and overarching social and governmental institutions, such as the predominant school organization, the justice system, the manner in which people acquire goods and services, and the Internet.

Magistrate a judicial officer of some limited jurisdiction, sometimes having the responsibility of presiding over a *settlement conference.*

Mandatory Mediation any mediation program promulgated by a court or other governmental entity, in which participation is made mandatory to some degree, in which nonparticipation is penalized, or in which the right to pursue litigation is denied or postponed to permit mediation to proceed.

Maslow's Needs Theory the psychological theory advanced by Abraham Maslow, proposing that basic human needs are arranged in a hierarchy, with *deficiency needs,* such as for air and nourishment, taking precedence over higher-level needs, such as for love and belongingness.

Master an adjudicator used in some court systems to decide legal issues that arise during litigation. The decision of a master is subject to review by a judge before becoming effective.

Matter of First Impression a legal issue not covered by statute and not previously decided by an appellate court of the jurisdiction in which the matter has come up. Thus, existing law does not control the situation.

Med-Arb a *hybrid dispute resolution process.* The disputants enter *mediation* with an agreement to *arbitrate* if the mediation process does not result in a settlement. The mediator may act as the arbitrator ("med-arb-same"), or the arbitrator may be a different person ("med-arb-different").

Mediation *assisted negotiation* in which the disputants, either alone or assisted by agents or advocates, negotiate in the presence of a neutral professional (or panel of professionals), called a *mediator* (or mediation panel). The mediator's role is to assist the disputants in their negotiation.

Mediator a neutral professional third-party whose role is to assist disputants in negotiating settlements of interpersonal conflicts. A mediator does not have the power to impose a binding settlement on the disputants.

Memorandum of Understanding (MOU), Memorandum of Settlement, Memorandum of Agreement a document memorializing an agreement worked out in mediation; generally, not considered binding. Occasionally, it is called a *stipulation.*

Meta-Conflict (Meta Dispute) an interpersonal conflict (dispute) over the way another interpersonal conflict is being handled.

Michigan Mediation a form of nonbinding evaluation provided by the Michigan State Courts for certain cases filed in the court system.

Minitrial a form of *nonbinding evaluation* and/or *hybrid ADR process.* With persons with authority to settle the interpersonal conflict (such as the chief executive officers of corporate disputants) in attendance, attorneys for the disputants put on an abbreviated version of what would be taken to trial if the matter were litigated. A neutral is usually present to moderate; occasionally, the neutral will also issue an advisory opinion. Following case presentation, the observing representatives for the disputants meet to negotiate a settlement. In some variants of this process, the neutral will act as mediator in this negotiation.

Mixed or Hybrid Process dispute resolution process combining elements of arbitration, mediation, and nonbinding evaluation.

Mixed-Motive Situation a conflict situation characterized by a combination of contrient and promotive interdependence.

Motions requests for judicial action. Motions are brought in the context of a pending lawsuit. The sorts of requests that may be brought up via a motion include a request to have a case determined without trial, to have the litigation dismissed, to compel one of the litigants to produce information, and to penalize a litigant for misconduct in relation to the pending litigation. Motions may be brought before, during, and after trial.

MOU   see **Memorandum of Understanding (MOU).**

Multimodal Process   an *ADR* program featuring a variety of ADR processes. For example, a multimodal court ADR program might feature mediation for some litigants and a choice of binding or nonbinding arbitration for others.

Muscle Mediation   mediation that features a great deal of pressure and coercion applied to the disputants to induce settlement.

N

Need   the most deeply seated underlying motive of a disputant in an interpersonal conflict. See also **Maslow's Needs Theory.**

Negotiation   the process in which disputants seek to resolve an interpersonal conflict through dialogue or another form of communication. In negotiation, the disputants themselves decide mutually whether, and on what terms, the conflict should be resolved.

Neutral   in alternative dispute resolution, a third party who adjudicates the dispute, or assists the disputants and/or their agents and advocates in resolving the dispute.

Neutrality   the ADR neutral's refusal to express opinions, feelings, beliefs, or values concerning the subject matter of the interpersonal conflict or to allow such opinions, feelings, beliefs, or values to color his or her conduct.

Night Baseball Arbitration   a form of *final offer arbitration.* The disputants submit their final, best offers for settling the case in confidence to the arbitrator, who takes custody of both offers without reading them. Then the arbitrator renders a decision and, subsequently, opens and reveals both offers. The ultimate arbitration award is required to be the offer that comes closest to the arbitrator's decision.

Nonadministered Process   the form of *arbitration* that does not rely on an established arbitration organization for procedural structure, support, or assistance. See also **Administered Arbitration.**

Nonbinding Evaluation   *assisted negotiation* in which the disputants present their conflict to a third party or a panel of third parties. The third party's role is to render a nonbinding decision or opinion about the conflict.

Nonspecific Compensation   a type of *integrating tactic.* Nonspecific compensation involves the trading of some-

thing of great value to the recipient for something unrelated, such as the trading of an item of great sentimental value for additional cash.

Normative Power   the ability to exert purposive influence that results from one's moral rectitude, either with the general population or with the group of people over whom the influence is sought.

O

Obliging   one of the five negotiation styles posited by the *Dual-Concern Theory;* disputants using this style give in to the demands of others. Disputants employing this style are thought to be combining a high level of concern for the other disputant with a low level of self-assertion.

ODR   see **Online Dispute Resolution (ODR).**

Ombuds   persons retained by a large organization, such as a corporation, government agency, or municipality, whose function is to resolve and prevent conflict using personal engagement, flexible dispute resolution, advice and advocacy for reform and cutting through bureaucracy.

Ombudsman   see **Ombuds.**

Ombudsperson   see **Ombuds.**

Online Dispute Resolution (ODR)   *ADR* processes that use the Internet as a communication platform.

Ouster Doctrine   an old, and now discredited, legal rule that invalidated *executory arbitration agreements,* on the theory that they "ousted" the jurisdiction of the courts.

Overcommitment   one's incremental investment of time and resources in contesting an interpersonal conflict. Over time, the disputant may overinvest, given the stakes. The overinvestment produces a psychological unwillingness to settle, because the disputant sees settlement as wasting what has been invested.

P

Pareto-Efficiency   the quality of a settlement agreement or another social arrangement to improve overall value of resources to the participants, as a group, without reducing the value of allocated resources to any one participant.

Pareto-Optimal   the most *Pareto-efficient* possible allocation of resources between persons.

Pareto-Superior   more *Pareto-efficient* than another arrangement.

Party (plural, **Parties**)   in the law, a litigant.

Pecuniary Disinterest   the absence, on the part of an ADR neutral, of a financial stake in the dispute or in other matters in which the disputants are involved.

Perceived Self-Efficacy   a person's beliefs about his or her ability to carry off a contemplated action—his or her belief about how well he or she can use a given tool from his or her toolbox of strategies and tactics.

Plaintiff   the party who initiates a lawsuit; the claiming litigant.

Positional Bargaining   a common type of negotiation style characterized by the negotiators taking firm stands using a series of demands or positions.

Positions   the stances or demands taken by disputants (or their agents or advocates) in an interpersonal conflict.

Positive-Sum Situation   a promotively interdependent situation. Efforts by each disputant to help themselves effectively improve joint resources and meet both disputant's underlying interests.

Power   deliberate or purposive influence.

Precedent   the outcome of a lawsuit that stands for a particular legal rule, hence being determinative of other lawsuits that present the same, or an equivalent, situation.

Principled Bargaining   a step-by-step strategy used to achieve the integrating negotiation style, first proposed by Roger Fisher and William Ury in their popular 1981 book *Getting to Yes: Negotiating Agreement Without Giving In.*

Principles   fundamental precepts, values, or assumptions that underlie a disputant's positions, aspirations, and interests.

Private Judging   see **Rent-a-Judge.**

Privilege   the right of a participant in an *ADR* process to lawfully enforce and protect the *confidentiality* of the process, using the courts to do so if necessary.

Problem-Solving Mediation   see **Pure Mediation.**

Procedural Justice   the perceived fairness, justness, and equity of a dispute resolution process, regardless of outcome. Contrast **Distributive Justice.**

Proficiency   the ability of an individual to carry out an intended action; synonymous with **Actual Self-Efficacy.**

Promotively Interdependent   a state of interdependence in which improvements to one party's needs, goals, or interests tend to improve or enhance the needs, goals, or interests of the other party.

Psychological Ownership   a phenomenon in which a disputant feels that the outcome of a conflict is psychologically "his or her own." A disputant is said to have a high degree of psychological ownership of a conflict outcome if he or she feels as if he or she had a strong hand in crafting, developing, and adopting it. High psychological ownership is associated with enthusiasm about the outcome, with high compliance rates, and with low rates of future conflict over the settlement. See also **Quality of Consent.**

Punitive Damages   a type of monetary remedy given in some civil litigation. Punitive damages are a money award over and above the losses suffered by the *plaintiff* and meant to punish the *defendant* for egregiously or outrageously wrongful behavior.

Pure Mediation   (also sometimes known as **Problem-Solving Mediation**) a facilitative form of mediation characterized by the mediator's efforts to promote constructive negotiation by the disputants.

Q

Quality of Consent   the extent to which the conflict resolution process and outcome are freely consented to by the disputants. Processes that possess a high quality of consent tend to yield outcomes that are *psychologically owned* by the disputants.

R

Reactive Devaluation   a phenomenon present in escalating conflict, in which a suggestion made by one disputant, or members of his or her team, is met with suspicion or incredulity by the other disputant, or members of his or her team.

Referent Power   the power that comes from being personally likeable or charismatic.

Relationship Power   the use of *power* to get one's interests addressed by affecting or influencing the behavior of other people.

Remedy (Legal Remedy)   an outcome that, by law, a court can provide to a party in litigation, such as a legal pronouncement or money damages.

Rent-a-Judge   a form of adjudication, in which disputants enter into a contract to hire a judge to decide their legal dispute. The effect of the hired judge's determination is identical to what would have occurred had the dispute been litigated, in terms of enforceability, appealability, and so on.

Response   see **Answer.**

Reviewability   the circumstances under which an arbitration award may be challenged and overturned in court.

Reward Power   the ability to deliberately influence others through the conferring of rewards and benefits.

Rights Arbitration   in labor relations, the use of arbitration to resolve active labor grievances. Contrast **Interest Arbitration.**

Ripeness   the personal quality of being ready to resolve a conflict due to the perceived unpleasantness of not immediately resolving it.

S

Salience   the quality of being noticeable, seemingly important, or patently obvious. For example, a woman's sex would be more *salient* if she were in a large group of men than if she were in a large group of women.

Settlement (Settlement Agreement)   see **Contract.**

Settlement Conference   the process in which a judge meets with litigants and their attorneys prior to a scheduled trial. Settlement conferences are typically used to streamline and plan the trial process and to determine whether action is needed on pre-trial matters. Many judges also use a settlement conference to attempt to settle the overall dispute.

Settlement Facilitation   a term sometimes used to denote a form of *mediation* in which the disputants' lawyers, but not the disputants themselves, participate in negotiation.

Simple Negotiation (Unassisted Negotiation)   negotiation in which the only participants are the disputants.

Social Ecology   Uri Bronfenbrenner's theory of human development, which proposes a bidirectional causal relationship between individual development and events and occurrences taking place in the person's immediate surroundings, larger community, and greater social and cultural context.

Social Stimulus   a *stimulus* that consists of a social event—that is, of one or more people behaving in a way that intentionally affects others.

Sociogram   a diagram or chart that shows individuals and their relationships to one another.

Splitting the Difference   see **Compromising.**

Stakeholder   a *constituent* who is powerful enough to significantly alter the course of a conflict.

Stay   in ADR law, the temporary suspension of the progress of a lawsuit to allow an ADR process to proceed.

Stereotype   the attribution of thoughts, qualities, behaviors, and attitudes to others, based on their categorization by the perceiver, into a social group.

Stimulus   in the field of psychology, any event or circumstance that elicits a response in someone who experiences it.

Stipulation   see **Contract; Memorandum of Understanding.**

Strong Category   a social category associated with a particularly strong likelihood of stereotype application. Strong categories tend to be those associated with obvious physical attributes and rigid social roles.

Sufficiency Principle   a principle that specifies when perceivers will apply stereotypes, and other heuristics, to understand a social event. The sufficiency principle provides that (1) people use complex, systematic processing to try to understand other people only if (a) they have plenty of time and resources to devote to the task *and* (b) they are highly motivated to understand the situation accurately, whereas (2) in the absence of these two requirements, people will use categories, such as stereotypes, to draw inferences about people.

Summary Jury Trial   a form of *nonbinding evaluation.* In this ADR process, a mock jury is assembled, often from the local jury pool. The mock jury hears a shortened version of the legal dispute to be decided and issues an advisory (nonbinding) opinion, which is then used by the disputants and their teams in subsequent negotiation.

Supplementary Proceedings   court proceedings that follow issuance of a money judgment for a plaintiff. In supplementary proceedings, the court requires the defendant to produce information under oath about his assets. The plaintiff uses the information to engage in further legal proceedings to obtain property held by the defendant to satisfy the judgment. Supplementary proceedings are used when a defendant is subject to a court judgment for money, but fails to pay.

Synchronous Communication   communication that occurs in real time, such as face-to-face discussion, telephone conversation, instant messaging, and videoconferencing.

T

Third-Party Neutral the third party in an *ADR* process, such as the *mediator, arbitrator, facilitator,* or *neutral evaluator.*

Tort a civil (noncriminal) wrong upon which a disputant can get compensation from a court. Examples: medical malpractice, negligence in causing an auto accident, civil assault.

Transactions interpersonal conflicts in which disputants work to create arrangements that transfer resources, delineate responsibilities, or otherwise create or adjust an interdependent relationship. Transactions are characterized by disputants' emphasis on mutually complementary needs, goals, and interests and a deemphasis on incompatible goals, needs, and interests.

Transformative Mediation a form of facilitative mediation in which the mediator's goal is to provide opportunities for each disputant to become empowered and to provide recognition to the other.

Triage Mediation a form of mediation characterized by the mediator's efforts to close the case and get a settlement as quickly as possible.

True (Veridical) Conflict conflict situation in which there are real incompatibilities of goals, needs, and interests between the parties to a conflict.

Trust a state of mind in which a person believes that another person intends to be helpful and, accordingly, that it is appropriate to take risks in the relationship.

U

Unassisted Negotiation see **Simple Negotiation.**

V

Vacatur the overturning of an arbitration award by a court.

Veridical Conflict see **True (Veridical) Conflict.**

Virtual Room software that, installed on networked computers, allows individuals in diverse locations to communicate, either *synchronously* or *asynchronously.* Their communications are private as to those persons not privileged to use the "room."

Z

Zero-Sum a term applied to interpersonal conflict situations that predominantly feature incompatible interests, without any significant countervailing *complementary interests.* In a zero-sum situation, the more one person gets, the less the other has.

Index